SPAIN

GUIDE

BE A TRAVELER - NOT A TOURIST!

OPEN ROAD TRAVEL GUIDES SHOW YOU
HOW TO BE A TRAVELER – NOT A TOURIST!

*Whether you're going abroad or planning a trip in the United States, take Open Road along on your journey. Our books have been praised by **Travel & Leisure, The Los Angeles Times, Newsday, Booklist, US News & World Report, Endless Vacation, American Bookseller, Coast to Coast,** and many other magazines and newspapers!*

Don't just see the world – experience it with Open Road!

ABOUT THE AUTHOR

Ron Charles is a travel writer whose Open Road travel guides include *Spain Guide, Portugal Guide, Holland Guide, Bahamas Guide,* and *Bermuda Guide.*

BE A TRAVELER, NOT A TOURIST - WITH OPEN ROAD TRAVEL GUIDES!

Open Road Publishing has guide books to exciting, fun destinations on four continents. As veteran travelers, our goal is to bring you the best travel guides available anywhere!

No small task, but here's what we offer:

•All Open Road travel guides are written by authors with a distinct, opinionated point of view – not some sterile committee or team of writers. Our authors are experts in the areas covered and are polished writers.

•Our guides are geared to people who want to make their own travel choices. We'll show you how to discover the real destination – not just see some place from a tour bus window.

•We're strong on the basics, but we also provide terrific choices for those looking to get off the beaten path and experience the country or city – not just see it or pass through it.

•We give you the best, but we also tell you about the worst and what to avoid. Nobody should waste their time and money on their hard-earned vacation because of bad or inadequate travel advice.

•Our guides assume nothing. We tell you everything you need to know to have the trip of a lifetime – presented in a fun, literate, no-nonsense style.

•And, above all, we welcome your input, ideas, and suggestions to help us put out the best travel guides possible.

SPAIN

GUIDE

BE A TRAVELER - NOT A TOURIST!

Ron Charles

OPEN ROAD PUBLISHING

This book is respectfully dedicated to Deidre Hahn, Pierre Bousset, Rafael Aguirre, and all of the wonderful people of Spain who helped make my travels and research so memorable.

2nd Edition

TABLE OF CONTENTS

SIDEBARS

ACKNOWLEDGMENTS

The author wishes to thank the following people in the travel industry without whose help this book would not have been possible:

Ignacio Ducasse (Tourist Office of Spain-Canada), Margarita Ramon (Tourist Office of Spain-Canada), Enrique Alda (Commercial Office of Spain-Canada), Anna Ursini (Consulate of Spain-Canada), Nancy Carlesso (Vinos de España), Rafael Foley (Tourist Office of Spain-USA), Alfred Loddo (Info Bureau-Gibraltar), Maxine Hurter (Iberia Airlines-Canada), Wim Bless (Iberia Airlines-Canada), Derek Mc Quarrie (Rail Europe-Canada), Cecile Campeau (Rail Europe-USA) Andrew J. Lazarus (A.J. Lazarus & Associates-USA), Imad Khalidy (Auto Europe USA), Kelly McGonagle (Auto Europe-USA), Deidre Hahn (ITVA-Valencia), Juan Ramon Bertomeu (ITVA-Valencia), Rafael Aguirre (CAT-San Sebastian), German Alarcon Martin (EPT-Sevilla), Constantino Ramirez de Frias (EPT-Sevilla), Jesus Diaz Nogueras (STPB-Sevilla), Rafael Perez de la Concha Camacho (OMTC-Córdoba), Leigh Warnick (Legado Andalusi-Granada), Adolf Luna (Fundacio Arqueologica Clos-Barcelona), Carlos Martinez Bujanda (Bodegas Martinez Bujanda-Rioja), Antonio Fernandez Casado (Tryp-Madrid), Ian Mc Farland (Marbian Prod. Intl-Canada), Gretta Staskiewicz (Utell-USA), Geoff Andrew (Utell-USA).

And for all their countless hours of assistance:

Antonio Lorenzo Deperte (CIGA-The Luxury Collection-USA), Carla Gaita (CIGA-The Luxury Collection-USA), Giovanna Colleto (CIGA-The Luxury Collection-USA), David Maranzana (NH Hotels-Barcelona), Sharon L. Barlow (Hyatt International-USA), Barbra Sutman (Utell-Canada), Rosann Valentini (Relais & Chateau-USA), Nina Chung (Hostelling International-Canada), Patricia Vallejo (Marbella Club-Marbella), Isabel Villavecchia (Hotel Alfonso XIII-Sevilla), Pierre Bousset (Hotel Claris-Barcelona), Juan Mari and Elena Arzak (Restaurante Arzak-San Sebastian), Alexander Bell (Palacio Gaviria-Madrid), Katrin Holtknott (Small Luxury Hotels-UK), Felix Garcia (Hotel Villa Real-Madrid), and the hundreds of local *Turismo* officers that showed me the places in their regions that weren't listed on the maps.

1. INTRODUCTION

With its historic cities, walled medieval towns, traditional mountain villages and seaside resorts, Spain offers visitors countless opportunities for exciting travel, incredible cultural encounters, or rest and relaxation. It's not easy to decide how to plan your trip to beautiful Spain with so many options.

Most cities, towns, and villages can be reached in comfort by plane, train, bus or rental car. You can stay in luxurious palaces, rustic farm houses, opulent villas, country inns, hillside castles, seaside resorts, deluxe hotels or romantic bed & breakfasts. The good news is you'll probably spend a lot less money than you might imagine.

Spain is home to some of the world's top museums, finest designer boutiques, prettiest beaches, reputable wines and top gourmet restaurants. In just one or two weeks, you can enjoy tours through castles and royal palaces which are centuries-old, walk around beautifully preserved Roman ruins, take day trips to ancient stone villages, ride horseback along mountain passes or dine on a romantic picnic lunch in beautiful lush gardens. You can stroll through bustling city neighborhoods, hunt for local crafts and antiques, join in unique festivals, play a game of soccer with the locals, or just relax on a quiet beach. At night the possibilities for fun are endless: enjoy delicious *tapas,* see a lively *Flamenco* show, try your luck at a casino, or dance the night away with friendly locals. No matter what you choose, always do as the Spanish do: Enjoy!

This book gives you all of the information necessary to create your own itinerary. You will find many recommendations included in each chapter to point you in the right direction. With a little reading and a taste for adventure, your trip to Spain will be unforgettable.

2. OVERVIEW

The beautiful country of Spain is one of Europe's most popular vacation destinations for a variety of reasons. Hundreds of thousands of people come here throughout the year just to soak up the sun and bathe in the warm waters of the seemingly endless Atlantic and Mediterranean coastlines. An endless stream of tourists spend their time mostly in the major cities in order go on sightseeing excursions, shop in one of a kind boutiques and outdoor markets, dine on regional gastronomic delights, and party till the early morning hours.

Others visit Spain just to view its unparalleled art collections and historic architectural landmarks. An ever-growing number of visitors come to see Spain's more remote regions boasting unspoiled natural beauty and their own special festivals that date back to ancient times. Planning your agenda just depends on how much time you have to do the things you most want to do.

In order to help guide you through the following chapters, I have included the following brief summary of what there is to see and do in a few of the most commonly visited major destinations covered in this book. These are just partial listings, and are designed to give you an idea of what you can find in more detail in the upcoming chapters of this guide.

There are also literally hundreds of smaller and less commonly visited areas discussed throughout this book which should also be considered while touring *España*, especially for those who want to get off the beaten path and find their own special hideaways.

DETAILED CITY WALKING TOURS

In each chapter you'll find in-depth walking tours for all the major cities, and many of the smaller towns as well. If you like to walk and explore, you'll enjoy these very detailed walks, where I point out great shopping, relatively unknown restaurants and cafes, architectural marvels, and of course all the well-known tourist attractions. So put on your walking shoes and let's get going!

MADRID

Spain's capital and largest city is the main point of arrival for the vast majority of visitors here. This bustling metropolis of well over three million residents, situated in the Comunidad de Madrid region in the geographic center of the country, has enough sights and attractions to keep you busy for several days. Many of the nation's finest museums, art galleries, live theater and music venues, designer boutiques and busy central squares are located within easy walking distance to each other.

For evening activities there is also a great selection of *tapas* bars, restaurants in all price ranges, amusing cafes and night clubs for people of all ages and tastes. While far from tranquil, this wonderful (and surprisingly safe) city is packed with smaller neighborhoods that each have their own special ambiance. From Madrid it is also easy to take excursions or self guided day trips by train, bus, or car to the enchanting nearby cities of **San Lorenzo de El Escorial**, **Toledo**, **Segovia** and **Ávila**.

BARCELONA

The sprawling city of Barcelona in the country's northeastern **Catalunya** region is a must-see for all visitors to Spain. Much more liberal, laid back, and artistically inclined than most other major Spanish population bases, every one of this magnificent city's unique districts, historic churches, shop-lined side streets, Modernist buildings, and seafront esplanades is a monument to civic planning and innovative architecture. From your first leisurely stroll down the **Ramblas**, you can't help but notice that this is one of the world's best places to sight-see and people-watch.

Most famous for its awesome 19th century structures designed by masters like Gaudí, Domènech i Montaner, and Puig i Cadafalch, Barcelona also has dozens of well preserved buildings, some even dating back as far as the Roman era. There are several excellent restaurants, chic bars and night clubs, and a rather active cultural scene to enjoy after hitting the museums and boutiques deep inside the older parts of the downtown sector. If the weather is warm, I can also suggest taking a day trip or guided tour to the close by attractions at **Montserrat**, **Sant Sadurní d'Anoia**, and the beach communities of the **Costa Brava** and **Costa Dorada**.

SEVILLA

This mesmerizing destination in southern Spain's **Andalucía** region is undoubtedly one of the most romantic places imaginable. For such a major city, Sevilla feels like a small medieval village full of friendly people that really know how to enjoy life. Maybe it's the intoxicating smell of the ever-present orange blossoms, the incomparable beauty of its residents, or just the vast magnificence of its centuries-old architecture and neighborhoods, but there is undeniably something unique about this city that makes visitors never want to leave!

Perfect for travelers in all budget ranges, this is one of the best places to enjoy fantastic *tapas* while strolling through ancient stone topped plazas. As the sun goes down, you have a good chance of hearing the sounds of students (usually dressed in centuries-old costumes) serenading pretty women on their way to delightful bars and taverns where the crowds will spill out onto the streets and mingle with each other all night long. The opulent cathedral and its adjacent neighborhood full of monumental Moorish-era buildings are enough to keep you busy for more than a few days.

The most spectacular time periods to visit the city are in March (and/or April) during the yearly **Semana Santa** and **Feria de Abril** festivities, but book accommodations for these specific time periods well in advance! If you happen to have the time for a side trip, you should arrange to get to the unforgettable nearby attractions at **Italica, Jerez, Cádiz, Córdoba, Carmona** and **Ronda**.

GRANADA

With it's bold architectural treasures like the incredible Moorish palace and gardens of the **Alhambra**, this city located in the nation's southern Andalucía region is a great place to spend a few days wandering around. While visiting Granada you should take full advantage of the area's abundance of fantastically affordable gourmet restaurants, memorable accommodations, and beautifully produced handicrafts. The festive outdoor markets, excellent boutiques, intriguing little Arab-style tea houses, peaceful riverside parks and out of the way caves, and *flamenco* singing and dancing in the many small taverns throughout the city, will make this a memorable place.

The town's older residents are delightfully friendly and have a strong sense of old world culture that continues to influence local traditions. Granada is relatively close to the massive snow capped **Sierra Nevada** mountain range, and only about an hour's drive from the sea. This area is also a good base for day trips to several of the region's most traditional villages, especially those in the picturesque **Alpujjaras** mountains.

VALENCIA

Located on the sunny eastern coast of the country's **Valencia** region, the youthful residents of this city have become world famous for really knowing how to have a great time. In fact, when Spaniards want to enjoy incredible *paella* and then party till the cows come home, this is the place they go. Valencia is also home to spectacular beach areas, beautiful palaces, Roman ruins, fantastic museums, wonderful outdoor markets, and impeccably maintained gardens.

When darkness falls each weekend night, thousands of locals can be found wandering the stone lanes of the old city in the pursuit of happiness. The most outrageous time to come here is during the annual **Las Fallas de San Jose** festival that takes place between the 9th and 19th of March each year. Up to half a million people from around the globe descend on the city to witness a series of bizarre processions, pyrotechnic explosions, cooking contests, and barn fires of satirical papier-mache sculptures. While in the vicinity it is also a good idea to check out the breathtaking beaches and attractions over at the **Costa del Azahar** and around **Alicante**.

SAN SEBASTIÁN

The impressive old seaside city of San Sebastián is located near the French border in the **Pais Vasco** region of northeastern Spain. This beautiful resort area has become internationally known for both its fine sandy beaches and superb culinary offerings. Once you have finished seeing the sights and museums of the old part of town, swimming in the sea, or shopping to your heart's content, even more delightful activities await you. This city has many fantastic restaurants, cider houses, *tapas* bars, discos, and pubs; it is perhaps the best place in the country to dine.

Each summer the town's incredible crescent shaped sandy beaches begin to fill up with tens of thousands of fun-loving northern Europeans. It is during this time when the downtown district hosts many special events, including an outdoor **Jazz Festival**, an international **film festival**, and a superb **fireworks** competition. During the off season months, San Sebastián offers even more spectacular cultural activities such as the Patron Saint's parades, a great international film festival, and fantastic Carnival processions. While staying in town you can take really nice day trips to the beautiful rural countryside of the Pais Vasco, and even stop off for a few hours in the famed city of **Pamplona**.

SANTIAGO DE COMPOSTELA

The deeply religious and historic city of Santiago de Compostela in the nation's **Galicia** region is one of the most enchanting destinations in northwestern Spain. Known for its giant cathedral and adjacent central square and its monumental buildings, this is a fantastic place to spend at least a few days. The best thing to do here is to just get lost for a while as you walk down ancient stone lanes surrounded by spectacular and well preserved structures dating back to the 10th century.

Visited by countless Christians on the 24th and 25th of July of each year as the highlight of the centuries-old **Camino de Santiago** (The Way of St. James) pilgrimage, Santiago de Compostela is the final resting place for the remains of this beloved Apostle. Each morning the city's church bells coincide with the sound of the university students rushing off to make it to their classes on time via the old streets. The boutiques here offer much lower prices than in most major cities in the country, and the local cuisine is hearty and a great value for the money. While in town make sure to get over to the incredible all-but-deserted beaches of the nearby Galician coastline, and explore the harbor city of **La Coruña**.

THE COSTA DEL SOL & COSTA DE LUZ

If you're a real sun worshipper, the **Costa del Sol** and **Costa de Luz** sections on the southern Andalucia region's coastline is the best place to head for. This part of the country is blessed with minimal rainfall and maximum sunlight throughout the year, and is lined with everything from cute little traditional villages, to giant internationally known beach resort areas with mega hotels and apartment complexes.

Depending on the ambiance you prefer, it is possible to find remote beaches where you will have the unspoiled sand dunes all to yourself near places like **Tarifa** and **Nerja**. Or take in the more bustling vacation resort areas such as **Marbella**, **Málaga**, **Torremolinos**, **Benalmádena Costa**, and **Fuengirola** with long sandy beaches. While prices are at a real premium in many of the more developed zones, you can still find charming accommodations and restaurants a bit off the beaten path where your dollar can go quite a long way. The summers here are extremely busy, and the accent is typically on hedonism, but during the off season the area becomes much more civilized and mature.

HOW TO USE THIS BOOK

The chapters in this book have been divided into logical and manageable sources for information on specific topics and localities. The first sections of this book deal with the vital information which a potential visitor needs before attempting to plan a vacation. You will find up-to-date information about passports, visas, and other documents and details that may need to be either considered or actually obtained before you depart for Europe, as well as information about entry requirements, customs regulations, and weather.

The next few chapters contain the necessary details that will explain the situations you may expect upon arrival in Spain. There are detailed descriptions regarding local time, electricity, business hours, currency, climate, medical services, post offices, communications, holidays, and tourist information resources. Also included are special sections for the physically challenged, what to do in case of an emergency, entertainment prospects, and a brief history of Spain.

After you know the basics, you'll find several chapters on how best to plan and book your vacation. You will find insider tips and detailed information on finding the best free tourist maps and brochures, booking the lowest international airfares, selecting the right travel specialist, and making sure that you end up with the kind of vacation that fits your needs. Additional sections will cover all the facts about traveling by rental car, bus, train, or plane within Spain, as well as which method of transportation may be best suited to your tastes and needs. Next there is an intensive chapter concerning what to expect from each classification of accommodations within Spain, including romantic deluxe castles, *paradores*, manor houses, seaside and golf resorts, bed & breakfast inns, farm houses, villas,

---

CURRENT EXCHANGE RATES

At press time, the value of $1 US is roughly equal to 152 pesetas, while the value of $1 Canadian dollar is about 106 pesetas.

apartments, pensions, youth hostels, camp sites, and even cheap rooms in private houses.

After the previous chapters have provided you with the basic information needed to get you to Spain, I have moved on to describe and explain the sights and infrastructure of each major city and charming rural historic village in northern, central, eastern, and southern Spain, as well as Spain's Mediterranean neighbor Gibraltar (which is a territory of the United Kingdom). These five chapters provide an in-depth look at where to stay and eat, and what to see and do while you are in Spain, and includes dozens of step-by-step walking tours to all the major attractions.

Additional information, such as local history and unique traditions, are also provided. The hundreds of listings and reviews in each region points you directly to the best local beaches, directions to every notable attraction, self-guided walking tours, enjoyable day trips and excursions, sporting activities, wineries, historical sights, parks and wildlife zones, and charming off the beaten path adventures and of course suggestions and reviews of many fine accommodations in all price ranges, regional restaurants, and evening diversions.

After reading this book, you will be a well-informed and culturally sensitive visitor who can travel throughout Spain with almost no stress. The best traveler is a well prepared traveler. Remember that phone numbers and prices are constantly changing in Spain, so be prepared to ask for help from Spain's many local *Turismo* tourist offices during your vacation.

3. SUGGESTED ITINERARIES

These are just a few of the many possibilities for a great vacation in Spain. All of these schedules can be altered to suit your specific needs. Unless otherwise noted, each itinerary can be followed by rental car or public transportation. Make sure to check for local markets, regional festivals, and special attractions that might coincide with each area you choose to visit.

THE LONG WEEKEND IN MADRID TOUR

(4 days/3 nights)
This tour is designed especially for those who have limited time in Madrid. Travel times are minimal, and flights should be via Madrid.

DAY 1
Arrive in Madrid. Take a full day by metro, foot, or bus to sightsee and tour in Madrid. Overnight in Madrid.

DAY 2
Take a full day by metro, foot, or bus to sightsee and tour in Madrid. Overnight in Madrid.

DAY 3
Use a car, train, bus, or excursion to get to Toledo. Take a half day by foot to sightsee and tour in Toledo. Return to Madrid. Overnight in Madrid.

DAY 4
Last minute shopping in Madrid before departure. No overnight. Depart Spain directly from Madrid.

THE QUICK TOUR OF MADRID & ENVIRONS
(7 days/6 nights)
This tour is especially designed for those who want to see Madrid, and would like to also visit a few of the nearby historic walled cities. (Minimal travel times).

DAY 1
Arrive in Madrid. Take a full day by metro, foot, or bus to sightsee and tour in Madrid. Overnight in Madrid.

DAY 2
Take a full day by metro, foot, or bus to sightsee and tour in Madrid. Overnight in Madrid.

DAY 3
Use a car, train, or bus to get to Toledo. Take a half day by foot and car to sightsee and tour in and around Toledo. Overnight in Toledo.

DAY 4
Take a full day by foot to sightsee and tour in Toledo. Overnight in Toledo.

DAY 5
Use a car, train, or bus to get to Avila. Take a full day by foot to sightsee and tour in Avila. Overnight in Avila.

DAY 6
Return to Madrid. Take the rest of this day to tour the museums of Madrid. Overnight in Madrid.

DAY 7
No overnight. Last minute shopping in Madrid before departure. Depart Spain directly from Madrid.

THE QUICK MADRID & ANDALUCÍA TOUR
(8 days/7 Nights)
This tour is designed for those who wish to see Madrid, and also experience some of the dramatic cities, seaside cliffs, beaches, and mountains of the southern Andalucía region. (Moderate travel times).

DAY 1
Arrive in Málaga direct or via a short transfer flight from Madrid.

Travel by car or bus to get to Marbella. Take a full day by foot to sightsee and tour in Marbella. Overnight in Marbella.

DAY 2

Travel by car or bus to get to Torremolinos. Take a half day by foot to sightsee and hit the beaches of Torremolinos. Return to Marbella. Overnight in Marbella.

DAY 3

Use a car or bus to get to Puerto Banús. Take a full day by foot to sightsee and hit the beaches of Puerto Banús. Return to Marbella. Overnight in Marbella.

DAY 4

Use a car, train, or bus to get to Sevilla. Take a full day by foot to sightsee and tour in Sevilla. Overnight in Sevilla.

DAY 5

Take a full day by foot to sightsee and tour in Sevilla. Overnight in Sevilla.

DAY 6

Use a car, train, or bus to get to Madrid. Take a half day by foot to sightsee and tour in Madrid. Overnight in Madrid.

DAY 7

Take a half day by foot to sightsee and tour in Madrid. Overnight in Madrid.

DAY 8

Last minute shopping in Madrid before departure. No overnight. Depart Spain directly from Madrid.

THE BEST OF NORTHWESTERN SPAIN TOUR

(9 days/8 nights)

This tour is designed especially for those who wish to travel to the major attractions of the northwestern corner of Spain. (Moderate to long travel times).

DAY 1

Arrive in Madrid. Take a half day by foot to sightsee and tour in Madrid. Overnight in Madrid.

DAY 2

Use a plane, car, train, or bus to get to Salamanca. Take a half day by foot to sightsee and tour in Salamanca. Overnight in Salamanca.

DAY 3

Take a full day by foot to sightsee and tour in Salamanca. Overnight in Salamanca.

DAY 4

Use a plane, car, train, or bus to get to Santiago de Compostela. Take a few hours by foot to sightsee and tour in Santiago de Compostela. Overnight in Santiago de Compostela.

DAY 5

Take a full day by foot to sightsee and tour in Santiago de Compostela. Overnight in Santiago de Compostela.

DAY 6

Use a plane, car, train, or bus to get to La Coruña. Take a few hours by foot to sightsee and tour in La Coruña. Overnight in La Coruña.

DAY 7

Take a full day by foot to sightsee and hit the beaches of La Coruña. Overnight in La Coruña.

DAY 8

Use a plane, car, train, or bus to get to Madrid. Take a few hours by metro, bus, or foot to sightsee in Madrid. Overnight in Madrid.

DAY 9

Last minute shopping in Madrid before departure. No overnight. Depart Spain directly from Madrid.

THE EXTENDED TOUR OF MADRID & ENVIRONS

(10 days/9 nights)

This tour is designed especially for those who want to see Madrid, and also see nearby cultural, historical, and rural areas. (Moderate travel times).

DAY 1

Arrive in Madrid. Take a full day by metro, foot, or bus to sightsee and tour in Madrid. Overnight in Madrid.

DAY 2
Take a full day by metro, foot, or bus to sightsee and tour in Madrid. Overnight in Madrid.

DAY 3
Use a car, train, or bus to get to Salamanca. Take a full day by foot to sightsee and tour in Salamanca. Overnight in Salamanca.

DAY 4
Take a full day by foot to sightsee and tour in Salamanca. Overnight in Salamanca.

DAY 5
Use a car, train, or bus to get to Avila. Take a full day by foot to sightsee and tour in Avila. Overnight in Avila.

DAY 6
Use a car, train, or bus to get to San Lorenzo del Escorial in the morning. Take a few hours to tour the palace of El Escorial. Return to Avila in time to check out of your hotel: Use a car, train, or bus to get to Segovia. Overnight in Segovia.

DAY 7
Take a full day by foot to sightsee and tour in Segovia. Overnight in Segovia.

DAY 8
Use a car, train, or bus to get to Toledo. Take a few hours by foot to sightsee and tour in Toledo. Overnight in Toledo.

DAY 9
Take a full day by foot or car to sightsee and tour in and around Toledo. Overnight in Toledo.

DAY 10
Return to Madrid before or after the heavy morning rush hour. Last minute shopping before departure. Depart Spain directly from Madrid.

THE HIGHLIGHTS OF ANDALUCÍA TOUR
(11 days / 10 nights)
This tour is perfect for those who are trying to find the most enchanting cities and villages in southern Spain and don't need the beaches. (Moderate travel times).

DAY 1

Arrive in Sevilla directly, or via a short transfer flight from Madrid. Take a half day by foot to sightsee and tour in Sevilla. Overnight in Sevilla.

DAY 2

Take a full day by foot to sightsee and tour in Sevilla. Overnight in Sevilla.

DAY 3

Travel by car or bus to get to Jerez de la Frontera. Take a half day by foot to sightsee and taste sherries in Jerez de la Frontera. Return to Sevilla. Overnight in Sevilla.

DAY 4

Travel by car or bus to get to Carmona. Take a half day by foot to sightsee and tour in Carmona. Take a few hours to tour the nearby Roman era necropolis. Overnight in Carmona.

DAY 5

Travel by car or bus to get to Córdoba. Take a half day by foot to sightsee and tour in Córdoba. Overnight in Córdoba.

DAY 6

Take a half day by foot to sightsee and tour in Córdoba. Take a car, taxi, or bus to tour the nearby Medina Azahara palace. Return to Córdoba. Overnight in Córdoba.

DAY 7

Use a plane, car, train, or bus to get to Granada. Take a few hours by foot to sightsee and tour in Granada. Overnight in Granada.

DAY 8

Take half a day to sightsee and tour in Granada. Take a bus, car, or walk up to tour the nearby Alhambra. Return to Granada. Overnight in Granada.

DAY 9

Travel by car or bus to get to the Alpujarras. Take a half day by foot, horse back, or car to sightsee in the Alpujarras. Overnight in Bubión.

DAY 10

Take a full day by foot, horseback, or car to sightsee in the Alpujarras. Overnight in Bubión.

DAY 11

Take a car or bus to Málaga. No Overnight. Depart Spain directly from Málaga, or via a short flight to Madrid.

THE BEST OF THE COSTA DEL SOL TOUR

(12 days / 11 nights)

This tour is designed especially for those who want to see the sunny beaches, fishing hamlets, white villages, and historical sights in and around the Costa del Sol. (Moderate travel times).

DAY 1

Arrive in Málaga directly, or via a short transfer flight from Madrid. Take a half day by foot to sightsee and tour in Málaga. Overnight in Málaga.

DAY 2

Travel by car or bus to get to Nerja. Take a full day by foot to sightsee and tour in Nerja. Overnight in Nerja.

DAY 3

Take a few hours to enjoy the beaches of Nerja. Travel by car or bus to get to the caves near Nerja. Take a couple of hours to enjoy the caves and return to Nerja. Overnight in Nerja.

DAY 4

Travel by car or bus to get to Granada. Take a half day by foot to sightsee and tour in Granada. Take a bus, car, or walk up to tour the nearby Alhambra. Return to Granada. Overnight in Granada.

DAY 5

Travel by car or bus to get to Marbella. Take a half day by foot to sightsee and hit the beaches in Marbella. Overnight in Marbella.

DAY 6

Travel by car or bus to get to Torremolinos. Take a half day by foot to sightsee and hit the beaches of Torremolinos. Use a car or bus to get to Puerto Banús. Take a half day by foot to sightsee and hit the beaches of Puerto Banús. Return to Marbella. Overnight in Marbella.

DAY 7

Travel by car or bus to get to Ronda. Take a half day by foot to sightsee in Ronda. Return to Marbella. Overnight in Marbella.

DAY 8
Take a full day by car to sightsee and hit the beaches near Tarifa. Overnight in Marbella.

DAY 9
Travel by car or bus to get to Sevilla. Take a half day by foot to sightsee and tour Sevilla. Overnight in Sevilla.

DAY 10
Take a full day by foot to sightsee and tour Sevilla. Overnight in Sevilla.

DAY 11
Travel by car or bus to get to Cádiz. Take a half day by foot to sightsee and hit the beaches of Cádiz. Return to Sevilla. Overnight in Sevilla.

DAY 12
Last minute shopping in Sevilla before departure. No Overnight. Depart Spain directly from Sevilla, or via a short transfer flight to Madrid.

THE BEST OF NORTHEASTERN SPAIN TOUR
(12 days / 11 nights)
This tour is designed especially for those who wish to travel to the major attractions of northern and eastern Spain. (Moderate to long travel times).

DAY 1
Arrive in Alicante directly, or via a short transfer flight from Madrid. Take a few hours by foot, or bus to sightsee and tour in Alicante. Overnight in Alicante.

DAY 2
Take a half day by foot, or bus to sightsee and hit the beaches of Alicante. Return to your hotel in time to check out. Travel by plane, car, or bus to get to Valencia. Take a few hours by foot, or bus to sightsee and tour Valencia. Overnight in Valencia.

DAY 3
Take a full day by foot, or bus to sightsee and tour Valencia. Overnight in Valencia.

DAY 4

Take a half day by foot, or bus to sightsee in Valencia. Travel by car or bus to get to El Salér. Take a few hours to hit the beaches and try the seafood restaurants of El Salér. Return and overnight in Valencia.

DAY 5

Travel by plane, car, train, or bus to get to Barcelona. Take a few hours by metro, foot, or bus to sightsee and tour in Barcelona. Overnight in Barcelona.

DAY 6

Take a full day by metro, foot, or bus to sightsee and tour in Barcelona. Overnight in Barcelona.

DAY 7

Travel by car, train, or bus to get to the Costa Brava. Take a full day to sightsee and hit the beaches of the Costa Brava. Return to Barcelona. Overnight in Barcelona.

DAY 8

Travel by plane, car, train, or bus to get to Zaragoza. Take a half day to sightsee and tour Zaragoza. Overnight in Zaragoza.

DAY 9

Take a full day to sightsee and tour Zaragoza. Overnight in Zaragoza.

DAY 10

Travel by plane, car, train, or bus to San Sebastián. Take a half day by foot or bus to sightsee in San Sebastián. Overnight in San Sebastián.

DAY 11

Take a full day by foot or bus to sightsee and hit the beaches of San Sebastián. Overnight in San Sebastián.

DAY 12

Last minute shopping in San Sebastián before departure. No Overnight. Depart Spain directly via San Sebastián, or via a short transfer flight to Madrid.

THE BIG CITY TOUR
(14 days / 13 nights)

This tour is designed especially for those who want to see several of Spain's most important cities in rapid succession. (Long travel times).

DAY 1

Arrive in Madrid. Take a full day by metro, foot, or bus to sightsee and tour in Madrid. Overnight in Madrid.

DAY 2

Take a full day by metro, foot, or bus to sightsee and tour in Madrid. Overnight in Madrid.

DAY 3

Take a full day by metro, foot, or bus to sightsee and tour in Madrid. Overnight in Madrid.

DAY 4

Take a full day by metro, foot, or bus to visit the museums of Madrid. Overnight in Madrid.

DAY 5

Travel by plane, car, train, or bus to get to Barcelona. Take a few hours by foot to relax and sightsee in Barcelona. Overnight in Barcelona.

DAY 6

Take a full day by foot to relax and sightsee in Barcelona. Overnight in Barcelona.

DAY 7

Take a full day by foot to relax and sightsee in Barcelona. Overnight in Barcelona.

DAY 8

Travel by plane, car, train, or bus to get to Valencia. Take a half day by foot to relax and sightsee in Valencia. Overnight in Valencia.

DAY 9

Travel by car or bus to get to the beaches of El Salér. Take a half a day to have fun in the sun and surf at El Salér. Return to Valencia. Overnight in Valencia.

DAY 10

Take a full day to sightsee in Valencia. Overnight in Valencia.

DAY 11

Travel by plane, car, train, or bus to get to Sevilla. Take a few hours by foot to relax and sightsee in Sevilla. Overnight in Sevilla.

DAY 12

Take a full day by foot to relax and sightsee in Sevilla. Overnight in Sevilla.

DAY 13

Take a full day by foot to relax and sightsee in Sevilla. Overnight in Sevilla.

DAY 14

Last minute shopping in Sevilla before departure. No overnight. Depart Spain directly from Sevilla, or via a short transfer flight to Madrid.

4. LAND & PEOPLE

The vast mainland of Spain takes up the majority of the **Iberian peninsula** of southwestern Europe. This nation covers 504,788 square kilometers (312,969 square miles) of mountains, hills, valleys, and plains. The heart of the country is centered around a huge central plateau known as the **Meseta**. The fertile Meseta is surrounded by a series of dramatic mountain ranges that in turn give way to well over 6,000 km (3,720 miles) of extraordinary beach and cliff-lined coasts.

Spain is bordered by **Portugal** to its west, the **Cantabrian Sea** and **France** to its north, the **Mediterranean Sea** to its east and south, and a small portion of the **Atlantic Ocean** on its extreme northwest and southwest corners. The country's territory also includes the **Balearic Island** chain starting about 80 km (50 miles) east of the mainland out in the Mediterranean, the **Canary Islands** some 1,100 kilometers (682 miles) southwest of the mainland out in the Atlantic Ocean, and a pair of port cities known as **Ceuta** and **Melilla** just to the south of the mainland at the very tip of Northern Africa.

CENTRAL SPAIN

Central Spain includes the regions of Comunidad de Madrid, Castilla y León, Castilla-La Mancha, and Extremadura.

Comunidad de Madrid

Situated in the very center of Spain, this smaller region is best known for surrounding the nation's capital city of **Madrid**. There are almost 5 million people who live in the cities and villages that are scattered amidst the 7,995 square kilometers (4,957 square miles) of plains and a few hilly areas. While Madrid itself has its own unique cosmopolitan ambiance, the rest of the region is home to large agricultural zones.

Castilla-La Mancha

This medium-sized region located in the eastern plains of central Spain is famous for both its historic walled city of **Toledo**, and the countless acres of hearty wine producing vineyards. A population of more than 1.7 million people reside in the tranquil villages and more active cities that are spread out near the rivers that cut through the region's 53,526 square kilometers (33,186 square miles).

Castilla y León

Located in the northern reaches of central Spain, this large region contains some of the country's most dramatic old cities, including **Ávila**, **Salamanca**, and **Segovia**. There are about 2.5 million people who inhabit the cities and villages along the rivers, high mountains, and fertile plains that can be found inside this 94,147 square kilometer (58,371 square miles) area.

Extremadura

This medium-sized isolated rural region occupies the western portion of central Spain along the border with Portugal. Full of barren plains, rocky outcrops, tumbleweed pastures, boulders, cork trees, and Roman-era roads, this 41,848 square kilometer (25,946 square mile) region of just over 1 million souls is hauntingly quiet most of the time. Although a few interesting cities can be found here, it is seldom visited by the vast majority of travelers and tourists.

NORTHERN SPAIN

Northern Spain includes the regions of Galicia, Asturias, Cantabria, País Vasco, La Rioja, Navarra, and Aragón.

Galicia

Located in the northwest corner of Spain, just above northern Portugal, this mid-sized region is home to the fascinating cities of **La Coruña**, **Salamanca**, and **Segovia**. There are about 2.5 million residents who inhabit the cities and villages along the rivers, high mountains, and fertile plains that can be found inside its 94,147 square kilometer (58,371 square miles) area.

While hit with heavy precipitation in the winter months, the hot summer days here are enjoyable the region is blessed with constant cool breezes.

Asturias

Situated in the extreme north, this small region of snow-capped mountains, traditional seaside villages, and lush hillside valleys is inhabited by just over 1 million hearty residents who follow more traditional lifestyles. With its remarkable selection of wildlife, scenery, and natural beauty, the Asturias has become an outdoor sportsman's paradise.

Cantabria

This is a tiny maritime region located in the center of northern Spain beneath the **Cantabrian Sea**. Mostly known for its charming mountain hamlets and fishing villages, the region's half a million or so people occupy a rough terrain of some 5,289 square kilometers (3,279 square miles). While seldom visited by most tourists, there is an abundance of enchanting little towns lined with beautiful old mansions and castle ruins.

País Vasco

Situated along part of northern Spain's border with France, this unusual region is known as the primary home for the **Basque** peoples with their own unique ancient language and cultural heritage. Most people come here to visit the wonderful city of **San Sebastián**, but the entire region is laced with medieval farming homesteads and a pretty selection of seaside villages. There are over 2 million people who live amid the 7,262 square kilometers (4,502 square miles) of inland and coastal areas. This is a great place to experience some of Spain's most enjoyable regional cuisine and fresh seafood after a long summer's day at the beach.

Navarra

The region of Navarra can be found below northern Spain's border with France. Although landlocked, this part of the country features a spectacular array of varying scenery and topography. Primarily visited by those wanting to tour the city of **Pamplona**, the entire region has a friendly population of about half a million residents that live in the cities and rural villages within its 10,420 square kilometers (6,460 square miles) of mountains, gorges, rolling hills, and small plains.

La Rioja

Located in the central part of northern Spain, this tiny region has about a quarter of a million residents who live primarily in small cities and farming villages on an area of just 5,033 square kilometers (3,120 square miles). While hardly ever visited by tourists, this is one of Spain's best **wine producing areas**, and contains many small traditional rural hamlets with extremely interesting people.

ARAGÓN

This large landlocked region sits below the border with France near the northeast corner of Spain. The huge **Ebro River** forms a wide fertile basin in the heart of this area, where the wonderful city of **Zaragoza** may be found. Large mountain ranges tower along the region's northern and southern edges.

There are over 1.2 million people living amid some 47,000 square kilometers (29,140 square miles) of assorted terrain. Aragón is known as a great destination for winter skiing, outdoor sports, game hunting, Romanesque churches, and a superb cuisine based on local meats such as goat and lamb.

EASTERN SPAIN

Eastern Spain includes the regions of Catalunya, Valencia, and Murcia.

Catalunya

Located in the northeastern corner of Spain's Mediterranean coast, just south of the border with France, this large and historic region has enough sights to keep visitors busy for several weeks on end. Besides containing the world famous city of **Barcelona**, the entire coastline of Catalunya is dotted with the seaside resorts and small fishing communities of the **Costa Dourada** and **Costa Brava**.

Within the region's interior there are dramatic snow-capped mountains, fantastic wineries producing champagne like **Cava** wines, and small villages where a unique dialect is still spoken by the locals. There are well over 6 million residents living within its 31,932 square kilometers (19,798 square miles) of memorable landscapes. This is a perfect place to go for people who enjoy sun worshipping, art and music, rural hikes, exciting cities, downhill skiing, crafts shopping, and water sports.

VALENCIA

The medium-sized maritime region of Valencia in the center of the country's east coast is usually drenched by sunshine all year long. Known for the magnificent and rather energetic seaside cities of **Valencia** and **Alicante**, this part of Spain attracts huge numbers of travelers – and for good reason. Besides having countless miles of incredible beachfront, there are numerous ancient villages, well- preserved castles, and absolutely breathtaking scenery that can be found in almost every corner of its 23,105 square kilometers (14,325 square miles) of coastal, plateau, and mountainous areas.

The 3.8 million or so inhabitants here are among the most outgoing and friendly in Spain, and the people of this region make a visit to Spain even more memorable. This is a great place to enjoy the sea, explore charming cities and villages packed with architectural masterpieces, participate in a full range of outdoor sporting activities, enjoy rich regional culinary delights (such as the famed *paella* rice dishes), take part in fabulous local festivals, and party with the locals until the sun comes up.

MURCIA

This quiet little region off the lower part of Spain's eastern coast is best known for its fine sandy beaches and the unusually peaceful cities of **Murcia** and **Cartegena**. Made up of 11,317 square kilometers (7,017 square miles) of inland and coastal areas, the region has become a home away from home for Spanish and Northern European vacationers who desire a fairly warm year round climate, and appreciate easy access to world class golf, fishing, and water sports facilities. While the official population is listed as being just over 1 million people, in the summertime this can swell greatly, especially in the seaside resort towns near **La Manga**.

SOUTHERN SPAIN

The main region of tourist interest in southern Spain is Andalucía.

Andalucía

Situated along the entire southern coast of Spain, the massive region of Andalucía is the gem of the country. Visited by enormous quantities of visitors from all over the world, there are dozens upon dozens of incomparably picturesque, romantic cities, towns, and villages here. Each place here will compel you to stay even longer than expected.

While most travelers plan to visit the awesome destinations of **Sevilla**, **Granada**, **Córdoba**, and the beaches of the **Costa del Sol**, this is only a small part of what this region has to offer. Andalucía is home to 6.7 million residents who live among 87,268 square kilometers (54,106 square miles) of plains, craggy mountains, Atlantic and Mediterranean coastline, and semi-tropical micro-climatic zones.

During your stay here you can visit fantastic Roman and Moorish structures, tour enchanting traditional "white villages," hike or ride horseback through the **Alpujarras**, ski in a world-class winter mountain resort, view impressive art collections and museums, shop for fine hand-made crafts and ceramics, day trip to historic castle towns, taste the best sherries in the world, witness spectacular festivals, watch dramatic bull-fights, become entranced with the sights and sounds of *Flamenco*, play golf and tennis with the best, and relax on breathtaking beaches.

About 96% of the roughly 40 million residents of Spain are Roman Catholic. With well over 60,000 churches, this is still considered a rather religious nation, although the mandatory Christian lessons at public schools have recently been done away with. The remaining small percentage of citizens are a mixture of Protestant, Muslim, Jewish and various other once persecuted sects who are now finally able to practice their beliefs under constitutional protection without fear of oppression. While not long ago it was unacceptable to even enter a church with shorts or a T-shirt, things have changed greatly since the mid-1970's when Franco's regime finally ended and Bourbon King Juan Carlos took the throne.

Nowadays families are smaller (unlike the old days when a family of seven children was commonplace), and divorce is becoming acceptable. I would also venture to say that the majority of those under the age of 25 do not attend church on a weekly basis. Based on my observations, the current generation of teens probably have a lot more sins to confess than their parents would want know about! What this means is that there are many different sides to life in Spain, and that the country is currently experiencing a dramatic change towards liberalization that will certainly affect future generations.

As one travels through the small villages in the heart of rural districts and regions, most of the older inhabitants can still be seen wearing vaguely traditional clothing or even riding around town atop a donkey. There are even a few scattered fishing villages remaining along the coast where many of the fishermen still hand-knit their nets and practice their trade in much the same way as their ancestors did. Unfortunately, many of the children of these traditional peoples are leaving these traditional little hamlets in favor of a more modern lifestyle and education in the huge cities throughout the nation.

The rapid influx of moneyed foreign tourists and the constant bombardment of US and northern European media has opened many Spaniard's eyes to the lifestyles of more liberal peoples. These new ideas have started to affect many people's perspectives on life and the pursuit of both happiness and material items. Even in cities that supposedly have economic problems, there are often still long lines at trendy boutiques, restaurants, and major discos. Most urban dwellers now have credit cards, and the idea of buying now and paying later has certainly caught on in a big way, much to the liking of major banks who have hiked up interest rates to well above 30 percent annually.

Some things that have managed to remain the same is the sense of pride, history, and culture that each separate region still maintains. There is not one Spain, but rather several smaller Spains, each with its very own dialect or language, seasonal festivals, cuisine, and ways of life.

Four official languages can be heard in Spain, the most common spoken by about 73% of the population and is called **Castillian** (what we normally refer to as "Spanish"). Another 16% of the country speaks **Catalan** which can be heard mainly in the eastern region of Catalunya. The Portuguese sounding **Galician** language is used by some 8% of the people who mainly come from the country's northwest. Finally, the strange and ancient **Basque** language of the northern rural regions below France (which historians cannot seem to accurately trace to any specific time or place of origin) is the least common of the languages, spoken by just about 3% of people in Spain. Newspapers, television programs, radio broadcasts, and films produced in each specific region will most commonly use the main language of that area.

Since most of the people living in this large country have bloodlines that come from a mixture of Visigothic, Arab, Roman, and other assorted European civilizations, even the look of the Spanish people varies greatly depending on how far north or south you travel. Most of the people living here also share a strong commitment to family, and a good balance of hard work and even harder play. Lunches are frequently enjoyed at home with loved ones and can take several hours (and usually include several bottles of local wine).

Locals of all ages can be seen partying through the wee hours of the morning in the process of the famed *La Marcha*, a method of enjoying a drink and a *tapa* in one bar before moving on to several more rounds of snacks and alcohol in one venue after another. Other noticeable characteristics of many (but not all) Spaniards is that they might be stubborn, usually never in a rush to get things done, and tend to be quite late for appointments and meetings. It is commonplace in the south of Europe to find whole towns and major city downtown zones completely deserted for most of the mid afternoon!

All in all, the Spanish are nice people who are usually happy to share some of their culture and stories with willing foreigners. If you make it a point to visit small communities during their unique festivals you may witness everything from tomato- throwing fights, a haunting pig slaughtering, and strange mystical parades.

The most dramatic of these events may very well be during *Semana Santa* (Easter Week), when strange processions with medieval monsters and icons are carried through the streets of each community accompanied by the smells of strong incense and hypnotic chants from spectators. Bullfights are also well worth the effort to view, and give visitors even more insight into the soul and traditions of Spain.

FLAMENCO

Flamenco is a unique form of traditional music that originated at least 200 years ago with the gypsies of the Andalucía region. Originally performed only at family celebrations within the gypsy community, the music's haunting tones often expressed bad luck and tragedy. With the highly stylized guitar riffs, a male or female singer belts out a beautiful yet sad story of fate, with a level of seriousness and gut wrenching intensity that defies comparison. In some cases, a Flamenco performance may include dances by mysterious women dressed in polka-dotted ruffled dresses who are known to play castanets, clap, and stomp their feet in rhythm with the guitarist. Even the audience can occasionally get so involved that they too clap along and shout with encouragement.

These days the whole event has often become commercialized. Most tourists have their first and only exposure to this amazing art form at organized flamenco shows held in dozens of specialized night clubs (**tablaos**) in Madrid, Sevilla, and Granada. While these tourist trap events that cost upwards of 3,000 ptas per person may be either enjoyable or just plain boring, the real practitioners of Flamenco can best be found (often playing for free) in out-of-the-way taverns, a handful of small local bars in Sevilla and Granada, or at master classes held in back alley dance studios that few tourists ever seem to find. There are also fantastic summertime festivals for this unusual cultural event held in various cities in **Andalucía**.

The best way to find out about more serious events is to keep your eyes and ears open while wandering around Spain's southern-most cities and villages, or by asking local people who are not part of the tourist trade. I was lucky enough to get myself invited to join a gypsy family during a birthday celebration, when the real heart and soul of Flamenco was revealed to me. Unfortunately, gypsies are understandably difficult to befriend since their culture and values are very different from the mainstream of European society. They have always lived on the fringe of this society and have generally been despised and mistrusted throughout their centuries of wandering, yet have left an incredible musical legacy which we are still lucky enough to hear today.

5. A SHORT HISTORY

WAY BACK WHEN

Not much is known about the prehistoric residents who roamed in what is now southern Spain as far back as over 1,000,000 years ago. These possibly tribal people have left little evidence of their existence besides a few scattered relics and well preserved examples of later **Paleolithic** period cave paintings and megaliths.

Sometime around 3500 BC, Neolithic peoples began to develop agriculturally based settlements along the eastern and southern coasts. The next wave of inhabitants were, to say the least, a mixed lot. As the newly arrived **Phoenicians** and **Greeks** began to establish their own major settlements along the southern and eastern reaches of the peninsula, **Iberian** tribes competed for control over the central and northern regions by the second millennium BC. Later, some time around the 8th century BC, invading **Celts** began to move down through Europe and integrate with the Iberians to form the new **Celt-Iberian** culture.

The next wave of inhabitants were, to say the least, a mixed lot. During the first millennium before Christ, the **Phoenicians** and **Greeks** both started to establish their own major settlements along the southern and eastern reaches of the peninsula. It was the Greek settlers who were responsible for the introduction of both olives and grapes, two crops which are still prevalent in Spanish agriculture to this day.

THE ROMANS COME & GO

The area was fairly stable until the 4th century BC when the **Carthaginians** crossed over from Northern Africa. Their plan was to create a huge empire by swallowing up southern Spain and then to advance as far in every direction as possible. To put it mildly, the **Romans** were not about to stand around and watch the Iberian Peninsula be taken over by the Carthaginians, and thus began the **Second Punic War**. Once victorious, the Romans began a long period of domination, and started to create a powerful cultural, political, military, and civil infrastructure throughout the land they called **Hispania**.

Soon Hispania became a vastly important trading colony and was soon covered by roads that helped to transport its rich wines, olive oils, and natural resources to many other destinations throughout the Roman empire. It was during the later part of this era that **Christianity** would find its way here via the words of Saint Paul. **Latin** became the official language of this sector, and major cities were constructed with the inclusion of arched stone bridges, aqueducts, and theaters. Today, many fine examples of these remarkable Roman era monuments and elaborate structures can still be seen standing in almost every region of Spain.

With the passage of more than 750 years in the region, the Roman Empire had finally started to decline. Owing to their vulnerability, by the 5th century AD they were forced to invite the help of the **Visigoths** to repel constant incursions by powerful **Germanic** forces. The Visigoths stayed after the collapse of the Roman empire, and began to build churches and cities throughout the center of what is now Spain. They ruled well, but were soon divided over which clans should be in charge of what territories.

THE MOORISH INVASION

As the disputes developed into full scale civil wars between Visigothic clans, the **Moors** from Northern Africa decided to invade this ravaged kingdom. By the year 718 the Muslim armies had conquered all of the south and were attempting to extend their reach as far north as possible. Churches in southern Hispania were soon replaced with Arabic mosques, new Muslim laws were instituted, and the nation of **Al-Andalus**, centered around what is now the region of **Andalucía**, remained firmly under Moorish control for over 750 more years. The Emirs and Caliphs had begun to establish universities, palaces, and new irrigation systems around their great southern cities that are now known as Granada, Sevilla, and Córdoba.

Many of the remaining Christians and Jews now found themselves living in Muslim controlled territories yet were able to find a way to live and work together with the Moors who were surprisingly tolerant of their differing cultural backgrounds. In fact, under the Arabs, many of these non-Islamic residents were permitted to practice their trade and religion much more freely than they had been allowed to under previous Roman and Visigothic rule, as long as they paid high taxes to the local authorities (taxes which were not imposed on their Muslim neighbors).

New sophisticated industries such as large scale agriculture, the production of silk, paper, filigree jewelry and finely crafted leather began to appear within Andalucia. Countless acres of fertile lands were planted for the first time with sugar cane, bananas, and date palms, crops which can still be found growing among several more recently transplanted crops along Spain's rural landscape.

For several centuries, art and culture in the Moorish society of Al-Andalus began to flourish. Muslim scholars brought new concepts and ideas with them to this newly acquired territory, along with massive libraries to help promote the study of the Sciences such as animal husbandry, astronomy, agricultural irrigation and (somewhat effective) medical procedures. Among the many fine civil and religious structures built during this era are the massive **Mesquita** mosque in Córdoba, the awesome **Alhambra** fortress in Toledo, and the fantastic **Giralda** prayer tower and regal **Alcázar** palace in Sevilla that are all embellished with unmistakable Moorish horseshoe arches and Arabic inscriptions, and all of which can still be viewed today.

During this time, the north of Hispania was still controlled by Christians who had vowed to repel any Muslim thoughts or influence in their lands. By the late 10th century, the powerful **Caliphate of Córdoba** sent his troops northwards, all the way to the Christian holy city of Santiago de Compostela and completely destroyed it.

THE CHRISTIAN RECONQUEST

While all this was taking place, the northern Christians had no desire to give up their way of life and historical claim to their lands, and thus began plans for a **Reconquista** (reconquest of the Christian Territories) of the entire Iberian peninsula. After the cities of Córdoba and Sevilla fell in 1236 and 1248 respectively, a series of battles continued on for hundreds of years in which the Christians were dedicated to capturing all of Hispania from the Muslims.

It was during this era that the Jews found themselves victims of violence and persecution in the Christian held areas. Although most of those who converted were allowed to remain members of Spanish society, many others were killed or exiled. At about the same time, many of the defeated Moors were allowed to remain Islamic (now referred to as *Mudejar*) and to work as artisans. It was not until the 15th century marriage of Queen Isabella of Castilla and King Fernando V of Aragón that the Christian population and armies of the north were consolidated. A series of bloody battles took place culminating in the capture of Granada on January, 2, 1492 when the Reconquest had achieved the goal of defeating the Arabs and re-taking control over all of what is still called **España**.

The royal family encouraged the expansion of their kingdom, and both international commerce and exploration began to be a main objective of this now unshakable Christian land. At about the same time that **Columbus** was being paid to find a new route to India (and found himself bumping into the Americas), the Catholic Monarchs, along with help from the Church, imposed a ruthless 200 year long **Inquisition** in which freedom of expression was totally restricted, intellectuals were either imprisoned or tortured, and all of the remaining 150,000 or so Jews were eventually expelled from the country.

THE HABSBURG DYNASTY

After the death of King Fernando in 1516, a successor was sought to sit on the throne and help the country continue to expand its global sphere of influence. After much debate and posturing, his teenage grandson, the heir apparent to the Austrian-based Habsburg empire was soon crowned as **King Carlos V**. The new and rather young king was raised mainly in the Netherlands and neither lived in Spain nor spoke a word of Spanish, and this greatly distressed most Spaniards. He in fact dispatched a series of Austrian and Flemish nobles and their troops to help him rule Spain with an iron fist and with little regard to the ways of life and politics that had preceded his rule, which in turn upset his subjects even more.

The result of this distrust was the failed **Comuneros rebellion** in the province of Castilla, where several disloyal residents, including the famed **Juan Bravo** of Segovia, were executed after their capture. However, as King Carlos V matured and began to realize Spanish ways and sense of pride, he was finally accepted as their true leader.

This period marked the real beginning of Spain's **Golden Age**, as King Carlos V sent out his unstoppable **conquistadores** who returned from the New World with incalculable wealth to the crown, as well as assuring the inclusion of much of the Americas (known in Spain as the "Indies") in his empire that already extended to such areas as Germany, Austria, Italy, and Holland. Many of the remaining historic maps and documents relating to the discovery (and sometimes ruthless exploitation) of these new lands and their peoples by explorers like Pizzaro and Cortes can still be viewed in the **Archivo General de Indias** in Sevilla. By 1578 the kingdom, now lead by Carlos V's son **King Felipe II**, had succeeded in absorbing Portugal and her rich colonies such as Brazil into the ever-growing power base.

THE EMPIRE BEGINS TO CRUMBLE

Other European nations were becoming increasingly suspicious of and uncomfortable with the powerful Iberian empire's seemingly endless greed for additional territories and global control. All of the demands of holding together a far-flung empire took a serious toll on the economy and military strength of Spain. First, the leader of the repressed Protestant peoples of the northern Netherlands, **Prince William of Orange**, declared his intention of leading his supporters in an uprising designed to end their domination by King Felipe II and his General, the Duke of Alba. The British navy began to assist the Protestants in order to help them try and break away from any form of Spanish rule. A decision was then made by King Felipe II to attack the British fleet to assure that they could no longer try to interfere with his repressive control of Holland.

On a hot summer's day in 1588, a huge **Spanish Armada** consisting of over 132 vessels and 30,000 troops departed for the English Channel. First a huge storm sank several of the Armada's ships before they even got half way to their targets, while most of the remaining warships were destroyed by their faster and better equipped British counterparts. The destruction of the Spanish Armada marked the slow and steady decline of the Iberian domination of Europe and the Americas. Even on the mainland, problems continued to build up.

When **King Felipe III** ascended the throne, he ordered the expulsion of the remaining 275,000 or so *Moriscos* (Moors who had converted to Christianity), leaving almost nobody left in Spain who was willing to do the basic jobs necessary to maintain factories, farms, and even the most basic construction projects. As economic conditions grew increasingly worse, Spain's entry in 1618 to the vicious **Thirty Years War** began to suck up all of the throne's remaining economic resources. The people of Portugal and the northern Netherlands won their independence, while continuing domestic revolts in the Catalunya region further weakened the now faltering kingdom.

THE BOURBON DYNASTY

When King Charles II died in 1700, leaving no heir apparent to the throne, the so-called **War of Spanish Succession** ensued, with claimants from several European royal families fighting for what they were sure was their rightful place as the new rulers of Spain and her diminishing territories. The 1713 **Treaty of Utrecht** led to the resolution of the conflict with the officially recognized coronation of **King Filipe V** (the grandson of France's King Louis XIV). The Bourbon dynasty had now firmly established itself on Spain's throne, but the empire lost control of the last remaining Flemish and Italian possessions, as well as control over Gibraltar, in the process.

Over the course of the next two centuries, major wars and struggles were necessary to keep a grip on those far away lands that had a few ideas about their own self-determination. It was also during this time when the British navy, under the direction of **Lord Nelson**, responding to a declaration of war from Spain, once again pummeled their fleet during the disastrous 1805 **Battle of Trafalgar**. Soon after this, **Napoleon** decided to get a piece of the action and began a four year occupation over much of Spain until his forces were repelled by General Wellington's English troops in 1813. By the end of the 19th century, almost all of Spain's distant colonies including those in South America achieved independence from the Spanish crown while the Philippines, Cuba, and Puerto Rico were then lost in the disastrous **Spanish American War.**

A series of contested royal successions caused the nation to become bitterly involved with three separate **Carlist Wars,** which in turn caused revolts that led to impositions of dictatorships. The resulting social and political instability that racked Spain at this point had serious consequences, including a long series of both major and minor uprisings and the struggle for power between rival liberal and conservative factions within the government.

King Alfonso XIII took the throne in 1902, and for a time things seemed to improve; but a coup in 1923 allowed the country to be ruled by the dictatorial regime of **General Primo de Rivera.** Although Spain remained neutral during **World War I,** the country's economy was still subjected to manic bouts of economic prosperity followed by dangerous recessions. In 1930 General Primo de Rivera died, and King Alfonso XIII was forced to call a new series of elections.

CIVIL UNREST & CIVIL WAR

As the liberal and anti-monarchist socialists came to power and created the so-called **Second Republic** in 1931, the King abdicated, and a new constitution guaranteeing enhanced political freedoms and the separation of church and state was instituted. The right wing politicians and their military cronies became furious and the political parties were further polarized. At about the same time the provinices of northern Spain began to seek their own independance, thus adding up to the pile of frustrations that finally broke out into what would become the start of the ruthless **Spanish Civil War.**

After a victory by the left-wing **Popular Front** party in the 1936 national elections, a long series of general strikes immobilized the nation's work force and fragile economy. During a mutiny by soldiers led by fascist troops on a Spanish military base in Morocco in July of 1936, **General Francisco Franco** flew in from his post on the Canary Islands to take charge of what was intended to become a rapid full-scale coup, with battles and military-led revolts quickly spreading throughout several sections of the country.

As the **Nationalist** forces began to succeed in taking over large parts of southern and western Spain, their troops and sympathizers began to wage a bloody war with **Republican** soldiers and citizens still faithful to their newly elected government. Since the revolting soldiers did not manage to take over all of the nation at first, a civil war broke out in which an estimated 250,000 people on both sides of the conflict may have been murdered in cold blood, although the official tally still rests at only 85,940 victims.

Those loyal to the government still held on to the capital of Madrid, while the Nationalists declared General Franco as their head of state for the duration of the conflict. Soon many foreigners got into the action, with over 100,000 poorly trained but highly motivated leftists siding up with the so-called **International Brigade** to help fight off the fascist Nationalist army, while Germany and Italy supplied well-seasoned troops and technicians to assist Franco's offensives. Atrocities were common on both sides: the government allied forces killed approximately 14,000 clergymen who spoke out in favor of the Fascists, and the Nationalists conspired with the Nazi airforce to carry out horrific German-led air bombing raids of **Guernica** and other defenseless Basque cities loyal to the Republicans, resulting in the first ever bombardment of a civilian population with little, if any, military or strategic significance.

In the long run, the Nationalists had the upper hand. After the fall of Madrid and Barcelona, they finally took control of what was left of Spain in less than three years, leaving over half a million dead in the process. By the end of the year the new leader and his government were officially recognized by almost all of the world's most powerful nations. Once in control, Franco's Fascist henchmen carried out a seemingly endless string of summary executions, politically motivated tortures, and the vengeful imprisonment and suppression of all those who supported the losing side. This marked the beginning of Franco's long and iron-fisted dictatorship of Spain.

Life for those living in Spain for the first decade after the war was extremely difficult due to the mass destruction of the infrastructure and economy that had occurred during the struggle. The nation would once again declare itself neutral in **World War II**, and by the 1950s Franco's government had secured a $1 billion deal with the Americans to allow US military bases to be built in Spain just after the country was allowed to become a member of the United Nations.

While most of the intellectuals who survived the war soon emigrated to more liberal European nations, the economy eventually re-stabilized, and new state-sponsored industries such as factories and tourism began to spread out over all of Spain. It was clear to all the citizens of Spain that if your community played by the rules and didn't denounce or question the current leadership, it would be among the first to benefit financially.

Since much of Franco's opposition came from Madrid, Barcelona, and especially the fiercely independent northern Basque-populated regions, they suffered the most during his long reign as a self-imposed ruler. Much of the profitable heavy industry was moved from these zones to districts that were more loyal during the war. As a result, these once staunchly Republican areas were racked with high unemployment, housing shortages, poor medical care, and insufficient transportation systems for many years to follow.

Following the suppression of a series of Basque separatist uprisings in northern Spain during the early 1970's, the **E.T.A.** revolutionary movement assassinated Prime Minister Carrero Blanco (Franco's heir apparent), in an act of political terror that still continues to this day. The Basques still feel that they have a right to their own separate homeland free from all of Madrid's constant interference, and have been known to shoot, bomb, and kidnap those who get in their way.

One recent scandal that may rock the current government has proven that Spanish secret police infiltrated southern France in an effort to assassinate underground E.T.A. members and financial supporters, while in the process perhaps killing some innocent civilians who had little if anything to do with the terrorists. While most of the Basque people publicly state they do not agree with E.T.A.'s tactics, some still will confide to their closest friends that they do not feel Spain has any right to govern them.

THE THRONE IS RESTORED

In 1975 Franco died, and Bourbon **King Juan Carlos** assumed the throne. The new King was immediately embraced by popular support, and the flood gates were lifted to allow for much more liberal socialization and individual freedoms. Democratic elections were held, a new constitution was soon drafted, freedom of the press was restored, and the nation was well on it's way to becoming an industrial and economic power.

In 1982, Spain joined NATO, and democracy was assured for the citizens of this now thriving nation. In 1990, Spain joined the **European Economic Community** and went on to secure the **1992 Olympic Games** for Barcelona, and gained unprecedented international publicity by hosting **EXPO 1992** in Sevilla.

SPAIN TODAY

The current Prime Minister of Spain, **Jose Maria Aznar**, and his P.P. political party, have once again been re-elected. Political violence is on the wane, although the Basque separatists still engage in high profile political kidnapping and assassinations throughout Spain. While he stays aloof from much of the controversial problems facing his nation, King Juan Carlos is still adored by the vast majority of his subjects.

6. PLANNING YOUR TRIP

BEFORE YOU GO

WHEN TO VISIT SPAIN

Your best bet is to visit Spain in the **spring**, from late March through June or early **fall**, September to early October. These times offer the visitor (generally) pleasant warm weather and the benefit of abundant available accommodations and airfare at low season rates. Just be careful to avoid the Easter or *Semana Santa* holidays, when all of Spain goes on vacation and hotels sell out well in advance – even with the 50% or higher surcharges they impose! Rain falls in generally low quantities during these months, with the possible exception of the northern regions of the country where you may need an umbrella.

If you are interested in visiting beaches when the ocean is warm and the sun is hot enough to bake under, you may prefer the **summer** season, June through August. During these months, almost all of Eastern and Southern Spain becomes burning hot and overcrowded with vacationing tourists from all over the globe. Since most Europeans receive a full month of vacation with pay (typically during August) the airlines and hotels have no problem increasing their rates by over 75% during these summer months. Although I have enjoyed the summers in Spain, they are typically not much of a bargain.

The **winter** season, November through February, is a great time to visit the southeastern and southernmost reaches of Spain and the major cities throughout the country. Rain and snow are not uncommon to all but the southeastern and extreme southern regions of Spain during this time of year. The roads in the northern regions are often closed to traffic, and most of the central zone is rather cold at night. The *Costa del Sol*, *Sevilla*, *Valencia*, and *Alicante* areas are still drenched with sunlight during much of the winter, but the climate is usually just warm.

AVERAGE HIGH & LOW DAILY TEMPERATURES

	Madrid High/Low	Barcelona High/Low	Sevilla High Low
Jan.	48F/36F 9C/3C	54F/42F 12C/05C	60F/44F 16C/4C
Feb.	52F/36F 12C/3C	57F/44F 14C/7C	63F/46F 18C/8C
Mar.	59F/41F 15C/5C	61F/47F 16C/8C	69F/48F 20C/9C
Apr.	65F/46F 19C/9C	65F/54F 19C/12C	76F/52F 24C/11C
May	70F/49F 21C/10C	70F/56F 21C/12C	82F/56F 28C/12C
Jun.	80F/59F 27C/15C	78F/65F 25C/19C	86F/65F 30C/19C
Jul.	88F/62F 31C/17C	82F/71F 28C/22C	96F/68F 35C/21C
Aug.	86F/63F 30C/18C	82F/71F 28C/22C	97F/68F 36C/21C
Sep.	76F/56F 24C/14C	78F/66F 25C/20C	90F/63F 33C/18C
Oct.	65F/50F 19C/10C	70F/58F 21C/14C	78F/56F 25C/13C
Nov.	54F/40F 12C/5C	62F/51F 17C/11C	67F/51F 20C/11C
Dec.	48F/36F 9C/03C	55F/45F 13C/7C	62F/44F 16C/6C

WHAT TO PACK

When visiting Spain there are several items that will come in handy, and others that you won't need. To begin with, most visitors will not need suits, ties, expensive dresses, and formal clothing. Only a handful of 5 star gourmet restaurants and snobby nightclubs will enforce a strict dress code. Any hotel will be pleased to welcome guests that are comfortably attired. Even the most important churches will never insist on visitors wearing long pants or long sleeve shirts.

The main concern about what to bring to wear should be based on the season. Since **summer** can be quite hot, I suggest lots of thin cotton clothing. In the **spring** and **fall** it would be wise to pack for mostly warm days and chilly nights, with the possibility of rain at any time. In the **winter** you should be prepared for anything from rain and snow to unexpected heat waves.

In all seasons, I suggest that you pack a money belt or sack, an umbrella, bathing suits, a sweater, comfortable walking shoes, sneakers, a waterproof wind breaker, extra glasses or contact lenses, necessary medications with copies of the prescriptions, personal hygiene items, sunglasses, an empty nylon bag for gifts and shopping, an electric converter, suntan lotion, lots of film and batteries, a waterproof key holder for swimming, photocopies of your passport, travel insurance documents, a list of travelers check numbers, good maps, the phone numbers of your travel provider your credit card companies in case of emergency and this book!

PASSPORTS & VISAS

Typically, all US and Canadian citizens require only a valid **passport** to enter Spain. I should however mention that a series of recent disputes between Canada and the Spanish fishing fleet have lead to the occasional requirement for a **visa**, so call the Spanish consulate in your country to double-check the current regulations. Visitors who intend to spend more than 90 days within Spain may need to register with the government to receive official permission to reside here longer, so please call the Spanish consulate for exact details.

Lost or Stolen Passports

Just in case you happen to somehow misplace your passport, or need the help and advice of your own government, please contact your country's embassy. They can also provide other services which your tax dollars are paying for, including travel advisories on other countries that you may wish to visit while overseas, lists of local English speaking medical specialists, and other valuable details.

NORTH AMERICAN EMBASSIES & CONSULATES

American Embassy in Madrid, Calle Serrano, 75. Tel. (91) 577-4000

American Consulate in Sevilla, Paseo de las Delicias, 7. Tel. (95) 423-1883

American Consulate in Barcelona, Passeig de la Reina Elisendra, 23. Tel. (93) 280-2227

Canadian Embassy in Madrid, Calle Nunez de Balboa, 35. Tel. (91) 431-4300

Canadian Consulate in Sevilla, Ave. de la Constitucion, 30. Tel. (95) 422-9413

Canadian Consulate in Barcelona, Via Augusta, 125. Tel. (93) 209-0634

SPANISH EMBASSIES IN NORTH AMERICA

Spanish Embassy in Canada, 350 Sparks Street, Ottawa, Ontario K1R 7S8, Tel. 613/237-2193

Spanish Embassy in the US, 2375 Pennsylvania Ave., NW, Washington, D.C. 20009, Tel. 202/452-0100

CUSTOMS REGULATIONS UPON ARRIVAL IN SPAIN

Customs and immigration officials are very relaxed in Spain, except for those working the ferry terminals from Africa where drugs are commonly smuggled. I have very rarely seen anyone subjected to a luggage search at an airport here.

The following is excerpted from the official Spanish customs regulations at press time. Check with Spain's consulates if you need further details.

North Americans arriving in Spain are allowed to bring an unlimited amount of cash for means of payment for tourist or travel expenses. Adults are each allowed to import into Spain the following amounts of these products:

- **Cigarettes**   200

or

- **Cigarillos**   100

or

- **Cigars**   50
- **Perfumes**   50 grams
- **Liquor**   1 liter
- **Wine**   2 liters

All North American visitors are allowed, for temporary importation, objects for personal use which must leave with them upon departure: personal jewelry, cameras and video cameras, a reasonable quantity of film and accessories, binoculars, sports equipment such as tents and camping gear, fishing gear, guns (check with airline for restrictions), non-motorized bicycles, tennis rackets, wind surfing boards, delta wings, musical instruments, sound recording equipment, radios and televisions, video recorders, typewriters, calculators, and personal computers.

If you have any additional questions, contact one of the Spanish embassies on this side of the ocean before you depart.

UPON YOUR RETURN TO NORTH AMERICA

All US citizens can return to America with up to $400 US without paying duty if you have left the US for over 48 hours and haven't made another international trip within the last 30 days. Each family member is eligible for the same limits, and these amounts may be pooled together. Normally a 10% duty will be assessed on goods which have exceeded the $400 US value, but are below $1400 in total value. Above this point the duty will vary with the specific merchandise being imported. Each adult may also bring in up to 1 liter of wine or alcohol and either 100 cigars (except from Cuba) or 200 cigarettes. There is no duty on antiquities or works of art which are over 100 years old. Bring all receipts with the merchandise to customs to avoid additional problems.

All Canadian citizens can return to Canada with up to $300 CD once each year if you have left Canada for over 7 days, or up to $100 CD several times each year if you have left Canada for over 48 hours. Each family member is eligible for the same limits per person. Normally a combination of federal and provincial taxes will be assessed on goods that have exceeded the $300 CD value depending on the specific items involved. Each adult can also bring in 1.14 liters of alcohol or 8.5 liters (24 cans or bottles each with 12 ounces) of beer. Also allowed for those at least 16 years old are up to 50 cigars, 200 cigarettes, and 400 grams of tobacco. Bring all receipts with the merchandise to customs to avoid additional problems.

NATIONAL TOURIST OFFICES OF SPAIN (LOCATED IN NORTH AMERICA)

Before you plan your vacation in Spain, it would be a good idea to contact the **National Tourist Office of Spain** in your country. If you ask a few questions relating to your specific interests, these offices will send you large manila envelopes full of maps, English language tourist information, artistically designed regional summaries, phrase books, and maybe even a few glossy brochures from the powerful and well connected major tour operators.

The receptionists at these offices are usually very informative Spaniards who are trying their best to keep up with the tidal wave of daily inquiries. If their line seems constantly busy, or if they don't seem to have the time to answer many questions, it's only because they are so understaffed. These are nice people who have a huge amount of work to do, so you must consider the fact that they just can't spend lots of time with call-ins.

On the other hand, a personal visit to one of the National Tourist Offices can result in a somewhat more intensive discussion and the chance to receive much more specific printed material. The Spanish government's **Ministerio de Comercio y Turismo** tourism division prints hundreds of useful documents in several languages, which are then eventually sent along to their tourist offices throughout the world.

Tourist Offices Addresses
- **National Tourist Office of Spain**, *665 Fifth Ave., New York, N.Y. 10022, Tel. 212/759-8822*
- **National Tourist Office of Spain**, *102 Bloor St. West, Suite 1400, Toronto, Ontario, Canada M5S 1M8, Tel. 416/961-3131*

BOOKING YOUR VACATION

Hopefully, with the help of this guidebook, you will have most of the information and suggestions necessary to begin planning your trip. The next step to create a near stress-free vacation is to start making your reservations. I strongly advise that after you have made your bookings, you consider prepaying your airfare, rental car(s), and some or all of your desired accommodations. Especially if you are traveling to Spain during Easter week or the summer months of June through September, do not expect to find much availability in the many tourist-preferred seaside and city hotels and inns by just showing up.

Book your most desired high-season accommodations well in advance. In the low seasons, I suggest that you book at least the first few and last few nights of hotels in advance, and then try to find a few places along the way on your own.

Travel Agents

Travel agents are hard working consultants who usually get paid on a commission basis. If a client desires a normal package tour, no additional fee should be charged, as the agent's commission of between 8% and 12% is built into the package's retail price. For special custom vacations (known in the industry as an F.I.T.), travel agents may charge as much as $150 extra per couple or family in advance to cover the extra hours of work involved and the many long distance calls or faxes which will be required. Each advance revision or cancellation may be heavily penalized with stiff fees, or just as often may be fully non-refundable. The only problem is that very few travel agents have much first-hand knowledge about the more exotic destinations and inns of Spain.

Travel agents do however, have access to somewhat helpful computer databases which can search out the least expensive regularly scheduled airfares or charter flights offered by leading international airlines, and also can look up basic information about over 16,500 hotels throughout the world. Travel agents (and a few savvy frequent travelers) also have access to industry only hotel information books such as the **Hotel and Travel Index** or the **Official Hotel Guide** that are published by the Reed Travel Group which gives somewhat detailed basic listings on tens of thousands of major hotels. Unfortunately, the best deals on airfare, and most remarkable accommodations in Spain are not necessarily going to appear in a travel agent's computer. What distinguishes a good agent from a great agent is quite clear. A good travel agent will either know first hand about the country you are visiting, or will offer to make a few calls and find out more. A great agent (and they are around if you look) will spend lots of time and energy researching their client's destination, and will work with you to book exactly what you want.

No matter whom you pick to assist you with your travel plans, make sure you are at least as equally well informed. The more specific that you can be about what type of trip and price range you want, the closer you'll get to matching your dreams with reality.

Tour Operators

These are the wholesale sources for well over 75% of the package tours and 35% of the F.I.T. custom vacations originating in North America. A good tour operator will specialize in just one or a few different countries, with a staff of experts who have been to hundreds of hotels and inns located in the countries that they represent. Unfortunately many tour operators do not sell directly to the public simply preferring to deal with travel agencies to avoid lengthy phone calls with uninformed travelers.

I have included a list of a few tour operators who are willing to sell directly to the public. Because the staff of most tour operators do not get paid by commission, their suggestions tend to be honest evaluations of first hand experiences. Unlike travel agencies, these companies often charge a much more reasonable penalty for each revision or cancellation made in advance. They usually offer discounted package rates on dozens of well known and even less famous Spanish hotels and rental apartments in all price ranges.

I have called all of these operators myself and have included a range of the ones I feel are the most honest, experienced, and informative based on different lifestyles, experiences, and needs of prospective visitors to Spain. They are listed below in order of their helpfulness and accuracy. While they all tend to work more often with travel agencies, they will all allow direct bookings from well informed individuals that know what they want.

RECOMMENDED TOUR OPERATORS WHO SELL DIRECT TO THE PUBLIC

MARKETING AHEAD, *Tel. 800/223-1356*

An excellent company representing hotels, paradores, haciendas, resorts, apart-hotels, and small luxury inns. They offer confirmed pre-paid reservations at reasonable rates, good airfare prices, rental car bargains, and much more. The staff have all been to both Spain and Portugal and can talk with plenty of first hand experience. Marketing Ahead is one of only a few official representatives for all of Spain's 80 or so wonderful *paradores* as well as all of Portugal's fine *pousadas*. Their service is first rate, prices quite competitive, and I highly recommend their services.

PETRABAX TOURS, *Tel. 800/367-6611*

Back when I was still active in the travel industry, I would refer my most serious clients to this great tour operator. Based in Los Angeles with additional offices in New York, Petrabax offers a full range of pre-packaged fly/drives, and excellent, yet affordable, escorted motor coach trips through all regions of Spain. Call and ask them to send you a free packet of detailed information on their impressive range of services. Highly recommended as the best and most impressive tour operator serving Spain!

ALTA TOURS, *Tel. 800/338-4191*

Based in San Francisco, this extremely good specialty tour operator has the right connections to book all sorts of customized and package travel itineraries throughout Spain. They have quoted me excellent prices on fly/drive packages, round-trip airfare, car rentals, and even escorted bus tours of various regions in Spain. Give them a ring and ask for one of their seasonal brochures to the Iberian Peninsula that will help you to plan a great vacation in any price range.

TAUCK TOURS, *Tel. 800/468-2825*

If you are the type of person who is looking for the most deluxe guided tours through Spain that money can buy, this is by far the best source. With many years of experience catering to an upscale bus-tour market of mainly 45+ year old clients, the people at Tauck continue to receive my highest ratings for customer service and exceptional value for the money. Among their several scheduled all inclusive itineraries are a 14 day trip through northern Spain, and a different 14 day trip combining both Spain and Portugal, using superb hotels, restaurants, guides, and excursions. Highly recommended as the finest deluxe bus tour operator for Europe!

SUN TOURS, *Tel. 800/387-9923*

For those looking for a vacation featuring a large range of 3 and 4 star hotels throughout Spain, as well as a huge selection of apart-hotels with kitchens in the Costa del Sol, they offer great prices. The staff has lots of specific details about each hotel and airline they represent, and can offer transfers, rental cars, airfare on major European carriers, escorted bus tours, and even can provide you with one of the industry's best trip cancellation and interruption insurance policies.

PERRYGOLF, *Tel. 800/344-5257*

An excellent golf program tour operator which offers a full range of one week or longer golf vacations in the Costa del Sol and eastern Spain's finest golf resorts and courses. They can provide airfare, accommodations, and golf. Excellent service from a staff of dedicated golf enthusiasts, some of which have been to Spain.

DISCOVER SPAIN, *Tel. 800/227-5858*

This company can help get you special rates on paradores, hotels, apart-hotels, rental cars, and airfares. Besides being honest and informative, this company will make life simple for you, if you know exactly where and what you want to book. The prices were also impressively low, especially during the off-season!

DELTA DREAM VACATIONS, *Tel. 800/872-7786*

A full service tour operator managed by Delta airlines which offers airfare, hotels, cars, and other services for the major Spanish resorts and large cities. They also have the ability to sell vouchers for hotels in some other regions. Some of the staff have been to Spain, the service is pretty good for such a big company, plus you get even more frequent-flyer points on Delta.

AMERICAN EXPRESS VACATIONS, *Tel. 800/241-1700*

A full service tour operator which offers airfare, hotels, cars, and other services to the Madrid and Barcelona areas only. Most of the staff have not ever been to Spain, and the service is efficient but not particularly informative. A good choice for businessmen on short city-center business trips.

MAJOR HOTEL REPRESENTATIVES

Thousands of experienced world travelers plan their own hotel stays after weeks of intensive research. The following is a partial listing of the best hotel groups and representatives that deal both with travel agents, and directly with the public in North America. There are hundreds of other good companies, but these are (in my experience of more than 10 years in the travel industry) among the very best.

First decide what your budget really is going to be, which nights you wish to be in which city, and have a good idea of the specific location and ambiance you are looking for in a hotel. After everything is listed on a piece of paper, call one of these phone numbers to reach an agent who can send a huge color brochure, make a reservation with a major credit card, request specific room categories, and perhaps even offer a special (corporate, weekend, off-season) rate that nobody else even knew existed.

Although these companies prefer to work via a travel agent, they will still help individuals book spectacular hotels all over the world.

RELAIS & CHATEAUX, *Tel. 800/735-2478* or *Tel. 212/856-0115*

This magnificent collection of unforgettable gourmet restaurants and charming little luxury properties around the world is perfect for those travelers expecting the highest standards of quality and service. While most of the properties are located in the northeast of Spain and fall into the higher price categories, you should consider spending at least a night or two in one of these truly memorable inns. Relais & Chateaux offers a dozen fine inns, converted castles, and superb restaurants in Spain.

LEADING HOTELS OF THE WORLD, *Tel. 800/223-6800*

With a wonderful selection of medium and larger-sized famous 4 and 5 star hotels throughout the world, their name says it all! They represent 11 of the highest quality luxury properties in the major city centers and nearby rural and coastal areas of Spain. All of these remarkable hotels offer a vast array of services and conference facilities, and provide a great setting for deluxe travelers and businessmen.

THE LUXURY COLLECTION, *Tel. 800/221-2340*

Now owned by ITT Sheraton Hotels, this select group of luxury hotels worldwide has a strong presence in Spain, with five excellent properties that were formerly part of the world famous Ciga hotel chain. Beautifully decorated rooms, top quality amenities, friendly multilingual staff, and gorgeous Old World style public spaces prevail in each and every one of their hotels.

HYATT INTERNATIONAL HOTELS, *Tel. 800/223-1234*

Hyatt's selection of stunningly beautiful modern deluxe resorts and hotels includes two fantastic properties in Spain. Besides offering wonderful spacious accommodations with every comfort, they also offer unique supervised children's activities programs and countless other services and facilities.

SMALL LUXURY HOTELS OF THE WORLD, *Tel. 800/525-4800*

This medium-sized company offers a selection of romantic manor houses, boutique style 4 and 5 star luxury hotels, and enchanting resorts on every continent. Their only two member properties in Spain can be found in Madrid and Barcelona, and both consistently receive my highest ratings.

UTELL INTERNATIONAL, *Tel. 800/44-UTELL*

This highly respected industry powerhouse offers instantaneous pricing, information, and reservations at well over 6,500 different 2 through 5 star hotels worldwide, including at least 250 in Spain in all price ranges. Their hard-working reservation agents just need to know what price you are looking for, and their advanced computer system selects several choices from which to choose.

GOLDEN TULIP HOTELS, *Tel. 800/344-1212*

When I want to book myself into a really good full-facility European hotel in the moderate price range, I make sure to give a ring to this great resource. Among the dozens of carefully selected properties they represent in Spain is a core group of excellent value 3 and 4 star city center hotels with huge rooms and extremely nice staff members.

BUYING FLEXIBLE VOUCHER BOOKLETS FOR HOTELS IN SPAIN

For those who wish to wait until their arrival to decide which cities, resorts, and hotels they wish to stay in, there exists a special voucher system for sale in Spain. The companies that create these voucher booklets are called **Hotel Color**, **Ibercheque**, and **Bancotel**. How it works is you pay an average of 37,500 *ptas* for a book of vouchers which will entitle the bearers to 5 nights of accommodations in double rooms (not including meals or taxes).

Holders of these vouchers can call one or more of the several hundred 3 and 4 star hotels that participate in this scheme, and after informing the hotel's reservation department that they will be using a specific brand of voucher, they can reserve a night for use with the voucher at 7,500 *ptas* per night per double room (often times a 40% or more discount to the hotel's normal posted rack rates). Of course some blackout dates apply, and a small minority of the hotels involved may still require a supplemental charge during certain high season months, but if you read the terms and conditions of these vouchers carefully you can save plenty of money year round. These vouchers are available at any good travel agency in Spain and usually expire on the 31 March of the year after they are purchased, do not generally include the hotel taxes, and are generally non-refundable. These vouchers may also be used to rent cars, take golf lessons, receive entrance passes to theme parks, and to get discounts on airlines and ferries. Almost all of these voucher programs also allow use of the same vouchers at a limited number of good hotels in several other European countries including neighboring Portugal.

For a free 50+ page booklet containing all included hotels, special services, blackout dates, and exact terms and conditions for use of the vouchers (available in Spanish only!) please visit each company's website, or pop into any major travel agency in Spain.

• *Hotel Color via the internet:www.mundicolor.es*
• *Bancotel via the internet: www.bancotel.es*
• *Ibercheque via the internet: www.ibercheque.es*

TRAVEL EMERGENCY & MEDICAL INSURANCE

One of the most important issues of any trip abroad is what to do in an emergency. Since the possibility of a medical problem is always a factor of risk, it is strongly advised that you take out an insurance policy. The best types of travel insurance are in the "Primary Coverage" category.

In an emergency, most of these policies will provide 24 hour toll-free help desks, lists of approved specialists, the ability to airlift you to a hospital with the proper facilities for your condition, and much more valuable assistance including refunds on additional expenses and unused hotel nights.

TRIP CANCELLATION & INTERRUPTION INSURANCE

Many special policies also cover vacation refunds if a family member gets ill and you must cancel your trip, if the airline you were supposed to be flying on goes out of business, if you must depart early from your trip due to sickness or death in the family, if the airline fails to deliver your baggage on time, if your luggage is stolen from your car, if your stay is extended due to injury, etc. Some elements, which are normally not covered, include airplane schedule changes, missed connections, and flight cancellations. Please check with your travel agent, tour operator, or the Canadian and American Automobile Agencies for further details.

Travel Insurance Companies
• **Mutual of Omaha (Tele-Trip)**, *Tel. 800/228-9792 in the US; Tel. 402/351-8000 in Canada*
• **Travel Guard**, *Tel. 715/345-0505 in the US and Canada*
• **Crown Life Travel Insurance**, *Tel. 800/265-0261 in Canada*
• **Access America**, *Tel. 800/284-8300 in the US and Canada*

NON-STOP FLIGHTS TO SPAIN

IBERIA AIRLINES, *Tel. 800/772-4642 in the US; Tel. 800/423-7421 in Canada; Tel. 900/100-223 in Spain*

The best way to get to Spain from North America is Iberia Airlines. They offer non-stop and direct flights scheduled several times weekly from Montreal, Toronto, New York, and Miami, the international carrier of Spain. For those in other major cities throughout North America, discounted add-on flight fares are available from Iberia on selected other airlines that allow for an easy connection via the above-listed hubs in both directions.

The lowest currently published round-trip prices (known in the travel business as promotional apex fares) to Madrid start at around $583 US plus taxes from New York, $648 US plus taxes from Miami, and $738 CD plus taxes from either Montreal or Toronto. Generally, when traveling with an adult, children under 12 years old may qualify for a 25% discount, while infants under two years of age sitting on the lap of the adult may be entitled to a 90% discount. There are also special fares for students, senior citizens, and young adults.

You can also choose Business Class or Gran Clase (First Class) seating. While tickets for these more spacious compartments are obviously more expensive, the benefits are significant. Besides having much more room to stretch out, those traveling in these specially designed sections are pampered from the moment they arrive at the airport. Among the many perks for deluxe and executive flyers are special VIP airport lounges with open bars and fax machines, special priority check-in and baggage services, complimentary limousine transfers, free valet parking at major Spanish airports, individual video movie screens (in Gran Clase only), incredible hotel discounts, great food (including items like smoked Scottish Salmon, giant prawns, rack of lamb, and filet of sole), vintage wines and much more. Round-trip promotional prices, special companion fares, and upgrade certificates on Preference Business Class and Gran Clase are usually available, so check with Iberia for more details.

Travelers desiring to continue on to other major Spanish airports can book conjunction round-trip add-ons within Spain for a small surcharge. Also available are the **City Plus** conjunction tickets (not applicable with US departures) and the great **Visit Spain** four-coupon flight booklets, which, when purchased along with an international ticket will allow for air travel anywhere in Spain and even to the Canary Islands at very low prices. If visiting other locations in Europe or the Middle East, the **Europass** conjunction fare can get you there and back much cheaper than buying a separate ticket. There are advance purchase requirements, specific dates of travel, and cancellation/revision penalties that may apply to all of the above.

Iberia's **Madrid Amigo** program is designed for passengers stopping over in Madrid while connecting to and from other European, Middle Eastern, and Far Eastern destinations. This program includes, depending on the fare paid, a wide variety of hotel accommodations, transfers, and local sightseeing options. Additional Iberia services include special boarding for the physically challenged, a wide variety of special meals, and fly/drive rental car programs to help you save some money while touring Spain. Once you've flown with Iberia, be sure to join their **Iberia Plus** frequent flyer program, where you can earn points towards free airline tickets on all member carriers of the Iberia group.

The overall service and amenities offered to all passengers on Iberia flights is simply outstanding. The in-flight cuisine is prepared by Iberswiss, a joint venture between Iberia Airlines and Swissair, so you know you're in for a special treat. First-run movies are offered on each transcontinental flight. Duty free shopping, renowned for offering some of the lowest prices compared to other international carriers, is also offered on-board.

IBERIA'S LOW RATES WITHIN SPAIN

If you wish to travel by plane to other Spanish cities after your arrival in Madrid, the carriers below usually cannot come close to matching the extremely low add-on rates which Iberia Airlines offers. This is because unlike the vast Iberia Airlines network, they do not operate their own flights within Spain.

AMERICAN AIRLINES, *Tel. 800/433-7300 in the US and Canada*
American offers daily non-stop flights between Miami and Madrid timed especially to link up with their ever-growing South and Central American gateways. Their lowest excursion fares usually start at just $667 US round-trip plus all applicable taxes. Their in-flight service is pretty good, and they also offer first and business class sections, non-smoking compartments, an assortment of special meals, package vacation deals, rental car discounts and frequent flyer award programs.

AIR CANADA, *Tel. 800/361-6340 in the US and Canada*
Air Canada offers fares in conjunction with the non-stop Iberia Airlines flights listed above from Toronto. Since the aircraft are the same as those listed above in the Iberia section, all the details remain the same with the one exception that frequent flyer miles can be accumulated for the Air Canada/Continental Airlines One Pass and En Route programs.

DELTA AIRLINES, *Tel. 800/221-2121 in the US and Canada*
Delta has non-stop service several times weekly between their hub in Atlanta and Madrid (and then to Barcelona via a stopover in Madrid).

Service on *Delta* is pretty good, and the planes are usually on time. The food is reasonable, but I still suggest that you consider ordering a special meal (vegetarian, low fat, low salt, fish only, etc.) as these are much better. Typical low season excursion fares start at about $ 628 US round-trip plus taxes, with business and first class tickets also available at much higher rates.

Delta has a generous frequent flyer program that at this time is connected to other airline programs such as Swiss Air.

CONTINENTAL AIRLINES, *Tel. 800/525-0280 in the US and Canada*

Continental has daily flights each week between Newark and Madrid. They tend to beat or at least match all the lowest fares offered by the competition. That means that the low season excursion tariff tends to start at about $558 US plus taxes round-trip, but the headache is that you have to find your way to their often less than convenient gateway in Newark, New Jersey. The service on Continental is first-rate, their frequent flyer program is among the industry's best, and they also have good deals on business class seats and larger city-oriented vacation packages.

TWA, *Tel. 800/892-4141 in the US and Canada*

TWA usually offers daily non-stop flights between JFK airport in New York and Madrid. Service on TWA is finally starting to match some of the above carriers, and the in-flight services may still be a bit more limited, but for low season excursion fares starting at around $558 US plus taxes, this airline is still worth strong consideration. TWA has a pretty good frequent flyer program, and offers vacation packages, a limited variety of large city and resort area hotel discounts, and special car rental rates for their clients.

FLIGHTS WITH CONNECTIONS TO SPAIN

Several international airlines offer European service through to Madrid, Barcelona, Málaga, and Sevilla from several North American cities. These flights take longer than the above-mentioned airlines because they require a change of planes in Europe before continuing on to Spain. The fares are often the same price as non-stop choices, but sometimes a free stopover in the city where you change planes is allowed.

The following is a partial listing of airlines with service to Spain via another European gateway.

Air France, *via Paris*
   Air France, *Tel. 800/237-2747 in the US*
   Air France, *Tel. 800/667-2747 in Canada*

ROCK BOTTOM PRICES FOR LOW SEASON PROMOTIONAL AIRFARES

Most years just after Christmas, during April, and usually again in October, the airfare price wars usually kick into high gear as tariffs may tumble to below $300 US round-trip plus taxes to Spain. Due to the fact that matching sale prices like this tend to make airlines lose money, these extremely limited (midweek) promotional fares commonly have many tough restrictions. Typical restrictions include a 7 day minimum and 21 day maximum stay, plenty of blackout dates, non-changeable and equally non-refundable ticketing policies, and no ability to combine the prices with any additional child or senior citizen discounts.

If you don't mind all the rules, super specials such as these are a great way to save some money for those who can wait until the last minute to travel during well off-season time periods. All of the carriers listed above have been known to match these rock bottom prices for a few short weeks, but there is no guarantee that this will be the situation at the time when you wish to visit Spain. The best advice is to keep reading your local newspaper's travel section, or call a good travel agent and ask them what their computer is offering.

Alitalia Airlines, *via Rome*
 Alitalia Airlines, *Tel. 800/221-4745 in the US*
 Alitalia Airlines, *Tel. 800/361-8336 in Canada*

British Air, *via London*
 British Air, *Tel. 800/247-9297 in the US*
 British Air, *Tel. 800/247-9297 in Canada*

KLM Airlines, *via Amsterdam*
 KLM, *Tel. 800/374-7747 in the US*
 KLM, *Tel. 800/361-5073 in Canada*

Lufthansa Airlines, *via Frankfurt*
 Lufthansa Airlines, *Tel. 800/645-3880 in the US*
 Lufthansa Airlines, *Tel. 800/645-3880 in Canada*

Sabena Airlines, *via Brussels*
 Sabena Airlines, *Tel. 800/955-2000 in the US*
 Sabena Airlines, *Tel. 800/955-2000 in Canada*

Swiss Air, *via Zurich*
>   **Swiss Air,** *Tel. 800/221-4750 in the US*
>   **Swiss Air,** *Tel. 800/267-9477 in Canada*

TAP Airlines, *via Lisbon*
>   **TAP Airlines,** *Tel. 800/221-7370 in the US*
>   **TAP Airlines,** *Tel. 800/221 7370 in Canada*

CHARTER FLIGHTS

Several charter operators offer airfare to the major destinations in Spain from New York, Boston, Chicago, Toronto, and other North American gateways. Be extra careful whenever booking a charter flight, as they are not bound by the same regulations as normal scheduled carriers.

It is not uncommon for these flights to be delayed for hours (or even days) waiting for replacement equipment, while you are stuck sleeping in the airport lobby. Charter flight tickets are normally non-changeable/non-refundable and are often not covered by travel insurance. For more details, call your travel agent.

DISCOUNT TICKET CONSOLIDATORS

There are many discount ticket brokers who offer last minute and special advance purchase round-trip fares, for airlines who have not sold enough seats on specific flights. I only suggest this method when you have not been able to find a reasonable deal for tickets directly with major airlines for the desired dates.

While some of these companies are in the habit of ripping off clients, several large companies have been doing a fairly good job in supplying the traveling public with good deals on highly restrictive tickets. It is advised that you first ask your travel agent for their recommendations, or call the local consumer protection agency or Better Business Bureau about any complaints on file about the consolidator you are considering.

Buy your consolidated tickets only from a travel agent or specialty tour operator. Be sure to use a major credit card to purchase this type of ticket. This way you will be better protected in case of any problems that may occur. These are a few consolidators with a good reputation:
• **Travac:** *Tel. 212/563-3303*
• **Air Travel Discounts:** *Tel. 212/922-1326*
• **Auto-Europe:** *Tel. 800/223 5555*
• **Unitravel:** *Tel. 800/325-2222*
• **World Travel:** *Tel. 800/886-4988*
• **Travel Cuts:** *Tel. 416/979 2406*
• **New Frontiers:** *Tel. 514/526-8444*

COURIER FLIGHTS

In many cases, a large company may need to send documents to Europe on a specific day. Agencies exist which book passengers on flights to Europe and use their luggage allotment to transport several documents to European clients. Since you are giving up your rights to your luggage compartment space, you are only allowed to bring whatever you can carry aboard. Upon arrival, a representative from the courier company will take possession of the stored documents.

These flights can run as low as $249 US round-trip and usually are valid for only one week. This is not the most recommended method of travel because you never know what is really in those suitcases, and you are completely responsible for their contents. Another major disadvantage is that you may be booked on a standby, or next available day basis. Travel agencies do not reserve these types of tickets, so please check the travel section of your local newspaper.

Some reasonably good courier agencies include:
• **D.T.I.**, *Tel. 212/362-3636*
• **Now Voyager,** *Tel. 212/431-1616*

GETTING AROUND SPAIN

BY AIR

There are several large commuter and tourist-based airports within Spain. Most of the air traffic tends to be between Madrid, Barcelona, Málaga, Sevilla, and the islands of the coast. Flights are cheap within Spain if booked at least 1 week in advance. For example flights between Barcelona and Sevilla can cost as little as 12,500 *ptas* round-trip. Without advance purchase the same flight would be very expensive. I once had to shell out over 29,000 *ptas* for a last minute one-way ticket from Madrid to San Sebastian. If you intend to fly into one Spanish airport, and fly out of another one, it is also best to include this segment on your international ticket.

Iberia Airlines, **Spanair**, and **Air Europa** fly between dozens of Spanish international, regional, and commuter airports around the country. If you buy special conjunction tickets and coupon books at the same time you make purchase the transcontinental segments, you will also save plenty of money. Please see the *Iberia Airlines* section a few pages back for more details about these special programs, or call your favorite travel agent.

BY CAR

Unlike some other countries in southern Europe, Spain is a delightful and relatively easy place to drive around. To begin with, the steering wheel and all other controls are placed exactly where they would be in your own car at home in America or Canada. While standard shift vehicles are most common, you can also get automatics if necessary. Before arriving in Spain, it's best to pre-plan your driving route by using a good Spanish road map (available at any National Tourist Office of Spain or your local travel book store) and marking out the roads with a yellow outliner pen. Please ask the rental car company or hotel staff to give you detailed directions to your next location, as maps tend to be inaccurate and may not point out many of the frequent and rather serious construction delays.

A good percentage of Spanish people seem to drive like maniacs. Expect more than a few other cars to pass on blind curves, pull multiple lane changes at high speeds, and generally disregard any form of manners on the road. If you drive very carefully, and stay in the appropriate lane for your desired velocity, you should be just fine. Be especially careful when driving into the mountainous and coastal reaches of Spain. Many roads do not have lights or reflectors, especially in and around small towns near the countryside. I have driven over 45,500 km. (28,210 miles) within Spain, and I have never had an accident although I recently received a traffic violation on the road. Official speed limits (unless otherwise posted) are 50 km/hr in towns and villages, 90 km/hr on most normal roads, and 120 km/hr on highways and motorways.

Most police cars now have laser aimed radar units that they use often, and foreigners must pay a minimum of a 20,000 *ptas* fine on the spot, in cash, or else the police will confiscate your car! Seat belts are mandatory, and should be used at all times while driving in Spain. Recently, those driving along the Costa del Sol have been stopped without reasonable suspicion by police using drug-sniffing dogs to catch narcotics and hashish smugglers coming from in Morocco.

Gasoline is extremely expensive in Spain. Until very recently, the government had a monopoly on all gas stations, and still controls the pricing. At press time, normal unleaded gasoline (95 octane) is called *Sin Plomo – Euro 95* and costs approximately 110 *ptas* and up per liter (about $3.40 US per gallon), super unleaded gasoline (98 Octane) is called *Sin Plomo - Super 98* and costs about 125 *ptas* per liter (about $3.90 US per gallon), and diesel fuel is called *Gasoleo A* and only costs about 90 *ptas* per liter (about $2.35 US per gallon). Since all of the rental vehicles are rather small in Europe, fortunately most cars' fuel efficiency is very high. Be careful not to use the wrong type of fuel. Most major brand gas stations accept a variety of major credit cards. Over the last few years, several hundred 24 hour 7 days per week service stations complete with repair shops, mini-markets, cafeterias, and bars have popped up throughout Spain and accept most major credit cards. Smaller service stations not located along major highways or in big cities may only keep limited opening hours that range from 8am until 8pm on Mondays through Sundays, but a small percentage of gas stations may also close during *siestas* and on Sundays.

It is important for me to explain that most roads in Spain are named using lettered prefixes. The super fast 3 or 4 lane in each direction motorways that usually charge tolls are known as *"Autopistas"* and are most commonly listed on maps and road signs with the letter *"A"* followed by either normal or Roman numerals. Most major toll roads in Spain accept Spanish cash as well as credit cards for tolls. Major 2 or 3 lane per direction highways tend to not have any tolls and are normally referred to as *"Autovias"* or *"Carreteras Nacional"* and are typically listed using the letter *"N"* followed by either Roman or regular numerals. Smaller rural or regional commercial roads of either 1 or 2 lanes in each direction are called *"Carreteras Comarcal"* and will either have a prefix of *"C"* or another letter not mentioned above, followed by a number.

While 90% of the major motorways in Spain cost nothing to travel on, a small number of them do charge tolls. You can always tell if the road you are going to take charges a toll if the sign marking the entrance to that road has a small white circle with a red border and a black horizontal line through it with the words *Peaje -Toll* written on it. These toll roads are mostly found in the Northeast and extreme Southern sections of Spain, and can easily rack up toll fees as high as 20 *ptas* per kilometer (which in some cases can add up to over 5,500 *ptas*), but most other normal road and bridge tolls are quite reasonable. It is a good idea to have a lot of 100 *ptas* coins handy in case you run into the unexpected tolls on the road you are traveling on, but as I mentioned above, many toll roads also accept major credit cards for payments. The high tech road traffic engineers in Spain have designed a computerized automatic toll paying system called the *Via Automatico* or *Tarjecta Tourista* for frequent commuters. Please do not use these specially marked lanes (generally located on the extreme right or left) or your car may be stopped by the police, and you will be in big trouble.

Since crime is still an issue for tourists in Spain, a rental car is easy prey. Please remember not to leave anything in your car when it is parked, and if possible it is advised to lock your gas cap. Since exposed hatchback cars have increased risks for potential pilferage, it is recommended to either cover the hatch, or avoid renting these categories of vehicles (usually the less expensive categories). Many companies (especially Europcar) maintain a very rapid car replacement service in the event that you incur a breakdown or an accident somewhere in Spain. It is important to find out where the branch offices of your rental car company are located, and their emergency phone numbers. The official representative in Spain for members of the AAA and the CAA auto clubs is called **RACE** (*Real Automobil Clube de España*) and if necessary they can be reached at by asking any *Turismo*, or policeman for their nearest location. Ask your rent a car company for exact listings of all major RACE offices, as well as their own emergency hotline number.

In case of an accident call the police and ask them to come to the scene of the accident, write down the license plate of the other car(s) involved, and if possible his license and insurance information. If no police arrive on the scene within 45 minutes or so, Immediately go to the closest police station and have them give you a copy of the accident report or the report number. Call your car rental company as soon as possible after you have obtained the above required documentation.

SAVE PLENTY OF MONEY BY RENTING A DIESEL CAR!

The average small rental 4 door or 2 door hatchback car running on the more frequently used unleaded gas costs about 5,250 ptas to fill up and gets somewhere around 475 kilometers per tank of gas on the highway. Therefor small unleaded cars average out at about 11 ptas per kilometer to operate plus rental charges, tolls, parking, and insurance costs.

The average small rental 4 door car running on the less frequently used (but still commonly available) diesel fuel costs only about 4,450 ptas to fill up and gets somewhere around 775 kilometers per tank of diesel on the highway. Diesel cars do however accelerate about 15% slower than the unleaded fuel cars. Therefor small diesel fuel cars average out at about 6 ptas per kilometer to operate plus rental charges, tolls, parking, and insurance fees.

As you can see from the above numbers, a diesel car costs almost half as much to operate, and is typically just a few dollars more per day to rent. I strongly suggest trying to book a diesel car such as the superb "category D" type 4 door SEAT Cordoba-Diesel in advance of your arrival. If your car rental agency says they cannot guarantee a diesel car, have them put the request for a diesel car in writing on the reservation voucher, and make sure to demand one upon your arrival at the car rental agency's pick-up location in Spain. I have always been able to get a diesel car from international car rental agency offices in Madrid, Barcelona, Sevilla, and Malaga.

CAR RENTALS

Most international airlines from North America fly into either Madrid, Málaga, or Barcelona. For those who want to immediately pick up a car upon arrival in Spain, many well-known international rental car companies operate both airport kiosks and downtown offices in these and many other locations. **Avis**, **Budget**, **National**, **Europcar**, **Hertz**, and several other lesser known companies maintain airport hours from early each morning until the last flight is scheduled to arrive.

If your flight is extremely late, you may have to camp out at the airport until the next morning to receive your car. International drivers licenses are not required for North Americans driving in Spain, but it's not a bad idea to visit the **AAA** (American Automobile Association) or **CAA** (Canadian Automobile Association) offices and get one for about $17.50 US. All that is required for car rental documentation is a major credit card, passport, and your valid US or Canadian driver's license.

If you intend to use a rental car in Spain, it is advisable to call a specialized tour operator to book and prepay in advance from within North America to save up to 45% of the normal rate. If you decide to rent a car only after you have arrived in Spain, rentals can be arranged from any Spanish travel agency or car rental company office but the prices are over twice as high as those offered from within the US. There are rental locations within most major Spanish cities. If you unexpectedly decide to rent a car while in Spain for at least 3 days, I strongly recommend that you call Auto Europe (toll free from any Spanish phone) at *Tel.* 900-990-011 and they can fax a voucher to your hotel and save you over a hundred of dollars in the process.

It is also important to call your credit card company before you leave for Europe to determine if any insurance is automatically included for car rentals in Spain. Recently American Express stopped automatically including international car rental insurance for most of their cardholders without much, if any, notification. Most forms of insurance (collision damage waiver, liability, vehicle theft, personal accident injury insurance, property theft insurance) will be offered upon your pick-up of the car and may add up to well over $20 US per day additional. Make sure that you are covered one way or another, or else you may wind up with a big problem after a collision of theft.

MAJOR CAR RENTAL COMPANIES IN NORTH AMERICA

- **Auto Europe,** *Tel. 800/223-5555, Canada Tel. 800/223-5555*
- **Avis,** *Tel. 800/331-1084, Canada Tel. 800/879-2847*
- **Budget,** *Tel. 800/527-0770, Canada Tel. 800/268-8900*
- **Hertz,** *Tel. 800/654-1101, Canada Tel. 800/263-0600*

With advance booking and prepayment from the US or Canada, prices range from below $125 US per week for a small two-door manual car (Opel Corsa hatchback or similar), $155 US per week for a four-door manual diesel car with a great stereo and air conditioning, or well over $285 US per week for any automatic car, plus insurance. Specialty rentals such as Mercedes Benz sedans and sporty little convertibles may also be available from $325 US per week and up. Also keep in mind that Spanish airports have a surcharge of about 1,500 *ptas* on all airport rental car pick-ups.

If you so desire, you can pick up a rental car in one major city in Spain and drop it off in another (usually no drop-off charges are added). If you want to drop off your car outside of Spain, large drop off surcharges of well over $350 US will apply. Please keep in mind that taking a rental car from Spain anywhere else in Europe is only allowed if you inform the rental company that you are doing so in advance, and ask the rental agent to provide you with a set of international insurance and registration documents.

MOPED & MOTORCYCLE RENTALS

Most major cities and coastal resort areas have small shops that rent mopeds, scooters, and smaller engine motorcycles. To drive these machines clients must be at least 16 years old, have a valid drivers license, and wear a helmet. Scooters and mopeds tend to cost around 4,500 *ptas* per day including insurance, while motorcycles can set you back upwards of 7,000 *ptas* per day. Please ask any tourist information office in the area you are staying in for further details about rental locations. I must state however, that these machines are responsible for a good percentage of serious accidents among tourists in Spain, and unless you have plenty of experience with them I suggest not renting one while visiting here!

BY TRAIN

The Spanish government owns and operates a fantastic national and regional rail company called **Renfe** (*Red Nacional de Ferrocarriles Españoles*) that operates trains on more than 13,000 kilometers (8,060 miles) of tracks throughout the country. The non-express train services offered are usually rather inexpensive (usually somewhere between 600 *ptas* to 950 *ptas* per 100 kilometers of travel). There are currently several different categories of trains to choose from depending on your routing, desired time of arrival, and budget.

The more expensive **AVE** high-speed express trains with a limited number of stops are an excellent method of longer distance travel between the major cities of Madrid, Córdoba, and Sevilla. The **Talgo** express trains service many more destinations than the AVE and are almost as comfortable, but are half as fast and half as expensive. Many other connections between major population centers may require the use of the inexpensive and frequently stopping **Electrotren** that costs a bit less than the Talgo.

The **Intercity** and **Expresso Estrella** trains are also well priced, but vary in each case as to speed and the amount of intermediate stops they achieve. For commuter and regional service, there are many other trains to choose from, including the slower and even less expensive **Diurno**, **Regional**, and **Regional Express**, as well as several other suburban commuter lines with slow service with many stops between smaller cities and villages.

RENFE PHONE NUMBERS
Renfe Headquarters in Madrid, Tel. (91) 429-0202
Renfe Headquarters in Barcelona, Tel. (93) 322-4142

Some trains require advance reservations (especially the AVE and Talgo trains) and some other trains have special facilities such as sleeping compartments and automobile compartments that must be booked in advance with supplemental charges applied to your fare. There are also many trains, which offer the often-crowded second class seats, as well as more expensive and comfortable first class seating.

Most of the trains in Spain offer reasonably good food and beverages in their dining cars, are fully air conditioned, and have small bathrooms. To get exact fare information, schedules, advice, reservations, and tickets please contact the expert agents over at **Rail Europe** (see below for phone numbers) before departing North America, or a Renfe station or a travel agency once you are already within Spain. All major train stations in Spain are open by 8am.

Several types of tourist train passes are only available directly from the Renfe train offices and stations if presented with proper identification. These Spain-only unlimited use (within a set number of days) first and second class train passes (**Tarjetas Turisticos**) are available in the following varieties, and must be purchased within Spain. Your choices are 8 days (about 55,500 *ptas* in first class and 43,250 *ptas* in second class), 15 days (about 99,500 *ptas* in first class and 75,250 *ptas* in second class), and 22 days (about 137,500 *ptas* in first class and 117,000 *ptas* in second class).

All passengers can receive up to 30% off on same-day round trips on any train, and may be eligible for off-peak specials for travel on over 325 **Dias Azules** (blue days) a year. Fare discounts are offered to different passengers with specific cases. For instance, if you are between the ages of 12 and 25, or are over 65 years old, or are traveling with children between the ages of 4 and 12 years old, or intend to travel on a *Dias Azules*, you can receive up to a 40% discount on the fare.

Official Renfe rail schedules are available for free from the Renfe stations in major cities and are called **Intercity** guides. If you intend to use the train system in Spain, you must get one of these books. Make sure to inquire about the **Suplemento** (supplemental section) of up-to-date revised schedules which comes with the normal guide.

Another good source may be to purchase either the monthly *European Rail Timetables*, or annual *On the Rails Around Europe* train travel guides published by **Thomas Cook**, which can be found in travel book shops in major cities throughout the world or by calling the **Forsyth Travel Library**, *Tel. 800/367-7984.*

Trains have a tendency to run late, so plan your connections with enough time to catch the next train if you have to. Occasional work stoppages and strikes may also affect your travel plans in rare circumstances. Since the train schedules change quite often, I have not listed most of the them in this book. It would be better for you to spend a few minutes planning your trip with the correct and up-to-date information. If you have trouble contacting any of the Renfe stations, visit any major travel agency in Spain and they will usually assist you. Please keep in mind that the stations may be several kilometers from the town centers, and transportation may or may not be provided into the heart of town.

In the regional chapters of this book I have included many listings of train station locations and phone numbers.

TAKE A SCENIC TRAIN RIDE!

There are a few remaining narrow gauge railways and waterfront rail road lines left in Spain. Some of these railroads include antique steam engines and railroad cars that date back to the late 1800's. Although the government is in the process of phasing out these lines, you may still find a few that run occasionally or are owned by private companies.

*The most famous of these is the deluxe **Al Andalus Express** that pampers its clients as they enjoy a five-day ride through the most dramatic cities of Andalucía. This is a wonderful experience if you have the time and money for it, but several more affordable normally scheduled train routes also offer incredible views through dramatic landscapes. The schedules and routes of these scenic train lines frequently change, so a visit to any Turismo, travel agency, or Renfe station or office will be necessary for more detailed information.*

EURAIL PASSES

Eurail passes are accepted on the *Renfe* train system and must be purchased before your departure from North America, although some services may require a supplemental surcharge. There are several types of youth and adult Eurail passes available for travel within a specific amount of time through 17 different countries in Europe, or solely within one specific country. When using a rail pass you may be allowed to upgrade your journey by reserving seats, couchettes, and sleeping cars for a supplemental charge.

The best place to buy these passes is directly from the prompt and reliable staff of **Rail Europe** in both the US and Canada, from a specialty tour operator, or your favorite travel agency. Once you have your Eurail pass (which will automatically expire in 6 months from the date of issue), any upgrades, specific reservations, or sleeping car requests should be made directly with Rail Europe before you depart North America, or if already in Spain with *Renfe* at one of their rail stations. Details of these passes are listed below.

Rail Europe's North American phone numbers are:
• **Rail Europe** *in the US, Tel. 800/438-7245*
• **Rail Europe** *in Canada, Tel. 800/361-7245*

Eurail Youthpass

These are **second class** train passes valid for people under 26 years old. These passes can only be purchased within North America before departure, and are valid from the first day you use it in Europe. They allow for unlimited train travel in 17 European countries (as well as certain bus and ferry routes) within a maximum number of predetermined days.
• **15 day pass**: *$418 US*
• **1 month pass**: *$598 US*
• **2 month pass**: *$798 US*

Eurail Pass

These are **first class** train passes that are valid for people of all ages. These passes can only be purchased within North America before departure, and are valid from the first day you use it in Europe.

They allow for unlimited train travel in 17 European countries (as well as certain bus and ferry routes) within a maximum number of predetermined days.
• **15 day pass**: *$522 US*
• **21 day pass**: *$678 US*
• **1 month pass**: *$838 US*
• **2 month pass**: *$1148 US*
• **3 month pass**: *$1468 US*

Accompanied children aged 4-11 can receive a discount of 50% off the above prices.

Eurail Saver Pass
These are special **first class** train passes for people of all ages traveling on the exact same schedule of train travel in 17 European countries (as well as certain bus and ferry routes). They are valid for unlimited travel during a predetermined length of time. Between the months of October through March these passes requires a minimum of 2 people traveling together, between the months of April and September this pass is valid for a minimum of three people traveling together.
• **15 day saver pass**: *$452 US*
• **21 day saver pass**: *$57 8US*
• **1 month saver pass**: *$712 US*
Accompanied children aged 4-11 can receive a discount of 50% off the above.

Eurail Youth Flexipass
These are **second class** train passes valid for people under 26 years old. They must be purchased within North America before departure, and are good from the first day you use it in Europe. They allow for unlimited train travel in 17 European countries (as well as certain bus and ferry routes) within a maximum number of predetermined days within a given time period.
• **10 days of travel within a 2 month period**: *$438 US*
• **15 days of travel within a 2 month period**: *$588 US*

Eurail Flexipass
These are **first class** train passes that are valid to people of all ages. They must be purchased within North America before departure, and are valid from the first day you use it in Europe. They allow for unlimited train travel in 17 European countries (as well as certain bus and ferry routes) within a maximum number of predetermined days within a given time period.
10 days of travel within a 2 month period: *$616US*
5 days of travel within a 2 month period: *$812US*
Accompanied children aged 4-11 can receive a discount of 50% off the above.

Europass
These are **first class** train passes valid for people of all ages. They must be purchased within North America before departure, and are valid from the first day you use it in Europe. They allow for unlimited train travel in

specific groupings of between 3 and 5 pre-selected European countries (as well as certain bus and ferry routes) within a maximum number of predetermined days in a given time period. Additional countries may be added to create a customized Europass valid for up to 9 pre-selected European nations in total, but the prices will increase with the number of nations you choose. This one gets a bit complicated to explain, so call Rail Europe for the exact country groupings they are offering.

Also, if you travel with a second passenger on the exact same schedule, you can each save about 25%. Prices range from $316 US for one person traveling to 3 pre-selected countries on any five days during a 60-day period, and go up to $736 US for one person traveling to 5 pre-selected countries on any 15 days during two months.

Europass Youth

These are **second class** train passes valid for people up to age 25. They must be purchased within North America before departure, and are good from the first day you use it in Europe. They allow for unlimited train travel in specific groupings of between 3 and 5 pre-selected European countries (as well as certain bus and ferry routes) within a maximum number of predetermined days within a given time period. Additional countries may be added to create a customized Europass Youth valid for up to 9 pre-selected European nations in total, but the prices increase along with the number of nations you choose. This one is also complicated, so call Rail Europe for the exact country groupings they are offering.

Prices range from $210 US for one young adult traveling to 3 pre-selected countries on any 5 days during a 60 day period, and go up to $500 US for one young adult traveling to 5 pre-selected countries on any 15 days during two months.

BY BUS

Spanish **Autobuses** offer a good alternative to driving in Spain, and have become competitive with the train system in terms of ticket prices for similar routes. Ask a *Turismo* for the best route to take, and for a photocopy of the appropriate schedule. The majority of inter-regional and inter-city buses are run by privately owned companies such as the **Enatcar** group.

Most major cities have bus stations and are covered by regularly scheduled express (**Expreso**) bus service. Local and regional buses can get you to smaller towns where there may be a bus stop instead of a bus station. These buses are usually slow since they make many more stops than an express bus. During weekends and holidays several routes may not operate, so make sure to stop by a bus station or local *Turismo* to ask for specific information and timetables before planning to travel. Many of these buses offer air conditioning and on-board videos, while some others play music throughout the journey. Just keep in mind that the place you will board or depart the bus may be rather far from the part of town you wish to visit.

The average fare on Spanish bus routes works out to around 780 *ptas* per 100 kilometers, but special deluxe or express service may be somewhat higher. In each regional chapter of this book, I have included several listings of bus station locations and phone numbers.

ACCOMMODATIONS

There are well over 1,000 government-licensed "accommodation providers" in Spain. For those of you who want to have a complete listing of every official accommodation in Spain, ask your country's branch of the Tourist Office of Spain to sell you a copy of the 1000+ page *Guida de Hoteles* (hotel guide) for about $8.50 US. Although the book uses ratings from 1 to 5 stars for most of the properties in the country, the system cannot be fully trusted.

I have included brief descriptions in this book's regional chapters of more than 200 of the properties throughout Spain that I have visited and reviewed. I have listed each destination's properties in up to four separate price categories. Within each of the price categories I have ranked my hotel choices from top to bottom.

While the quality and facilities of accommodations may change from season to season, I have given you the most up-to-date information currently available to help you select the best places to fit your requirements. The price guidelines for all types of accommodations which I have used in my reviews, are based on the lowest price room rate for 2 people staying in a double room, not including the 7% or so government-imposed tax. In some cases, I have listed either a year-round or weekend price. Please keep in mind that many hotels have up to 75% surcharges during special festival and holiday seasons, especially during Easter.

If you enter any establishment offering overnight accommodations that does not display a blue metal plaque with its rating in stars on or near the front door, it is not a government-licensed property! In the event that you have checked into a licensed property and feel you are being overcharged, ask the front desk manager for his **Libro de Reclamaciones** complaint book. Since the tourism authorities and local police seriously look into all written complaints, most managers would rather settle with you on the spot before having a complaint placed permanently on their record.

Also keep in mind that you will have to hand over your passport (and in some cases a credit card imprint) upon check-in. All registered guests must be placed on the property's occupant sheets that the government then uses for statistical analysis. Make sure that you get back your passport later the same day, and walk around with a photocopy of it until the original is returned. In Spain, all foreigners must always carry either a valid passport or a photocopy of one, or risk the possibility of arrest if stopped by police. This is a rare occurrence, but it does happen.

HOTEL INDUSTRY TERMS USED IN THIS BOOK

Almost all the hotel prices used in this book are taken from the officially approved rates for a double room with 2 people per night as listed in the most recent copy of the government publication known as the "Guia Oficial de Hotels de España," and usually do not include 7% IVA tax. Rates are subject to change and special seasonal or promotional prices are often available, so check directly with the hotel or its listed North American representative before booking your accommodations.

Low Season: *Usually from about October through March, excluding holidays.*

High Season: *Usually from about April through September.*

Rack Rate: *The full retail price of a room, special rates may also be available.*

Corporate Rate: *Available to almost anyone who presents a business card.*

Weekend Rate: *A limited number of discounted rooms available Friday through Sunday.*

Double Room: *A room designed and priced for 2 people staying together.*

Apartment: *A room or suite with cooking facilities built in.*

E.P.: *European Plan, no meals included in the price.*

C.P.: *Continental Plan, a small breakfast included in the price.*

B.P.: *Breakfast Plan, a full breakfast (typically a buffet) included in the price.*

M.A.P. *(a.k.a. H/B): Modified American Plan (Half Board/Half Pension), full breakfast and dinner included in the price.*

A.I. *(a.k.a. F/B): All-Inclusive Plan (Full Board/Full Pension), all meals (and sometimes cocktails as well as beverages) are included in the price.*

COMMON ACCOMMODATIONS

Hoteles

These are **hotels** and **resorts**, which run the full gamut of quality and accommodation levels and are available in several types of classifications. Hotel properties throughout the country can be housed in everything from multistory modern buildings to centuries-old convents and palaces. Any property that uses the word hotel in its name will be rated by a series of stars.

If a hotel offers **1** or **2 stars**, chances are that it will have private bathrooms and facilities such as a breakfast room and central heating. Properties of **3 stars** or more will often be loaded with additional facilities including a restaurant, parking, cable TV, an outdoor pool, in-room phones, and perhaps even mini-bars. Most **4** and **5 star** hotels may have gourmet restaurants, snack bars, lounges, air conditioning, health clubs, sports facilities, marble bathrooms, room service, multilingual staff, a concierge desk and bellboys.

Also in this general category are **Cuidades de Vacaciones** (resorts) that will offer special facilities and services that typically include either golf courses or a water sports center, heated indoor pools, supervised children's programs, state of the art conference halls, boutiques, and valet parking. **Aparthotels** are usually full service **2 to 4 star** hotels offering rooms with kitchens and either 1 or 2 bedrooms for family style use.

Hotel Residencias (motels) tend to run in the **2 to 3 star** range and do not usually have restaurants or a full range of facilities, but are great values when compared to a nearby hotel with affordable rooms. Bookings for these properties can be made from a specialty tour operator, travel agent, or directly from each specific hotel. **Estaciones Termales** (Hot Spring Spas) can be found throughout the country and have modern hotel facilities as well as medically supervised curative programs.

Paradores

These are a series of about 85 or so properties that are part of a government owned company known as *Paradores de Turismo*. Originally designed as inexpensive **inns** that hosted Spanish travelers, these inns have become a favorite of foreign visitors and are now much more expensive. They are often housed in castles, former mansions of civil engineers, well-located traditional homes, or modern resorts that have been converted into fashionable hotels with many facilities including private bathrooms. Each *parador* is unique, and the service quality can range quite substantially from one to the other.

I have listed only the best and most comfortable of these properties in this book. Reservations for these properties can be made from a specialty tour operator, travel agent, directly from each specific parador, or by calling their official US based reservations representative, **Marketing Ahead**, *in New York at Tel. 800/223-1356*. If you are already in Spain, call the **Paradores de Turismo** *in Madrid at Tel. (91) 559-0069 or Fax (91) 559-3233*. Be advised that prepayment will be requested at the time of booking, and that penalties may be applied for no shows and cancellations. Many of the *paradores* are sold out well in advance, and it can take several days to receive a confirmation from any source of these bookings. I suggest you contact your travel agent, or one of the tour operators listed in this book for further details.

Cortijos & Casa Rurales

These are **Farmhouses** and are akin to **Bed & breakfasts**. Usually they are private estates that offer guests a chance to stay in traditional manor homes and farmhouses. Using funds provided by E.E.C. economic development programs, many estate owners have found a low cost way to improve their properties for tourism purposes. These charming farmhouses can range from wonderfully ornate former palaces to wine producing mansions and rustic mountain lodges.

It is common for the host family to greet each guest personally and sometimes even offer a glass of wine. These properties can provide a memorable cultural experience for visitors as they often provide deluxe guestrooms filled with antiques and private bathrooms in unforgettable settings. Some farmhouses offer apartments and guestrooms with fireplaces, 4 poster beds, scenic patios, and even modern or antique style kitchens. Other more commercialized farmhouses can be rented as complete private estates for families or high-end groups and business meetings. Many of these properties have special features such as horseback riding, bicycles, jeeps, romantic gardens, TV rooms, priceless artwork, farm fresh meals and their own in-house wineries. I have only have listed the properties that I have either seen or have been a guest in, and can fully recommend.

There are a handful of associations that can book prepaid stays in farm houses. Among the best of these reservation companies are **Hoteles con Encanto** *in Malaga, at Tel. (95) 244-7789 and Fax (95) 244-5591*, **Cortijos & Haciendas** *in Sevilla, at Tel. (95) 422-2529 and Fax (95) 421-8764*, **Estancias de España** *in Madrid, at (91) 561-0170 and Fax (91) 561-0172*, and **R.A.A.R.** and **A.H.R.A** *in Almeria, at Tel. (950) 271-678 and Fax (950) 270-431*.

Keep in mind that full pre-payment will be requested at the time of booking, and that penalties will be applied for revisions, cancellations, or no-shows. Many farmhouses are sold out well in advance during the summer months, so book well ahead.

Villas & Apartamentos

Villas and **Apartments** are usually multiple bedroom houses or condo style apartments with all the comforts of home including private bathrooms and kitchens. Since these are usually private and not rated by the government, you must contact a travel specialist to ensure that you get what you pay for. These villas and apartments can range in quality from basic bungalows with 1 or 2 bedrooms, to modern 3 bedroom condos with sea views, and may even include a handful of 12 bedroom castles with dramatic sea views or vineyards.

Usually you must rent these properties for a minimum of one week, but in low season a 3 night stay is possible. If you are looking for a long-term rental, you will have almost no problem finding one from either a good tour operator in North America, or if necessary from an English-speaking real estate agent once you arrive in Spain. If you need long term housing in the Madrid area, you will have big problems, as the vacancy rate in this vicinity is about 1.25%.

To book a villa or apartment in Spain in advance from North America, you might start by giving a call to highly reliable villa representation companies like **Villas International** *in San Francisco, Tel. 800/221-2260* and **Vacances Provencales** *in Toronto, Tel. 800/263-7152.* You may also want to pick up a copy of the England based *Private Villas Magazine* if you're lucky enough to find a copy at a major North American city newsstand. This 150 page monthly lists all sorts of properties with pricing details, large color photos, and phone or fax contacts (usually of their London-based estate agents). Be advised that reservations for villas and apartments must be prepaid in full in advance, and penalties will apply for cancellations, revisions, and no-shows.

Albergues & Hostales

These are also inns, but typically ranked just below a hotel in quality and facilities offered. Many **residencias** are rather nice and offer most of the facilities of a smaller inn or motel. Almost all of these properties are rated between **2** and **4 stars** and will usually offer private bathrooms, a breakfast room, bar, heating, in room phones, a TV room, safe deposit boxes, nearby parking, and sometimes even a pool. Bookings for these properties can be made from a specialty tour operator, travel agent, or directly with their front desk.

Pensiones, Fondas, & Casas de Huéspedes

Guesthouses are the lowest rated classification of officially licensed accommodations in Spain. These basic and simple inns are rated from **1** to **3 stars** (although many of these are not licensed) and have minimal facilities. Most **pensiones** offer rooms with shared bathrooms, but some of these properties have a few guestrooms with private bathrooms as well. Some of these properties offer an optional breakfast. The furnishings tend to be rather minimal, and they may even lock their front doors well before midnight, creating a virtual curfew for their guests. Since these inns often do not pay commissions to travel agents and tour operators, you can only book most of them directly with their owner/manager.

Monasterios & Santuarios

Monasteries and **Retreats** offer a unique lodging experience for those looking for a tranquil place to unwind. Generally run by Benedictine, Cistercian, Franciscan, Hieronymite, or Dominican religious orders, many of these historic monasteries (especially the medieval ones in the northern and central Spain) allow members of the general public to stay for up to two weeks. The price of these accommodations is usually a small donation that works out to somewhere around 1,450 *ptas* per person per night (sometimes including meals).

While the architecture of these structures is quite dramatic, the rooms they rent out are often simple monastic cells without any frills. Excellent homemade meals might also be offered to guests at amazingly low prices. Please keep in mind that some of these structures are run by monks who only allow men to use their facilities, while others are run my nuns and may admit only female guests. House rules may include early curfews, and couples may be asked to inhabit separate quarters at night. For more details about monastic stays, contact any local *Turismo*.

Camas & Habitaciones

These are best described as **Simple Rooms in Private Houses**, essentially rooms for rent in private houses with shared bathrooms. These accommodations are not officially recognized by the government, and are usually part of the underground economy. I have not included listings of these units because they come and go each season and there is no quality assurance. The most common way to find a private room is to either inquire at a *Turismo* office, or go to a local train station and look out for either signs or the hawkers who earn a 15% commission to each tourist they successfully bring in.

Youth Hostels

For adults and youths alike, the vast network of good Youth Hostels (**Albergues de Juveniles**) provide a highly economical alternative to budget hotels. There are well over 110 Spanish hostels scattered throughout every major city and rural area in the country. Many of these hostels provide both separate dormitory accommodations for each sex, as well as a limited quantity of modern private double rooms for couples, and family sized multiple bedroom units. These properties welcome international guests of all ages, and are no longer used just by students and backpackers on budget road trips.

The hostels tend to be located in major resort and large population zones and are usually open from 9am until 12pm and from 6pm until midnight. Some, but not all, hostels have curfews that are strictly enforced, and may have an 8-day maximum stay limit. Each hostel is different, so expect anything from huge air conditioned rooms inside modern marble-floored buildings in the city center to spacious private bungalows and nice guest rooms with private bathrooms in old converted houses. The current price range is from about 1075 *ptas* to 2,250 *ptas* per person each night depending on the season and type of room requested. Many hostels offer inexpensive meals for a small surcharge.

All guests of these hostels must hold a valid hostel membership card which is available for about $25 US per year from any **IFYH (International Federation of Youth Hostels)** office, or if necessary, from the hostel's front desk. These cards also enable their holders to receive discounts on the hostels themselves, as well as on restaurants and sports rental equipment. Special cards may be available for people under 17 and families at differing prices. To book reservations, it is best to contact the official member of the (IFYH) in your country. Some hostels request a 10-day advance booking made via an IFYH branch office, but if space is available you can just walk in and stay.

A new computer system called the International Booking Network can often be used to reserve and print out confirmations for prepaid bookings in many hostels throughout the world for a mere $2.50 US fee plus the price of the accommodation chosen. Many Spanish hostels are open year round, but it is not uncommon for several of them to be sold out well in advance for the summer season, so book early. For specific location, pricing, and facility listings, please order a copy of Hostelling International's multilingual handbook.

Contact one of the following organizations or their many branches for more specific information:
- **American Youth Hostel Federation**, *Washington DC, Tel. 202/783-6161*
- **Canadian Hostelling Association**, *Ontario, Tel. 613/237-7884*
- **Spanish Association of Hostels**, *Madrid, Tel. (91) 347-7700*
- **Spanish Association of Hostels**, *Barcelona, Tel. (93) 483-8378*
- **Council Travel**, *New York, Tel. 212/661-1450*
- **Travel Cuts**, *Toronto, Tel. 416/979-2406*

Camping

With over 750 official public and private campgrounds throughout the country, Spain is a great place to **camp** and **caravan**. If you follow normal precautions and don't leave anything valuable in your tent or caravan you will have a wonderful time. One of the most important issues besides security should be where you decide to stay. If you intend to avoid the official campsites and try to stay on private land you may end up with buckshot in your rear end. If you attempt to illegally camp anywhere along the coast, you may very well be harassed or even arrested by the local police.

To put it simply, campgrounds are so numerous and cheap that there is almost no reasonable excuse to avoid them. If you happen to find a wonderful secluded rural spot that is not within 1 kilometer (.62 miles) of beaches, cities, or water sources you can always cross your fingers and chances are you will be okay.

Most of the campgrounds and caravan sights are fairly attractive and located in areas close to tourism spots, city centers, beach resorts and beautiful parks. Besides the (almost) hot showers and sanitary facilities, you may often find bungalows, mini-markets, snack bars, tennis courts, rental boats, laundry machines, telephones, on site parking, and swimming pools. Many sights are open year round and you can expect to pay between 475 *ptas* and 800 *ptas* per night for a 2 person tent site, 765 *ptas* to 975 *ptas* for a 4 person tent site, and 1,250 *ptas* to 1,975 *ptas* for a caravan site. Parking, showers, meals, sports facilities, and electrical hook-ups may be available at an additional fee. It would also be a good idea to get an **International Camping Card** from a local camping supply shop or from the National Campers Association, *Tel. 716/668-6242.*

Before departing for Europe you should make sure that you have bought all the camping supplies that may be needed. Don't forget to bring extra waterproofed tent flies and strong bug repellent as they will most certainly come in handy. If you need to buy camping supplies within Spain you can expect to pay double or triple what they cost at home. If you want specific information on every campsite in Spain, you can ask in a Spanish book shop for a copy of the current *Guia de Campings* guide for about 1,400 *ptas.*

The local *Turismos* may also offer either a listing of regional campsites, or a free copy of the *Mapa de Campings* map and listings. In any case you can always ask any Spanish National Tourist Office if they can send you some information before you depart.

7. BASIC INFORMATION

BUSINESS HOURS

Most retail stores are open from 9am until 1:30pm and then again from about 5pm until 8pm Monday through Friday, and 9am until 1:30pm or so on Saturday. There are some shopping centers in the major cities as well as tourist areas along the coast which may also be open until midnight 6 days a week, and also in a limited number of instances, they will open on Sundays as well. Banks are open from 8:30am until 4:30pm Monday through Thursday, and 8:30pm until 2pm on Friday, but during the summer months it is not uncommon for many banks to close at 2pm on weekdays. Government offices are generally open from 9am until 6pm (although many take lunch between 1pm and 3:30pm).

CRIME

I have only had a few problems in Spain, like being pickpocketed in Sevilla and Barcelona. Yet I have heard about theft of suitcases and radios from parked cars, and of stolen gasoline from unlocked gas tanks.

To begin with, if you're driving around, make sure to remove or at least cover any visible items in the luggage or hatch area of your car. If possible you should avoid any rental cars with an open uncovered hatchback. Do not leave luggage, cameras, or any type of valuable item within the grasp of unscrupulous people. Be extra careful around gypsies who surround you in the streets (especially if they are cute little 4 year olds!). Pay attention while in bus and train stations and never leave your bags unattended. If you have any special items you are traveling around with, leave them at the safety deposit box or in the room mini-safe at your hotel. Also, be careful about walking around deserted city neighborhoods at night.

If you take these simple precautions, you are almost sure to all but avoid the possibility of a major problem. In the case that you do have a problem with theft, visit the nearest police station to make an insurance claim. Assuming you have coverage on either your homeowner's or a special policy, you must have a copy of a detailed police report. For up to date advice in several languages on security issues, call *Tel. 900-150-000 toll free* from anywhere within Spain.

ELECTRICITY

Spanish outlets are designed for 220 Volts AC and 50 Hertz and the plugs are two round pins. If you are bringing electrical appliances or components, you should bring a transformer and a plug converter of the appropriate wattage. Many appliances such as hair dryers, razors, and personal computers already have a switchable transformer built in, and may require only an adapter for the plug. Check your owner's manual carefully.

HEALTH & MEDICAL CONCERNS

Spain currently requires no inoculations or special immunizations for visitors from America and Canada. In fact, there haven't been any outbreaks of major infectious diseases here in many years. The best thing to do in case you're worried about these things is to contact the State Department Information Center in the US and ask if there are any current travel advisories on Spain.

If you are currently under medication, you should bring a copy of your prescription (with the generic name for the drug) along with your medicine. If necessary, a local *Farmacia* (pharmacy) may be able to either refill it, or refer you to a doctor who can write a new prescription. To find a 24 hour drug store, or an emergency room, just call **directory assistance (1003)** or look in a local newspaper for listings. Hospitals are available in most major population areas, and can also be found by calling directory assistance (1003) or in case of an emergency calling **(091)** for an **ambulance**.

For a free listing of English speaking doctors in Spain, please contact **I.A.M.A.T.** *in North America, Tel. 716/754-4883.* I have also included listings of a few major medical and Red Cross centers in each regional chapter of this book.

INSURANCE COVERAGE IN SPAIN

Since you are not a Spanish citizen, health care will not be provided for free. Americans with private insurance may be covered for reimbursements under their current policy, but that may only help you after months of detailed paper work. Canadians may find that their provincial health insurance may cover or reimburse certain procedures, but don't count on it. Check the *Travel Emergency* and *Trip Cancellation Insurance* sections of Chapter 6 for important advice on this subject.

OFFICIAL HOLIDAYS IN SPAIN

New Year's Day	January 1
Epiphany	January 6
Semana Santa	Easter Week
May Day	May 1
Corpus Christi, San Juan Day	24 June
Santiago Day	July 25
Assumption Day	August 15
National Day	October 12
All Saints Day	November 1
Constitution Day	December 6
Immaculate Conception Day	December 8
Christmas Eve	24 December
Christmas	25 December

These dates change yearly and the government occasionally moves holidays around to form long weekends. Many additional regional holidays exist, which vary by province. During these days expect many museums, castles, restaurants, banks, government related offices, and several private companies to be closed. If a holiday falls on a Friday or Monday you can expect many of these places to close for the entire holiday weekend. Trains and buses will tend to run on limited schedules during these times.

MONEY & BANKING

The unit of Spanish currency is called the *peseta*. You should know that in this book, and usually throughout Spain the symbol for these units of currency is marked as *ptas.*. This money comes in denominations of coins at 1, 5, 10, 25, 50, 100, 200, and 500 *ptas* while bills are printed in denominations of 1,000 through 10,000 *ptas* At press time the value of $1.00 US is roughly equal to 152 *ptas* while the value of $1.00 Canadian is about 106 *ptas*. Be advised that these rates can fluctuate wildly, so I suggest checking the exchange rate section of your newspaper to know what the value is.

Converting your currency and travelers checks into Spanish *pesetas* is quite simple, and can be done in several ways. Converting foreign currency at international airports is recommended for small amounts only. If you're arriving into Madrid and need cash for airport tips and taxis, or if you are arriving on a holiday or weekend, you can make your exchange at the international airport's banks and exchange booth (almost always open). It is advisable to exchange enough money until you can reach an open bank. Rates at the many banks in major cities are usually much better. Some banks impose a very small commission (of up to 4% or so) or fee for exchanges. When entering a bank, look for the *Cambios* or exchange sign and wait in line. Private exchange bureaus also exist in the major shopping areas of Madrid, Sevilla, Barcelona, Valencia, and the Costa del Sol although the rate is not always as good as it would be at a bank. There is no black market in Spain, so don't even try to look for it. Computerized ATM machines and 24 hour automated currency machines are available in almost every town, city, and tourist zone. Most hotels also will exchange currency for guests, but their rates include high built-in commissions and are typically not nearly as good as at a bank.

Travelers' Checks

In most places travelers' checks are easily accepted. One suggestion is that you should try to keep the denominations fairly small so the cashier will have enough *pesetas* to give proper change. While Thomas Cook and Visa travelers' checks are usually not a problem, **American Express** travelers' checks are much more widely recognized. Another advantage to American Express is that if you have lost or stolen checks, their refund center is available 24 hours a day, and can be reached toll free from anywhere in Spain by dialing *(900) 994426*.

You can also call American Express in the United States collect, *Tel. 919/333-3211*, for a U.S. travelers check refund and replacement office location nearest to where you are.

NEWSPAPERS & MAGAZINES

There is a vast assortment of Spanish language daily and weekly newspapers that can easily be located at any newsstand, hotel lobby, or local tobacco shop. Of these, the majority of people tend to read the informative *El Mundo, ABC*, and *El Pais* daily papers from Madrid, and the progressive *El Periodico* from Barcelona. Excellent weeklys include the arts and entertainment laden *Cambio 16* which is a great source for things to do in Madrid.

There are also a handful of English language weekly and monthly papers, such as *Sol in English,* that can be found in major areas of the Costa del Sol. If you search around the Costa del Sol and the kiosks of Barcelona and Madrid, you may also find current copies of the *International Herald Tribune*, the *European*, and *US Today*. If you don't mind reading old news, backdated issues of the *New York Times*, *Wall Street Journal,* and the *London Times* may sometimes be collecting dust in hotel-based tobacconists and a few newsstands in the financial districts of the major cities. Special European editions of English language magazines such as *Time, Newsweek, Playboy, Penthouse* and *The Economist*, are also available at leading hotels.

PHYSICALLY-CHALLENGED TRAVELERS

Traveling in Spain for the physically challenged person can prove to be a bit complicated. Getting to the country is the easy part of your journey as most airlines offer special seating assignments, wheelchair storage, and boarding assistance to anyone who requests so in advance.

Upon arrival in Madrid, additional special airport assistance services are also offered free of charge by the airlines. Now that you have arrived in Spain, things get a little more difficult. Although well marked, reserved "handicapped" parking spaces can be found at the airport and in some cities, almost none of the major rental car companies offer specially adapted vehicles.

New regulations from the European Economic Community (E.E.C.) are finally starting to have a positive effect on the availability of special services and facilities, especially in the larger cities of Madrid, Barcelona, and Sevilla. The **Tourist Office of Spain** (listed in Chapter 6, *Planning Your Trip*) in Toronto and New York have listings of hotels with specially adapted rooms, and companies like **Viajes 2000** that book vacations for those with specific challenges.

About the best Spanish language publication on this subject is called "*Viajes para Minusvalidos*" and can be found in major city book shops for 1750 *ptas*.

Wheelchair accessible bathrooms, entrance ramps, and well designed elevators with Braille and chime features are starting to become more common in the larger 4 and 5 star hotels in resort areas and business centers. Whenever possible I have included a special notation in some hotel listings when special facilities are offered. Each regional *Turismo* office may be able to direct visitors to additional transportation services, accommodations, and restaurants which are properly equipped.

There are also new daily dial-a-ride door to door bus services in some cities that must be arranged at least two days in advance. A special card might be required from the bus operators. For dial-a-ride details, please call the tourist offices here, or in Spain itself.

Helpful organizations include:
- **Society for the Advancement of Travel for the Handicapped**, *New York, New York, Tel. 212/447-7284*. A members-only service with basic information about travel needs for the physically challenged. Yearly membership is $45 US for adults and $25 for students.
- **MossRehab Travel Information Services**, *Philadelphia, Pennsylvania, Tel. 215/456-9600*. A free information and referral service with valuable hints and suggestions on companies that offer travel services for the physically challenged.
- **Flying Wheels Travel**, *Owatonna, Minnesota, Tel. 800/535-6790*. A great full service travel agency and group tour operator that can provide

helpful information and reservations for the physically challenged. Services include all forms of special transportation and accommodation reservations, and guided group tours.

POST OFFICES & MAIL

Throughout the country there is a vast network of over 6,000 post offices (**Correos**) which are open from about 8am until 12 noon and again from about 5pm until 7pm on Monday through Friday, some with limited Saturday morning hours. In major cities it is possible to find a few main branch offices which remain open 24 hours a day. Letters sent via air mail (*por avión*) from Spain to North America normally cost around 120 *ptas,* and can take up to 2 weeks to arrive. Mail within Spain itself usually costs about 70 *ptas* and can find their way to the addressee in around 6 days.

Most post offices sell stamps and can help with normal postal needs. You can send and receive mail, make phone calls, place international money orders, faxes, telegraphs, and wire money transfers at several of the larger branches. If you wish to have a main post office hold mail for you, general delivery can be arranged. Let the postal clerk know who you are and that you will eventually be expecting mail to arrive at his branch.

NIGHTLIFE IN SPAIN

Each city and town in Spain has a vast assortment of evening entertainment. There are many establishments where you can enjoy rock concerts, jazz bands, symphonies, opera, theater, ballroom dancing, and casino gaming. There are also thousands of establishments which are similar to the bars, discos, and nightclubs which you are already accustomed to back home.

Although once thought of as an extremely conservative Catholic nation, the recent liberalization of Spain after the death of General Franco has changed the way the younger generations think, act, and dress. Most young people tend to get to the bars and clubs late on weekend nights. It's quite common for people between the ages of 17 to 35 or so to start off partying at midnight and keep on going at least until breakfast time the next morning, especially around Valencia. The bar scene is among Europe's most exciting, and one night stands are a frequent occurrence here these days.

Included in this guide are several lists of the local nightlife in each regional and major city chapter, but you should always try to ask a local student, resident, or hotel concierge to fill you in on the most happening spots.

Incoming letters must be marked **Poste Restante-Lista do Correos** and sent, with your last named boldly written and underlined, to the closest post office. When letters arrive, they can be picked up at the post office as long as you present the clerk with a passport or other ID.

You can also receive mail and telegrams via an **American Express** office, but you must contact them before you depart North America, *Tel. 800/221-7282*. These client mail services are free to American Express cardholders, vacation clients, and traveler's check holders, but can sometimes be obtained by others for a small fee.

Both **DHL** and **Federal Express** can deliver packages between North America and Spain, and visa versa, within 3 business days.

RADIO

The countless regional or major city AM and FM radio stations in Spain are wonderful sources of free entertainment, and most hotel rooms and rental cars have the equipment to receive them. There are hundreds of stations broadcasting every type of music and talk show imaginable.

One of the funniest things about hearing the radio here is that after several sets of unfamiliar local music, you will then be pelted with tasteless old American songs like *Yummy, Yummy, Yummy I've Got Love in My Tummy* or some all but forgotten disco tune. The stations in large cities and resort areas like Madrid, Sevilla, Barcelona, Marbella, and Valencia will sometimes offer great classical, rock, blues, or jazz shows. For those of you who are interested in finding English language programs, I suggest that you carefully search the dial for the BBC World Service and the US Armed Forces Radio broadcasts. There are also daily programs geared towards tourists and expatriates from England, that are broadcast on some stations in the Costa del Sol.

For under $200 US, you can purchase a great compact portable **short-wave radio receiver**, such as the top-rated **Grundig Yacht Boy 400** that will allow you to pick up a multitude of English (and other language) broadcasts originating from the country you are about to visit. This is a great way learn about special cultural events, weather conditions, festivals, important news and other helpful tips before you leave for your vacation or business trip . Once you have arrived in Europe, you will find it easy to keep in touch with the current events back home in Canada or the U.S..

Among the most enjoyable news, information, and entertainment programming in English on the short-wave bands are those broadcast several times daily by operations like **Radio Canada International, Voice of America**, **Swiss Radio International**, and the superb **Radio Netherlands**. For specific frequency locations for these and many other networks, ask your local book shop to order you a copy of *Passport to World Band Radio* published annually by International Broadcasting Services Ltd. in Penns Park, Pennsylvania.

Send a quick fax or letter to Marbian Productions International, *P.O. Box 1051, Pointe Claire, Quebec, Canada H9S 4H9 (Fax 514-697-2615).* Marbian's president, Mr. Ian McFarland, a former shortwave radio program producer and host, will be glad to send you current programming and frequency schedules for a variety of shortwave stations, including the above mentioned networks, directly to your home or office for free.

STUDENT TRAVEL & YOUTH ID CARDS

For full-time students under the age of 26 who can provide documentation of their current status, I strongly suggest the **International Student Identity Card (I.S.I.C.)**. It is valid for one year and should be obtained in North America before you depart for about $15 US. It allows its holder to have discounts on international flights, museums, public transportation and other services.

Included with the cost of these cards in the U.S., is special emergency medical insurance, which can cover about $3000 US in medical bills as well as approximately $100 a day in hospital bills for up to two months or so. Another card known as the **International Youth Card** is also available with similar features for young adults under 26 who are no longer in school.

To obtain one of these cards, contact on of the following student travel companies:

• **Council Travel**, *New York, Tel. 212/661-1450*
• **Travel Cuts**, *Toronto, Tel. 416/979-2406*

TELEPHONES, TELEGRAMS, & FAXES

The phone system in Spain is becoming as modern and convenient to use as any in North America. For example, most pay phones provide detailed multilingual instructions for local and international calling procedures if you press the button that displays an **L** inside a flag on the left side of the payphone. Now the vast majority of public payphones in Spain accept Visa, Mastercard, Diners, and American Express cards. The standard street corner pay phones also accept Spanish *Tarjecta Telephonica* phonecards (see below) as well as multiple coins of 5 *ptas*, 25 *ptas*, 50 *ptas*, 100 *ptas*, 200 *ptas*, and in some cases 500 *ptas*, but the older 50 *ptas* and 200 *ptas* coins may not always work.

Over the last few years the major phone companies in Spain offer prepaid phone cards for use in specially marked phones. The *Tarjeta*

Telefónica card is the most commonly used such card, and can be bought in denominations of 1000 and 2000 *ptas* at most newsstands and/or tobacconists. They are generally useful in the major cities, but not always in some smaller secluded villages and towns.

You could always place a local or long distance call from your hotel, but you can expect to get hit with a surcharge of up to 250%. About the only time I suggest using a hotel's equipment is when I need to send or receive a fax. Another suggestion is to place calls (or even faxes and telegrams) during normal business hours from a main post office's *Correro* telephone and communications department, or ask the *Turismo* tourist office for the location of a *Telefónica* phone company office, where you are shown to a small cabin. After making your call you pay a somewhat higher than normal rate that is still much less than the typical hotel surcharge. Most of these telephone company offices will accept Visa and Mastercard.

SAVE MONEY CALLING HOME!

*A couple of small new telecommunications companies have started offering prepaid international calling cards for sale in Spain. These reusable discounted telephone cards are marketed under the names **Fon-Olé** or **Printel Card** and are available in 1,000 ptas and 2,000 ptas denominations. When using this type of card you must first dial a toll free number in Spain, then using the touch tone pad of any public or house phone you must first enter in a special access code, then your destination country code, area code and phone number. While the whole process takes an extra minute or so, you can count on **saving 60%** or so off the usual daytime and evening payphone (and tarjeta telefonica) rates to the U.S. or Canada. These cards are a bit tough to find at first, but they are getting more popular and are available in select newsstands and tobacconists in major cities and tourist resorts such as Sevilla, Madrid, Barcelona, Malaga, Marbella, and Sitges.*

PHONE TIPS

To reach the U.S. and Canada from Spain:
Dial 07, wait for the high frequency response tone, then dial 1 (for North America) followed by the desired area code and phone number.

To reach Spain from the US and Canada:
Dial 011 - 34 and then the area code and phone number
(Make sure to include a nine (9) as the first digit of the regional area code).

To call between two Spanish cities within the same area code:
Dial the area code and phone number
(Make sure to include a nine (9) as the first digit of the regional area code).

To call between two Spanish cities in different area codes:
Dial the area code and phone number
(Make sure to include a nine (9) as the first digit of the regional area code).

A typical call within one region or city should cost around 30 *ptas* per minute. Calling outside the same city or region can bring the cost up to about 50 *ptas* per minute. Calling a GSM cell phone within Spain will cost about 145 *ptas* per minute. Calling internationally can cost 170 *ptas* or more per minute. In general, calling long distance or internationally from Spain is cheaper after 11pm on weekdays and after 2pm on weekends. If you need to call internationally, you can use MCI, Sprint, ATT, and a variety of private phone company's access codes from within Spain to reach English speaking operators for collect, credit card, and third party calls. It is even possible to use these cards in the hotel's lobby pay phone.

IMPORTANT PHONE NUMBERS

Local Information	*1003*
International Operator Assistance	*1005*
Municipal Police	*092*
Civil Guard	*062*
Red Cross Emergencies	*061*
US Country Code	*1*
Canada Country Code	*1*
U.K. Country Code	*44*
ATT USA Direct Access Number	*900/990-011*
MCI CALL USA Access Number	*900/990-014*
SPRINT USA Direct Access Number	*900/990-013*

Cellular Telephones
Cellular telephones are quite popular in Spain, but your North American cell phone will not function in Europe's totally different *GSM* cellular operating system. If you're like me, and like to have some means of communication while on the road, your best option is to buy a GSM in Europe and carry it with you. I have even been able to connect to the

Internet and send most of my faxes via GSM cell phones and my portable notebook computer. While major rental car companies offer rather expensive European cell phone rentals, they have always screwed up my reservation, and no phone was available when I went to get it.

GSM cell phones are available for purchase from just $50 US if you sign up for a 12-month contract in Spain, but that is of no use for vacationers. On the other hand the same type of cell phone can be purchased for under $250.00 US without the usual 12 month mandatory activation contract. You can purchase the phone anywhere in Europe without an activation contract and then just spend and additional 5,500 ptas to receive a special instant non-contracted incoming phone number which is valid for 6 months, and receive a credit of some 2,500 ptas for outgoing calls (you can always add more outgoing call credit to your phone in increments of 5,000 ptas) from any cell phone shop in Spain.

The two major cell phone service that provide these non-contracted instant service packages are Airtel and Movistar, and they charge about 175 ptas per minute of peak time outgoing calls, 30 ptas per minute per minute of outgoing off peak calls within Spain and the rest of the European Economic Community. Calls to America cost upwards of 300 ptas per minute, and there is absolutely no charge to receive incoming calls on your phone. If you only answer calls on your GSM cell phone, you can talk to anyone from anywhere on Earth, and it's absolutely free.

TELEVISION

Take advantage of the selection of media (some is in English) available in Spain. To begin with, the national government offers two of their own TV stations that are managed by the **TVE** broadcasting company. These stations transmit their signal to most parts of the country, and tend to offer a combination of locally produced game shows, soap operas, talk shows, news programs and poorly dubbed international movies. The prospect of seeing a Mel Brooks movie being shown on the tube in Spanish may seem unbearable, but I find it rather amusing.

There are also a few private television stations and satellite channels including **Tele 5**, **Antena 3**, and the **Canal Plus** movie channel. Most of the better hotels also offer a selection of other European satellite TV programs from Germany France, Italy, and in some cases you will find CNN International. Usually at least one of these stations will be the SKY news network from England which is quite entertaining. You should know that the Canal Plus and German networks have a tendency to show hardcore porno flicks on weekend evenings.

TIME

Spain usually follows the same daylight savings time system as the US and Canada from April through October. Technically these time zone are Greenwich Mean Time (GMT) + 1 hour from November through March, and Greenwich Mean Time (GMT) + 2 hours from April through October.

The time difference between the North American Eastern time zone (New York, Boston, Montreal, Toronto) and mainland Spain is 6 hours, 7 hours from Central time, 8 hours from Mountain time, and 9 hours from Pacific time.

TIPPING

There are many situations in which a gratuity may be appropriate. In most cases you are free to use your judgment based on the quality of services rendered. Many Spaniards do not tip for some services that in our culture may be commonplace. If someone gives you back a tip, do not take it as an insult.

Below are the standard amounts to tip in Spain:
- **Taxi Driver** *8% of the meter's rate*
- **Hotel Porter** *150 ptas per bag*
- **Hotel Concierge** *500 ptas per small favor, 1,500 ptas per big favor*
- **Room Service** *250 ptas per person per meal*
- **Hotel Doorman** *200 ptas per taxi*
- **Bartender** *100 ptas per round*
- **Waiter** *10% to 15% of the bill, in cash*
- **Ushers** *150 ptas*
- **Private Guide** *1,800 ptas per person per day*
- **Private Drivers** *1,250 ptas per person per day*
- **Tour Guides** *1,400 ptas per person per day*
- **Tour Bus Drivers** *850 ptas per person per day*

TOURIST INFORMATION OFFICES - TURISMOS

Once you have arrived in Spain, there are many places to pick up vital tourist information in several languages. Each major city, tourist destination, and rural town hall (**ayuntamiento**) usually operates at least one office to assist visitors to their region. These tourist information offices are usually marked with a sign that says **Turismo**.

Many of these offices are open during typical business hours, so during Saturday afternoons and all day on Sundays they may be closed. These *Turismos* are normally staffed by just one or two local residents who have the ability to communicate in multiple languages.

Turismos are managed by the local and/or regional government, and most of them are extremely friendly and helpful with handing out free maps, walking tour brochures, hotel listings, transportation schedules, and much more. I suggest that when you arrive in a city or town you should first pop into the local *Turismo* and find out if they can offer any suggestions to help you better enjoy and understand your visit. If you are both specific and nice to them, the staff of these tourist offices will often alert you to off-the-beaten-path attractions and unique accommodations that only local residents would know about.

I have included address and phone listings of many *Turismos* in their corresponding city listings.

8. SPORTS & RECREATION

The following is a brief description of the most popular sports and recreational activities available in Spain. Golf is particularly big here, as you can see from the long list of courses. Have fun!

BICYCLES

During the last several years, the sport of **bicycling** has become more popular in Spain. It is now possible to plan either long or short-range cycle excursions for both on and off-road adventures. Many hotels, farmhouses, and local bike shops offer bicycle rentals for those who are interested in a few hours or days of two-wheeled fun. Use the reflectors, flags, and lights for cycling in Spain, as your safety may depend on them. Cars may often not give a bicycle the right of way. I have included a partial listing of places that rent bicycles in some of the regional chapters, but for further information please contact a local *Turismo* office.

If you intend to travel extensively by bicycle in Spain, consider the following items: Most airlines will permit the transportation of bikes, but may charge the passenger for so-called extra baggage. Trains in Spain also permit the transportation of bikes with a small additional fee. Buses will often not allow for bikes on-board owing to limited luggage capacity. Most spare parts are quite expensive in Spain, so bring them with you.

For people interested in group bicycle tours, there are a few companies such as **Cycling Through the Centuries** in the US, *Tel. 800/245-4226*, who offer guided cycling tours in Spain.

BULLFIGHTS - LOS TOROS

One of the most exciting spectator sports throughout the country is the typical Spanish **bullfight** (**corrida**). These events have been enjoyed in Spain since the 14th century, and follow a strictly enforced set of customs and rules set forth by the famed Romero family in **Ronda**. Many cities and towns all over Spain will hold weekly or monthly bullfighting events from around March through October in a specially designed circular bullring (**Plaza de Toros**).

Tickets for these events can range from between 1,250 *ptas* and 6,750 *ptas* per seat depending on the seat's location. Many bullrings that hold daytime events will sell the cheap tickets in the section facing the sun (*sol*), while the more expensive seats tend to be closer to the action and in the shady (*sombra*) sections.

Before the start of the evening's events, there is usually a traditional parade of the ornately costumed and highly trained horses with their costumed mounted warriors accompanied by music from the bandstand. When the ring is cleared, an angry bull is released from the ringside bullpen. A bullfighter (**matador**) enters the ring and provokes the bull using his brightly colored capes. After a determination is made as to how aggressive the bull is, the bullfighter leaves the ring for a few minutes.

After this, a gate soon opens and well-trained horses with mounted fighters (**picadores**) begin to taunt the bull into action using spears. The object of this activity is for the bull to charge towards the padded bodies of the horses in order for the *picador* to poke his spear into the bull's body and tire it out a bit. After a few minutes, the mounted fighters depart the field.

Soon after, three of the bullfighter's assistants (**banderillas**) walk into the ring and attempt to lodge a series of colorful spears into the bull's shoulders. Once this is done, the *matador* walks onto the field, salutes the presiding officials with his hat, and takes his red cape out to begin prodding the bull to charge at him. While these charges are taking place, the band strikes up a tune while enthusiastic audience members shout out, "*Ole!*" A perfect fight would end with the *matador* striking the bull with a spear to its heart. In many cases the direct hit to the heart is not achieved, and a spear is used to slit the bull's spine and kill it quickly.

The dead bull is then dragged out of the ring by a mule team while the crowd applauds the *matador*. These events can take several hours, and some include several *matadores* each with two separate fights.

CAR RACES & RALLIES - AUTOMOVILISMO

Major car races include the **Rallye Costa Brava** in **Gerona** each February, the **Rallye de Catalunya** in **Barcelona** each March, the **Rallye R.A.C.E. de Costa Blanca** in March, and the **Rallye de Austrias** in **Oviedo** each September.

FISHING - PESCA

The rivers, lakes, reservoirs, and seacoast of Spain contain a vast array of fine **fish**. A special license issued by the government is generally required for deep sea, river, and underwater fishing. For lake and seashore fishing, you should check with the local *Turismo* office and make sure there are no local laws forbidding the activity.

Each season presents opportunities to catch a different assortment of wonderful fresh and salt-water fish. The most common targets for sea fishing include grouper, bass, bream, swordfish, shark, bluefish, tuna, sole, mackerel, rays, and dolphin fish. For those who are interested in river and lake fishing, expect to find trout, salmon, bass, shad, and pike. Many companies offer excursions by boat into the most famous fishing areas of Spain.

For more details, contact the nearest Tourist Office of Spain or the **Spanish Fishing Federation (Federacíon Española de Pesca)** in Madrid, *Tel. (91) 413-9951.*

GOLF

Golf is a tremendously popular pastime in Spain for visiting British, German, and North American visitors. Due to the excellent climate year-round, many courses have sprung up throughout the country, and several more are in the planning and construction stages. Many courses have been designed by the world's leading professionals such as Robert Trent Jones, Gary Player, and Mackenzie Ross. Although Golf in Spain is not particularly inexpensive, the unique conditions and dramatic views make this an unbeatable location for world-class facilities. Most clubs offer a full range of services including access to opulent clubhouses.

A brief description of the best of Spain's 159 major courses is listed below, but please contact the National Tourist office of Spain in your country to receive a free copy of the *Mapa de Golf* golf course map and directory. The **Spanish Royal Federation of Golf** (**Real Federacíon Española de Golf**) can provide you with specific course maps and green fee listings. They can be reached in Madrid, *Tel. (91) 555-2682 or Fax (91) 555-2757.*

You will find that most golf courses (even private clubs) will offer rates for non-members to use their facilities. The major cities and the coastal areas are studded with a vast array of choices for all levels of skill, and there are other courses in most regions of the country. Just because everything else in Spain seems like a bargain, don't expect golf to be cheap. I have spent over 10,000 *ptas* per person for a round of golf on a nice course this year. Electric carts, equipment rental, locker rooms, lessons, and caddies are usually available at additional cost.

Many hotels offer discounts and preferred tee times on local courses to their guests, so please at the front desk for details. Some regional chapters of this book contain the listings of available courses.

HORSEBACK RIDING

With a long equestrian tradition, Spain offers a wide variety of **horseback** and carriage riding facilities. Many stables, hotels, resorts, farms, and riding centers can offer hourly riding on wonderful pure and mixed breed horses for as little as 1,350 *ptas* per hour. Each region offers several different places to ride horses, but the **Alpujarras** section of **Andalucía** may be the most dramatic area for scenic rides.

I have listed a selection of my favorite riding establishments in some regional chapters of this book. If you need further details please contact your hotel's front desk or a local *Turismo* office. For detailed information on the full range of horseback riding schools and exhibitions, contact the **Spanish Equestrian Federation (Federacíon Hipíca Española)** in Madrid, *Tel. (91) 319-2003 or Fax (91) 319-0233.*

HUNTING - CAZA

Spain offers fine **hunting** for visitors who have obtained a hunting license from the **ICONA** *in* Madrid *at Tel. (91) 347-5956.* To receive the license each foreigner must present a passport and a gun license from their country of origin. If arriving in Spain with firearms, you may have to leave a deposit for each gun and get a special permit at the customs area when you first arrive in the country.

If you are not bringing your arms, finding equipment is not always an easy task. Expect to find sanctioned hunting areas for quail, rabbit, partridge, pheasant, duck, and wild boar. For tips and regulations on hunting in Spain, contact the **Spanish Hunting Federation (Federacíon Española de Caza)** in Madrid, *Tel. (91) 553-9017.*

JAI-ALAI - VASCO PELOTA

This popular betting sport based on an old Basque game takes place in a venue known as a **frontón**, where one of several variants of this sport may be scheduled.

The most exciting version pits two teams of two men each on a three walled court. During a normal game, the teams serve and return a small hard ball (**pelota**) that has been bounced off the walls at a high rate of speed. Each time a serve is missed, or a bounce has not been returned before it hits the floor, a point for the opposing team is scored. The game can be played using bare hands, leather paddles, rubber paddles, rackets, and most dramatically with curved wood and wicker baskets attached to the players' stronger hand. Ask your hotel's front desk or a nearby *Turismo* office for game schedules and locations.

OFF-ROAD VEHICLES

You can rent jeeps by the hour or day from several large car rental agencies in major tourist zones. Since this sport entails an increased element of danger, your insurance may not cover you in case of an accident. Check with your hotel or local *Turismo* office for a listing of good excursion companies that may offer more specialized off-road adventures.

SOCCER - FUTBOL

Like the rest of Europe, **soccer (futbol)** is a major national pastime in Spain. In the months between September and May there are many serious soccer league matches within the country (especially in Madrid, Barcelona, Zaragoza and Sevilla) that can each draw upwards of 95,000 spectators. Since these matches are so faithfully attended, the tickets (which range in price from 850 *ptas* to 4,250 *ptas* per seat) are often completely sold out well in advance.

The games featuring the leading teams (**F.C. Barcelona**, **Real Madrid**, **Real Zaragoza**, **F.C. Sevilla**) often create huge all-night traffic jams due to the tendency of the spectators to use the highways and streets of the host city as giant parking lots. If you are interested in seeing a match, you can check with the hosting stadium's box office to see if there are any seats available. Be extremely careful not to cheer too loudly for the visiting team, as fans can get a bit rough with their adversaries. Soccer matches are generally accompanied by a series of events not unlike our pro football half-time and pre-game festivities.

TENNIS - TENIS

You can find both private and municipal **tennis** centers and courts in most major tourist resorts and large cities. As with golf, there is a higher concentration of these facilities in both the southern and eastern coastal areas. Many hotels also offer a few courts for the exclusive use of their guests, but sometimes they can be persuaded to welcome others. If you are looking for lessons or court time, you can inquire at either the front desk of your hotel, or at a local *Turismo* office for details and suggestions.

I have included a listing several tennis centers in the regional chapters of this book. For complete details and listings on all of the country's tennis facilities, contact the **Spanish Royal Federation of Tennis (Real Federacíon Española de Tenis)** in Madrid, *Tel. (91) 519-5008 or Fax (91) 416-4504.*

WATER SPORTS

With hundreds of miles of superb coastline, Spain offers visitors many opportunities to **swim**, **sail**, **windsurf**, **water-ski**, **jet-ski**, **surf**, **dive**, and **snorkel**. Since there are so many different areas to enjoy water sports throughout the country, I have included a listing of the best facilities in each regional chapter.

For the most part, you can expect to find world-class surfing and wind surfing in the **Costa del Sol**, **Costa de Almeria**, and **Costa de la Luz**. Fine sailing, diving, snorkeling, jet skiing and water-skiing can be enjoyed all along the southern and eastern coastlines. There are also countless spots for swimming and sailing in lakes scattered around almost all of the interior regions of the country. Check with the local *Turismo* office for details on additional sights and equipment rentals.

SKIING - ESQUI

That's right, Spain is a great place to hit the slopes and cross-county trails in the wintertime. There are over 30 licensed ski resorts located in varying regions of the country. For specific information about trail and lift specifications, private lessons, world class alpine and downhill competitions and months of operation get in touch with the **Tourist Ski and Mountain Resort Association** (**ATUDEM**) in Madrid, *Tel. (91) 350-2020.*

The most notable Spanish ski areas include the Pyrenees mountain range in the upper reaches of the eastern **Catalunya** region where you can find resorts like Baqueira Beret, Vallter 2000, Marsella, La Molina, Tuca Betren, Vall de Nuria, Port Aine, Super Espot, Port de Compte and Rasos de Peguera. Nearby, in the part of the Pyrenees Mountains that heads into the northern **Aragón** region there are the resorts of Formigal, Cerler, Astun, Candanchu, and Panticosa.

The **Cordillera Cantabrica** mountains in the northern and central **Cantabria, Asturias**, and **Castilla y León** regions are home to ski areas such as Alto Campo, San Isidro, Picos de Europa, Manzaneda, and Valgrande-Pajares. Over in the **Iberian Mountains** in the northern and central **La Rioja** and **Castilla y León** regions you can also enjoy the slopes of Lunada and Valdezcaray. In the heart of the country in the **Comunidad de Madrid** region there are a handful of ski areas like the Navacerrada, Valdesqui, La Pinilla, and Valcotos. Last, but certainly not least, is the fine Sierra Nevada ski resort in the **Sierra Nevada** mountain range in the southern region of **Andalucía**.

SWIMMING

Spain has countless fine **beaches**, **lagoons**, **rivers**, and **lakes** where you can enjoy a great swim. Keep in mind that most swimming areas do not have full time lifeguards, so it's important to take the proper precautions. When you swim in the ocean there may be strong undertows and cross currents that must be considered. Also worth noting are the blue flags that can be seen in main beach resort areas. These blue flags ensure that the area has passed current E.E.C. safe water requirements for purity.

Other options for swimming include the hundreds of **municipal swimming pools** in the major towns of Spain. These public pools are normally open during the warmer months of each year and often provide lifeguards, showers, changing rooms, lockers, and pool side lounge chairs which are available for locals and visitors alike. Some public pools may charge a small admittance fee. Check with a local *Turismo* office for hours and locations of public pools and municipal beaches.

Remember: the sun is often hot here. Be sure to bring a good waterproof sunscreen to block out the sun's dangerous rays, whether you're on land or sea.

SPAIN'S MOST BEAUTIFUL BEACHES

Playa Las Genovas: San Jose, Cabos de Gato, Almeria Province.
Crescent shaped 800 meter long beach with fine virgin white sand, no development at all, and bordered on either side by bold little mountains.
Playa Calblanque: Calblanque, La Manga, Murcia Province.
Over one kilometer of protected parkland beach with plenty of nearby dunes full of migrating birds and beautiful semi-tropical foliage.
Playa de Carabeillo: Nerja, Costa del Sol, Aldalucia Province.
Tiny sheltered cove beach with rocky cliffs isolating the entire area from the rest of the world. Well worth the cliff hike to find this secluded spot.
Platja de Boadella: Lloret de Mar, Costa Brava, Girona Province.
Secluded and romantic little crescent shaped silky white sand beach two kilometers south of town on an unmarked access road. No services here.
Playa de Galizano: Ajo, Costa Verde, Cantabria Province.
Almost unknown remote 75 meter long tidal beach on a dry river bed near Santander. Bordered by pine cliffs and strange geometric rock formations.

9. SHOPPING

BOUTIQUES

Shopping in Spain is a pleasure. Each region produces different items ranging from hand-painted ceramics to finely tailored designer clothing. Fine shoes, shirts, sweaters, dresses, handbags, belts, suits, linens, ceramics, tiles, embroidery, vintage wines, jewelry and all sorts of additional items can be found at a fraction of their export price. Many larger size items of clothing and footwear may not be available (including any North American shoe size over ten and a half).

Most jewelry is made with 10 to 20-karat gold (*ouro*) or sterling silver (*plata*), but many filigree items are only offered in gold or silver plate. Remember that most boutiques and other stores are generally open from about 9:30am until 1:30pm, and again from 4:30pm until at least 8pm on weekdays, and on Saturdays from about 9:30am until 1pm.

Since Spain has joined the EEC, a program of tax refunds on selected export items has begun. What this **Tax Free for Tourists** program really does is quite simple and worth taking advantage of. Over 1100 shops in Spain display the black and blue "Tax Free" sticker on their door. When you make a purchase of over 15,000 *ptas*, you can ask for a Tax Free voucher check for your refund. The unsigned check is made out to the tourist (you must have your passport with you), which can only be cashed at the airport upon exiting the country.

The value of the check depends on what percentage of tax was placed on the specific item you have purchased. Clothes are usually taxed around 10%–15%, while some luxury items such as jewelry and electronics are taxed as high as 25% or more.

At the airport, go to the information booth and they will direct you to the cashier (7 days a week) before you reach the gates. For more details, pick up an English version of the *Tax Free For Tourists* brochure at either the airport or a participating boutique, or if necessary call the Madrid office of the *Tax Free for Tourists* offices, *Tel. (91) 435-4822.*

ANTIQUE HUNTING

For those of you interested in **antiques** (**antigüedades**), the best places to find good values are at the outdoor markets. Most major cities have a few select antique shops that can provide a fun browsing experience. Bargaining is not uncommon. Among the best antique values are old paintings, estate jewelry, rare books, old lamps, ancient doorknockers, centuries-old ceramic tiles, and wonderful wooden picture frames. Spanish furniture is also a good bargain, but the shipping, insurance, and customs hassles can be discouraging. The less reputable shops may display reproductions of antique objects without explaining the true age of the item.

REGIONAL HANDICRAFTS

Each town and village in Spain offers many unique regional **crafts** (**artisanías**) which can easily be found in shops, markets, crafts fairs, and artisan's kiosks. Several local *Turismo* offices throughout Spain have copies of a pamphlet that give complete listings of all the regional crafts fairs and exhibitions each year.

The most sought-after examples of regional crafts include these fine products that are made and then sold in the following places:

• *Barcelona, Catalunya*	Hand blown glass and pottery
• *Benalmádena, Andalucía*	Fine wrought iron pieces
• *Córdoba, Andalucía*	Hand crafted leather and filigree jewelry
• *Granada, Andalucía*	Ceramics, wrought iron, furniture, guitars
• *Jerez de la Frontera, Andalucía*	Hand sewn leather saddles
• *Lanjarón, Andalucía*	Wicker baskets
• *Madrid, Comunidad de Madrid*	Lace goods, guitars, and much more
• *Murcia, Murcia*	Pottery, wooden goods
• *Ronda, Andalucía*	Leather saddles and packsacks
• *Salamanca, Castilla y León*	Fine hats
• *Santiago, La Coruña*	Silver goods, beads
• *Segovia, Castilla y León*	Chandlery
• *Sevilla, Andalucía*	Ceramics, *Flamenco* dresses, and more
• *Toledo, Castilla-La Mancha*	Replica weapons, inlaid jewelry, leather goods
• *Valencia, Valencia Fallas*	Figurines, guitars, leather goods
• *Zaragoza, Aragón*	Wine sacks

EUROPEAN SIZE CONVERSIONS

These sizes are an approximate conversion and may not be accurate in certain cases. Ask for a free measurement or try on items before you purchase them.

Men's Shoes

North America	7	7.5	8	9	10	11
Spain	39	40	41	43	44	45

Women's Shoes

North America	4	5	6	7	8	9
Spain	35	36	37	38	39	40

Men's Suits

North America	34	36	38	40	42	44
Spain	44	46	48	50	52	54

Women's Dresses

North America	6	8	10	12	14	16
Spain	36	38	40	42	44	46

Men's Shirts

North America	15	16	17	18
Europe	38	40	42	44

10. MAJOR FESTIVALS

Each region of Spain hosts several festivals, fairs, religious processions and special celebrations every year. The following list contains some of the most important religious, cultural, historical and agricultural festivities. To receive information on the exact dates of each specific event, contact either one of the National Tourist Offices of Spain, or the *Turismo* office in the region you are visiting. Several more fairs and festivals are also listed in each regional chapter.

JANUARY
Epiphany celebrations throughout Spain include the giving of gifts to children, and large parades down main avenues.

FEBRUARY
Carnival festivities throughout Spain. Outrageous street dancing, all night parties, and crowded parades take over whole cities and towns. The city of **Cádiz** is the best place to take part in the fun.

MARCH
Las Fallas de San José fireworks and parades in the city of **Valencia** take place for a week before large papier-mache statues are lit up in a huge barn fire.

Semana Santa are strange yet enchanting religious processions of masked men carrying revered icons and altars through the streets of Spanish cities and towns on the week prior to Easter Sunday. This is especially dramatic in **Sevilla**.

Drama Festival of Madrid has dozens of unique theater performances featuring a cast of world famous actors.

Antique Car Rally in the coastal city of **Sitges**.

APRIL

Feria de Abril week-long celebrations on the outskirts of **Sevilla** that include bullfights, *flamenco* singing and dancing by costumed residents, equestrian parades, and plenty of drinking for all.

MAY

Equestrian Festival in Jerez, featuring several days of shows and special events featuring the amazing skills of the trained horses of *Jerez de la Frontera*.

Fiesta San Isidro in **Madrid** when a week of bullfights and parades gets the city into a much livelier mood than normal.

Fiesta de los Patios in the city of **Córdoba** when the most beautiful inner courtyards are judged for prizes and open to the public for inspection.

Romero de Rocio in the city of **Almonte** in **Andalucía** when strange processions of altar pieces are brought across the river by horse drawn wagons.

JUNE

Corpus Cristi is a series of religious processions taking place all over the nation.

International Festival of Dance and Music celebrates the world's top performers in both indoor and outdoor venues around the city of **Granada**.

Fiesta de San Juan celebrations throughout Spain include odd parades, concerts, and superb fireworks.

JULY

Fiesta San Fermin in the city of **Pamplona**, where you'll find the famous running of the bulls, preceded by a week of parties and bullfights.

Fiesta Mayor in **Santiago de Compostela** is a giant festival that coincides with the completion of the pilgrimage on the Road of St. James.

San Sebastian International Jazz Festival has indoor and outdoor jazz concerts from the best musicians in the world.

International Guitar Festival features fine concerts of world famous guitarists for weeks on end in **Córdoba**.

AUGUST

El Misteri de Elchi, a world renowned performance of the oldest known Christian mystery play in the town of **Eleche** in **Valencia**.

Semana Grande in **San Sebastian** is a week-long celebration including fireworks, ball games, parades and plenty of huge parties.

Greek Theater Festival in **Barcelona** has outdoor theater, music, and dance shows held at the Greek Theater up on **Montjuic**.

Tomato Fights are held in the hamlet of **Bunol, Valencia** where residents pelt each other with the season's pick of ripe juicy tomatoes!

SEPTEMBER

Grape Harvest Festivals are held throughout Spain to celebrate the year's harvest.

La Merced parades and huge street parties are held in **Barcelona**.

Festival of Ancient Music of Daroca in **Zaragoza** provides a great cultural experience for those who love Renaissance and Baroque music.

NOVEMBER

Barcelona International Jazz Festival highlights over a week of heart-pounding jazz concerts by both masters and new talent on the jazz scene.

Madrid Jazz Festival is a three week festival including shows all over town, midnight jam sessions, and special events.

11. SPANISH CUISINE

I have included brief descriptions in the regional chapters of more than 100 restaurants throughout Spain that I have enjoyed and can appropriately review. I have listed each restaurant in four separate price categories that cover the average price per person for a full meal not including tax, wine, or tips. Within each of the price categories, I have ranked the restaurants from the top of my list to the bottom. All menu selections and prices may be subject to change without notice.

REGIONAL CUISINE

Each region of Spain offers visitors a huge selection of unique traditional foods. While wandering through the country you can enjoy sumptuous dishes in small local restaurants and taverns at reasonable prices. The following is a listing of some of the most commonly prepared soups, appetizers, main courses, and desserts from around Spain. Many of these regional items have become so popular that they can be found throughout the country.

Make the effort to try a few of these at least once during your visit to Spain:

Angulas a la Bilbaina - baby eels sautéed in garlic sauce
Arroz con Camarones - fried rice with shrimp
Arroz con Leche - rice pudding
Arroz con Mariscos - a tomato based rice and seafood stew
Avo Blanco con uvas - white garlic soup with grapes
Bacalao a la en salsa - codfish in tomato sauce
Calamar en su tinto - squid in their own ink
Caldo Verde - a filling cabbage soup (often with bits of sausage)
Campinion al Ajillo - mushrooms sautéed in garlic
Chuletas de Cordero al la Pamplona - lambchops with ham and sausage
Churrasco - meat cooked on a barbecue grill
Cochinillo asado al horno - roasted suckling pig
Conejo en Salmorejo - rabbit roasted and then marinated in tomato sauce
Empanadilla de Carne - meat filled pastries

Empanadilla de Bonito - tuna filled pastries
Escalivada - a roasted vegetable medley
Fabada Austriana - a spicy bean and meat stew
Fiedos Negras – black pasta with seafood
Flan - a caramel custard
Gambas al Ajillo -shrimp sauteed with chunks of garlic
Gazpacho - a chilled tomato and cucumber soup
Jamon Serrano - cured ham
Mojama – cured tuna
Paella -rice flavored with saffron and assorted meats and/or seafood
Patatas Bravas - spicy roasted potatoes
Perdiz con chocolate - partridge with a sauce infused with chocolate
Pimentos Piquillo - roasted red peppers
Pimentos Rellenos - stuffed red peppers
Pinchos – Spanish kebabs
Queso Manchego - aged sheep's milk cheese
Sardinas a la Espanol - sardines baked with fresh spices and garlic
Sopa de Ajillo - garlic soup
Sopa de cocido - meat soup
Tortilla Espanol - potato egg frittata
Trucha a la Navarra - whole trout stuffed with ham
Zarzuela de Mariscos - a hearty seafood casserole

BEVERAGES

Throughout Spain it is common to find the same selection of beverages. During breakfast, the most common drink is **coffee** *(cafe)* which can be ordered as either an **espresso** *(café solo)*, coffee with lots of warm milk *(cafe cortado)*, or a coffee with just a bit of milk *(café con leche)*. Decaffeinated instant coffee *(Descafinado)* is available in most larger cities and is often called by its brand name, **Nescafe.** The tea here is known as *Té,* and it is reasonably good. Those looking to satisfy their sweet tooth may either want to sample hot chocolate with fried strips of dough known as *Chocolate con churros,* or enjoy a sugary beverage known as *Horchata* made from small nuts.

As the day progresses, a much more varied selection of beverages will be available for consumption. Tap water in any foreign country can be risky, so I suggest always drinking **bottled water**. In Spain there are many brands of great tasting spring and mineral waters, including my favorite brand called *Laranjon*. These waters cost about 135 *ptas* per liter in a store and as much as 340 *ptas* in a restaurant. Most mineral waters and can be ordered with bubbles *(agua con gas)* or without bubbles *(agua sin gas)* and are always best when served cold *(fresca)*. There is also an assortment of carbonated soft drinks like Coca Cola and *Fanta Naranja* (orange soda) and they cost about 110 *ptas* per can or bottle in stores, and 190 *ptas* in most restaurants.

There are also some great brands of Spanish **beer** (*cerveza*) including *Mahou, Cruz Campo, San Miguel,* and many others. Beer usually costs about 135 *ptas* per bottle or can with a refundable deposit included at a store, and can cost between 150 *ptas* and 400 *ptas* per glass (usually called a caña) at a bar or restaurant. A normal sized glass of beer is called a *caña*, while those who want a large glass of beer should ask for a *tubo*. Whenever possible, ask for your beer on tap as it is much fresher tasting. Other major European brands such as Kronenburg, Heineken, Bass and Beck's may also be available by the bottle at the more upscale clubs and bars for a premium. If you really want a strong kick, try a taste of the infamous **hard apple cider** (*sidra*).

Of course **wine** (*vino*) is another major beverage during afternoon and evening meals. There are so many different types and brands of white wines (*vino blanco*), red wine (*vino tinto*), rosé wines (*vino rosado*), sparkling wines (*cava*), Sherry (*fino*) and fruit infused wines (*sangria*) that I have included in the next chapter. A bottle of good house wine (*vino de casa*) or table wine (*vino de mesa*) should cost under 750 *ptas* in a normal restaurant, and about half that much in stores. For more information about wine, please see the next chapter, *The Wines of Spain*.

RESTAURANTS

Throughout Spain you'll find many good eating establishments in all price ranges. In almost every city chapter of this book you will see listings for several restaurants that I can fully recommend, but I still suggest that you try to find a few gems of your own. It is easy to find great restaurants serving either regional or different international cuisine by simply asking at your hotel's front desk for a suggestion.

Many restaurants accept Visa and Mastercard and have their logo on the front door. American Express is often not accepted. Many restaurants are rated with a crossed fork symbol on a plaque near the front door, which has from 1 to 5 forks. I have not found this official rating system to be particularly accurate, so trust your own instincts.

Usually a full Spanish-style breakfast with an omelet, toast, and coffee in a local restaurant costs about 425 *ptas* per person. If you instead choose a typical American style breakfast with eggs, bacon, or pancakes at a hotel, expect to get hit for about 995 *ptas per person* , or at least 1,900 *ptas* for a buffet. A typical Spanish three or four course lunch can easily range between 1,050 *ptas* and 2,950 *ptas* per person depending on what main dish and how fancy a restaurant you select.

Spanish multiple course dinners with wine can cost somewhere from 1,650 *ptas* to well over 5,750 *ptas* per person depending again on what you choose and where you eat. Hotels may charge much higher prices (especially 5 star hotels), while hole-in-the-wall eating establishments may charge a fraction of these prices. If you want to reduce your expenses, you will have no problem in most of Spain. Also remember that some hotels include either a continental breakfast (little more than juice, rolls, and coffee), or a buffet American breakfast with all the trimmings in their weekend prices.

Generally the hours that meals are served are from 7am until 10am for breakfast (**desayuno**), from 2pm until 4:30pm for lunch (**almuerzo**), and from 9pm until 11:30pm for dinner (**cena**). I should point out that during breakfast most Spanish people tend to have just bread, cheese, and coffee. Lunch is a major meal here, and many people will take well over an hour to consume multiple courses and wash them down with a fair quantity of wine. Dinner is a late event that can consist of several courses and more wine.

Restaurants come in many types, each with a different typical ambiance. Many cities will have several full service restaurants (**restaurantes**) and dining rooms (**comedores**) with a large selection of either regional or international cuisine. Most seaside areas have fine seafood restaurants (**marisquerías**) which have large tanks of live shellfish. For those who like self-service cafeterias (**cafeterías**) with reasonable prices, they're all over the place.

For a little more genuine regional atmosphere you may want to visit a quintessential local restaurant (**meson**). Many cities offer a wide range of simple taverns (**tabernas**) where only a few inexpensive selected dishes may be offered. You can also find snacks and sandwiches in pastry shops (**pastelerías**), cafes (**cafes**), and assorted fast food joints. When it's time for dessert (**postres**) you can head for the nearest local bakery (**confitería**) or teahouse (**tetería**). If you need help translating a menu, consult the Glossary in the back of this book.

There are also some wonderful bars (**cervecerías**) that serve great finger foods (**tapas**) at moderate prices in a variety of sizes for those of varying appetites. At these informal bars in every major city you can order assorted sandwiches (**bocadillos**) and fish, meat, salad and cheese appetizers in sizes that range from normal **tapas** (also known as **pinchos**) starting at around 175 *ptas* each, to larger sized **raciones** of the same items that may cost double the price. It is common for most of these establishments to have normal prices to stand and eat, and surcharges for either tables or outdoor seating.

In most restaurants you can find selections that are either totally a la carte, two or three course daily specials (**menú del día**), and multiple course combination plates (**platos combinados**). Several restaurants offer their shellfish items by the kilogram (2.2 pounds), so you may want to ask for a half of a kilogram (*media kilo*) at the very most. Also most restaurants will bill your table a small cover charge if you indulge in the assortment of bread, cheese, olives, and smoked meats presented to you before your meal arrives.

When you have finished your meal and have gotten the bill (**la cuenta**) you may notice a 7% charge added in at the end for **IVA**. This is a government tax, and is not a service charge or gratuity. If service is not also added or included in the bill already, I suggest that you consider a 10% tip for good service and a 15% tip for extraordinary service, left in cash on the table when you depart. If you put a tip on your credit card, I can assure you that your waiter will never get it.

12. SPANISH WINE

Spain is Europe's third largest producer of wines. More than 80 different varieties of grapes are cultivated here. I am confident you'll agree with me that there are many fantastic Spanish wines that deserve the highest praise, at prices usually lower than most French wines. The trick, of course, is finding the right wine for you!

The history of wine production in Spain can be traced back to the Phoenicians, Greeks, and Romans, who established the first vineyards in what is now Spain. During the Moorish domination of the Iberian Peninsula, all wine-making had officially been terminated for centuries due to Muslim laws forbidding the use of alcohol. As the Christian Reconquest took shape, medieval monks reintroduced traditional wine making techniques to Spain that exist to this day.

By the late 15th century, many northern European wine merchants had established trade routes to bring home large vessels full of wines (especially sherry). As the influx of phylloxera disease began to destroy the vineyards of France during the late 19th century, a decrease in the supply of high quality wines began to affect the world's wine trade. At about this time, many rich foreign merchants invested in Spanish wineries (known as **bodegas**) to produce large quantities of respectable vintages that could fill the huge gap left by the lack of available French products.

At the turn of this century, the Spanish government realized the need for serious research and quality control in this blossoming industry that was beginning to have a profound positive impact on the nation's delicate economy. A new system of quality assurance was enforced by official councils of regulators that created a series of specific wine growing zones, each known as a **Denominacion de Origen** or simply **D.O.** Special rules regarding the cultivation, grape selections, fermentation, aging, and bottling of wines from each of these zones would now be written and strictly enforced.

Today, there are 39 different D.O. areas, each creating an abundance of red, white, rosé, sparkling, and fortified wines that all are marked with an official seal indicating that is has been tested and approved by its D.O.

control board. These range in price from 475 *ptas* per liter for good table wines that can be found at casual Spanish restaurants and supermarkets, to 69,500 *ptas* per bottle for grand reserves from world famous wineries that can be found only at the most expensive hotels and restaurants, or at one of the large wine specialist shops in Spain listed below.

If you are interested in the science and art of wine production, call the North American offices of **Vinos de España** in New York, *Tel. 212/661-4814* or in Toronto at *Tel. 416/967-2862* and ask them to send you a copy of their 550-plus page *"Guide to the Wines of Spain"* book. This fine publication gives detailed information about every Spanish winery's annual production, vineyard sizes, grape varieties, crushing and storage equipment, fermentation processes, aging techniques, bottling machinery, retail prices and presence in the world market.

It also gives invaluable contact information for hundreds of *bodegas* that will gladly welcome you (with an advance request via phone or fax) to either tour their facilities while enjoying free samples of their most noble wines, or perhaps allow you to buy direct small quantities of fine vintages that you may never be able to find anywhere outside of Spain!

The following is a summary of the most famous of these D.O. zones in alphabetical order. I explain a bit about each vineyard, and suggest a few of their best wines that you should try before leaving Spain. I have also included (in each regional chapter) listings of the wineries that offer some of the best tastings and tours.

For serious collectors, I have noted a few choice vintages that may be well worth the effort to search around for.

SOME OF SPAIN'S BEST WINES

D.O. CAVA

Located on 39,000 hectares of vineyards found mostly in, but not limited to, the **Catalunya** region near the town of **Sant Sadurni d'Anoia**. This region mainly produces excellent sparkling wines using Macabeo, Xarello, Chardonnay and Paradella grapes.

Recommended D.O. Cava Labels

Cava Parxet Chardonnay - sparkling produced by Parxet SA

Reserva Heredad Gran Reserva - sparkling produced by Segura Viudas

Cava Gramona Tres Lustros - sparkling produced by Gramona SA

Cavas Hill Reserva Oro - sparkling produced by Cavas Hill

Rovellats Brut Nature - sparkling produced by Cavas Rovellats

Brut Zero - sparkling produced by Castellblanch SA

Cava Parxet Brut Nature - sparkling produced by Parxet SA

Freixenet Brut Nature - sparkling produced by Freixenet SA

D.O. JEREZ

Located on 18,000 hectares of vineyards in the **Andalucía** region near the city of **Jerez de la Frontera**. This region mainly produces world famous fortified Sherries blended from Palomino and Pedro Ximenez grapes.

Recommended D.O. Jerez Labels

Carlos I Imperial - sherry produced by Pedro Domecq
Mentidero - sherry produced by Miguel M. Gomez SA
Amontillado del Duque - sherry produced by Gonzalez Byass SA
Dos Cortados - sherry produced by WIlliams & Hubert Ltd.
Capitan - sherry produced by Manuel Fernandez SA
Etiqueta Amarilla - sherry produced by Antonio Borbadillo SA

D.O. LA MANCHA

Located on over 170,000 hectares of vineyards in the **Castilla-La Mancha** region near the city of **Ciudad Real**. This region mainly produces good quality white and red wines using mostly Airen, Cencibel, and Garnacha grapes.

Great vintage years for red wines from here include '77, '89, '93, '90, '84, '82, '80.

Recommended D.O. La Mancha Labels

Torres Filoso - white produced by Bodegas Torres Filoso
Don Fadrique - white produced by Julian Santos Aguado y Cia
Estola Gran Reserva - red produced by Fermin Ayuso Roig
Senorio de Guadianeja Cencibel - red produced by Vinicola de Castilla

D.O. MONTILLA-MORILES

Located on 15,000 hectares of vineyards in the **Andalucía** region below the city of **Córdoba**. This region mainly produces a series of wonderful sherry style wines. Unlike the Sherries of Jerez, these wines use only Pedro Ximenez grapes and are much higher in natural alcohol content, thus requiring no fortification.

Recommended D.O. Montilla-Moriles Labels

Carlos VII - sherry produced by Alvear SA
Flor de Montilla - sherry produced by Carbonell y Cia de Córdoba SA
Abuelo Diego 27 Pedro Ximenez - sherry produced by Alvear SA
Nectar TG - sherry produced by Tomas Garcia SA
Gran Barquero - sherry produced by Ortega Marin Hermanos SA

D.O NAVARRA

Located on 18,000 hectares of vineyards in the **Navarra** region surrounding the town of **Olite**. This region is best known for producing fine rose wines, as well as good reds and whites from Tempranillo, Garnacha, Graciano, Mazuelo, Cabernet Sauvignon, Merlot, Viura, Palomino, Malvasia, and Moscatel grapes.

Great vintage years for red wines from here include '81, '82, '73, '83, '91, '90, and '94.

Recommended D.O. Navarra Labels

Gran Feudo - rose produced by Julian Chivite Marco
Principe de Viana - rose produced by Bodegas Principe de Viana
Castillo de Javier - rose produced by Vinicola Navarra SA
Senor de Cascante Gran Reserva - red produced by N.S. del Romero
Ochoa - red produced by Bodegas Ochoa SA
Vina Rubican - red produced by Bodegas Corellanas
Agramont - white produced by Bodegas Cenalsa

D.O. PENEDÉS

Located on 22,500 hectares of vineyards in the **Catalunya** region below the city of **Barcelona**. This region is best known for producing high quality red, white, rose, and sparkling wines from Macabeo, Garnacha, Parellada, Monastrell, Xarello, Carinena, Tempranillo, Cabernet Sauvignon, Merlot and other grapes.

Great vintage years for red wines from here include '78, '76, '81, '90, '87, '89. '93.

Recommended D.O. Penedés Labels

Vin Nature Blanc de Blancs —white produced by Marques de Monistrol SA
Jean Leon Chardonnay —white produced by Jean Leon SA
Olivella Sadurnin - white produced by Can Bas de Lavern
Penedes Gran Blanc - white produced by Masia Vallformosa
Conde de Caralt - red produced by Conde de Carralt SA
Gran Coronas Mas la Plana - red produced by Miguel Torres SA
Reynal - rose produced by Bodegas Pinord

D.O. RIBERA DEL DUERO

Located on 12,000 acres of vineyards in the **Castilla y León** region near the city of **Burgos**. This region produces some of Europe's finest (and often some of Spain's most expensive) vintage red wines made from Tinto Fino, Garnacha, Cabernet Sauvignon, and Merlot grape varieties.

Great vintage years for red wines from here include '81, '76, '86, '89, '82, '85, '95.

Recommended D.O. Ribera del Duero Labels
Vega Sicilia Unico - red produced by Bodegas Vega Sicilia
Vega Sicilia Valbuena - red produced by Bodegas Vega Sicilia
Pesquera Consecha Especial - red produced by Alejandro Fernandez
Marques de Velilla - red produced by Grandes Bodegas SA
Vina Pedrosa - red produced by Bodega Hnos. Perez Pascuas
Protos Gran Reserva - red produced by Bodegas Ribera Duero

D.O. RIOJA
Located on 46,000 hectares of vineyards in the regions of **La Rioja**, **Navarra**, and the **País Vasco**, near the city of **Zaragoza**. These regions produce amazingly delicious red and some good white reserve wines using Tempranillo, Garnacha, Mazuelo, Graciano, Viura, and other types of grapes. These wines are a great bargain when compared with French vintages of similiar quality and composition.

Great vintage years for red wines from here include '82, '76, '81, '89, '90, '83, '94.

Recommended D.O. Rioja Labels
Conde de Valedemar Gran Reserva - red produced by Bodegas Martinez Bujanda
Reserva Vendimia Seleccionada - red produced by Bodegas Martinez Bujanda
Castillo de Ygay Gran Reserva - red produced by Marques de Murrieta
Marques de Riscal Gran Reserva - red produced by Marques de Riscal SA
Vonde de los Andes Gran Reserva - red produced by Federico Paternina SA
Faustino I Gran Reserva - red produced by Bodegas Faustino Martinez
Marques de Murrieta Reserva - white produced by Marques de Murrieta
Muria Gran Reserva - red produced by Bodegas Murua SA
Marques de Murrieta Reserva - red produced by Marques de Murrieta
Conde de Valdemar Finca Alto - white produced bt Bodegas Martinez Bujanda
Ondarre - white produced by Bodegas Ondarre SA

D.O. VALDEPEÑAS

Located on 21,000 hectares of vineyards in the **Castilla-La Mancha** region near the city of **Valdepeñas**. This region produces nice, simple, and inexpensive red and white wines from Cencibel and Airen grapes. Great vintage years for red wines from here include '81, '84, '86, '89, '88, '93.

Recommended D.O. Valdepeñas Labels

Vega de Moriz - red produced by Casa de la Vina
Marques de Gastanaga -white produced by Luis Megia SA

OTHER D.O. AREAS

These areas all produce fine wines and spirits in every concievable variety. If you are near any of these zones, you should try to sample some of their local wines as well:

Alella, Alicante, Almansa, Ampurdan, Bierzo, Binisalem, Catayud, Carinena, Cmpo de Borja, Chacoli de Getaria, Cigales, Conca de Berbera, Condado de Huelva, Costers del Segre, Jumilla, Málaga, Mentrida, Navarra, Priorato, Rias Baixas, Ribeiro, Rueda, Somotano, Tarragona, Terra Alta, Toro, Utiel-Requena, Valdoerras, Valenica, Vinos de Madrid, Yecla.

13. SPAIN'S BEST PLACES TO STAY

After staying in well over 285 different Spanish hotels, resorts, inns, farmhouses, and family-run *pensions*, these are the 25 establishments that I will never be able to forget. My selections for this chapter have been based solely on my opinion of each property's unique qualities, including overall level of personalized service, interior and exterior design, location, special features, value for the money, and my own personal sense of what a good hotel or simple inn should offer its guests. There are, of course, many other great places to stay that are listed in the various chapters of this book, but these are the gems that you should try not to miss if at all possible.

I have divided my picks into four different categories: **Grand Hotels**, **Seaside Resorts**, **Small Luxurious Hotels**, and **Charming Affordable Inns**. In each separate category I have listed the properties in the order I would suggest them to a good friend. For further details about most of the accommodations described in the following section, please also look in each regional and city chapter of this book where another complete review of these places can also be found.

Let me know what you think of my choices. If I haven't included one of your favorite hotels or inns on the next several pages, forward me details about them and I will consider including them in future editions of this book.

GRAND HOTELS

HOTEL CLARIS, *Pau Claris, 150, Barcelona. Tel. (93) 487-6262, Fax (93) 215-7970. Represented in North America by Small Luxury Hotels, Tel. 800/ 525-4800. Year round rack rates from 34,100 ptas per double room per night (E.P.). Weekend rates from 19,500 ptas per double room per night (B.P.). All major credit cards accepted.*

If you are going to visit Barcelona, I could not possibly suggest a more luxurious and comfortable hotel than the fantastic Hotel Claris. Situated just a few short blocks above downtown's central Plaça de Catalunya square, this one-of-a- kind boutique style five star property has done everything to assure that it's guests are all treated like VIPs and will never think of staying anywhere else while visiting this wonderful city. The structure was once a 19th century nobleman's palace that recently underwent a massive five year top to bottom renovation by the country's leading master architects and craftsmen.

With rates costing only about half the price of their competition, every single room and suite here has been uniquely designed using rare hardwoods, plush tapestries, imported marbles, exceedingly comfortable custom designed furnishings, the latest in high-end consumer electronics, immense deluxe private bathrooms, the most powerful air conditioning and heating systems I have ever seen, an assortment of Europe's finest amenities, and in many cases there are even priceless original Roman mosaics and one of a kind ancient Egyptian relics.

While the Claris is the home away from home for visiting heads of state and high power executives, travelers will feel equally at ease here due to the fact that it is actually a rather casual place. Every member of the exceptionally talented staff here smiles effortlessly, and will help to provide you with anything needed to make your stay as delightful as possible. Additional on-premises facilities include an excellent gourmet grill room, a champagne and caviar restaurant, a peaceful bar with top shelf imported and domestic liquors, room service, the best rooftop swimming pool in the city, a great sauna, deluxe business meeting rooms, a private museum of Egyptian art, a Japanese garden, express laundry and dry cleaning services, excursion and rental car reservations and indoor parking.

Make sure to say hello to Pierre Bouisset, the extremely personable Swiss manager and co-creator of the Hotel Claris, whose concepts have made this hotel so memorable.

HOTEL VILLA REAL, *Plaza de las Cortes, 10, Madrid. Tel. (91) 420-3767, Fax (91) 420-2547 Represented in North America by Small Luxury Hotels, Tel. 800/525-4800. Year round rack rates from 39,600 ptas per double room per night (E.P.). Corporate rack rates from 35,650 ptas per double room per night (C.P.). All major credit cards accepted.*

Located in the heart of downtown Madrid, this excellent medium sized luxury hotel was always a real gem. Now with its recent extensive renovations and the addition of a museum of ancient Greek and Egyptian artifacts, it is an even better place to stay while visiting Madrid. What has always made the Hotel Villa Real so memorable is that even though there are plenty of movie stars and political world leaders staying here, manager Felix Garcia and his hard working multilingual staff treats every guest as a VIP. All of the hotel's 96 spacious air conditioned double rooms have opulent marble bathrooms stocked with the finest amenities, beautifully designed sunken living rooms with spare sofa beds, hardwood parquet floors, soundproof windows, a fully stocked mini-bar, multiple direct dial telephones, a mini-safe, remote-control satellite televisions, beautiful hardwood furnishings, plush cotton bathrobes and individual hair dryers. The hotel also offers an additional junior suites, several duplex suites, and two royal suites that all contain private outdoor terraces and sun decks with superb views out over the city, giant bathtubs with Jacuzzi whirlpools, a collection of fine art and antiques and in some cases a private sauna.

During the past few years the hotel has redesigned several tranquil sitting rooms which are now beautifully embellished with a collection of museum quality ancient Greek vases and Roman era mosaic panels. There are also many additional services and facilities offered here, including two nice restaurants, 24 hour room service, complimentary sherry upon check-in, 24-hour room-service, an indoor garage, several business-meeting rooms, tranquil public sitting rooms, a health spa with massage therapy and sauna, beauty salon and plenty of rooms with fine views of the Paseo del Prado. This is a fantastic city center hotel dedicated to providing the highest levels of customer attention, comfort, and satisfaction.

THE PALACE HOTEL, *Plaza de las Cortes, 7. Madrid. Tel. (91) 429-7551; Fax (91) 429-8266. Represented in North America by ITT Sheraton's Luxury Collection, Tel. 800/325-3589. Year round rack rates from 59,000 ptas per double room per night (E.P.). Special promotional rates from 37,500 ptas per double room per night (E.P.). All major credit cards accepted.*

This newly renovated baroque-style hotel, conceived by King Alfonso XIII, has been lovingly transformed into the best hotel in all of Madrid. Situated steps away from the Prado museum in the heart of downtown Madrid, this large, fabulous four- star luxury hotel is among my favorite places to stay in Europe.

As soon as you arrive, a formally dressed doorman greets you and you are then led up to one of the most dramatic lobbies found anywhere. Every detail has been thought of, and the extremely talented staff here make sure that you are treated as well as the many kings, presidents, and film stars that call the Palace their home while visiting Madrid. Each of the 476 large and beautifully decorated rooms and suites offer individually controlled air conditioning, marble-lined private bathrooms, mini-bars, direct dial telephones, satellite televisions, plush furnishings, huge closets, in-room music systems, and large marble bathrooms with the best amenities in town.

Services and facilities at the hotel include 24 hour fax services, an in-house travel agency, valet parking, a full service concierge desk which can usually find tickets for even sold-out events, a wonderful attached luxury shopping arcade with over three dozen upscale boutiques, all-night room service, business meeting rooms, laundry and dry cleaning facilities and much, much more.

Dining at the Palace is also a great experience, with the best buffet breakfast in all of Spain served under a stained glass dome. Other meals are offered in both the El Ambigu restaurant and the remarkably intimate La Cupola Italian restaurant, which will only seat 48 people at a time to ensure absolute culinary perfection. Since the hotel has completed its far-reaching renovation, some say it surpasses such other well known properties as the Ritz and the Santo Mauro.

HOTEL ALFONSO XIII, *Calle de San Fernando, 2, Sevilla. Tel. (95) 422-2850, Fax (95) 421-6033. Represented in North America by ITT Sheraton's Luxury Collection, Tel. 800/325-3589. Low Season rack rates from 40,000 per double room per night (E.P.). High season rack rates from 68,000 per double room per night (E.P.).*

If you have a little extra money and really want to stay in a simply outstanding deluxe hotel while visiting Sevilla, there is no doubt in my mind that this is the place to go! The Hotel Alfonso XIII was built in 1929 for King Alfonso XIII by hundreds of talented artisans to evoke Mudéjar and Baroque styles in both its opulent public and equally impressive guestrooms. Every inch of this palatial structure in the heart of the old city is filled to the brim with unique tapestries, carpets, chandeliers and custom made furnishings. The service here is top notch, and the guests tend to wear the finest haute-couture fashions.

This five-star hotel features some of Europe's most elegant old world style rooms and suites that feature huge super deluxe private bathrooms, exquisite furnishings, remote control satellite television, mini-bars, direct-dial telephones, air conditioning, comfortable bedding, and fine art.

The list of facilities includes a superb formal gourmet restaurant, the world famous inner-courtyard, a tranquil lounge with live piano music daily, 24-hour room-service, a wonderful outdoor swimming pool, lounges lined with impressive galleries, designer boutiques, several conference and business-meeting rooms, valet parking, excursion and car rental services, a beauty salon and full concierge service.

PARADOR DE CARMONA, *Alcázar de Arriba, Carmona. Tel. (95) 414-1010, Fax (95) 414-1712. Represented in North America by Marketing Ahead, Tel. 800/223-1356. Year round rack rates from 18,500 ptas per double room per night (E.P.). All major credit cards accepted.*

Finally reopened after a major two year refurbishment project, the amazingly beautiful Parador de Carmona is among my favorite places to stay in all of Spain. Originally built in the 14th century as a fortress and later used as a royal residence during the Reconquest, this luxurious hotel is embellished by countless examples of superb *Mudejar* craftsmanship including bold columns, arches, hand-crafted tiles, mosaic flooring, regal tapestries, and an unforgettable inner courtyard with a fountain.

While the structure itself is awesome, the superb manager (Sr. Ronda) and his fine staff work rather hard to insure that the level of service and hospitality here is the finest of any parador in Spain! The accommodations consist of 63 beautifully furnished rooms and suites that all have powerful air conditioning, large private marble bathrooms, remote control satellite television, mini-bar, direct dial telephone, Spanish tile flooring, period style tapestries, hand-carved hardwood furnishings and either large picture widows or private terraces with unforgettable views out over the countryside and nearby villages. For a small surcharge guests may wish to consider reserving room 306 or 406 which have a Jacuzzi as well.

Besides offering a wonderful gourmet restaurant featuring delicious regional cuisine with a Moorish twist, the parador also has a magnificent terrace with great views out over the Carbones river valley, a giant outdoor swimming pool and sun deck, several opulent lounge areas lined with antique tiles from Sevilla, a tranquil cocktail bar, business meeting rooms, and well manicured gardens. Once you stay here you will soon realize why many guests return time and time again. If you are visiting Carmona, this is by far the best place to both sleep and dine.

PARADOR DE RONDA, *Plaza de España, Ronda. Tel. (95) 287-7500, Fax (95) 287-8188. Represented in North America by Marketing Ahead, Tel. 800/223-1356. Low season rack rates from 15,000 ptas per double room per night (E.P.), High season rack rates from 18,500 ptas per double room per night (E.P.). All major credit cards accepted.*

Situated on the edge of the famous Tajo gorge and overlooking the most picturesque districts of Ronda, the hotel was built in 1994 within the walls of the city's 17th century former town hall. The Parador de Ronda was lovingly created using a combination of stone, marble, modern designer furnishings, classic Spanish decorations, and accents of exotic hardwoods.

The majority of the parador's 78 superbly spacious rooms and suites have marbled tiled private bathrooms, mini-bar, electronic mini-safe, executive style desks, direct dial telephones, remote control cable television, hair dryers, rather comfortable double bedding, an additional sofa bed, and plenty of closet space. The rooms and suites on the top (third) floor also offer fantastic oversized private balconies with incredible views over the city and the nearby mountain-lined countryside. For those with a bit more money to spend, the luxurious duplex suites feature king beds, dual sofa beds, and a great Jacuzzi.

The property also offers a great Adalucian style gourmet restaurant with fine cuisine, inexpensive garage parking, complete elevator access, international currency exchange services, elaborate lounge and sitting areas with giant panoramic windows, 2 bars including one that hangs directly over the famous gorge, an indoor glass domed atrium, a small yet relaxing outdoor swimming pool and sun deck, lots of business meeting and reception rooms, a cafe, available baby sitting, a tour desk that can help arrange all sorts of private excursions including horseback rides to delightful nearby sights, and a great young staff that love to work here. I highly recommend the Parador de Ronda for those looking for a special place to stay while enjoying this tranquil and awesome section of Spain.

Make sure to ask the front desk for a free copy of the English brochure called *Activities around the Parador of Ronda*, which features fun recommendations for day trips (by car, foot, hot air balloon, and horseback) to nearby sights, including caves with 20,000 year old drawings, national parks, and Roman era ruins.

HOTEL LOS REYES CATOLICÓS, *Praza do Obradoiro, Santiago de Campostela. Tel. (981) 582-200, Fax (981) 563-094. Represented in North America by Marketing Ahead, Tel. 800/223-1356. Low season rack rates from 15,000 ptas per double room per night (E.P.), High season rack rates from 18,500 ptas per double room per night (E.P.). All major credit cards accepted.*

The fine five-star Hotel Los Reyes Catolicós is situated across from the city's world famous cathedral in the main square of the old quarter. This converted 16th century former royal convent and hospital has 136 uniquely decorated rooms and suites that all feature huge private marble bathrooms, mini-bar, hardwood floors, extremely comfortable furnishings, direct dial telephone, and remote control satellite television.

Several of the most impressive accommodations may contain plush velvet curtains, canopy beds, exposed stone beams, Gothic-style iron chandeliers, antique tapestries, private terraces, fireplaces, antique oil paintings, original medieval religious icons, wood panel ceilings, extremely comfortable furnishings, a Jacuzzi, and great views out over either the dramatic inner courtyard or the cathedral.

There are also many beautiful public areas, sitting rooms with antiques and peaceful courtyard views, an original medieval chapel, the best semi-formal gourmet regional restaurant, a private royal dining room, opulent meeting rooms, a fully equipped auditorium, and free parking. Service here is prompt and efficient, and the ambiance is powerful. It is still hard for me to believe that this is actually a government-owned establishment.

SEASIDE RESORT HOTELS

HYATT REGENCY LA MANGA, *Los Belones, La Manga Resort. Tel. (968) 331-234. Fax (968) 331-235. Represented in North America Hyatt International, Tel. 800/233-1234. Low season rack rates from 36,000 ptas per double room per night (B.P.). High season rack rates from 38,000 ptas per double room per night (B.P.). Special sports & leisure packages are available upon request. Half Board Meal Plans are available from 4,650 ptas per person per night upon request. All major credit cards accepted.*

Hyatt Regency La Manga is situated in the heart of the world famous La Manga Club Resort which in turn is bordered by both the sea and a peaceful mountain valley on over 1,400 acres of beautifully landscaped gardens planted with olive trees, bougainvillea, and palms. Located just a few minutes drive away from the popular beach area of *La Manga*, this superb world class golf, tennis, and casino resort is perhaps the finest five star hotel and sporting center in all of Spain.

The hotel is embellished with a seemingly endless array of fine marbles, Moorish style stone carvings, regional ceramic tiles, original Spanish works of art, and a series of ornate yet relaxing public rooms. Here there are some 192 beautifully designed and wonderfully decorated rooms and suites that all feature private marble bathrooms with dual basins and hair dryers, golf course or pool view balconies, individual air conditioning systems, remote control satellite television with international stations and pay per view movies, a mini-bar, mini-safe, executive style desks, direct dial telephones, internet access, 24-hour room service, and extremely comfortable bedding. During meal times, guests can choose to dine in one of seven different restaurants that range from opulent gourmet dining rooms to casual seaside dining terraces with amazing sunset views.

The Hyatt Regency features a brand new casino, a large heated outdoor swimming pool and sun deck, several casual gourmet dining establishments, a tranquil library and cigar bar with a working fireplace, a few different lounges with scheduled live pianists and live music acts, a unisex beauty salon, designer boutiques, optional excursions and scheduled (high season) daily activities, car rental services, free outdoor parking, laundry and dry cleaning services, a newsstand and tobacconist, and half a dozen business meeting or private reception rooms.

Many guests stay at the Hyatt Regency due to its full range of sporting and recreation facilities. The resort is home to three championship 18 hole golf courses that have a world class golf academy, the La Manga Club Tennis Center with 18 professionally surfaced courts and a superb tennis academy, a private cove beach, European football pitches, a good workout room with both sauna and Jacuzzi (and optional massages), a pitch and putt course, mini golf, a children's activity club, two more swimming pools, pro shops, mountain bike rentals, and affiliated nearby horse back riding and scuba/wind-surfing centers. If you are looking for a truly deluxe resort with more than enough world class services and facilities to keep anyone more than busy for over a week, this is the place to go. Perfect for stressed out executives, golf and tennis enthusiasts, families looking for some quality time together, and couples trying to put some romance back in their lives.

HOTEL PUENTE ROMANO, *Carretera de Cadiz kilometer 177, Marbella. Tel. (95) 282-0900, Fax (95) 277-5766. Represented in North America by Leading Hotels of the World, Tel. 800/223-6800. Low season rack rates from 24,200 ptas per double room per night (E.P.). High season rack rates from 42,900 ptas per double room per night (E.P.). All major credit cards accepted.*

This is certainly the most comfortable deluxe seaside resort hotel in the entire country. Built in 1976, this amazingly beautiful five-star hotel and country club offers some 229 superbly decorate and rather spacious deluxe rooms and suites contained in a series of 26 three story Andalucian style lodges set amidst several acres of dramatic tropical gardens. Located steps away from a wide stretch of white sand beach on the edge of Marbella, the Puente Romano is the perfect getaway for vacationers, honeymoon couples, sports enthusiasts and business travelers from all over the globe.

All of the huge rooms and lavish suites offered here feature private terraces, marble bathrooms, satellite televisions with movie channels, powerful air conditioning systems, electronic mini-safe, fully stocked mini-bar, hair dryer, direct dial telephones, brightly colored furnishings with designer fabrics, and some of the best bedding I have found in all of Spain. The property also offers its guests three outdoor swimming pools (two are heated), award winning tennis club with ten courts and a great team of pros, a state of the art health and fitness center, optional message therapy, a beach-front water-sports area, 2 saunas, a children's game room, available child-care, a complete range of excursions, available horseback riding, guest membership privileges at two dozen area golf clubs, a high season supervised kids club, 24-hour room service, a posh high season disco, and plenty of lounges and sitting rooms.

The Puente Romano has three restaurants that range from casual buffet breakfast and lunch venues, to a fine Beach Club dining terrace and the outstanding Roberto's gourmet Italian restaurant. This terrific resort easily receives my highest rating of any beach area hotel in all of Spain.

HOSTAL DE LA GAVINA, *Platja de S'Agaro, S'Agaro, Costa Brava. Tel. (972) 321-100, Fax (972) 321-573. Represented in North America by Relais & Chateaux, Tel. 212/856-0115. Low season rack rates from 23,000 ptas per double room per night (E.P.). High season rack rates from 35,000 ptas per double room per night (E.P.). Closed from November through March. All major credit cards accepted.*

Perched above a small hillside just above one of the best beaches in all of northern Spain, the magnificent Hostal de la Gavina sets the standard by which all other full service European luxury hotels should be measured by. Originally built back in 1932 as a small inn for the friends of wealthy local homeowners, over the years it has grown to its present capacity of 56 fabulous rooms and 16 regal suites. This magnificent 5 star property is set amidst several acres of semi-tropical gardens that terminate at an elegant outdoor salt water swimming pool and sun-deck which rest just above the deep blue Mediterranean ocean. The three-story structure itself is an architectural delight in its own right with convent style ceilings, Romanesque mosaic floors, limestone columns, huge terraces, opulent fireside salons and an endless array of museum quality objects d'art from the 16th through 20th century.

Each of the property's spacious rooms and suites are uniquely decorated in a variety of old world styles that remind me of a combination of interior design styles found in Spanish castles and Venetian palaces. All accommodations here feature large dual basin marble covered private bathrooms, rare antique walnut and mahogany furnishings with mother of pearl inlays, remote control air conditioning/heating systems, ceiling fans, remote control satellite television, Murano glass lamps, big picture windows with views out over either the dramatic seaside of the pristine gardens, mini-safe, mini-bar, plenty of closet space, executive style desks, direct dial telephones, freshly cut flowers, beautiful works of art, and either wood parquet or Spanish tile floorings. Many of the accommodations here also offer huge ocean-view terraces, while a limited number boast a wonderful Louis XV decor complete with Italian silk wall coverings and hand-carved wooden moldings. There is also a truly spectacular Royal Suite that is definitely fit for a king and includes antique Venetian chandeliers, gilded wooden walls, a working fireplace, mosaic marble flooring, and a huge Jacuzzi (although when King Juan Carlos stays here he opts for a smaller suite).

The hotel also has five of the finest Catalan restaurants I have ever had the pleasure to dine in. Guests can choose (depending on weather conditions) to dine in the sumptuous Candlelight restaurant, the informal Villa d' Este dining room, the Las Conchas and El Barco al fresco patios, the pool-side luncheon terrace, or in their own rooms via 24-hour room service. Even the breakfast here is a gourmet delight with both a fine continental buffet and cooked to order omelets and pastries. Each night the pastry chef cooks up a new batch of tiny delights which are placed inside the rooms as an evening treat. Other facilities include a health club with both sauna and Jacuzzi, two tennis courts, free outdoor parking, a garage, currency exchange, available health and beauty treatments including invigorating massages, a nearby semi-private beach, large inner courtyards dotted with fantastic fountains, and a well staffed concierge desk to help you arrange rounds of golf or suggest a variety of day trips and excursions around this unspoiled sector of the Costa Brava.

The level of hospitality here is extremely high, and both the management and staff believe in the concept of service with a smile. Perfect for couples, honeymooners, or executives that need to get away from it all, this is one of the finest deluxe hotels in Europe.

RIGAT PARK HOTEL, *Platja de Fenals, Lloret del Mar, Costa Brava. Tel. (972) 365-200, Fax (972) 370-411. Represented in North America by UTELL International, Tel. 800/44-UTELL. Low season rack rates from 15,000 ptas per double room per night (E.P.). High season rack rates from 19,800 ptas per double room per night (E.P.). Closed from November through March. All major credit cards accepted.*

Owned and operated by the Rigat family for five generations, this magnificent beachfront four-star hotel surrounded by 20,000 square meters of pinewood forest is one of the best places to enjoy the sea anywhere in Spain. This famous full service deluxe hotel is beautifully situated right above the picturesque Platja de Fenals beach on the edge of Lloret del Mar, the Costa Brava's most popular seaside resort town. Favored by celebrities, rock stars, politicians, and wealthy international businessmen, the Rigat Park is fully booked during most nights in the summer. The good news is that in the months of April, May, September and October (when the weather is still usually great) there is plenty of availability at reduced rates.

While many of the hotel's 105 spacious and beautiful rooms and suites (decorated in several different classical styles including Elizabethan, Victorian and Louis XIV) boast huge sun terraces with spectacular views out to the beach, air conditioning, original or reproduction antique furnishings, marble lined private bathrooms, remote control satellite television, mini-bar, executive style desk, mini-safe, direct dial telephone, hair dryer, original local art work, and lots of natural sunlight.

The hotel also offers facilities such as direct beach access, a large swimming pool with underwater music and a pool bar, three different restaurants with open air terraces, plenty of business meeting rooms for up to 700 people, boutiques, billiards, ping-pong, a tennis court, a solarium, secure parking, and some wonderful sitting rooms with fine oil paintings and fireplaces. The service here is world class, with a great front desk staff that will be glad to help arrange rounds of golf at several nearby courses, horseback riding, yacht and boat rentals, and all sorts of exciting excursions. Their main seaview semi-formal dining room offers wonderful regional cuisine with white linen and silver service. This is a great place to stay if you want to be near Barcelona and enjoy the Costa Brava in high style. For a large hotel, this unique establishment feels rather like a small family owned inn with an extremely high level of hospitality, comfort, and personalized service.

MARBELLA CLUB HOTEL, *Boulevard Principe Alfonso von Hohenlohe, Marbella. Tel. (95) 282-2211, Fax (95) 282-9884. Represented in North America by Leading Hotels of the World, Tel. 800/223-6800. Low season rack rates from 26,000 ptas per double room per night (E.P.). High season rack rates from 51,500 ptas per double room per night (E.P.). All major credit cards accepted.*

When I am asked to suggest a great seafront hotel, the Marbella Club is one of the first places that comes to mind. Situated on a long sandy beach on Spain's famed southern Costa del Sol, this unique vacation resort paradise is so inviting that many guests never want to leave. Once a private royal retreat, the hotel and its newly expanded beach club are the center of a 42,000 square meter property that is the playground for many world famous celebrities, politicians, and rather deluxe vacationers. Every aspect of this property's lavish accommodations, cuisine, facilities, amenities, and service, assures the highest standards of comfort.

All of the 119 air conditioned rooms and spectacular suites are housed in either the newly built beach-front wing or a series of low rise Andalucian cottages that are surrounded by lush semi-tropical gardens. The all feature deluxe marble private bathrooms, remote control satellite televisions with pay per view movies, electronic mini-safes, mini-bar, direct dial telephones, and fine furnishings. There are also 10 or so villa style two and three bedroom bungalows with their own private plunge pools for those desiring additional privacy and space.

Among the countless stream of facilities offered here are two incredible gourmet restaurants, an opulent champagne bar, a beach-view dining patio, a pool-side snack bar, two huge swimming pools, a fully equipped health club with sauna and private massage therapies, business meeting rooms, available child care, 24 hour room service, plenty of secure car parking, a year round open-fire lounge, and full guest access privileges to nearby tennis, golf, and horseback riding clubs. The hotel's staff are extremely friendly locals (many of whom have been here for decades!), and the ambiance at the hotel is rather refined yet still quite welcoming.

SMALL & LUXURIOUS HOTELS

HOTEL TORRE DEL REMEI, *Carretera de Bolvir de Cerdanya a Puigcerda, Cami Reial, Bolvir de Cerdanya. Tel. (972) 140-182, Fax (972) 140-449. Represented in North America by Relais & Chateaux, Tel. 212/856-0115. Year round double room rack rates from 26,000 ptas per double room per night (E.P.). Year round suite rack rates from 40,000 ptas per double room per night (E.P.). Half board meal plan available from 7,650 ptas per person per night. All major credit cards accepted.*

While all the hotels included inside this special chapter are fantastic, the breathtakingly beautiful Hotel and Restaurant Torre del Remei is far and away the finest small luxurious hotel in Spain. This superb property is situated just a few minutes south of the French border, on a fertile valley deep within the majestic Pyrenees mountains near Andorra. This unique castle was built in 1905 by famed architect Freixa de Llivia for a wealthy Catalan family who spent their summers here.

After a painstaking conversion project which was completed in 1991, the castle soon became the country's best and most memorable little luxury hotel and restaurant. The regal three-story facade is highlighted by a pair of fine towers, hand-etched stained glass windows, and several dramatically carved stone terraces. Inside guests will find beautiful architectural elements including Arabesque archways bordered by stained glass panels, Romanesque marble columns, sky lights, top floor glass enclosed observation deck, and a bold central rotunda.

The five acre property surrounding the hotel is also blessed with a two hectare landscaped garden complete with seasonal flowering plants, tranquil walking paths, a nice outdoor swimming pool, fine orchards, a putting green, and a private reception tent. For those seeking adventure, the extremely helpful multilingual front desk staff can help to arrange expertly guided mountain hikes, unforgettable horseback rides through the countryside, and all sorts of sporting activities such as fly fishing trips along nearby rivers, transfers to nearby 18 hole golf courses, and great winter Alpine skiing. Even King Juan Carlos has been known to pop up here on his private helicopter just to enjoy the hotel and its surroundings.

Torre del Remei's owner, Sr. Josep-Maria Boix (one of Europe's top master chefs), labors for countless hours each day in both the hotel and the restaurant to insure that his guests are offered the finest quality of luxury accommodations, world class gourmet cuisine, and personalized service. Without a doubt his lifelong dream of a creating a luxurious, yet completely warm and welcoming, home away from home for both Spanish and foreign travelers has been fully realized here. The hotel features seven lavish suites and four strikingly beautiful double rooms.

During my recent stay here, I slept in a two room suite that had large crescent shaped balconies bordered by art nouveau wrought iron grillwork from which I viewed the nearby snow capped mountains. Inside my suite there was a master bedroom with the most comfortable king size bed I have ever slept in, a wonderful separate sitting room filled with fine designer furnishings and fresh flowers, several pairs of French doors that opened onto large picture windows, a gigantic deluxe marble bathroom with an oversized Jacuzzi stocked with exclusive Catalan bath oils and herbal shampoos, exquisite hand-carved ceiling moldings, two remote control Bang & Olufsen satellite color televisions with VCR, computer controlled reverse cycle air conditioner/heaters, an electronic mini-safe, direct dial telephones, a nice collection of original art and interesting books, a mini-bar, and an impressive selection of fine antique and modern furnishings.

Other rooms and suites here also contain working fireplaces, sloped beam ceilings, and either old lithographs or modern art. The two rooms on top of the tower have one of a kind bathrooms featuring pinnacle ceilings with windows offering unparalleled 360 degree views of some of Spain's prettiest rural spaces. The full American breakfasts here, all custom cooked to order, are a great way to start the day, and can be ordered on the sundeck or up to your room at no extra charge.

The Torre del Remei is also home to one of Spain's top gourmet restaurants, which has been awarded with one well deserved Michelin star. Sr. Boix and his staff of talented Spanish chefs offer a wonderful menu full of seasonal gastronomic delights. Whether dining al fresco on the sun terrace or inside one of two opulent dining rooms, guests are surrounded by candlelight and imported crystal, Villeroy & Boch porcelain, and Christofle silver set perfectly on white linen topped tables. Their inventive menu offers over two dozen delicious gastronomic delights such as lobster bisque, carpaccio of Parma ham and caviar, fresh pasta with seasonal wild mushrooms, lobster salad, braised beef steak stuffed with garden fresh green peas, free range chicken with mushrooms, shrimps and scallops au gratin, lentils stuffed with black and white local sausage, duck breast in sweet and sour sauce, prime cut of beef slowly cooked in advance for six hours, ravioli of pate and truffles, passionfruit mousse in lime sauce, black and white chocolate mouse and ice cream delight and much more.

The wait staff here is the finest I have had the pleasure to meet any where in the country, and the excellent head waiter, Sr. Joan Ibanez will gladly help you to select the perfect wine from a wonderful list of over 20 pages of the best Spanish and French vintages and below market prices ranging from below 1,100 *ptas* to over 175,000 *ptas* per bottle. I strongly suggest that any deluxe visitor to Spain make the Hotel and Restaurant Torre del Remei a mandatory part of their travel plans.

MAS DE TORRENT, *Estrada de Torrent, Torrent, Costa Brava. Tel. (972) 303-292. Fax (972) 303-293. Represented by in North America by Relais & Chateaux, Tel. 212/856-0115. Low season rack rates from 29,000 ptas per double room per night (C.P.). High season rack rates from 35,000 ptas per double room per night (C.P.). Half board meal plan available from 6,500 ptas per person per night. All major credit cards accepted.*

Mas de Torrent is a spectacular exclusive five star hotel housed in a wonderfully converted 18th century mansion surrounded by sumptuous gardens. Located just about six kilometers southwest from the medieval town of Begur, this picture perfect oasis of tranquillity is situated just a few minutes drive away from several areas of extreme natural beauty including secluded crescent shaped beaches and lush valleys. This deluxe tranquil hotel offers some 26 suites and four double rooms in both its beautiful three level main building (originally built in 1751) and a series of adjacent one story connecting bungalows that have their own private garden patios. Each spacious room here is beautifully decorated with a selection of antique rural furnishings, and feature amenities such as powerful individual air conditioning systems, large marble lined private bathrooms, excellent twin double or king bedding, remote control satellite television, fully stocked mini-bar, direct dial telephone, oversized closets, electronic mini-safe, fresh fruit baskets and windows with superb views out over the adjacent pristine countryside.

The hotel is also home to a superb semi-formal restaurant, featuring huge picture windows and a sloped ceiling of exposed hardwood beams. The main dining room's walls are embellished by a series of priceless sketches drawn on lace panels which were created by Catalan artists such as Miro and Tapies to celebrated the 90th birthday of Pablo Picasso in 1991. During the warmer months the garden-side al fresco dining patio opens as well and is one of the prettiest places to enjoy a wonderful gourmet lunch or dinner. The overall ambiance here is unusually relaxed yet somewhat sophisticated, with an affluent international clientele that tend to enjoy socializing with each other over cocktails and dinner.

Additional facilities here include a stunning outdoor swimming pool with sun-deck, a tennis court, a snooker room, mountain bicycles, a game room, business meeting rooms, several opulent chandelier lit salons filled with fireplaces and a fine collection of fine antiques and rare works of art, and much more. Nearby there are several golf courses, horseback riding stables, fine sandy beaches, and quaint little towns where local ceramics can be purchased. The service here is quite good, and the overall experience is best enjoyed by those seeking a private and sophisticated place to stay while visiting this beautiful coastal section of Catalunya.

HOTEL VILLA MEDITERRÁNEA, *Calle Leon, 5, Jávea. Tel. (96) 579-5233, Fax (96) 579-4581. Low season rack rates from 25,000 ptas per double room per night (B.P.). High season rack rates from 31,500 ptas per double room per night (B.P.). All major credit cards accepted.*

The Hotel Villa Mediterranea is dramatically situated along the hills just above the small coastal resort town of Javea, just a five minute drive away from the town's wonderful sandy cove beach area. Housed in a wonderfully converted sea-view mansion full of fine antiques and stunning works of art from all over Europe, the entire property is surrounded by lush semi-tropical gardens full of singing birds, fruit bearing plants, and towering Cyprus trees.

The hotel has some seven superbly decorated and designed deluxe rooms and luxurious suites that all feature deluxe dual basin private marble bathrooms, remote control satellite television with video machines and movie channels, powerful air conditioning and heating systems, mini-bar, mini-safe, local azulejos tiles and tapestries, direct dial telephone, extremely comfortable custom designed beds and furnishings, and in a few cases even a private Jacuzzi or a working wood burning fireplace.

Besides offering a spectacular restaurant with a menu and wine list that will impress even the most difficult patron and delicious 24-hour room service, this amazing little hotel also features a freeform outdoor swimming pool with a tranquil sun-deck and luncheon terrace, a glass enclosed indoor swimming pool, a sauna, a health club, optional massages, a brand new jazz club with scheduled live entertainment, plenty of free parking, and a breakfast that will start your day off on the right foot. Service here is top notch, with a multinational staff that will be glad to offer their advise on local outings and nearby sights worthy of a short drive. This is one of the best new hotels in the country, and although refined, it is both friendly and casual. If you are heading in this direction and you really want to experience the finest quality of hospitality, service, and cuisine in a property with breathtaking views, the Hotel Villa Mediterranea is well worth the money.

HOSTERIA DE MONT SANT, *Subida al Castillo, Xativa, Valencia. Tel. (96) 227-5081, Fax (96) 228-1905. Represented in North America by Marketing Ahead, Tel. 800/223-1356. Year Round rack rates from 17,500 ptas per double room per night (B.P.). All major credit cards accepted.*

This superb small luxury inn and gourmet restaurant is a fantastic place to stay while visiting the eastern coast of Spain. The property is dramatically situated on a dramatic mountaintop below an awesome 13th century Arab palace, just a 25 minute ride from the pristine beaches of the Mediterranean coast. The beautiful Hosteria de Mont Sant is without the slightest doubt one of Europe's most beautiful, tranquil, charming, and welcoming deluxe properties. This delightful hotel features some seven beautifully decorated rooms that all have a carefully selected assortment of regional antiques, central heating and air conditioning, deluxe private bathrooms stocked with the finest quality imported hair and skin care products, direct dial telephone, remote control satellite television, executive style desks, mini-bar, mini-safe, artistic hand-made ceramic flooring and French doors leading out to some of the most incredible views imaginable.

The inn and its equally outstanding regional restaurant are both surrounded by shady moonlit courtyards full of singing birds, dramatic sections of Moorish era defensive walls, hundreds of palms and fruit bearing orange trees, magnificent paths that lead to nearby medieval monasteries, and panoramic terraces that look out over the historic city of Xativa below. Here the guests can enjoy one of the country's finest regional restaurants (a culinary experience that should not be missed by any visitor to this country) complete with age old decorative arts and an unusually pleasant relaxed ambiance, live weekend jazz and classical music concerts, an outdoor swimming pool, one of the best daily complimentary breakfasts anywhere on the planet, plenty of free parking and over 15,000 square meters of impeccably maintained gardens.

The young multilingual staff are extremely friendly. Owned and operated by Sr. Javier Andres Cifre, whose family has owned this former noble manor house for many decades, this truly special getaway receives my highest recommendation.

HOTEL SAN ROMAN DE ESCALANTE, *Carretera de Escalante a Castillo, km. 2, Escalante. Tel. (942) 677-745, Fax (942) 677-643. Represented in North America by Relais & Chateaux, Tel. 212/856-0115. Low season rack rates from 13,000 ptas per double room per night (E.P.). High Season rack rates from 16,000 ptas per double room per night (E.P.). Half board meal plan available from 5,200 ptas per person per night. All major credit cards accepted*

Close your eyes and try to imagine the perfect secluded getaway filled with an amazing collection of fine antiques and awesome works of art. The image that you may be imagining could easily fit the superb 13 room Hotel and Restaurant San Roman de Escalante. Situated within several acres of ornate gardens and housed in a beautifully converted 17th century manor house near the peaceful Cantabrian village of Escalante, this luxurious yet relaxed property is a real gem. Owned and expertly managed by the ever-present Juan Melis and Victoria Reynes, service here is of the highest level.

The hotel is located within a half hour's drive to dozens of exquisite beaches, traditional mountain villages, countless historic sights, and even the brand new Guggenheim Museum of Modern Art, all of which are well worth a visit. This extremely peaceful and romantic little luxury hotel features 11 stunningly decorated rooms, one cozy cottage, and a suite, which have all been individually designed with deluxe marble lined private bathrooms, a wonderful selection of very comfortable canopied beds, exposed hardwood beams or original stone walls (even a boulder protruding from the wall in one), lavish antique furnishings, remote control satellite television, rare works of art, mini-safe, mini-bar, direct dial telephone and plush wall-to-wall carpeting.

The hotel also boasts several acres of nicely manicured gardens dotted with sculptures and fountains, their own antiques shop, a private art gallery featuring captivating expositions, an adjacent 12th century chapel (a great place for a wedding) and several impressive sitting rooms stacked with rare leather-bound books and embellished by selections from the owners' vast collection of 16th-20th century European art.

The hotel boasts a fantastic gourmet restaurant (officially awarded with one Michelin star just steps away in a converted 17th century stable. The two main dining rooms both rest below exposed wooden beams and are surrounded by an impressive hand painted ceramic tiled fireplace and walls adorned with priceless works of art. Lunch or dinner here is an unforgettable experience with Basque chef Jorge Martinez and his staff preparing some of the best meals I have ever had the pleasure to enjoy. Although the menu changes seasonally, during my recent visit it offered cream of codfish soup with garlic croutons, garden fresh salads with white asparagus, rice with clams from Escalante, home-made pate, filet of duck in a sesame crust, grilled red mullet, prime cut steak served with wild mountain mushrooms, and six different desserts that were all beyond comparison. There is an 18-page Spanish and French wine list. The overall level of personalized service and comfort here are truly first class.

HOTEL CASA IMPERIAL, *Calle Imperial, 29, Sevilla. Tel. (95) 450-0300, Fax (95) 450-0330. Internet: www.casaimperial.es. Low season rack rates from 22,500 per double room per night (B.P.).High season rack rates from 28,000 per double room per night (B.P.). All major credit cards accepted.*

Located in a quiet residential section of the old part of Sevilla, this stunningly restored 16th century mansion (originally designed by the same architect as the adjacent Casa de Pilatos) is simply the best small luxury hotel in town! Originally known as the Casa de Don Alonso de Villafranca mansion, the five star Hotel Casa Imperial is a fantastic little gem that is simply breathtaking in every aspect.

This delightfully luxurious little property features less than a dozen individually designed and decorated duplex suites and large super-deluxe rooms that all feature Moorish style tiled bathrooms with unusual antique fixtures and huge bathtubs, an enormous array of fine marbles and granites, hand painted azulejos tiles and ancient artwork, a fully equipped kitchenette (although the guests never seem to use it!), electronic mini-safe, mini-bar, direct dial telephone, air conditioning and heating systems, opulent custom designed furnishings covered by beautiful imported and local fabrics, remote control satellite televisions (with audio/video systems in some cases), direct dial telephones, one-of-a-kind hardwood trimming, Andalucian tapestries and in several cases either spiral staircases or huge terraces leading out to either one of the 16th century inner courtyard patios or fine views over the historic heart of Sevilla.

The mansion has several peaceful inner patio-gardens that are lined by galleries bordered by Roman-era columns topped by Corinthian capitals. Every inch of the hotel is covered by yet another ancient object d'art or rare artifact. The stairways are covered by Pisan tiles that date back to the structure's origins, and the woodwork that can be seen throughout the hotel is a true masterpiece. Besides numerous fountains and sitting rooms scattered around this ideal oasis from the noise and bustle of town, there are unforgettable roof-top sun decks, a cafe, and a fantastic antique breakfast room that you will certainly never forget.

Favored by discreet movie stars and well-to-do travelers from all over the world, this new and enchanting five star hotel (technically listed as an Apart-Hotel) specializes in the highest levels of personalized service and hospitality, two items that have long been missing from the hotel business in Sevilla. If you are looking for a small, refined, relaxing, and absolutely romantic getaway to spend your nights in the heart of Sevilla, the Hotel Casa Imperial is the first place to call.

CHARMING YET AFFORDABLE INNS

HOTEL AIGUA BLAVA, *Platja de Fornells, Aiguablava, Costa Brava. Tel. (972) 622-058, Fax (972) 622-112. Low season rack rates from 10,800 ptas per double room per night (E.P.). High season rack rates from 13,000 ptas per double room per night (E.P.). Half board meal plans available from 2,100 ptas per person per day. Closed from December through February. All major credit cards accepted.*

The beautiful Hotel Aigua Blava is one of my favorite beachfront getaways anywhere on earth. Comprised of several small low-rise Mediterranean lodges at the water's edge along one of Spain's prettiest coves, the hotel feels much like a tranquil seaside village. After just one minute of sitting in the lobby and hearing the comments of departing guests, I knew this was a special place. Owned and managed by four generations of the same family since its inception as a small restaurant and cozy inn back in 1932, these days it is looked after by the exceedingly charming Sr. Juan Gispert Lapedra, his wife Caty, his daughter Mercedes, and a superb multilingual staff that all really know how to graciously provide the absolute highest levels of true hospitality. During my recent visit here I heard guest after guest tell various staff members that they can't wait to return next year, and that says it all in the hotel business!

The Aigua Blava offers a total of 89 standard rooms, deluxe rooms, and junior suites that in most cases have wonderful patios with amazing views out over the nearby bays and beaches and are drenched in warm Spanish sunlight during most of the year. While each spacious and extremely comfortable accommodation here is uniquely decorated, they all feature a casual yet elegant styling complete with deluxe marble or tile lined private bathrooms, large double or king size beds (and extra sofa beds in some cases), hand carved hardwood furnishings, direct dial telephones, mini-safe, mini-bar, pastel serigraphs with rural themes, individual air conditioning systems, and all day room service. There are also a series of special units adapted for family use that have a separate children's bedroom, and a nice big sitting room.

Within the "pueblo" itself there are several idyllic inner courtyards, a huge Olympic sized swimming pool with snack-bar and sun-deck, sofa-lined reading rooms and lounges, a selection of private reception and meeting rooms, a small bar with live entertainment in the summer evenings and a quaint cove beach with crystal clear water that is perfect for a cool afternoon swim. There are also three fine restaurants serving wonderful gourmet cuisine on outdoor terraces as well as in casual seaside dining areas and a formal candlelit dining room. While some of Spain's best beaches are just a five minute walk away, several other world class golf courses, tennis clubs, scuba sights, hiking trails, horseback riding stables, and water-skiing facilities are a mere 25 minute drive from the hotel's front door. If all that wasn't enough, the well-preserved medieval stone villages of Pals and Begur, embellished with dramatic castles and Gothic churches, are just a few miles down the same road.

HOSTAL SANCHO DEL ESTRADA, *Castillo de Villaviciosa, Solosancho, (Avila). Tel. (920) 291-082, Fax (920) 291-082. Low season rack rates from 9,310 ptas per double room per night (E.P.). High season rack rates from 9,775 ptas per double room per night (E.P.). All major credit cards accepted.*

The wonderful little Hostal Sancho del Estrada is a converted 14th century turreted castle located some 15 minutes away from Avila. Strikingly set at the base of the Pico Zapatero mountains (less than 1 hour from Madrid), this dramatic castle features an impressive array of salons, sitting rooms, turreted tower tops, delightfully furnished accommodations, and dining areas that have all been filled with one of a kind antiques and rare works of art which in many cases date back well over half a millenium.

The project of renovating the castle into a deluxe hotel took 22 years to complete when it opened in 1995. Nowadays the hotel offers its guests 12 extremely comfortable double rooms and two amazing suites (located in the towers) which all have modern private bathrooms, remote control satellite television, direct dial telephone, mini-bar, antique furnishings, three-foot thick exposed stone walls, and in some cases there are also incredible canopied brass beds and wonderful stone window ledges lined with benches. While all of the rooms are of the four star quality lever or better, those looking for a romantic evening should give strong consideration to renting the cozy circular duplex mini-suite 103 (a mere 13,000 *ptas* per night) which is located in one of the three tower tops.

Besides wonderful rooms and truly personalized service at the highest levels, the castle also can provide superb gourmet meals in their magnificent and rather intimate candlelit dining room surrounded by some of Spain's best preserved tapestries and authentic Mudejar carved wooden ceilings. Other facilities include private guided horseback rides up to the nearby Celtic era villages (call in advance to reserve), mountain bikes, buffet breakfast, private dining and meeting facilities, plenty of free parking, and great advice on self-guided valley hikes and excursions to the nearby city of Avila. Staff is extremely friendly and helpful, and for the price there is no better place to stay in all of central Spain. This is the perfect place to stay while taking day trips by car to Avila, Madrid, Toledo, Segovia, Salamanca, and El Escorial.

PALACETE DE CAZULAS, *Carretera Vieja de Granada, Otivar, Granada. Tel. (958) 644-036. Fax (958) 644-048. Year round rack rates from 14,000 per double room per night (C.P.). Self-contained three bedroom, three bathroom villa-annex from 70,000 ptas per week (E.P.). Half board meal plan available from 3,000 ptas per person per day. Most major credit cards accepted.*

The Palacete de Cazulas is a lovingly restored manor house situated on a peaceful rural farming valley some 35 minutes drive north of the coastal town of Almunecar. Originally built centuries ago as a regal manor house, resident managers Brenda Watkins and Richard Russell-Cowan spent the last four years creating a wonderful and impressively welcoming bed and breakfast inn.

The property offers its guests a total of 12 spacious guest-rooms and a quaint three bedroom, three bathroom detached casita that all come complete with individual full private bathrooms, twin or double bedding, original antique tiles, delightful period furnishings, nice picture windows with views out over the countryside and an unusual selection of modern art. The manor is flanked by a pair of old towers that may soon be transformed into two fantastic rooms. All accommodations are bright, cozy, and full of authentic Spanish country charm. Guests receive a complimentary home baked continental breakfast each morning, and if requested special candlelit dinners can also be arranged in either their delightful master dining room or on their pretty little al fresco terrace. The hotel can also either be rented in its entirety for a minimum of one week to host small exclusive meetings for up to 20 or so participants, or in some cases on a daily basis for receptions, private dinners, and special conferences.

This casual and unassuming regal manor house (who's land deed dates back to 1492) and its adjacent old chapel are surrounded by 5,000 square meters of well manicured Moorish styled gardens dotted with rare palms and fruit trees as well as box hedges. Here guests can choose to relax alongside a large outdoor swimming pool, sit back and read a novel in one of several grand fireside sitting rooms, hike along nearby waterfalls, or take great day-trips by car to either Granada or picturesque beaches along the Costa Tropical. Those more adventurous may ask Brenda and Richard to arrange a horseback ride through the adjacent pristine Adalucian landscape. While private and tranquil, guests here really do get the feeling that they are completely at home visiting at the vacation home of a rich and perhaps slightly eccentric uncle. Perfect for romantic couples, families, small groups and private executive seminars, this is a special little country inn.

HACIENDA DE LOS GRANEROS, *Carretera de Sevilla, Carmona. Tel. (95) 595-3020, Fax (95) 595-3020. Year round rack rates from 7,500 ptas per one bedroom apartment per night (E.P.). Low season rack rates from 66,000 ptas per 2 bedroom apartment per week (E.P.). High season rack rates from 87,000 ptas per 4 bedroom apartment per week. Cash only - no credit cards accepted.*

For my money, this extremely welcoming and comfortable converted farmhouse just outside of the walled city of Carmona, is the best value in Spain. The property is owned and operated by the delightful Spanish-German Fernandez family who really understand hospitality and service. Converted from an 15th century olive farming estate house on 1100 square meters, the Hacienda de Los Graneros offers five amazingly spacious and well decorated one to four bedroom self-catered apartments in a unique rural setting that seems to make every guest want to stay here forever. Still all but unknown to the vast majority of both Spanish and foreign visitors to Andalucia, this is without any doubt a real hidden treasure. Every time I stay here, I bump into a handful of guests from all over the world that all tell me that this place is their own little paradise.

All five of their individually decorated apartments (equivalent in overall quality to rooms in the very best three and four star hotels in Spain) have been wonderfully decorated with a combination of modern furnishings and antique trimmings, and feature hotel quality private bathrooms, nice bedrooms with great beds, individual heating systems, fully equipped modern kitchens, and more space than you could ever need. The big abide bedroom apartment also has a wonderful salon and a working fireplace. Perfect for small groups, couples, and even adventurous families with children of any age, the Hacienda features an outdoor swimming pool, an antique meeting room and lounge, available nearby horseback riding, a wonderful rooftop sun-deck, some of the most romantic views out over fertile Andalucian farms and so much more.

Make sure to first call before arriving to get specific directions (via phone or fax), as it is located on an old unpaved farm road that is not so easy to find at first.

PENSION EL TORREON, *Calle de Jazmin 4, Mojacar. Tel. (950) 475-259, Fax (950) 475-259. Low season rack rates from 5,000 ptas per double room per night (E.P.). High season rack rates from 6,000 ptas per double room per night (E.P.). Cash Only - No credit cards accepted.*

This is my favorite one-star pension in the whole country. Located on the ancient hilltop village of Mojacar just a ten minute drive or bus ride to some amazing beaches, this is a cute little bed and breakfast inn in the typical Spanish tradition. Situated in the enchanting Barrio Vieja district this sleepy town with incredible views out over both the sea and the countryside, this simple yet extremely charming inn is just adorable.

Set within the walls of an antique Moorish style mini-mansion resting on the mountain's edge, the El Torreon boasts some of the best views you could ever imagine. The owner and manager (a wonderfully friendly local woman named Charro) offers five beautifully decorated traditional bedrooms that all contain antiques, curiosities, old tiles, and in some cases a view you will never forget. Although the bathrooms are shared, in this case it is not a problem at all. The inn also has a stunning sun terrace that is covered by bougainvillea and looks right out over the sea, optional continental breakfast, nearby free parking and access to outside telephone lines if necessary. The owner also rents out a cozy casita (small house) with a kitchen and space for either three adults or two adults with two small children, as well as a nearby one bedroom fully equipped apartment (both for similar prices as the rooms at the pension but long stay rates can be negotiated).

APARTHOTEL TRES PINOS, *Camino de la Escuela, San José. Tel. (950) 380-212, Fax (950) 380-213. Low season rack rates from 5,000 ptas per studio apartment per night (E.P.). High season rack rates from 9,000 ptas per studio apartment per night (E.P.). Visa and Mastercards accepted.*

Located on a hill just a few minutes walk or ride away from the heart of the quaint little town of San José, this amazingly friendly and beautifully designed sea-view apart-hotel is the best place to stay in the dramatic Cabo de Gata National Park. The Tres Pinos is a traditional yet modern styled three floor structure that offers a half dozen or so nicely designed studio and one bedroom apartments (several have great seaviews) with fully stocked kitchens, television, comfortable bedding including extra sofa beds in some cases, daily housekeeping and nice furnishings of rattan. The hotel also has plenty of free parking, a nice outdoor swimming pool, a sun deck and a really nice staff. Perfect for those that wish to drive or hike around one of Europe's most amazing natural spaces.

ALBERGUE JUVENIL DE CÓRDOBA, *Plaza de Juda Levi, Cordoba. Tel. (957) 290-0166, no fax. Represented in North America by Hostelling International, Tel. 202/783-6161. Year-round rack rates from 4,350 ptas per double room per night (E.P.). Most major credit cards accepted.*

This is one of Europe's most luxurious youth hostels and is perfect for people of any age who are looking for a fun, safe, and perfectly located inexpensive place to stay. This modern marble floored structure offers 44 private and shared double rooms that all have surprisingly comfortable furnishings, shared or private bathrooms, air conditioning, and large windows. Facilities here include a television room, a good inexpensive restaurant, and absolutely no curfew.

Packed year round with both students and adults from all over the world, all you have to do is present a valid Hostelling International card or purchase one here for about 3,000 *ptas*. Those over 26 who wish to stay at this hostel will be asked to pay a 20% surcharge. This is, without a doubt, the best budget place to stay in Cordoba.

14. MADRID

Madrid is located in the geographical center of mainland Spain, in the heart of the small urban and suburban region known simply as the Comunidad de Madrid. From the center of the city, no town or village in this country is more than 730 kilometers (453 miles) away.

In fact, most of the cities, villages, beaches and attractions listed in this book can be reached from Madrid in well under two hours by plane, seven hours by car, nine hours by train or 12 hours by regular bus service.

History

Archaeological excavations in and around the city of **Madrid** have shown proof that humans first inhabited the area over 16,000 years ago. Evidence suggests that back in prehistoric times, a large settlement of primitive dwellers lived alongside the Manazanares River on the city's western edge.

Later the zone was occupied by **Iberian** tribes in the first millennium B.C., who eventually joined together with invading **Celtic** peoples to form the basis of the **Celtiberian** civilization. The next major wave of inhabitants to live in and around what is now Madrid were the **Romans** who started to colonize this part of their empire by the 2nd century B.C. or so. The Romans were responsible for creating many roads which passed through this area as they developed trading routes and military strongholds across the Iberian peninsula.

After the decline of the Roman empire in the 5th century, the Visigoths established a short lived presence here, but some three centuries later were easily overpowered by the invading Moorish troops from northern Africa. By the 9th century, the powerful Arab ruler known as Mohammed I (the Emir of Cordoba) decided to establish a major military fortress and palace known as the Alcázar here, calling this new town Magerit. Under his leadership and protection, a civilization of skilled Muslim, Visigoth, and Roman blooded citizens lived and worked together in relative harmony within the defensive walls of this important strategic community.

As the Christians pushed their way south through what is now Spain during the Reconquest, King Alfonso VI finally captured the town and it's fortress in 1083. By 1202 the town's name was converted from the Arabic sounding Magerit to the more Castillian sounding Madrid and it was granted its official charter by King Alfonso VIII. By the early 16th century, this ever growing municipality grew into a city with a population of over 15,500 Madrileños (the name local residents proudly call themselves). With the city now growing in importance, the Royal family began to take up residence here, transforming the old Alcázar into a Palacio Real (Royal Palace). In 1561 the Parliament and other government officials were moved here by the Habsburg monarch King Felipe II and the city became the new capital of his empire.

Through the so-called Golden Age of the 16th and 17th centuries, Madrid began to experience a great surge in population, encouraging the construction of fantastically ornate squares and buildings like the platteresque Casa de Cisneros, the neo-classical Casa de la Villa, the gothic Parroquia de San Andrés chapel, the baroque Palacio de Santa Cruz court prison and the delightful Plaza Mayor square. It was also about this time that the cultural scene began to develop here with Spanish writers like Cervantes and Lope de Vega, as well as artists such as Velázquez and Coello living and working alongside other masters of their craft, finding their way here from all over the world.

During the late 18th century Age of Enlightenment, Madrid's appearance changed dramatically as brilliant urban planning projects were undertaken under the reign of Bourbon King Carlos III who would be remembered fondly as the King-Mayor of Madrid. These projects were to create a new layout for much of the city including the addition of many new monuments, public parks, botanical gardens, libraries, museums and beautiful buildings which were designed by the King's favorite architects such as Francisco Sabatini of Italy. These included the Puerta de Alcalá, the Centro de Arte Reina Sofia, and the Casa Real de la Aduana. As the city's cultural and architectural renaissance continued, the appearance of the city changed forever as it developed it's own unique style which is still quite evident today.

When Napoleon's troops started to occupy the city in early 1808, they were not at all appreciated by the local population. During a May 2, 1808 protest by local residents against the removal of the Queen from the Palacio Real, French troops opened fire into the unarmed crowd. Now encouraged to fight against these invaders for their freedom, a small segment of the population began a series of brutal street clashes which took place later that same afternoon. These small battles were brutally retaliated against by the French during the massacre that occured the next day on the third of May when French soldiers shot any Madrileño on sight who was carrying a gun. This horrible event has been revealingly chronicled in the paintings entitled *Dos de Mayo* and *Tres de Mayo* by Francisco de Goya, which still hang proudly in the Prado as some of the museum's most notable works.

The Spanish Civil War broke out in 1936, and the city suffered greatly during a more than two year siege. As General Franco's repressive dictatorship continued for almost four decades, massive construction projects were undertaken to extend the downtown sector further northward. With dozens of unique neighborhoods, each from a different era with its own identity, the city has retained much of its vibrant historical context and monumental vestiges. While still continuing its expansion, and modernization becoming a major economic power-base, the municipality was honored to be declared the "1992 Capital of European Culture."

ARRIVALS & DEPARTURES
By Air
The main international airport that services Madrid-bound flights is called the **Aeropuerto de Madrid – Barajas**. Located 13 kilometers (about nine miles) northeast of Madrid near the small village of Barajas, this large and well-designed facility has separate domestic (*terminal nacional*) and international (*terminal internacional*) wings. Since the airport has more flights than it can possibly park alongside the gate areas, most flights will park just off the tarmac, and you will most likely be transported between the terminal gate and the airplane via shuttle bus. With its current annual passenger load of over 17 million people, this is a rather busy airport by any standards.

Among the many services offered in the airport are free luggage carts, wheelchairs for the physically challenged, 24-hour currency exchange desks, banks with ATM machines, a tourist (*Turismo*) office, luggage storage at 450 *ptas* per bag each day, restaurants and cafés, a chapel, a beauty salon, boutiques featuring designer goods, a pharmacy, a newsstand and cigarette shop, soda machines, dozens of pay phones that accept coins and credit cards, child care services, a Renfe train ticketing and reservation office, a full service post office, a multilingual information desk, a hotel booking kiosk, duty free shops, car rental offices, tour operator and excursion desks and VIP lounges for business and first class passengers.

There is also a message board and well-marked meeting point if you're trying to contact fellow travelers who have been delayed. For those of you trying to pick up or drop off passengers at the airport, parking is available at 150 *ptas* per hour and 950 *ptas* per day. If you want to leave your rental car at the airport while you explore Madrid for a few hours or days, ask at your rental company's kiosk in the airport. Most major car rental companies will let you park in their officially assigned airport parking areas for free.

GETTING TO TOWN FROM THE AIRPORT
By Bus

You have several options available that should take between 25 and 55 minutes each way depending on local traffic conditions. A special airport shuttle bus marked Aeropuerto-Madrid takes passengers and their luggage to and from the airport and the underground taxi stand underneath Madrid's central Plaza de Colón for 365 *ptas* each way with scheduled stops all along the route. These buses depart daily every 12 minutes during normal airport operating hours (no service from 2am until 5am) in both directions and can be found at the bus stop directly in front of the international terminal's door #2.

Upon arrival at the downtown Plaza de Colón bus depot, there is a good local travel agency called Brujula which is open 8am until 10pm daily and can book hotels, excursions, and sightseeing tours as soon as you arrive in town. Another more local municipal bus marked Linea 101-Barajas-Canillejas can take you between the airport and the less central Canillejas area of Madrid for 125 *ptas* each way with departures every 16 minutes or so until about midnight.

By Taxi

Taxis are white sedans with bold red stripes on the doors marked with the *Taxi* sign, and can be found in abundant supply at well indicated taxi stands at the airport. Keep in mind that 99% of the taxis are fairly small sized four-door cars. Generally, their trunks can only hold two large sized suitcases, but those with roof racks can secure two more medium pieces of luggage, and perhaps a couple of carry on bags inside as well. Unfortunately, no station wagon or van type taxis are available in Madrid.

Expect to pay somewhere between 1,700 and 2,300 *ptas* per ride from the airport to most downtown locations, but rip-offs do occur with non-Spanish speaking arrivals. If you think you are being overcharged, if the driver tells you he uses a flat rate, or if he takes the longest possible route to the requested destination, ask for an official receipt (*recibo oficial*) and then write down the licence number of the taxi which must be posted near the meter, and call *Tel. (91) 447-0704 to register your complaint*. The police take tourism related complaints rather seriously. Also be wary of hawkers soliciting their services as taxi drivers to disembarking passengers inside the terminals; they often charge you double the going taxi rate, and are not licensed.

By Bus

Most, but not all, of the bus lines between Madrid and other parts of Spain as well as the rest of Europe tend to stop at the busy modern Estación Sur bus depot at the south side of the city. Be sure to call in advance to find out exactly where and when your bus comes in. From here, a municipal bus or *metro* will cost 125 *ptas* to almost any location in town, or you can hail down a taxi which can be expected to charge about 540 *ptas* to reach most downtown destinations.

By Car

A vast array of high speed national and international motorways runs throughout Spain and most of Europe. The city is surrounded by both a wide circular ring road known as the M-30, and a more suburban M-40 semi-circular high speed access route, upon which many of the major **Autopistas** (toll motorways), **Autovias** (usually non-toll highways), and **Carretera Nacionals** (normal non-toll national roads) of Spain cross-connect and extend out to and from their various destinations.

From these major points of intersection, it is rather easy to follow detailed directions (ask for these instructions in advance!) into almost any part of downtown or suburban Madrid. Once inside the city you will have a difficult time finding free street side parking. Many private garages can be found throughout the city, but you can expect to pay somewhere around 2,900 *ptas* and up per day.

Keep in mind that while the road conditions of almost every Spanish *Autovia* (highway) are quite impressive, high tolls of up to 8,000 *ptas* or more may be imposed on some of these journeys, especially from regions north and east of the Madrid. Additional non-toll roads can also be used to get here, but expect travel times to be double those found if utilizing the vast highway system. With the recent abolishment of controlled border crossing points between most European Economic Community member nations, it may no longer be necessary to present passports or even wait on line while entering Spain via Portugal and France.

Additional passenger and car ferry connection services also exist to and from the Canary Islands, the Balearic Islands, and various other international locations such as the northern tip of Africa, southern Portugal, and England, but valid international travel documents may still mandatory for many of these sea-based routes.

By Train

Madrid is linked to almost every other point in Spain and Europe by an exhaustive series of rail lines. Madrid contains several different rail stations, each with its own series of daily arrivals and departures.

The most common location for service to and from the northern, eastern, and a few southern regions of Spain, as well as from France and other European countries, is at the large and modern Estación de Chamartin station at the north edge of the city. For arrivals and departures for the majority of southern and western regions of Spain (as well as Portugal), and high speed AVE trains to Cordoba and Sevilla, the normally utilized structure is the ornate Estación de Atocha station in the southern section of downtown. Less commonly requested routes via the northwestern regions of Spain may call at the smaller Estación de Principe Pio (also called Norte) station on the west side of town.

Use the train information phone numbers listed in the section further below to reconfirm, in advance, the exact time and station which you may need. All of these stations offer such facilities as ticket/reservation booths, nearby currency exchange, luggage storage areas, restrooms, and cafés, while *Chamartin* even offers such unique features as a bowling alley, disco, shopping center, skating rink and even a hotel reservation desk. Connections between these stations and any other point in Madrid can generally be made by public bus or *metro* for 125 *ptas* each way, or via taxi for roughly 650 *ptas* or so depending on how much luggage you have.

ORIENTATION

Madrid is a huge, and at times overwhelming, major metropolis. With more than three million residents and the steady sound of grid-locked traffic, it can a take a few days to adjust to the pace and energy level of this intense destination. With a seemingly endless array of fantastic museums, monumental buildings, awesome churches, peaceful gardens, public squares, world-class designer boutiques, fine restaurants and a thriving nightlife scene that lasts at least until sunrise, it's really a shame that most visitors will choose to stay only a few nights in Madrid. But you can see a fair amount of the city in a limited time, since the vast majority of the most famous historic, cultural, and architectural attractions can be found within a small area of less than 40 square blocks.

I have designated Madrid's largest and most central square, the hyperactive Puerta del Sol, as a starting point for most of the walking tours that follow in this chapter. This plaza is the real crossroads of the town, and people watching, shopping, and transportation options are in abundance here. Depending on how much time you have, select at least a few of the tours listed below to see some of the highlights that should not me missed. Just before going home after sunrise, a fair amount of these provocatively dressed night-crawlers can be found enjoying a cup of *chocolate*, Spain's infamous liquid chocolate pudding, with *churros* (long sticks of fried dough).

GETTING AROUND TOWN

By Bus

This city's municipal bus company, known officially as La Empresa Municipal de Transportes (EMT), offers an abundant supply of large red or smaller yellow painted Autobuses (buses) that criss-cross almost every neighborhood. With over 160 different bus lines, all numbered for convenience, and thousands of well marked bus stops, each with it's posted corresponding route map, getting around above the ground in this town is fairly easy.

Pick up a free pocket *Plano* (map) and bus system timetable. These can be found, for free, during business hours at the EMT bus information kiosks in three of the city's largest municipal bus stations, the Plaza de Callao, Puerta del Sol, and the Plaza de Cibeles. What you will find upon reading these multilingual maps is that the operating hours for most buses is from 6am until 12midnight. Just in case you party 'till the wee hours of the morning, two dozen or so special (Buhos) nightowl buses run from both the Puerta del Sol and nearby Plaza de la Cibeles central bus stops. These special buses to various locations throughout the city operate on a 30 to 60 minute frequency when the normal buses have stopped and usually have the letter "N" preceding their route number.

The price for a single use ticket is currently 130 *ptas* each way and can be bought directly from the bus driver who will be glad to make change for small bills. A special bonobus 10 ride ticket may be purchased for the discounted price of only 670 *ptas* from any bus information kiosk listed above, or at hundreds of newsstands throughout the city. For those of you who board the buses with a pre-purchased ticket, use the validation machines next to the driver to stamp it before each ride. If you ask politely, the driver will try to call out the name of your desired stop upon arrival.

Another great aspect to taking the bus instead of the *metro* (subway) is that you get to see lots of side streets that you wouldn't have ordinarily taken. The major drawback is that during rush hours, you may find yourself packed in like a sardine, and getting off at your stop can be difficult.

By Subway

After spending three months in Madrid recently, I came to love using the *metro* and I am sure you will also grow to enjoy the experience. It's great to know that you're zipping under the streets of the city at 45 kilometers per hour while the cars above you are stuck in grid-lock.

The subway system here is a well planned series of ten separate lines that are both numbered as well as color coded and call at over 120 separate stations throughout the city. At every *metro* station there is a ticket booth where you can pick up a wonderful free Plano system map, a must for every visitor to town.

Although some stations require the use of multiple escalators (some of which tend to break at inconvenient times) to access different platforms, there are easy-to-read signs always around to point you in the right direction. Since the interior transfer signs indicate the name of the line's termination station in each direction of the line, make sure you know where you are, where you are going, and the last stop of the train you wish to take.

Transfers are fairly easy, and do not cost extra. With the use of the free map, it will generally take less than 18 minutes to reach any destination in town. The subways are fairly clean, graffiti free, relatively safe at all hours, and a great way to get around. Smoking is not permitted in the stations, but many commuters tend to smoke with impunity until their train arrives.

The trains cost the same amount as the municipal buses, although the tickets are not interchangeable at this point. A single fare costs 130 *ptas* per person, and a 10 ride bonometro ticket costs 670 *ptas*. You can buy either of these types of tickets at any *metro* station's ticket window or automated ticket-dispensing machine. Be sure to insert your ticket with the arrow pointing into the turnstile, pass through the gate, and retrieve your ticket at the other end.

The subway system starts operating at 6am and the last train out is at 1:30am each day. Train frequencies average about every six minutes during business days, and every 17 minutes or so during late evenings, holidays, and weekends. A recent increase in the number of both panhandlers, con artists, illegal vendors and pick-pockets during the packed rush hours (7am–10am and 4pm–9pm) are on the rise, and I expect the police will start cleaning up the situation if pressure continues. Still, the *metro* system is certainly the best way to get around town during weekdays.

By Taxi

There are well over 15,000 licensed taxis which roam the streets and major passenger arrival points of this large capital city during all hours of the day and night. Drivers are typically polite, humorous, great sources of inside information and quite honest in comparison to those currently found in either New York or Toronto.

To find a taxi, either hail an unoccupied taxi (they often will display a small sign which says *Libre*) driving by, go to one of the dozens of obvious taxi stands throughout the city, or call Madrid Radio Taxi Companies, *Tel. (91) 447-5180* or *(91) 445-9008* for a radio response pick up on demand.

TAXIS FOR THE PHYSICALLY CHALLENGED

*A new service has come on line which offers specially designed taxis for those with special needs. The price is identical to normal taxi rates, and considering the obvious lack of access for those in wheelchairs to reach the municipal buses and metro, this is the way to go. Just call Tel. (91) 547-8200 or (91) 547-8600 and reserve a pick up with a **Taxi para Minusvalidos**.*

During rainy days, festivals, trade fairs, or weekday morning and evening rush hours (6am until 10am and 6pm until 9pm) it may be quite a wait until you get lucky. Taxis tend to charge somewhere around 300 to 800 *ptas* per ride (not per person!) between most downtown locations depending on exact distance and traffic conditions. All licensed taxis have electronic meters which start at 170 *ptas* and click away at roughly 80 *ptas* per kilometer (50 *ptas* per mile) when the taxi is travelling at over 21 kilometers per hour (13 miles per hour), or will click away at about 30 *ptas* per minute when the taxi is going slower than the above velocity, or is totally stuck in traffic. Normally this works out to somewhere around 8 *ptas* per city block during non-rush hour city rides.

Legally chargeable supplements are posted on a sticker in the taxi's interior and are reflected in the meter rate include an additional 350 *ptas* for airport pick ups, 150 *ptas* for bus and *Renfe* train station pick ups, 150 *ptas* for trade fair pick ups, 150 *ptas* extra on public holidays, another 150 *ptas* between the hours of 11pm and 6am daily and 50 *ptas* extra for each piece of luggage.

These extra charges can be combined, but are occasionally illegally utilized, so pay attention. If for any reason you think you are being overcharged, ask for an official receipt (*recibo oficial*), write down the license number of the taxi (posted near the meter), and call *Tel. (91) 447-0704* to register your complaint. You might actually get a refund in a year or so.

WHERE TO STAY

Expensive

THE PALACE HOTEL, *Plaza de las Cortes, 7. Tel. (91) 429-7551; Fax (91) 429-8266. US & Canada Bookings (The Luxury Collection), Tel. 800/325-3589 Year round rack rates from 59,000 ptas per double room per night (E.P.). Special promotional rates from 37,500 ptas per double room per night (E.P.). All major credit cards accepted.*

Recently restored into Madrid´s finest 5 star deluxe hotel, this Baroque-style hotel, conceived by King Alfonso XIII, is an absolute delight! Situated steps away from the Prado museum in the heart of downtown Madrid, this large, fabulous luxury hotel is among my favorite places to stay in Europe.

As soon as you arrive here you are greeted by a formally dressed doorman and led up to one of the most dramatic lobbies found anywhere. Every detail has been thought of, and the extremely talented staff here make sure that you are treated as well as the many kings, presidents, and film stars that call the Palace their home while visiting Madrid. Each of the 476 large and traditionally decorated rooms and suites offer air conditioning, mini-bars, direct dial telephones, satellite televisions, plush furnishings, huge closets, in-room music systems and large marble bathrooms with the best amenities in town.

Services and facilities at the hotel include 24-hour fax services, an in-house travel agency, valet parking, a full service concierge desk which can find tickets for even most sold-out events, a wonderful attached luxury shopping arcade with over three dozen upscale boutiques, all-night room service, business meeting rooms, laundry and dry cleaning facilities, and much, much, more. Dining at The Palace is also a great experience, with the best buffet breakfast in all of Spain served under an unforgettable stained glass dome. Other meals offered in both the El Ambigu restaurant, and the remarkably intimate La Cupola Italian restaurant – which will only seat 48 people at a time to ensure absolute culinary perfection. The hotel is scheduled for a far reaching renovation that will make it even more deluxe, and is sure to scare its competition. Selected as one of my best places to stay (see Chapter 13).

HOTEL VILLA MAGNA, *Paseo de la Castellana, 22. Tel. (91) 576-7500; Fax (91) 431-2286. US & Canada Bookings (Hyatt), Tel. 800/233-1234. Year-round rack rates from 55,000 per double room per night (E.P.). All major credit cards accepted.*

Located in the exclusive embassy row section of town just a couple of blocks north of the Plaza de Colón, this thoroughly modern five-star property has set the standard for comfort and service in Madrid. All of the 164 double rooms, eight junior suites, 12 executive suites, and two giant presidential suites contain deluxe marble bathrooms, powerful air conditioning systems, electronic mini-safes, stereo satellite televisions with VCR, hand-carved oak furnishings, direct dial phones, soundproofed window, mini-bars, and luxurious bathrobes.

Guests here tend to be visiting American and European bank executives and international celebrities who are treated to a wide variety of services, including a 24- hour valet, room service, indoor parking, an expert multilingual concierge desk, beauty salon, designer boutiques, sauna, and even a special business center with available secretarial services, fax machines, computers and translators.

Dining here is a magnificent experience with a full American buffet breakfast being offered daily in the tranquil Lobby Lounge, as well as fine lunches, afternoon tea, and gourmet dinners being served at either chef Carmelo Valverde's fantastic Berceo restaurant, or on one of several lounges and outdoor terraces. Under the leadership of Philippe Bloch, the hotel's superb French general manager, the staff here are among the most professional in all of Spain and understand how to cater to even the most demanding guests. I couldn't imagine a more comfortable hotel for either business or leisure travelers who expect only the best that money will buy.

SANTO MAURO HOTEL, *Calle Zurbano, 36. Tel. (91) 319-6900, Fax (91) 308-5477. US & Canada Bookings (UTELL), Tel. 800/44-UTELL. Year-round rack rates from 37,500 ptas per double room per night (E.P.). All major credit cards accepted.*

This 37 room boutique hotel was once the best hotel in Madrid, but they really have begun to lose their concept of what customer service is all about! Situated on a quiet side street in the embassy row zone just a few blocks north of Plaza de Colón, the Santo Mauro is so opulent, deluxe, and private that it seems to think that it is the Royal Palace.

The main section of this ornate structure was originally constructed as a mansion for the Duke of Santo Mauro in 1894 by famed French architect Louis Legrand. After a painstaking conversion, the old structure, along with its extravagant new addition, houses the most remarkable collection of rooms and suites found just about anywhere. Each accommodation is fully air conditioned, has giant marble bathrooms with translucent doors, large satellite color televisions, CD/cassette/radio/ stereo systems, direct dial phones, modern furnishings, mini-bars, mini-safes, beautiful furnishings and lots of space.

The restaurant offers a continental buffet breakfast, and is then transformed into an intimate and formal venue with fine cuisine. The hotel also has overnight shoe-shine service, room service, laundry and dry cleaning and newspapers delivered daily to each room. Guest facilities include an indoor pool, a fitness center, sauna, peaceful lounges and much more. Simply put, this is for the super deluxe visitor or businessman who expects the finest quality, doesn't mind inconsistent service, and is willing to pay whatever it costs to stay in the snobbiest hotel in town.

THE RITZ, *Plaza de la Lealtad, 5. Tel. (91) 521-2857, Fax (91) 532-8776. US & Canada Bookings (Leading Hotels), Tel. 800/223-6800. Yea-round rack rates from 53,000 ptas per double room per night (E.P.). Special weekend rates from 40,000 ptas per double room per night (E.P.).All major credit cards accepted.*

If money is no object and you are looking for the most aristocratic place to stay in town, join the hundreds of visiting celebrities and heads of state who have chosen The Ritz. Although it has recently been surpassed in both quality and luxury by the nearby Palace Hotel, this stunningly elegant five-star hotel rests at the foot of Retiro Park just across from the famed Prado museum. The property offers 154 super-deluxe rooms and opulent suites that all have marble bathrooms with dual basins, high quality hair and skin care products, direct-dial telephones, remote control satellite television, beautiful furnishings and powerful air conditioners.

The hotel also offers a new upper floor health club with sauna and optional massages, the formal Goya Restaurant and terrace, a serious concierge, beauty salon, 24-hour room service and secured underground parking. Service here is formal and geared towards VIP guests, and it's famed lobby lounge and piano bar is certainly still the choicest place to meet other high-end travelers and famous personalities.

CASTELLANA INTER-CONTINENTAL HOTEL, *Paseo de la Castellana, 49. Tel. (91) 410-0200; Fax (91) 319-5853. US & Canada Bookings (Inter-Continental), Tel. 800/327-0200. Low season rack rates from 37,500 ptas per double room per night (E.P.). High season rates from 56,200 ptas per double room per night (E.P.). Low season rates from 43,600 ptas per double room per night (E.P.). All major credit cards accepted.*

With its excellent location in the city's most famous business district, the beautiful four-star Castellana is a truly memorable hotel. The property boasts 311 bright and spacious air conditioned rooms and suites each with deluxe marble bathrooms, direct dial telephones, satellite television, available in-room fax, mini-bar, hair dryer, am-fm clock radio and rather impressive interiors.

Facilities here include several cafés and restaurants which feature both live music and afternoon tea, a fully equipped health club, 24-hour room service, express laundry and dry cleaning, sauna, marble floored public lounges, safe deposit boxes, sun terrace, jogging track, non-smoking rooms, baby-sitting, business meeting rooms, boutiques, excursion desk, concierge desk, rental cars and a great staff of true professionals. Mostly used by top business executives, the hotel is a great choice for those who can afford these rates!

HOTEL VILLA REAL, *Plaza de las Cortes, 10. Tel. (91) 420-3767; Fax (91) 420-2547. US & Canada Bookings (Small Luxury Hotels), Tel. 800/525-4800. Corporate rack rates from 35,650 ptas per double room per night (C.P.). Year-round rack rates from 39,600 ptas per double room per night (E.P.). All major credit cards accepted.*

This newly renovated, fantastically luxurious, and unusually friendly mid-sized hotel is the best place to stay in this price category. Located within easy walking distance to all the most important museums, shops, and nightlife in town, this 115 room super-deluxe four-star (it really deserves to have five) hotel has some of the nicest rooms available in the whole country. The new addition of a museum displaying Greek and Roman antiquities has added even more charm to this amazing hotel.

Each of the 96 superb double rooms has extremely comfortable bedding, state-of-the-art air conditioners, totally soundproofed windows, fine European designed fabrics, sunken living rooms with spare sofa beds, electronic key pass doors, mini-bars, mini-safes, three telephones, 14 channel remote control satellite televisions with English stations, beautiful hardwood furnishings and floral prints. Even the huge wall-to-wall marble bathrooms are unbelievably opulent, and are stocked to the brim with German skin care products, French perfumes, the finest bathrobes money can buy, and powerful hair dryers. If you want even more spacious accommodations, the hotel also offers several additional junior suites, penthouse duplex suites, and two royal suites which may contain grand staircases, huge panoramic private outdoor terraces and sun decks, circular bathtubs with built in whirlpools, private sauna systems, antiques and more.

What really makes this beautiful hotel so memorable is that the staff (under the expert direction of Sr. Felix Garcia Hernan) is remarkably helpful and friendly. Even though there are plenty of movie stars and world political leaders staying here, every guest is treated like a real VIP. Among the many services featured are complimentary bottles of Sherry upon check-in, 24-hour room-service, an affordable indoor garage, the best bell boys and doormen I have ever seen, sunny business meeting rooms, a wonderful bar and lounge lined with priceless Roman mosaics and an excellent daily breakfast featuring freshly squeezed orange juice and home-made pastries.

There is also a great restaurant, one of the city's best snack shops, ornate public sitting rooms, a tourist information library, a health spa with massage therapy and sauna, a full service beauty salon, and plenty of rooms with fine views overlooking the Cortes parliament buildings and peaceful Paseo del Prado. If you are looking for a hotel that is dedicated to providing the highest level of customer attention and comfort, this is the place to go! Selected as one of my Best Places to Stay (see Chapter 13).

N.H. HOTEL EUROBUILDING, *Calle Padre Damian, 23. Tel. (91) 345-4500. Fax (91) 345-4576. US & Canada Bookings (UTELL), Tel. 800/ 44-UTELL. Year-round rack rates from 43,000 ptas per double room per night (E.P.). Weekend rates from 28,000 ptas per double room per night (E.P.). All major credit cards accepted.*

The Eurobuilding hotel is understandably the first choice of many mid-budget businessmen and vacationers looking for a full service hotel with great prices, huge rooms, and even complete apartments with kitchens. Situated in the northern business sector of Madrid, just off of the

Paseo de la Castellana, this is a fine hotel at a bargain price. All of the 420 or so huge double rooms are nicely designed and include large king or double bedding, terraces, multilingual satellite televisions, mini-safes, mini-bars, marble bathrooms stocked with amenities including cologne, direct-dial phones with automated wake-up call services, plenty of sunlight, and plush furnishings. There are also 70 one-bedroom apartment suites in the adjacent "Las Estancias" apartment building, which share all of the hotel's facilities, as well as more upscale suites.

The hotel is packed with facilities, including several restaurants and bars, a huge outdoor pool and garden area with a snack bar, lobby level boutiques, an adjacent shopping center, an Iberia airlines ticket office, a large room service menu, 20 different meeting rooms with world class conference facilities and available secretarial services, underground parking for hundreds of cars, baby-sitting upon request, a health club with sauna and workout room, excursion desk, express check-out and a great staff of hard-working people.

HOTEL WELLINGTON, *Calle Velázquez, 8. Tel. (91) 575-4400. Fax (91) 576-4164. US & Canada Bookings (Golden Tulip), Tel. 800/344-1212. High season rack rates from 34,250 ptas per double room per night (E.P.). Low season rack rates from 23,500 ptas per double room per night (E.P.). All major credit cards accepted.*

If shopping in the exclusive nearby boutique-lined **Salamanca district** is your cup of tea, this is the best place to stay. This great five-star hotel is an oasis of tranquility in the heart of town. The Wellington has some 300 beautifully furnished and air conditioned rooms and giant suites with large private bathrooms, plenty of marble, mini-safes, cable television, in-room music systems, direct-dial phones and soundproofed windows. Facilities here include parking, multiple restaurants, a snack bar, coffee shop, two bars, room-service, outdoor pool, sauna, gardens, solarium, meeting rooms, secretarial services, excursion desk, boutiques, newsstand, tobacco shop and much more. With its traditional Madrid style and atmosphere, this is a good choice, especially during the low season price specials.

HOTEL MELIA CASTILLA, *Calle de Capitan Hoya, 43. Tel. (91) 571-2211, Fax (91) 571-4411. US & Canada bookings (UTELL), Tel. 800/44U-TELL. Year-round rack rates from 35,400 ptas per double room per night (E.P.). All major credit cards accepted.*

If you are looking for a modern full-service deluxe hotel with countless facilities to accommodate huge groups and conventions near the convention center, this is certainly the best place in town. The Melia Castilla offers a staggering 936 air conditioned rooms and suites (making it one of southern Europe's largest downtown hotels) that all feature remote control satellite television, large deluxe marble floored bathrooms with high quality hair and skin care products, direct-dial telephone with voice mail and computer modem connectors, electronic mini-safe, mini-bar, large picture windows and much more.

The hotel features four different restaurants, 24-hour room-service, special executive and non-smoking floors, a huge array of business and congress meeting rooms, optional secretarial and child care facilities, boutiques, newsstand, concierge and excursion desks, limousine rental and the famed panoramic La Scala theater and showcase where you can catch international recording stars performing almost daily.

HOTEL OCCIDENTAL MIGUEL ANGEL, *Calle de Miguel Angel, 29. Tel. (91) 442-0022, Fax (91) 441-6911. US & Canada bookings (UTELL), Tel. 800/44UTELL. Year-round rack rates from 35,700 ptas per double room per night (E.P.). All major credit cards accepted.*

Situated just off the central Paseo de la Castellana in the heart of Madrid's commercial and banking district, this modern eight-floor executive class 4 star hotel is a good choice for both businessmen and travelers. There are 271 air conditioned rooms and suites each with large private bathrooms, direct-dial telephones, satellite television, nice but simple furnishings and either interior or city view windows.

There are business meeting rooms, a swimming pool, boutiques, a newsstand, room-service, a car rental and excursion desk, nearby parking, a tranquil bar and lounge, two full service restaurants offering three optional meals daily, baby-sitting and a friendly staff.

HOLIDAY INN MADRID, *Plaza Carlos Trias Beltran, 4. Tel. (91) 597-0102, Fax (91) 597-0292. US & Canada Bookings (Holiday Inn), Tel. 800/465-4329. Special weekend rates from 16,500 ptas per double room per night (B.P.). Special weekday rates from 32,675 ptas per double room per night (B.P.). All major credit cards accepted.*

Located just across from Madrid's main convention center in the northern edge of the city's business district, this modern towering four-star business class hotel is a good choice for travelers and executives, especially during their incredible weekend promotions. The hotel features 313 nicely decorated air conditioned rooms with large private bathrooms, remote control satellite television with movie channels, mini-bars, and extremely comfortable furnishings. The hotel also has a great rooftop outdoor swimming pool, two restaurants, two pools, room-service, a fully equipped fitness center, baby sitting, business meeting and convention rooms, direct bus service to the heart of the city, and several boutiques. The staff here are true professionals, and are sure to make your stay here a memorable one.

HOTEL TRYP FÉNIX, *Calle de Hermosilla, 2. Tel. (91) 431-6700. Fax (91) 576-0661. US & Canada Bookings (UTELL), Tel. 800/44UTELL. Year-*

*round rack rates from 30,050 ptas per double room per night (B.P.). All major
credit cards accepted.*

This large and unattractive four-star hotel rests on the edge of Plaza
de Colón. Its 216 rooms and 20 suites all come with air conditioning,
private bathrooms, mini-bars, electronic mini-safes, direct dial telephones,
satellite televisions, radios, and either king or double beds.

Primarily used by European businessmen for short trips to Madrid,
the hotel features grand public rooms, nearby parking, porters, room-
service, a travel agency, a hair salon, boutiques, meeting rooms, a
restaurant and a bar. Included in the daily rate is a full buffet breakfast
featuring eggs, pastries, cheeses, fresh fruits, strong coffee, juices and
cereals. The guest rooms vary in size and view, but since they all cost the
same amount, I suggest asking to see a few first.

HOTEL BARAJAS, *Calle de Leganitos, 13. Tel. (91) 747-7700, Fax (91)
747-8717. US & Canada Bookings: (Golden Tulip), Tel. 800/344-1212.
Special weekend rates from 21,500 ptas per double room per night (B.P.). Year-
round rack rates from 29,000 ptas per double room per night (E.P.). All major
credit cards accepted.*

If you want to be just a few minutes away from Madrid's main
international airport at Barajas, this is the best place to stay. This beautiful
five-star deluxe hotel offers its guests 230 of the nicest rooms and suites
in town, all featuring powerful air conditioning, private bathrooms with
high quality amenities, direct-dial telephones, satellite televisions with
movie channels, extremely comfortable furnishings, large picture windows and mini-bars. The hotel also has a great swimming pool, free
airport shuttle service, executive and no smoking floors, solarium, free
parking, Jacuzzi, boutiques, two excellent restaurants, a coffee shop,
gardens, business meeting and convention rooms, beauty salon and much
more. This is really a great choice for those of you who need to be close
to the airport.

Moderate

GRAN HOTEL CONDE DUQUE, *Plaza Conde Valle de Suchill, 5. Tel.
(91) 447-7000. Fax (91) 448-3569. Weekend rates from 14,500 ptas per double
room per night (B.P.). Corporate rack rates from 23,500 ptas per double room per
night (E.P.). US & Canada Bookings (UTELL), Tel. 800/44UTELL. All major
credit cards accepted.*

This friendly four-star hotel is so comfortable that you may never
want to check out. Situated on one of the quietest and most secure squares
in all of Madrid, the property is close to every sight and attraction in town.
Since the completion of a fantastic multi-million dollar top to bottom
renovation in 1992, the Gran Hotel Conde Duque has become one of my
favorite places to stay.

Each of the 142 large and beautifully decorated rooms offer air conditioning, the highest quality furnishings, plush designer fabrics, deluxe marble bathrooms, electronic mini-safes, mini-bars, multilingual satellite television, direct-dial phones, in-room music systems, scales, magnetic key card locks, hair dryers, and a huge array of complimentary amenities. There are also seven special rooms with sitting areas and Jacuzzi whirlpools as well as a gigantic suite with a private sun terrace.

The multilingual staff here are delightfully courteous, and provide excursion reservations, laundry and dry cleaning, currency exchange, 24-hour room-service and fax machine and computer rentals. Other great features here include a welcoming lobby area, a great breakfast room featuring a superb full American- style buffet, a cafeteria/snack bar and a popular Italian pasta and pizza restaurant. This is one the top of my list in the moderate price accommodations category.

GRAN HOTEL REINA VICTORIA, *Plaza de Santa Ana, 14. Tel. (91) 531-6000. Fax (91) 522-0307. US & Canada bookings (UTELL), Tel. 800/44UTELL. Year-round rack rates from 25,000 ptas per double room per night (E.P.). All major credit cards accepted.*

Situated on the edge of charming Plaza de Santa Ana, this fine four-star hotel is a great place to stay. Its prime location is just a few minutes walk away from Madrid's most famous museums, attractions, restaurants, nightclubs, and historical sights. The hotel offers 201 spacious and well-appointed rooms and suites, many of which have full views over either the Plaza de Santa Ana or the Plaza del Ángel.

All of the guestrooms are individually heated and air conditioned and contain deco-era furnishings, large private marble bathrooms, huge closets, mini-safes, mini-bars, direct-dial phones, satellite televisions with CNN and local movie channels, currency exchange and new electronic door locks. With the help of a fantastic multilingual staff, the hotel offers many convenient services including porters, room-service, excursion reservations, and optional indoor parking. A la carte lunches and dinners are available at the hotel's El Ruedo restaurant which also serves a large buffet breakfast from 7:30am until 11am each morning. Drinks can be enjoyed inside the intimate Bar Taurino Manolete.

This landmark property has also become the home-away-from-home for bullfighters (who can be seen dressed in full costume), especially during the Fiera de San Isidro festival in May. This hotel is recommended for younger more active travelers.

HOTEL MAYORAZGO, *Calle de Flor Baja, 3. Tel. (91) 547-2600. Fax (91) 541-2485. Year round rack rates from 17,000 ptas per double room per night (E.P.). All major credit cards accepted.*

With its central location only steps away from the Gran Via, this new five-story hotel offers 224 nice spacious rooms. Each of the rooms is air conditioned and has private bathrooms, television, direct dial telephones, sound proofed windows, am-fm radios and city street or interior views. The hotel also has parking facilities, a restaurant, bar, laundry facilities, mini-safes, room service, special converted accommodations for the physically challenged, an excursion desk, business meeting rooms, and porters. A good selection for those with a limited amount of time to wander around downtown Madrid.

N.H. HOTEL EMBAJADA, *Calle de Santa Engracia, 5. Tel. (91) 594-0213. Fax (91) 447-3312. US & Canada Bookings (UTELL), Tel. 800/ 44UTELL. Weekend rack rates from 13,500 ptas per double room per night (E.P.). Weekday rack rates from 24,940 ptas per double room per night (E.P.). All major credit cards accepted.*

The Embajada is by far the best value in the affordable selection of Madrid's most distinctive hotels, especially during the weekends (Friday through Sunday). This extremely comfortable and uniquely designed three-star hotel boasts a great location within steps of a major metro station, and only a two block walk to the heart of the Plaza de Colón, with its abundance of museums and nearby boutiques.

The guests here are mostly European, North American, and Japanese tourists or businessmen who return to this property year after year. Each of the 101 single and double air conditioned rooms have plush ultra modern furnishings, marble and tile bathrooms loaded with the highest quality amenities, mini-bars, electronic keys, satellite television, am-fm radios, soundproofed windows, hair dryers, and in many cases, separate sitting areas at no additional charge. The hotel also has a breakfast room serving a daily European style buffet, a tranquil bar, and a full-service restaurant. Other services include currency exchange, room-service, and business meeting facilities. Considering the superior location, comfort level, service, and creative interior design, this is a gem of a hotel at a great price.

N.H. HOTEL LAGASCA, *Calle de Lagasca, 64. Tel. (91) 575-4606. Fax (91) 575-1694. US & Canada Bookings (UTELL), Tel. 800/44UTELL. Weekend rack rates from 11,500 ptas per double room per night (E.P.). Weekday rack rates from 18,600 ptas per double room per night (E.P.)*

Situated in the heart of the fine Barrio Salamanca high end shopping district just a few blocks above Retiro Park, the three- star Hotel Lagasca is another great value, especially during the weekends (Friday through Sunday). This modern and rather comfortable property contains 100 simple yet spacious rooms with pine furnishings, marble private bathrooms, mini-bars, electronic keys, satellite television, am-fm radios, soundproof windows, and hair dryers. The hotel also has a breakfast room serving a daily European style buffet, a tranquil bar, and a full- service restaurant. Other services include currency exchange, room-service, and business meeting facilities. Considering the supeb location and level of affordable comfort, this is a real bargain.

HOTEL CARLTON, *Paseo de las Delicias, 26. Tel. (91) 539-7100, Fax (91) 527-8510. Year round rack rates from 22,000 ptas per double room per night (E.P.). Special weekend rates from 15,750 ptas per double room per night (C.P.). All major credit cards accepted.*

The newly renovated Carlton Hotel is located in a bustling commercial district just a few minutes walk away from the Prado museum. This modern four-star hotel offers 133 spacious air conditioned and sound-proofed rooms that have nice private bathrooms with hair dryers, direct dial telephones, color satellite television, mini-safe, comfortable pine wood furnishings, plenty of natural sunlight, and nearby parking. This is an excellent value for the money, especially during the weekends when their special rates make it much more affordable.

HOTEL EMPERADOR, *Gran Via, 53. Tel. (91) 547-2800, Fax (91) 547-6000. Year-round rack rates from 21,325 ptas per double room per night (E.P.). All major credit cards accepted.*

If you are looking for reasonably priced accommodations right on the main avenue in the center of town, the Emperador is one of the better choices. After completing a recent renovation, this nice three-star hotel has 232 fully air conditioned rooms that each contain private bathrooms, direct-dial telephones, cable television, comfortable bedding, nice but simple furnishings, and either courtyard or exterior views. The hotel also offers its guests a rooftop outdoor swimming pool and terrace, a nice piano bar, two restaurants, private parking, business meeting and convention rooms and good service for the money.

HOTEL AROSA, *Calle de Salud, 21. Tel. (91) 532-1600, Fax (91) 531-3127. US & Canada Bookings: (Best Western), Tel. 800/528-1234. Year round rack rates from 19,680 ptas per double room per night (E.P.). All major credit cards accepted.*

Simple but comfortable, this four-star is a good bargain in the city-center. Just a few blocks off the main Gran Via, this hotel has 139 rooms each with private bathroom, mini-bar, mini-safe, hair dryer, cable television, in-room radio, air conditioning, heating and simple furnishings. The Arosa also offers a restaurant, lounge, nearby parking, business meeting rooms, room service, laundry service, and a good staff.

Inexpensive

HOTEL INGLÉS, *Calle Echegaray, 8. Tel. (91) 429-6551. Fax (91) 420-2423. Year-round rack rates from 10,950 ptas per double room per night (E.P.). All major credit cards accepted.*

This modern and well designed three-star hotel near the Plaza Santa Ana is a good choice for travelers who want to be near the heart of town without spending a fortune. All of the 58 single and double rooms feature private bathrooms, direct- dial phones, television, heating, and simple but comfortable furnishings. Other facilities include a breakfast room, laundry services, nearby parking garage, meeting rooms, safe deposit boxes, and a front desk staff that can book excursions and give plenty of tourist information. Since the street it fronts is rather busy at night, you may wish to request a quiet interior-view room.

HOTEL EL COLLOSO, *Calle de Leganitos, 13. Tel. (91) 559-7600. Fax (91) 547-4968. US & Canada Bookings (UTELL), Tel. 800/44UTELL. Low season rack rates from 9,750 ptas per double room per night (E.P.). High season rack rates from 14,500 ptas per double room per night (E.P.).*

Within walking distance to both the Palacio Real and the Gran Via, this four-star hotel is a great deal during the summer months. All of its 84 single and double air conditioned rooms have modern private bathrooms, mini-bars, hair dryers, large windows and wall-to-wall carpeting. During the last major renovation of the hotel back in 1991, the facilities and accommodations improved and now include a restaurant, snack shop, bar, lounge, nice public rooms, nearby parking, and a large lobby. The staff here is polite and hard-working, and will be glad to provide tourist information, restaurant suggestions, and even book bus tours and reconfirm your airplane's departure time.

HOTEL FRANCISCO I, *Calle de Arenal, 15. Tel. (91) 548-0204. Fax (91) 542-2899. Low season rack rates from 9,700 ptas per double room per night (B.P.). High season rack rates from 11,250 ptas per double room per night (B.P.). All major credit cards accepted.*

With an excellent location just two blocks away from the Puerta del Sol and rather competitive prices, this nice two-star hotel is a good choice for budget-conscious travelers. The hotel has 60 single, double, and triple rooms (many with air conditioning), which have spotless private bathrooms, telephones, television, plenty of light, simple wooden furnishings, and big closets. Unlike some less expensive properties, there are elevators to each floor, large public spaces, a nice 6th floor restaurant that serves an inclusive breakfast, and an unusually friendly front desk staff. Some rooms even come with patios overlooking the street.

HOTEL RESIDENCIA CORTEZO, *Calle de Dr. Cortezo, 3. Tel. (91) 369-0101, Fax (91) 369-3774. US & Canada Bookings: (Best Western), Tel. 800/528-1234. Year-round rack rates from 14,500 ptas per double room per night (B.P.). All major credit cards accepted.*

Although not very dramatic from the outside, this nice little three-star city center hotel within easy walking distance to the Puerta del Sol offers a good deal on modest, air conditioned rooms that all have private bathrooms, mini-safe, mini-bar, direct dial telephone, and basic furnishings that are more comfortable than I had expected. There is a restaurant, lounge, solarium, laundry, room service and nearby parking.

HOTEL CARLOS V, *Calle de Maestro Victoria, 5. Tel. (91) 531-4100, Fax (91) 531-3761. US & Canada bookings: (Best Western), Tel. 800/528-1234. Year-round rack rates from 13,000 ptas per double room per night (C.P.). Most major credit cards accepted.*

The cute Carlos V is a simple three-star classic style hotel located about 75 meters away from the famed Puerta del Sol on a small side street near the world famous downtown Madrid branch of the El Corte Ingles department store. The hotel's 67 medium-sized interior and exterior view rooms feature satellite television, private bathroom, air conditioning and heating systems, telephones, mini-safe, in-room music and simple but comfortable furnishings. There is also a bar, nearby garage parking, breakfast room, laundry service and a helpful front desk staff.

HOTEL AUSTRIAS, *Calle de Sevilla, 2. Tel. (91) 429-6676, Fax (91) 429-4036. US & Canada Bookings: (UTELL), Tel. 800/44-UTELL. Special weekend rack rates from 8,750 ptas per double room per night (C.P.). Year-round rack rates from 12,750 ptas per double room per night (E.P.)*

While far from deluxe or opulent, this fairly nice two-star property is only a few minutes walk away from the heart of the Puerta del Sol in the city center. Here you can choose one of 175 rooms that have all been renovated in 1993 and contain private bathrooms, direct dial telephone, remote control cable television and simple but comfortable furnishings. The hotel also has a restaurant, room service, laundry service, heating and nearby parking.

HOTEL MARÍA CRISTINA, *Calle de Fuencarral, 20. Tel. (91) 531-6300. Fax (91) 531-6309. Year round rack rates from 5,975 ptas per double room per night (E.P.). American Express and Visa cards accepted.*

This clean and comfortable two-star hotel just above the Gran Via in central Madrid has 18 single and double rooms with private bathroom, telephone, and heating. The interior is nice and simple, and is a good selection for this price range. Don't expect much in the way of facilities.

RESIDENCIA DUCAL, *Calle de Hortaleza, 3. Tel. (91) 521-1045, Fax (91) 521-5064. Year round rack rates from 6,750 ptas per double room per night (E.P.). Cash only.*

Just a short walk from the Gran Via, this friendly, safe, clean, and comfortable budget inn has a few dozen single and double rooms with either private or shared bathrooms that are a good value. Try and look at a few units to choose the one you will be happiest with. No facilities, but the staff and guests are rather pleasant.

RESIDENCIA ZAMORAN, *Calle de Fuencarral, 18. Tel. (91) 532-2060, No fax. Year round rack rates from 5,250 ptas per double room per night (E.P.). Cash only.*

When you're on a tight budget and still want a clean comfortable room in a good location, this basic no-thrills inn is worth consideration. You can choose between 11 simple heated rooms that have either a private, or shared bathroom. No real facilities but still a decent place to stay in the center of the city.

HOSTEL RICHARD SCHIRRMAN, *Casa de Campo. Tel. (91) 463-5699, Unlisted fax. Year round rack rates from 2,250 ptas per dormitory bed per night (C.P.). Cash only.*

This is the larger of the two official R.E.A.J. Hostelling International affiliated youth hostels and is quite close to the Royal Palace. It's a great place to sleep for people of all ages who are on extremely tight budgets, and a perfect place to meet other travelers. The hostel has a somewhat early curfew and some other basic regulations, but at these prices what do you expect? The hostel offers 134 bunk beds in an assortment of large rooms with semi-private toilet and shower facilities . They also offer a nice complimentary continental breakfast.

Make sure to lock up your valuables in the available lockers before heading out to do your sightseeing. A hostel card must either be presented or purchased to be admitted into this facility.

WHERE TO EAT

Expensive

RESTAURANT ZALACAÍN, *Calle de Alvarez de Baena, 4. Tel. (91) 561-5935. All major credit cards accepted.*

Chef Benjamin Urdiain creates fantastic gourmet menus in this elegant and formal three Michelin star French restaurant above the Paseo de la Castellana. Known as one of Europe's finest restaurants and a member of Relais & Chateaux, Zalacain is popular with the most demanding executives and politicians that live and work in Madrid. Their seasonal offerings always include the absolute freshest prime cuts of meat, filets of fish, rare game, and seafood all prepared and presented with the highest degree of care.

The ambiance is relaxing with several of the intimate dining rooms adorned with dark paneling and beautiful oil paintings . Please be sure to call well in advance for reservations, especially if you want to be seated in the wonderful terrace area. Even their extensive wine list is hard to match, and includes vintages from around the globe. Expect to pay somewhere between 10,000 *ptas* and 16,000 *ptas* per person, plus wine, for the meal of your life.

SUNTORY, *Paseo de la Castellana, 38. Tel. (91) 577-3733. All major credit cards accepted.*

Suntory is a serious Shusi and Sashimi restaurant for those who want the finest quality and service. As soon as you step inside the dramatically decorated modern interior, you can't help but notice the scores of traditionally dressed Sushi chefs preparing roll after roll of freshly caught raw fish and seafood surrounded by rice and crispy black seaweed. This is still the premier Japanese dining establishment in Spain, and the high prices are equally famous. I spent well over 10,000 *ptas* per person, plus wine, for my meal here, and I'm told that I got away cheaply.

RESTAURANTE JOCKEY, *Calle Amador de los Rios, 6. Tel. (91) 319-1003. Most major credit cards accepted.*

This great posh little restaurant in a quaint residential area of the city offers its patrons a chance to unwind in the civilized atmosphere of a private club while enjoying extremely delicious international cuisine and an immense selection of fine wines. The understated formal interior lined with antique paintings of thoroughbred horses (the restaurant was formerly known as the Jockey Club) has enchanted both locals and visitors alike for over 50 years, and the service is absolutely first rate.

The chef prepares a large assortment of seasonal Spanish-style meals. The veal, seafood, and steak courses are made with the freshest and finest available ingredients including truffles and caviar used to add a slightly French accent. A meal here (before adding wine) will cost somewhere around 11,000 *ptas* per person, but its well worth it if you're used to this type of conservative ambiance. Jacket and tie is requested, and reservations are usually a necessity.

RESTAURANTE HORCHER, *Calle Alfonso XII, 6. Tel. (91) 522-0731. All major credit cards accepted.*

If more restaurants in Madrid could be this impressive, I think I would have stayed here a few more months (and gained a few extra kilos in the process). This opulent continental gourmet-dining establishment is not an easy place to get a reservation, but it's well worth the effort. Once inside, you can't help but be overpowered by the savory smells wafting out from the award-winning kitchen. With its fine European menu and crystal/silver settings, Horcher offers its fortunate guests an assortment of local and international favorites with a special German style twist.

Since the menu changes regularly I won't get too specific, but dress formally, call a week in advance for a table, and prepare yourself to spend at least 12,500 *ptas* a head, plus wine, for a fabulous culinary experience.

RESTAURANTE BOTÍN, *Calle de Cuchilleros, 17. Tel. (91) 366-4217. All major credit cards accepted.*

Named after the chef who created it, this Madrid landmark was first opened in 1725 making it the world's oldest restaurant. Now owned and operated by the delightful Gonzalez family, this Old World style restaurant has become one of the busiest places in town. Upon arrival, patrons have their choice of dining in an original 16th century vaulted brick cellar, an intimate kitchen side salon, or the larger upper floor dining rooms which feature exposed beams, old paintings, and *azulejos* tiles.

Since the days when Hemingway would stagger in here, it has become a favorite eating establishment of Americans and Europeans alike who are looking for the famed oven-roasted suckling pig or their marvelous roasted baby lamb, which are both carefully cooked in the restaurant's original three hundred year old wood-fired oven.

Other worthy dishes include the baked Cantabrian hake with a secret ingredient (it turns out to be veal juice), the best smoked salmon in town, freshly roasted peppers with codfish, their famous quarter of an hour fish soup, garlic soup with egg, fried trout Navarra style, filet mignon with mushrooms, and a selection of great desserts. One dessert suggestion: upon arrival, order the special soufflé (not listed on the menu) to top off a perfect meal. Expect to spend an average of 5,950 *ptas* per person plus wine here.

TABERNA ALKALDE, *Calle de Jorge Juan, 10. Tel. (91) 576-3359. All major credit cards accepted.*

Although it doesn't look like much from the outside, this pricey little restaurant in the trendy Salamanca district above the Retiro park attracts formally attired patrons who often arrive in chauffeur driven BMW and Mercedes sedans. Once inside, the tranquil tan interior with exposed wood is eclipsed only by the impressive menu that changes daily.

On my last visit here, featured dishes included mostly seafood items such as endive and avocado salads, prawns with garlic, filet mignon, salmon with Bernaise sauce, whole grilled or stuffed filet of sole, and raspberries with fresh whipped cream. Expect to spend an average of 6,075 *ptas* per person plus wine here.

TEATRIZ, *Calle de Hermosilla, 15. Tel. (91) 577-5379. Most major credit cards accepted.*

This stunning bar and restaurant about a block away from the Plaza de Colón is an architectural masterpiece. The designers have taken an old theater and remodeled it into an opulent and somewhat futuristic fine Italian restaurant with the highest level of service imaginable.

People here tend to be extremely well dressed (although jackets and ties don't seem to be required) and are treated to an eclectic selection of inspired dishes such as fresh mozzarella with tomato and virgin olive oil, salads with goat cheese and endive, spaghetti carbonara, salmon filled ravioli in cream sauce, assorted carpaccios, osso bucco with pasta, tiramiso, homemade ice cream and several more seasonal meat and seafood items. This is a wonderful restaurant that could only exist in the new Europe! An average three course a la carte dinner here will set each person back at least 4,975 *ptas* plus wine.

RESTAURANTE DE HOTEL RITZ, *Plaza de la Lealtad, 5. Tel. (91) 521-2857. All major credit cards accepted.*

The lavish ground floor restaurant and terrace of the Hotel Ritz is encircled by marble and antique paintings and I recommend trying their elegant 1:30pm to 4pm Sunday brunch buffet. This features over 60 different hot and cold items such as Waldorf salads, paella, black noodles with seafood, grilled seasonal fish, sirloin burgers, Iberian ham, Manchego cheese, omletes, smoked salmon and tuna, fresh regional beans and vegatables, homemade tarts and ice cream, and the best rice pudding in town. There is also often a live pianist playing soothing music during the meal. Reservations are always a good idea, and the brunch price is 7,900 *ptas* per person (kids under 12 free). Simply the best brunch in Spain.

FORTUNY, *Calle de Fortuny, 34. Tel. (91) 308-3267. All major credit cards accepted.*

Housed in a delightful antique mansion in the Embassy row district just behind the Paseo de la Castellana, this snobby and long established formal Continental restaurant (and chic nightclub) is a rare treat even for those who can afford it. Patrons are served by a staff of elegantly attired waiters who will upon suggestion bring your choice of incredibly pre-pared game and fish selections served on the finest china in town. Expect to find items like soufflés, roasted lean duck, filet of sole stuffed with crab, grilled sirloin, and shrimp or lobster with rich creamy sauces and farm fresh vegetables. The bill here can start at about 8,750 *ptas* per person and go sky high from there, but if you need to ask about prices, this is not the place to go. Reservations are essential, and regulars tend to get the best tables.

LÚCULO, *Calle de Genova, 19. Tel. (91) 419-4029. Most major credit cards accepted.*

Located a couple of blocks behind the Plaza de Colón, this incredible gourmet restaurant is run by a Catalunya born and raised executive chef who has brought his own interpretations of nouveau Spanish regional cuisine to Madrid. The ever changing menu features choice cuts of meat and fish that are first cooked with rare spices from all over Europe and then delicately blended with rich creams and farm fresh vegetables before being presented in the finest style at your table. A typical three course a la carte meal here can cost upwards of 8,500 *ptas* per person before adding a bottle of excellent wine from the cellar. The interior and ambiance here is somewhat refined and usually formal, and is the perfect venue to have a long romantic meal with someone you really care about.

EMBASSY, *Paseo de la Castellana, 12. Tel. (91) 575-6633. Most major credit card accepted.*

I first came to this beautiful teahouse and restaurant because a friend told me that it had the best hot chocolate in town. While he was correct, I soon discovered that the small and somewhat elegant restaurant here also offered great traditional Spanish cuisine served in a most pleasant setting amid chandeliers and marble floors. The menu here on any given day might feature a wide assortment of local meat and seafood specialties that cost around 5,900 *ptas* per person and are expertly prepared.

Moderate

RESTAURANTE BOMARZO, *Calle de Jorge Juan, 16. Tel. (91) 431-5840. Most major credit cards accepted.*

Located in a small storefront on the trendy Calle de Jorge Juan in the Barrio Salamanca, this superb and affordable little dining establishment offers great cuisine and plenty of charm. The small bi-level interior is embellished with blue and gold trim as well as several antique mirrors. My recent visit here was during July, when they were offering a superb 2,500 *ptas* per person (plus wine) three course summer menu. It featured choices such as cold melon cream soup, exotic shrimp salad, veggie pastas, trout carpaccio, chicken marinated in soya sauce, duck in a wine and onion glaze, passionfruit and lemon sorbet, a dark chocolate mousse, and much more. Call in advance for reservations and dress fairly well if possible.

CAFÉ DEL ORIENTE, *Plaza Oriente. Tel. (91) 541-3974. All major credit cards accepted.*

Besides being a fine café, this opulent Madrid restaurant near the Palacio Real is a wonderful place to enjoy superb cuisine at reasonable prices. Small tables and sofas highlighted by turn-of-the-century decorations and antiques surround the bar area. They prepare some of the classiest *tapas* I have ever seen, including huge canapés with smoked salmon and black caviar, fresh cheese and anchovies with olives, and pate with pimientos, for only 260 *ptas* each. For those who prefer to sit down and enjoy table service, you can dress as casual or formal as you wish and be treated to offerings such as chicken sandwiches for 575 *ptas*, waldorf salad at 945 *ptas*, assorted pizzas from 800 *ptas*, and a four course daily menu at 1,475 *ptas*. A great place, especially during the summer months when they open an outdoor dining area.

LA TRUCHA, *Calle de Manuel Fernández y Gonzales, 3. Tel. (91) 429-5833. Most major credit cards accepted.*

This pretty seafood restaurant just two short blocks from the the Plaza de Santa Ana is well worth the effort locate so you can enjoy a casual meal (no jackets or ties required) while being served by a friendly staff who will suggest the day's freshest offerings. Among the unusual items on the bilingual menu are red mullet, grilled swordfish, pickled partridge, a half chicken sautéed in garlic, oxtail, several typical Spanish desserts, and wonderfully fresh seafood selections that change seasonally. Expect to spend an average of 3,150 *ptas* per person plus wine here.

TABERNA DA QUEIMADA, *Calle de Echegaray, 15. Telephone unlisted. Visa cards accepted.*

Over the years this little authentic Spanish meat and seafood restaurant has grown so popular with locals that they have added an annex across the street. Once inside you will find a menu that offers good value on huge portions of Caldo Gallego soup, large shrimp with garlic, huge mixed salads, steamed mussels with vinegar, fried fish, and sometimes a huge dish of paella. The typical three course a la carte meal here costs around 2,775 *ptas* per person plus wine. A good choice for down to earth dining in this busy area.

ARCIMBALDO, *Calle de Lope de Vega, 37. Tel. (91) 429-6760. All major credit cards accepted.*

Arcimbaldo is a small Italian restaurant with a bright and airy interior full of designer fabrics and fine paintings. Patrons here dress fairly well, and enjoy delicious house specialties like their fresh mozzarella with basil and olive oil, vegetable minestrone soup, assorted gourmet pizzas, pasta with pesto sauce, meat and cheese filled cannelloni, tender osso bucco and mouth-watering desserts. At about 2,560 *ptas* per person or so for a filling three course meal, this place is a good value for this level of food quality and service.

EL PABELLÓN DEL ESPEJO, *Paseo de Recoletos, 31. Tel. (91) 319-1122. All major credit cards accepted.*

Set on the wide promenade across from the Biblioteca Nacional, this unique glass-enclosed turn of the century style café and restaurant offers rather good Spanish cuisine at prices that are far less than one would expect. Among the better selections on the menu are consommé, large house salads, avocado and prawn salad, squid in its own ink, grilled salmon, entrecote with Gorgonzola sauce, grilled filet of sole, and a daily special menu for just 950 *ptas*. The bar itself may also be a good choice for a strong coffee after visiting the area's attractions. Expect to spend an average of 2,550 *ptas* per person plus wine here.

EL CORTE INGLÉS *(7th floor caféteria), Calle de Preciados, 5. Tel. (91) 532-1800. Most major credit cards accepted.*

Believe it or not, this major department store just off the Puerta del Sol offers a couple of excellent choices for regional cuisine on its top floor. Although their more private (and expensive) Las Trébedes restaurant is also quite good, I would suggest you try the La Rotonda caféteria first. On my last visit to the self-service buffet line, I was able to make my own huge salad, order a hamburger platter with fries, enjoy great lobster salad and delicate seafood *paella*, and munch on several different pastas and pizzas. My lunch here set me back around 2,195 *ptas* a person, but my friends spent half as much for theirs. This is a great place to stop for a snack or a meal while shopping and sightseeing in this area.

D'ABUTINI, *Calle de Barbara de Braganza, 4. Tel. (91) 319-9490. All major credit cards accepted.*

Located about two blocks south of the Plaza de Colón, this Mediterranean style restaurant has a simple but good menu. The pastel interior is adorned with beautiful paintings and an almost elegant atmosphere, and there is no dress code to speak of. Their talented chefs prepare such classic dishes as capriccio salads, veal marsala, entrecote, pasta carbonara, spaghetti bolongese, lasagna verde, assorted pizzas and gelati. Expect to spend an average of 2,300 *ptas* per person plus wine here.

THE HARD ROCK CAFE, *Paseo de la Castellana, 2. Telephone unlisted. All major credit cards accepted.*

When you've seen one Hard Rock Cafe, you've seen them all. This loud American import displays everything you would expect, including famous rock star's guitars, an upside down '55 Cadillac, and even Madonna's leather bra and panties. The menu is bilingual and includes Buffalo wings, bean and cheese nachos, chef salads, B.L.T. sandwiches, cheeseburgers with fries, veggie or chicken fajitas, hot fudge sundaes, and all sorts of strange mixed drinks. A good hearty American lunch or dinner will set you back around 3,850 *ptas* a head plus drinks. If you're in need of a burger to satisfy your fix, this is about the best spot to find a real one in Spain.

CASA LUCIO, *Cava Baja, 35. Tel. (91) 265-3252. Some credit cards accepted.*

This typical Castillian style restaurant gets totally packed on weekends with locals and visitors alike who know all too well that excellently prepared seafood at reasonable prices is hard to find. Its semi-casual atmosphere and smiling wait staff will be glad to assist you in selecting the best of the day's catch, or if you prefer, there are also meat dishes available, but not as highly suggested. Situated on one of the more historic streets in the heart of town, this is a great place to sit back and relax while taking in some of the local gossip. Expect to spend around 4,500 *ptas* or so per person for a huge meal of fresh fish with vegetables or roasted meats cooked in clay pans in the region's traditional manner.

TABERNA DEL ALABARDERO, *Calle de Felipe V, 6. Tel. (91) 241-5192. Most major credit cards accepted.*

This traditionally decorated restaurant near the Royal Palace has several intimate dining rooms that are reminiscent of its beginnings as a highly regarded 19th century tavern where off duty Royal Soldiers once drank and ate. Nowadays the tavern serves up superb northern Spanish cuisine in the Basque style. For around 4,000 *ptas* or so a head you can enjoy whatever your waiter says is the day's best bet, and you will want to come back the next day for more. Service here is wonderful, and the desserts are incredible.

HANG ZHOU, *Calle Lopez de Hoyos, 14. Tel. (91) 563-1172. Most major credit cards accepted.*

After you have had your fill of typical Spanish cuisine and want to try something with a lot more spice, this nice and simple Chinese restaurant is a good bet. Here you can find recognizable Cantonese and Szechuan dishes like wonton soup, crunchy egg rolls, prawn toast, chop suey, general Tzao's chicken, pork lo mein, spare ribs, vegetables with pan fried noodles, shrimp with black bean sauce, Peking duck, sautéed lobster with hot sauce, and about 30 other choices starting at under 2,450 *ptas* each. I've really enjoyed my meals here, and the dress code is fairly casual.

HYLOGUI, *Calle de Ventura de Vega, 3. Tel. (91) 429-7357. No credit cards accepted.*

Packed most of the time, this huge and simple Spanish restaurant specializes in roasted meats and simple Castillian fish dishes that could easily cost double in most other establishments than what they charge here. Don't expect elegance or good table manners because that's not what this place is all about. My last three course meal here cost under 3,000 *ptas* and I was completely satisfied.

Inexpensive

CASA RODRIGUEZ, *Calle de las Maldonadas, 5. Tel. (91) 266-1134. Cash only - no credit cards accepted.*

If you desire an excellent but simple local dining experience while in the La Latina district, look no further than this wonderful little casual restaurant. Although its 14 small tables get packed during the adjacent El Rastro Sunday outdoor market, normally you won't have to wait to sit down and enjoy a tasty and unbelievably inexpensive lunch or dinner here. On my last visit, the large menu included fish soup, vegetable soup, mushrooms with garlic, mixed Spanish style vegetables, shrimp omelets, fried whole trout, half a chicken with garlic sauce, shrimp with garlic, veal cutlets, tripe and half bottles of red or white house wine. A great three course tapa meal will cost only around 1,900 *ptas* a head including wine.

LA COSTA DE VEJER, *Calle de Nuñez de Arce, 16. Telephone unlisted. Cash only - no credit cards accepted.*

Just a few doors away from the Gran Hotel Reina Victoria, this simple little restaurant offers a dozen or so small tables behind its bar. The prices here are an absolute bargain, especially considering how good the food is. Try the shrimp smothered in garlic and oil, sautéed mushrooms, fried calamari, or the Iberian cured ham. A few tapas will set you back around 1,375 *ptas* a head.

RODILLA, *Calle de Preciados, 25. Tel. (91) 544-8828. Cash only - no credit cards accepted.*

Although not much more than a glorified snack shop and caféteria off the Puerta de Sol, Rodilla serves up some of the most delicate sandwiches in town. For 95 to 145 *ptas* each, you can get a half sandwich (white bread with the crust cut off) with a cheese filling laced with your choice of tomato, vegetables, shrimp, ham, anchovy, salami, or pate. They also have excellent pastries from 120 *ptas*, croissants from 125 *ptas*, and coffee, soda, beer and juice. Nothing fancy, but good for a quick bite on the run.

SANABRESA, *Calle de Amor de Dio, 12. Tel. unlisted. No credit cards accepted.*

This is an unpretentious restaurant to sit back and eat with the locals. The menu is limited but tends to feature complete meals such as roasted meat, grilled chicken, *paella*, cured ham, and fried fish specials that cost around 1,750 *ptas* during lunchtime when the place is at its best (and most crowded). Jeans and t-shirts are no problem, and forget about even trying to make a reservation.

MUSEO DE JAMON, *Carrera de San Jeronimo, 8. Tel. (91) 521-0340. Cash only.*

This branch of the famous local chain known for the hundreds of ham legs hanging from its ceiling is the best one to experience. The restaurant and takeout counter both offer a dazzling array of cured hams, assorted roasted meats, Spanish cheeses, cold salads, and even desserts at reasonable prices. The place gets extremely busy during lunch time, so try and check it out on an off hour. If you love deli sandwiches made with Iberico or Serrano ham, this is the place to go, and it's relatively cheap too! My last big lunch here was only 1,870 *ptas* a person.

SEEING THE SIGHTS

The sights are arranged by various walking tours. You can start each tour at the beginning, or pick it up along the way – your call.

TOUR 1

The Palacio Real, the Catedral de Nuestra Señora de la Almudena, and the Ermita de San António de la Florida.

Approximate duration (by foot) is about 6.5 hours including church and palace visits. Start from the Sol metro station.

The Puerta del Sol

After arriving at the Puerta del Sol, you will notice several fine sights worth investigating which surround this central square's bronze statue of

King Carlos III sitting gallantly on his horse. The Baroque facade of the **Casa de Correos** rests at the south side of the square and was originally built as a post office in 1766 Jaime Marquet of France. Over the years it was converted into government administration offices, and its bold clock tower was added in 1866.

Embedded into the pavement directly in front of the former post office is an important bronze plaque (mile marker) with a relief of Spain stating that this is the *Origen de las Carreteras Radiales–Km. 0*. This indicates that several of this country's major highways and national roads officially commence at this spot, known as kilometer zero, and is the point from which their distances are measured.

Across the square's north side is the famed bronze statue of Madrid's official emblem, a bear standing up against a small fruit tree, which has become a popular meeting place for both tourists and residents alike.

It is from the north side of the Puerta del Sol that a series of small streets and *pedestrian only* lanes radiate towards the north. Of these, the **Calle de las Preciados** offers the best possibilities for window browsing and shopping. Here as you head up the street you will find the massive seven-floor **El Corte Inglés** department store, several small boutiques and shoe shops, a few cafés and restaurants, and finally end up at the **Plaza de Callao** with its local bus depot.

Westward towards the Palacio Real

At the western edge of the Puerta del Sol, two streets fork off the plaza, each leading further westward into the section of the city known as **Habsburg Madrid** (the **Madrid de los Austrias** area). On this first walking tour I suggest bearing to the right hand side of the fork and following the **Calle de Arenal**.

The first block of this street is lined with shops and boutiques, but is primarily known for its assortment of bridal shops. On the corner of this block is **Ferpal**, one of Madrid's finest stops for a quick sandwich to go. Continuing down the second block of Calle de Arenal you can't help but notice the facades of **Palacio Gaviria**, a wonderful nightclub with an illustrious history as the mansion of a former king's mistress, and a converted theater known as the **Teatro Joy Eslava**, now the city's premier disco.

At the next corner, turn right onto Calle de San Martin and follow it to the end which will bring you into the **Plaza de San Martin**. A few steps away from the beginning of the plaza is the not-to-be-missed **Convento de las Descalzas Reales**. This convent and museum, filled with fine art, was created in 1559 as a retreat for women of nobility (including St. Teresa and Empress Maria of Austria), and has been transformed into an award winning museum. It's one of the true gems of culture in Madrid.

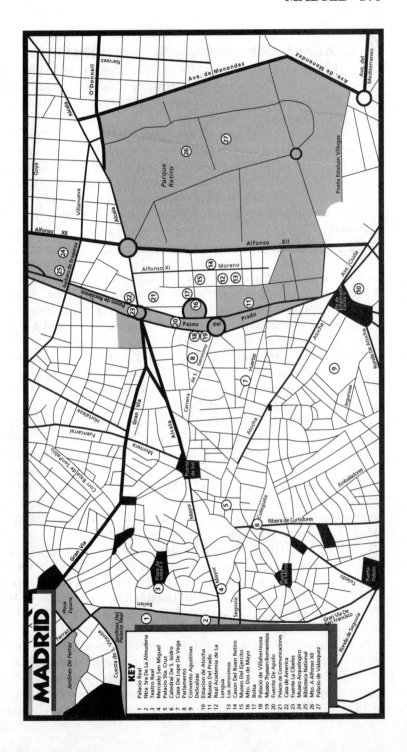

MADRID

KEY

1. Palacio Real
2. Ntra. Sta. De La Almudena
3. Teatro Real
4. Mercado San Miguel
5. Palacio Sta. Cruz
6. Catedral De S. Isidro
7. Casa De Lope De Vega
8. Parlamento
9. Convento Agustinas
10. DeScalzas
11. Estacion de Atocha
12. Museo Del Prado
13. Real Academia de la Lengua
14. Los Jeronimos
15. Cason Del Buen Retiro
16. Museo Del Ejercito
17. Mto. Dos de Mayo
18. Bolsa
19. Palacio de Villahermosa
20. Museo Thyssen-Bornemisza
21. Fuente De Apolo
22. Palacio de Communicaciones
23. Casa de America
24. Fuente La Cibeles
25. Museo Arqueologico
26. Biblioteca National
27. Mto. A Alfonso XII
28. Palacio de Valasquez

GREAT HOT CHOCOLATE, SPANISH-STYLE!

One of Spain's most satisfying traditions is to pop into a **Chocolateria** *to enjoy an order of* **chocolate con churros** *(thickened hot chocolate served with a thin piece of fried dough) before heading home from a hard day's work or after a long night of partying.*

Perhaps the most famous of these establishments is the beautiful 100 year old **Chocolateria San Ginés**, *located on a small alleyway called the Pasadizo de San Ginés just off of the Calle de Arenal (next to the Teatro Joy Eslava disco). Open from 7pm until 10pm and once again for the massive rush from 1am until 7am from Tuesday through Thursday, and 7pm until 7am on weekends, I strongly suggest at least one visit here during your stay in town.*

As you enter the museum, you will be taken on a tour of the many treasures here including paintings by **Zurbarán** and **Titian**, tapestries based on drawings by **Rubens**, frescoes by **Carducci**, dozens of elaborate cloisters, one of the most ornate stairways in existence, and a treasury laden with jewels and unusual objects. *The museum is open from 10:30am until 12:30pm and 4pm until 5:30pm on Tuesday, Wednesday, Thursday and Saturday, as well as from 10:30am until 12:30pm on Saturdays, and 11am, until 1:30pm. Admission including the guided tour is 650 ptas per adult or 250 ptas for students with an International Student ID Card.*

Just across the street from the convent is a wonderful exhibition space run by the **Caja de Madrid** bank. This small but enchanting three-floor museum features an array of constantly changing collections including antique paintings, tapestries, glassware, china, and silver settings produced throughout the centuries by Europe's finest artisans. Although most of the events are both free and open to the public, the hours have been known to alter from those posted which state Tuesday through Friday from 11am until 4pm.

Now return to the Calle de Arenal and continue heading west where you will pass by one of the city's scattered 24-hour ATM cash machines that accept Visa, Mastercard, Amex, Diners Club, Plus, and Cirrus cash cards, near the corner of Calle de los Donados. Soon the **Plaza de Isabel II** comes into sight, and the street changes its name to the Calle de Carlos III which in turn ends at the **Plaza de Oriente**. If you make a right turn before entering the plaza, you will pass the luxurious **Café del Oriente** with its fine selection of gourmet *tapas* and surprisingly reasonable menu.

A few steps away from the café is the main entrance to the **Teatro Real**. Construction began under the direction of António López Aguado in 1818, and was completed in time for its first Operatic production in

1850. The theater is still undergoing a massive renovation and structural overhaul, and thus is not currently open to the public. From here you can wander around the sculpture-laden **Plaza de Oriente** to view dozens of bronzes including the much touted rendering of King Felipe V on his horse before crossing the Calle de Bailén and turning left.

The Palacio Real

Also called the **Palacio del Oriente**, about half a block south on the Calle de Bailén is the main entrance to the absolutely fantastic **Palacio Real** (**Royal Palace**) of Spain. The palace occupies a site that started out as a Moorish fortress known as the **Alcazár**. In the early 16th century, the Habsburg Emperor Charles V ordered the construction of a new building to serve as the principal royal palace for his dynasty (and later for the Bourbon dynasty). Unfortunately, this first palace completely burned down on Christmas Eve of 1734, destroying almost all of its treasures, including over 500 irreplaceable paintings.

In 1738, construction began on a new fireproof palace on the same site for King Felipe V which was designed in the Baroque style by Juan Bautista Sachetti of Italy. Since this king died before the 26 year construction project was completed, his successor King Carlos III was the first occupant of this majestic building. Although still used occasionally by King Juan Carlos for official state visits (during which time it may be closed to the public for weeks at a time), the palace is open to the public and truly must be seen by all visitors to Madrid.

Upon entering the quadrilateral complex, you will first pass through the east wing entry point with its extremely tight security check points, metal detectors, and x-ray machines. Since photos are allowed (but not flashes), you might want to have the necessary high speed film hand-inspected to avoid any radiation damage to your photos.

The first section that can be visited in the palace is the **Real Farmacia** (**Royal Pharmacy**), which is also located in the eastern extension of the palace. The museum contains several rooms filled with porcelain and glass jars stamped with 18th century royal coats of arms used to store herbs and medicinal substances. There are also wooden drawers which are painted with the Latin names of the herbs and extracts they once contained. A few steps away is an 18th century distillation room.

After the self-guided tour of the pharmacy, you will depart the eastern courtside wing, and walk through the massive courtyard known as the **Plaza de la Armería** to reach the main structure of the palace itself. Here you must wait in the lobby near a gift shop until the next scheduled 45 minute guided tour (offered in either English of Spanish several times per hour) departs through the dozens of rooms which include the **Salónes Oficiales**, (**Official Staterooms**), **Biblioteca Real** (**Royal Library**), the

Sala del Trono (**Throne Room**), and other breathtaking areas. The tour-guides themselves are typically rather amusing, and some of them have been working here for decades.

The walking tour brings visitors up a flight of stairs to see such highlights as tapestries by Flemish master Van de Goth who was appointed as the head of the royal tapestry factory; the opulent banquet room which hosted the Israeli-Arab peace conference; the royal portraits by **Goya**; Venetian and Spanish chandeliers; and frescoes by **Tiepolo** and **Mengs**. Also shown during the tour are the former apartments of royal family members, various antique clocks and furnishings, a music room laden with Stradivarius stringed instruments as well as several antique pianos and guitars, fine paintings by **El Greco** and **Rubens**, and **Zurbarán**, a rare "Christmas set" china collection painted with landscapes from around Europe, famed La Granja royal crystal, glass cases full of gold and silver coins, the King's billiard room and the fantastic Throne Room.

After this guided tour is finished, you can walk across the **Plaza de Armería** courtyard to the protruding western wing extension of the palace grounds to view the **Real Armería** (**Royal Armory**). The armory exhibits one of the world's finest collections of European swords, rifles, armored suits (including a few made for children) and mounted warriors dressed in full 17th century combat fatigues. *The palace and its museums are open from 9am until 6pm from Monday through Friday, and 9am to 2:30pm on Sundays. Tickets are available until about one hour prior to closing, when the last tour of the main palace commences. Admission price is 950 ptas per adult, 350 ptas for students with International Student ID Cards, and children under 5 are admitted for free.*

Also included in the price of admission is entrance to the Royal Pharmacy and the Armory. Unlike many other attractions here in Madrid, special facilities have been created for those who are physically challenged. Again, I'd like to stress that during special royal events the palace may be closed to the public without prior notice.

After leaving the palace compound, you should turn right, back onto Calle de Bailén and take the first right to reach Calle de la Goya. Here you will find the entrance to the towering, but less than inspiring, neo-classical **Catedral de Nuestra Señora de la Almudena** cathedral. Designed by the Marques de Cubas in 1880, the church named after Madrid's patron saint was not completed until just this past year. It can be visited for free each morning during hourly masses until about 1pm, and in the early evenings after 5pm.

Another great nearby side trip would be to return to the Calle de Bailén, and turn left. Just after passing the Royal Palace, you can descend down a flight of stairs to view the formal **Jardines de Sabatini** gardens. *The gardens are open daily from sunrise to sunset, and there is no entrance fee.*

After the gardens, return to Calle de Bailén and turn left. A block or so up you will bear left onto the Cuesta de San Vicente and follow it as it curves around the **Estación Principe Pio** Renfe train station. Here the street name now changes to the Paseo de Florida where at #5 you can't help but notice the **Ermita de San António de la Florida** church. Built in 1798 by Felipe Fontana of Italy, this fantastic small church is covered by frescoes by **Goya**, whose body is now entombed here. *The church is open Tuesday through Friday from 10am until 2pm and again from 4pm until 8pm, weekends from 10am until 2pm. Admission is free.*

TOUR 2

La Ciudad Antigua (old town) & La Latina district.
Approximate duration (by foot) is about 5 hours, including church visits. Start from the Sol metro station.

Towards Plaza Mayor

After entering the Puerta del Sol, head towards its western edge and follow the Calle de Mayor as it forks off the to the left. At the next corner take a left turn onto Calle de Esparteros, and a few steps further you should turn right onto Calle de Postas. The major attraction of this small lane is the hilarious **Museo del Jambon** restaurant and deli, which features hundreds of hams hanging from the ceiling of its two floors.

Continue straight ahead until the next corner at Calle de San Cristobal, and bear left to take this "pedestrian only" street for a couple of blocks until reaching the **Plaza de Santa Cruz**. This plaza is surrounded by upscale boutiques and the unique facade of the **Palacio de Santa Cruz**. This Baroque structure was designed by Juan Bautista Cresenci from Italy in collaboration with Spaniard Juan Gómez de Mora during the early 17th century when its primary function was to serve as a prison for the local courts. The palace is not open to the public, and now is home to the **Ministerio de Asuntas Exteriores (Foreign Affairs Ministry)**.

From the front of the palace, follow the Calle de Gerona and pass under one of the several archways leading into the heart of Habsburg Madrid, the unforgettable **Plaza Mayor**. Built by Juan Gómez de Mora using an earlier design by Juan de Herrera, this huge quadrilateral plaza was completed in 1617 to serve as the social gathering point for the residents of Madrid. The entire plaza is enclosed by buildings with hundreds of balconies facing into the center of the square. These were once were filled with spectators waiting here to witness bullfights, plays, proclamations and even occasional public executions during the horrid Inquisition.

On the north side of the plaza, facing the central bronze statue of King Filipe II, is the curious facade of the restored **Casa de la Panaderia** whose unusual spires and colorful paintings have become one of the most famous sights in all of Spain. The building now houses government offices and is unfortunately not open to the public, but the exterior paintings alone are well worth a look.

On nice days, the plaza still serves as a meeting place for the city's residents, during which time it is possible to experience a hint of what 17th century urban gatherings here must have felt like. Sunday mornings are particularly interesting since a small coin and stamp market takes place within the square. The many souvenir and handicraft shops, cafés, and restaurants which now line the plaza are rather overpriced, and even the *Turismo* (tourist information office) here offers little in the way of helpful advice or printed material.

On to the Plaza de la Villa

From the southwest corner of the plaza, pass under the famed **Arco de Cuchilleros** archway and walk down the steps leading onto the restaurant-packed Calle de Cuchilleros. This old street is home to a superb eating establishment that may very well be the oldest restaurant in the world, **Restaurante Botin**, which dates back to 1725 and was yet another of Ernest Hemingway's favored haunts.

At the end of this street, turn right and head into the small **Plaza de Puerta Cerrada**. A few steps later when the road forks, follow Calle de San Justo and soon you will find the extraordinary rounded exterior of the **Basilica Pontifica de San Miguel**. This ornate Baroque church was designed by Santiago Bonavia of Italy, and its construction was completed in 1745. The church is open to the public only during its several daily masses.

From the church, continue up Calle de San Justo until turning right onto Calle del Cordon. After a few steps up this narrow passageway, you will find yourself in the heart of the dramatic **Plaza de la Villa** square. Three magnificent buildings form this square, each with its own illustrious history. The east side of the square is flanked by the fine Mudéjar 15th century **Torre de los Lujanes** tower which originally was part of a much larger mansion whose noble owner's coats of arms still adorn the doorway. Once used to imprison Emperor Carlos V's arch enemy, François I, the tower now ironically houses the Academy of Moral and Political Sciences and cannot be entered by the general public.

Across the square, on its western border, is the Juan Gómez de Mora designed 17th century former **Casa de la Villa** (**City Hall**). Even though the city hall has moved across town to a much larger structure, this slate and granite building is topped with forceful spires and still contains the offices of fairly high ranking municipal officials, so the ever-present security guards will not let you in. The one building that is open for tours is the 16th century Platteresque style **Casa de Cisneros**. If you arrive here during non visiting hours, try to get a good peek through the iron bars into its exquisite gateway entrance and tranquil courtyard. *The building is open to the public on Monday nights only, at 5pm for a free 35 minute guided tour (in Spanish) and is well worth the effort to see.*

Depart the plaza and turn left onto the Calle de Mayor. About a block up this wide commercial street you can follow your nose towards the smell of freshly baked almond cakes from one of Madrid's best pastry shops called the **Horno la Santiaguesa** at #73. This is one of my favorite places to stop in for a fantastic cookies and tarts starting at only 100 *ptas* each.

At this point I suggest turning left onto Calle de Bailén. After crossing the modern **El Viaducto** viaduct, continue straight for 3 blocks to reach the front of the elaborate **Iglesia de San Francisco**. Here you can enjoy a good look at this huge 18th century neo-classical church which was designed by Fray Francisco Cabezas. Since a major renovation project is currently under way, it may be difficult to view some of its fine features including a huge dome and memorable chapels decorated with paintings by Goya, Coello, and other major artists. *The church can be visited for free from 11am until 2pm and again from 4pm to 7pm from Tuesday through Saturday, or during public masses throughout most of Sunday.*

Towards the La Latina District

From directly in front of the church, cross the street and head straight along the Carrera de San Francisco for about 5 blocks before passing the **Plaza de Puerta de Moros**. At the edge of the plaza is the 17th century **Parroquia de San Andrés**, which has a spectacular Baroque chapel and an unusual domed ceiling lined with golden cherubs. You can wander in during one of the many daily masses, and be awe struck by its beauty. Just behind this church, you will find the 16th century **Capilla del Obispo** chapel which is the only Gothic building left standing in Madrid. The Capilla contains a passionate altarpiece depicting *Christ and the Virgin* by Francisco Giralta, but is now closed to the public for a major restoration project.

After visiting the church, return to the Carrera de San Francisco and keep going straight, passing through the **Plaza de la Cabeda** to reach the Calle de Toledo where you will turn left. A block or so up you will find the 17th century **Catedral de San Isidro** that was designed by Pedro Sanchez and Francisco Bautista. Originally a Jesuit church, it can be visited during daily public masses to see the tomb of its namesake, the peasant who became the patron saint of Madrid, as well as some fine stained glass windows.

EL RASTRO FLEA MARKET

Each Sunday from about 10am until 3:30pm, thousands of sleepy-eyed urban residents and visitors head to the Latina and Tirso de Molina metro stations to attend the enchanting **El Rastro** *flea market, a 500 year old tradition. Most of the small streets surrounding the Plaza de Cascorro near the Catedral San Isidro are lined with hundreds of stalls offering everything from handicrafts and silver jewelry, to used leather jackets and cheap sunglasses.*

This is as good a place as any to see how the Madrileños unwind, and to perhaps chance upon an unusual souvenir. Expect to be squeezed and bumped on several occasions, and perhaps have a long wait to get in area restaurants during these hours. The tourist office advises visitors to be extra careful while wandering through the market as pickpockets are known to ply their trade here. To be honest, after over a dozen visits to this market, nobody has ever attempted to steal my wallet.

TOUR 3

The Plaza de Santa Ana area, Calle de las Huertas, & Plaza de las Cortes.
Approximate duration (by foot) is about 4 hours, including museum visits. Start from the Sol metro station. Note: This tour is best enjoyed in the afternoon, so afterwards you can take advantage of the area's many restaurants and some of Madrid's best nightlife.

Around Plaza Santa Ana

From the **Puerta del Sol**, turn right (south) to follow the boutique-lined Calle de Carretas down for a couple of minutes until it merges with the **Plaza Jacinto Benavente**. As soon as you enter this small plaza, immediately turn left onto a small lane which first bisects tiny **Plaza del Ángel** before leading straight into the **Plaza de Santa Ana**.

This is certainly one of the most entertaining zones in the entire city. During the day it is common to find locals playing cards and relaxing on the benches found in the center of the square. The plaza (with its own underground public parking lot) is surrounded by a series of interesting buildings including the beautiful 18th century **Teatro Español** theater on its eastern border of Calle Principe, which offers plays on most evenings. Across the way on the plaza's western edge is the unmistakable tower topped facade of the **Gran Hotel Reina Victoria** which offers impeccable mid-priced accommodations.

The most compelling reason to visit this square is for its fantastic selection of traditional *Cervecerias*. Each weekend night from about 10pm until 2am, the plaza becomes filled with hundreds of the city's most spirited younger residents who pack these bars to order delicious (and reasonably priced) *tapas* with glasses of beer or sherry.

On the south side of the plaza, you can stroll along Calle del Prado and pop into the popular **Cerveceria Alemana**, adorned with photos of bullfighters and was once one of Ernest Hemingway's favorite local watering holes, and the equally compelling **Cerveceria Santa Ana**. Perhaps my favorite of these unique tapas bars is the less crowded **Naturbier**, which brews its own silky smooth lagers and dark ale.

The Calle de las Huertas area

Just one block below (south of) the plaza is the infamous Calle de las Huertas. During the day this street seems tranquil enough, but late at night it completely changes character and becomes a hotbed of the "under 25" singles scene. There are well over 40 bars, disco-pubs, jazz clubs, cafés, and restaurants within sight of each other. They're particularly packed on Friday and Saturday nights after 11:30pm or so.

As you head along the strip, you will find several intersecting side streets with a nice selection of entertaining bars and live music offerings. These include Calle de Echegaray, where you should stop at the incredible **Los Gabrieles** tapas bar at #17 to view its dramatic antique tile murals, and the more peaceful Calle León, where at #3 you can pop into the opulent **Casapueblo** jazz bar. Many of the bars here serve *Mojitos* which are herb infused cocktails with a real kick.

Nearby Historical Sights

The tiny winding lanes that can be found just above (north of) the bar and club zone also have some interesting historical attractions. Follow Calle de las Huertas down for a few blocks before making a left turn on Calle León, and then the first right turn onto a small street called Calle de Lope de Vega. A half a block up you will soon see the **Convento de Trinitarias** at #18 where writer **Cervantes'** body is entombed and can be visited for free, *only during daily mass at 9am weekdays and 7:30am on weekends*. At # 21 on the same street there is a fine antique store called **Almonedo del Convento**, and at # 29 you can pop into the **Becara** shop which sells fine housewares, lamps, old world fabrics, and is usually filled with interior designers looking for unusual accessories.

Now I suggest returning to the Calle León where you will turn right and head up another block before again turning right onto Calle de Cervantes. This is one of the stranger streets in this part of town. Besides hosting a few discreet brothels indicated by small red litter bugs, you can also find the private former home of the great 17th century Spanish writer **Cervantes** over at #2 (currently closed to the public).

More worthy of attention is the beautifully restored 17th century house of famed Spanish writer **Lope de Vega**. The so-called **Casa de Lope de Vega** house & museum at #11 on the same street features the writer's original master bedroom, a fantastic little chapel, the original kitchen and cauldron, a library filled with centuries-old books, and a tranquil courtyard garden and well. This is one of the few buildings in Madrid that can really give you an idea of what middle class life was like in this city 300 years ago. To enter, you may have to first ring the doorbell, and then follow a guide (they usually speak Spanish only) for a 15 minute tour through the various rooms packed with period furnishings and housewares on three separate floors.

The house & museum are open from Monday through Friday from 9:30am until 3pm and Saturdays from 10am until 2pm. Admission is 200 ptas per person, 50% off for students with international student ID, and is free on Saturdays.

The Plaza de las Cortes

From Calle de Cervantes, turn left onto Calle de Agustin that leads into the **Plaza de las Cortes**. Office buildings as well as the Fantastic Hotel Villa Real, which is my absolute favorite hotel in town, flank this small tree lined square,. Just across the square are the bold 19th century and bizarre 20th century wings of the **Cortes Españoles**, Spain's parliament.

Although not all official parliament sessions are open to the public, it is worth checking with the guards at the gatehouse near the new wing to see if it is possible to view an open session or join in on a scheduled free tour on most Saturday mornings. Since the Cortes was the scene of a violent failed coup attempt in 1981 by deranged soldiers, security here has become a serious matter.

TOUR 4

Calle de Alcalá, Parque del Retiro, the Atocha rail station, & the Centro de Arte Reina Sofia.

Approximate duration (by foot) is about 6.5 hours, including museum, park, and building visits. Start from the Sol metro station.

The Calle de Alcalá area

After departing the **Puerta del Sol** plaza, walk east along the bustling Calle de Alcalá for a half a block or so until passing next to Casa Real de Aduana on your left hand side. This huge structure was built under the reign of King Carlos III during the city's Age of Enlightenment by Francisco Sabatini of Italy in 1761. Its neo-classical facade has housed Spain's Ministry of Finance office for the past century and a half, but is not open to the public.

A bit further down the same side of the street at #13 is a more exciting building which houses the small but worthwhile **Real Academia de Bellas Artes de San Fernando** museum. After entering the rather dull facade, you will ascend a flight of stairs leading past an antique printing press. To the left of the first landing near this press, there is a small shop and gallery called **Calcografia Nacional Cabinete Francisco de Goya.** Here you can browse through or purchase fine coffee table books and collections of historic scenic prints, lithographs, and beautiful thermographic works from the 19th century.

An additional flight of stairs bring visitors into the main entrance and waiting lounge of the museum, covered by copies of masterworks as well as antique tapestries and assorted precursors to what is waiting inside. The tiny rooms that follow are introduced by a legend which does its best to explain (in Spanish) the pieces which are displayed. Among the more remarkable 17th through 20th century items on two large floors include paintings by **Goya, El Greco, Mengs, Alvarez, Zubarán, Murillo, Sorolla, Ribera, Lopez, Lucas, Cano, Vassano, Raphael, Rubens, Correggio, Diaz, Bellini,** and others. There are also special rooms containing Oriental sculptures, Muslim ceramics, Egyptian bronzes, vintage cigarette boxes and jewelry, chandeliers, silver, and a set of story board type sketches by **Picasso.**

One of the most touted items on display here is the original official portrait of President George Washington by **Perovanni**, a copy of which still hangs in the White House. Since the layout of the museum is less than logical, and rooms are not always arranged in sequential order, I strongly recommend that you fork over the 100 *ptas* extra for a descriptive brochure which should still be available in English. *The museum is open from Tuesday through Friday from 9am until 7pm as well as Mondays and weekends from 9am until 2:30pm with admission at 300 ptas per person.*

Across the street from the Real Academia museum is a rather odd looking **Circulo de Bellas Artes** building, with an art deco statue up top, which was designed and built in 1919 by António Palacios. Originally a men's social club, the center still maintains an almost elite ambiance, but is now a private club dedicated to the presentation of art, plays, and music in its theaters and side galleries. A period style café and bar can also be enjoyed, but all non-members will be forced to shell out 100 *ptas* just to get through the door of this complex.

A bit further down the street you will arrive at the intersection of Calle de Alcalá with the **Paseo del Prado**. At the near corner is the French-roofed **Banco de España** building which was built by Eduardo Adaro in 1882 to create a new commercial district in this part of the city. Some 28 years after this bank was completed, the fantastic **Palacio de Comunicaciónes** was built across the plaza by António Palacios and its

marvelous exterior and dramatic interior are home to postal and electronic wiring services which are frequently used by many residents of
Madrid. This is my favorite 20th century structure in town, and is a great
place to send and post mark all your international correspondence from.
The lovely fountain in the plaza between these two buildings is the work
of Ventura Rodriguez, and is known as the **Fuente de Cibeles** after the
Greek goddess of Cybele which it lovingly depicts atop a chariot pulled by
lions. *The post office is open from 9am until 10pm on weekdays, 9am until 8pm
on Saturdays, and 10am until 1pm on most Sundays, and admission is free.*

From this point, continue up the Calle de Alcalá and just a few steps
past the prior intersection you will find the **Puerta de Alcalá** gate situated
in the middle of the **Plaza de la Independencia** traffic circle. This
monumental gateway dates back to the city's Age of Enlightenment in the
18th century, when famed King Carlos III asked Francisco Sabatini of Italy
to design a prominent entrance way into Madrid via the frequently
utilized roads from the northern regions of Spain.

The Retiro Park area

After passing by the traffic circle, continue down the right hand side
of Calle de Alcalá for a few dozen steps until seeing an entrance into the
beautiful **Parque del Retiro** public park. Originally built as a private royal
garden for the former **Palacio Buen Retiro** palace, it was donated to the
citizens of Madrid as a gift from Queen Isabella II in 1868. This peaceful
diversion from urban noise and stress features well over 120 hectares with
over 15,000 trees lining the pristine grounds, benches, lakes, sporting
fields, public gardens, recreation trails, cafés and historical buildings.

The main access road into the park from Calle de Alcalá is known as
the Avenida de Mejico (although no sign will indicate the name). During
the weekends it is full of vendors and street performers trying to make a
few bucks. As you are lead deeper into this massive park, this road passes
by a series of overpriced cafés and snack kiosks and eventually intersects
with the scenic waterside **Paseo Salón del Estanque** promenade.

The reason I mention water is that you can't help but notice the
beautiful man-made lake called the **Estanque del Retiro**, where row boats
can be rented for about 550 *ptas* per 45 minutes. There is also a high
season motor boat tour that can take up to 36 passengers on a quick zip
around the lake for 150 *ptas* a head. The boat rental facilities are located
along the Paseo de Columbia just a few steps away from the columns of
the large semicircular **Monumento a Alfonso XII** monument and unofficial meeting point. The park has a bright and cheery ambiance, with
young couples having secluded, romantic picnics, and large families
dressed to kill as they stroll along from one part of the park to another,
especially on Saturday and Sunday afternoons during warmer weather.

Besides hosting a series of spring and summer fashion shows, outdoor movie screenings, children's activities, art exhibitions, book fairs and sporting events, the park also has several fine buildings which really should been visited while in the area. A good suggestion would be to follow the lakeside promenade south as it ends at the Plaza de Honduras and turn to the left along the **Paseo de Venezuela**. From this road there are several signs pointing the way to the famed **Palacio de Velázquez** which was constructed by Ricardo Velázquez Bosco to host the 1883 Mining Exhibition and has beautiful hand glazed ceramic tiles by Daniel Zuloaga. Now the structure is primarily used as a gallery with assorted temporary exhibitions from around the world.

Just a few minutes south of the Plaza de Honduras off the **Paseo de la Republica de Cuba** is the even more impressive **Palacio de Cristal**. Built by Ricardo Velázquez Bosco and Alberto del Palacio in 1887, this glass enclosed series of vaulted chambers supports a delightful dome. The tile work here too was created by Daniel Zuloaga. Although admission prices for both of these art laden buildings range from being free to costing upwards of 200 *ptas* or so, they are each worth at least a quick look. *The galleries are generally open from Tuesday through Sunday from 11am until 7pm.*

The Atocha Rail Station

After visiting the glass palace, continue south through the park along the Paseo de la Republica de Cuba until it ends at the bizarre **Glorieta del Ángel Caido** statue in honor of the devil. From here turn right onto the Paseo Duque which leads to the park's southwestern most exit and onto the wide Calle de Alfonso XII where you will turn left and walk a few blocks until passing in front of the spectacular **Estación de Atocha** train station.

This is the masterpiece of all Spanish train stations, and you must at least walk through once before you leave the city. Based on plans devised by Alberto del Palacio in the late 19th century, this beautifully preserved example of glass and iron architecture remains one of the country's busiest train stations. A recent addition to the station has allowed for the conversion of some of the original hangar style structure into a semi-tropical greenhouse. *The station is almost always open, and there is no admission charge to walk around.*

The Centro de Arte Reina Sofia

After exiting the train station, turn left onto the Avenida Ciudad de Barcelona and follow it for a block or so until it meets up with the Plaza de Emperador Carlos V. If you cross through the plaza to reach Calle de Atocha, you will soon find the entrance to the **Centro de Arte Reina Sofia** art museum off of Calle de Santa Isabel. Located on the sight of the former San Carlos hospital designed by Francisco Sabatini of Italy in 1776, this quadrilateral structure and inner courtyard garden was named after the current Queen and contains a museum of 20th century Spanish modern works. The museum contains a great collection of cubist and surrealistic art on three floors from masters like **Miró**, **Chillida**, **Gris**, **Tapies**, **Dali**, and of course **Picasso** whose famed *Guernica* denouncing Franco's involvement in the Nazis' massive bombing of a northern Spanish town, which is one of the most important pieces on exhibit. There is also a schedule of temporary exhibitions, lectures, videos, movie theater, art library, boutiques, restaurant, and café.

The museum is open Monday (rather unusual in Spain) and from Wednesday through Saturday from 10am until 9pm, as well as Sunday from 10am until 230pm. Admission is 500 ptas per person.

TOUR 5

The Prado Museum & the Asón del Buen Retiro annex.

Approximate duration (by foot) depends on your specific level of artistic interest, but expect to spend at least 5 hours visiting these two buildings. Start from the Banco de España metro station.

THE PRADO MUSEUM

After exiting the *metro* station, turn right onto the Paseo del Prado and follow it south for a few blocks until you reach the large statue of Neptune in the **Plaza Canovas de Castillo**. At this plaza, cross the street and continue further down the eastern side of the Paseo del Prado for another block or so until reaching the unmistakable facade of the **Museo del Prado** museum.

While there are three separate main entrances to the museum, the easiest one to access from this direction would be the large *Puerta de Goya* doorway just off Calle Filipe IV, which is up a flight of stairs from ground level. The main or upper floor is known as the *Planta Principal* and is divided by a series of some 50 delightful rooms. The ground floor or *Planta Baja* contains an additional 42 or so rooms as well as museum shops and public restrooms. Keep in mind that the Prado only displays works between the 15th and 18th century, and its **Cáson del Buen Retiro** annex exhibits only 19th century art.

Entrance Details & Prices

The Prado and the Cáson del Buen Retiro are both accessible from the same ticket. Their hours are from Tuesday through Saturday, 9am until 7pm, and Sundays and holidays from 9am until 2pm. Admission is 500 ptas for adults, 250 ptas for students with their international student ID card, and free for people over

65 from Spain (but I have heard some foreign senior citizens have also gotten in for free).

Entrance to the museums is free every Saturday from 2:30pm until 7pm, all day on Sundays, as well as on December 6, October 12, and May 18.

The Museum's Turbulent History

This masterpiece of neo-classical architecture was originally designed by **Juan de Villanueva** in 1785 to house the Spanish Academy and Museum of Natural Sciences. With the massive construction project taking over two decades to complete, followed by additional delays and damage caused by the invasion of Napoleon's troops, the science academy never actually moved in to the building. With the wisdom and personal guidance of King Fernando VII and Queen Isabella, a decision was made to repair the structure and convert it into a Royal Museum.

Soon work began on the restoration and installation of 311 fine works of art from collections in the royal palaces of **El Escorial**, **Aranjuez**, and **La Granja**. These included pieces by Spanish artists such as Velázquez, Goya, Ribera, Madrazo, Bayeu, Coello, Juanes, and others.

After hurried last minute preparations, the first floor of this new so-called Royal Museum was opened to the public on November 19, 1819. As time progressed, additional works from all over Europe were installed in other parts of the building, and by 1843 there were over 1,900 items in the museum's 458 page official catalogue.

The Revolution of 1868 gave way to the museum being stripped of royal ownership, and by 1872 when most of the abundant collection housed in the nearby former Museo Nacional de Trinidad were moved here, the museum was renamed the **El Prado**.

Currently the museum boasts one of Europe's finest collections of art, with over 6,000 items in its possession, over 1,850 of which can be seen on display at any one time. There are two huge floors with 75 spacious viewing galleries dedicated to various artists divided by both eras and nationality. The King recently broke ground on a project to convert an adjacent convent into an additional wing of the museum, slated to open up by the year 2000.

In addition, the museum offers a wonderful 19th century annex called the **Casón del Buen Retiro** (see section below), as well as fantastic temporary exhibitions and monthly lectures and conferences by world renowned art historians, many of which can be attended for free by visiting art enthusiasts.

The Spanish School Collections

Spread out over 38 different rooms on both floors of the museum, the **Escuela Española** collection makes up the vast bulk of the Prado's

THE PRADO MUSEUM - A FEW HELPFUL HINTS

It would take a whole book just to be able to give you any truly insightful and detailed historical criticism about the majority of this museum's prized contents. What I have decided to do instead is to list basic information as to the location and creators in order of nationality and antiquity of the most significant masterpieces to point you in the right direction. I strongly suggest that you purchase one of the many fine 300+ page photo guides about the Prado available in the museum's bookshops (and throughout the world). Some of the works I've described may not be on display at all times. Many of the most visited sections of the museum also have small racks which offer brief English language fact sheets about the most important artists for 100 ptas each.

Another good idea may be to come here during the free Saturday afternoon and Sunday opening hours when dozens of groups are led through the galleries each hour by official guides who give lengthy descriptions and criticisms about the works on display. Even though these groups are paying big money for the guides, there is no law against tagging along and listening to what is being told to them. Just wait around for a few American, Canadian, or English groups to pass by, select your favorite guide, and pretend you are part of the group.

During these free admission times the museum gets totally packed. It may not be a bad idea to return here once again during a normal weekday morning to get a better chance at enjoying a more detailed inspection of the masterpieces that are not easily accessible during the busiest days. Also worthy of note is the self-service caféteria in the basement which serves excellent café con leche for only 125 ptas and reasonably palatable lunch items from 550 ptas.

intensive permanent exhibition space. As you begin to explore rooms #8B through #39, #49 through #51C, and #66 through #67 you will undoubtedly have plenty of company. These works, many of which were acquired by the royal family, are the single best and largest collection of Spanish art found anywhere on earth.

I suggest spending plenty of time here to see almost all the works included. All visitors to the Prado must spend a fair amount of time to see and understand such important works as *Christ in Majesty* by **Gallego** (1467-1507), *Presentation in the Chapel* and *Virgin and Child* by **Morales** (1500-1586), *The Infanta Isabella* and *The Mystic Marriage of St. Catherine* by **Coello** (1532-1588), and the entire collections on display by **El Greco** (1541-1614), **Ribera** (1591-1652), **Velázquez** (1599-1660), **Zubarán** (1598-1664), **Cano** (1601-1667), **Murillo** (1618-1682), **Valdes Leal** (1622-1660), and **Goya** (1746-1828), including his exceptionally haunting series of so-called *Black Paintings* which he completed just before his death.

After nine different visits to this museum, these are the works that keep bringing me back. Be sure to pick up the English language versions of the information pamphlets on some of the above painters (100 *ptas* each) before continuing through their respective exhibits.

The Flemish School Collections

Perhaps almost as important as the Spanish collections available for viewing at the Prado, is the extraordinary display of the **Escuela Flamenca** or Flemish school art. With a large section of the museum dedicated to these sublime masters of scenic and religious art, you will have to set aside plenty of time to browse through rooms #56 through #58 and #60 through #75.

The best offerings in these galleries include *Deposition* by **Van Der Weyden** (1400-1464), *Presentation in the Temple* and *Adoration of the Kings* by **Memling** (1433-1494), the entire collection on display by **Bosch** (1450-1616), *Ecce Homo* by **Matsys** (1465-1530), *Charon Crossing the Styx* and *Rest on the Flight* by **Patinir** (1480-1524), *The Triumph of Death* by **Brueghel the Elder** (1525-1569), and all included works by **Brueghel de Velours** (1568-1625), **Rubens** (1577-1640), **Synders** (1579-1657), **Van Dyck** (1599-1641), **Jordaens** (1593-1678), and **Teniers** (1610-1690).

The Italian School Collections

Just off both sides of the upper floor's *Puerta de Goya* entrance, and extending back to the left part of the building, are the majority of rooms that are dedicated to the **Escuela Italiana** or the Italian School.

Here in rooms #2 through #10A as well as room 18A, pay special attention to *Adoration of the Kings* and *Annunciation* by **Fra Angelico** (1387-1455), *The Story of Nastagio* panels by **Botticelli** (1443-1510), *Noli Me Tangere* by **Correggio** (1494-1534), *Bacchanal, The Fall of Man, Venus with the Organ Player*, and *Charles V with his Dog* by **Titian** (1489-1576), *The Holy Family* and *Portrait of a Cardinal* by **Raphael** (1483-1520), *Joseph and Potiphar's Wife* and *Susanna and the Elders* by **Tintoretto** (1518-1594), *Venus and Andonis* and *The Finding of Moses* by **Veronese** (1528-1588), *David and Goliath* by **Caravaggio** (1573-1610), *Pieta* by **Crespi** (1590-1630), *Christ and the Traders of the Temple* by **Panini** (1691-1765), and *Olympus* by **Tiepolo** (1696-1770).

The French School Collections

Scattered to the immediate front and the left mid-section of this upper floor are a few rooms filled with art from the **Escuela Francesa** or the French School. While visiting these rooms marked #15A, 16A, and 40,

I suggest giving a good look at paintings like the *Landscape* series and *Parnassus* by **Poussin** (1594-1665), *Temptation of St. Anthony* and *Embarkation of St. Paula at Ostia* by **Le Lorrain** (1600-1682), *Louis XIV* by **Rigaud**, and *Festivities in a Park* by **Watteau** (1684-1721).

The Dutch School Collections

On the middle and rear sections of the ground floor in rooms 59, 64, and 65 is a small but dramatic **Escuela Holandesa** series of Dutch works. Since most of the pieces here are utterly amazing, I will point out a few specific canvases that you've got to see: *The Money Changer and his Wife* and *Virgin and Child* by **Van Reymerswaele** (1500-1567), *The Painter's Wife* by **Van Dashorst** (1520-1576), *The Incredulity of St. Thomas* by **Van Honthorst** (1590-1656), and of course *Artemisa* by **Rembrandt** (1606-1669).

The German School Collections

With only two rooms (#17A and #54) dispersed between two different floors currently containing the museum's not-so-abundant holdings of their **Escuela Alemana** collections of German art, most people don't even bother to give these pieces a good look. What they would find if they spent the time and effort might just surprise them.

Try to take a few extra minutes to peek at these beautiful paintings, including *Adam and Eve* and *Self Portrait* by **Durer** (1471-1528), *The Three Graces* and its haunting counterpart *The Stages of Human Life* by **Grien** (1484-1545), and *Charles III* and *Maria Louisa of Parma* by **Mengs** (1728-1779).

The Casón del Buen Retiro

Located only about a two minute walk behind the Prado, this lovely former ballroom of the long gone **Palacio del Buen Retiro** palace rests just off of Calle de Alfonso XII. The two floors of this small but worthwhile museum of mainly 19th century Spanish art and sculpture (although some foreign pieces exist here too) contain two dozen or so rooms dedicated to various artist and themes.

Although far less challenging than its big brother, this annex features pieces from such artists as **Madrazo, Esquivel, Fortuny, Beruete, Zuloaga, Rico, Degrain, Rosales, Sorolla, Pradilla, Gimeno, Riancho, Regoyos, Chicharro, Sala, Carbonero, Gisbert, Zubiaurre, Gris**, and others from across the country as well as Europe. The entire building is topped off by a beautiful central dome that was frescoed by **Giordano**. This may be a bit difficult to appreciate after a long day at the Prado, but is almost never busy (even during the free admission times).

If you check at the front door, the guard may let you use your entrance stub from the Prado to enter here on a different day. All in all, it's a fairly nice place to spend an hour or so to understand 19th century trends in the complex world of Spanish art.

TOUR 6

The Thyssen-Bornemisza Museum & the Jardin Botánico.
Approximate duration (by foot) including museum and garden visits is about 4 hours. Start from the Banco de España metro station.

The Thyssen-Bornemisza Museum

After exiting the *metro* station, turn right onto the Paseo del Prado and follow it south for a few blocks until you reach the **Fuente de Apolo** fountain. Just after the next corner, on the right hand side of the Paseo del Prado is the main entrance to the museum. Now housed inside the beautiful 18th century **Palacio de Villahermosa** palace, this superb art museum was opened to the public in 1992.

The contents of the museum consist of the private collections of millionaire industrialist **Baron Hans Heirich Thyssen Bornemisza** and his father, who took their acquisitions rather seriously. Arranged on four separate floors, this is a great place to spend a few hours at most. Besides a constantly changing temporary exhibition held on the basement level, the other three floors hold a vast assortment of works from all over the globe that span the 13th through 20th centuries. You will find that all the items have been logically arranged in thematic rooms that have well-marked plaques for each piece and era.

The second (top) floor is the best way to start your visit, and here you can view rooms #1 through #21 which contain 13th through 17th century European masterpieces by such artists as **Jan Van Eyck**, **Van der Weyden**, **Ghirlandaio**, **Durers**, **Raphael**, **Carpaccio**, **Caravaggio**, **El Greco**, **Tintoretto**, and **Titian**. The first floor showcases 17th through 19th century European and North American works on rooms #22 through #40 by artists like **Van Gogh**, **Homer**, **Whistler**, and **Munch**.

Another level down to the ground floor will reveal a series of modern art pieces in rooms #41 throgh #48 from the likes of **Picasso**, **Miró**, **Magritte**, **Dali**, **Pollack**, and **Rauschenberg**. The basement level has a changing seasonal exhibit that can also be visited for an additional fee. Other facilities here include a self service caféteria, elevators between all floors, restrooms, museum gift shop, advance ticket purchases, a great bookshop and facilities for the physically challenged.

The museum is open from Tuesday through Sunday from 10am until 7pm. Admission for adults is 900 ptas for the museum and 500 for the temporary exhibit, or a combined ticket for both will cost 1,200 ptas Students and senior citizens with valid internationally recognized ID can enter the museum half price.

The Real Jardin Botánico

From the museum, walk across to the other side of the Paseo del Prado and turn right to head south for a couple of blocks until reaching the well marked entrance off the Plaza de Murillo to the **Real Jardin Botánico (Royal Botanical Gardens)**. These gardens were originally opened to the public by order of King Carlos III in 1781 during Madrid's Age of Enlightenment and contain an absolutely amazing collection consisting of thousands of species of flora from almost every continent. It is among my favorite places to relax during a sunny day.

As you pass through the entrance gate, ask for a free *plano* (map) which will explain the exact location of each type of plant, flower, and tree as well as other specific points of interest. The gardens are laid out in three separate outdoor sections which contain ornamental, medicinal, aromatic and exotic plant life, Scattered through these zones are a fantastic collection of indigenous and imported trees. A large indoor pavilion known as the **Pabellón Villanueva** also contains additional tropical plants, a herb garden, a vast archive of antique floral prints, and a huge research library. Benches are scattered through the gardens, and services such as public restrooms and telephones are available on the site. *The gardens are open every day from 10am until sunset and admission is 300 ptas per person.*

TOUR 7

The Plaza de España, the Gran Via, & the Museo de Artes Decorativas.
Approximate duration (by foot) is about 4.5 hours including museum visits. Start from the Plaza de España metro station.

The Plaza de España

The *metro* station will leave you off right next to the plaza and its small urban park. The focal point of the park is the **Monumento A Cervantes** and its adjacent fountain which depicts Don Quixote and Sancho seemingly ready to embark on another adventure. The plaza is rung by a series of skyscrapers including the **Edificio de España** which was built by José Maria Otamendi and his brother Joaquin in 1948 during the reign of Franco, and its nearby neighbor known as the **Torre de Madrid**.

On the rear side of the park is a shorter, but much more inspiring, structure called the **Real Compania Austriana de Minas**, which was built in 1899 by Manuel Martinez. Designed to look like a palatial mansion, this French four story pavilion- topped building has always been just an expensive office and apartment building. Formerly a place of drug dealing and crime, the police have done a wonderful job in once again making the Plaza de España a safe and enjoyable place to stroll around during daylight hours.

From the front of the plaza, turn right onto the wide **Gran Via**, the Broadway of Madrid. Once the most prominent address for corporate headquarters, these days the street is better known for its movie theaters, dance halls, souvenir shops, and fast food joints. As you walk down the Gran Via there are several examples of innovative turn-of-the-century architecture.

A few blocks down on the right hand side of the street (just off the Plaza de Callao) is the Art Deco **Edificio Capitol** built in the 1930's by Louis Martinez Feduchi. Another several blocks down on the left hand side of the street off the corner of Calle de Fuencarral is the **La Telefónica** building which was built in 1926 by Ignacio de Cárdenas and maintained its classification as the tallest building in Madrid during the 1930's. If you now cross the Gran Via and keep following it down, you can't help but be enchanted by the fantastically ornate **Edificio Metropolis** that rests at the junction of Calle de Alcalá. Built in 1905 by Raymond and Jules Fevrier of France, I can't think of any other building in the city that better typifies turn-of-the-century design. With its wonderful position at the merger of two major thoroughfares and its great dome topped with a winged statue, it's a real stunner.

The Museo Nacional des Artes Decorativas

From the end of the Gran Via, merge onto Calle de Alcalá and bear left. Continue straight ahead until reaching the Puerta de Alcalá where you should now turn right onto Calle Alfonso XII. Two blocks on, take a right turn onto Calle Montalbán where on #12 will be the entrance to the **Museo Nacional des Artes Decorativas**.

For some reason that I can't understand, this wonderful five floor collection of some of Europe's finest 13th through 19th century furnishings and decorative arts is not high on most visitor's lists. Do not miss the opportunity to come here for a couple of hours, especially on Sundays when it is free to get in and not very crowded. While you stroll through the dozens of thematic rooms, you can find hundreds of unique handmade *azulejos* tiles, canopy beds, the finest European crystal and porcelain, an authentic 18th century kitchen, fantastic clocks, irreplaceable tapestries and paintings dating back over 300 years and countless other treasures. *The museum is open Tuesday through Friday from 9am until 530pm, and weekends from 10am until 2pm. Admission is 400 ptas per person during the week, free on Sunday.*

TOUR 8

The Plaza de Colón, the Barrio de Salamanca district, & the Museo Lázaro Galdiano.

Approximate duration (by foot) is about 6 hours including museum visits. Start from the Colón metro station.

The Plaza de Colón area

After arriving at the Colón *metro* station, bear right and head west along the wide Calle de Génova. At the next corner you will cross the wide Paseo de Recoletos and enter **Plaza de Colón**. The plaza's highlight is the **Jardines del Descubrimento** gardens and sculpture park with its statue of Christopher Columbus and other odd monuments to the Age of Discoveries.

A large fountain partially covers the entrance to the subterranean **Centro Cultural Villa de Madrid**, which hosts plays, concerts, art exhibitions and other special events throughout the year.

After a short rest around this delightful garden full of young lovers and unusual sculptures, return to the Paseo de Recoletos and walk one block south to find the **Biblioteca Nacional**. This immense structure was designed in 1865 by Francisco Jareño with a bold colonnade in the center of its facade. The large staircases leading up to the library past statues of San Isidro, Cervantes, Lope de Vega, and Luis Vives are about as far as you'll get before being promptly turned away by the ever present security guards. *The library itself is closed to the general public, but it does offer a small adjacent art exposition gallery that can be visited for free from 10am to 9pm from Tuesday through Saturday, Sundays and holidays from 10 am to 2 pm.*

If you walk around to the other side of this fine building via the Plaza de Colón, you will soon find a massive staircase flanked by two statues of bare breasted half woman/half lioness that lead up to the **Museo Arqueológico Nacional** museum. Among the many exhibits here are examples of prehistoric, Visigothic, Celt- Iberian, Moorish, and Christian era artifacts. An underground pathway can be taken to view replicas of the famed *Altimira* cave paintings. *The museum is open 9:30am to 8:30pm from Tuesday through Saturday, and Sunday from 9:30am until 2:30pm, and admission is 500 ptas but there is free entry to all on Saturday afternoons, and all day on Sundays & Holidays.*

One of the least notable attractions in this general vicinity, is the **Museo de Cera (Wax Museum)** *at #41 Paseo de Recoletos.* If you want to see the likeness of over 450 famous entertainers, politicians, and historical figures, this is the place. *Admission is 750 ptas per adult, and 500 ptas for kids between 4 and 12 years old. Hours are 10:am until 2pm and 4pm until 8:30pm daily.*

The Salamanca District

After a good look around the museum, turn left onto **Calle de Serrano**, and cross over the street to follow Calle de Jorge Juan to browse and window shop in the many designer boutiques, art galleries, and antique shops which line the upscale **Barrio de Salamanca** district. This exclusive neighborhood was originally built by railroad Spanish magnate Marquis José de Salamanca in the late 19th century. It was the hope of the Marquis to promote a modern French style of urban development within his new district, and consequently he bankrolled the construction of opulent mansions that were among the first in the city to feature elevators, street lights, and electrical systems.

The original boundaries of this zone were from Calle de Serrano eastward until Calle Velázquez, and from Calle Villanueva northward until Calle Don Juan Ramón de la Cruz. Soon the district began to expand in all directions and is now almost 10 times its original size. It is however the original heart of the quarter which still contains the most interesting shops and architecture.

Be sure to check out the larger streets here such as **Calle Jorge Juan** and **Calle Goya**, as well as the small newly developed lanes full of salons, retail shopping, chic clothing shops, and art galleries, like Calle de Puigcerda, **Calle de Alaya**, **Calle Nunez de Balboa**, and **Callejon Jorge Juan 14 y 14 Bis**. Another street in this area is called the **Calle de Claudio Coello** where there are a fwe more reasonably priced shops as well as a traditional covered marketplace called the **Mercado de la Paz** where you can buy great fresh veggies, meats, cheese, and smoked fish for an unforgettable picnic in nearby Retiro park.

Northward along Calle de Serrano & Beyond

Now return to the **Calle de Serrano** and turn right onto its busy sidewalks to visit block after block of fine jewelry shops, designer boutiques, cafés and department stores. The first few blocks of this avenue are lined by well known designer shops such as **Caramelo**, **Ermengildo Zegna** (the snobbiest shop in the city!), **Bally of Switzerland**, **Modit**, **Cartier**, and also features department stores such as **Marks & Spencer** and **El Corte Ingles**. Over near the intersection of this avenue with the Calle Goya is the exclusive **El Jardin de Serrano** shopping center with such famed boutiques as **Bvlgari**, **Beverly Hills Polo Club**, **Prada**, and the great **Café Mallorca** cafateria and pastry shop. About another dozen streets up the avenue near the intersection of Calle de León is the **American Embassy** complex, followed by even more fine retail shops and galleries.

Just before reaching the corner of Calle Maria de Molina is the unmistakable (and not to be missed!) 18th century mansion housing one of the finest art collections in the world, the **Fondacion Lázaro Galdiano Museo** *at # 122.* The museum is comprised of the once private collection of priceless treasures contained in 37 opulent rooms on four separate floors. While the rooms themselves are spectacularly embellished with gold leaf, marble, and frescoes, they each contain countless works of art. Among the most notable pieces exhibited are 13th through 16th century Catholic icons and religious artifacts from all over Europe, 18th century jewelry, one-of-a-kind furnishings, Celtic and Iberian bronze relics, antique pocket watches, medieval swords, 17th century navigational instruments, silk tapestries, ivory inlaid rifles, and paintings by **Goya**, **Maella**, **Romney**, **Rembrandt**, **Gainsborough**, **Velázquez**, **El Greco**, **Murillo** and many others.

This is a fine place to spend a cloudy morning, and although the exhibits are poorly marked, you can get up close to the pieces without being bothered by the security guards. *The museum is open from 10am until 2pm from Tuesday through Sunday and costs 400 ptas per person, half price for students.*

TOUR 9

The Templo de Debod, Parque de Oeste, & the Casa de Campo park.
Approximate duration (by foot) is about 4.5 hours including park visits. Start from the Ventura Rodriguez metro station. Note: Be advised that these parks are best enjoyed during warmer weather, and that many attractions included in this tour are subject to limited winter schedules.

After leaving the *metro*, take the Calle de Princesa up one block and then turn left onto Calle Luisa Fernanda. A block later, at the end of this street, you will first cross carefully across the rather busy Calle de Ferraz and then notice the entrance-ways that lead into the **Parque del Oeste** public park area. The park itself is full of small hills, walking paths, benches, and a strangely out of place Egyptian temple. The unmistakable ruins of the 2,300 year old **Templo de Debod** temple which was shipped to Spain and reassembled in this park before the controversial Aswan dam was built in Egypt and flooded many historical areas. Now open to the public, the temple and its adjacent *loggia* are worth a quick look at, especially to see its interior hieroglyphics. *The temple is open Tuesday through Friday from 10am until 1pm and 3:45pm until 6:30pm, and on Saturdays and Sundays from 10am until 1pm. Admission into the temple's interior is 300 ptas per person.*

After seeing the temple and park, return to Calle de Ferraz and follow it for a couple of blocks until the fork in the road. At this point, bear left onto the café lined Paseo Pintor Rosales where signposts mark the way to the nearby **Teleférico (cable car ride)** across the **Manzanares** river and into the gigantic **Casa de Campo** park. This is the largest park in Madrid and it offers a seemingly endless array of activities for the whole family. Once the private property of King Filipe II and his descendants, this delightful 4,275 acre recreation area boasts several walking and running paths, an outdoor municipal swimming pool, and even the tranquil **El Lago** lake with rowboats and peddle boats for rent at about 400 *ptas* per hour during the warmer months. Also located in the park is the **Parque de Atracciones** amusement park complex where you can enjoy roller coaster rides, and the nearby **Zoo** with over 3,000 animals on display and a great dolphin show.

The Teleférico cable car's daily summer schedule is from 11:30am until 9pm or later. During the winter: Friday through Sunday only from 11am until about 7pm. The trip costs 425 ptas round trip per person. The park itself is open daily year round from sunrise to sunset and there is no entrance fee. The amusement park complex is open during the summer from about 10am until at least midnight daily, while in the winter it opens on weekends only from about 12noon until 7pm or later depending on the month. Admission is now 850 ptas per person, with additional charges for some rides and special events. The zoo is open daily from 10am until 8pm and admission is 380 ptas per adult and 200 ptas per child.

GUIDED CITY TOURS OF MADRID

The typical city tour of Madrid is provided by large tour operators who have big air conditioned buses and either a live guide (in the language of your choice) or a multilingual tape recorded guide. Expect to be offered a variety of half and full day trips which generally cost between 3,000 ptas and 5,000 ptas per half day, and between 6,000 ptas and 8,000 ptas per full day without meals. Special interest excursions that include specific history, art, nightlife, or cultural events may cost upwards of 13,000 ptas including dinner and drinks.

The best bargain in town may be the half day and full day **Madrid Vision** *guided tours which cost less than half the price of their competition. Their multilingual bus trips depart from the Prado museum's bus stop several times each day from Tuesday through Sunday. The companies listed below offer a wide range of these trips, and may actually be able to pick you up directly from your hotel lobby with advance notification. Contact either the companies below directly or via a travel agent to make the mandatory advance reservations.*

Madrid Vision, *Ave. de Manoteras, 14, Tel. (91) 302-4526*
Pullmantour, *Plaza de Oriente, 8, Tel. (91) 541-1807*
Juliá Tour, *Gran Via, 68, Tel. (91) 559-9605*
MadridTurismo, *Calle Mayor, 69, Tel. (91) 588-2906*

NIGHTLIFE & ENTERTAINMENT

The Puerta del Sol area

PALACIO GAVIRIA, *Calle de Arenal, 9. Tel. (91) 526-6069.*

This has got to be the most intriguing nightspot in the world! Housed in a fantastic 19th century palace built as a love nest for Queen Isabella II by her noble lover, this wildly luxurious nightclub must be seen to be believed. After ascending a regal flight of stairs, you enter a series of ornate parlors and antique-filled lounges, each of which has its own unique ambiance.

Of the many rooms, each connected by secret passageways and a grand hall, you will find some of Madrid's most refined singles and couples socializing without any attitude or snobbery. The highlights of this unbelievable club include a fresco adorned ballroom where people waltz and salsa the night away, a fantastic billiard parlor featuring rock and dance music, and over a dozen intimate sitting rooms where you can actually hear the person you're sitting with. This place gets packed on weekend nights after midnight. The cover charge of about 1500 *ptas* and up is well worth paying, especially considering the free caviar and salmon canopies offered after midnight. A must-see for all visitors to Madrid!

TEATRO JOY ESLAVA, *Calle de Arenal, 11. Tel. (91) 366-3733.*

This massive converted theater turned glitzy disco is home to a nightly parade of over 1500 of the city's most serious party people. The mixed crowd of 20-40 year old singles arrives here after about 2am and stay until the sun comes up. Between the huge dance floor, pumping hot Euro dance mixes, multimedia light show, modern ballet performances and red jacketed waiters, this is the in place for aggressive singles looking to meet someone to spend the night with. I got the definite feeling that this is where the not-so-famous arrive dressed to kill in order to meet the real rich and famous guests who often dress in jeans. Expect to pay about 2000 *ptas* to get in on weekend nights with one drink included, and 1200 *ptas* for any cocktail from a simple soda to a straight whiskey.

ELTEMPLO DEL GATO, *Calle de Trujillos. Telephone unlisted.*

Simply the most laid-back and comfortable venue for live music and fine wines in the whole city. This somewhat hidden club bills itself as a California music bar, and the description is right on the ball. Besides offering excellent live bands from all over the globe, the bar also features avant-garde movie screenings, small theatrical performances, a great pool table, and a good selection of California wines. Beers are only 375 *ptas*, and wines and strong mixed drinks start at about 550 *ptas* each. Not your typical Spanish bar, but that's why I love it.

The Plaza de Santa Ana area
CERVECERÍA ALEMANA, *Plaza de Santa Ana, 6. Tel. (91) 429-7033.*
This is a fantastic little *tapas* bar and restaurant, once frequented by Ernest Hemingway, that has a casually dressed crowd of friendly young singles and couples. Especially busy after 11pm on weekends, you can stand at the lively bar surrounded by bullfighting statues and photos and meet lots of other people while ordering superb *tapas*.

Expect to pay about 155 *ptas* for an *empanadilla*, 750 *ptas* for a small plate of shrimp, 700 *ptas* for fried calamari, 450 *ptas* for surprisingly tasty pan fried sardines, 225 *ptas* for two German style sausages, 225 *ptas* for a *tortilla Español*, 150 *ptas* for a small beer, and from 300 to 700 *ptas* for a glass of sherry or a mixed drink. If you're really hungry, large *raciones* are available at the bar, or with waiter service from one of the two dozen or so small tables for 1100-2300 *ptas* per portion. Among the most charming of Madrid's *Cervecerias*.

NATURBIER, *Plaza de Santa Ana, 9. Tel. (91) 429-3198.*
This is a beautiful two floor micro-brewery with exposed brick walls and wooden beam ceilings. The crowd here is a mix of both young and middle aged beer lovers who spend hours socializing over beers while munching on the tastiest *tapas* on the plaza. The brewery is located in the rear of the building, and creates what I believe to be the best lagers and ales available in Spain.

The food here is wonderful and features *tapas* such as canapes with either Roquefort cheese, salmon, tuna, caviar, ham, pate or trout for about 200 *ptas* each, as well as more substantial *raciones* like bratworst for 325 *ptas*, Manchego cheese for 850 *ptas*, mussels for 600 *ptas*, pork loin for 1,650 *ptas*, and much more. This may very well be the best beer and *tapas* bar in Madrid.

CAFÉ CENTRAL, *Plaza del Ángel, 19. Tel. (91) 468-0844.*
Just around the corner from Plaza de Santa Ana, this large café offers a relaxing atmosphere to enjoy a drink during the day, as well as live jazz bands on most nights. The café has both a bar area facing the stage, and several small tables. The music here tends to be loud, and you may want to sit at a rear table to avoid hearing loss during the shows. Cover charges start at about 800 *ptas*, and during the evenings there may also be a small minimum. The last time I was here there was an excellent local quartet that played three sets of songs by Miles Davis, Chick Corea, and Weather Report , almost as good as the originals.

VILLA ROSA, *Plaza Santa Ana, 15. Tel. (91) 521-3689.*
The colorful *azulejos* tile exterior of this wildly successful late night disco is a throwback to its earlier days as a Flamenco club when such celebrities as Frank Sinatra and Ava Gardener would spend their nights trying to out-drink the Spaniards. Nowadays this unusual dance club

offers both techno and house music and packs in hundreds of casually dressed night crawlers who range in age from 16 to 25. The interior features tile murals, four separate bars, and a huge dance floor that can be fitted with long tables on nights when cabarets and other special events take place. The doors open at about 1am, and since there normally is no cover charge, this place gets completely packed from 3am until 5am. Once inside expect to pay 450 *ptas* per beer, and up to 950 *ptas* for each mixed drink.

CARBONES 13, *Calle Manuel Fernández y Gonzalez, 13. Telephone unlisted.*

If you happen to be looking for a cool and comfortable place to mingle with the 30-40 year old crowd of urban professionals, this small popular watering hole just off the Calle de Echegaray strip may be your best bet. The laid-back bartenders serve up potent drinks at fairly reasonable prices (beer is 300 *ptas* a glass, mixed drinks are around 550 *ptas* each), and the talented deejays play classic funk and soul music at a manageable volume. Even though the people here may be much more sophisticated than several other area bars, everything from Armani suits to jeans are acceptable. The best times to enjoy this nightspot are from Thursday through Saturday nights starting at 11pm.

The Calle de las Huertas area

CAFÉ JAZZ POPULART, *Calle de las Huertas, 22. Tel. (91) 429-8407.*

Every night starting at about 11pm, this charming bar and small live music venue offers a fine lineup of talented bands that belt out two sets of great music. Depending on the night of the week, and the band on the schedule, you might hear some of the best blues, jazz, country, reggae, soul, samba, African or even flamenco music from around the world.

There is usually a small cover charge of about 600 *ptas* or so, and a great selection of imported beers and liquors starting at 300 *ptas* each. On nights with no cover charge they double the beer and drink prices to help pay for the band, so ask what the drinks here will cost before ordering them. The crowd is a great mix of young and old alike, and the ambiance is quite relaxing and is highlighted by small white marble tables and several hanging antique tubas.

LOS GABRIELES, *Calle de Echegaray, 17. Tel. (91) 429-6261.*

Of all the places to sit down and enjoy a great beer or fine sherry in Madrid, this is by far the most impressive. The casually dressed crowd here tends to be between 20 and 40 years old and prefer to sit at small tables beneath a series of fine 19th century tile murals from sherry-producing companies in the Jerez de la Frontera area of Andalucia. As you explore the walls of this small treasure you will find even more unusual tiles that depict skeletons and other odd scenes. Although completely packed on weekend nights after 11pm, the bar unfortunately has rather hefty prices after 7pm. I strongly urge you to at least pop inside this place for a few minutes, perhaps during the day when the drinks are much cheaper and they serve free *tapas*.

TABERNA DE DOLORES, *Calle de Lope de Vega, 31. No telephone.*

A nice simple local bar with a typical ceramic exterior and plenty of international beer bottles lining the walls. Each night starting at about 10:00pm you will find area residents sitting either at the bar or the 14 or so wooden tables in the rear, spreading gossip about their neighbors. Besides a good selection of canapes and other *tapas*, they also serve salads and good *raciones* of meat and seafood.

CASAPUEBLO, *Calle de Leon, 3. Tel. (1) 429-0515.*

Besides playing soft jazz music throughout the night, the cute little bar has a huge selection of exotic liquors, *cavas*, wines, coffees, hot chocolate and mixed drink combinations at reasonable prices. As one of the most tranquil places to settle in after a busy day of sightseeing, this bar is uniquely mature and civilized for this general area. The crowd here tends to be dressed in a casual yet elegant manner, and settle into long conversations. A romantic spot for couples that appreciate the finer things in life. Try a glass of *cava*, and relax here all night.

The Plaza de Colón area

TEATRIZ, *Calle de Hermosilla, 15. Tel. (91) 577-5379.*

Of all the nightspots in Madrid, this converted theater is perhaps the most memorable. The well dressed patrons have a choice of three floors of exotic ultra- modern lounges, small dance floors, and plenty of avant-garde ambiance. On weekend nights, this fantastic club is packed with some of the city's most beautiful people who pay up to 1,500 *ptas* for a mixed drink. The bizarre architecture even extends to the lower floor stainless steel and glass-laden bathrooms that seem to have been inspired by a UFO. Although there is no cover charge, the doorman may be a bit picky about who gets in on busy nights.

The Atocha Area

LA ESTACION VIEJA, *Estacion de Atocha, Tel. (1) Unlisted.*

Madrid´s newest hip spot for late weekend night disco dancing. The cover charge may exceed 2,000 *ptas* but its well worth the money. Located in a open air terrace at the edge of the Atocha train station, this disco also has chill-out rooms inside of old train cars, several lounge areas, a huge dance floor, and even karaoke, this is the place to see and be seen these days. Drinks cost upwards of 950 *ptas* each.

SPORTS & RECREATION

Amusement Parks
- **Parque de Atracciones**, *Casa de Campo, Tel. (91) 463-2900*
- **Aquapalace**, *Paseo de la Ermita del Santo, 48, Tel. (91) 526-1779*

Bicycle Rentals & Bicycle Excursions
- **Bicibus**, *Puerta del Sol, 14, Tel. (91) 522-4501*
- **Munoz Garcia**, *Calle Perlajo, 17, Tel. (91) 792-0823*
- **Karacol**, *Calle Montera, 32, Tel. (91) 532-9073*

Boat Rentals
- **El Estanque**, *Parque del Retiro*
- **Lago de Casa de Campo**, *Casa de Campo*

Bowling
- **AMF Bowling**, *Paseo de la Castellana, 77, Tel. (91) 555-0379*
- **Chamartin Bowling**, *Estación de Chamartin, Tel. (91) 315-7119*

Bullfights
- **Las Ventas Bullring**, *Calle de Alcalá, 237, Tel. (91) 356-2200*

Gambling

   Casino Gran Madrid, *N-VI-Km, Torrelodones, Tel. (91) 856-1100*. Free shuttle bus service several times daily from Plaza de España. Ask your hotel for a complimentary invitation and be sure to bring your passport!

Golf
- **Club de Campo**, *Carretera de Castilla-Km.2, Tel. (91) 357-3635. 18 holes + 9 holes, par 72*
- **Golf La Herreria**, *(San Lorenzo de el Escorial), Tel. (91) 890-5111. 18 holes, par 72*
- **Golf La Moraleja**, *Carretera de Burgos,-Km.8, Tel. (91) 650-0700. 18 holes, par 72*
- **Puerta de Hierro**, *N-IV-Km.4, Tel. (91) 316-1745. 18 holes x 2, par 72*
- **Campo de Golf**, *(Somosaguas), Tel. (91) 352-1647. 9 holes, par 68*

Gyms & Health Clubs
- **Aluche**, *Avda. del General Fanjul, 14, Tel. (91) 706-2968*
- **Chamartin**, *Prazuela de Peru, Tel. (91) 350-1223*
- **Deporte y Salud**, *Calle Guzmán el Bueno, Tel. (91) 543 1165*
- **El Presidente**, *Calle Profesor Waksman, 3, Tel. (91) 458-6759*
- **New Life**, *Avenida de Osa Mayor, 32, Tel. (91) 307-0988*
- **Votre Ligne**, *Calle COnde del Valle Suchil, 17, Tel. (91) 446-9015*

Horseback Riding
• **Club de Campo**, *Carretera de Castilla-Km. 2, Tel. (91) 357-3635*
• **Esquela de Equitacion**, *(Somosaguas), Tel. (91) 212-1247*
• **Hipica Villafranca**, *(Villanueva de Canada), Tel. (91) 815-0836*

Horseracing
• **Hipodromo Zarzuela**, *N-VI-Km. 7800, (Zarzuela), Tel. (91) 307-0140*

Outdoor Markets
• **El Rastro**, *Sunday Flea Maket, Plaza de Cascorro area*
• **Sunday Coin and Stamp Market**, *Plaza Mayor*

Soccer Teams & Stadiums
• **Real Madrid**, *Estadio Santiago Bernabeu, Calle Concha Espina, 1, Tel. (91) 457-1112*
• **Atletico de Madrid**, *Estadio Vicente Calderon, Paseo Virgen del Puerto, Tel. (91) 266-4707*

Squash
• **Castellana Squash**, *Estación de Chamartin, Tel. (91) 733-8898*
• **Club Canoe**, *Calle Pez Volador, 30, Tel. (91) 237-3501*
• **King's Squash**, *Calle Andrés Mellado, 88, Tel. (91) 543-4311*
• **Palladium Sports**, *Calle Carlos Mauras, 5, Tel. (91) 350-8805*

Swimming Pools
• **Canal Isabel II**, *Calle Islas Filipinas, 54, Tel. (91) 533-9642*
• **San Vicente de Paul**, *Calle Pelicano, 4, Tel. (91) 469-7404*

Tennis
• **Federacion de Tenis**, *Calle San Cugat de Valles, Tel. (91) 735-1154*
• **Tenis Chamartin**, *Calle Federico Salmon, 4, Tel. (91) 345-250*

Zoos & Aquariums
• **Acuario de Madrid**, *Calle Maestro Vitiria, 8, Tel. (91) 531-8172*
• **Zoo Parque Grande**, *Casa de Campo, Tel. (91) 677-7060*

EXCURSIONS & DAY TRIPS
If you have a full or half-day to kill while visiting Madrid, I'd suggest seeing **San Lorenzo de El Escorial**, **Aranjuez**, and **El Pardo**. These are just a few of the best day-trips. In most cases the sightseeing and excursion companies listed below provide guided tours to these destinations on a set schedule.

There are also additional half and full-day guided tours to such destinations as Toledo, Segovia, and Ávila, as well as multiple day tours that visit the Costa del Sol, Granada, Sevilla, Cordoba, Jerez, Fez, Tangier, Lisbon, and Fatima on a seasonal schedule.

Prices start at about 5000 *ptas* for a short local bus tour, and go up to over 9,000 *ptas* on full day tours with lunch, and well over 155,000 *ptas* per person for a 13 night tour with meals and hotels included. More independent travelers may wish to save money and read the corresponding chapters about the Spanish cities listed above to follow the directions via train, bus, or rent a car to get to these places. If you intend to visit Portugal, make sure to purchase my *Portugal Guide* (Open Road Publishing, New York) for more detailed sightseeing information and cost saving tips. More independent travelers may wish to save money and follow the directions via train, bus, or rent a car to get to these places.

Bus Excursions

Tickets for the dozens of guided tours operated daily by the following operators can be purchased from most hotels, travel agencies, or directly from the companies listed below. Call in advance to determine the exact times and days of the week for your preferred excursion, which language the tour will be narrated with, and where the pick-up location nearest to you will be for that specific outing.

• **Pullmantour**, *Plaza de Oriente, 8, Tel. (91) 541-1807*
• **Julia Tour**, *Gran Via, 68, Tel. (91) 559-9605*
• **Trapsatur**, *Calle San Bernardo, 23, Tel. (91) 542-6666*

SAN LORENZO DE EL ESCORIAL

Situated 54 km (33.5 miles) northwest of Madrid at the base of the **Guadarrama** mountain range, the bustling town of **San Lorenzo de El Escorial** is one of the most popular excursions. The town itself offers little of interest other than the famous **El Real Monasterio de El Escorial** (often abbreviated as El Escorial).

After Spanish forces won a decisive victory over the French at San Quentin on St. Lawrence day (August 10) of 1557, King Felipe II decided to erect a gigantic pantheon to honor St. Lawrence. He entrusted the project to the great architect Juan Bautista de Toledo, who agreed to create a royal palace and Hieronymite monastery here in the shape of the gridiron upon which St. Lawrence was martyred. With a crew of over 1,500 men, construction of this huge granite structure began in 1563. After Juan Bautista de Toledo's death in 1567, his protege, Juan de Herrera was then called in to finish the building, and added many of his own designs into the project which was finally completed in 1584.

Upon entering the main gateway on the western side, you line up for tickets, go through a metal detector, and are immediately lead through the complex. You have many possible routes to follow in order to see the most important sights. Take a free floor plan and map from the ticket window and if necessary, zig zag your way between the different sections of the building to avoid the biggest crowds and lines inside.

Among the most impressive sights within the complex include the following sections which should no be missed, beginning with the **Patio de los Reyes (King's Courtyard)**, with its six statues of the Kings of Judea. Just behind the courtyard lies the magnificent dome-topped **Basilica (Church)** that contains several sculptures by Leone and Pompeo Leoni, and the beautiful fresco of the Martyrdom of St. Lawrence by Titan. Nearby in the downstairs **Panteón Real (Royal Pantheon)** you can view the 26 identical marble sarcophagi resting along the walls with the bodies of most of Spain's Kings since the early 16th century on one side of the gallery, as well as all of the Queens who gave birth to a future king on the opposite side. Interestingly enough, three of the sarcophagi are still empty and are awaiting the death of present and/or future monarchs.

The upstairs **Panteón de las Infantas (Pantheon of the Princes)** is the final resting place for children of royalty and Queens who did not produce a future King. Also of considerable interest is the opulent fresco covered **Biblioteca (Library)** on the second floor where you can still find thousands of irreplaceable leather bound books, some dating back several centuries. In the basement you can tour the **Nuevos Museos (New Museums)** with a wonderful collection of paintings by **Ribera**, **Van Dyck**, **Velázquez**, **Titian**, **El Greco** and others.

For me, the most impressive part of my tour was in the **Palacio Real (Royal Palace)** section complete with throne room, battle room, and the former apartments of the Kings.

Hours

The El Escorial complex is open from Tuesday through Sunday from 10am until 1:30pm and again from 3pm until 6pm. Admission is 600 ptas.

Guided walk-through (more like run-through) tours are available, but the schedule is somewhat erratic.

Directions

To get here by car, take the N-VI highway northwest from Madrid, following the exits for "El Escorial" near the town of Las Rozas.

Departures are from Madrid's Atocha and Chamartin Renfe train stations almost two dozen times per day for about 850 *ptas* round trip. The train station is about about two kilometers (1.3 miles) from the heart of town, with a connecting shuttle bus service to and from the center of town.

Bus service here is provided by the Empresa Herranz bus company via their station on Calle Isaac Peral, 10, and runs about twice per day in each direction. Round-trip costs 1,100 *ptas*.

The excursion companies listed above run bus tours here throughout the year for approximately 5,200 *ptas* per person for a half-day trip with guide and admission included.

Major Local Festivals

Contact the local Turismo office, *Tel. (91) 890-1554*, for exact details.
• **Semana Santa**, *April – Strange Processions*
• **Festa Santa**, *Mid-August – Processions*
• **Festa Virgen de Gracia**, *Mid-September – Parade of Carts*

ARANJUEZ

Located about 47 km (29 miles) south of Madrid is the royal town of **Aranjuez**. Way back in the 16th century, King Filipe II decided to build a summer retreat and palace in this town that is located on the **Rio Tajo** river in a lush and fertile plain. The original palace was completely devastated by fire and rebuilt twice during the 18th century.

During the reigns of King Fernando VI and King Carlos III, the **Palacio Real de Aranjuez** grew in both size and beauty as luscious gardens and new wings were added. The town and its attractions have long been a major tourist attraction of Mardileños who need a break from the hot and humid summer days. Thousands of people flock here daily during July and August to stroll through the brick and stone block palace's gardens, shady outdoor paths, and numerous opulent rooms. There are dozens of beautifully decorated salons open to the public that are each full of unique antiques, tapestries and decorative arts.

The highlights here include a former audience chamber lined with 18th century *azulejos* tiles, a Moorish style smoking lounge, and a vast assortment of fine paintings, chandeliers, and hand carved wood trimmings. Once you have seen the interior of this luxurious royal residence, expect to spend an hour or two wandering through the hundreds of acres of stunning grounds.

Make sure to stroll through the adjacent **Jardin de la Isla** gardens with their exotic fruit trees and bold statues until crossing the canal to reach the huge **Jardines del Principe** gardens and recreation park. Walk through the formal gardens, the relaxing foot paths, the old **Casa de Marinos** royal boat museum with a fine collection of royal gondolas, and even a nearby paddle boat rental kiosk.

Also inside the park is the inspiring 19th century **Casita del Labrador** (**Laborer's Cottage**) that is actually a miniature palace full of hand embroidered silk hangings, fine paintings, unforgettable Roman mosaics, antique timepieces, and plenty of marble statues. After a long day of walking around the palace and its grounds, most visitors line up at roadside kiosks and cafés to enjoy the refreshing local specialty of *fresas con nata* (strawberries with rich cream).

Hours

Marinos and Casita del Labrador are open Tuesday through Sunday from 10am until 1pm. The palace is open Tuesday through Sunday from 10am until 1pm and again from 3pm until 6pm. The gardens are open Tuesday through Sunday from 10am until sunset. Combined admission for both the palace and gardens is 450 ptas per person. The Casa de and again from 3pm until 6pm, with combined admission costing 350 ptas.

Free guided tours are usually available (in Spanish only), and commence about once per hour.

Directions

By car, follow the N-IV motorway south from Madrid for 46 km (29 miles) before exiting at the "Aranjuez" exit and follow the signs to the palace.

If you prefer taking the train, there are between 6 and 19 trains per day to and from the Atocha Renfe train station in Madrid and the cost is around 750 *ptas* round trip. The local train station is about one kilometer (.62 miles) from the center of town, and the walk to the palace takes 10 minutes or less. A special antique Renfe steam locomotive called *El Tren de la Fresa* (The Strawberry Train) runs from May through October only from the Atocha Renfe train station in Madrid about 9:40am and returns to Madrid at 8pm. The price is about 1,950 *ptas* per adult and 1,375 *ptas* per child, including admission to the palace and its grounds. Please call Renfe or visit any travel agency, as advance booking may be required.

Bus service is mainly provided by the Aisa bus company, and there are about 6 buses in each direction per day via Madrid's Sur bus station for some 975 *ptas* round trip.

All these excursion companies run bus tours here (usually with a stop at Chinchon) throughout the year for approximately 7,650 *ptas* per person for a full day trip with lunch, guide, and admission included.

Major Local Festivals

Contact the local Turismo office, *Tel. (91) 891-0427,* for exact details.
• **Fiesta San Fernando,** *May 30 – Processions and Feasts*
• **Fiesta Motin,** *Early September – Processions*

EL PARDO

The lovely village of **El Pardo** rests in a peaceful wooded area some 9.5 kilometers (6 miles) northwest of Madrid. The major draw of the town is undoubtedly the 16th century **Palacio de El Pardo** palace.

Originally built for King Filipe II on the sight of an old royal hunting lodge, it was destroyed by fire and subsequently rebuilt in 1604 and then totally renovated in 1772. The palace is most famous for its use as Franco's residence during his decades as Spain's dictator. While visiting the interior of the palace and its chapel you will be guided past the hundreds of tapestries based on designs by artists such as Goya and Bayeu.

Also worthy of note are the fine collections of porcelain, crystal, silver, clocks, and fine paintings that can be viewed in each of the rooms. You should also take the time to visit the adjacent 18th century **Casita del Principe (Prince's Pavilion)** that was beautifully designed by Juan de Villanueva for Queen Maria Luisa.

Hours

The palace and its grounds are open Monday through Saturday from 9am until 12:30pm and again from 3pm until 6pm, Sundays from 10am until 2pm. Combined admission for both the palace and Casita is 400 ptas per person.

Free guided tours are available in Spanish at least twice per hour.

Directions

By car, you should hop on the tiny local route C-601 north from Madrid for 9.5 km (6 miles) before following the signs to the palace.

Municipal bus service is available dozens of times daily in both directions via bus #601 that departs from, and returns to, the front of Madrid's Montcloa *metro* station for 125 *ptas* in each direction.

PRACTICAL INFORMATION

- **Main City Tourist Office** - *TURISMO - Plaza Mayor, 3 - Tel. (91) 266-5477*
- **Regional Tourist Office** - *Calle Duque de Medinacelli, 2 - Tel. (91) 429-3705*
- **Airport Tourist Office** - *Aeropuerto de Madrid-Barajas - Tel. (91) 305-8656*
- **Madrid-Barajas Airport** - *Barajas - Tel. (91) 305-8343*
- **Airport Luggage Storage area** - *Barajas - Tel. (91) 305-6112*
- **Airport Lost and Found Office** - *Barajas - Tel. (91) 393-6000*
- **Iberia Airlines at the Airport** - *Barajas - Tel. (91) 329-5767 or Tel. (91) 587-3723*
- **Iberia Airlines Reservations** - *Calle Velázquez - Tel. (91) 587-8156*
- **Airport Bus Information** - *Plaza de Colón - Tel. (91) 431-6192*
- **Spanish Customs Offices** - *Calle Guzmán el Bueno, 137 - Tel. (91) 554-3200*

- **Canadian Embassy** - *Calle Nunez de Balboa, 35 - Tel. (91) 431-4300*
- **U.S. Embassy** - *Calle Serrano, 75 - Tel. (91) 577-4000*
- **Regional Train Info** - *RENFE - Tel. (91) 530-0202*
- **Atocha Train Station** - *Avenida Ciudad de Barcelona - Tel. (91) 527-3160*
- **Chamartin Train Station** - *Calle Agustin de Foxá - Tel. (91) 323-2121*
- **Principe Pio Train Station** - *Paseo del Rey, 30 - Tel. (91) 547-0000*
- **Regional Bus Info** - *ESTACIÓN SUR - Calle Canarias,17 - Tel. (91) 468-4200*
- **Madrid's Municipal Bus Info** - *EMT - Calle Alcántara, 24 - Tel. (91) 401-3100*
- **Madrid's Municipal Subway Info** - *METRO - Tel. 552-4900*
- **Highway Assistance Hotline** - *Tel. (91) 742-1213*
- **Madrid Radio Taxi Companies** - *Tel. (91) 447-5180 or Tel. (91) 445-9008*
- **Central Post Office** - *Palacio de Comunicaciónes - Tel. (91) 521-8195*
- **Madrid's Municipal Event Hot Line** - *Tel. 010*
- **Hotel Info Hot-line** - *Tel. (91) 902-2020*
- **Tourist Help Line (In English)** - *Tel. (91) 559-1393*
- **Municipal Lost and Found Office** - *Plaza de Legazpi,7 - Tel. (91) 588-4346*
- **Pre-Recorded Weather Forecast** - *Tel. 094*
- **Madrid Directory Assistance** - *Tel. 098*
- **Regional Directory Assistance** - *Tel. 1003*
- **National Directory Assistance** - *Tel. 1009*
- **Medical Emergencies Hot Line** - *Tel. 061*
- **Late Night Pharmacy Listings** - *Tel. 098*
- **Burn Center** - *Tel. (91) 544-5207*
- **La Paz Hospital** - *Paseo de la Castellana, 261 - Tel. (91) 734-2600*
- **Universidad Medical Center** - *Calle Vallehermoso, 1 - Tel. (91) 466-2675*
- **Red Cross (Ambulances)** - *Tel. (91) 522-2222*
- **National Police** - *Tel. 091*
- **Municipal Police** - *Tel. 092*

MADRID'S MAJOR FESTIVALS

Contact the local Turismo office, Tel. (91) 366-5477, for more details.

Carnival	*Late February*	*Processions, All Night Parties*
Semana Santa	*Easter*	*Strange Processions*
Fiesta Sant Isidro	*15 May*	*Outdoor Fair on the River*
Fiesta La Paloma	*15 August*	*Outdoor Fair and Parades*
Fiesta La Almudena	*Early August*	*Processions*
Festivales Otono	*October*	*Live Music, Theater*

15. CENTRAL SPAIN

Including the regions of Castilla y León,
Castilla-La Mancha, & Extremadura

ÁVILA

If you need either a break from or an alternative to Madrid (also in Central Spain), **Ávila** might be the perfect diversion. The old city itself is surrounded by some of the most spectacular and complete turreted defensive walls in all of Europe, and they date back to the late 11th century when King Alfonso VI assigned his son in law to fortify what was then a small village.

By the time Saint Teresa was born here in 1515, the city had grown significantly in both importance and population, and began to attract noble families such as the parents of Queen Isabella. Many of these rich residents went on to build magnificent palaces that still stand to this day.

ARRIVALS & DEPARTURES

By Bus

The AutoRes bus company offers daily scheduled bus service to Ávila from Madrid and other nearby locations. The city's main bus station is located on the Avenida de Madrid, which is only about one kilometer (half a mile) east of the old part of town. Expect a taxi to cost about 590 *ptas* to almost any hotel or sight in town.

By Car

The best way to reach Ávila by car is to leave Madrid via the A-6 highway northeast. After about 68 kilometers (42 miles), you will be lead through a high speed tunnel with a toll of 675 *ptas* which cuts through part of the dramatic Sierra de Guadarrama mountain range. About 20 kilometers (12 miles) after the tunnel, exit the highway at Villacastin, and follow the indications towards Ávila, which lies about 24 kilometers (15 miles) southeast on route N-110.

Once inside the city you will find plenty of parking on the streets with electronic self-service machines that issue parking coupons for about 100 *ptas* per hour. If the coupon is not visible, expires, or has not been bought, expect a ticket to be waiting for you on the car's windshield.

By Train

Ávila's Renfe rail station is situated on Avenida José António on the eastern edge of the city, approximately two kilometers (1.5 miles) from the historic center of town. There are several daily arrivals and departures between this city, and dozens of other locations throughout the country via the extensive national rail system. From the station, a taxi to just about anywhere in town is about 490 *ptas*.

ORIENTATION

The walled city of Ávila rests above the Rio Adaja river in the southern portion of central Spain's Castilla y León region, a 112 kilometer (68 mile) drive northeast of Madrid. The city's population is 44,651.

GETTING AROUND TOWN

Once inside Ávila, you can walk anywhere. If you need to use a bus, the well marked stops for the Avilabus company can point the way towards other parts of town for just 90 *ptas* per ride. Taxis can be called at *Tel. (920) 211-959*, or by walking to the taxi stands at the major plazas in town, but don't expect them to be in abundance. Typical taxi fares almost never cost more than 600 *ptas* within city limits.

WHERE TO STAY

Expensive

HOTEL PALACIO DE LOS VELADA, *Plaza de la Catedral, 10. Tel. (920) 255-100, Fax (920) 254-900. Internet: palaciov@isid.es. Year round rack rates from 17,700 ptas per double room per night (E.P.). All major credit cards accepted.*

This majestically converted 15th century palace once known as the Torreon de los Velada is simply the best place to stay in town. Located steps away from the main cathedral, this stunning 85 room hotel (with a solid 5 star rating!) was originally the home of Queen Isabella's treasurer. After being converted into a convent chapel for some time, the building was purchased by a local duke who entertained various members of royalty here, and has recently been restored into on of the city's most beautiful hotels.

The property centers around a three story glass enclosed courtyard which in turn is surrounded by arched columns and some of the finest exposed beam ceilings found in this province. All of the rooms here feature deluxe tile lined private bathrooms with marble basins, air conditioning, remote control satellite television with international channels, ornate hand-painted furnishings in antique motifs, superb king or double bedding, mini-bar, electric mini-safe, trouser press and in some cases the top floor units have amazing views out over the town walls and cathedral. In some rooms there are sloped ceilings, four-poster king beds, and original convent nuns' window ledges. For a mere 85% surcharge, guests can choose to stay in the unique "Torre" suite which is a super deluxe duplex accommodation built into the old tower and it has a wonderful spiral staircase as well as two of the cutest bathrooms (one has a big Jacuzzi) you will find in Europe, all topped by a dome ceiling. The hotel also offers plenty of business meeting rooms, multiple restaurants, and live piano music in the enclosed courtyard bar and cafe.

PALACIO VALDERRÁBANOS, *Plaza de la Catedral, 9. Tel. (920) 211-023, Fax (20) 251-691. Year round rack rates from 14,000 ptas per double room per night (E.P.). All major credit cards accepted.*

With its prime location in a 14th century palace just next to the cathedral, this is the best and classiest place to stay in town. As soon as you enter this refined hotel you will find the original family coat of arms, a beautiful lobby area with exposed beam ceilings, marble floors, and large glass exhibition cases filled with antiques for sale.

The palace offers its guests 73 rooms and suites that are all air conditioned and have electronic door locks, cable television, direct dial telephones, reasonably large private bathrooms, mini-bars, mini-safes, comfortable furnishings, hairdryers. Many of the best rooms, including the amazing duplex suite #229, with great picture windows, have fantastic views of the cathedral and old town walls. There is also a fine restaurant, a peaceful bar, a few sitting rooms, and a staff of real professionals.

PARADOR DE ÁVILA, *Calle de Marques de Canales de Chozas, 2. Tel. (920) 211-340, Fax (920) 226-166. US and Canada Bookings (Marketing Ahead) Tel. 800/223-1356. Low season rack rates from 13,500 ptas per double room per night (E.P.). High season rack rates from 17,500 ptas per double room per night (E.P.). All major credit cards accepted*

This nicely refurbished 16th century nobleman's palace in the heart of the old city is also a great place to stay. This government owned property is packed with some of the best services and facilities in the area. The sun drenched *parador* has 61 large and beautifully decorated rooms and suites, all with deluxe marble private bathrooms, heating, tile and hardwood flooring, hair dryers, satellite color television, mini-bar, modern hardwood furnishings, direct dial telephones, windows with views out of the old streets or beautiful gardens, executive-styled desks and canopied beds in some cases.

Facilities here include an excellent regional restaurant, bar, fireside lounges, meeting and convention rooms, gardens, plenty of free parking, foreign currency exchange and an indoor garage. Service here is first rate, and the people working here are really nice.

Moderate

HOSTAL SANCHO DEL ESTRADA, *Castillo de Villaviciosa, Solosancho, (Avila). Tel. (920) 291-082, Fax (920) 291-082. Low season rack rates from 9,310 ptas per double room per night (E.P.). Low season rack rates from 9,775 ptas per double room per night (E.P.). All major credit cards accepted.*

The superb Hostal Sancho del Estrada is a regal 14th century restored castle, stunningly set at the foot of the Pico Zapatero mountains some 20 kilometers (13 miles) south of the walled city of Avila and less than one hour from Madrid! The castle was originally built for General Sancho de Estrada as a gift for valiantly defending Avila from Moorish invaders. This lavish yet relaxing property features an impressive array of salons, sitting rooms, turreted tower tops, delightfully furnished accommodations, and dining areas that have all be filled with museum quality suites of armor. There are one of a kind Iberian objects de art, priceless chandeliers, and amazing portraits and tapestries which date back as far as 700 years.

Owned and operated by the charming Sr. Avelino Mayoral Hernandez, a successful historical preservationist who has restored several world famous cathedrals and palaces throughout Spain, the project of converting the semi-ruined castle into a deluxe hotel took him some 22 years to complete when it opened in 1995. Nowadays the hotel offers its guests 12 extremely comfortable double rooms and two amazing suites (located in the towers) which all have modern private bathrooms, remote control satellite television, direct dial telephone, mini-bar, antique furnishings, three foot thick exposed stone walls, and in some rooms there are also incredible canopied brass beds and wonderful stone window ledges with nun style benches. While all of the rooms are of four-star quality or better, those looking for a romantic evening should give strong consideration to renting the cozy circular duplex mini-suite # 103 (a mere 13,000 *ptas* per night) which is located in one of the three tower tops.

Besides wonderful rooms and truly personalized service at the highest levels, the castle also can provide superb gourmet meals in their magnificent and rather intimate candelit dining room surrounded by some of Spain's best preserved tapestries and authentic Mudejar carved wooden ceilings. Other facilities here include private guided horseback rides up to the nearby Celtic era villages (call in advance to reserve), mountain bikes, buffet breakfast, private dining and meeting facilities, plenty of free parking and of course great advice on self guided valley hikes and unforgettable excursions to the nearby city of Avila. All of the locally based staff here are extremely friendly and helpful, and for the price there is no better place to stay in all of central Spain. This is a good place to stay if you have a rental car and want to stay somewhere special near Avila or Madrid, and take day trips to Avila, Madrid, Toledo, Segovia, Salamanca, and El Escorial.

GRAN HOSTAL SAN SEGUNDO, *Calle de San Segundo, 28. Tel. (920) 252-590, No Fax. Year round rack rates from 8,000 ptas per double room per night (B.P.). All major credit cards accepted.*

Situated just outside the old town walls, this delightful 14 room hotel offers an unusual assortment of modern and comfortable rooms. All of the spacious rooms here are modern and have television, direct dial phones, private bathrooms, in-room music, air conditioners and pine furnishings. There is a caféteria and a nearby restaurant. This is a good mid-priced lodging choice close to all of the town's sights.

HOSTERIA DE BRACAMONTE, *Calle de Bracamonte, 6. Tel. (920) 251-280, No Fax. Year round rack rates from 8,000 ptas per double room per night (E.P.). All major credit cards accepted.*

Located near the parador, this cozy looking, but rather confused, little historic mansion turned hotel and restaurant has some dozen or so antique styled rooms that are actually nice looking. The only problem here is that they are fully booked most of the time, and the staff have absolutely no clue at all about how to provide the necessary level of service (its a real shame because the place is so cute). Anyway, here the rooms in most cases feature tile floors, private bathrooms, four-poster beds, television, heating and great views of the old town.

Inexpensive

PENSION CONTINENTAL, *Plaza de la Catedral, 6. Tel. (920) 211-502, Fax (20) 251-691. Year round rack rates from 4,500 ptas per double room per night (E.P.). No credit cards accepted.*

This bright and clean family-run basic inn offers some 53 single and double rooms, as well as a six person family suite. While some of the rooms have shared bathrooms, many offer private bathrooms, hardwood floors, balconies with great views of the cathedral, simple furnishings, plenty of light and lots of charm for this price range. This is about the best choice for budget minded travelers who would like to be close to everything in town.

WHERE TO EAT

Expensive

EL MOLINO DE LA LOSA, *Bajada de la Losa, 12. Tel. (920) 211-102. All major credit cards accepted.*

The Molino de la Losa, certainly Avila's finest and most welcoming restaurant, rests peacefully alongside the far banks of the city's rambling Rio Adaja river. Located just 250 meters from the fortified walls surrounding the oldest part of town, this wonderful little oasis of gastronomic delights is one of the most relaxing places to dine out anywhere in Europe. The restaurant was built inside a wonderfully converted 500 year grain mill that used the rapidly moving river water to churn its huge gears. These age old gears can still be seen throughout both floors of this wonderful establishment which serves some of the best regional Spanish cuisine I have had the pleasure to sample.

Although there is a tranquil outdoor patio for casual afternoon and evening al fresco dining (the views out over Avila's walls are truly breathtaking!), I strongly suggest that you instead ascend towards the top floor dining room and open kitchen where jackets and ties are never required. During most evenings, about three dozen or so locals and a few well informed travelers fill up the river-view tables to begin a two hour (or more) feast of the most delicious gourmet food in all of Castilla La Mancha. Owned and operated by Sr. Venancio de Andres Matias, the Molino de la Losa employs a staff of local residents that really know how to transform even the most typical Spanish dishes into something quite special. All the ingredients here are market fresh and of the absolute highest qualities, and the meats, vegetables, and cheeses come directly from farms in the surrounding mountains.

Among the best dishes to try (feel free to ask for an English menu) while dining here are the amazing local wild herbs with anchovies in garlic infused Spanish extra-virgin olive oil, the delicious platter of four different aged local goat cheeses, smoked pork sausages in casserole, the freshly grilled bonito tuna salad with roasted red peppers and olives, partridge and bull's tail soup, their famous meat stuffed onions (a real treat!), Barco de Avila beans stewed in smoked pork sausage, filet of striped bass in orange sauce, a quarter of a newly roasted suckling pig, prime mountain steak baked inside earthenware, roasted lamb, a rich chocolate tart, homemade creme caramel, and a great rice pudding. The wine list here features a great assortment of Spanish vintages at reasonable prices, including their excellent house wine which costs a lot less than I would ever guess (try the Reserva 1992 in red). The typical price for an unforgettable three course a la carte lunch or dinner here would be about 4,250 *ptas* per person plus wine.

EL MESON DEL RASTRO, *Plaza del Rastro, 1. Tel. (920) 211-219. Most major credit cards accepted.*

For those looking for reasonably priced regional cuisine in nice humble surroundings, this famed local restaurant does a good job. The simple whitewashed interior is embellished with old wood beams, antlers on the walls, and simple wooden tables. Popular with businessmen during lunch, and tourists at dinner time, the menu here includes gazpacho, garlic soup, sautéed mushrooms, ham with melon, consommé, pork chops, artichokes with mayonnaise, shrimp with wild mushrooms, tuna omelet, beef steak in wine sauce, roasted chicken, veal cutlets and tasty desserts. A typical three course a la carte lunch or dinner here costs upwards of 3,300 *ptas* per person, but the best deal is their 1,700 *ptas* per person daily lunch and dinner menu with 2 courses plus dessert and wine. A nice place for local food with good service.

Moderate

LA POSADA DE LA FRUTA, *Plaza de la Fruta, 8. Tel. (920) 254-702. Some credit cards accepted in the main dining room only.*

Located just off the central Plaza de Pedro Davila square, this good restaurant has three separate areas to eat and drink in, all with different menus and prices. The most impressive sections are the mid-priced outdoor courtyard, and the more refined main dining room. The main restaurant menu here includes such memorable offerings as Castellanian soup, fish soup, white asparagus, mixed salad, shrimp in garlic, entrecote, stuffed partridge, filet of sole, and salmon with shrimp. The nice and casual glass enclosed courtyard cafeteria section offers a cheaper menu featuring ham and cheese sandwiches, hamburgers, various salads, fried calamari, sautéed mushrooms, and several combination plates.

Expect an a three course la carte dinner here to average about 2,800 *ptas* per person plus drinks, a daily cafeteria menu with two courses plus dessert and wine or bottled water is under 1,500 *ptas* per person, and a quick snack will cost around 800 *ptas* a person.

RESTAURANTE EL TORREÓN, *Plaza de la Catedral, 11. Tel. (920) 213-171. All major credit cards accepted.*

This converted 15th century house contains one of Ávila's nicest informal restaurants. The lower floor dining rooms have original arched ceilings and stone walls that recall a cave style ambiance. Their friendly staff serve such classic dishes such as cream of mushroom soup, cream of asparagus soup, zesty garlic soup, gazpacho, Spanish sausages with eggs, grilled hake, fried local trout, shrimp with garlic, entrecote, veal chops, roasted lamb, garlic chicken and good desserts. A typical three course la carte dinner here will cost about 2,950 *ptas* per person plus drinks, while a special house menu with two courses plus dessert and wine is available for 1,700 *ptas* per person.

Inexpensive
BOCATTI, *Calle de San Segundo, 26. Tel. (920) 251-080. No credit cards accepted.*

If you want a great little snack and don't want to pay through the nose, try this modern salad and sandwich shop just across the town walls behind the cathedral. Here you can sit down or even take out such fresh items as bacon and cheese sandwiches, potato omelet subs, tuna salad sandwiches, salami and fresh cheese subs, seafood salads, giant capriccio salads with salmon and swordfish, big burgers, croissants and delicious waffles. A filling lunch here will set you back under 750 *ptas* a person including a can of soda or mineral water.

SEEING THE SIGHTS
Approximate duration (by foot) is about 4 hours, including church, museum, rampart, plaza, and side street visits.

If you're driving, follow the signs that lead to the *"Centro Ciudad"*. As you start to notice the massive walls with their 90 or so circular towers, you will begin your walking tour at the **Parroquia de San Vicente** church across from the walls at the Plaza de San Vicente. This unusual basilica was built on a site formerly occupied by a tiny hermitage that might have dated back to the 4th century.

When its construction was begun in the 12th century, it was designed in the Romanesque style and resembled the shape of a cross. Dedicated to the memory of San Vicente and his two sisters who were executed by the Romans on this very site, the church offers several unique features including the **tomb of San Vicente**, with its rendering of his execution. Also worth noting are the golden main altar, the Gothic 13th-14th century transept tower and nave, and even the odd new age music which is piped in when mass is not in progress. *The basilica is open from 10am until 2pm and again from 4pm until 8pm each day and admission is 50 ptas.*

From the basilica, walk into the **Plaza de San Vicente** to get a close-up view of the old walls and gardens before continuing down the Calle de San Segundo for about two blocks. At the corner of Calle de Leales turn left into the Plaza de Italia, and soon you will pass the small Romanesque 12th century **Iglesia de Santo Tomé el Viejo**, open only during masses. The more interesting sight in this area is on the other side of the church at the great **Mansion de los Deanes** and its **Museo de Ávila** museum on the Plaza Navillos. Here you can wander through several rooms surrounding the courtyard of this 16th century mansion that now features exhibits of artifacts and reconstructions from the Paleolithic, Neolithic, Iron Age, Celtic, Roman, Moorish, Gothic, and other time periods. Among the most impressive items are ancient ceramics and tools found in this province. *The museum is open Tuesday through Saturday from 10am until 1:45pm and again from 3:30pm until 7:30pm, and Sundays from 10am until 2pm and admission is 200 ptas*

When you're done with the museum, return to the Calle de los Leales, and pass under the arch cut into the wall which then leads into the Plaza de la Catedral. The huge structure on your left side is the famous **Catedral**, the apse of which is actually integrated into the old town walls. As soon as you see the bizarre lion sculptures chained by their mouths into the main entrance door, you know you're in for something special. Construction of this massive cathedral started in the Romanesque style during the 12th century but during the process of 300 years of different architects imposing their ideas for updates and renovations it began to also include many Gothic elements.

The interior is comprised of both granite as well as pink and white stone which lead up to high trapezoid vaults which culminate in keystones that have been carved with floral patterns. Of note inside the structure are bold gothic windows, a beautiful series of 16th century Renaissance marble and walnut choir stalls, several side chapels of various time periods, 15th century paintings by , and a 16th century alabaster altar piece by Vasco de la Zarza. A small museum contains wonderful Gothic grillwork, huge choir books, 15th-18th century paintings, gold and silver religious plate, embroidery, sculptures and an unforgettable 16th century silver monstrance by Juan de Arte.

The cathedral is open daily from 10am until 1:30pm and again from 3:30pm until at 5pm during winter and 3:30pm until 630pm in the summer. Admission to the cathedralis free, but the museum and a few other small sections have a charge of 250 ptas per person.

After leaving the cathedral, immediately bear left and cross through the plaza until turning left onto the Calle de la Cruz Vieja. This small street winds its way into the dramatic **Plaza de la Calvo Sotelo**, which is enclosed by a few bank buildings and is centered around a pretty fountain. It is from the edge of this plaza that a fantastic rampart walk called the **Accesso a la Muralla** can be enjoyed above the old fortified walls. *Unfortunately you must pay 200 ptas for the privilege of getting to the top of the walls, and they are only open from about 10:30am until 1:30pm, and again from 5pm until 7:30pm from Tuesday through Sunday.*

Once you have experienced the old wall walk, return to the plaza and turn left onto the Calle de Generalismo Franco, then turn left at the next intersection which then will take you into the **Plaza del Teniente Arevalo**. Walk through this plaza and then bear right onto Calle Pedro Lagasca and

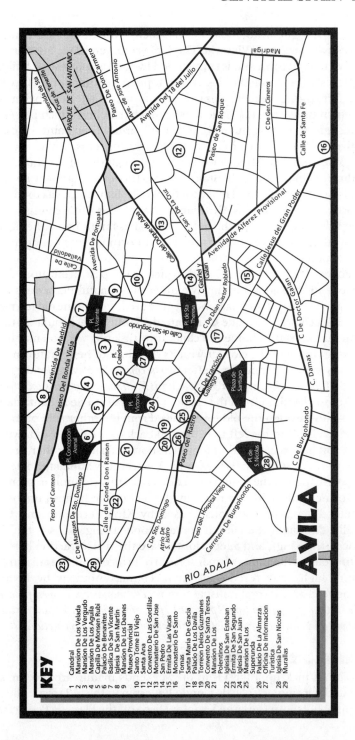

AVILA

RIO ADAJA

KEY

1. Catedral
2. Mansion De Los Velada
3. Mansion De Los Verdugo
4. Mansion De Los Aguila
5. Capilla De Monsen Rubi
6. Palacio De Benavites
7. Basilica De Lon Vicente
8. Iglesia De San Martin
9. Mansion De Los Deanes
10. Museo Provincial
11. Santo Tome El Viejo
12. Santa Ana
13. Convento De Las Gordillas
14. Monasterio De San Jose
15. San Pedro
16. Ermita De Las Vacas
17. Monasterio De Santo Tomas
18. Santa Maria De Gracia
19. Palacio De Davila
20. Torreon Delos Guzmanes
21. Convento De Santa Teresa
22. Mansion De Los Polentinos
23. Iglesia De San Esteban
24. Ermita De San Segundo
25. Iglesia De San Juan
26. Mansion De Los Superunda
27. Palacio De La Almarza
28. Oficina De Informacion Turistica
29. Iglesia De San Nicolas
30. Murallas

again turn right onto Calle de Caballeros which will lead into the impressive **Plaza de la Victoria**. This large commercial square is truly the heart of the old town and is surrounded by several interesting buildings, shops, restaurants and the clock tower topped **Ayuntamiento** (City Hall).

After visiting the main plaza, return down the Calle de Cabelleros and soon turn right onto the Calle de Martin Carrmolino which passes next to the **Iglesia de San Juan** where mystic and writer Saint Teresa was baptized in 1515. The church is only open during masses in the mornings and some evenings. After viewing at least the exterior of the church, keep heading down the Calle de Blasco Jimeno (no street sign may be visible, but just head straight) and make a left on Calle Sancho Dávila to reach the fantastic **Torreón de los Guzmánes** tower. This 15th century Gothic tower was once owned by the noble Guzmánes family before being taken over by the provincial government, and unfortunately is not open to the general public.

Follow Calle Madre Soledad, which leads past even more private palaces and mansions and finally ends at the tranquil **Plaza de la Santa**. The main feature of this plaza, besides the great view of the old town walls, is the 17th century baroque **Convento de Santa Teresa**, built on the site of this famous saint's home as a child. If you ask politely, you may be able to get a glimpse of the cloister with its paintings of her paranormal acts, as well as some of her personal effects. *The convent is open daily from 9:30am until 1:30pm and again from 3:30pm until 7:30pm and admission is free.*

Across the plaza from the convent is the **Puerta de la Santa** gateway that passes through the old town walls. From the other side of the gate, a road leads off to the left to bring you back to the center of town.

If you have a car, or don't mind a short taxi ride, another fine sight just south of the old town is the Gothic 15th century **Monasterio de Santo Tomás**. Shaped in the design of a Latin cross, this Dominican monastery and former university was not only the seat of the Inquisition, but also contained a palace occasionally used by King Fernando and Queen Isabella. Although the church contains only a singular isle, the Three Novices, the Kings, and Silent cloisters are the real attraction here. Also worth seeing is the alabaster mausoleum of Prince Juan, the amazing 15th century high altar reredos of Saint Thomas Aquinas by Pedro de Berruguete, and several unusual tombs. *The monastery is open from 11am until 1:00pm and again from 4pm until 7pm; admission is 150 ptas for the both the choir and cloisters, and another 200 ptas for the museum sections.*

NIGHTLIFE & ENTERTAINMENT

Things pick up after 11pm on weekends mainly around the small pubs and bars along Calle de Conde Vallespin in the old town. The great late night hotspot is the large **Xanofer Disco** off the Plaza de Pedro Davila.

PRACTICAL INFORMATION

- **Main City Tourist Office** – *Turismo, Plaza de la Catedral, 4, Tel. (920) 211-387*
- **Bus Station** – *Avenida de* Madrid, *Tel. (920) 220-154*
- **Avilabus** - *Tel. (920) 252-411*
- **Train Station** – *Avenida José Antônio, Tel. (920) 220-188 or (20) 250-202*
- **Municipal Police** – *Tel. 091*

Major Local Festivals

Contact the local Turismo office, *Tel. (920) 211-387,* for exact details.
- **Semana Santa,** *Easter Week, Strange Processions*
- **Fiesta Santa Teresa,** *Mid-October, Parades and Festivals*

SEGOVIA

Few cities in Europe offer so many fine structures dating from the 1st through the 15th centuries in such a concentrated area. **Segovia** is a delightful place where in the space of one or two days you can really become familiar with the entirety of the magnificent old town.

Each plaza has yet another great church that awaits your visit, while every side street seems to be lined with one opulent mansion after another. Plus, all along the tour I've laid out for you below you will find plenty of great bakeries and cafés, so take your time and bring some extra film to really enjoy a trip through the centuries in this memorable city.

ARRIVALS & DEPARTURES

By Bus

Most bus lines between Segovia and other parts of Spain arrive at the Estación de Autobuses bus station off the Paseo Ezequil Gonzalez that is 18 blocks or so southeast of the old city. From here, municipal bus #3 goes to the Plaza Mayor for 85 *ptas*, or you can hire a taxi for about 565 *ptas*.

By Car

From Madrid, the fastest way here is to take the high speed A-6 motorway northwest for 71 kilometers (44 miles). Exit near the town of Vilacastin where you will connect onto the smaller route N-110 northeast for about 36 kilometers (22 miles) before reaching the signs directing you to city. If coming here from Ávila, just follow the N-110 northeast for some 68 kilometers (42 miles).

Once inside the city you will have to spend a fair amount of time looking for metered street side parking, or pull into the private and municipal parking lots that charge about 1,650 *ptas* or more per day.

By Train

Segovia is connected to the rest of Spain by extensive rail service via Renfe. The large **Estación de** Renfe is located well outside of the old town walls on the southeast part of the suburbs at the Plaza de la Estación. From here you can either take municipal bus #3 to the Plaza Mayor for 85 ptas., or pay around 720 *ptas* for a taxi into the heart of the old town.

ORIENTATION

Segovia with a population of 69,327 rests above the Eresma river in the Castilla y León region of north central Spain, 93 kilometers (58 miles) northwest of Madrid.

GETTING AROUND TOWN

By Bus

Segovia's municipal bus company has several Autobuses that criss-cross the city and its suburbs. Most people will have no need to use any transportation here other than their feet. For those who wish to walk a little bit less, getting around town and its outskirts by bus is relatively easy.

The city has several different bus lines, all numbered for convenience, and dozens of well-marked bus stops. Ask anyone standing at a nearby bus stop or the helpful *Turismo* tourist office for route details. Most buses operate every 15 minutes in both directions from about 6:30am until 9:30pm daily, with less frequent service on weekends and holidays. The fare is 85 *ptas* per ride, and tickets can be paid for on the bus.

By Taxi

A couple of hundred taxis roam the streets, plaza side taxi stands, and major passenger arrival points of this the city 24 hours a day. To find a taxi, either hail an unoccupied taxi that happens to be driving by, call for a radio taxi pick up, or go to one of the dozens of obvious taxi stands throughout the city. Taxis charge customers using meters and the fare usually will cost somewhere around 510 *ptas* per ride (not per person between most downtown areas. Legally chargeable supplements are posted on a sticker in the taxi's interior.

WHERE TO STAY

Expensive

PARADOR DE SEGOVIA, *Carretera de Valladolid. Tel. (921) 443-737, Fax (921) 437-362. US & Canada bookings (Marketing Ahead), Tel. 800/223-1356. Year round rack rates from 18,500 ptas per double room per night (E.P.). All major credit cards accepted.*

This wonderful modern (chalet-style) four-star hotel is a great place to stay for deluxe visitors who have a rental car. Located about three minutes drive from the heart of the old town with great views out over the city, this government owned property is packed with the best services and facilities in the area. The sun-drenched *parador* has 113 large and beautifully decorated rooms and opulent suites, all with deluxe marble private bathrooms, air conditioning, tile and hardwood flooring, electronic key pass locks, hair dryers, satellite color television, mini-bar, modern furnishings, direct dial telephones, outdoor terraces with great panoramic views and nice artwork.

Facilities include indoor and outdoor swimming pools, an excellent regional restaurant, bar, fireside lounges, meeting and convention facilities, trails, gardens, plenty of free parking, sauna, health club, tennis courts, massage rooms, sun deck, foreign currency exchange and an indoor garage. Service here is first rate, and the people working here are really nice. This is the best hotel in town.

Moderate

HOTEL INFANTA ISABEL, *Calle de Isabella Catolica. Tel. (921) 443-105. Fax (921) 433-240. US & Canada Bookings (Golden Tulip), Tel. 800/344-1212. Year round rack rates from 12,100 ptas per double room per night (E.P.). All major credit cards accepted*

Situated less than half a block off the central Plaza Mayor, this romantic little three-star hotel (it really should have four) is the best place to stay downtown! The magnificently decorated property offers guests some 29 superb rooms that all have air conditioning, remote control color satellite television, in-room music, mini-bar, direct dial telephones, mini-safe, extremely comfortable furnishings, cute floral lithographs, excellent beds, and several of the best rooms offer fantastic views of the cathedral from their small balconies.

Facilities include a nice restaurant, laundry and dry cleaning services, foreign currency exchange, nice public rooms and a really friendly staff that can assist you with suggestions on sightseeing and local restaurants. Call well in advance for reservations, as they are sold out much of the time.

Inexpensive

RESIDENCIA DON JAIME, *Calle de Ochoa Ondategui, 8. Tel. (921) 444-787, no Fax. Low season rack rates from 5,000 ptas per double room per night (E.P.). High season rack rates from 5,400 ptas per double room per night (E.P.). Some credit cards accepted.*

This new one-star inn near the old aqueduct offers an excellent value for its 16 double rooms, each with feature either private or shared bathrooms, heating, simple but comfortable furnishings, and radios. Not much here in the way of facilities besides the television room, but the accommodations are clean and well decorated for the price.

WHERE TO EAT

Moderate

MESON DE JOSÉ MARÍA, *Calle de Cronista Lecea, 11. Tel. (921) 462-111. Most major credit cards accepted*

This medium-sized regional restaurant just off the Plaza Mayor is packed with local families that come here on every weekend. Their large main dining room is lined with murals and features Castellana soup, fish soup, large vegetable salads, white asparagus, smoked salmon, shrimp with garlic, baked filet of sole and entrecote of beef. A good and solid three-course meal here costs around 2,450 *ptas* a person plus beverages.

LA CONCEPCION, *Plaza Mayor, 15. Tel. (921) 433-693. All major credit cards accepted*

With its prime location, this nice little eating establishment and outdoor café in the town's main square is usually full of European tourists looking for a nice environment and a simple meal. Their menu contains such internationally favored items as cream of onion soup, chickpea soup, eggs with ham, assorted omelets, Russian salad, smoked fish, calamari, Osso Bucco, red peppers stuffed with crab, squid in their own ink, and a good selection of Spanish wines and regional desserts. Expect a lunch or dinner to set you back around 2,35 *ptas* per person plus wine.

Inexpensive

HAMBURGERCERIA LA GRANJA, *Calle de la Alhondiga, 6. Cash only - no credit cards accepted*

Although far from fancy, this small restaurant near the Plaza de Juan Bravo offers an assortment of sandwiches, and combination plates including hake, pork cutlets, burgers or chicken served with salad and French fries for between 600 and 995 *ptas*. A good choice for those on tight budgets.

SEEING THE SIGHTS

Approximate duration (by foot) of the walking tour below is about 5 hours, including church, fortress, aqueduct, mansion, museum, monument, and side street visits.

Start at the central Plaza Mayor square. Besides being lined by delightful outdoor cafés, candy kiosks, and even a couple of ATM electronic banking machines, this great plaza is also home to the main *Turismo* office where you really should pick up a free map of the old town. The other notable attraction in the square is Segovia's elaborate 16th century Gothic **Catedral** cathedral. Topped by imaginative spires and supported by a series of flying buttresses, this huge structure was designed by Juan Gil de Hontanon and finished off by his son Rodrigo Gil de

Hontanon. On most weekend afternoons, a band of local gypsy women sell their not-so-hand-made embroidered tablecloths in front of the cathedral's main entrance.

Inside there are three naves with an assortment of side chapels between its buttresses, an ambulatory, a semicircular apse, radial chapels, and a huge tower. Just beside the door leading into the cathedral is the **Capilla La Piedad** chapel with a wonderful 16th century altarpiece by Juan de Juni. The **Capilla Mayor** main chapel contains a dramatic 18th century neo-classical altarpiece made from marble and bronze, designed by Francisco Sabatini of Italy. A wrought iron screen closes it off. Other chapels hold fine paintings by masters from the Renaissance period. Inside the Coro choir area there are choir stalls (originally from the older cathedral that once stood near the Alcázar before it burned down in the 16th century), and two hand-crafted 18th century organs.

Pass through the **Claustro** cloister (transported here stone by stone from the ruined old cathedral) to enter inside the **Sala Capitular** chapter house, where there are several 17th century Flemish tapestries beneath its spectacular ceilings. Also worth a visit is the **Museo Catedralico** religious art museum with its fine collection of gold and silver objects, 16th through 18th century paintings and sculpture, and other treasures.

The cathedral is open daily from 9am until at least 7pm in the Summer, and during the Winter it can be entered on weekdays from *9:30am until 1pm and again from 3pm until 6pm, while during the Winter weekends it is from 9:30am until 6pm, all with no entrance charge. The museum is open during pretty much the same hours and costs 200 ptas to enter.*

After leaving the cathedral via its main facade overlooking the plaza, bear right, and then turn right on the next street called the Calle de San Frutos. After another block, turn left onto the Calle de Juderia Vieja that once marked the center of the old Barrio Juderia Jewish quarter. A block or so up this street cuts through the **Plaza del Corpus** square where on the right hand side is a small church with a doorway marked *Corpus Cristi*. Before the Inquisition, this was the sight of a 13th century Jewish **Sinagoga** (synagogue), and was severely damaged by a fire in 1899, thus is still being reconstructed and is currently not open to the public.

Now cut through the plaza and continue ahead as the street merges into the **Calle de Juan Bravo**. This wide, interesting lane is home to countless boutiques and bakeries on the ground floors of beautiful old mansions. In another block or so on the left hand side, you will find the fantastic **Plaza de Juan Bravo Square** named in honor of its former resident who was executed after leading a revolt against the high taxes imposed by the new Emperor Carlos V.

The plaza is home to several amazing structures including the 17th century Baroque **Antigua Carcel** former prison that is now a library, the

12th century Romanesque **Iglesia de San Martin** church and bell tower with its unique front porch, a large statue of Sr. Juan Bravo holding up a sword in defiance, and behind it is the 14th century **Torreón de Lozoya** tower where local art exhibitions may be open to the public. If you're lucky, Sr. Ramon will pose with his mural of traditionally costumed figures (with their heads cut out in order to insert yours) while his antique instant camera captures the humorous image for a mere 1,000 *ptas*. Keep walking along the same street until then passing the 15th century **Casa de los Picos** mansion (now a school of applied arts) with its one-of-a-kind facade of diamond shaped ornaments.

Soon the street merges into the Calle de Cervantes and cuts through the old town walls before leading into the **Plaza del Azoguejo** square. This large plaza is the best place to see the remarkable 1st century Roman **Acueducto** aqueduct. It spans some 728 meters (2,392 feet) in length and still carries fresh mountain water along its elevated path towers that reach up over 28 meters (92 feet) above ground level. There is a set of stairways on the left side of the plaza that will bring adventurous hikers on a stunning panoramic walkway above the old town walls and is open daily for free from sunrise to sunset. There is also a small *Turismo* office in the square for those entering the city from this access point.

Cross beneath the spans of the aqueduct and turn left onto the Calle de San Juan as it ascends and then curves to the left as it passes in front of the Romanesque **Iglesia de San Sebastian** church. At this point the street changes its name to the Calle de San Augustin and cuts throughout the **Plaza del Conde de Cheste**, where several noblemans' mansions including the stunning **Casa de los Marqueses de Moya**.

On the right side of the street at the far edge of the plaza take a right turn onto the Calle de los Zuloagas and head straight to the imaginative portico, full of interesting carvings, at the 11th century Romanesque **Iglesia de San Juan de los Caballeros** church, the oldest house of worship still standing in town. The building also contains the **Museo Zuloaga** art museum and former studio of famed 20th century Spanish ceramic artisan Daniel Zuloaga and his son Igancio's paintings. *The museum is open Tuesday through Saturday from 10am until 1:30pm and again from 4pm until 6pm, Sundays from 10am until 2pm. Admission is 175 ptas*

Now retrace your steps back to the Plaza del Conde de Cheste and turn right to once again follow the Calle de San Agustin. A few blocks later, bear right at the fork in the road onto the Calle de San Nicolás and follow into the picturesque **Plaza de San Nicolás** where no less than three majestic structures will capture your attention. On the right side of the square is the 12th century Romanesque **Iglesia de San Nicolás** church that can be visited for free during daily masses to see a series of medieval paintings in its main and side chapels.

On the right side of the plaza is the 12th century **Iglesia de las Trinidad** church that contains beautiful Romanesque porticos. Almost adjacent to the church is the magnificent 13th century **Torre de Hercules** defensive tower that was later taken over by the adjoining Dominican monastery.

After passing through the plaza, continue along the same road (it's renamed the Calle de San Quirce here). At the next block you will pass by a couple of nice churches just before turning left onto the Calle de Capuchinos Alta and a few steps later turning right onto the Travesia Capuchinos that will lead straight towards the amazing **Plaza de San Esteban**. This square is flanked on top by the unforgettable 12th century Romanesque **Iglesia y Torre de San Esteban** church and dramatic tower. Just across the square is the 18th century Renaissance **Palacio Episcopal** church office building. From the bottom of the square, follow the nearby Calle del Escuderos right back into the **Plaza Mayor**.

Walk to the left side of the cathedral and follow the Calle de San Frutos down for a block or so before making a wide right turn onto the Calle de Barrio Nuevo that will lead you around the rear of the cathedral. This street more or less merges into the Calle de Martinez Campos that now leads beyond the back of the cathedral and passes alongside the old town walls. A block or so later you will find the charming little **Plazuela de Socorro** with its 13th century **Puerta de San Andrés** gateway that was once the main entrance to the Jewish quarter of town.

These days the gateway has a small chapel on top of it, and the adjoining building at #1 is for sale (you wouldn't believe the price!). Keep following the side of the old walls as the street name now changes to the Calle de Socorro and passes by the peach colored 14th century stone **Casa del Sol** fort house built right into the defensive walls. Recently the structure was modified to accommodate the **Museo de Segovia** provincial art and archaeology museum with a good collection of fine arts and locally found relics. *The museum is open Tuesday through Saturday from 10am until 2pm and again from 5pm until 7pm, Sundays from 10am until 2pm, and costs 100 ptas to enter.*

After the museum, keep following the old walls as the street name once again changes, this time to the Ronda de Don Juan II, and then leads past the well-manicured gardens of the **Plaza del la Reina Victoria Regina**, a panoramic promenade off to the left. Just behind the promenade you can miss the stunning turreted silhouette of the incomparable 12th through 14th century **Alcázar** fortress. Built on the sight of a Roman era fortress, this amazing structure had to be completely rebuilt from the ground up in the 19th century after a devastating fire.

This was the place from which Isabella emerged and walked into the Plaza Mayor to be crowned as the Queen of Spain. Inside you can see several rooms and chambers that contain 16th century furnishings, suits of armor, *Mudéjar* woodwork, antique Flemish tapestries, royal thrones, stained glass windows, murals, royal portraits, 16th century altarpieces, old guns, military objects and the former jail housed inside the tower. There are various balconies, patios, and windows that look outward across the riverbed towards the **Monasterio de El Parral**. *The fortress is open from daily from 9am until at least 6pm, and the entrance fee is 400 ptas.*

EXCURSIONS & DAY TRIPS

If you have seen all the major sights in Segovia and want to spend at least a few hours visiting the area outside of the city, here a few of the best day-trips. Since few excursions are offered by major companies, you may need to take a bus, train, rent a car, or private guide with a sedan to get to the following destinations.

LA GRANJA DE SAN ILDEFONSO

Located about 11 kilometers (7 miles) southeast of Segovia, with a population of 4, 940, the 18th century royal palace known as **La Granja** is the best to visit on a nice day. Surrounded by luscious gardens amidst a peaceful mountainous backdrop, this luxurious summer palace was built for King Filipe V to remind him of his upbringing at Versailles, France.

While still not completely restored after a disastrous fire at the turn of this century, you can still admire several lavish rooms laced with fine antique furnishings, Flemish tapestries, frescoes, locally produced chandeliers, chapel and the adjacent fountain-lined formal gardens.

Hours

The La Granja palace is open Tuesday through Saturday from 10am until 1:30pm and again from 3pm until 5pm, Sundays from 10am until 3pm, and admission is 400 ptas per person. The gardens are open are open daily from 10am until at least 6pm; the fountains are turned on only during Thursdays, Saturdays, and Sundays, sometime around 5:15pm or so.

Directions

To get here by car, take the N-601 highway south towards Madrid, following the exits for "La Granja" after traveling about 11 kilometers (7 miles).

Bus service here is provided via Segovia about 8 times per day in each direction, with a round-trip cost of some 950 *ptas*.

Major Local Festivals

Contact Segovia's Turismo office, *Tel. (921) 430-328,* for exact details.
- **Festa San Luis**, *Late August – Young Bull Fights*

PALACIO DE RIO FRIO

The 18th century **Palacio de Rio Frío** royal summer palace was built for **Queen Isabel Farnese**. This odd pink palace offers guided tours through its occasionally dramatic rooms. Later used as a noble hunting lodge, there is also a museum of hunting with some interesting portraits of royal hunters, and a selection of stuffed animals that live in the nearby park. Far from enchanting, but it makes a reasonably decent side trip on a rainy day.

Hours

The Rio Frío palace is open Tuesday through Saturday from 10am until 1:30pm and again from 3pm until 5pm, Sundays from 10am until 3pm, and admission is 300 ptas per person to enter the building and drive through its nearby park preserve area.

Directions

To get here by car, take the N-603 highway south towards Madrid, following the exits for "Rio Frio" after traveling about 11 kilometers (7 miles).

PRACTICAL INFORMATION
- **Regional Tourist Office**, *Turismo, Plaza Mayor, 10. Tel. (921) 440-302*
- **Regional Train Office**, *Renfe. Tel. (921) 420-774*
- **Regional Bus Info**, *Estación de Autobuses. Tel. (921) 427-725*
- **Segovia Radio Taxi Companies**, *Tel. (921) 445-000*
- **Central Post Office**, *Plaza de Doctor Laguna, 5. Tel. (921) 431-611*
- **Regional Directory Assistance**, *Tel. 1003*
- **National Directory Assistance**, *Tel. 1009*
- **Red Cross Ambulances**, *Tel. (921) 430-311*
- **National Police**, *Tel. (921) 426-363*
- **Municipal Police**, *Tel. 431-212*

Major Local Festivals

Contact the local Turismo office, *Tel. (921) 430-328,* for exact details.
- **Semana Santa**, *March or April, Eight Religious Processions*
- **Fiesta San Juan & Pedro**, *Late June, Processions and Feasts*
- **Fiesta Musica**, *July, Folklore and Concerts*
- **Fiesta San Frutos**, *Late October, Processions*

SALAMANCA

The historic university city of **Salamanca** is the most enchanting place to visit in this entire large region. Originally settled by Celtiberian tribes, the area was transformed into a strategically important city while under the control of the Romans. Centuries later, after passing through hands of the Moors, it began a new life as a major center of education and commerce.

There are hundreds of beautiful mansions, churches, and university buildings to explore throughout the old quarter of the city, all of which seem to compete for attention. This is a city that deserves at least a couple of days to experience. If you get lost, just ask a student for directions – many of them are foreign and may speak better English than we do!

ARRIVALS & DEPARTURES

By Air

Salamanca's small regional airport is called the Aeropuerto de Salamanca-Matacan and is located just off route N-501, 14 kilometers (9 miles) east of town.

Buses between the Airport & Downtown

The special bus service between the airport and downtown is currently under revision. Check with the Turismo for up to date information, prices, and schedules.

Taxis from the Airport to Downtown

Taxis are usually marked with the *Taxi* sign, and can be found at the taxi stand at the airport. Almost all of the taxis are fairly small four-door cars. Normally, taxi's trunks can hold about two large suitcases, but those with roof racks can secure two more medium pieces of luggage, and perhaps a couple of carry-on bags inside as well. Expect to pay between 1,650-1,950 *ptas* per ride from the airport to most downtown locations.

By Bus

Most of the bus lines between Salamanca and other parts of Spain arrive at the Estación de Autobuses bus station on the northwestern outskirts of town. From here you might have to take a taxi for sabout 525 ptas. to reach the old quarter of the city.

By Car

From Madrid, the best way here is to take the A-6 highway northeast. After about 68 kilometers (42 miles), you will be led through a high speed tunnel that cuts through part of the dramatic Sierra de Guadarrama mountain range (there's a toll of 675 *ptas*). About 20 kilometers (12 miles) after the tunnel, exit the highway at "Villacastin," and follow the indications towards Ávila, about 24 kilometers (15 miles) southeast on route N-110. After reaching Ávila, look for signs pointing to route N-501 west upon which you will drive about 97 kilometers (60 miles) to reach Salamanca.

Once inside the city you will have a tough time finding street-side metered parking, so ask your hotel or look for one of several parking lots charging about 1,850 *ptas* per day.

By Train

Salamanca is connected to the rest of Spain and Europe by extensive rail service via Renfe. Travelers will find themselves using the much larger Estación de Ferrocarril just off the Plaza de Estación on the northeastern outskirts of town. From here you may have to take a taxi for about 480 *ptas* or so into the old quarter.

ORIENTATION

Salamanca, population 159,342, is situated in the western part of central Spain in the Castilla y León region, some 212 kilometers (131 miles) northwest of Madrid, and about 97 kilometers (60 miles) northwest of Ávila.

GETTING AROUND TOWN

By Taxi

A few hundred licensed taxis roam the streets, plaza-side taxi stands, and major passenger arrival points 24 hours a day. To find a taxi, either hail one on the street, go to one of the dozens of obvious taxi stands throughout the city, or call Salamanca Radio Taxi Companies, *Tel. (923) 230-000,* for a radio response pick up on demand.

Taxis charge customers using meters and the fare usually will cost somewhere around 450 *ptas* per ride (not per person) between most downtown areas. Legally chargeable supplements are posted on a sticker in the taxi's interior.

WHERE TO STAY

Expensive

N.H. PALACIO DE CASTELLANOS, *Calle de San Pablo, 58. Tel. (923) 261-818, Fax (923) 261-819. US & Canada Bookings (UTELL), Tel. 800/44-UTELL. Year round rack rates from 18,200 ptas per double room per night (E.P.). All major credit cards accepted.*

The fantastic Palacio de Castellanos is a converted nobleman's mansion in the heart of the old quarter, just across the street from the San

Esteban Convent. The structure itself dates back to the 15th century, and has been declared a protected historic monument. After minor structural renovations, and a sophisticated interior refitted to further expose the centuries-old masonry, the four-star hotel now boasts some of Spain's most exquisite public rooms and guest accommodations.

Here you can choose between one of 67 deluxe sun-drenched rooms and duplex suites that all offer air conditioning, marble bathrooms stocked with fine European amenities, remote control satellite television with VCR, mini-bar, fine designer furnishings, am-fm clock radios, direct dial telephones and beautiful art.

The hotel also offers beautiful lounges, a rather exceptional restaurant, an outdoor patio and bar, business meeting rooms, private dining facilities, an indoor garage, complimentary video tape rental service, currency exchange, laundry and dry cleaning services, child care and much, much, more. Service here is first class, and the youthful professional staff even smile while assisting the guests. If you want the best possible place to stay in town, at a price that is well below what might be expected, this is the place to consider. This former palace gets my highest recommendation for luxury, service, facilities and rooms.

GRAND HOTEL R, *Calle Poeta Iglesias, 3. Tel. (923) 213-500, Fax (923) 213-501. Year round rack rates from 19,500 ptas per double room per night (E.P.). All major credit cards accepted*

Located just below the central Plaza Mayor, this medium-sized old world hotel is the second best bet in the upper price range. Completely renovated in 1992, the hotel now features 100 or so nice rooms that all have air conditioning, private bathrooms, satellite televisions, mini-bar, in-room music systems, and comfortable furnishings. Facilities here include a regional restaurant, meeting rooms, parking, concierge and a helpful front desk.

Moderate

HOTEL SAN POLO, *Calle Arroyo de Santo Domingo, 3. Tel. (923) 211-177, Fax (923) 211-177. Year round rack rates from 13,500 ptas per double room per night (E.P.). All major credit cards accepted*

With its tranquil position on the edge of the old town, this brand new three- star executive class hotel is the winner in this price range. Its 36 large modern rooms are air conditioned, have beautiful private bathrooms, and feature soundproof walls, direct dial telephones, satellite television, mini-safe, and either interior or more dramatic exterior views. Their facilities include a restaurant, parking, meeting rooms and a helpful staff.

PARADOR DE SALAMANCA, *Calle Teso de la Feria, 2. Tel. (923) 268-700, Fax (923) 215-438. US & Canada bookings (Marketing Ahead), Tel. 800/*

223-1356. Low season rack rates from 14,000 ptas per double room per night (E.P.). High season rack rates from 16,500 ptas per double room per night (E.P.). All major credit cards accepted.

Although not as dramatic as some of the other government-owned inns listed in this book, this moden *parador* across the Roman bridge from the old part of the city is a reasonably friendly and comfortable alternative to some of the more expensive hotels listed above. Here you can stay in one of one hundred single and double air conditioned rooms (some are wheelchair accessible) that all have nice private bathrooms, remote control cable television, mini-bar, am-fm clock radios, direct dial phones and nice interior or exterior views. The *parador* also has a good regional restaurant, parking, outdoor swimming pool and a tennis court.

HOTEL REGIO, *Carretera de Salamanca, Km. 4. Tel. (923) 138-888, Fax (923) 138-044. Year round rack rates from 13,500 ptas per double room per night (E.P.). Most major credit cards accepted*

Located less than a five minute drive from the historic heart of downtown Salamanca, this modern four-star full service hotel is a good consideration for those who are traveling by car and want to save a bit of money while sightseeing in the area. The hotel has 121 air conditioned modern rooms with private bathrooms, color satellite television, direct dial telephones, rather comfortable furnishings, and large balconies. There are also meeting rooms, a good regional restaurant, free outdoor parking, tennis courts, a large outdoor swimming pool and safe deposit boxes available to all guests.

Inexpensive

HOSTAL EMPERATRIZ, *Rua Mayor, 18. Tel. (923) 219-156. Low season rack rates from 7,000 ptas per double room per night (E.P.). High season rack rates from 8,000 ptas per double room per night (E.P.). Most major credit cards accepted*

This small hostel is connected to a more expensive hotel of the same name offers a dozen large, well maintained rooms with private bathrooms on the old quarter's main street. Although far from fancy, it's a good choice for those on a tight budget.

RESIDENCIA CUZCO, *Calle de Canalejas, 166. Tel. (923) 265-745, No Fax. Year round rack rates from 5,500 ptas per double room per night (E.P.). Most major credit cards accepted*

The newly designed Cuzco is a simple full service two-star hotel in the heart of Salamanca, with more facilities and services than any other hotel in this price range. There are 18 nicely furnished rooms with central heating, satellite television, private bathroom, and telephones. There is also a nice terrace, a good restaurant, nearby parking, 24-hour room service, foreign currency exchange, and a nice staff.

HOTEL PASAJE, *Calle de Espoz y Mina, 25. Tel. (923) 212-003, Fax (923) 214-261. Year round rack rates from 6,950 ptas per double room per night (E.P.). Cash only.*

Located just off the central Plaza Mayor, the Pasaje is a basic two-star hotel offering 62 pleasant but air conditioned and heated simple rooms with private bathrooms, direct dial telephone, and television. Nothing fancy, but a good value in this section of the city.

WHERE TO EAT

Moderate

CHEZ VICTOR, *Calle de Espoz y Mina, 26. Tel. (923) 213-12. Most major credit cards accepted.*

Expert chef and proprietor Victor Salvador Macias has created a wonderfully romantic and welcoming little restaurant where the French inspired cuisine is simply outstanding. Here you can sit in the beautifully rustic styled dining room and enjoy an assortment of seasonal fish, meat, and game dishes prepared from ingredients that have been brought straight from the local markets and farms. Expect to spend somewhere around 5,500 *ptas* per person for a wonderful gourmet meal with superb service. Reservations are often necessary, and I suggest you consider dressing up a bit before coming here.

ASADOR ARANDINO, *Calle de Azucena, 5. Tel. (923) 217-382. All major credit cards accepted.*

Located in the heart of Salamanca, this nationally famous dining establishment has perfected the art of cooking traditional Castillian style regional cuisine. Here you can enjoy a fine meal for around 4,850 *ptas* per person, that might include oven roasted meats and freshly caught fish, all with a great bottle of reasonably priced Ribero del Duero wine. The service is great, and if you love huge portions of hearty meats, this is the place to check out first.

LE SABLON, *Calle de Espoz y Mina, 20. Tel. (923) 262-952. Most major credit cards accepted.*

This cute little French restaurant features a good assortment of fish and meat dishes that start at about 2,100 *ptas* and up. With its relaxing decor, affordable menu, and proximity to the Plaza Mayor, it has become a favorite of visitors and locals alike.

RIO DE LA PLATA, *Plaza del Peso, 1. Tel. (923) 219-005. Most major credit cards accepted.*

Operating in a quaint location near in the center of the city, the Andres family has continued to present its simple yet imaginative regional cuisine at the Rio de la Plata restaurant since 1958. With affordable prices (approximately 3,850 *ptas* and up per person for a 3 course meal) and friendly service, this dining establishment is among the favorites of the local businessmen and families. Call in advance for reservations as they get pretty busy, especially during the warmer months.

Inexpensive

EL BARDO, *Calle de Compania, 8. Tel. (923) 219-089. Cash only.*

When you're in the mood for budget meals, join half of the university students as they head for this hole in the wall restaurant that features super cheap daily specials and an assortment of *tapas*. The last time I ate here, a complete lunch with three courses cost only 1,350 *ptas* or so. Nothing fancy, but still a real good place.

RESTAURANTE ROMA, *Calle de Ruiz Aguilera, 12. Tel. Unlisted. Cash only.*

Another good budget place for both students and tourists alike. Daily special plates with soup and salad may cost as little as 975 *ptas* each and are relatively good for the money.

SEEING THE SIGHTS

Approximate duration (by foot) is about 5 hours, including church, cathedral, university, museum, monument, and side street visits.

While there are dozens of possible places to start off your adventures through the old lanes of this fascinating city, I suggest using the Baroque central **Plaza Mayor** town square as your jumping off point. Built in the early 18th century by Alberto and Nicolás Churriguera (for whom Spain's unique *Churriguesque* style of design has been named for), this constantly active plaza is surrounded by a series of four story mansions and government buildings whose facades are embellished with fine iron balconies, sculpted images of famous Spaniards between each of the ground floor archways, and pinnacle-topped roofing.

This was also once the sight of large public functions including the occasional bullfight. The city's dramatic **Ayuntamiento** town hall building designed by Andrés Garcia de Quiñones on the north side of the square is the most obvious highlight here. During warm days, the entire populace seems to stroll through the Plaza Mayor at least half a dozen times to check out the scene and perhaps indulge in an overpriced coffee at one of several outdoor cafés located in front of the arches.

After passing through the main square's south exit via the El Corrillo gateway, you will find yourself on the Calle de El Corillo. At the next corner, bear left and walk a few paces until passing in front of the 12th century Romanesque **Iglesia de San Martin** church. Besides noticing the fine Baroque window and older spires, take a good look up towards the church's tower where pairs of storks have been known to build their nests.

From the front facade of the church, walk directly across onto the wide Rua Mayor. As one of the major streets through the old quarter of town, here you will find a good selection of boutiques, souvenir shops, and moderately priced restaurants. Keep walking down the Rua Mayor for a few blocks before turning right onto the Calle de Compañia and passing the 15th century **Casa de las Conchas** just off the corner. This mansion was owned by the local chancellor of the Order of Saint James, and he had several hundred carvings of scallop shells placed on its stone block facade, a motif representing the yearly pilgrimage to **Santiago de Compostela**. Also worth seeing is the carving of the royal crest above its main arched doorway, the exquisite Gothic iron window grilles, and the ornate second floor window frames. Once inside the house you can see its delightful inner courtyard, grand staircase, and artistic wooden ceilings.

Entry is free on weekdays from 9am until 9pm, and on weekends from 10am until 2pm and again from 4pm until 7pm.

Just across the street from here is the Baroque 17th century **Universidad Pontifica** Jesuit college complex. Designed by famed architect Juan Gómez de Mora, it can be entered through its beautiful central cloister. *Limited sections of the college can be visited for free on weekdays only from 9am until 2pm and again from 4pm until 8pm.*

If you get here just after the one or two posted daily masses, you will also be permitted to enter the **Iglesia de la Clerecia** church that contains beautiful altarpieces. Walking one more block along the Calle de Compañia you will find the 15th century **Iglesia de San Benito** church just off to the right. Surrounded by stunning mansions once owned by powerful local families who killed each other's members during 14th century conflicts, the church became the premature final resting place for many of these feuding family's members caught up in the violence. You can enter the church for free during regular daily masses to see its simple single nave and fine altarpiece.

Now retrace your steps back down the Calle de Compañia until you pass the house with the scallop shells and then bear sharply to the right onto Calle Serranos. After a block and a half, make a left turn onto the Calle de Libreros and walk another block or so until finding the **Patio de Escuelas** student's courtyard on the right side of the street. This is the main access area into the **Universidad de Salamanca** university, founded in 1243 by King Alfonso IX, and is centered around a large Italian bronze statue of **Fray Luis de León**, a famed professor, poet, and leader of the school during the 16th century. Legend has it that after being imprisoned during the Inquisition for his works, Fray Luis returned to his classroom, blurted out the words, "As we were saying yesterday", and finished off the lecture that he had begun some five years earlier.

Both sides of the street are surrounded by a series of exceptional university buildings that can be visited by the general public. Just behind the Patio de Escuelas' statue is the fantastic Platteresque main entrance that has been covered by outstanding pinnacle-topped friezes. From top to bottom they are carved with exceptional decorative motifs that surround the royal crest of King Carlos V, medallions with images of King Ferdinand and Queen Isabella along with a Greek inscription that translates to *"The Monarchs to the University, The University to the Monarchs,"* and scenes of the Pope in the process of exhorting his clergymen.

Once inside the main entrance you can view a series of old lecture halls, the original **Sala de Frey Luis** classroom of Fray Luis de León, the **Paraninfo** assembly room with antique Belgium tapestries and a portrait of King Carlos IV by Goya, a marble-filled 18th century baroque **Capilla** chapel with the tomb of Frey Luis, a series of fine staircases carved with medieval themes, and an amazing 18th century **Biblioteca** (library) stocked with over 150,00 rare volumes and hand-crafted baroque shelves.

Also off the Patio de Escuelas is the **Antiqua Rectorado** (old rectory) building of the university that now houses the **Casa Museo Unamuno** with recreations of former school rector Miguel de Unamuno's apartment, as well as his personal papers and manuscripts. Another less interesting museum known as the **Museo de la Universidad** (university museum) contains a collection of old books, tests, classroom furnishings and related objects. Nearby are the so-called **Escuelas Menores**, Platteresque 16th century university buildings with even more period classrooms, a beautiful ceiling decorated with zodiac motifs, and a smaller courtyard. Finally, the city has taken over the adjacent 16th century **Casa de los Doctores de la Reina** mansion once belonging to Queen Isabella's private physician, and installed a less than exciting **Museo Provincial de Bellas Artes** art and archaeological museum within its walls.

The university's main building can be entered Monday through Saturday from 9:30am until 1:30pm and again from 4pm until 8pm, as well as Sundays and holidays from 10am until 2pm. Admission to most parts of the complex is 200 ptas per adult, or 100 for senior citizens. The Unamuno museum is open Tuesday through Friday from 11am until 1:30pm and again from 4:30pm until 6:30pm and entry is free. The university museum is open from 9:30am until 1:30pm and again from 4pm until 6:30pm daily and entry is free. The Museo Provincial de Bellas Artes is open Tuesday through Saturday from 9:45am until 1:45pm and again from 5pm until 7:45pm, Sundays from 10:15am until 1:45pm. Admission is currently 200 ptas per adult, and 100 ptas for children and senior citizens.

After leaving the university area, continue heading along the Calle de Libreros and make the first left turn onto the Calle Nueva, which in turn leads to the exterior of the city's Gothic **Catedral Nueva** new cathedral. Originally designed by architect Juan Gil de Hontanon and built during the 16th through 18th centuries, this vaulted house of worship contains several luxurious side chapels, a central dome, a baroque tower, a Platteresque 16th century organ, lovely choir stalls designed by the Churriguera brothers, delicate stained glass and a Renaissance cloister.

Adjacent to, and supported by, this building is the more impressive **Catedral Vieja** that dates back to the 12th century and is fashioned in the Romanesque style. Back in the 14th century, those wishing to graduate from the nearby university with a Doctorate had to take their grueling examinations inside this building's chapels. With its fine **Torre de Gallo** tower, 15th century Italian altarpiece with its 53 paintings by Nicolás Florentino, Gothic mural lined chapels, amazing 15th century organ, cloisters and unique sepulchers, this cathedral may take over an hour to really examine in detail. Within the structure is the **Museo Diocesano**, a religious art museum that displays a collection of paintings by locally born 15th century artist Fernando Gallego. *The cathedrals and museum are open daily from 10am until 2pm and again from 4pm until at least 6pm. Admission is free for the new cathedral, and 200 ptas per person for the old cathedral and its museum.*

From the new cathedral, walk into the **Plaza Anaya** and bear right onto Calle de el Tostado for a block or so until turning left at the main Calle de San Pablo. Just off the right side is the exterior of the 16th century **Convento de las Dueñas** convent featuring a wonderful Renaissance cloister and Gothic church with seven domes. *Open daily from 10:30am until 1pm and again from 4pm until 7pm for 65 ptas per person.* Just across the way is the 16th century **Convento de San Esteban** convent with a church that features a massive wooden altar carved by José Churriguera, a nice cloister, and a highly decorated main facade. *This convent can be entered 9am until 1pm and again from 5pm until at least 6:30pm for 200 ptas per person.*

Now continue heading up the Calle de San Pedro for another block or two until reaching the **Plaza de Colón** where you will cut through the upper part of the plaza to reach the octagonal **Torre del Clavero** tower. Once part of a 15th century castle, this tower is the only part that still stands today. Entrance is currently not permitted, but you should take note of its dramatic exterior turrets. Now return to the Calle de San Pedro and follow it up and back into the Plaza Mayor, and you're done!

PRACTICAL INFORMATION
- **Regional Tourist Office**, *PPTS, Gran Via, 41. Tel. (923) 268-571*
- **Municipal Tourist Office**, *Turismo, Plaza Mayor, 10. Tel. (923) 218-342*
- **Salamanca Airport**, *Matacan. Tel. (923) 306-031*
- **Regional Train Info**, *Renfe. Tel. (923) 212-454*
- **Regional Bus Info**, *Estación de Autobuses. Tel. (923) 236-717*
- **Salamanca Radio Taxi Companies**, *Tel. (923) 230-000*

· **Central Post Office**, *Gran Via, 25. Tel. (923) 243-011*
· **Regional Directory Assistance**, *Tel. 1003*
· **National Directory Assistance**, *Tel. 1009*
· **Red Cross**, *Tel. (923) 214-134*
· **Ambulance**, *Tel. (923) 240-916*
· **National Police**, *Tel. (923) 262-750*
· **Municipal Police**, *Tel. (923) 265-311*

TOLEDO

The historic walled city of **Toledo** is one of the most enjoyable cities to just wander around in. As this strategic city passed hands between the Romans, Visigoths, Moors, and the Christian Kings, it grew larger and more concentrated.

In each separate neighborhood of the old town there are hundreds of fine structures that remain from various eras of the past. Besides having two of the only remaining Jewish synagogues in all of Spain, the city is also home to unique Arab mosques and countless churches, including the incredible 12th century **Catedral**. The city has also always been obsessed with defense (for good reason) and the fortress of the **Alcázar** remains a monument to this attitude and the town's strong political will.

Besides art, culture, and history, this great city also offers a huge range of local crafts, excellent shopping, quaint shady parks, good regional restaurants and unique hotels. To best enjoy a trip to Toledo, expect to spend a bare minimum of two full days exploring its narrow lanes and architectural treasures.

ARRIVALS & DEPARTURES

By Bus

Most of the bus lines between Toledo and other parts of Spain and Europe arrive at the Terminal de Autobuses bus station off the Calle Castilla–La Mancha, one kilometer (.62 mile) away from the old town in the more modern section. From here, municipal bus #5 goes to the *Turismo* for 70 *ptas*, or you can hire a taxi for about 520 *ptas*.

By Car

From Madrid, the fastest way here is to take the fast N-401 highway south for some 71 miles (44 miles) before reaching town. Once inside the city you will have to spend a fair amount of time looking for free streetside parking, or pull into the lots next to the Alzacar or Puerta de Sol that charge about 1,550 *ptas* or more per day. There is also a free lot just in front of the Hostal del Cardinal.

By Train

Toledo is connected to the rest of Spain by extensive rail service via Renfe. The large Estación Renfe is about two kilometers (1.5 miles) northeast of the old town across the river on the Paseo de la Rosa. From here you can either take municipal bus #5 to the *Turismo* office for 70 *ptas*, or pay around 695 *ptas* for a taxi into the heart of the old town.

ORIENTATION

Toledo rests on a hill above the Tajo river in the Castilla–La Mancha region of central Spain, 71 kilometers (44 miles) southwest of Madrid. The population is 60,242.

GETTING AROUND TOWN

By Bus

Toledo's municipal bus company has several Autobuses (buses) that criss-cross the city and its suburbs. Most people will have no need to use any transportation here other than their feet. For those who wish to walk a little bit less, getting around town and its outskirts by bus is relatively easy.

The city has over a dozen different bus lines, all numbered for convenience, and hundreds of well marked bus stops. Ask anyone standing at a nearby bus stop, or the helpful Turismo tourist office for route details. Most buses operate every 30 minutes in both directions from about 6am until 10pm daily, with less frequent service on weekends and holidays. The fare is 70 *ptas* per ride, and tickets can be paid for on the bus.

By Taxi

About one hundred licensed taxis roam the streets, plaza-side taxi stands, and major passenger arrival points of this the city during 24 hours each day. To find a taxi, either hail down an unoccupied taxi that happens to be driving by, call Toledo Radio Taxi Companies for a radio taxi pick up, *Tel. (925) 222-396*, or go to one of the dozens of obvious taxi stands throughout the city. Taxis charge customers using meters and the fare usually will cost somewhere around 425 *ptas* per ride (not per person!) between most downtown areas. Legally chargeable supplements are posted on a sticker in the taxi's interior.

WHERE TO STAY

Expensive

PARADOR CONDE DE ORGAZ, *Paseo de la Cigarrales. Tel. (925) 221-850, Fax (925) 225-166. US & Canada bookings (Marketing Ahead), Tel. 800/*

223-1356. Year round rack rates from 18,500 ptas per double room per night (E.P.). All major credit cards accepted.

Located across the Tajo river five minutes away by car from the old part of town, with great terraces featuring gardens and panomaric views out over the city, this four-star government-owned inn is a great place to stay for travelers who can afford it. The hotel features 76 nicely furnished rooms that all have private bathrooms, ceramic tile flooring, direct dial telephone, and reproduction antique furnishings. The *parador* also offers a good regional restaurant, tranquil gardens, foreign currency exchange, a nice outdoor pool, fantastic gardens and meeting rooms.

Moderate

HOTEL DOMENICO, *Cerro del Emparador. Tel. (925) 250-040, Fax (925) 252-877. US & Canada Bookings (Golden Tulip), Tel. 800/344-1212. Year round rack rates from 14,850 ptas per double room per night (E.P.). Special weekend rack rates from 12,250 ptas per double room per night (B.P.). All major credit cards accepted.*

For my money, this is by far the best hotel in Toledo. Situated up near the *parador* in a peaceful panoramic residential zone, this absolutely fantastic new four- star hotel blows the competition away. This modern deluxe hotel offers 50 huge air conditioned rooms with great private bathrooms, remote control satellite television, direct dial telephone, extremely comfortable bedding, designer fabrics, impressionist lithographs, mini-bar, electronic key pass locks, mini-safe, am-fm clock radios, hairdryers, and wonderful terraces.

Facilities here are being expanded every month, but even now include a large outdoor pool, cappuccino bar, casual patio restaurant, gourmet dining room, business meeting rooms, large screen televisions, reading lounges, dry cleaning and laundry services, foreign currency exchange, plenty of free parking, baby sitting, and a great staff.

HOTEL MARIA CRISTINA, *Calle Marques de Mendrigorria,1. Tel. (925) 213-202, Fax (925) 213-650. Year round rack rates from 12,500 ptas per double room per night (E.P.). Special Weekend rates from 9,000 ptas per double room per night (E.P.). All major credit cards accepted.*

Situated just a few blocks outside the walls of Toledo, this fantastic medium sized three star hotel is also one of the best bargains in town. The hotel has been creatively converted from an old hospital and mansion near the bus station and features some 65 mid-sized air conditioned rooms that all feature private bathrooms with hair dryers and ecologically friendly hair and skin care products, mini-bars, remote control satellite color televisions, comfortable furnishings, in-room music systems, and direct dial telephones. There is also a very good restaurant and laundry service. Ask about the special domed suite in the tower with breathtaking views and a unqiue interior design.

HOTEL PINTOR EL GRECO, *Alamillos del Transito, 13. Tel. (925) 214-250, Fax (925) 215-819. US & Canada Bookings: (ALTA TOURS) Tel. 800/338-4191. Year round rack rates from 13,000 ptas per double room per night (C.P.). Special weekend rates from 11,500 ptas per double room per night (C.P.). All major credit cards accepted.*

Located on a small side street just steps away from the old Synagogue, this fantastic little three-star hotel is one of the best bargains in town. The Pintor El Greco has been beautifully converted from a gorgeous 17th century mansion, and maintains many of its original architectural elements, including a wonderful patio. There are 33 cute air conditioned rooms that all feature deluxe private bathrooms, mini-bars, remote control satellite color televisions, comfortable furnishings, and direct dial telephones. There is also a good restaurant and laundry service. The hotel offers some of the best personalized service in all of Toledo.

HOSTAL DEL CARDINAL, *Paseo de Recaredo, 24. Tel. (925) 224-900, Fax (925) 222-991. Year round rack rates from 11,800 ptas per double room per night (E.P.). Most major credit cards accepted.*

This historic former 18th century Archbishop's mansion in front of the old town walls near the Puerta Vieja de Bisagra is full of old world charm. This three-star inn features 27 small but quaint rooms with private bathrooms, antiques, direct dial telephones, and heating systems. Public rooms here are filled with an unusual collection of old paintings, tapestries, and furniture. Surrounding the inn are peaceful gardens with beautiful fountains where visitors and guests can sit in the sun and reflect on the magnificent structures that can be seen in all directions. Facilities include a formal regional gourmet restaurant, a casual breakfast room, free parking and a helpful front desk staff.

HOTEL ALFONSO VI, *Calle General Moscardo, 2. Tel. (925) 222-600, Fax (925) 214-458. Low season rack rates from 12,970 ptas per double room per night (E.P.). High season rack rates from 14,060 ptas per double room per night (E.P.). All major credit cards accepted.*

For those of you who want to be near all the old town sights, this reasonably nice old world four-star hotel across from the Alcazár is a good choice. There are 88 medium-sized air-conditioned double rooms with private bathrooms, color television, marble floors, direct dial telephones, and simple but comfortable furnishings. Make sure to ask for a room with a patio and a view. Facilities include a casual restaurant, a nice lobby, nearby parking and a gift shop.

Inexpensive

PENSION MADRID, *Calle Marques de Mendigorria, 7. Tel. (925) 221-114. Low season rack rates from 4,800 ptas per double room per night (E.P.). High season rack rates from 5,250 ptas per double room per night (E.P.). Cash Only - no credit cards accepted.*

This small 10 room pension is a bit far from most of the major sights – but for clean rooms with private bath at this price, it's a fairly good choice.

WHERE TO EAT

Expensive

RESTAURANTE DE HOSTAL DEL CARDINAL, *Paseo de Recaredo, 24. Tel. (925) 224-900. Most major credit cards accepted.*

Located in a wing of the famed hotel, this extremely popular (make sure to call ahead for reservations), opulent restaurant features casual lunches and formal dinners. Although their large menu changes seasonally, expect to spend at least 2,700 ptas. for a multiple course mid day meal, or more than 4,200 *ptas* for a complete four course dinner that might include dishes such as large salads, oven roasted suckling pig, filet mignon with mushrooms, lamb chops, braised rabbit, roasted chicken, grilled swordfish, baked hake, Iberian ham, codfish, sirloin steak and a vast assortment of other local recipes.

Moderate

RINCON DEL BOHEMIO – PASTA NUEVA, *Calle Sierpe, 4. Tel. (925) 213-732. Most major credit cards accepted.*

If you're looking for a break from the hearty Spanish cuisine, try this reasonably priced Italian joint right near the Plaza Zocódover. Their menu features consommé, gazpacho, mixed salads, mozzarella and tomato with olives, endives with salmon and Roquefort, melon with Iberian ham, grilled salmon, filet of sole meuniere, entrecote of beef with pimentos, pasta Alfredo, green lasagna, and assorted pizzas. The typical three-course meal here will set you back around 3,100 *ptas* a person plus drinks.

MESON VILLA MAXIMA, *Calle del Trinidad, 6. Tel. (925) 225-270. Most major credit cards accepted.*

This cute restaurant near the Cathedral offers affordable snacks and meals in a friendly local environment. Their limited menu contains items like gazpacho, huge green salads, nachos, salmon canopies, anchovy canopies, assorted omelets, lamb chops with fries and beefsteak in pepper. Although far from fancy, the local crowd loves this place! A typical three tapa meal here will set you back around 2,050 *ptas* per person plus drinks.

Inexpensive

TELEPIZZA, *Calle Comercio. Tel. (925) 223-100. Cash only - no credit cards accepted.*

Whether you're in the mood for a quick bite in the small dining room, or prefer to have them deliver a hot snack to your hotel, this is about the best pizza in town. The price is just 675 *ptas* for individual pizzas, 975 *ptas* for medium pizzas, or 1500 *ptas* for family-sized pizzas, plus about 125 *ptas* for the addition of each extra item including peppers, tuna, shrimp, anchovies, olives, onion, mushrooms, pepperoni, capers, bacon, pineapple, or extra cheese.

The most amazing part of the deal is that there is a 2 for 1 offer on weekdays, so that you get two of the above for the same price if you ask for it, at no additional cost. A great place when you just don't feel like leaving the hotel but don't want to pay hotel prices to eat informally. Their several other central locations within town might be more convenient.

SEEING THE SIGHTS

Approximate duration (by foot) is about 8.5 hours, including church, synagogue, castle, museum, monument, and side street visits.

No matter how well you follow my (or anyone else's) directions, you will get lost at some point. But I also assure you that by the time you are back on track, you'll have discovered many interesting sights not listed here.

The Old Town

The most obvious starting place for anyone trying to explore Toledo is the fantastic 16th century **Puerta Nueva de Bisagra** principal gateway through the old quarter's defensive walls. Surrounded by two large semicircular towers, this gateway's main arch is topped off by a sculpture of a double-headed crowned eagle with the city's coat of arms, and a statue of a guardian angel that holds up a sword. Before even considering walking through the arch and heading up into town, first turn around and carefully cross the street to reach the *Turismo* tourist office building on the far edge the traffic circle. Since there are no straight roads in the historic part of town, the free large maps of town given out by the *Turismo* will help you to avoid getting lost less frequently while wandering around. After asking a few questions and picking up your map, once again cross the street, this time walking through the Puerta Nueva de Bisagra gateway.

Now that you have passed through the old walls, follow everyone else as they bear slightly to the left to head up the Calle Real de Arrabal towards the heart of town. On your right side just a few steps after walking up this street is the *Mudéjar* 13th century **Iglesia de Santiago del Arrabal** church and bell tower that were built on the sight of an older ruined mosque. You can enter the church for free during its posted daily mass hours to view its fine Gothic pulpit, from which Saint Vincent Ferrer is believed to have preached.

Further along, the same main road will curve first to the left, and then to the right before inclining more steeply as it merges into the Cuesta de las Armas. After another couple of minutes the street now leads straight into the city's bustling central **Plaza de Zocódover** square. This is the major gathering point for the townsfolk, especially at night when commuting locals pop into the bakeries to pick up great pastries on their way home. Meanwhile, the kids hang out in the new McDonalds, and the tourists enjoy snacks at several overpriced outdoor cafés.

On the left side of the plaza you will find the **Arco de Sangre** archway leading down the stairs and onto the Calle de Cervantes. A block or so later on your left hand side is the Platteresque entrance to the 16th century **Hospital de Santa Cruz**. This enchanting former children's hospital was designed by Enrique Egas, and is among the most opulent structures in the city. Built in the form of a Greek cross, the building contains several finely arcaded Renaissance cloisters, *Mudéjar* cupolas, sculpted wooden ceilings, superb staircases, and a Gothic chapel. The building has been converted to house the **Museo de Santa Cruz** art and archaeology museum.

Among the most memorable items to be seen here are the hundreds of 15th through 18th century paintings by masters like **Berrruguete**, **Morales**, **Ribera**, **Gallego**, **El Greco**, **Goya**, and **Coello**. Additional galleries display antique Belgian tapestries, gold and silver coins, Roman mosaics, historical documents, furnishings, sculptures, pocket watches and other assorted archaeological findings. The museum is a great place to spend several hours, and is well worth the price of admission. *Open from Monday through Saturday from 10am until 6:30pm (closed for lunch on Mondays only between 2pm and 4:30pm), Sundays from 10am until 1:45pm, and it costs 350 ptas to enter.*

The El Alcázar Fortress

Walk back up to, and then along, the left side of the plaza and follow the Cuesta de Carlos V up for a couple of blocks until reaching the stairway on your left that leads up and around into the massive **El Alcázar** fortress and its **Museo del Ejercito** military museum. The strategic hill that the present fortress now occupies is the highest point in town, and has been the home of countless previous defensive structures dating back to Roman times.

It was during the 16th century that **Emperor Carlos V** decided to build his royal summer palace on this spot, and work began under the

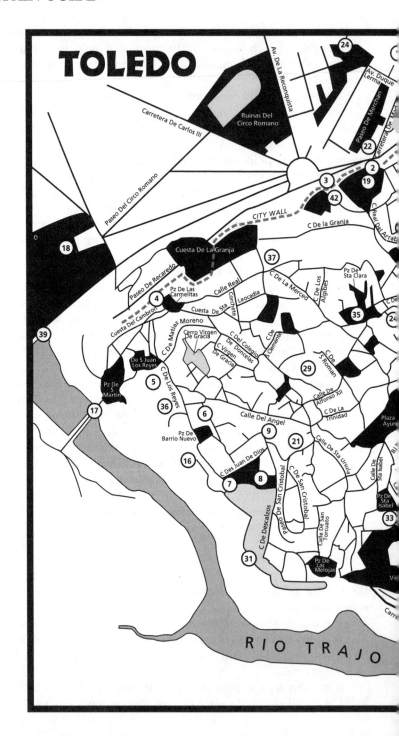

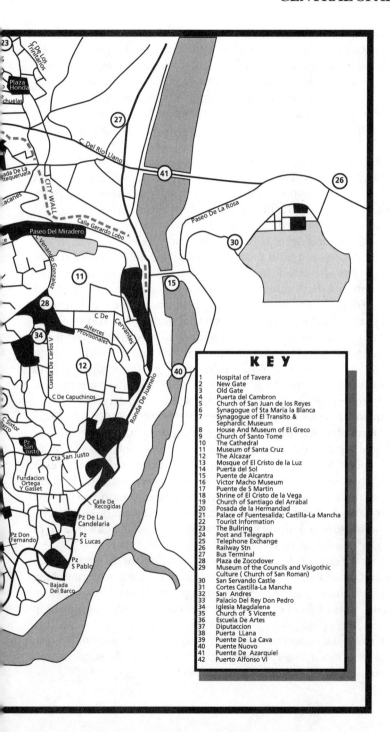

C. De Los Trinitarios

Plaza Honda

23

huelas

27

C. Del Rio Llano

41

ada De La itequeruela

acanes

CITY WALL

Calle Gerardo Lobo

26

Paseo De La Rosa

Paseo Del Miradero

30

Venancio Gonzalez

11

15

28

C De Alferces Provisionales

Cervantes

34

12

40

Cuesta De Carlos V

C De Capuchinos

Ronda De Juanelo

C Sixtor ro

Pz San Justo

Cta San Justo

Fundacion Ortega Y Gasset

Calle De Recogidas

Pz De La Candelaria

Pz S Lucas

Pz Don Fernando

Pz S Pablo

Bajada Del Barco

KEY

1	Hospital of Tavera
2	New Gate
3	Old Gate
4	Puerta del Cambron
5	Church of San Juan de los Reyes
6	Synagogue of Sta Maria la Blanca
7	Synagogue of El Transito & Sephardic Museum
8	House And Museum of El Greco
9	Church of Santo Tome
10	The Cathedral
11	Museum of Santa Cruz
12	The Alcazar
13	Mosque of El Cristo de la Luz
14	Puerta del Sol
15	Puente de Alcantra
16	Victor Macho Museum
17	Puente de S Martin
18	Shrine of El Cristo de la Vega
19	Church of Santiago del Arrabal
20	Posada de la Hermandad
21	Palace of Fuentesalida; Castilla-La Mancha
22	Tourist Information
23	The Bullring
24	Post and Telegraph
25	Telephone Exchange
26	Railway Stn
27	Bus Terminal
28	Plaza de Zocodover
29	Museum of the Councils and Visigothic Culture (Church of San Roman)
30	San Servando Castle
31	Cortes Castilla-La Mancha
32	San Andres
33	Palacio Del Rey Don Pedro
34	Iglesia Magdalena
35	Church of S Vicente
36	Escuela De Artes
37	Diputaccion
38	Puerta Llana
39	Puente De La Cava
40	Puente Nuovo
41	Puente De Azarquiel
42	Puerto Alfonso VI

direction of master architect Alonso de Covarrubias. Progress was slow in the construction of the project due partly to the abdication of the Emperor, and it was not until more than 100 years later (when it no longer would be needed as a palace) that it was finished off with the help of Juan de Herrera and others. Over the next three centuries the building would be destroyed by fire and rebuilt several times, to be used as everything from a prison to a poor house until finally being converted into a military academy.

During the Spanish Civil War local military leader Colonel Moscardo and over 600 Nationalist sympathizers including women and children were besieged in the fortress for nine weeks with a limited supply of food, water, and ammunition. During the siege, Republican forces telephoned the colonel to demand a prompt surrender or else they would murder his captured son. Vowing never to surrender, the colonel's son was in fact executed, and it was not until several weeks later that Nationalist troops captured the city and saved the lives of those held up in the fortress.

Upon entering the Alcázar and its museum you will be led into a huge column- lined two story inner courtyard that surrounds a bronze of Emperor Carlos V in battle. Along the ground floor off the courtyard are several rooms containing expositions of ancient arrowheads and tools, old swords with ivory handles, antique hand-crafted firearms from around the world, bayonets, modern machine guns, photographs and scale models of the fortress's renovations, gold and silver medallions, military uniforms, and statues of military and royal leaders.

The main attraction here for Spaniards is the bullet ridden office that Colonel Moscardo used during the siege, complete with a recorded tape reenacting his dramatic last phone call to his captured son who was about to be executed. Sets of staircases then lead down to the fortress's basement where you can look at the 18th century kitchen with its huge oven, an explosives assembly room, vintage Harley motorcycles, the sleeping quarters of the besieged women and children, a small royal chapel, and the tombs of those killed during the siege as well as the crypt of the heroic colonel himself.

Another set of stairs head up to the second floor of the fortress that now displays thousands of hand-painted miniature soldiers in marching formation and in scenes of warfare, topographical models of famous battle sights, suits of amour, the personal effects of soldiers stationed in Africa.

The fortress and museum are open Tuesday through Sunday from 10am until 1:30pm and again from 4pm until 5:30pm (6:30 during the winter months) with an admission charge of 125 ptas per person.

The Cathedral

After seeing the interior and walking around the outside of the fortress, return back down to the **Plaza de Zocódover** where you will make a left turn onto the boutique-lined Calle de Comercio. All along this street you will find small shops offering the gold and black engraved jewelry typical of the city and a huge assortment of replica guns. A few blocks down, you will bear slightly to the left onto the Calle de la Chapineria that will take you straight in front of the city's most spectacular attraction.

The huge 13th century **Catedral** (cathedral) and its magnificent spire-topped tower are visited each day by an average of about 1,600 people from all over the world. Originally built by King Fernando III in 1227 and designed by Petrus Perez, this is truly one of the most compelling structures of its type in all of Europe. Built on the sight of both a former Visigoth church and its preceding Moorish era mosque, construction and modifications to the cathedral took over 250 years during which it began to take on Gothic, Renaissance, and Baroque features.

Supported by a series of exterior flying buttresses as well as 88 columns that rise up to the vaulted ceiling above its 120 meter (131 yard) long and 59 meter (65 yard) wide interior, this unforgettable house of worship boasts over 750 stained glass windows from the 14th through 16th centuries. In the very center of the building is the fantastic **Coro** (choir) area enclosed by a fine wrought-iron grill that closes off the area to the visiting public. Behind the grill are several amazing works of craftsmanship, including two rows of 15th through 16th century choir stalls carved in solid walnut by Rodrigo Aleman (the bottom row), Alonso de Berreguete (the upper left row), and Felipe de Borgona (the upper right row).

Also worthy of note here are the alabaster carvings on the back of the Archbishop's chair, the 18th century pipe organs, and the 16th century alabaster sculpture of the *Transfiguration of Jesus on Mount Tabor* by Alonso de Berreguete. Just behind the choir area is the opulent **Capilla Mayor** (main chapel) that features a magnificent Gothic gold leaf altarpiece that almost touches the ceiling and displays the most famous scenes from the New Testament and took more than two years to be completed by a team of over two dozen artisans. The main chapel also contains side tombs of notable people including King Alfonso VII, King Sancho III, King Sancho IV, and Cardinal Mendoza. The entire chapel is closed off by a unique metal grill created by Francisco de Villalpando that is among the finest found on earth. Behind the main chapel you will find the 18th century **Transparente**, a marble, alabaster, and bronze baroque altarpiece by Narciso Tomé that's loaded with cherubs and biblical figures. The central bronze sculpture of the sun is often illuminated by sunshine from the pierced roof above.

Further exploration of the cathedral will lead you past dozens of chapels and side chambers that are all worthy of attention. The most dramatic of these include the 16th century **Capilla Mozárabe** chapel beneath the dome where ancient Visigothic masses are held daily at about 9:30am in a setting surrounded by frescoes by Juan de Borgona, a cornice and cupola by Jorge Theotocopouli (El Greco's son), and an 18th century altar with fine mosaics by Juan Manzano. The **Capilla de San Juan** chapel that rests below the giant tower is now the home to the cathedral's **Tesoro** treasury collection which includes a fantastic 16th century gold and silver monstrance by Enrique de Arfe decorated in jewels and ceramic pieces.

Queen Isabella's royal crown, a 15th century wooden crucifix by Fra Angelico, a bible full of incredible artwork donated by French King Louis in the 13th century, and countless medieval gold and silver works of art. Over by the 16th century **Sala Capitular** chapter house you can take note of the wooden *Mudéjar* doorway and carved ceilings while viewing portraits of the local archbishops and a few somber frescoes. If the weather is good, pop inside the 14th century **Claustro** cloister with its galleries full of saintly portraits.

The **Sacristia** (sacristy) is home to the **Museo Catedralico** art museum where you will find a huge frescoes by **Jordan** and **Coello**, as well as other fine paintings by El Greco, Goya, Raphael, Bassano, Titian, Carvaggio, Van Dyke, and Ruebens among others. There are also additional works on exhibit in the so called **Nuevas Salas** or new rooms, that are part of the museum's collection. There are at least a dozen other fantastic chapels that each deserve some of your time, so expect to spend at least two hours inside this incomparable cathedral.

The cathedral itself is open daily from about 8:45am until 1pm and again from 3:30pm until 8pm or so with no admission charge. The museums, treasury, and chapter house can be entered Monday through Saturday from 10:30am until 1pm and again from 330pm until 7pm, Sundays from 10:30pm until 1pm and again from 4pm until 6pm with a combined admission charge of 350 ptas.

Towards the Jewish Quarter

After exiting through the main doors of the cathedral, turn left to follow the exterior of the building around until you reach the **Plaza del Ayuntamiento** square where you will find the city's twin spire topped Renaissance **Ayuntamiento** town hall building designed in the 17th century by Juan de Herrera and Jorge Theotocopouli, the son of El Greco. Walk past the front of the town hall, and bear slightly to the right onto the Calle de El Salvador. Follow this for a couple of blocks until it cuts through a square. The road will then more or less merge into the boutique, café, and bakery-lined Calle de Santo Tomé.

On the left side of the street you will find a small lane leading off to the left side called the Travesia del Conde that leads a few steps further to the **Plaza del Conde**, where you will find the main entrance of the 12th century **Iglesia de Santo Tomé** church with its adjacent *Mudéjar* tower. The church is most often visited by travelers who wish to look at its world famous 16th century painting by **El Greco** entitled *The Burial of Count Orgaz* in which the artist used the portraits of notable people of his day. The young boy in the bottom left side of this magnificent work of art is actually El Greco's son, Jorge Theotocopouli, who later went on to design many of the most impressive structures in Toledo.

The church's small art museum where this and other works are kept is open Tuesday through Saturday from 10am until 1:30pm and again from 3:30pm until 5:45pm or later, Sunday from 10am until 1:30pm, and it costs 100 ptas to enter.

Another fine building just behind the church is the **Taller del Moro** just around the corner from the Plaza del Conde on the Calle Taller del Moro. This former 14th century palace with *Mudéjar* ceilings, doorways, and inscriptions from the Koran is now home to a small museum of Moorish style arts and craftsmanship. *Open Tuesday through Saturday from 10am until 2pm and again from 4pm until 6pm, Sunday from 10am until 2pm, with an entrance fee of 100 ptas per person.*

After visiting the church and museum, walk back up to the top of the plaza and turn left onto the Calle de San Juan de Dios, where the merchants walk up to you and almost demand that you visit their shops. This street now descends some stairs past the beautiful old houses with iron railings that are typical in this area that was once the heart of the old **Juderia** (Jewish) district. A block or so later on your left hand side is the 14th century **Sinagogo del Transito** Jewish synagogue. Currently home to the **Museo Sefardi** Jewish culture and artifacts museum, this opulent house of worship was originally founded by Samuel Levi (the treasurer of King Pedro I).

Here you will find *Mudéjar* style walls with Hebrew inscriptions, unusual vaulted wooden ceilings, antique silk tapestries, and polychrome stucco lattice work. After the Inquisition saw to it that the Jews were either converted or more frequently expelled, the synagogue was taken over to eventually be used as a church. *The museum and synagogue are open Tuesday through Saturday from 10am until 1:30pm and again from 3:30pm until at least 6pm, Sundays from 10am until 1:30pm, and admission is currently 200 ptas per person.*

After leaving the front entrance of the temple, immediately bear left on the small Calle de Samuel Levi and a few steps away you can't help but notice the reconstructed 16th century **Casa y Museo El Greco**. It was in this house that Crete born painter Dominicos Theotocopoulos (better known as "El Greco" which translates to "The Greek") came to live at the age of 36 after studying in Venice, Italy. After walking through the house's entrance hall and adjacent patio, you are led into a series of rooms that include dozens of El Greco original paintings, a selection of high quality copies, period furnishings, the artist's reconstructed living quarters and studio, and additional canvases and sculptures by his Spanish born contemporaries.

This museum is open Tuesday through Saturday from 10am until 2pm and again from 3:30pm until at least 6pm, Sundays from 10am until 2pm, and entrance costs 400 ptas per adult and 200 ptas for children under 12.

Just in front of the museum's courtyard is the **Mercado de Artesania** traditional crafts market where artisans create inlaid jewelry, leather goods, and wood carvings for sale in their shops.

After leaving the craft market, walk down the lane and bear right onto the park lined Calle de los Reyes Catolicas and just after passing the **Plaza de la Barrio Nueva** on your right hand side you will find the late 12th century **Sinagoga de Santa Maria la Blanca**. Inside this lovely old structure you will find four rows of eight octagonal pillars with unique ceramic tiles on their bases that each support fine *Mudéjar* horseshoe arches. If you are wondering how a synagogue became named after a Christian saint, the answer is quite simple.

In the 15th century, as the Inquisition was about to begin, local cleric Saint Vincent Ferrer stirred up his congregation with a horrific sermon about the evils of the Jews. After the service was over, those participating in this service at the Iglesia de Santiago de Arrabal on the other end of town left the church and confiscated the temple from the Jewish community. Soon after, it was converted into a sort of convent for wayward women dedicated to the saint, whose name it now reflects.

The former synagogue is open to the public Tuesday through Saturday from 10am until 1:30pm and again from 3:30pm until at least 6pm, Sundays from 10am until 1:30pm, and admission is currently 150 ptas per person.

Continue along the same street as it passes several jewelry and antique shops for a couple of blocks until passing by the massive 15th century Gothic **Convento de San Juan de los Reyes**, a former Franciscan convent. Commissioned by King Fernando and Queen Isabella to celebrate their victorious battle over the Portuguese at the town of Toro, this impressive structure was designed by Juan Guas and later finished off by Alonso de Covarrubias. Inside there is an amazing two floor cloister with sculpture-lined arcades and *Mudéjar* ceilings, a fine **Capilla Mayor** main chapel with royal coats of arms of the King and Queen who originally intended to be entombed here, and stunning tile work. The chains just in front of the main facade were once used to shackle the Christian prisoners held captive in dungeons during the battle with the Moors in Granada.

Back through the Old Town

After seeing the convent's interior, continue along the same road as it descends and then passes next to the 16th century **Puerta del Cambrón** gateway. This fantastic twin tower topped gate leading through the town's defensive walls was built on the site of a much older Visigoth version, and is fronted by a statue of Saint Leocadia by Berreguette. From this side of the gate, turn right into the Calle de Carmelitas Descalzas as it cuts through the Plaza de las Carmelitas and changes its name to the Calle Real.

If you look carefully at the facades along this street, you will find that every meter (yard) or so up the type of stone and brick seems to change, evidence of various construction and renovation projects during the past 500 years. Make a right turn a couple of blocks or so up into the **Plaza de Santa Leocadia** where you will find the 12 century *Mudéjar* tower connected to the **Iglesia de Santa Leocadia** church and just behind it the more interesting 16th century **Monasterio de Santo Domingo el Antiguo** monastery, built by Nicolás de Bergara and Juan de Herrera. The altars of this monastery contain paintings by El Greco (although some are copies), who is entombed here. There is also a small museum of religious arts located in the former choir area. *The monastery and its museum can be visited daily from 11am until 1:30pm and again from 4pm until 7pm, Sundays from 4pm until 7pm only, and costs 150 ptas per person.*

After exiting the plaza just in front of the monastery, take the second right to walk along the Calle Real which changes its name to the Calle de la Merced as it leads into the **Plaza de la Merced** square. Walk through the square and continue straight ahead for another block and a half before turning right onto the Calle Alfonso X El Sabio, and follow it until it ends at the foot of the twin towered **Iglesia de San Ildefonso** church. Now walk around the far side of the church and head up the Calle de San Roman for a block, and you will find a small square. Although several fine buildings line the square, the most impressive sight is the absolutely breathtaking 13th century Mudéjar **Iglesia de San Roman** church and tower which is now home to the **Museo de la Cultura Visigoda** (Visigoth art and culture museum).

Upon entering the building you will find a series of fine Moorish style marble columns topped by horseshoe arches, dramatic Romanesque frescoes, ancient burial urns, Visigothic jewelry, historical documents, and plenty of other unusual relics. *The museum is open Tuesday through Saturday from 10am until 2pm and again from 4pm until 6pm, Sunday from 10am until 2pm, and the entrance fee is 200 ptas per person.*

After leaving the museum, walk back down to the end of the Calle de San Roman and turn left onto the **Calle de Alfonso X El Sabio**. Keep walking up this street for a few blocks until passing through the **Plaza de**

San Vicente with its old church, and turn right onto the Calle de los Alfileritos which you will follow for a few blocks into the charming little **Plaza de San Nicolás.**

From this plaza, turn left onto the Calle de Nunez de Arce and walk down its curved way until it ends at an elevated point above the main access road into the old city. Now make an extremely sharp left turn onto the Calle de las Carreteras and pass beneath the dramatic 12th century **Puerta del Sol** *Mudéjar* gateway whose 14th century restoration unmasked the Moorish keyhole style portal. Walk through the parking lot in front of the gateway and then ascend the stairs leading up and to the left until reaching the Cuesta del Cristo de la Luz.

At #22 on this street you will find the remains of the 10th century Mezquita **de la Cristo de la Luz** mosque. This amazing brick building was built by the Moors atop the sight of an older Visigoth church. Although entry is often impossible to due an iron gate surrounding its exterior, you can check with the mosque's caretaker who lives at #11 of the same street to let you in (tip him a few hundred *ptas* for the favor). Even from outside the gates you can still see most of its amazing columns, arches, and exterior walls that have Arabic inscriptions from the Koran.

From the mosque, walk back down to the parking lot in front of the gateway, and turn left to head down the Calle Real de Arrabal and pass under the Puerta de Bisagra gateway. Carefully cross the traffic circle and continue straight ahead passing the *Turismo* and a block behind it, you will find the 16th century Renaissance **Hospital de Tavera** former hospital. Designed by a team of skillful architects, this building contains a fine church by Alonso de Berreguete where the remains of Cardinal Tavera are entombed. After being turned over to the noble Lerma family to be used as a palace, it was later converted to house the **Museo de la Fundacion de Duque de Lerma** arts museum that contains paintings by great European artists from the 16th through 18th centuries such as **Titian**, **Coello**, **El Greco**, **Zubarán**, **Ribera**, and **Tintoretto.**

Other rooms like the old library and apothecary include fine antique tapestries, and rare medieval books. *This museum is open daily from 10:30am until 1:30pm and again from 3:30pm until 6pm, and the entrance fee is 250 ptas.*

NIGHTLIFE & ENTERTAINMENT

To begin with, this is not the most happening place at night in Spain. However, for those with a car (or for a 1,000 *ptas* taxi ride), the place to go is the inviting **Venta del Alma** tavern. Located on the other side of the river *at Carretera de Piedrabuena, 35,* this historic converted manor house features great music, relaxing fireside chairs, and a great crowd of casually dressed singles and couples from 20 to 35 years old.

Inside the old town itself, your choices are pretty much limited to the **La Abadia** bar on the Calle de los Alfileritos or **Sithon's Disco** on Calle de Lucio.

PRACTICAL INFORMATION
- **Regional Tourist Office**, *Turismo, Puerta de Bisagra Neuva, Tel. (925) 220-843*
- **Regional Train Info**, *Renfe, Tel. (925) 221-272*
- **Regional Bus Info**, *Terminal de Autobuses, Tel. (925) 215-850*
- **Toledo Radio Taxi Companies**, *Tel. (925) 222-396*
- **Central Post Office**, *Calle de Plata, 1. Tel. (925) 223-611*
- **Regional Directory Assistance**, *Tel. 1003*
- **National Directory Assistance**, *Tel. 1009*
- **Red Cross Ambulances**, *Tel. (925) 222-900*
- **Medical Emergencies Hot Line**, *Tel. (925) 225-500*
- **Municipal Police**, *Tel. (925) 213-400*

FOR GREAT VIEWS & SOME EXERCISE ...

*For those of you who are looking for a great hour-long hike, cross over the fantastic Roman **Puerta y Ponte de Alcantara** bridge and towered gateway on the northeastern edge of the old city to access the other side of the **Tajo** river. If you turn left after the bridge you can walk up to the majestic 13th century **Castillo de San Servando** fortress (now home to a youth hostel), or if you turn right after crossing the bridge, you can leisurely stroll along to the ruins of the **Acueducto Romano** Roman era aqueduct. Either way, the road leads past some of the most photogenic views out over the old city.*

*If you happen to have a car, the modern **Puerta Nueva** bridge can get you across to the far side of the river, from which you can turn right onto the **Carretera de Circunvalacion**. This route merges with the scenic Paseo de la Cigarrales, that in turn takes you past the wonderful gardens and panoramic lookout points near the distinguished **Parador** where families enjoy extended hikes on sunny weekend afternoons.*

16. NORTHERN SPAIN

Including the regions of Galicia, Asturias, Cantabria,
País Vasco, La Rioja, Navarra & Aragón

SANTIAGO DE COMPOSTELA

The historic university city of **Santiago de Compostela** is one of the most beautiful places to visit in all of the **Galicia** region. This is a fantastic place to spend at least a few days walking down ancient stone lanes surrounded by spectacular and well preserved structures from the 10th through 18th centuries.

Visited by countless Christians on each July 24th and 25th as the highlight of the centuries old **Camino de Santiago (The Way of St. James)** pilgrimage through northern Spain, the city is best known as the final resting place for the remains of the Apostle. Each morning, a seemingly endless ringing of the city's church bells coincide with the sound of the university students rushing off to make it to their classes on time through the old streets.

ARRIVALS & DEPARTURES

By Air

Santiago de Compostela's busy regional airport is called the Aeropuerto de Labacolla. Located some 12 kilometers (7 miles) east of Santiago de Compostela off route N-544 on the outskirts of Labacolla.

Buses between the Airport & Downtown

Bus service via the Enpressa Friere line operates in both directions between the Airport's arrival area and the Rúa de General Pardinas a couple of blocks from the city's centrally located Plaza de Galicia. The price is about 200 *ptas* each way, and it runs about 9 times per day in each direction from Monday through Friday, and much less frequently on weekends and holidays.

Taxis from the Airport to Downtown

Taxis are usually marked with the *Taxi* sign, and can be found at the well-indicated taxi stand at the airport. Almost all of the taxis here are fairly small 4 door cars. Normally, a taxi's trunks can hold about two large suitcases, but those with roof racks can secure two more medium pieces of luggage, and perhaps a couple of carry-on bags inside as well. Expect to pay somewhere between 1,350 and 1,600 *ptas* per ride from the airport to most downtown locations.

By Bus

Most of the bus lines between Santiago de Compostela and other parts of Spain and Europe arrive at the Estación de Autobuses bus station, located off the Rúa de Angel Casal about 1 kilometer northeast of the old quarter of downtown. From this station, municipal bus line #10 can take you to the Praza de Galicia area for 65 *ptas*, or a taxi can be hired for about 425 *ptas*.

By Car

From Madrid, the best way here is to take the fast N-VI highway north for 498 kilometers (309 miles) until reaching the Lugo, where you will exit onto route N-640 south for 20 kilometers (12 miles) before finding Guntin. Turn off onto the windy little route N-547 west for the last 84 kilometers (52 miles) and then follow the signs into Santiago de Compostela.

For those arriving here via La Coruña, just take the high speed A-9/E-1 toll motorway south for 63 kilometers (39 miles) before exiting for Santiago de Compostela. Since much of the downtown historic zone is closed to automotive traffic, once inside the city you may have to drive around for a quite some time to find metered street-side parking. You can easily find private garages that charge about 1,750 *ptas* per day.

By Train

Santiago de Compostela is connected to the rest of Spain and other points in Europe by extensive rail service via Renfe. The large Estación de Ferrocarrils train station is located off the bottom of Rúa Horreo near the Avenida de Lugo about 1.5 kilometers south of the old quarter of downtown. From here there is no municipal bus service in the heart of the city, but you can find a taxi just in front of the station; the average charge is about 495 *ptas* to most downtown hotels and sights.

ORIENTATION

Santiago de Compostela is in the northwest corner of Spain, about 602 km (374 miles) northwest of Madrid, and 63 km (39 miles) south of La Coruña. The population is about 106,000.

GETTING AROUND TOWN

By Taxi

A couple of hundred licensed taxis roam the streets, plaza side taxi stands, and major passenger arrival points of this the city during 24 hours each day. To find a taxi, either hail an unoccupied taxi that happens to be driving by, call for a radio taxi pick up Santiago de Compostela Radio Taxi Companies, *Tel. (81) 561-028 or (81) 580-173)*, or go to one of the dozens of obvious taxi stands throughout the city. Taxis charge customers using meters and the fare usually will cost somewhere around 450 *ptas* per ride between most downtown areas. Legally chargeable supplements are posted on a sticker in the taxi's interior.

By Bus

Santiago de Compostela's municipal bus company, known as Trapsa, has several Autobuses (buses) which criss-cross the city and its suburbs. Most people will have no need to use any transportation here other than their feet. For those who wish to walk a little bit less, getting around town and outskirts by bus is relatively easy. The city has over a dozen different bus lines, all numbered for convenience, and hundreds of well marked bus stops.

Ask anyone standing at a nearby bus stop or the helpful Turismo tourist office for route details. Most buses operate every 10 to 20 minutes in both directions from about 6am until 9:30pm daily, with less frequent service on weekends and holidays. The fare is 65 *ptas* per ride, and tickets can be paid for on the bus.

WHERE TO STAY

Expensive

HOTEL LOS REYES CATOLICÓS, *Praza do Obradoiro. Tel. (981) 582-200, Fax (981) 563-094. US & Canada bookings (Marketing Ahead), 800-223-1356. Year round rack rates from 26,500 ptas per double room per night (E.P.). All major credit cards accepted.*

The deluxe five-star Hotel Reyes Catolicós is without a doubt one of the finest hotels in all of Spain. Located just across from the city's dramatic cathedral in the main square of the old quarter, this 16th century structure is well worth the extra money.

There are 136 uniquely decorated rooms and suites that feature huge private marble bathrooms, mini-bar, hardwood floors, extremely comfortable furnishings, direct dial telephone and remote control satellite television. Some of the most requested rooms and suites contain plush velvet curtains, canopy beds, exposed stone beams, Gothic style iron chandeliers, antique tapestries, private terraces, fireplaces, antique oil paintings, religious icons, wood panel ceilings, extremely comfortable furnishings, Jacuzzi and great cathedral views. The public spaces are even more delightful, including luxurious courtyard view sitting rooms packed with antiques, a medieval chapel, beautifully designed sofa-lined lounges, a cafeteria, and the best gourmet restaurant in town. Facilities include private parking, currency exchange, a concierge, a private royal dining room, opulent meeting rooms, a fully equipped auditorium, and much more. Service here is equally impressive, with the white gloved staff making themselves available to all guests.

If you have only enough room in your budget to stay in one deluxe hotel in Galicia, this is where you should spend the night. Advance reservations are strongly suggested.

Moderate

HOTEL COMPOSTELA, *Rúa de Horreo, 1. Tel. (981) 585-700, Fax (981) 563-269. Low season rack rates from 12,750 ptas per double room per night (E.P.). High season rack rates from 15,500 ptas per double room per night (E.P.). Most major credit cards accepted.*

This nice four-star hotel is situated near the main university campus just across from the Praza de Galicia square. The property offers some 99 mid-sized rooms with private bathrooms, satellite remote control color television, direct dial telephones, mini-bar, wall to wall carpeting, mini-safe, hair dryer, electronic key pass locks, interior or old town views, heating and comfortable furnishings. Facilities include a breakfast room, nearby parking, and a nice staff who can help with car rentals and directions to the major sights in town.

HOTEL GELMIREZ, *Rúa de Horreo, 92. Tel. (981) 561-100, Fax (981) 563-269. Low season rack rates from 9,950 ptas per double room per night (E.P.). High season rack rates from 13,750 ptas per double room per night (E.P.). Most major credit cards accepted.*

The Hotel Gelmirez is a modern three-star executive style hotel just down the block from the Praza de Galicia, near all the major sights of the old town. There are 138 comfortable rooms with private bathrooms, direct dial telephones, satellite color television, and basic wooden furnishings. They also have meeting facilities, nearby parking, a breakfast room, safe deposit boxes, and a good staff.

Inexpensive

HOTEL UNIVERSAL, *Praza de Galicia, 2. Tel. (981) 585-800. Low season rack rates from 6,000 ptas per double room per night (E.P.). High season rack rates from 7,500 ptas per double room per night (E.P.). Visa and Mastercard accepted.*

While nothing fancy, this two-star hotel on a somewhat noisy plaza, well within walking distance to the old city's sights, is a real bargain. They have 54 single and double rooms with private bathroom, color television, telephone, and basic furniture. Facilities are limited but include nearby parking and a full service front desk.

HOSTAL SAN ROQUE, *Rúa de San Roque, 8. Tel. (981) 581-647. Low season rack rates from 3,950 ptas per double room per night (E.P.). High season rack rates from 4,900 ptas per double room per night (E.P.). Cash only.*

This is your best basic no-frills hostel with shared bathrooms and clean rooms in the heart of town. No real facilities except for an optional breakfast, but then again, what can you expect for these prices?

WHERE TO EAT

Expensive

HOTEL LOS REYES CATOLICÓS, *Praza do Obradoiro. Tel. (981) 582-200. All major credit cards accepted.*

Located in the basement floor of this 16th century structure just beside the cathedral, this *parador's* superb gourmet restaurant is the finest in the region. Expertly designed using original stone walls, antique tapestries, fine hardwood ceilings, period furnishings, and fine china and crystal, this unique restaurant is equally favored by local executives and visiting travelers who expect and receive the best possible service and cuisine. Although rather fancy, a suit and tie are not needed to enjoy a meal here.

Executive chef Daniel Turrado de la Huerga has created one of the finest menus in Spain. Their offerings change seasonally, but when I recently enjoyed lunch here I just asked José Iglesias Gonzalez (perhaps the finest *Maitre* in Spain) for his suggestions. Featured dishes often include a cream of pumpkin and corn soup served in a hollowed pumpkin, baked onion soup, terrine of smoked salmon with local cheese, stuffed crepes with scallop oysters and jumbo shrimp, spinach with cream and duck liver, grilled rib of Galician veal, roasted duck with orange sauce, an amazing soufflé of roasted vegetables and smoked meat, lamb with garlic sauce served on top of a waffle, shellfish salad with spiny lobster, baked spider crab, hake with clams, grilled filet of sole with scallop oysters and a fantastic dessert tray with half a dozen mouth-watering items

Be sure to ask about their selection of fine wines by the full and half bottle. The typical four course meal here will cost around 5,700 *ptas* a person plus drinks.

Moderate

RESTUARANTE 0 42, *Rúa do Franco, 42. Tel. (981) 581-009. Most major credit cards accepted*

This excellent restaurant in the old part of town has an informal bar and dining area, a glass enclosed patio, and an outdoor terrace. Filled with modern art and old photographs, it is one of my favorite spots for a good meal and good people- watching.

Specialties include Galician soup, veggi empanadas, homemade sausages, roasted hot green peppers, sardines, grilled mushrooms, stuffed papayas with meat, steamed mussels, sautéed scallops, grilled cod, spider crabs, grilled hake, battered hake and chips, sirloin steak, entrecote, and a nice sampling of desserts. A great three course meal here will set you back around 2,900 *ptas* a person plus wine.

BODEGON DE XULIO, *Rúa do Franco, 24. Tel. (981) 584-639. All major credit cards accepted.*

Located in the center of the old quarter, this cute little traditional and casual restaurant is a great place to sit down and enjoy a great lunch or dinner after visiting the Cathedral. Specialties include Galician soup, consommé, fish soup, garden salads, melon with ham, clams marinara, shrimp with garlic sauce, hake with mayonnaise, grilled salmon, cod fish served in several styles, marinated octopus, pork cutlets, grilled chicken with garlic and potatoes, and Spanish omelets. They also have a good selection of pastries and affordable local wines. The typical three course meal here will set you back around 2,960 *ptas* a person plus wine.

SEEING THE SIGHTS

Approximate duration (by foot) is about 6 hours, including church, castle, museum, monument, and side street visits.

The Catedral facade

To start your tour of this wonderful city, begin at the world famous Romanesque **Catedral** (Cathedral) in the heart of the old quarter. Construction of this fantastically ornate granite block house of worship started way back in 1075 and took almost 700 years of additional work to take its present-day form. The Cathedral was built atop an old basilica reportedly housing the bones of Saint James the Apostle. Before entering the building, take a walk around the entire exterior, surrounded by four separate plazas, each with its own equally compelling facades from different eras.

The main Baroque **Obradoiro** facade off the huge **Praza do Obradoiro** square was created by locally born Fernando de Casas y Novoa and finally completed in 1747. Among the most memorable elements of this facade are the Torre de la Carraca and Torre de las Campanas towers on either side of the main entrance. Between these two towers is the central facade that is topped off by a statue of Saint James ("Santiago" in Spanish). Below the image of the saint is an urn that contained his bones, statues of his parents and his disciples, large windows, and the cathedral's front entrance doors.

While facing the Obradoiro facade, bear right and follow the exterior of the cathedral around to left until reaching the **Las Platerías** facade off the **Praza de las Platerías** (also known as **Las Praterías**) square. This Romanesque facade was built in the early 12th century and contains two additional entrance doors into the cathedral. Above these doors is an unusual frieze carved by Esteban and Maestro del Cordero depicting several biblical characters including Adam and Eve's banishment from paradise. Just to the left of the portico is the cathedral's Renaissance treasury section that is topped off with a large pyramidal tower. To the right of the portico is the giant Baroque **Torre de Reloxio** clock tower built by Domingo de Andrade. The plaza itself also contains a fine granite equestrian fountain, and the fine 18th century Baroque **Casa de Cabildo**, a church chapter's mansion at #5.

Now continue around the corner to follow the exterior of the cathedral into the **Praza de la Quintana** square. The first doorway you will see, just adjacent to the clock tower's base, is the 17th century **Puerta Real** built by José Pena de Toro. This is where official parades and processions emerge from the cathedral to enter the city streets. The top of the doorway is adorned with a royal coat of arms. A bit further down is the more dramatic **Puerta Santa** doorway. Designed and constructed in 1616 by Francisco Gonzalez, the door is topped by a statue of Saint James the Apostle surrounded by two smaller figures of his disciples Theodore and Athanasius that were all carved by Pedro de Campo. The 24 square figures on the sides of this doorway were carved by Maestro Mateo are copies of similar figures that can be found inside the cathedral's choir.

This entrance is only opened on the 25th of July on Jubilee Years (the years when the 25th of July falls on a Sunday) and only for those participating in the pilgrimage. The plaza also is home to several outstanding structures including the Baroque 18th century **Casa de Conga** and **Casa de Parra** mansions, as well as the side of the 16th century **Convento de San Paio de Antealtares** convent.

Continue around the next corner until reaching the **Azabachería** facade off the **Praza de la Inmaculada** square with its two simple doorways. This Neoclassical facade was created in the late 18th century by Lucas Ferro Caaveiro. Although not as impressive as the preceding facades, the overall view of the cathedral's many domes and towers from this square is quite impressive. Just across the square is the Baroque 16th century **Monasterio de San Martíno Pinaro** monastery built by Fray Gabriel de Casas. From here, walk along the exterior of the cathedral and continue through the tunnel until it leads back out towards the front of the building.

Inside the Cathedral

Walk through the iron gates and up the stairs leading to the doorway in the middle of the astonishing Baroque **Obradoiro** facade. As soon as you pass through the outer doors, you will find the beautiful Romanesque sculpted arches of the **Pórtico de la Gloría**. Built by Maestro Mateo in 1188, this is one of the most dramatic examples of medieval art in all of Europe.

Originally the exterior entrance of the cathedral, it was later masked by the 18th century addition of the Obradoiro facade. The marble frieze above the door's center is carved with a large figure of Jesus surrounded by the four evangelists, and just below rests a seated Saint John the Apostle intricately carved into the central column. It is below this image that pilgrims traditionally touch the sculpture with their fingers to mark their safe arrival, thus creating large indentations in the surface of the marble. Well over 100 other images of angels, 24 musical apostles, saints, and even Adam and Eve can be found on every inch of three arches that make up this amazing portico.

After passing through the arches, head straight into the heart of the cathedral. Most of the vaulted interior is of Romanesque design, and, although altered in subsequent centuries, contains many original medieval elements. Once you have made your way past the aisles, keep walking towards the incredibly beautiful **Capela Maior** main altar surrounded by fine Baroque gold-coated wooden carvings, and topped by an angel-supported canopy upon which rests an exquisite statue of Saint James clothed in a fine jeweled robe. A small staircase on the side of the altar leads up to the top floor where pilgrims and worshippers usually kiss the saint's robe, and visitors can see into the aisles out above the priest's head. Another staircase on the side of the altar area leads down into the original 9th century **crypt** of Saint James and his two disciples.

There are plenty of fine Baroque and Gothic chapels to visit here including the 16th century **Capilla de Mandragon**, the **Capilla de San Fernando**, and the **Capilla de Corticella**. The cathedral's **Museo Catedralicio** religious art museum contains gold and silver works, antique tapestries, and the Botafumeiro swinging incense burner that is used during the pilgrimage services on Jubilee Years. There is also a wonderful cloister, library, and treasury wing that can be entered upon presentation of an admission ticket to the museum section.

The cathedral itself is open daily from sunrise to sunset and there is no entrance fee. The museum is open daily from 10:30am until 1pm, and again from 4pm until 6:30pm every day except Sunday. Admission to the museum and several other parts of the building is currently 300 ptas per person.

Around the Old Quarter

After spending an hour or so touring the cathedral, exit through its main facade and out into the **Praza do Obradoiro** square. In this square itself there are several historic buildings that are open to the public.

Facing away from the cathedral, the large rectangular structure to your right is the Renaissance **Hostal de los Reyes Catolicós**. Originally built by Enrique de Egas in 1501, this magnificent two-story building served as a royal hospital before being first converted into a pilgrimage inn and later remodeled as a super deluxe *parador*. The hotel's facade is lined by a fine wrought-iron balcony, while its main entrance is surrounded by a spectacular frieze carved with the likeness of the 12 Apostles, King Ferdinand and Queen Isabella, and dozens of intricate motifs. Several parts of the hotel's interior can be visited even if you're not staying here, including its fine Gothic chapel, antique-filled public rooms, four beautiful patios, and one of the finest restaurants in the region (see reviews above). During highly promoted festivals, internationally known musicians perform concerts in the acoustically perfect chapel.

The next building you should take a peek at is the adjacent 18th century Classical **Pazo de Raxoi** (also known locally as the **Casa Consistorial**). This structure was built by Lucas Ferro Caaveiro under the commission of Archbishop Raxoi who wanted a seminary built across from the cathedral. Today this building houses local government offices, including those of the city council. Entry is somewhat restricted, but you can still appreciate the facade's many arches and frieze depicting an historic battle and the statue of Saint James on horseback atop the main entrance.

The last important sight to visit in the Praza do Obradoiro square, directly opposite from the hotel, is the 17th century **Pazo de Xerome**. This simple building is now home to the offices of the city's **Colegio de San Xerome** university. The 15th century facade was actually removed from an old hospital and placed here to make the building more dramatic.

From the university building, depart the main square, and follow the fun Rúa do Franco into the heart of the old town. A few steps down this street on the right hand side you will find an entrance to the **Colegio de San Xerome's** amazing inner garden courtyard. Just next door is the 16th century Renaissance **Colegio de Fonseca** university building. After seeing the peaceful courtyard, continue up the Rúa do Franco and peek inside the many boutiques and student cafes that line the street. When you reach the second intersection a couple of blocks further down, bear left and then immediately turn left again onto the quaint Rúa do Vilar to head back towards the side of the cathedral.

While walking down this street, notice the fine assortment of archways and interesting buildings dating from the 16th through 18th centuries that house fine boutiques on their ground floors. I suggest popping into the city's busy Turismo tourist office at #43 to get a free historic map and walking tour map of town. For those interested in details about the yearly pilgrimage, the second floor of #1 Rúa do Vilar contains the public information offices for the festivities and processions.

At the bottom of the street you will find yourself once again at the edge of the **Praza de la Platerías** square from where you will make a sharp right turn onto the Rúa de Gelmirez. Just after turning you will see the Baroque 18th century **Casa del Dean** on your right hand side. This dean's mansion is fronted by granite block balconies and a fine doorway carved with scrolls. At the next corner, turn right onto the Rúa Nova where you can window shop in the stores. About a block down on the left hand side of the street is the 18th century **Iglesia de Santa María Salome** church. Built in the middle ages and completely altered to suit the Baroque styles of the 18th century, this originally Gothic church is topped by a dome above its octagonal lantern. Inside, the main altar dims in comparison to the more lavish gold side altar.

Also along the sides of this street you will find several vendors with kiosks selling leather goods and local crafts. At the end of the street you will make a left turn onto the Canton do Toural and a few steps later make a right hand turn onto the Rúa das Orfas.

The Rúa das Orfas leads a block or so further down and into the heart of the major **Praza de Galicia** square. At the beginning of the square, turn left onto the wide Rúa de Fonte de Santo Antonio. About a block and a half later on your right hand side is the 17th century **Convento de las Mercedarías** convent that is now closed to the public. Now cross the street and head up the unnamed side road's ramp, which leads up an embankment towards the large rectangular Neoclassical building that is home to the History and Geography Collage campus of the **Universidad Compostelana**. After walking around to the front of this structure you will find yourself in the **Praza da Universidade**.

Walk along the exterior of the university building until once again reaching the wall at the edge of the embankment, and follow it for a couple of blocks until passing the back of the wonderfully alive indoor and outdoor **Mercado** marketplace. This is a good place to stock up on picnic supplies or to grab a snack.

Cut between the two main market pavilions and bear right onto the **Praza de Abastos** that then merges into the Rúa de Santo Augostino. The large rectangular building, an imposing tower on the right corner of this street, is the 17th century Jesuit **Convento de San Agostino** convent. Just after the convent's tower, turn left onto the Rúa de San Bieito and follow it for a couple of blocks until running smack into the lovely **Praza de Cervantes**, with a large statue in the middle.

Walk directly across the plaza and then along the Rúa da Acebicheria until you hit the **Praza de Immaculada** and the side of the cathedral. Now head down the steps and through the archways back into the **Praza do Obradoiro** square to end your tour of this enchanting city.

NIGHTLIFE & ENTERTAINMENT

Bars and clubs are scattered around the old town, but be advised that since most of the university students leave for their homes outside the city on Friday afternoons and return on Monday morning, Thursday night is the big night to party here.

Good bets along the **Rúa do Franco** are the **Cafe Dakar** and the **O'Barril** bar. The happening **Cafe Literarios**, over near the **Praza de Immaculada**, is the in place for students to hang out.

PRACTICAL INFORMATION

- **Regional Tourist Office**, *Turismo, Rúa do Villar, 43, Tel. (981) 584-081*
- **Santiago de Compostela Airport**, *Labacolla, Tel. (981) 597-400*
- **Airport Bus Info**, *Empresa Freire, Tel. (981) 588-111*
- **Iberia Airlines**, *Tel. (981) 572,028 or (81) 594-104*
- **Regional Train Info**, *Renfe, Tel. (981) 520-202*
- **Regional Bus Info**, *Estación de Autobuses, Tel. (981) 587-700*
- **Municipal Bus Info**, *TRAPSA, Tel. (981) 581-815*
- **Santiago de Compostela Radio Taxi Companies**, *Tel. (981) 561-028 or (81) 580-173*
- **Central Post Office**, *Travesia Fonseca, Tel. (981) 582-028*
- **Regional Directory Assistance**, *Tel. 1003*
- **National Directory Assistance**, *Tel. 1009*
- **Red Cross Ambulances**, *Tel. (981) 585-454*
- **Medical Emergencies Hot Line**, *Tel. 085*
- **National Police**, *Tel. (981) 589-000*
- **Municipal Police**, *Tel. (981) 581-678*

MAJOR LOCAL FESTIVALS

Contact the local Turismo office, *Tel. (925) 220-843*, for exact details.
- **Semana Santa**, *March or April, Religious Processions*
- **Corpus Cristi**, *June, Processions and Feasts*
- **Fiesta de la Virgen**, *August, Bullfights and Festivals*
- **Fiesta Padre Jesus**, *Late August, Parades, Bullfights, Music*

LA CORUÑA

The busy port city of **La Coruña** is the second largest in all of the **Galicia** region. Although slightly less rainy and windy than in other parts of the region, it can still be damp during any time of the year.

The faces of many older local residents show how hard life has been for them. Still, for visitors, there is something for everyone to enjoy in this fun city. The beaches and nightlife possibilities are exceptional – but be sure to always have an umbrella handy just in case. The only other caution I have for you is that the locals don't drive with any respect for other cars or pedestrians, so be careful.

ARRIVALS & DEPARTURES

By Air

La Coruña's small regional airport is called the Aeropuerto de La Coruña – Alvedro. Located 9 km (6 miles) south of La Coruña off route N-550 on the outskirts of the hamlet of Alvedro. Since this is just a small airport with limited runway length, it primarily services domestic flights.

Buses between the Airport & Downtown

Bus service via the Autos Sigras line operates in both directions between the Airport's arrival area and the city's centrally located Estación de Autobuses. The price is about 250 *ptas* each way, and it runs about three times per day in each direction from Monday through Friday, and much less frequently on weekends and holidays.

Taxis from the Airport to Downtown

Taxis are usually marked with the *Taxi* sign, and can be found at the well-marked taxi stand at the airport. Almost all of the taxis here are fairly small sized four door cars. Normally, taxi's trunks can hold about two large sized suitcases, but those with roof racks can secure two more medium pieces of luggage, and perhaps a couple of carry on bags inside as well. Expect to pay somewhere between 1,550 and 1,900 *ptas* per ride from the airport to most downtown locations.

By Car

From Madrid, the best way here is to take the fast N-VI highway north for 596 km (370 miles) until reaching the end at the La Coruña exit.

From Santiago de Compostela, you can take the high speed A-9/E-1 toll motorway north for 63 km (39 miles) before exiting for La Coruña.

Once inside the city you may have to drive around for a few minutes to find metered parking, or put it in a private garage charging about 1,300 *ptas* per day.

By Train

La Coruña is connected to the rest of Spain, Portugal, and other points in Europe by extensive rail service via Renfe. While some commuter lines arrive at the smaller Estación de Mercantias off of the Avenida del Ejercito, most travelers will use the much larger Estación de San Cristobal train station located off the Praza de San Cristobal, near the Ronda de Outero about two kilometers southwest of downtown.

From here, the municipal bus line #5 goes to the Calle de San Andrés in the heart of the city at 90 *ptas* per ride. Taxis can also be found just in front of the station, and the average charge is about 525 *ptas* to most downtown hotels and sights.

By Bus

Most of the bus lines between La Coruña and other parts of Spain arrive at the Estación de Autobuses bus station on the Calle de Caballeros, about five blocks away from the main train station. From this station, municipal bus lines #1 or #1A can take you to the Darsena marina area and its nearby Turismo tourist info center for about 120 *ptas*, or a taxi can be hired for about 485 *ptas*.

ORIENTATION

La Coruña and its beaches sit at the edge of the Atlantic Ocean along the extreme northwestern coast of Spain, 596 kilometers (370 miles) northwest of Madrid and 63 kilometers (39 miles) north of Santiago de Campostela. The population is 248,887.

GETTING AROUND TOWN

By Bus

La Coruña's municipal bus company, known as C.T.C., has several Autobuses that criss-cross the city and its suburbs. With over a dozen different bus lines, all numbered for convenience, and hundreds of well-marked bus stops each with its posted corresponding route map, getting around is fairly easy. Ask anyone standing at a nearby bus station or the helpful Turismo tourist office for route details.

Most buses operate every 10 to 25 minutes in both directions from about 6am until 10pm daily, with less frequent service on weekends and holidays. The fare is about 120 *ptas* per ride, and tickets can be bought on the bus.

By Taxi

A couple of hundred licensed taxis roam the streets, plaza-side taxi stands, and major passenger arrival points 24 hours a day. To find a taxi, either hail an unoccupied taxi (they often will display a small sign which says *Libre*) driving by, go to one of the dozens of obvious taxi stands throughout the city, or call La Coruña Radio Taxi Companies, *Tel. (981) 243-377 or Tel. (981) 287-777*, for a radio response pick up on demand.

Taxis charge customers using meters and the fare usually will cost somewhere around 650 *ptas* per ride (Not per person!) between most downtown areas. Legally chargeable supplements are posted on a sticker in the taxi's interior.

WHERE TO STAY

Expensive

TRYP MARÍA PITA HOTEL, *Ave. Pedro Barrie de la Maza, 1. Tel. (981) 205-000, Fax (981) 205-565. US & Canda Bookings (UTELL), Tel. 800/44-UTELL. Low season rack rates from 16,500 ptas per double room per night (E.P.). High season rack rates from 18,500 ptas per double room per night (E.P.). All major credit cards accepted.*

This is certainly the best seafront hotel in town. Situated just off the Playa del Orzan beach with its famed esplanade, the brand new ultra-modern four-star María Pita offers 183 deluxe rooms and suites. Each room has marble tiled private bathrooms stocked with amenities, air conditioning, mini-bar, hair dryers, satellite televisions, mini-safes, hard-wood floors, in-room music, am-fm radios, direct dial telephones and comfortable furnishings.

All of the public spaces have been beautifully designed and decorated, and there are plenty of sunny areas to just sit down and relax while reading the complimentary international newspapers available at the reception area. The hotel also has valet and garage parking, boutiques, a sauna, two restaurants, business and conference facilities, baby sitting, hair salon, game room, a piano bar and a lower floor art gallery. Service here is absolutely fantastic, and the staff go well beyond the call of duty to assure that each guest has everything necessary for a great stay. With its prime location and large rooms, this is a great selection for deluxe travelers and businessmen.

Moderate

HOTEL RIAZOR, *Ave. Pedro Barrie de la Maza, 29. Tel. (981) 253-400, Fax (981) 253-404. Low season rack rates from 9,750 ptas per double room per night (E.P.). High season rack rates from 12,500 ptas per double room per night (E.P.). All major credit cards accepted.*

If you're looking for a good three-star seafront hotel, the Riazor is a good selection. This fairly modern three-star property in front of the Playa del Riazor has some 180 rooms that have private bathrooms, satellite televisions, one or two beds, direct dial telephones, and in-room music.

Other facilities include a good restaurant, ocean-view lounges, a nice bar, a snack bar, meeting rooms and nearby parking.

Inexpensive

HOSTAL MAYCAR, *Calle de San Andrés, 159. Tel. (981) 226-000, Fax (981) 229-208. Low season rack rates from 6,500 ptas per double room per night (E.P.). High season rack rates from 7,500 ptas per double room per night (E.P.). Most major credit cards accepted.*

Located in the heart of the downtown shopping and nightlife zone on the famous San Andrés Street, this clean 63 room *hostal* is a real bargain. Here you can choose between nicely maintained interior and exterior view rooms that all have private bathrooms, color televisions, direct dial telephones, and comfortable pine furnishings. There is also elevator service to all nine floors, nearby parking, a breakfast restaurant, and a nice staff.

WHERE TO EAT

Moderate

RESTAURANTE NORAY, *Plaza de María Pita. Tel. (981) 220-371. All major credit cards accepted.*

In the center of the old quarter, this medium-sized restaurant has both a cafeteria and more spacious sit-down dining room that share the same menu. Specialties include such mouth-watering items as Galician soup, marinated octopus, clams marinara, grilled jumbo shrimp, fried calamari, beefsteak with potatoes, entrecote with pimentos, roasted meats, grilled filet of sole, grilled hake and cod fish. This place gives you the opportunity to sample some home style cooking that is specific to this region. The typical three course meal here will cost around 3,200 *ptas* per person plus drinks.

PIZZERIA CAMBALACHE, *Plaza de María Pita. Tel. (981) 205-834. All major credit cards accepted.*

If you're not in the mood for seafood, this cute little pizzeria and fresh pasta restaurant is one of the better places to check out. Their large menu includes spaghetti Bolognese, pasta with pesto sauce, gnocchi with pesto, green lasagna, ravioli carbonera, as well as an assortment of both half and whole pizzas. Expect to spend around 2,050 *ptas* per person for a filling meal here. A real good stop!

Inexpensive

PAREDES, *Calle Olmos, 17. Cash only.*

This excellent stand-up *tapas* bar in the old part of the commercial district just off of the Calle de San Andrés is a good place to hit between 7pm and 10pm on weekday nights. Their small menu features such delicious snacks such as calamari, oysters, sardines, local boiled shrimp, marinated octopus, omelet sandwiches and other tapas. Nothing fancy, but good for a quick snack between bars. A hearty three tapa meal will cost around 1,250 *ptas* per head here.

TELEPIZZA, *Ave. Pedro Barrie de la Maza, 23. Tel. (981) 222-232. Cash only.*

Whether you're in the mood for a quick bite in the small dining room, or prefer to have them deliver a hot snack to your hotel, this is about the best pizza in town. The price is just 675 *ptas* for individual pizzas, 975 *ptas* for medium pizzas, or 1500 *ptas* for family sized pizzas, plus about 125 *ptas* for the addition of each extra item including peppers, tuna, shrimp, anchovies, olives, onion, mushrooms, pepperoni, capers, bacon, pineapple, or extra cheese. The most amazing part of the deal is that there is a 2 for 1 offer on weekdays so that you get two of the above for the same price if you ask for it, at no additional cost. This is a great place when you just don't feel like leaving the hotel, but don't want to pay hotel prices to eat informally.

SEEING THE SIGHTS

Approximate duration (by foot and optional taxi) is about 7 hours, including church, castle, waterfront, museum, monument, and side street visits.

Start your trip over by the **Darsena de la Marina** port and harbor area. This is where many of the fishing boats dock that head for the North Atlantic to catch huge quantities of codfish for the Spanish market. The marina is always full of fishermen checking their nets and washing their boats. The city's *Turismo* office is located in a modern building just across the port on the **Paseo de la Darsena** esplanade. Here you can get plenty of free maps background information on this lovely city. The wide avenue almost adjacent to the *Turismo* is called the Avenida de la Marina, and is lined on one side by beautiful white buildings with superb glass-enclosed galleries, and on the other side by the lovely **Jardines de Mendez Nuñez** park and gardens.

From the tourist office, cross the street and head directly up the small lane called Calle de Luchana that leads away from the waterfront and into the old **Barrio Pescadería** (Fisherman's) quarter of the city. On the next corner, turn right onto the quaint Calle de Riego de Agua with its many boutiques and seafood restaurants. This street will now lead you through an archway and into the awesome **Praza de María Pita** square. The plaza was named after a local woman who saw Sir Francis Drake's ships sailing towards the city in 1589, and saved the city from an English invasion by firing a cannon blast, thus alerting the local defense forces.

The square is rung by a series of fine structures including the **Palacio Municipal** town hall building, built in 1904, with its three red tiled domes.

The Modernist style town hall can be entered for free from 5pm until 7pm on weekdays to view its fine assembly hall and small museum of clocks. Most of the other buildings around the square house nice moderately priced restaurants and outdoor cafes on their ground floors.

After cutting through the main plaza and passing under yet another archway you will find yourself on the Avenida de Los Angeles. Follow this avenue until it ends in a few blocks, and turn left onto Calle de Damas and its centuries old uneven stone pavement. About one block up the street, on the right hand side is the enchanting **Praza de la General Azcarraga** square. Tucked away on the far right hand corner of the plaza is the wonderful 12th century Romanesque **Iglesia de Santiago** church. This is the city's oldest church, and was renovated and expanded during later centuries. There are Gothic features, including a beautiful nave, bell tower, and several 16th century tombs. *The church can be visited daily for free from 8:30am until 1pm and again from 6pm until 8pm.*

Now return to the Calle de Damas and head another two blocks up until reaching the 13th century **Colegiata de Santa María del Campo** collegiate church. Standing on the highest point of the old quarter, this medieval church should be visited to view its large rose window, Gothic aisles, and its adjacent pillory. *The church can be seen for free daily from 8:30am until 1pm and again from 5pm until 7pm.* Almost next to the church is a small side street known as the Calle de Puerta de Aires, where at #23 visitors can enter the almost unmarked **Museo de Arte Sacra** religious arts museum that contains paintings, sculptures, and treasures taken from several of the city's oldest churches.

The museum is open Tuesday through Friday from 10am until 1pm and again from 5pm until 7pm, and on Saturday from 10am until 1pm. There is no entrance fee to see its impressive collections.

After leaving the museum, once again return to the Calle de Damas and continue heading up the street until it ends at the Calle de Herrerías where you will make a right turn and follow the old stone walls that lead into the **Plazuela de Santa Barbara**. This charming little plaza is centered around a medieval stone cross and is surrounded by a series of dramatic old houses and the remarkable facade of the 15th century **Convento de Santa Barbara** (closed to the public). Make sure to look up at the convent's main portico that is topped by ornate stone carvings.

Walk through this plaza, and then bear to the left to head into the **Plazuela de Santo Domingo** square with its central old stone fountain, mosaic pavements, palm trees, and peaceful gardens. At the edge of this plaza you can't miss the giant bell tower and Baroque facade of the 18th century **Iglesia de Santo Domingo** church, with its chapel dedicated to the city's patron saint. It's open daily, no charge, from 8am until noon and again from 5:30pm until 8:30pm.

After departing the church, turn left onto the Calle de San Francisco and keep your eyes out for the blue **Arquivo Galicia** archives building. Just behind this building is the walled **Jardin de San Carlos** gardens. Besides containing beautiful flowers, this former bastion has been converted into a tranquil garden surrounding the **Tomb of Sir John Moore**, an English General who died in 1809 while battling Napoleonic troops. Other plaques are dedicated to the 172 British Royal Navy officers of the *H.M.S. Serpent* that was shipwrecked on a nearby cape in 1890. *The park is open from sunrise to sunset.*

Just across and down the same street you can pop into **Praza de San Carlos** and peek inside the **Museo Militar Regional** (military museum) where over 1,400 guns, shells, cannons, medallions, and uniforms from the 18th through 20th century are on display. *The museum is open with free admission Monday through Friday from 10am until 2pm year round, and again from 4pm until 7pm during summer only, and 10am until 2pm on Saturdays.* Strangely enough, just next to the military museum is the 18th century Baroque **Iglesia de la Venerable Orden Tercera** church with many Platteresque interior elements. *This church is open from 8am until 2pm and again from 4:30pm until 8:30pm daily with no entrance fee.*

After visiting the church, walk back to the garden and turn left to follow its side fence towards the waterfront. In one block or so you will turn left onto the Paseo del Parrote and follow it past the old 16th century **Puertas del Mar** (old town walls) and cross over to the other side of the street. In a minute or so you will find the entrance the **Castillo de San Anton** fortress with its fine panoramic lookouts. Built during the 16th through 18th centuries on a small peninsula and once used as a political prison, the fortress is now home to the **Museo Arqueológico de la Coruña** that displays ancient stone carvings, local artifacts, and historical exhibitions. *The museum costs 250 ptas to enter and is open daily from 10am until 2pm and again from 4pm until at least 7pm.* A small fishing fleet is moored just below the fort, and a high class yacht club can be found a bit further along the seafront from here.

Now turn back towards the harbor area by following the Paseo Marítimo around for a few minutes until you once again end up in front *Turismo* office on the Paseo de la Darsena. From the tourist office, cross the street and turn left onto the Avenida de la Marina. After about a block or so you will make the first right turn onto Calle de Agar, and then make the next left turn onto boutique-lined Calle Real. This nice wide street is where you can find the best quality clothing and jewelry shops in town. After window shopping for a few more blocks, turn right onto the busy Calle de Santa Catalina and walk upon it for about two more blocks until bearing right left the famous Calle de San Andrés, the center of the city's commercial zone. In a handful of blocks you will be led into the busy **Plaza de Pontevedra** square, where hundreds of cafes, restaurants, and shops stay open until at least 9pm on weekdays. From the far end of the plaza, bear right onto Calle Samoza and follow it until it ends at the Avenida de Pedro Barrie de la Maza just across from the sea.

Now that you are in front of the city's beachfront, you can enjoy the two fine sandy crescent-shaped beaches and the adjacent seaside promenade that are filled to the brim with sun worshipping singles and couples on hot days in the summer. To the right is the windswept **Playa del Orzan** beach, and to the right is the **Playa de Riazor** beach. After the sun has set on these well-maintained beaches, the nearby restaurants, bars, and discos just inland a block or two behind this zone are packed until the early morning hours.

Before leaving town there are two other nice sights that may be of interest. The first of these is the excellent **Museo de Bellas Artes** on Calle de Panaderas #58. This beautiful building located off the old quarter's Praza de San Augustin is well worth a side trip. Here you can view a fine collection of antique paintings, and sculptures by Spanish and other European artists, as well as a series of etchings by Goya. *The museum is open Tuesday through Sunday from 10am until 2:30pm, and admission is currently 450 ptas per person.*

The other impressive sight is the **Torre de Hercules** tower situated way out of the downtown zone along the northwestern edge of the city's upper peninsula. This was originally built by the Romans as a lighthouse in the 2nd century, but was totally rebuilt from the ground up some 200 or so years ago. Since this is so far out of the way, you must either take a municipal bus to get here (#3 stops near the Jardin de San Carlos), or pay a taxi to take you here and ask the driver to wait about 10 minutes to take you back into downtown. The last time I went all the way to the tower, it was closed for repairs, so ask the tourism office if its open before wasting your time and money traveling this far out of the way.

NIGHTLIFE & ENTERTAINMENT

If you want some liquid refreshments and company after a long day at the beach, walk along the Ave. Pedro Barrie de la Maza and choose between the **Brigadon Pub** or the **Boca Chica Disco**. Near the beach on the Calle Sol, youthful party animals head for places like the **Cafe Bar Puerta del Sol**, the **La-La Disco**, the **Tatrabis Bar**, the **Tatraplan Club**, the **Latrec Cocktail Cafe**, the **Grietax Disco**, the **Picasso Bar** and the **Cats Pub**.

Along the central Calle de San Andrés itself is one of town's the most happening and sophisticated cafe/bars called the **El Cafe Macondo** at

#106. On the fun little side streets near the Calle de San Andrés you can pop into places like the youthful **Cafe Museo** on Travessia de Santa Catalina, the **Cervecería Otros Tiempos** on the Calle Jaleria or the **Memphis Disco Pub** on Calle Torreiro.

PRACTICAL INFORMATION
- **Regional Tourist Office**, *Turismo, Paseo de la Darsena, Tel. (981) 221-822*
- **La Coruña Airport**, *Alvedro, Tel. (981) 232-240*
- **Airport Bus Info**, *Autos Sigras, Tel. (981) 231-234*
- **Iberia Airlines**, *Tel. (981) 293-855 or (81) 297-3755*
- **Aviaco Airlines**, *Tel. (981) 247-966*
- **Regional Train Info**, *Renfe, Tel. (981) 232-240 or (81) 237-299*
- **Municipal Bus Info**, *C.T.C., Tel. (981) 250-100*
- **Regional Bus Info**, *Estación de Autobuses, Tel. (981) 239-099 or (81) 239-644*
- **La Coruña Radio Taxi Companies**, *Tel. (981) 243-377 or (81) 287-777*
- **Central Post Office**, *Calle M. Casas, Tel. (981) 221-956*
- **Regional Directory Assistance**, *Tel. 1003*
- **National Directory Assistance**, *Tel. 1009*
- **Red Cross Ambulances**, *Tel. (981) 222-222*
- **Medical Emergencies Hot Line**, *Tel. 085*
- **National Police**, *Tel. (981) 122-260*
- **Municipal Police**, *Tel. (981) 184-223*

SAN SEBASTIÁN - DONOSTIA

No one can really say for sure when this dramatic strip of seafront nestled between sheltering mountains was actually settled, but experts believe it was at least 500 years before Christ. During the Middle Ages, the hard working residents here consisted mainly of fishermen, whale hunters, and merchants who lived in peaceful harmony. As time progressed, the inhabitants became quite skilled at long sea voyages and were known to have journeyed thousands of miles in pursuit of codfish.

By the 14th century, they established trade routes to northern Europe. Even though the town was heavily fortified against invasion from its hostile French neighbors, war and siege were the order of the day throughout the turbulent 17th and 18th centuries. This all came to a peak in 1808 after the city was invaded and subjected to several years of occupation under Napoleonic forces.

When the joint English-Portuguese army repelled the French troops from **San Sebastián** in 1813, they proceeded to commit countless atrocities upon the local population, culminating in the destruction of nearly the entire city by fire. The local residents came together after this terrible destruction and began to rebuild the city around what is now know as the **Plaza de la Constitución**.

In the mid-19th century, **Queen Isabella II** began to come here during the summer to take advantage of the seawater's curative powers. It was most likely that her well publicized visits here, along with the corresponding influx of governmental and aristocratic visitors, helped make San Sebastián a well known beach resort. By the late 19th century, the population had increased so much that it was necessary to dismantle most of the city's original defensive walls to make room for the expansion of the downtown sectors.

During World War I, wealthy Europeans fleeing from advancing German troops started to settle here, bringing with them vast sums of money. Construction of palatial estates and seaview mansions became commonplace, and the city had begun to evolve into a seaside playground for the rich and famous. Although the many of the wealthiest ex-patriots began to leave town after the war was over, the newly expanded city maintained its excellent infrastructure and continued to attract additional development, especially with the industrialization of its suburbs under the years of Franco's dictatorship.

Along with Franco came the attempted suppression of the Basque language and culture. It was during this time that the **E.T.A.** separatists began their campaign of terror that once was marked by car bombs and murders here in town. Although their activity here has pretty much ceased, and has moved onto the larger cities of Madrid and Barcelona, they still have a small base of support among the city's poorest residents who continue to hang banners in protest of the Spanish government.

On many Friday nights, a group of about 100 friends and relatives of imprisoned or assassinated E.T.A. guerrillas can be seen marching through the streets of the old town, carefully watched by heavily armed Basque police force units looking for any suspected terrorists. Don't be fooled by what looks like a show of public support for terrorism; most of the 180,000 local residents are thoroughly fed up with the tactics used by both sides of this conflict, and would much prefer to see peace come to their region. Despite what you might hear, San Sebastián is perhaps the safest city to visit in all of Spain. Try to include San Sebastián in your plans for a perfect vacation in Spain, no matter what time of the year you decide to arrive.

ARRIVALS & DEPARTURES

By Air

Aviaco airlines usaually offers one flight per weekday into San Sebastián's small national airport to and from Barcelona, and two per flights per day to and from Madrid. The airport lies 21 kilometers (13 miles) northeast of the city, on the way to France.

Buses between the Airport & Downtown

A local green colored private airport bus labeled *San Sebastián-Irun-Fuenterrabia (Hondarribia)* goes from the front of the airport to the city center every 15 minutes or so from 7am until 10pm daily, and costs about 170 *ptas* each way.

Taxis between the Airport and Downtown

Numerous taxis can be found at the arrivals building, and charge about 3,775 *ptas* to take you into any part of the town.

By Bus

An abundance of local companies list daily bus schedules connecting San Sebastián with many other regional and national cities and villages. Although there are a few other small depots, the main bus station is found at the Plaza de Pio XII, less than two kilometers (1.3 miles) south of the downtown zone.

From here you can take a taxi to most downtown destinations for somewhere around 690 *ptas*. From the front of the bus station, public bus line #8 will take you into the center of the city for about 120 *ptas* and runs about every 10 minutes from around 7am until 11pm.

By Car

The best way to drive to San Sebastián from Madrid is to take the fast N-1 highway north for 469 km (286 miles), ignoring all signs that may suggest alternative routes to this city. While a series of smaller roads can be taken to shorten the trip, don't even think about attempting to use them, as they are extremely difficult, especially at night!

By Train

Daily scheduled train service on Renfe links San Sebastián with the rest of Spain via this city's main rail station on the Paseo de Francia just east the heart of town across the Urumea river. Additional local and international (usually French) trains arrive and depart at the town's other rail station on Calle Easo, just south of the city center. It is possible to walk from these stations to most hotels and sights, but taxis are also available and can cost around 550 *ptas* to most destinations in San Sebastián.

After walking across the river via the María Cristina bridge, you can catch public bus line #8 that will take you into the center of the city for 90 *ptas*, and it runs about every 10 minutes from around 7am until 11pm.

ORIENTATION

San Sebastián is located on the Cantabrian Sea along the northern border of Spain in the tiny Guipúzcoa province of the País Vasco region, close to the French border. The road trip from Madrid to this lovely seaside resort city is only about 484 kilometers (295 miles) to the north-northeast, or just a 21 kilometer trip west from the French border town of Hendaye.

This remarkable seaside community, called Donostia in the Basque language of *Euskara*, is a fantastic place to spend at least a few days. Situated at the confluence of the Urumea River and the Bay of Biscay, this beautiful resort area has become internationally known for both its great sandy beaches and superb culinary offerings. During the off-season months, when hotel prices are surprisingly reasonable, the city bustles with cultural activities such as the Patron Saint's Festival on the 19th and 20th of January when thousands of costumed children and marching drum bands fill the streets in a spectacular parade, and of course February's fantastic Carnival processions.

When the weather gets warm and the beaches begin to fill up with scantily dressed Europeans, the city's focus becomes somewhat more hedonistic. During July, the town hosts a small but enchanting Jazz Festival featuring top recording artists from around the globe. In September the city becomes full of starlets and autograph seeking fans during the famous International Film Festival. And finally during the middle of August, the whole town gets swept up in the Semana Grande or "Big Week" celebrations, during which an action-packed daily schedule of sporting and cultural events are capped off by a nightly barrage of pyrotechnics that are known as the International Fireworks Competition. No matter when you decide to come here, you must take the time to see many of the historic, gastronomic, and cultural attractions that make San Sebastián one of the most delightful destinations in all of Spain.

Once you have finished seeing the sights, swimming in the sea, or shopping to your heart's content, even more delightful activities await you. This city has so many fantastic restaurants, cider houses, *tapas* bars (known locally as *pinchos*), discos and pubs that each evening promises to be another terrific adventure.

WHERE TO STAY

Expensive

HOTEL MARÍA CRISTINA, *Paseo República Argentina, 4. Tel. (943) 424-900, Fax (943) 423-914. US & Canadsa Bookings (The Luxury Collection)) Tel. 800/325-3589. Low season rack rates from 31,500 ptas per double* *room per night (E.P.). High season rack rates from 44,100 ptas per double room per night (E.P.). All major credit cards accepted.*

With its perfect location just steps away from the old part of town, and some of the finest rooms in all of northern Spain, this is a fantastic place to stay and well worth the price. Originally built in 1912, this lavish oasis of luxury offers some of the best public lounges and sitting areas I have ever seen. During my last visit here I shared a floor of the hotel with the Rolling Stones (although I have a few good stories from that week, I have been sworn to secrecy!) Each of the 136 huge and beautifully decorated Belle Époque style rooms and suites have reverse cycle air conditioners, huge marble bathrooms stocked with the highest quality amenities, turn-of-the-century rich wooden furnishings, designer wall fabrics, direct dial telephones, in-room music, mini-bars, remote control satellite televisions, extremely comfortable bedding and splendid views over either the old town, the new town, or the water.

Unique features at this deluxe hotel include six superb business meeting rooms, 24-hour room service, safe deposit boxes, free outdoor secured parking, and full concierge and business services. The staff here is among the most helpful and professional in Europe, and under the skillful direction of Sr. Ramon Felip have become known throughout the world for their attention to quality and customer satisfaction.

While here you may want to enjoy either the opulent Easo restaurant that offers a romantic Saturday night candlelight dinner with live piano music, or the relaxing Gritti piano bar where the more affluent locals come for early evening drinks. Be sure to ask about their special weekend rates and packages, and you may be able to get a great deal.

Expensive

HOTEL LONDRES Y INGLATERRA, *Calle Zubieta, 2. Tel. (943) 426-989, Fax (943) 420-031. Low season rack rates from 17,800 ptas per double room per night (E.P.). High season rack rates from 20,000 ptas per double room per night (E.P.) Most major credit cards accepted.*

Consisting of six floors, this modern seafront hotel offers 45 modern and reasonably sized air conditioned rooms, each with white marble bathrooms, color satellite television, direct dial phones, dark wooden furnishings, hair dryers, in room music systems and many amenities.

Facilities include limited room service, a full service restaurant, nearby parking, coin operated shoe shine machines, and a front desk that will be glad to book restaurant reservations and excursions. If you specifically request it, you can have a terraced room with an excellent view of the beach at no additional price. The city's casino is located just steps away from the front door.

Moderate

HOTEL RESIDENCIA PARMA, *Calle de General Jauregi, 11. Tel. (943) 428-893, Fax (943) 424-082. Low season rack rates from 10,500 ptas per double room per night (E.P.). High season rack rates from 14,500 ptas per double room per night (E.P.). Most major credit cards accepted.*

In terms of a well-located and reasonably priced hotel with all the necessary facilities, this two-star hotel near the seafront promenade is about the best choice. The modern Parma has 27 rooms, each with wooden or marble flooring, color television, private tiled bathrooms, simple furnishings, direct dial phones, and heating. If you would like good view of the sea, expect to pay about another 2,000 *ptas* or so. A good selection in a city where hotels are not usually this affordable.

WHERE TO EAT

Expensive

RESTAURANTE ARZAK, *Calle Alto de Miracruz, 21. Tel. (943) 278-465. All major credit cards accepted.*

This is simply my favorite gourmet restaurant in all of Europe. After half a dozen different people from all over the world told be about this small gourmet establishment on the edge of the city, it was obviously time to give it a try. As soon as we got to the door, owner and master chef Juan Mari Arzak and his beautiful and equally talented daughter Elena greeted us. Upon being escorted to the table amidst antique oil paintings and fine crystal and porcelain settings, we were then asked if we would prefer to have a menu featuring traditional Basque cuisine or the new menu offering their own special nouveau style offerings. I chose the latter, and from the first course of this amazing meal until the last I was in total heaven. The well dressed clientele here are pampered by a great staff of patient waitresses and wine stewards.

The menu itself features over 50 items prepared with the best ingredients available, and changes daily depending on what Sr. Arzak has selected from the market. On the day I dined here, the offerings included warm oysters with seasonal vegetables, mousse of codfish with pimento juice, prawns with broccoli and artichoke hearts with a coffee vinaigrette, fish soup in the new style, sirloin with herb sauce, glazed pigeon cooked with ginger, filet of ox with potatoes cooked in white port wine, filet of fresh sole, pistachio cream with pastry and cheese flavored ice cream, chocolate cake with orange and raspberry ice cream, and at least 35 other tempting selections.

The two huge wine lists are outstanding, and offer bottles from every major Spanish winery as well as some of the best French vintages. If you can only enjoy one special meal during your trip to Spain, this restaurant should most certainly be the place to have it. This superb Relais &

Chateaux affiliated restaurant gets my highest recommendation and should not be missed! A superb four course a la carte gourmet meal here will cost about 8,800 *ptas* per person plus wine, and is truly worth every penny.

RESTAURANTE JUANITO KOJUA, *Calle de Puerta, 14. Tel. (943) 420-180. Mastercard accepted.*

This may very well be my favorite restaurant in the old town. The interior is laden with maritime antiques, stained glass windows, and other delightful accessories. This is one place where you should ask your very friendly waiter or waitress what the best items are for that specific day.

The serious semi-formally attired patrons are served large portions of such delicious items as fish soup, mixed salads, green salads, seafood paella for two, Iberico ham, mouth watering grilled prawns, freshly caught filet of sole, stewed pigeon, baked whole partridge, entrecote with pepper sauce, and a huge selection of homemade desserts and fine Spanish wines. A great place for those who can afford it: a great three course a la carte meal will be about 4,050 *ptas* per person plus drinks.

Moderate

RESTAURANTE JOSETXO, *Calle San Jeronimo, 20. Tel. (943) 422-098. Most major credit cards accepted.*

A modern and semi-casual old town restaurant offering high quality meals. The dining room is nicely decorated and the service here is outstanding. Among the best dishes available are the consommé, fish soup, Russian salad, asparagus with two sauces, shrimp with garlic, grilled prawns, tuna steak with tomato, grilled salmon, and shrimp cocktails. A great three course a la carte meal will set each person back around 2,850 *ptas*.

RESTAURANTE LA VINA, *Calle de 31 de Agosto, 3. Tel. (943) 427-495. Most major credit cards accepted.*

Besides offering great *tapas* at the bar, the rear dining room of this down-to-earth seafood restaurant serves rather tasty and moderately priced meals. Service here is prompt, friendly, and first rate. Their comprehensive menu features mixed salad, green salads, Russian salads, asparagus with two sauces, classic fish soup, prawn and shrimp cocktails, fish and shrimp pastries, octopus vinaigrette, smoked salmon, filet of sole, codfish with vizcania sauce, entrecote with green peppers, and assorted tarts. A good three course meal will set you back around 2,800 *ptas* per person plus drinks.

AMARA BERRI, *Calle de Isabel II, 4. Tel. (943) 464-684. Cash only.*

Newly opened, Amara Berri is the only cider house located in the downtown zone of the city. Packed on weekends with small groups of both young and old locals, this is a great place to experience. During the

THE CIDER HOUSES OF SAN SEBASTIÁN

Another unique type of dining establishment in San Sebastián and throughout the País Vasco region are the cider houses, known locally as **Los Sidrerías.** *These are special restaurants that only offer one meal – a cod fish omelet, cod fish with green peppers, a thick grilled steak, and cheese with nuts. The most famous aspect of these merry places is that the clientelle come here to stand up every few minutes and wait in front of a huge barrel of fermented apple cider (Sidra). When their turn comes, a small tap is opened and they must stand about a meter (1 yard) away and let the cider squirt at a rather high velocity into their glass. Its also important to drink the cider immediately or else it will lose its desired level of carbonation.*

A typical cider house will be open only during the January through April fresh cider season, and charge about 3,0800 ptas per person for a huge meal with unlimited glasses of cider. Although packed on weekends, I strongly suggest enjoying an evening at a Sidreria during the middle of the week. In the past, cider houses were located a fair distance from town, which led to some intoxicated driving on area roads! Fortunately a great new Sidreria, **Amara Berri,** *has opened in the heart of downtown (see review immediately above), and you can even walk here from most hotels in the city.*

January through April fresh cider season, they have four giant barrels full, and instead of closing down for the rest of the year, they serve bottled cider and remain open.

Their menu is rather typical of these establishments, and for about 2,900 *ptas* per person you get lots of codfish and a cooked to order three inch thick steak that is sure to leave you filled to the gills. The food here is wonderful, and the ambiance is very friendly. A great place to visit at least once during your stay in this exciting city.

RESTAURANTE LA CUEVA, *Plaza de la Trinidad. Tel. (943) 425-437. Most major credit cards accepted.*

Located in an ancient stone building studded with beautiful old wooden beams, this small but impressive restaurant features excellent local seafood meals. After passing their open kitchen you will be promptly seated at one of only a dozen or so simple wood tables.

The best selections at this simple establishment include mixed salads, fish soup, smoked salmon, grilled shrimp, shrimp with garlic, grilled squid, filet of sole, veal cutlets, filet mignon, grilled salmon, and beef entrecote. A typical three course a la carte meal will cost around 2,850 *ptas* per person plus drinks.

RESTAURANTE URBIA, *Calle de Puerto, 7. Tel. (943) 425-782. Most major credit cards accepted.*

Located on one of the main streets of the old part of town, this wonderfully relaxing seafood and steak restaurant is a real gem. I actually came here twice because both the food and service was so good. The large menu features large salads, excellent foie gras, a rich red fish soup, fried hake, lamb chops with mint, roasted partridge, sirloin steak, roast beef, paella for two, and dozens of other house specialties. A great three course a la carte meal will set you back around 3,050 *ptas* per person plus drinks.

RESTAURANTE TOYKO, *Calle Euskalherria, 8. Tel. (943) 431-602. Most major credit cards accepted.*

If you've been in town for a few days and are looking for something different than seafood and steak meals, I suggest trying this cute Chinese and Japanese restaurant on the edge of the old town. I liked their nori-maki, California rolls, spring rolls, Chinese style hot and sour soup, chicken and corn soup, yakitori chicken, seafood tempura, fried rice, sweet and sour shrimp, chicken with curry, and rice noodles with assorted meats. A hearty threecourse a la carte meal will cost around 3,100 *ptas* per person plus drinks.

Inexpensive

TORTALETAS, *Calle de Puerto, 8. Tel. (943) 424-272. Cash only.*

This casual little bar offers some of the freshest seafood and meat *pinchos* (*tapas*) in town for between 125 and 250 *ptas* each. Their best offerings include mussels with either garlic or tomato sauce, and small sandwiches made with your choice of shrimp, tuna, tortilla, sausage, calamari, or ham.

SEEING THE SIGHTS

Approximate duration (by foot and cable car) is about 6.5 hours, including museum, side street, church, mountain, and beach visits.

The Sea-front & the Monte Urgull area

The best place to begin your walking tour of San Sebastián is at the **Puente Zurriola** bridge that crosses the swiftly flowing **Rio Urumea** river before it finally reaches the sea. From the bridge, follow the **Paseo de Salamanca** seaside promenade past the spectacular tunnel shaped waves pounding the breakers.

As you head up along the promenade, you can turn to your right to view the **Playa de Gros** beach that lies just across the river. This beach has a strong undercurrent, and is not recommended for swimming. As you walk along the promenade, be careful not to get splashed by the giant waves that tend to sneak up above the sea wall and soak pedestrians who are not paying attention.

Soon the walkway curves to the left and takes the name of Paseo Nuevo at the point where it passes the northernmost blocks of the city. Rising steeply above you at this point is the dramatic **Monte Urgull** mountain, where you can see some of the last remaining segments of the town's original defenses. Here you can take a stair path up the mountainside to view the remains of the 12th century **Castillo de Santa Cruz de la Mota** castle, several sections of the old fortified walls and defensive batteries, an old church cemetery, and a huge statue of Jesus. *The municipal park that contains these sights is open from sunrise to sunset daily, and admission is free.*

After returning down to the seafront walkway, continue heading around the tip of this small peninsula to reach the **Punta del Castillo o Zurriola** patio where you can have a great view without much fear of getting drenched by the waves. Further along the promenade you will find the **Ermita**, a small shrine that has been dedicated to the memory of those who have been lost at sea. Another entrance to the mountaintop park and castle can been found on the uphill road just to the left of this solemn shrine.

As the seafront walkway twists to the left for the last time, passing several outdoor cafes and bars, you can't help but notice several interesting sights in and around the fine **Bahía de la Concha** bay. First of all you will find the small **Isla de Santa Clara** island sitting in the heart of the bay. Access to the island is by the Ciudad de San Sebastián ferry from the town's port area with scheduled service every half hour during daylight hours in the high season only. Surrounding the bay are the crescent shaped beaches called the **Playa de la Concha** and the **Playa de Ondarreta** that are the main attractions of this city during the summer.

As the walkway ends, take the small flight of stairs down into the old part of town. The first building you will pass on your right hand side is the **Palacio del Mar**. This beautiful harborfront structure is the home of the **Donostia-San Sebastián Aquarium** that is privately owned and operated by the Oceanographic Society of Gipuzkoa. As you pass though the doorway, marked by a pair of salvaged cannons, you will find three separate floors of exhibits. The basement (sea level) floor is home to the 28-tank aquarium that offers visitors a chance to see live examples of sea creatures commonly found along the local seacoast, including a Large Spotted Dogfish and even some species of shark.

The ground floor contains an oceanographic museum that displays information on the town's history of whaling, along with an old whale skeleton and other collections of shells, stuffed sea birds, exotic shells, and a marine research laboratory/library section. The top floor has been devoted to naval history and has an assortment of materials relating to fishing, shipbuilding, maritime trade and cartography.

The museum is open 10am until 1:30pm and again from 3:30pm until 7:30pm daily during the summer and from Tuesday until Sunday the rest of the year. Admission is 450 ptas per person.

After visiting the aquarium, head down yet another flight of stairs to the Paseo del Muelle next to the harbor and port area that shelters the small but lively fishing fleet. About a block further down, you will find a white building on the left side that contains the public **Museo Naval** museum. Once inside this modern museum and research library, wander around the museum's three floors packed with historical exhibits on wooden ship building methods, antique tools, scale models of ships, food and wine storage containers, old anchors, beautifully preserved navigational instruments, a huge maritime research library, and a series of small video rooms showing films on related topics.

The museum is open from Tuesday through Saturday from 10am until 1:30pm and again from 4pm until 7:30pm, and on Sunday from 11am until 2pm. Admission is always free.

When you're done with the museums, continue down the same street passing a series of old wooden fishermen's houses and casual fresh seafood restaurants. During most afternoons you'll see fishermen hand-knitting their nets in preparation for a long day or night at sea. After walking past the **Capilla de Sao Pedro Apostol**, the street turns to the right and is renamed Calle Muelle de la Lasta.

Parte Vieja – Old Town

From the Calle Muelle de la Lasta, a small gateway to your left leads onto the Calle del Puerto in the remarkable **Parte Vieja** (old section). This particular street is an excellent place to stop for a quick, affordable lunch of assorted meat and seafood *pinchos* (the local word for what you already know as *tapas*). As you continue down this street, you can smell the scent of freshly caught fish and seafood smothered with garlic and sweet peppers. There is also a large selection of tacky tourist souvenir shops and small boutiques lining this and almost every other block in this zone.

A few blocks further up on the same street you will find yourself entering the charming **Plaza de la Constitución** that was built as the center of the new "Old Town Center" after the devastating fire of 1813. In bygone days, the plaza, surrounded by a series of four-storied buildings with numbered balconies (147 of them to be exact) and the huge **Biblioteca Municipal** library (formerly the city hall building), was where bullfights and other social events took place. Now it has become a gathering place for the younger residents of town, who start their all-night vigil of bar and disco hopping on most weekend nights.

POPULAR SOCIETIES - COOKING CLUBS FOR MEN ONLY!

One of the most interesting traditions in San Sebastián (and elsewhere in the province of Guipúzcoa) that dates back to the mid-18th century, are the unique gastronomic social clubs for men only that are based on the art of cooking and socializing without any class barriers. These so called **Sociedades Populares** *(Popular Societies) are gathering places for members and their friends to relax and enjoy amazing home-cooked meals with fine local wines and good conversation (except for politics).*

To join one of the 100 or so gastronomic clubs around town, one might be on a waiting list for up to four decades or more. Once you have either been approved or have been invited for a group meal by a member, the group selects a few people to act as the chefs, and they will arrive several hours in advance to prepare a wonderful five or six course meal. All of the ingredients are purchased by the participants, except for wine, oil, and most spices that are provided by the society and must be paid for using the honor system. The kitchen equipment and utensils rival those found in the best restaurants of the world, and much of the annual membership fees go for the upgrading of the facilities.

On my first visit to one of these great institutions, the **Sociedad Gaztelubide** *on Calle Subida al Castillo, I saw a well-known bank president cooking alongside two fishermen and a shopkeeper, all relating to each other on equal ground without any snobbery or pretension. Women are permitted only on two special nights per year. Upon asking these casually dressed men if they ever cook at home, they all answered that they would never even consider it, "because that is the job of a wife." In any case, even though these societies are usually not open to the public, it is well worth the effort to ask permission at the door during the hours before lunch or dinner to be allowed to just take a peek inside. The dishes that these highly skilled non-professional chefs create is as good as anything you're likely to have in the better restaurants in town.*

From the far end of the plaza, take a left turn onto the Calle de Narrica and soon you will find the Gothic edifice of the 16th century **Iglesia San Vicente**, one of a handful of structures that survived the fire of 1813. Not only is this the oldest building in town, but for some reason, its tower was never actually completed. The interior is fairly basic aside from a beautiful altar, and it is only open to the public during daily masses.

After visiting the church, keep following the same street until it ends. Here you should take a right turn onto the wonderful Calle de 31 de

Agosto. Because the English-Portuguese army had a field office on this street, it was not burned down when they torched the rest of the town. The result is that it has retained much of its historic and original atmosphere.

About half a block up this street is an entrance to the **Plaza de Zuloaga** that is home to the fantastic **Museo de San Telmo**. Inside the redesigned yellow Neo-Renaissance facade (the building was formerly a Dominican monastery dating from the 16th century, designed by Martín de Santiago), this great museum offers three floors full of beautiful art and artifacts. As you enter the building you are led into a pretty inner courtyard surrounded by vaulted hallways packed with medieval funeral stones and archaeological findings.

Nearby is the original 16th century church that was painted earlier this century with bold scenes of Basque historical moments and famous local legends by famed artist J.M. Sert. A few small rooms off the beautiful cloister on the ground floor contain modern sculptures, but it's the second floor art gallery, divided into a series of small rooms each with a superb collection of masterpieces from different centuries, that is the real attraction here.

Among the most notable works on display include paintings by **El Greco**, **Rubens**, **Cano**, **Domingues Becquer**, **Ribera**, **Valdes Leal**, **Jordan**, **Collantes**, **Borgona** and dozens of works marked *Desconocido* (painter unknown). Interspersed with the paintings are a vast assortment of antique furnishings and sculptures taken from the monastery itself, as well as from several other local sources. Another side gallery is completely dedicated to **Antonio Ortiz-Echague**, an early 20th century local painter whose work shows a wonderful talent for colorful landscapes and portraits that seem to pop off the canvas. A special ethnography wing displays embroidered fabrics, framing implements, and even a reconstruction of a Basque farmhouse. The top floor of the museum is dedicated to Basque artists from the 19th and 20th centuries. *The museum is open from Tuesday through Saturday from 9:30am until 1:30pm and again from 4pm until 7pm, Sundays from 10am until 2pm. Admission is 400 ptas per person.*

When you're done, head back to the Calle de 31 de Agosto, this time bearing right. A couple of blocks further up this street, after passing the quaint **Plaza de la Trinidad**, the gorgeous Baroque facade of the 18th century **Iglesia de Santa María** basilica comes into view. If you're lucky enough to pass by this church during mass, make sure to peek inside to view its famous image of the *Virgin of the Choir* at the altar. Even the exterior is fantastically ornate, and its clock still keeps perfect time.

From the front of the church, follow the **Calle Mayor** down into the central part of town, heading towards the giant spire of the city's main cathedral. About four blocks down this street you'll hit a major intersection at the wide Alameda del Boulevard.

The Centro – Town Center

Across the Alameda del Boulevard is the 19th century **Ayuntamiento (City Hall)** that actually started as a casino for wealthy visitors until gambling was made illegal in 1924. After many years of abandonment and disrepair, the city decided to move its official headquarters here from the older structure in the Plaza de la Constitución. Although not usually open to the general public, this is a fine example of turn-of-the-century architecture. After seeing the city hall building from across the street, turn left on the boulevard and follow it past the central park and bandstand until reaching the corner of the Calle de San Juan. At this corner you can visit another exciting attraction, the town's **main market** where amusing vendors offer everything from flowers and fruits to dried spices and other provisions. Behind the indoor sections of the market is an outdoor courtyard market and nearby a fish market.

Across the boulevard from the market is the ornate **Teatro Victoria Eugenia** theater that first opened its doors in 1922. Besides being the sight of many fine performances, the theater is the headquarters of the International Film Festival, and also is home to the excellent **Oficina Municipal de Informacion, Centro de Atracción y Turismo** that is without doubt the finest Turismo office in all of Spain. This office is a wonderful place to get all the latest tourist information and cultural activity schedules, and their multilingual staff is amazingly polite and helpful. I wish all tourist offices in Spain were required to send their staff here for a few weeks of on-the-job training with Sr. Rafael Aguirre, who has been at the forefront of tourist promotion in this region for over 30 years and still loves his work.

From the *Turismo*, follow the boulevard back down for half a block until turning left onto Calle Oquendo where the bold facade of the deluxe **Hotel María Cristina** welcomes the most famous celebrities to San Sebastián. After passing the hotel, keep heading down the same street for a block or so until bearing left onto the Avenida de la Libertad that marks the beginning of the city's most concentrated commercial and shopping district. A small and somewhat helpful provincial **Oficina de Informacion Turistica** can be visited just off the Plaza de España for additional maps on other nearby cities.

If you turn around and then walk up the Avenida de la Libertad in the opposite direction, and turn left onto Calle Loyola, the impressive spire of the late 19th century **Catedral del Buen Pastor** cathedral will soon come into view. The streets that line this part of town are all filled with boutiques offering good prices on European clothing, jewelry, cosmetics and other items.

Other Diversions

If you have enough time to wander around the old and new quarters of this fun city, and are looking for more things to see and do, you're in luck! Take a ride on the cable car that operates from the area around the **Real Club de Tenis** tennis club in the west end of the city to the top of the windy **Monte Igüeldo** mountain. The ride takes about 15 minutes each way and during its summer operational season costs less than 300 *ptas*.

If you're looking for a good walk, stroll along the **Playa de la Concha** beach to view the **Palacio y Parque de Miramar** palace and gardens. In the mood to gamble? Walk to the downtown **Casino Gran Kursaal** on Calle Zubieta (bring your passport to enter), or take a ride over to the suburban **Horse Track** that offers scheduled races in both winter and summer seasons with good purses. Most of all, the superb cuisine and exhilarating nightlife here may be all you need to keep busy.

NIGHTLIFE & ENTERTAINMENT

The vast majority of action takes place on weekend nights in the bars and pubs of the old town. Here you will find over 80 places to hang out, including the cavernous **Iguana Bar**, and the more intimate **Charleston Club**, both off Calle de los Estailines, or the packed **Soriketa Bar** and the **Curaitz Club** (more local color here) on Calle Fermín Calveton.

A small jazz club known as the **Galleria** offers occaisional live music nights without a cover charge and can be found at the edge of the old town on the Alameda del Boulevard. As the night progresses past 1am or so, much of the action moves to the center of the newer part of town around the Calle de los Reyes Catolicós with packed bars and small clubs like **Splash** and **Adaberi-Beri**, or on nearby Calle de San Bartolemeu where you will find **Rash**, **Cine**, and **Bar Yaba-Daba**.

By 4am (if you've got the stamina), the most fanatical party animals head over to one of the discos like the world-famous **Bataplan Disco** on the Playa dle Concha with its sea-view dance floor and outdoor terrace. Discos likes these will charge about 2,000 *ptas* just to get in, and the action is aggressive.

PRACTICAL INFORMATION

· **San Sebastián Airport**, *Hondarribia-Fuenterrabia, Tel. (943) 642-144*
· **Iberia Airlines Ticket Office**, *Calle Bengoetxea, 3, Tel. (43) 423-586*
· **Main City Tourist Office**, *Turismo, Calle Reina Regente, Tel. (43) 481-166*
· **Regional Tourist Office**, *O.T.G.V., Paseo Fueros, 1, Tel. (43) 426-282*
· **Main Bus Station**, *Estación de Autobuses, Plaza de Pio XII, Tel. (43) 469-074*
· **Main Train Station**, *Estación de Norte, Paseo de Francia, Tel. (43) 283-599*

- **Municipal Bus Information**, *C.T.S.S., Calle Ataritzar, 24, Tel. (43) 287-100*
- **Municipal Police**, *Tel. (43) 451-946*

PAMPLONA

The city of **Pamplona** is the capital of the **Navarra** region. Made famous throughout the world by Ernest Hemingway's novel *The Sun Also Rises*, this town really comes to life during its July **Fiesta de San Fermín** "running of the bulls" and parades. If you are here at any other time of year, the best sights to check out are mostly in the old quarter.

ARRIVALS & DEPARTURES

By Air

Pamplona's busy regional airport is called the Aeropuerto de Noain, located 7 km (4 miles) south of Pamplona off route N-121 on the outskirts of the town of Noain.

Buses between the Airport & Downtown

There is currently no scheduled bus service between the airport and downtown. You must take a taxi or rent a car to get downtown.

Taxis from the Airport to Downtown

Taxis are usually marked with the *Taxi* sign, and can be found at the well-indicated taxi stand at the airport. Almost all of the taxis here are fairly small 4 door cars. Normally, a taxi's trunks can hold about two large suitcases, but those with roof racks can secure two more medium pieces of luggage, and perhaps a couple of carry-on bags inside as well. Expect to pay somewhere between 1,250 and 1,700 *ptas* per ride from the airport to most downtown locations.

By Bus

Most of the bus lines between Pamplona and other parts of Spain and Europe arrive at the Estación de Autobuses bus station off the Calle de Conde Oliveto, near the Plaza de la Paz on the southwestern edge of downtown. From this station, you can either walk about 12 blocks to the central Plaza de Castillo, or a taxi can be hired for about 525 *ptas*.

By Car

From Madrid, the best way here is to take the fast N-1 highway north for 237 km (147 miles) before reaching Burgos., where you will exit onto the small route N-120 east for 115 km (71 miles) until getting to Logrono, where you will make your final connection onto the windy route N-111 north for 88 km (54 miles) before reaching the exit for Pamplona.

From San Sebastián, take route N-240 south for 92 km into Pamplona. Once inside the city you may have to drive around for a few minutes to find metered street-side parking. You can easily find private and municipal garages that charge about 1,750 *ptas* per day.

By Train

Pamplona is connected to the rest of Spain and other points in Europe by extensive rail service via Renfe. The large Estación Renfe train station is located off the Avenida de San Jorge about two km northeast of the old quarter of downtown.

From here you can hop on municipal bus #9 to the Paseo de Sarasate for about 120 *ptas* and walk a few blocks north to reach the central Plaza del Castillo. Taxis can also be found just in front of the station, and the average charge is about 750 *ptas* to most downtown hotels and sights.

ORIENTATION

Pamplona, population 182,951, is on the edge of the eastern section of northern Spain, quite close to the French border. It is located 407 km (252 miles) northeast of Madrid, and 92 km (57 miles) south of San Sebastián.

GETTING AROUND TOWN

By Bus

Pamplona's municipal bus company has several Autobuses that criss-cross the city and its suburbs. Most people will have no need to use any transportation here other than their feet. For those who wish to walk a little bit less, getting around by bus is relatively easy. The city has over a dozen different bus lines, all numbered, and hundreds of well-marked bus stops.

Ask anyone standing at a nearby bus stop or the *Turismo* tourist office for route details. Most buses operate every 10 to 20 minutes in both directions from about 6am until 11pm daily, with less frequent service on weekends and holidays. The fare is about 120 *ptas* per ride, and tickets can be paid for on the bus.

By Taxi

A couple of hundred licensed taxis roam the streets, plaza side taxi stands, and major passenger arrival points of this the city during 24 hours each day. To find a taxi, either hail down an unoccupied taxi that happens to be driving by, call for a radio taxi pick up (Pamplona Radio Taxi

Companies, *Tel. (48) 232-300)*, or go to one of the dozens of obvious taxi stands throughout the city.

Taxis charge customers using meters; the fare usually will cost somewhere around 630 *ptas* between most downtown areas. Legally chargeable supplements are posted on a sticker in the taxi's interior.

WHERE TO STAY
Expensive
HOTEL TRES REYES, *Jardines de la Taconera. Tel. (948) 226-600, Fax (948) 222-930. Low season rack rates from 20,000 ptas per double room per night (E.P.). Fiesta San Fermín rack rates from 37,000 ptas per double room per night (E.P.). All major credit cards accepted.*

This giant modern tower four-star hotel in the gardens near the old fortress at the edge of downtown is the best hotel in Pamplona. While far from charming, the hotel offers 350 or so of the best-equipped rooms and suites available in town. All units are air conditioned and come with private bathrooms, direct dial televisions, mini bar, electric trouser press, mini-safe, and great terraces looking out onto the city. Facilities include a full health club, squash courts, sauna, room service, laundry and dry cleaning, secretarial service, private garage, outdoor pool and solarium, business meeting rooms, piano bar, cafeteria, restaurant, beauty salon, boutiques and much more.

Moderate
N.H. HOTEL CIUDAD DE PAMPLONA, *Ave. Iturrama, 21. Tel. (948) 266-011, Fax (948) 173-626. US & Canada Bookings (UTELL), Tel. 800/44-UTELL. Low season rack rates from 14,900 ptas per double room per night (E.P.). Fiesta San Fermín rack rates from 24,700 ptas per double room per night (E.P.). All major credit cards accepted.*

This three-star executive class hotel, on the edge of town in a residential area across from the university, is the best place to stay here. The hotel features 117 rooms and suites with air conditioning, satellite color television, deluxe private bathrooms stocked with amenities, mini-bar, direct dial telephone and comfortable modern furnishings. Facilities include nearby parking, cafe, restaurant, room service, laundry and dry cleaning, business meeting rooms, public bus service to downtown and more. Ask about their special weekend rates including buffet breakfast.

HOTEL ORHI, *Calle Amaya, 4. Tel. (948) 228-474, Fax (948) 228-318. Low season rack rates from 15,500 ptas per double room per night (E.P.). Fiesta San Fermín rack rates from 29,750 ptas per double room per night (E.P.). Most major credit cards accepted.*

Located well within walking distance to the old town, this decent three-star hotel offers 55 rooms that all feature private bathrooms, remote control satellite television, hardwood floors, mini-bar, direct dial telephone, halogen lights and basic furnishings. Facilities here include a cafeteria, nearby parking, and laundry service on request. Nothing special, but a good backup possibility.

Inexpensive
CASA HUESPEDES DE SANTA CECILIA, *Calle Navarreria, 17. Tel. (948) 222-230. Low season rack rates from 5,750 ptas per double room per night (E.P.). Fiesta San Fermín rack rates from 10,600 ptas per double room per night (E.P.). Cash only.*

This converted mansion in the heart of the old town near the cathedral offers large rooms with and without private bathrooms in an attractive setting. No real facilities, but plenty of charm and personalized service.

WHERE TO EAT
Moderate
MESON DE CABALLO BLANCO, *Calle de Redin. Tel. (948) 211-508. Most major credit cards accepted.*

This beautiful converted farm building, just a few blocks from the cathedral near the old town walls and park, is a great place to enjoy a snack or meal while in town. Downstairs you can sit at the bar and join the locals listening to classical music and enjoying mixed drinks, while upstairs the somewhat more formal medieval dining room is filled with period antiques, stone walls, and exposed beams. Their menu features cream of mushroom soup, rice salad, endive and Roquefort salad, entrecote, lobster, grilled daily fish, baked rabbit and several other seasonal specialties. A good three course a la carte meal will cost around 2,850 *ptas* per person plus drinks.

SEEING THE SIGHTS
Approximate duration (by foot and optional taxi) is about 5.5 hours, including church, castle, museum, monument, and side street visits.

The best place to begin your wandering around town is at the centrally located **Plaza del Castillo** square in the heart of downtown. This huge and sometimes noisy plaza has a bandstand in its center, and is surrounded by trees and cafes on its perimeter. Most of the city's workers arrive in this plaza by bus each morning from the newer suburban areas that surround the downtown sector.

The first place you should visit while near the plaza is the somewhat overwhelmed and often less than helpful Turismo tourist office on the Calle de Duque de Ahumada #3, just off the corner of the square's southeast corner. If they have any left (and they usually don't!), ask for a free city map and historical brochure.

Cross through the plaza and follow the Calle de Chapitela and make the next right turn onto the Calle de las Mercaderes. Follow this charming street for a few blocks until it changes its name to the Calle de la Curia and runs smack into the city's Gothic 14th century **Catedral** (Cathedral). Built in the typical Latin cross floor plan, this major house of worship has three different naves, each with dramatic *reredos* of differing styles and ages. The main Baroque facade that you will enter through was actually added by Ventura Rodriguez in the late 18th century, but does not fit in with the rest of the structure. Once inside, you pass beneath a series of fine silver chandeliers and stained glass windows until reaching the simple central nave where you can find the 15th century **tomb** of King Carlos III and his Queen, carved by Janin Lomme from a block of alabaster.

The fantastic 14th century gabled cloister on the right side of the cathedral should also be viewed to see its beautifully carved *Puerta de la Preciosa* doorway, with its images of the Virgin Mary, and the adjacent *Capilla de Barbazan* chapel, whose ceiling is vaulted in a star shaped pattern. Just to the side of the main entrance is a passageway that leads into the **Museo Diocesáno** religious arts museum that has both permanent and temporary collections that are displayed in a wonderful environment including piped in medieval choral music.

The cathedral is open daily from 8am until 1:30pm and 4pm until 8pm with no admission charge. The museum is open daily from May 15 until October 15 from 9am until 2pm, and sporadically open from October 16 until May 14 on Tuesday through Friday from 10am until 1pm. Admission is usually 200 ptas per person, but they often let people in for free during special events.

Once you have exited the cathedral, make a right turn through the tranquil mansion-lined **Plazuela de San José**. Cut through this small plaza and turn left onto the **Calle de Redin** that then leads past several 16th century stone buildings with ancient iron grilles that are connected by wooden overhead archways. A few steps along this block you will find yourself at the medieval **Murallas** (old town walls) and the remains of an old fortress that has been converted into a beautiful park with panoramic river views. This is a wonderful spot to enjoy a picnic, or to stop in at the historic **Meson del Caballo Blanco** tavern for a quick snack.

After resting by the old town walls, return to the front of the cathedral and follow the Calle de la Curia back towards the heart of town. A few blocks after it changes its name to the Calle de las Mercaderes, you will be led into the quaint little **Plaza Consistorial** square with its fine Baroque **Ayuntamiento** city hall building that is lined by fantastic balconies. Continue through the square and bear towards your right onto the shop-lined Calle de Santo Domingo. On the next corner, and just off the right

THE RUNNING OF THE BULLS

The city of Pamplona is now known throughout the world as the location of the famed **La Fiesta de San Fermín** festival that runs (no pun intended!) from July 6th through July 14th of each year. Popularized by Ernest Hemingway's novel "The Sun Also Rises," this wild 8 day party is celebrated by tens of thousands of people from all over the world. While parades, drunken parties, concerts and bullfights are held throughout all hours of the days and nights, the obvious highlight is the **Encierro** bull runs that take place each morning at 8am.

Crowds of anxious spectators get here up to eight hours in advance to line the route between the Plaza Santo Domingo and the old town lanes that lead up to the Plaza de Toros bullring. For about three minutes a bunch of angry bulls run rampant down the streets as crazed runners dressed in white garments push each other into and out of the way of these oncoming beasts and try their best to hit them with rolled-up newspapers without getting killed. This is a dangerous prospect as there are always several major casualties, including one American student that was killed in 1995. Once the bulls reach the bullring, they are again released into crowds, this time inside the ring itself.

The Pobre De, a quiet candlelit midnight parade through the old quarter, marks the final night of this celebration. Tickets for the festivities inside the bullring are sold out well in advance, and hotels still have no choice but to turn away thousands of advance reservation requests. Even so, these hotels still get away with charging surcharges of 250% for rooms booked during these dates! If you didn't plan your trip here during festival time at least nine months in advance, stay about 100 km away and drive into the city at about 3am the day before you want to either run or watch. In the evenings after the bull runs, drunken party animals hop from one bar or party to another, and fights are known to break out rather frequently, so be alert.

along the Calle de Mercado, you will find the city's central **Mercado Santo Domingo** covered marketplace where you can stock up on items for a picnic.

Continue along the Calle de Santo Domingo until finding the **Museo de Navarra** art and archeology museum. Housed in a converted 16th century Renaissance hospital, the museum contains an excellent collection of Roman mosaics and stonework, 14th through 18th century paintings by Spanish masters, regional costumes, and several unusual murals. *The museum is open from Tuesday through Saturday from 10am until*

2pm and again from 5pm until 7pm, Sundays and Holidays from 11am until 2pm. Admission is 300 past per person, except for Saturdays when it is free.

From the museum, return back up the Calle de Santo Domingo and pop into the 16th century **Iglesia de Santo Domingo** church just before turning left through the Plaza Consistorial and once again finding yourself heading down the Calle de las Mercaderes. This time, when you reach the bizarre street called Calle de Calderia, you're in the center of the once bustling **Juderia** (Jewish Quarter) that was abandoned after the inquisition. These days it is home to squatters, hippies, punks, and a collection of the strangest bars in town. Walking around here during the day is quite safe, but at night be a bit more careful! Keep walking along this street as its name changes to the Calle de San Agustin and at the next major intersection, turn right onto the Paseo de Hemingway and cross the street to get a good look at the **Plaza de Toros** bullring. *Olé!*

From the bullring, continue walking up the Paseo Hemingway until reaching the next intersection where you will turn left on Calle de Amaya and follow it down for a few more blocks, until bearing right onto the main Avenida de Baja Navarra. Walk up the right side of this wide avenue for several blocks while passing a few major traffic circles until it changes its name to the Avenida de Conde Oliveto.

When you pass the bus station on the **Plaza de la Paz**, cross over to the other side of the avenue and look for a large municipal parking lot. Just behind the lot is a path leading up to the **Parque de la Cuitadela** park that surrounds the well- preserved 17th century walls of the even older **Citadel** fortress.

NIGHTLIFE & ENTERTAINMENT

While new bars seem to pop up all over town, the grunge and alchemist crowds seem to hang out along the *Calle de San Agustin* in places like **Baska**, the **Aska Blues Bar**, and the **Alegria Club**. Over by the **Plaza de Toros** you can pop inside the late night **Cavas** and **Katos** discos, while crazies hop over to the dozen or so hot spots around the Calle de San Nicolas.

For those of you looking for less youthful hangouts, try the civilized **Cafe Iruña** off the **Plaza del Castillo**.

PRACTICAL INFORMATION

- **Regional Tourist Office**, *Turismo, Calle Duque de Ahumada, Tel. (948) 220-741*
- **Pamplona Airport**, *Noain, Tel. (948) 317-551*
- **Regional Train Info**, *Renfe, Tel. (948) 130-202*
- **Regional Bus Info**, *Estación de Autobuses, Tel. (948) 213-619*

- **Pamplona Radio Taxi Companies**, *Tel. (948) 232-300*
- **Central Post Office**, *Paseo Sarasate, Tel. (948) 221-263*
- **Regional Directory Assistance**, *Tel. 1003*
- **National Directory Assistance**, *Tel. 1009*
- **Red Cross Ambulances**, *Tel. (948) 226-404*
- **Medical Emergencies Hot Line**, *Tel. 088*
- **National Police**, *Tel. 091*
- **Municipal Police**, *Tel. (948) 255-150*

ZARAGOZA

The huge city of **Zaragoza** is a friendly place heavily reliant on industry. The compact old districts are steeped in beautiful historic landmarks from the Roman, Arab, Gothic, and Renaissance eras. In the modern commercial zones of the town, there are countless designer boutiques, excellent restaurants, exciting nightlife, and inexpensive museums that draw both rich suburbanites and local university students.

ARRIVALS & DEPARTURES

By Air

If you are arriving by air, there is a small national airport located about 14 km (9 miles) west of town. There are flights scheduled each day to and from Madrid and other major Spanish cities. If you take a taxi from the airport to the center of town, expect to pay about 1,750 *ptas*. Buses can also be found just outside the terminal that are scheduled to coincide with arriving and departing flights. The airport bus that is marked Ebrobus will take you to and from the airport and the city's central Plaza de Aragón and costs about 175 *ptas* each way.

By Bus

There several bus companies offering inexpensive daily service to Zaragoza from a huge variety of nearby cities, towns, and resort areas. The city's main bus station is situated off the Paseo de María Augustin (there are other smaller terminals elsewhere) just a few blocks east of the train station. A taxi from here to almost any downtown hotel or sight will cost under 600 ptas.. The #35 public bus line stops on this avenue, and will take you to the Plaza de España or even further into the heart of the city for just about 125 *ptas* each way.

By Car

From Madrid, the fastest way here is to follow the high speed N-II Autovia east for 325 km (202 miles) until reaching the exits for Zaragoza.

If coming here via Barcelona, take the wide E-15 highway south for 67 km (42 miles) and then merge onto the A-2 Autopista west for about 231 km until it leads to the exit for the city. Once inside the city you will have little problem finding free street-side parking.

By Train

Zaragoza's main rail station is only about 1.5 km (1 mile) west of the city center just off Avenida de José Anselmo Clave. There are multiple daily arrivals and departures between Zaragoza and dozens of other locations throughout the country via the extensive national rail system. From the station, a taxi to just about anywhere in town is about 720 *ptas*, while the #22 public bus can take to the centrally located Plaza de España for about 120 *ptas*.

ORIENTATION

Zaragoza, population 571,355, is both the capital and largest city in the Aragón region, situated in the northeast section of Spain. It is located almost halfway between the two most famous Spanish cities, at about 326 km (202) miles northeast of Madrid, and some 298 km west of Barcelona.

GETTING AROUND TOWN

Once inside Zaragoza, you can walk to almost anywhere. If you prefer to reduce your time on foot, take advantage of the three dozen or so public bus lines (run by the municipal Transportes Urbanos de Zaragoza – TUZSA) that offers single use fares of about 100 *ptas*, or a booklet of 10 trip *Bobobus* tickets for a reduced rate of about 750 *ptas*, available from the major bus stop kiosk at Plaza de España. Maps and other information are available on bus stop signs, in each bus, or from the tourist information offices.

Taxis are also relatively easy to find roaming the streets. Just look for any cab that is exposing the *Libre* (unoccupied) sign in its front window and wave to the driver. The drivers here are typically more honest than in most other cities, and can sometimes provide good tips on nightlife and local restaurants if you try to speak with them in even the most crude Spanish. Typical taxi rides rarely cost more than 775 *ptas* within city limits.

WHERE TO STAY

Expensive

N.H. GRAN HOTEL, *Calle Joaquin Costa, 5. Tel. (976) 221-901, Fax (976) 236-713. US & Canada Bookings (UTELL), Tel. 800/44UTELL. Year round rack rates from 14,000 ptas per double room per night (E.P.). Special* *weekend rates from 10,000 ptas per double room per night (E.P.). All major credit cards accepted.*

The Gran Hotel is a fantastically ornate four-star deluxe hotel offering the finest accommodations in *Zaragoza*. Originally built in the early part of this century, the hotel has been the home away from home for some of Spain's highest level V.I.P. clients, including the current king and prince who both lived here for a year while they were in school.

Besides having an excellent staff, the hotel hosts some of the city's most elaborate social functions. All of the 140 wonderfully large and comfortable rooms and suites offer air conditioning, huge marble bathrooms packed with amenities, mini-bars, hair dryers, direct dial telephones, soundproofed windows, in-room music systems, remote control satellite television and superb furnishings.

World class facilities here include laundry and dry cleaning services, a fantastic buffet breakfast room, chandelier-filled public rooms, business meeting rooms, indoor parking, an electronic tourist information system, a rather good restaurant, and room service. This classic old world hotel is located in the heart of the downtown zone and is surrounded by designer boutiques and peaceful plazas.

HOTEL PALAFOX, *Calle Casa Jimenez. Tel. (976) 237-700, Fax (976) 234-705. Year round rack rates from 19,000 ptas per double room per night (E.P.). All major credit cards accepted.*

This is currently the city's only five-star executive class hotel. Located on a nice downtown street, this serious deluxe hotel offers more services and facilities than any other place in town. The Palafox has 200 beautifully decorated air conditioned rooms and suites featuring deluxe private bathrooms, remote control satellite television, in-room music, mini-bar, direct dial telephones, and great amenities. The facilities here include 24-hour room service, a fully equipped business center, meeting rooms, a rooftop outdoor pool, a good restaurant and two bars, sauna, private garage, and a great staff of real professionals.

Moderate

N.H. ORUS HOTEL, *Calle de Escoriaza, 45. Tel. (976) 536-600. Fax (976) 536-163. US & Canada Bookings (UTELL), Tel. 800/44UTELL. Year round rack rates from 11,000 ptas per double room per night (E.P.). Special weekend rates from 8,000 ptas per double room per night (E.P.). All major credit cards accepted.*

This is a real gem of a hotel, located near the main train station. Housed in an unusual turn of the century building, the Orus represents the best boutique style hotel in the whole city. All of its 38 air conditioned rooms and suites feature beautiful modern furnishings, deluxe private bathrooms stocked with high quality hair and skin care products, remote control televisions with VCR machines built in, direct dial telephones and great beds.

If available, ask the reservations department about one of the special duplex suites – they are truly amazing. The hotel also features plenty of parking, a huge buffet breakfast, special meeting rooms, laundry service, and the best staff in town.

HOTEL TIBUR, *Plaza de la Seo, 3. Tel. (976) 202-000, Fax (976) 202-002. Year round rack rates from 9,750 ptas per double room per night (E.P.). Most major credit cards accepted.*

If location is what you're looking for, no other hotel can beat this place. with its vantage point just in front of the cathedral. The Tibur has 50 larger-than-normal air conditioned rooms with soundproofed windows, marble and tile private bathrooms stocked with amenities and hair dryers, remote control color satellite televisions, in-room music systems, electronic key pass door locks, subtle artwork, modern Formica furnishings, direct dial telephone, mini-bars, a full room service menu, and wall to wall carpeting. There is also a great restaurant, a coffee shop, nearby indoor parking and mini-safes. Make sure to ask for one of the rooms with a view over the plaza.

HOTEL VIA ROMANA, *Calle Don Jaime I, 54. Tel. (976) 398-215, Fax (976) 290-511. Low season rack rates from 10,000 ptas per double room per night (E.P.). High season rack rates from 12,000 ptas per double room per night (E.P.). Most major credit cards accepted.*

Located just a block from the Plaza de N.S. del Pilar, this nice little downtown hotel offers 48 air conditioned rooms with small private tiled bathrooms, satellite color television, direct dial phones, pine furnishings, and either one large or two small beds. Some of the rooms have mini-bars and views over the plaza while some others don't. Facilities here include nearby indoor parking, a coffee shop, a bar, and a restaurant. The staff is extremely nice here, and will be glad to recommend local restaurants and excursions. At these prices, its a great deal.

SPORT HOTEL, *Calle Moncayo, 5. Tel. (976) 398-061, Fax (976) 398-302. US & Canada Bookings (UTELL), Tel. 800/44UTELL. Year round rack rates from 11000 ptas per double room per night (E.P.). All major credit cards accepted.*

Located in the new residential section of town, within walking distance of the main train station, this modern three-star business style hotel is a great find. All of its 64 large air conditioned rooms are beautifully designed with modern furnishings, and have large private marble bathrooms, satellite televisions and video recorders, extremely comfortable beds that tilt at the touch of a button, mini-bars, direct dial phones, colorful artwork, wall to wall carpeting, double glazed windows and environmentally friendly amenities. The hotel also has a nice breakfast room, a modern cafe, a full service restaurant, indoor parking, and meeting rooms. A good choice for this price range.

HOTEL EL PRINCIPE, *Calle Santiago, 12. Tel. (976) 294-101, Fax (976) 299-047. High season rack rates from 11,000 ptas per double room per night (E.P.). Low season rack rates from 8,000 ptas per double room per night (E.P.). Visa and Mastercard Accepted.*

With its great location just seconds away from the Basilica de N.S del Pilar and one of the friendliest front desk staffs in town, this is modern three-star hotel is a great budget selection. The hotel has 45 comfortable air conditioned rooms, each with wall to wall carpeting, nice wooden furnishings, direct dial phones, satellite color televisions, in-room music systems, and spotless private bathrooms. Facilities include a business meeting room, nearby underground parking, and a good restaurant offering inexpensive breakfasts year round, and other meals during the summer.

Inexpensive

HOSTAL PLAZA, *Plaza del Pilar, 14. Tel. (976) 294-830. Year round rack rates from 4,100 ptas per double room per night (E.P.). Cash only.*

Although far from fancy, this basic 13 room hostel offers a series of rooms with either shared or private bathrooms, basic furnishings, and few other facilities. It's clean and is located in the most central part of the historic section of town. Nothing special, but a great deal for those on a tight budget.

WHERE TO EAT

Expensive

RESTAURANTE MONTAL, *Calle de Torre Nueva, 29. Tel. (976) 298-998. Most major credit cards accepted.*

All I can say is that I have been to many excellent restaurants during the research for this book, but none of them (except for Restaurante Arzak in San Sebastián and El Pilar del Toro in Granada) can compare to this amazing establishment. Located inside the luxurious interior of a 15th century tower and an adjacent 17th century palace, this formal gourmet dining room opens its doors from Monday through Friday to a select clientele of the world's most serious gourmets.

The lucky patrons who gather here for lunch or dinner have called several days in advance to reserve a table for a superb five course meal that can be customized to the tastes of each guest. As you enter the restaurant, you are greeted by owners Julián and Rafael Montal who will invite you for an aperitif in a private cellar before being guided through a small museum in the basement of the tower that contains very old bottles of fine

Rioja wines. Then you are led upstairs into one of several ornate dining rooms, featuring Limoges china, imported crystal, and silver cutlery, to view the day's suggested menu that includes vintage Spanish wines. If you don't want anythging from the menu it's no problem, just tell your waiter what you're in the mood for and it will magically appear. The service is perfect and the ambiance is refined but not at all snobby.

The price for this fantastic meal is 7,750 *ptas* per person and is well worth it. Make sure to call at least two days in advance if possible, and dress appropriately. If you can't afford a wonderful meal here, at least try some of their more reasonably priced take-out items from the downstairs gourmet shop. A meal here is one of the true highlights of Zaragoza.

RESTAURANTE ALDABA, *Calle de Santa Teresa de Jesus, 26. Tel. (976) 356-379. All major credit cards accepted.*

A professor from the nearby university recommended this charming place. What I found was a serious gourmet restaurant that featured dishes from this province that were not available anywhere else. Their excellent menu offers prawn salad, marinated mixed fish with fresh herbs, filet of sole with mustard and fresh pasta, sirloin steak with Roquefort cheese, mixed vegetables, and a complete *Carta Aragónesa* menu that is comprised of many of their specialties for only 3,500 *ptas*a person plus wine.

Moderate

RESTAURANTE FORO ROMANO, *Plaza de lo Seo, 2. Tel. (976) 202-000. Most major credit cards accepted.*

After walking around the Plaza de N.S. Del Pilar for a couple of hours, it's good to know that there is a good restaurant nearby. The Foro Romano is a beautiful little establishment with marble floors and plenty of sunlight to help you enjoy a fine lunch or dinner. The menu here is surprisingly affordable, considering the picture perfect location, and during the summer they even set up outdoor tables.

Among their offerings are seafood soup, consommé, vegetable salad, smoked salmon salad, tuna and pimento salad, endives with Roquefort cheese, asparagus au gratin with salmon, saffron rice with mixed seafood, paella for two, filet of sole, sirloin brochette, entrecote, and a vast assortment of desserts. A great 3-course a la carte meal will set you back around 2,850 *ptas* per person plus drinks.

Inexpensive

CASA PASCUALILLO, *Calle de la Libertad, 5. Tel. (976) 397-203. Most major credit cards accepted.*

This casual and somewhat dark *El Tubo* restaurant serves some of the best meals in this price range. Among the extensive menu are both *tapas* and full size *raciones* like bean soup, consommé, paella for one, grilled and marinated seasonal vegetables, house salads, asparagus with vinegar, mushrooms with garlic, eggs with potatoes, calamari, Roman style hake, fried codfish with tomatoes, fresh anchovies, Serrano ham, beefsteak with potatoes, and really good flan. A wonderful three tapas meal heer will set you back around 1,250 *ptas* per person.

LA CAFETERIA DE LA UNIVERSITARIA, *Ciudad Universitaria. No telephone. Cash only.*

If you're looking for the best deal on lunch time food and drinks in town, head over to the city's university and pop into the student cafe and restaurant that is open to the public. Just ask anybody to point out the *Edificio Interfacultades* building and you will be amazed at how cheap and good the grub is.

The menu changes often, but on my last visit I was able to get pizza for 155 *ptas*, potato omelet sandwiches at 95 *ptas*, hot dogs for 120 *ptas*, calamari at 290 *ptas*, sodas for 95 *ptas*, big beers at 125 *ptas*, and a full three course menu of the day for only 650 *ptas*. This place is lots of fun, better than you would expect, and made me want to go back to school for a while.

SEEING THE SIGHTS

Approximate duration (by foot) is about 7.5 hours, including museum, church, plaza, historic ruin, castle, and side street visits.

The Plaza de Nuestra Señora del Pilar

For the sake of convenience, we will begin our walking tour at the pedestrian only **Plaza de Nuestra Señora del Pilar** that is at the northern edge of the old downtown quarter just below to the **Rio Ebro** river. The square itself, built atop Roman ruins, was thoroughly modernized just a few years ago to better accommodate the hundreds of thousands of pilgrims who flock here yearly to visit its principal attraction, the 18th century Baroque **Basilica de Señora Señora del Pilar**.

This fantastically ornate basilica, designed by Philipe Sanchez Francisco de Herrera and later built by Ventura Rodriguez, is famous for its beautiful domed pillar that is located on the very spot where St. James the Apostle was visited by an apparition of the Virgin Mary. Above the pillar, now the primary sight of daily masses that are usually accompanied by a fantastic choir, are a series of frescoed cupolas by such masters as **Goya**, **Velázquez**, **Bayeu**, and **Stolz**.

Just behind the pillar is a small golden frame that contains a piece of stone upon that the apparition descended and people line up to kiss or touch this stone and then leave a small donation in the adjacent box. There are even a pair of bombs on display on the side of the pillar that were dropped on the church during the Spanish Civil War in 1936.

Also in the unusually bright and inviting basilica is a small **Museo Pilarista** museum, which contains a collection of additional paintings and sketches of the painters above, as well as silk religious vestments, intricately designed 19th century pocket watches, precious stone covered crowns and jewelry, Arabic artwork, chalices donated by Queen Isabella II, plenty of silver plate, and beautiful woodwork. Further into the basilica you can also view the central altar with its fine 16th century alabaster *ratable* by Damien Forment.

Additionally, there is a wonderful gated choir area with finely carved wooden seats and massive choir books, a dozen or so impressive side chapels, the solemn *Sacristia Mayor* featuring fine paintings and impressive woodwork, and even a small gift shop selling guide books and souvenirs. Make sure to get a good look at the colorful Spanish tiles that have been placed on the exterior of the many cupolas on top of the basilica, as well as the towers whose clock still keeps perfect time.

The basilica is open to the public from 5:45am until at least 8:30pm daily and admission is free. The basilica's museum is open from 9:30am until 2pm and again from 2pm until 4pm daily and admission is 150 ptas

From the basilica, walk back out into the plaza and take a good look around you. The best place to start is right across the street, at the city's main *Turismo* (tourist information office) housed in a modern black glass building. Here the friendly but overworked staff can supply you with maps and English language sightseeing brochures. After getting some good information at the Turismo, leave the building and turn right. The structure located just next to the basilica is the **Ayuntamiento** (City Hall), not open to the general public.

The building just next to the city hall, called the Lonja (exchange hall) dates back to the 16th century and its spectacular vaulted interior with golden decorative emblems usually contains a free art exhibit of some sort.

Typical exhibition hours here are from Tuesday through Saturday from 10am until 2pm and again from 5pm until 9pm, as well as Sundays from 10am until 2pm.

In front of the exchange hall you can take a quick peek at the **Monumento A Goya**, a statue and monument dedicated to the world famous artist Francisco Goya who was born in a nearby town. Although not really impressive, the monument gives visitors an idea of how well respected his works are in this city, the place where he painted his first canvases.

Continue eastward past the monument to Goya. The **Plaza de N.S. del Pilar** ends and merges into the **Plaza de la Seo**. Here you will find the brand new **Espacio Arqueológico del Foro** museum in a modern building in the middle of this plaza. Once inside this unusual structure, you will descend a flight of stairs that lead to a series of Roman ruins dating back to the era of Caesar Augustus. On display are recently excavated market areas, sewer systems, a Tiberius-era forum, several small buildings that once may have been shops, and some columns. The ruins are quite interesting, but for me, it's the bizarre contrast of the newly built ultra-modern steel and concrete shell that now surrounds these ancient remnants that makes this museum so strange.

What is even more captivating is that there are most likely more ruins form this era buried under many of the buildings in this part of town. There are some property owners around here that are afraid that if they dig anywhere near their buildings, something ancient might be found that will delay their construction project for several years. *The museum is open with no entrance charge from 10am until 2pm and again from 5pm until 9pm on Tuesday through Saturday, and from 10am until 2pm on Sunday.*

Just behind the Roman ruin museum is the imposing facade and giant bell tower of the 12th century **Catedral de la Seo** that is closed for repairs and excavation studies and may not re-open until about the year 2000. The cathedral has elements ranging from Gothic to Platteresque style, and can only be viewed from the outside. Walk around the entire exterior of the building for a view of other interesting structures including the 16th century Casa y Arco del Dean archway and house.

After walking around the cathedral, it's time to head for the other side of the plaza. The next sight that comes into view is the Baroque 17th century **Iglesia de San Juan de los Panetes** church that is now closed to the public. Just behind this church is a fantastic 15th century Mudéjar tower known as the **Torreón de la Zuda** that houses the regional government's *Turismo* office. If you need details about other cities and villages in the Aragón region, this is the place to go. *The office is open from Monday through Friday from 8:30am until 2:30 pm and again from 4pm until 8pm, and on Saturdays from 9am until 1:30pm.*

Other Downtown Attractions

From the western edge of the Plaza de N.S. del Pilar, you should follow the less than impressive 3rd century **Murallas Romanas** (Roman walls) down until they end at a series of more modern archways. Just across the street from these old walls is the covered **Mercado Central** that is the best place in Zaragoza to buy fresh produce and other picnic supplies.

Now exit through the rear doorway of the market and turn left onto Calle de Torre Nueva. After walking a short distance up this small street with several antique shops and inexpensive boutiques, you will run right into the fantastic **Plaza de San Felipe**. For such a small plaza, there are many incredible sights and diversions to be seen here. Once dominated by a huge leaning tower called the Torre Nueva that was destroyed about 100 years ago before it could fall down, this area still contains some of the finest 15th–18th century palaces and mansions in all of Spain. On the left hand side of the plaza is the 15th century *Mudéjar* **Torreón de Fortea** tower that now houses municipal offices and occasional art exhibitions.

Just next to this building is the venerable **Montal**, an absolutely fabulous delicatessen and wine shop first established in 1919, featuring some of the finest take-out food I've eaten in Europe. Housed in part of the adjacent tower as well as in a private 17th century **palace**, offering room after room of freshly cooked regional specialties sold by weight, as well as a giant selection of Spain's highest quality provisions, wines, and spices. Their opulent private upstairs **restaurant** is so fantastic that it ranks as one the world's best, and is a must for all serious gourmands who visit this region.

Across the plaza from the tower is the 17th century Baroque **Iglesia de San Filipe** that is worth a quick look to see its unique spiral stone columns at its front portico and around its main gold leaf altar, and is open during masses. Next door to the church is the 17th century Renaissance **Palacio de los Condes de Argillo** with its excellent **Museo Pablo Gargallo** art museum – the real attraction on this side of the plaza. This fine museum contains hundreds of sculptures and sketches by its namesake who was born in this province back in 1881. His early 20th century works in bronze, lead, and pencil show significant journeys into the worlds of expressionist, modernist, and cubist art and are displayed on three floors of this magnificent palace and inner courtyard. Additional exhibitions of other artists such as **Antonio Saura** may also be open when you visit.

The museum is open Tuesday through Saturday from 10am until 2pm and again from 5pm until 9pm, and Sundays from 10am until 2pm. Admission is free, but you must present either a passport or a driver's license to be allowed inside.

After seeing the sculpture, head back on to the Calle de Torre Nueva and make a left turn onto the boutique-lined Calle de Alfonso I, where the shopping possibilities are endless. About three streets down, make a right turn onto the Calle Espoz y Mina and a bit down this street will be the fantastic **Museo Camón Aznar** fine arts museum. This wonderful museum offers several floors full of paintings and sculptures by 15th-20th century European masters including El Greco, Metsys, Ribera, Cano, Rubens, Zurbarán, Herrera, Velázquez, Rembrandt, Lucas, Lopez, Manet, Bayeu, Pissarro, Renoir, Ruosseau, Dalí, and others.

These were part of the private collection of more than 800 works owned by local academic José Camon Aznar who died a few years ago. A local bank has helped to renovate the lovely 16th century Renaissance **Palacio de los Pardo** mansion to house this simply awesome museum.

The museum is open from Tuesday through Friday from 10am until 2pm, Saturdays from 10am until 1pm, Sundays from 11am until 2pm, and admission is an unbelievably low 100 ptas – but again, you must show either a passport or a driver's license to enter.

This is one of the best museums in the country and should not be overlooked! After visiting the museum you can walk across the street to peek inside the solemn **Iglesia de Santa Cruz** and then continue down the same street, turning right onto the Calle de Don Jaime I.

The El Tubo District

From Calle Don Jaime I, take a right turn onto Calle de Mendez Nuñez that will lead right into the heart of the charming lanes of the **El Tubo** district. While some visitors to Zaragoza will end up spending much of the night in the small *tapas* bars and disco clubs scattered in this area, everybody should at least walk through this district once. The most logical way to stroll along this bizarre collection of bohemian cafes and inexpensive eating establishments is to zig-zag your way through its two main streets, stopping to check out a few nearly hidden side lanes.

Most of the other streets that intersect here are also worthy of a quick look. There are one of a kind hand-made jewelry and exceptional deals on antiques in some of the small shops in this district. After walking down Calle de Mendez Nuñez all the way until reaching the zone's western border at Calle de Alfonso I, turn left and, after reaching the next corner, turn left again onto Calle Estebanez. This street cuts right back into more bars, boutiques, and restaurants, ending once you reach this zone's eastern edge of Calle Don Jaime I, where you will now turn right.

The City Center

Follow Calle Don Jaime I southward for a block or so until it ends at the major intersection of Calle Coso, where you will cross the street and bear right. A few steps away you will then bear left into the **Plaza de España** with its central winged monument, which in turn merges into the **Paseo Independencía** that is the most prestigious business address in town. At the next corner, turn left onto the boutique-lined **Calle de San Miguel** and shop 'till you drop for the next handful of blocks.

At the intersection of Calle Sancho y Gil, turn right until reaching the tranquil **Plaza de los Sitios**, where there might be children playing among the trees. Many of the historic buildings and former palaces that surround this plaza are closed to the general public, but one of the largest is a municipl museum. The **Museo de Zaragoza, Seccion de Arqueologia y Bellas Artes** displays a vast selection of interesting prehistoric and ancient artifacts as well as several galleries full of religious art. Upon entering the museum's turn of the century building, you will be led into the archaeological section with Paleolithic hand tools of stone, arrow heads, bronze age cups and pottery, crude metal hatchets, skeletal remains, funeral stones, gold jewelry, ancient art and sculptures, Roman statues, coinage, Arabic artifacts, and much more.

After entering the beautiful column-lined inner courtyard with huge Roman mosaics and early Iberian commemorative stones, a flight of stairs takes you up to the fine arts museum. Here, there are several rooms, each dedicated to either a specific century or artist. The most impressive works include a series of 14th century icons whose origin is unknown, and other biblical, potrait, and scenic paintings by Bernat, Jimeniz, Abadia, Forment, Pertus, Cosida, Mois, Mengs, Bayeu, Goya, Velázquez, Fortuny, Nicanor, and Unceta. Additional paintings and sculptures also line the hallways.

The museum is open from Tuesday through Saturday from 9am until 2pm and Sunday from 10am until 2pm. Admission is 200 ptas and you must have either a driver's license or a passport to be allowed inside the complex.

Further Afield

There are a few other attractions that you may want to consider taking a taxi to visit. Among the most interesting of these is the 11th century Palacio de la Aljafería that now is home to the region's parliamentary offices. This bold castle, rung with towers, features a Moorish mosque and Arabesque archways that are rather delightful. The palace is in the northwestern edge of the city, just across from the train station. *Entrance to the palace's inner courtyard is free and hours here are from Tuesday through Saturday from 10am until 2pm and again from 4:30pm until 6:30pm or later, and from 10am until 2pm on Sundays.*

The other possible excursion near here is a visit to the Sunday morning open air **El Rastro** flea market that is held alongside the bullring a couple of blocks southeast of the palace. An additional flea market that offers only fabrics and clothing can be found on Wednesday and Sunday mornings along the Calle de Eduardo Ibarra, way out in the southeast section of town a few blocks away from the university.

NIGHTLIFE & ENTERTAINMENT

People in this town really know how to party, especially on the weekends. The nights here start out quiet enough, with people flocking to the **El Tubo** district for small glasses of wine to wash down their *pinchos* (*tapas*).

The most promising of the relaxing hotspots are the wonderful Cafe **Tango** on Calle Mendez Nuñez that displays local art, plays great jazz tunes, and serves the best coffee and beer in the city. Also worth checking out is the adorable little *tapas* bar called the **Bodeguilla de la Santa Cruz** on the Calle de la Santa Cruz, serving great food and beer for really low prices in a unique old world atmosphere.

From there, most people head off around 10pm to other bars on the same street, including **Naíf**, **Cafe Recuerdo**, **La Fondación**, the **Neutral Cafe**, and later on the Taberna **Henry McNamara**, an English-style pub. For still later-night action, go just a few blocks further west to the action-packed Calle Temple, deep within the **Coso** zone, where you'll find fun bars and small dance clubs such as the **El Balcón**, **La Cucaracha**, **Corto Maltes**, **La Encantadora**, **La Recogida**, **Buscon Cafe**, and **Me Mata Zaragoza**.

For live jazz and blues, check out the **Real Club** directly across the street from the basilica.

PRACTICAL INFORMATION
- **Main City Tourist Office**, *Turismo, Plaza de N.S. del Pilar, Tel. (976) 201-200*
- **Regional Tourist Office**, *D.P.D.A., Torreon de la Zuda, Tel. (976) 393-537*
- **Zaragoza National Airport**, *Garrapinillos, Tel. (976) 349-050*
- **Iberia Airlines Offices**, *Aeropuerto, Tel. (976) 326-262*
- **Inter-Regional Bus Info**, *AGREDA, Paseo María Agustin, 7, Tel. (976) 229-343*
- **City Bus Info**, *TUZSA, Plaza de España, Tel. (976) 226-471*
- **Regional Train Info**, *RENFE, Ave. José Anselmo Clave - Tel. (976) 280-202*
- **Radio Dispatched Taxis**, *Radio-Taxi Zaragoza, Tel. (976) 424-242*
- **Municipal Police**, *Tel. 092*

17. BARCELONA & EASTERN SPAIN

Including the regions of Catalunya, Valencia, & Murcia

BARCELONA

Although evidence points to its orginal inhabitation by the Phonecians 3,100 years ago, this area was not permanently settled until a millennium later when the Carthaginians arrived. By the 3rd century BC, they founded a large village here and called it **Barcino**. Soon after, the Romans took control of this growing city and began to create the infrastructure and defensive walls that helped to shape the original city of **Barcelona**, within the boundaries of the district that is now called the **Barri Gòtic** (Gothic Quarter).

In 801 the city was freed from Muslim rule and incorporated into Charlemagne's own territories by the successful invasion of the Christian Franks. Although subject to constant attacks by the Moors, the city finally began to feel a sense of security, when in 988 Count Borrell II declared the city as capital of a new independent state. By the 13th century it had become the dominant partner in the confederation of Catalunya and Aragón.

During the next several centuries, Barcelona became a large and powerful center of commerce. Soon the city outgrew the limits of its original Roman defensive walls and expanded further down towards the waterfront. Making full use of its prime location on the Mediterranean Sea, the state built up an unparalleled naval force and local merchants began to develop superiority in maritime trade. All was going well for Barcelona until it sided with Charles of Austria during the 18th century Spanish War of Succession. As their side was being defeated, the city was besieged for well over a year by Bourbon troops. As the victorious Bourbon forces took control of Barcelona, the Catalonian language was outlawed.

The 19th century saw many changes in the layout of Barcelona. The industrial revolution brought huge factories and mills to the city and money seemed to start to pour into the local economy. By 1860 the old defensive walls were pulled down in order to allow for the expansion of the city, and new neighborhoods like the **Eixample** district began to pop up. The construction of Modernist palaces and mansions in these new urban spaces led to the beginning of the city's **Renaixenca** (Renaissance) era.

During this period, the architectural designs of Gaudí, Domènech i Montaner, and Puig i Cadafalch forever changed the face of Barcelona. The selection of this burgeoning city for the 1888 Universal Exhibition and 1929 Expo also signified to the world that Barcelona had come of age.

The vast majority of local residents sided with the Republicans during the Spanish Civil War, and sadly the people once again suffered greatly as they found their language and unique culture officially suppressed under Franco.

After the Republicans lost, Franco's Nationalist henchmen took Catalunya's president to the Montjuïc castle and had him brutally executed. After the repressive dictator died in 1975, the autonomous government of Catalunya once again ruled in Barcelona. With massive improvements in the infrastructure built for the 1992 Olympic Games, Barcelona has once again become one of the world's great cities.

ARRIVALS & DEPARTURES

By Air

Barcelona's main international airport is the Aeropuerto de Barcelona. Located 12 km (7 miles) southwest of Barcelona off the C-246 highway near the industrial town of El Prat de Llobregat, this modern and beautifully designed airport has separate international (Terminal A), domestic (Terminal B), and Madrid air shuttle (Terminal C) wings. This well-managed facility is responsible for the trouble-free movement of approximately 10 million passengers yearly, and generally services more than 2,600 flights per week! Since this airport is so much less congested than its counterpart in Madrid, the ambiance and comfort level here is actually much more impressive.

The many services at the airport include luggage carts for 25 *ptas*, wheelchairs for the physically challenged, currency exchange desks (open 7am until 11pm), banks with ATM machines, a tourist (*Turismo*) office, luggage storage at 475 *ptas* per bag each day, a lost and found office, self-service and sit-down restaurants, cafés, boutiques featuring designer goods, a pharmacy, a newsstand and cigarette shop, soda machines, a florist, a mini-market, a *Cava* bar, dozens of pay phones that accept coins and credit cards, a Renfe train station, a full service post office, a multilingual information desk, a hotel booking kiosk, duty free shops, car rental offices, tour operator and excursion desks, and VIP lounges for business and first class passengers.

For pick up or drop off of passengers at the airport, parking is available at 200 *ptas* per hour and 1,200 *ptas* per day via a series of automated coin and credit card operated payment stations. If you want to leave your rental car at the airport while you explore Barcelona for a few hours or days, ask your rental company's kiosk in the airport. Most major car rental companies will let you park in their officially assigned airport parking areas for free.

Buses between the Airport & Downtown

There are three bus options available which should take between 35 and 55 minutes each way depending on local traffic conditions. A special air conditioned airport shuttle bus marked Aerobús A1 takes passengers and their luggage to and from the airport and Barcelona's central Plaça de Catalunya plaza with its taxi stand and nearby metro station for 435 *ptas* each way, with additional stops along the way. These buses depart every 15 to 20 minutes during normal airport operating hours daily (no service from about 11pm until 6am) in both directions and can be found at the well-marked bus stops directly in front of terminals A, B, and C. The friendly drivers can make change of small bills, accept Visa cards, and will be glad to announce the requested stop in advance for your convenience.

The local tourist office has recently informed me of an excellent airport and city tour bus package fare called the Travelcard. This card includes four journeys on the Aerobus and two tickets for the Tomb Bus sightseeing bus for only 1,000 *ptas* Ask the driver before boarding the Aerobus if this excellent promotion is still being offered!

Other less expensive municipal buses may also be used to go back and forth between Terminal B and Barcelona's large Plaça d'Espanya square on the west side of the city on a daily basis. Between 6:20am and about 10pm, the bus marked Linea EA-Aeropuerto-Pl. Espanya can take you past several stops between the airport and Plaça de Espanya (with a nearby metro station) for 120 *ptas* each way, with departures every 80 minutes or so. Between 11pm and about 3am, the night bus marked Linea EN-Aeropuerto-Pl. Espanya travels between the airport and Plaça d'Espanya for 120 *ptas* each way with departures every 65 minutes. Have exact change ready for the driver.

Trains between the Airport and Downtown

There is a new Renfe train station that can be reached via a walkway above the parking lot from Terminal B. Here you can find scheduled service daily between the airport and several locations in the city. These commuter-style trains are marked Aeropuerto-Barcelona Sants and run every 30 minutes or so in each direction from 5:45am until about 10:15pm. Since they are not subject to road traffic congestion, the typical running time from the airport is under 18 minutes to the Sants Estació just a few blocks above the Plaça d'Espanya for 275 *ptas* each way.

For a little more money, there may also be additional service offered along the same line that leads further onward to the Plaça de Catalunya, Arc del Triomf, and Clot-Aragó train stations.

Taxis from the Airport to Downtown

Taxis are generally yellow and black sedans marked with the *Taxi* sign, and can be found in abundant supply at well-indicated taxi stands at the airport. Please note that almost all of the taxis here are fairly small sized 4 door cars. Normally, a taxi's trunk can hold about two large suitcases, but those with roof racks can secure two more medium pieces of luggage, and perhaps a couple of carry-on bags inside as well. Unfortunately, there are no station wagon or van style taxis available in Barcelona.

Expect to pay somewhere between 1,850 and 2,300 *ptas* per ride from the airport to most downtown locations, but rip-offs do occasionally occur. If you think you are being overcharged, ask for an official receipt (*recibo oficial*), write down the license number of the taxi (usually posted near the meter), and call *(93) 301-9060* to register your complaint. The police tend to take these complaints seriously.

By Bus

Most, but not all, of the bus lines between Barcelona and other parts of Spain and Europe tend to stop at the busy Estació d'Autobuses Barcelona Nord bus depot, a few blocks above the Parc de la Ciutadella park in the east part of downtown. Be sure to call in advance to find out exactly where and when your bus comes in. From here, a municipal bus, or subway from the nearby Arc de Triomf *metro* station will cost 120 *ptas* to almost any location in town.

Another major point of arrivals and departures for private buses servicing this city is over at the Estació d'Autobuses Sants, situated a handful of streets northwest of Plaça d'Espanya in the west zone of downtown. From this station, a city bus or even a subway from the nearby Sants Estació *metro* station will set you back 120 *ptas* You can also hail a taxi from either of these two bus stations, which can be expected to charge about 670 *ptas* to reach almost any downtown destination desired.

By Car

From Madrid, the fastest way here is to follow the high speed N-II Autovia east for 325 km (202 miles) until reaching Zaragoza, where you should connect to the adjacent A-2 toll motorway east for about another 257 km (159 miles) until it ends and you are forced to merge onto the E-15 expressway north for the final 39 km (24 miles) to Barcelona.

Once inside the city you may have a difficult time finding free street-side parking. Many private garages can be found throughout the city, but you can expect to pay somewhere around 2,400 *ptas* and up per day.

By Ferry & Sea

Since Barcelona is situated along the ocean, several ferries and luxury liners make this city one of their ports of call. Ferries to and from the **Balearic Islands** – Palma de Mallorca, Ibiza, and Mahon – call in over at the Moll de Barcelona ferry landing over on the southeast side of downtown below the Ramblas. From here you can pretty much walk to all of the downtown sights, or take a subway from the nearby Drassanes *metro* station for 120 *ptas*.

If you arriving on one of the regularly scheduled cruise ships that stop briefly in town while navigating the Mediterranean, you'll end up at the international cruise port of Moll de Adossat a few blocks further south. Most cruise liners provide courtesy buses to points downtown upon arrival, but a taxi will bring you anywhere in town for 520 *ptas* or so.

By Train

Barcelona is linked to the rest of Spain and Europe by an extensive series of rail lines. This city has several different Renfe rail stations, each with its own series of daily arrivals and departures. The most common location for service to and from most cities in Spain and border villages in France, is the large Estació Sants, about six blocks northwest of the Plaça d'Espanya square in the western sector of downtown.

For other long distance Spanish and international trains including those servicing Paris, Milan, Zurich, and Geneva, you may need to utilize the Estació de Franca station across from the Parc de la de la Ciutadella park in the eastern part of downtown.

Additional local services and commuter trains may be found at either the Plaça de Catalunya depot located in the square it is named after; the Clot-Aragó station over by the Parc de Clot park in the northeastern part of town; or at the Passeig de Gràcia terminal in the upper zone of downtown a few blocks above the Gran Via Cortes Catalanes. There are smaller commuter rail stations at several other locations throughout the city and suburbs.

Make sure to use the train information phone numbers listed in the *Practical Information* section at the end of the Barcelona entry to recon-firm, in advance, the exact time and station that you may need. Both the Estació Sants and Estació de Franca stations offer such facilities as ticket/

reservation booths, nearby currency exchange, luggage storage areas, restrooms, showers, bookstores, travel agencies, and cafés, while the others are somewhat more basic in terms of facilities.

Connections between these stations and any other point in Barcelona can generally be made by public bus or *metro* for 120 *ptas* each way, or via taxi for roughly 790 *ptas* or so depending on how much luggage you have and where you are going.

ORIENTATION

Barcelona, population 3,096,800, is the capital the **Catalunya** region. The city faces the Mediterranean Sea in the northeast corner of Spain. It lies 621 km (385 miles) east-northeast of Madrid, and about 128 km (79 miles) south of the French border.

There are few cities in the world that can compare in either beauty and excitement to the spectacular metropolis of Barcelona. Every district, street, monument, mansion, park, and seafront esplanade seems to take on an enchanting glow. More liberal, laid back, and artistically inclined than Madrid, this city has enough to keep a visitor occupied for at least five days. Since about half of the most important attractions are well within walking distance from each other, those with just a couple of days here can still get a good idea of what this city is all about.

For people who have a limited time to see the sights, I strongly recommend hopping on either a half-day guided city tour, or a self-guided **Bus Turístic** journey to get the feel of the city. Be aware that pickpockets are in abundance here, and if you're not careful you could easily become a target.

For the sightseeing part of this section, I have used the bustling **Plaça de Catalunya** as a starting point for the walking tours. This plaza and the **Ramblas** that adjoin it are the focal point of town, where you'll find great people watching, shopping, and transportation choices.

GETTING AROUND TOWN

By Bus

Barcelona's municipal bus company, known officially as Transportes Municipal de Barcelona (**TMB**), offers an abundant supply of large red, green, or yellow colored **Autobuses** (buses) that criss-cross almost every neighborhood. With dozens of different bus lines, all numbered for convenience, and hundreds of well-marked bus stops each with its posted corresponding route map, getting around above the ground is fairly easy.

First pick up a free, multilingual pocket **Guida del Transport Public** (public transportation system map and timetable). These can be found, for free, during business hours at the TMB bus information kiosk at the

Plaça de Catalunya, or at any local *Turismo* tourist office in town. The operating hours for most buses is from 5am until about 10:30pm daily. If you're out late at night, several special (**Nitbus**) nightowl buses, indicated by the letter "**N**" preceding their route number, run from the *Plaça de Catalunya* to several other major bus stops in town from about 10:30pm until 4:30am. These special buses to various locations throughout the city run on a 40 to 60 minute frequency when the normal buses have stopped, and are usually painted blue on the outside. Keep in mind that these special night buses do not accept normal single use or multiple use tickets.

The price for a single use normal bus ticket is currently 140 *ptas*. A single use night bus ticket is 150 *ptas* each way and can be bought directly from the driver who will be glad to make change for small bills. New passes called **T-Dia** cost 575 *ptas* each and can be used for unlimited access on all public transport within a 24 hour period. A special **T-1** 10 ride bus and *metro* ticket may be purchased for the discounted price of only 775 *ptas* from any *metro* station ticket window. For those of you who board the buses with a pre-purchased ticket, please use the validation machines next to the driver to stamp it before each ride. If you ask politely, the driver will try to call out the name of your desired stop upon arrival.

TAKE THE #100-BUS TURISTIC!

*Another interesting **TMB** managed bus program designed especially for tourists is the wonderful **#100-Bus Turistic** sightseeing bus. This high season only (mid-June through mid-October) program allows visitors to enjoy unlimited express bus service for either one or two days between 15 specially designed stops adjacent to almost every major attraction in the city. You just hop on the red colored #100 bus and jump on and off again at your whim. Locations covered include **Plaça de Catalunya, Las Ramblas, Plaça de Palau, Moll de Barcelona, Parc de la Ciutadella, Vila Olímpica, Sagrada Familia, Passeig de Gràcia, Park Guell, Tibidabo Tram, Poble Espanyol, Montjuïc,** and more. Service is daily from 9am until 9:30pm and starts every 20 minutes from the Plaça de Catalunya.*

Another added advantage is that you get between 30% and 50% discounts with your pass at attractions, amusement parks, museums, tram rides, and boat excursions that are located just seconds away from the above stops. Best of all, a local tourist information officer will be aboard each bus to explain the sights and hand out information along the route. The current fare is 1,700 ptas for a one day pass or 2,300 ptas for a two day pass. Children under 12 can get a 30% discount from the above rates. In the summer, this is the best way to see all of the city's best sights. You also have a great chance to become friends with other travelers from around the globe.

Another great aspect of taking the bus as opposed to the *metro* is that you get to see lots of side streets that you wouldn't normally see. The major drawback is that during rush hours, you may find yourself packed in like a sardine, and getting off at your stop can be difficult.

Barcelona also offers a fantastic express bus program for local businessmen and those interested in serious shopping. The **TMB** municipal transit company runs a series of blue painted **Tomb Bus** 18-seat air conditioned coaches that cover many of the city's most important downtown shopping zones in a circular route. This fantastic downtown bus route stops every 6 to 12 minutes at each of 27 locations between Plaça de Catalunya and Plaça Piu XII. The tickets can be bought for 150 *ptas* each ride on the bus itself. *Hours of operation are Monday through Friday from 7:30am until 9pm, and Saturdays from 10am until 9:30pm.*

In theory, the **T-1** passes should be accepted, but I had trouble using mine on this route for some strange reason. There is however, a special deal for this bus that includes four one-way tickets to and from the airport via the Aerobus and two tickets on the Tomb Bus for only 1000 *ptas* Ask the driver for details and tickets.

By Subway

The pubic *metro* train system here is a well-designed and easy to use series of four separate subway lines (as well as one connecting commuter train routes). All of the lines are noted by the letter "L" followed by a number, and are color coded as well. There are more than 80 separate stations throughout the city and nearby suburban areas.

At every *metro* station there is a ticket booth where you should be able to obtain a free little **Guia de Metro** system map upon request, and it is a must for every visitor to town. The diamond-shaped red signs on their maps indicate the location of the street level access stairways to the stations. Since the transfer signs indicate the number and color of each line and name of the line's termination station in each direction, you must make sure to know where you are, where you are going, and the last stop of the train you wish to take.

These transfers are fairly easy, and do not cost anything additional. With the use of the free map, it will generally take less than 16 minutes to reach any destination in town. The subways are clean, graffiti-free, relatively safe at all hours, and a great way to get around. Smoking is not permitted in the stations, and most people obey this regulation.

The trains cost the same amount as the municipal buses, although the tickets are not interchangeable at this point. A single fare costs 140 *ptas* per person, a ten ride **T-1** ticket for *metro*, bus, and some commuter lines costs 775 *ptas* New passes called **T-Dia** cost 575 *ptas* each and can be used for unlimited access on all public transport within a 24 hour period.

Longer term passes from 2 through 30 days are also available at additional cost. You can buy either of these types of tickets at any *metro* station's ticket window or automated ticket dispensing machine. Be sure to insert your ticket with the arrow pointing into the turnstile. Pass through the gate and retrieve your ticket at the other end. If you get caught inside the system without a recently stamped ticket, you will be fined 5,000 *ptas* on the spot!

The *metro* system operates at different hours depending on the day of the week. On Monday through Thursday the hours are from 5am until 11pm. On Fridays, Saturdays, and evenings immediately before a public holiday, the system operates from 5am until 1am. On Sundays the hours of service are from 6am until midnight. Finally, on holidays that fall on weekdays, the subway runs between 6am and 11am. Train frequencies average about every five minutes during business days, and every eight minutes or so during late evenings, holidays, and weekends. Although packed during the rush hours (8am until 10am and 6pm until 9pm), the *metro* system is still the best way, besides walking, to get around town.

By Taxi

There are more than 11,000 licensed taxis that roam the streets and major passenger arrival points during all hours of the day and night. Drivers here are generally polite, humorous, and great sources of inside information. To find a taxi, either hail an unoccupied taxi (when empty they will illuminate a small *Taxi* light above the car) that is driving by, go to one of the dozens of obvious taxi stands throughout the city, or call Barcelona Radio Taxi Companies, *Tel. (93) 357-7755 or (93) 490-2222,* for a radio response pick up on demand. During rainy days, festivals, trade fairs, or weekday morning and evening rush hours (6am until 10am and 6pm until 9pm) it may be quite a wait until you get lucky.

Taxis for the Physically Challenged

A new service offers specially designated taxis for those with special needs. The price is identical to normal taxi rates, and considering the obvious lack of access for those in wheelchairs to reach most municipal buses and the *metro*, this is the way to go. Just call *Tel. (93) 358-1111* and reserve a pickup for a **Taxi para Minusvalidos**.

WHERE TO STAY

Expensive

HOTEL RITZ, *Gran Via de les Cortes Catalanes, 7. Tel. (93) 318-5200, Fax (93) 318-0148. US & Canada Bookings (Leading Hotels), Tel. 800/223-6800. Weekend rates from 32,000 ptas per double room per night (B.P.). Normal rack rates from 48,000 ptas per double room per night (E.P.). All major credit cards accepted.*

This opulent, ornate grand five-star hotel is the most famous place for movie stars and top executives to stay. There is a formal and old world ambiance here. There are 160 beautifully decorated rooms and suites, each offering sitting areas, air conditioning, luxurious bathrooms, satellite television, mini-bar, direct dial telephone and mini-safe.

Facilities include a gourmet restaurant, piano lounge, boutiques, newsstands, car rental and excursion desk, valet, 24-hour room service, available secretarial assistance, valet parking, laundry and dry cleaning, meeting rooms, and an older staff that remembers the repeat clients and takes good care of them.

HOTEL ARTS, *Carrer de la Marina, 19, Port Olímpic. Tel. (93) 221-1000, Fax (93) 221-1070. US & Canada Bookings (Ritz Carlton), Tel. 800/241-3333. Weekend rates from 24,000 ptas per double room per night (E.P.). Normal rack rates from 30,000 ptas per double room per night (E.P.). All major credit cards accepted.*

Located in the Olympic Village area of Barcelona, this ultra-modern deluxe hotel is located in a 44-story glass and exposed steel beam skyscraper. Operated by the famous American-based Ritz-Carlton com-

---

FIGURING OUT BARCELONA'S TAXI RATES!

Taxis charge somewhere around 390 to 720 ptas per ride (not per person) between most downtown locations, depending on exact distance and traffic conditions. All licensed taxis have electronic meters that start at 295 ptas that should last about four minutes, or the first 1.8 km (1.1 mile), and click away at differing rates depending on the time and day. The basic weekday price is roughly 101 ptas per kilometer from 6am until 10pm daily, and 122 ptas per kilometer from 10pm until 6am, as well as all day during weekends and holidays. You may also be charged at about 38 ptas per minute when the taxi is going slow, or if it's totally stopped. Normally this works out to somewhere around 11 ptas per city block during non-rush hour city rides.

*Legally chargeable **supplements**, posted on a sticker in the taxi's interior and reflected in the meter rate, include an additional 300 ptas for airport pickups and 100 ptas extra for each piece of luggage. There is also a minimum fee of 1,000 ptas for airport service. These extra charges can be combined, but are occasionally illegally utilized, so pay attention. If for any reason you think you are being overcharged, ask for an official receipt (**recibo oficial**), write down the license number of the taxi (posted near the meter), and call Tel. (93) 301-9060 to register your complaint. By the way, over 1,000 taxis in this city are equipped to accept credit cards for their tariffs.*

pany, this five-star hotel has 455 rooms and suites (some with outstanding city and ocean views) that are very modern style, featuring marble-filled deluxe private bathrooms with deluxe amenities, powerful air conditioning, mini-bars, mini-safes, Bang & Olufsen audio/video systems, plush furnishings, multiple direct dial telephones, motorized curtain blinds, and bath robes. Mostly used for large groups and conventions, the hotel is a favorite among visiting heads of state and celebrities.

Facilities here include an outdoor swimming pool, a health club, boutiques as well as a nearby shopping center, a newsstand, limousine service, special top floor Executive Club floors, several restaurants and lounges, a grand ballroom, huge business meeting rooms, indoor valet parking, room service, laundry and dry cleaning services, free video rentals, high security, a full service concierge desk, and plenty of staff to point you in the right direction. The ambiance here is quite formal, and male guests are requested to wear sport jackets after 8pm each night. The Hotel Arts is about the best place in the city to book accommodations for conferences or large business meetings, but is unfortunately far from perfect for vacationers.

HOTEL REY JUAN CARLOS I, *Avenida Diagonal, 671. Tel. (93) 448-0808, Fax (93) 448-0607. US & Canada Bookings (Leading Hotels), Tel. 800/223-6800. Special weekend rates from 25,500 ptas per double room per night (B.P.). Year-round rack rates from 38,000 ptas per double room per night (E.P.). All major credit cards accepted.*

The modern Rey Juan Carlos I is a fine five-star deluxe property situated in the northern section of downtown Barcelona's financial district. The hotel features 375 rooms and 37 opulent suites with either city, mountain, or port views. These are all air conditioned and have large private bathrooms, remote control cable television, mini-bar, am-fm clock radio, direct dial telephone, and extremely comfortable modern furnishings.

Facilities include a fully equipped health club with jogging track and tennis courts, a huge outdoor swimming pool, concierge and excursion desks, limousine service to the airport, optional child care and secretarial services, gourmet French and Japanese restaurants as well as a nice cafe and a tranquil bar/lounge. There is also secure private parking, boutiques, a newsstand, a putting green, business and convention rooms, a valet, 24-hour room service, car and cellular phone rental on the premises and a really nice young professional staff who are as patient as they come. Good for businessmen, deluxe travelers, and demanding groups.

HOTEL DUQUES DE BERAGA, *Carrer de Beraga, 11. Tel. (93) 301-5151, Fax (93) 317-3442. US & Canada Bookings (Meridien), Tel. 800/543-4300. Normal rack rates from 23,100 ptas per double room per night (E.P.). All major credit cards accepted.*

Housed in a beautifully restored 19th century Modernist mansion just off the central Plaça de Catalunya square, this great little four-star hotel is a real gem. As soon as you pass through the hotel's front doors and enter the opulent lobby area filled with fine tapestries, marble floors, handcrafted coffered ceilings, period furnishings, and a grand staircase and skylight, you know you are in for a special stay. There are 55 rooms and one serious suite that all have a mixture of antique and modern furnishings, private bathrooms, cable television, nice artwork, and windows with either interior or city street views. Facilities here are fairly limited, but you can enjoy a good meal at the quaint gourmet restaurant, and ask the nice staff here for suggestions about excursions and sightseeing. A good place to stay if you want to be close to everything Barcelona has to offer.

CONRAD INTERNATIONAL BARCELONA, *Avenida Diagonal, 661. Tel. (93) 448-0808, Fax (93) 448-0607. US & Canada Bookings (Hilton), Tel. 800/445-8667. Normal rack rates from 32,000 ptas per double room per night (E.P.). All Major credit cards accepted.*

This modern five-star deluxe hotel towers 15 floors above the upper limits of downtown Barcelona to reveal wonderful sea and mountain views. The hotel offers 412 beautifully decorated rooms and suites (some are wheelchair accessible) each with large marble bathrooms, high quality hair and skin care products, air conditioning, one or two queen sized beds, mini-safe, mini-bar, executive desk, fax and computer modem jacks,

BARCELONA'S LOCAL FESTIVALS

Contact the local Turismo office, Tel. (93) 410-2570, for more details.

Carnaval	*Mid-February*	*Processions, Parties*
Semana Santa	*April*	*Strange Processions*
Festa Sant Jordi	*23 April*	*Giving of Books and Roses*
Verbena de Sant Joan	*23 June*	*Bonfires, Fireworks on Montjuïc*
Festes Grec	*Late June-July*	*Live Theater throughout the city*
La Diada	*11 September*	*War Remberance Celebrations*
Festa Major	*Late September*	*Processions, Music, Fireworks*
Jazz Festival	*October/Nov.*	*Live Jazz Concerts*
Festa Santa Lucia	*Late December*	*Fair near Sagrada Familia*

remote control satellite television with optional movie channels, large picture windows and comfortable new furnishings.

The hotel is a favorite among visiting American executives because of the many facilities which include a massive outdoor swimming pool, jogging track, formal and casual restaurants and bars, a coffee shop, secretarial and child care services, room service and business meeting rooms.

HOTEL CLARIS, *Pau Claris, 150. Tel. (93) 487-6262, Fax (93) 215-7970. US & Canada Bookings (Small Luxury Hotels), Tel. 800/525-4800. Weekend rates from 21,800 ptas per double room per night (B.P.). Normal rack rates from 34,100 ptas per double room per night (E.P.). All major credit cards accepted.*

This is among my top hotel picks in all of Spain. This amazing five-star property is so luxurious, beautiful, well managed, and welcoming, that I checked out of a much more expensive hotel so that I could spend another two nights here instead! Located on an exclusive tree-lined street above the Plaça de Catalunya, it's only a four minute walk to most of the best museums, shops, restaurants, and nightlife in town. The best part is that the Claris is at least as luxurious as some of the much more expensive hotels listed above, but is not snobby, stiff, or overly formal. The whole idea here is that guests are expected to feel at home, relaxed and casual.

Originally a 19th century palace, the process of rebuilding the interior took more than five years of back-breaking work. This unique hotel contains over 120 of the most opulent rooms and suites rooms available in the world, each individually designed. Every inch of the impeccably decorated guest rooms and massive public spaces have been filled with the finest quality marble, exotic woods, furnishings, tapestries, and in some cases, Roman mosaics and priceless ancient Egyptian art.

My suite was a fantastic split level unit with its own private sauna, Jacuzzi, suede sofa, hand-carved wooden furniture, a fully remote controlled Bang & Olufsen audio/video system, rare tapestries, a selection of ancient artwork, and totally sound proofed windows. Rooms and suites are each different and feature ultra- deluxe marble bathrooms with gold and chrome fixtures, the highest quality hair and skin care products, plush bathrobes, hair dryers, powerful air conditioners, comfortable beds, unique inlaid hardwood furnishings, satellite televisions, mini-bars, security safes, electronic key pass locks, and direct dial telephones.

Amenities include a rooftop swimming pool, a sauna, an excellent gourmet grill restaurant, a champagne and caviar restaurant, a peaceful bar with an outstanding array of top-shelf liquors, deluxe business meeting rooms, a special private museum of Egyptian art, a Japanese garden, laundry and dry cleaning services, a front desk excursion reservation center, indoor garage and a remarkably beautiful lobby.

The multilingual staff are young but experienced, and do an excellent job. The hotel's esteemed and friendly Swiss trained manager, Pierre Bouisset, insists on greeting as many of the guests as possible, and keeps the customer service at the highest possible standards and the rates are half the price one would expect.

LE MERIDIEN BARCELONA, *Rambla dels Estudis, 111. Tel. (93) 318-6200, Fax (93) 301-6200. US & Canada Bookings (Meridien), Tel. 800/ 543-4300. Weekend rates from 19,000 ptas per double room per night (B.P.). Normal rack rates from 31,500 ptas per double room per night (E.P.). All major credit cards accepted.*

Situated right on the Ramblas, the lovely four-star Meridien has 208 spacious rooms and suites, some with terraces overlooking the old town, each with air conditioning, deluxe bathrooms with heated floors and hair dryers, satellite televisions, in-room movie channel, radios, mini-bars and direct dial telephones. The well-designed hotel features a small health club, garage, 24-hour room service, a good restaurant, a piano bar, a newsstand, boutiques, laundry and dry cleaning services, child care, business meeting rooms, and an excursion desk in its reception area. This hotel is a real bargain, especially if booked with its great summer and weekend special rates.

MELIA BARCELONA SARRIA, *Avenida Sarria, 50. Tel. (93) 410-6060, Fax (93) 321-5179. US & Canada Bookings (UTELL), Tel. 800/44-UTELL. Year-round rack rates from 30,050 ptas per double room per night (E.P.). All major credit cards accepted.*

The upscale Melia Sarria is a nice executive class four-star hotel that is mainly frequented by European executives doing business while in Barcelona. The hotel offers 312 individually decorated huge rooms with spacious private bathrooms, remote control satellite television, am-fm clock radio, mini-bar, mini-safe, extremely comfortable furnishings, executive desks, and nice views out over the city streets. The hotel has a fantastic health club, executive club floors, non-smoking rooms, a good restaurant, secure parking, luxurious bar and lounge areas, the best Sunday brunch in town, business services and electronic office equipment for the guests use, car rental and excursion desks, a polite concierge, child care, room service and a friendly staff.

HOTEL CONDES DE BARCELONA, *Passeig de Gracia, 75. Tel. (93) 484-8600, Fax (93) 488-0614. Normal rack rates from 29,000 ptas per double room per night (E.P.). All major credit cards accepted.*

Housed in a famous modernist mansion on the city's most famous block, this unusual medium sized four-star hotel gets books months in advance. The hotel features 109 modern styled (but a bit small) rooms with private bathrooms, direct dial telephones, remote control cable television and simple furnishings. It is the hotel's amazing modernist masterpiece of a lobby, peaceful colonnaded courtyard, and the several balconies facing Gaudi's unique *La Pedrera* housing complex, that keep many of the same guests coming back year after year. Although the facilities are limited to a restaurant and a few nice lounge areas, a nearby health club can be used for a small additional fee.

HOTEL MAJESTIC, *Paseo de Gracia, 72. Tel. (93) 488-1717, Fax (93) 488-1880. US & Canada Bookings (Supranatural), Tel. 800/843-3311. Special weekend rates from 17,500 ptas per double room per night (E.P.). Normal rack rates from 30,000 ptas per double room per night (E.P.). All Major credit cards accepted.*

With an excellent central location in the best shopping and sightseeing district of the city, near to everything important to see and do, this old world style four-star hotel is certainly worth consideration. The property has recently gone through a major renovation and now includes 355 air conditioned rooms and suites that all have private bathrooms with hair dryers, simple but comfortable furnishings, direct dial telephone, remote control cable television, mini-bar and either city or courtyard views. Facilities here include nearby parking, a restaurant, a bar/lounge, health club with rooftop swimming pool, sauna, excursion and car rental desk, business meeting rooms, and more. If you can book the difficult to find weekend special rates, the Majestic is a great choice.

GRAN PASSAGE SUITES HOTEL, *Carrer de Mutaner, 212. Tel. (93) 201-0306, Fax (93) 201-0004. Rack rates from 24,750 ptas per double room per night (E.P.). Most major credit cards accepted.*

For those looking for spacious downtown accommodations that include a complete living-room, this is a really good choice. Located on a quiet side street in the wonderful Eixample district, the Gran Passage has become a favorite for long stay clients as well as families with small children. The rooms are well equipped and include deluxe private bathrooms, mini-bars, climate control systems, hair dryers, and comfortable bedding.

Why get a small room elsewhere when you can get a complete suite for the same price at this modern and friendly establishment?

Moderate

HOTEL BALMES, *Carrer de Mallorca, 216. Tel. (93) 451-1914, Fax (93) 451-0049. US & Canada Bookings (Planet Hotels), Tel. 800/337-4685. Weekend rates from 12,600 ptas per double room per night (B.P.). Corporate rack rates from 18,500 ptas per double room per night (E.P.). All major credit cards accepted.*

The Balmes is a superbly designed medium-sized three-star hotel a few blocks up from the Plaça de Catalunya on a nice quiet side street in the heart of downtown Barcelona's most luxurious shopping district.

There are 100 large rooms and suites that have been built to provide true comfort and a tranquil ambiance. A favorite of visiting businessmen and tourists alike, this hotel is a very good value. Each of the spacious guestrooms and lavish duplex suites has air conditioning, private deluxe marble bathrooms stocked with amenities, satellite television, direct dial telephone, mini-bar, in-room music, mini-safe, dramatic lithographic art, extremely comfortable furnishings and in some cases private patios and balconies. The peaceful inner courtyard has a great outdoor swimming pool and snackbar, while the interior offers a good restaurant, meeting rooms, a wonderful café, garage parking, and a pleasant staff. An excellant good choice in this price range, and a great place to spend a few nights.

N.H. HOTEL PODIUM, *Carrer de Bailen, 4. Tel. (93) 265-0202, Fax (93) 265-0506. US & Canada Bookings (UTELL), Tel. 800/44-UTELL. Weekend rates from 12,000 ptas per double room per night (E.P.). Year-round rack rates from 16,000 ptas per double room per night (E.P.). All major credit cards accepted.*

Located in a tranquil downtown neighborhood just above the Arc de Triomf, the Podium is a delightful small hotel with excellent accommodations. The hotel has 145 huge modern rooms and great junior suites each featuring air conditioning, beautiful furnishings, marble bathrooms stocked with high quality amenities, hair dryers, remote control satellite television, electronic key pass locks, mini-bar, and direct dial telephones. Whether you decide to reserve a terraced city view room or a quiet split-level interior view room, the price remains the same. The junior suites have an additional sitting lounge with their own television and business-style office desk and telephone.

The facilities include a wonderful rooftop swimming pool and sundeck, a fully equipped health club, sauna, an unusually affordable restaurant serving great meals, a nice bar with a big screen television and plush sofas, several business meeting rooms, safe deposit boxes, a black marble lobby area with a piano lounge, laundry and dry cleaning services, parking, and a great front desk staff offering good advice and assistance in booking local excursions, sightseeing, and dining reservations. Under the direction of Sr. Santiago Cabre Ortiz, this nice affordable place has become a truly memorable hotel.

HOTEL ASTORIA, *Carrer de Paris, 203. Tel. (93) 209-8311, Fax (93) 202-3008. US & Canada Bookings (UTELL), Tel. 800/44-UTELL. Special weekend rates from 11,500 ptas per double room per night (E.P.). Normal rack rates from 17,500 ptas per double room per night (E.P.). All Major credit cards accepted.*

Originally built in the 1950's this superb and moderately priced three-star hotel has recently been restored to fine condition. Complete with lavish art nouveau lounges and one of the nicest lobbies in Barcelona, the Astoria is a friendly medium-sized hotel just steps from the Avenida Diagonal, right in the heart of downtown. The hotel offers 117 single, double, duplex, suite, and penthouse accommodations that have been beautifully furnished and include air conditioning, spacious private bathrooms, direct dial telephones, cable television and comfortable modern furnishings.

Fully renovated in 1992, this classic hotel has plenty of charm and a nice staff. Health club services, nearby parking, a bar, business meeting rooms, express laundry and dry cleaning, and a restaurant are available to guests at a small additional charge. Recommended for anyone looking for nice rooms at affordable rates.

N.H. HOTEL CALDERON, *Rambla de Catalunya, 26. Tel. (93) 301-0000, Fax (93) 412-4193. US & Canada Bookings (UTELL), Tel. 800/44-UTELL. Weekend rates from 17,000 ptas per double room per night (E.P.). Year round rack rates from 25,000 ptas per double room per night (E.P.). All major credit cards accepted.*

The modern four-star Calderon towers above the upper Ramblas just a few minutes away from the heart of downtown. It offers 264 nicely designed sun- drenched rooms and suites each with electronic key pass locks, satellite televisions, marble bathrooms stocked with amenities, air conditioning, bedside radios, mini-bars, one king or two double beds, lithographic art, direct dial telephones, and nice furnishings. There is a special executive floor, dozens of balconied and connecting rooms, and the three upper floors have sea views. With its mixed clientele of international businessmen and travelers, and plenty of in-house facilities, this is one of the city's best large hotels in the moderate price range.

The many facilities here include a panoramic rooftop swimming pool and sun deck, a small indoor heated swimming pool, a workout room, sauna, a business center with free use for the guests, large business meeting rooms, safe deposit box rental, indoor garage, 24 hour porterage and security, rental car and excursion desk, a good restaurant and bar, big screen TV lounge, laundry and dry cleaning service, and a great staff.

HOTEL PRINCESS SOFIA, *Plaça Pius XII, 4. Tel. (93) 330-7111, Fax (93) 330-7621. US & Canada Bookings (SRS Hotels), Tel. 800/223-5652. Weekend rates from 17,000 ptas per double room per night (E.P.). Normal rack rates from 21,000 ptas per double room per night (E.P.). All major credit cards accepted.*

Located uptown just off the Avinguda Diagonal, this large four-star modern tower hotel is another good choice. The hotel has 500 nice big rooms and suites, many with city views, all offering air conditioning, huge marble bathrooms, mini-bar, in-room movies, direct dial telephones, satellite television, hair dryer, bathrobes, mini-safe, radio, and nice interiors. Facilities include both indoor and outdoor swimming pools, sauna, massage, steam bath, health club, two good restaurants, bar, lounge area, newsstand, boutiques, indoor parking, laundry and dry cleaning, 24-hour room service, meeting rooms and child care. It's a good hotel a little bit outside of the central downtown zone.

HOTEL RIVOLI RAMBLAS, *Rambla dels Estudis, 128. Tel. (93) 302-6643, Fax (93) 317-5053. Rack rates from 19,750 ptas per double room per night (E.P.). All major credit cards accepted.*

You couldn't ask for a more central location in the heart of the Ramblas, and this thoroughly modern four-star hotel is a real gem. This charming hotel offers 87 tastefully decorated rooms with marble bathrooms, air conditioning, mini-bar, remote control cable television, am-fm clock radio, and nice artwork. There is also a health club, rooftop bar, breakfast room, health club, solarium, nearby parking, and a nice staff. If you don't want a noisy room, ask for an interior view if they have any left.

Inexpensive

HOTEL GRAVINA, *Carrer de Gravina, 12. Tel. (93) 301-6868, Fax (93) 317-2838. US & Canada Bookings (Golden Tulip), Tel. 800/344-1212. Weekend rates from 9,900 ptas per double room per night (E.P.). Corporate rack rates from 14,900 ptas per double room per night (E.P.). All major credit cards accepted.*

The Gravina is located a few blocks from the heart of downtown on a nice quite side street. This is a small three-star full service hotel with 60 nicely decorated rooms featuring air conditioning, private bathrooms, mini-bars, direct dial telephones, mini-safes, hair dryers, trouser press, satellite television, and sound proofed windows. Facilities include a restaurant, snack bar, lounge, and indoor parking. A good budget choice, especially on weekends.

HOTEL ALEXANDRA, *Carrer de Mallorca, 25. Tel. (93) 487-0505, Fax (93) 486-0258. US & Canada Bookings (Best Western), Tel. 800/528-1234. Special weekend rates from 14,500 ptas per double room per night (B.P.). Normal rack rates from 19,750 ptas per double room per night (E.P.). All major credit cards accepted.*

Located in the heart of town, this modern four-star hotel offers 81 nicely furnished air conditioned rooms at good prices. All units are well sound proofed and feature simple private bathrooms, remote control cable television, mini-bar, direct dial telephone and comfortable twin or king sized bedding. Facilities at the Alexandra include a small but convenient exercise room with sauna, restaurant, bar/lounge and a nice staff. A pretty good value, especially during the weekend specials.

HOTEL REDING, *Carrer de Gravina, 5. Tel. (93) 412-1097, Fax (93) 268-3482. US & Canada Bookings (Supranatural), Tel. 800/843-3311.*

Weekend rates from 7,900 ptas per double room per night (E.P.). Normal rack rates from 11,300 ptas per double room per night (E.P.). Most major credit cards accepted.

This basic but nice three-star hotel downtown near the Plaça de Catalunya has 44 comfortable rooms with private bathroom, air conditioning, television, and nice but simple furnishings. Services offered include laundry, breakfast room, lounge, nearby parking and a meeting room. Nothing special, but good for this price range.

HOTEL TABER, *Carrer de Aragon, 256. Tel. (93) 487-3887, Fax (93) 488-1350. US & Canada Bookings (Best Western), Tel. 800/528-1234. Special weekend rates from 10,500 ptas per double room per night (B.P.). Normal rack rates from 13,500 ptas per double room per night (E.P.). All major credit cards accepted.*

This simple three-star hotel near all of Barcelona's major attractions is well priced for both quality and location. Here you will find 91 medium sized air conditioned rooms with small private bathrooms, mini-bar, and either interior or exterior views. There is also a television room, breakfast room, nearby parking, and safe deposit boxes at the front desk.

HOTEL ROMA REIAL, *Plaça Reial, 11. Tel. (93) 302-0366, Fax (93) 301-1839. Weekend rates from 4,500 ptas per double room per night (E.P.). Normal rack rates from 5,500 ptas per double room per night (E.P.). Most major credit cards accepted.*

Although far from deluxe, this well-located one-star hotel in the heart of town has 52 clean and comfortable rooms with private bathrooms and telephones. A good selection for those on a tight budget.

PENSION PALACIOS, *Gran Via de Cortes Catalanes, 629. Tel. (93) 301-3792, No Fax. Normal rack rates from 3,750 ptas per double room per night (E.P.). Most major credit cards accepted.*

Located near the heart of town on a busy main avenue, this extremely basic budget inn offers about two dozen single and double rooms with heat and simple furnishings as well as either private or shared bathrooms (with even cheaper rates). Not a bad choice, but don't expect any real facilities.

HOSTEL DE JOVES, *Passeig Pujades, 29. Tel. (93) 300-3104, No Fax. Year round rack rates from 1,850 ptas per dormitory bed per night (C.P.). No credit cards accepted.*

This most central of the four official R.E.A.J. Hostelling International-affiliated youth hostels in town. It is a great place to sleep for people of all ages on extremely tight budgets, and is a perfect place to meet fellow travelers. The hostel has a somewhat early curfew and some other basic regulations, but at these prices what do you expect! The hostel offers 68 bunk style beds in an assortment of large rooms with semi-private toilet and shower facilities quite close to the Parc de la Ciutadella area. Make sure to lock up your valuable possessions in the lockers before heading out to sightsee, and enjoy their complimentary continental breakfast. A Hostel card must either be presented, or purchased to be admitted into this facility.

WHERE TO EAT

Very Expensive

RESTAURANT NEICHEL, *Carrer de Beltran y Rozpide, 16 bis. Tel. (93) 205-6369. Most major credit cards accepted.*

Affiliated with the prestigious Relais & Chateaux organization, this elegant and sophisticated gourmet restaurant in the Pedralbes district is one of the finest dining establishments in all of Barcelona. Frequented by fashionable locals, executives, and well dressed visitors from around the globe, Restaurant Neichel's beautiful garden-side dining room (and adjacent bar) have recently won top awards for their superb modern interior styling and design.

Jean Louis Neichel, the Alsatian born master chef and owner, continues to set new standards for fine Mediterranean cuisine in Spain. Patrons are offered two different menus that feature absolutely mouth watering dishes such as consommé with fresh herbs, onion tarts, salmon cooked in a pesto and truffle flavored oil, scallops and shrimp with cold noodles, pork loin with rhubarb in grape and pepper sauce, hake gratinee with herbs and black rice, braised country chicken with shrimp, stuffed pheasant, tournedos of lamb with olives and red peppers, scallops in curry sauce and dozens of other great selections that are prepared using the freshest possible ingredients. The wine list is equally impressive, with hundreds of French and Spanish vintages that can be found no where else in the region. The candle-lit tables create a magnificent setting, and the personalized service here is outstanding.

Expect to spend at least 7,200 *ptas* per person (excluding wine) for a superb multiple course gourmet lunch or dinner that is well beyond comparison. Make sure you are dressed to kill, and have made reservations as far in advance as possible.

ELDORADO PETIT, *Carrer de Dolors Monserda, 51. Tel. (93) 204-5506. All major credit cards accepted.*

This internationally acclaimed Mediterranean-style nouvelle cuisine restaurant features outstanding culinary delights prepared by chef Mariano Gonzalvo and his highly trained staff. The casual yet elegant setting in a converted antique villa in the Sarria district of town has brought the trendy set here for years, and continues to be among the most memorable dining establishments in the whole city. Every course from starters and salads to the impressive seafood and meat dishes are dramatically prepared and presented. Although the menu changes seasonally, for around 6,900 *ptas* per person you can enjoy a delightful four course meal that may feature such delicious items as tarragon and arrugula salad, jumbo prawns in rice, foie gras, roasted duck with wine sauce, and diet busting desserts. The wine list is also immense, and this is certainly a great place to spend an entire evening in the pursuit of fine dining without the need to dress too formally. Reservations are a must.

TALAIA MAR RESTAURANT, *Carrer de Marina, 16, Port Olímpic. Tel. (93) 221-9090. All major credit cards accepted.*

A great choice in the Olympic port area, this semi-formal and ultra modern seaview establishment is an excellent gourmet dining experience. The dark wooden interior and red vested waiters really give you the feeling that you're somewhere special. Their huge menu has a wonderful selection of specialties including minestrone soup with shellfish, salad of cured duck with artichokes and foie gras, codfish and spinach, marinaded octopus, mushrooms with pine nut vinaigrette, vegetable casserole with truffles, hake in red wine sauce, stuffed squid, stuffed lobsters, grilled lamb's head and feet with snails and an assortment fine desserts. The typcial cost here is around 6,200 *ptas* per person for a great four course a la carte meal .

Expensive

RESTAURANTE LLEVATAPS, *Palau del Mar, Plaça de Pau Vila. Tel. (93) 221-2433. All major credit cards accepted.*

This modern relaxing harborside dining establishment in the Barceloneta district's most famous building offers a soft pastel interior with exposed wood beams, as well as outdoor seating for 100 patrons. A favorite of families heading back from an afternoon of sightseeing, this cute restaurant is a favorite lunch spot. The fine menu here includes fresh fruit and Roquefort cheese salads fried calamari, assorted croquets, huge oysters, mussels marinara, filet of sole, roast beef, entrecote steak with wine sauce, smoked salmon, rice with lobster bits, beach shrimp and clams with marinara sauce, steak tartar and a rich chocolate mousse with fresh cream. A typcial three-course a la carte meal here will cost around 4,980 *ptas* per person plus drinks.

AGUT D'AVIGNON, *Carrer de Trinitat, 3. Tel. (93) 302-6034. All major credit cards accepted*

Located in the Barri Gothic section of downtown just a stones throw away from the city hall, this highly respected restaurant is frequented by politicians, power brokers, and those looking for the finest in typical regional cuisine. The executive chef, Pedro Falagan Giralt, and his brother Javier have been famous for their incredible dishes, such as langostinos in hot sauce and roasted wild duck in fig sauce, for years now. The older conservative clientele show up at lunch and dinner to spend about 5,250 *ptas* a head for a gastronomic delight, and stay for hours at a time. Reservations are necessary, and the dress code is semi-formal.

BOTAFUMEIRO, *Mayor de Gracia, 81. Tel. (93) 218-4230. Most major credit cards accepted*

Not all of Barcelona's great seafood restaurants are located in the Port Olympic section, and this bustling downtown establishment near all the major attractions is a really good alternative. Botafumeiro's dark wood paneled, nautical-inspired interior is the perfect place to try shrimp, lobster, and fish caught earlier the same day and prepared by chef Moncho Neira in the northern Spanish tradition. My last dinner here cost about 5,450 *ptas* and was as good as any I have ever had anywhere in the world. The restaurant's dress code is not too rigid, and I didn't even have an advance reservation.

7 PORTES, *Passeig Isabel II, 14. Tel. (93) 319-3033. All major credit cards accepted*

Celebrating 160 years of continuous operation, this remarkably busy and casual Catalan restaurant on the edge of Barceloneta specializes in local *paella* style fish and seafood dishes, as well as a vast selection of roasted and grilled meats. The portions are huge, and the place gets packed at all hours of the day until they close sometime after midnight. Service is pretty good and the huge kitchen delivers their entrees at a furious pace to keep the hundreds of patrons moving through their doors, especially during the extremely busy lunch hours. Expect to pay around 4,950 *ptas* a head for a great four-course meal here. The 7 Portes (the name translates to the 7 doors) is a must visit dining establishment for those looking for some local color and good food at reasonable prices. Advance reservations are a good idea, but if you don't mind a long wait you can just show up.

EL RACO D'EN FREIXA, *Sant Elies, 26. Tel. (93) 209-7559 Most major credit cards accepted*

Owned and operated by the remarkably friendly Freixa-Riera family of fine local chefs, this wonderful little regional restaurant features a warm and relaxing ambiance as well as magnificent cuisine. For 5,300 *ptas* and up you can sit in splendor surrounded by fine paintings and an old chimney while being served delicious steak, fowl, and seafood specialties that have a definite Catalan flair. Just tell your waiter or one of the chefs what you are in the mood for, and they will keep bringing huge plates of their seasonal offerings or more complicated house specialties featuring fresh aromatic herbs and other unique seasonings found nowhere else.

EL REY DE GAMBAS, *Moll de Mestral, 22, Port Olímpic. Tel. (93) 221-0012. Visa and Mastercard accepted.*

This is one of the best of the moderately priced restaurants along the port area of the Olympic Village and the staff here try to make every meal special. After passing by the small bar-style entrance and huge aquariums loaded with fish, you are led into either a bustling indoor dining room filled with marble tables, or out onto one of the dozens of yacht-side outdoor tables. This Barcelona institution has a giant menu loaded with freshly caught fish meals and top quality meats.

On my last visit here, the offerings included fish soup, Russian salad, tomato salad, sauteed mushrooms, fresh steamed artichokes, meat kebobs, octopus Galician style, salt crusted prawns, Serrano ham, a huge mixed fishermen's platter, large grilled prawns, broiled crab, filet of sole, Norwegian lobster and strawberries with cream. A nice three course seafood meal here will cost around 5,100 *ptas* per person plus beverages.

Moderate

LES QUINZE NITZ, *Plaça Reial, 6. Tel. (93) 317-3075. All major credit cards accepted.*

As the current hot spot for trendy downtown dining, this relaxed and informal restaurant gets the 25 to 40 year old yuppie crowd each night for an affordable gourmet dining experience. The large bistro-style dining room is delightfully decorated, and is a bit noisy at times. Once inside you will discover a great menu offering gazpacho, a superb vichyssoise, rockfish crepes, cannelloni, grilled endives, steamed rock mussels, grilled salmon, grilled entrecote, and plenty of seasonal specials. At around 3,800 *ptas* per person for a four course meal, it is a great bargain and has lots of local ambiance.

RESTAURANTE SALAMANCA, *Carrer de L'Almirall Cervera, 34. Tel. (93) 221-5033. Most major credit cards accepted.*

Located in the interior of Barceloneta, this is the best home-style seafood restaurant in the city. Packed on weekends and holidays with large families waiting in line for as long as an hour, this wonderful two floor establishment is a real treat. If you get here around 4pm on Saturdays and Sundays, there should be no problem being seated immediately.

The giant menu is full of superbly prepared items like white asparagus, huge mixed salads, fish soup, noodles with clams, fried filet of hake, calamari Roman style, seafood paella, assorted grilled fish, fresh oysters by the dozen, lamb chops with mint, roast leg of kid, stuffed veal loin, beefsteak with french fries, roasted chicken, sirloin steaks and a good assortment of delicious desserts. A hearty three course meal here will set you back around 4,050 *ptas* a person plus wine. This is a great place!

BRASSERIE FLO, *Carrer de Jonqueres, 10. Tel. (93) 317-8037. Most major credit cards accepted*

This is a simple but rather good French brasserie style restaurant where the patrons range from families of tourists wearing Levis and t-shirts to more upscale and well suited locals. The point here is to relax and enjoy good basic French cuisine while watching hundreds of other people and absorbing the lively and somewhat noisy ambiance complete with piped in soft rock music. Among the many items on their large menu are onion soup with melted cheese, pate, barbecued meats, steak with fries, assorted omelets, crepes, grilled salmon, roasted chicken, bouillabaisse, cafe au lait and filling desserts. Lunch or dinner here averages about 2,950 *ptas* per person, and the place is open late on many nights to grab the after theater crowd.

RESTAURANTE EMPERADOR, *Palau del Mar, Plaça de Pau Vila. Tel. (93) 221-0220. Most major credit cards accepted.*

The Emperador is a nice and simple water-side restaurant that offers a great selection of freshly caught fish at good prices. Its extensive menu features such delicious dishes as fish soup, seafood salad, *paella*, black rice with seafood, swordfish kebobs, grilled tuna, filet of sole with citrus sauce, turbot grilled with garlic, veal steaks, grilled prawns, broiled lobster, veal entrecote in green pepper sauce, and lots of good desserts. Dinner here averages about 3,350 *ptas* per person plus drinks.

LA FONDA, *Carrer del Escudellers, 10. Tel. (93) 301-7515. Most major credit cards accepted.*

As another one of downtown's most appreciated new restaurants, La Fonda is a big hit with the under 30 crowd. It has a plush cafe-style interior with huge picture windows looking out onto this odd little street. Make sure to get here before 8pm and avoid the long lines of romantic couples waiting to get in. Typical offerings include a fish soup, assorted omelettes, mixed vegetables, beef carpaccio, meat filled cannelloni, mixed rice casserole, black noodles with seafood bits, mussels marinara, filet of sole meuniere, gulf shrimp platter, entrecote, and plenty more. A hearty three course meal here will cost around 2,250 *ptas* a person plus wine.

RESTAURANTE L'ESCAMARLA, *Passeig Marítim, 40, Platja Bogatell. Tel. (93) 221-1366. All major credit cards accepted.*

You can walk to the beachview L'Escamarla from the Port Olímpic when the crowds gets too big. I had a wonderful feast of a meal at an outdoor table with a great view, for about half of what some other places were charging in the port itself, and the quality was equally high. I suggest trying the house salad, fresh turbot, grilled pork chops, beefsteak, fried calamari, black rice with seafood, clams marinara, grilled langostinos with lemon and a great whiskey tart with ice cream for dessert. Expect a good three course meal here to cost 2,050 *ptas* a person plus wine.

RESTAURANTE PERU, *Passeig de Don Joan de Borbo, 16. Tel. (93) 310-3709. Most major credit cards accepted.*

This is a typical old world restaurant just across the seafront on Barceloneta's main street. Although far from gourmet, this is a nice little place to sit indoors in the simple dining room, or outdoors on one of a dozen small tables and enjoy home-style lunches and dinners. Among the items available here are mixed salads, tuna salad, bouillabaisse, deep fried prawns, roasted chicken, mussels in red sauce, grilled razor clams, seafood paella, entrecote with Roquefort cheese sauce, assorted fish platter, hake with green sauce, monkfish marinara, filet of sole, grilled prawns as well as several daily specials.

Ask your waiter or waitress for suggestions. Typically a good three course al la carte meal here will set you back around 2,650 *ptas* per person plus wine.

Inexpensive

TEXTIL CAFÉ, *at the Museu Téxtil i d'Indumentaria, Carrer de Montcada 12. Tel. (93) 268-2590. Cash Only.*

A small café located on the ground floor of the museum that is managed by students from its school of design. Open from 10am until midnight, this is the prefect place to stop in for a great snack, coffee, or full meal while hopping around the area's many museums and palaces. They feature a full breakfast, lunch, and dinner menu at reasonable prices and a down-to-earth atmosphere with great music. The last time I was here the menu featured such items as croissants for 130 *ptas*, French bread with Manchego cheese at 300 *ptas*, Tuna and tomato sandwiches for 300 *ptas*, excellent salads from 325 *ptas*, guacamole with chips for 575 *ptas*, and a huge array of vegetarian specials starting at just 450 *ptas* each.

EGIPTE, *Carrer de Jerusalem, 12. Tel. (93) 317- 8037. Cash Only.*

Known to budget minded locals and tourists alike, this unusual little Catalan restaurant near the edge of the less than sophisticated Barri Xines district behind the Mercat de la Boqueria market features strangely decorated dining rooms and balconies with dozens of tables pulled way too close to each other. The whole idea here is to eat homemade local cuisine as cheaply as possible, in a strange setting that is loud, packed, and somewhat bizarre. A complete three course meal centered around the day's fish, meat, and chicken entrees will only cost about 2,350 *ptas* a person, and is usually well worth the money. This is a great place to people-watch as everyone from students to well-dressed families of all ages have found their way to the line that starts at the front door. There is no dress code, and you can all but forget about even trying to make a reservation. What an experience, and the food isn't bad either.

AGUT, *Carrer de Gignas, 16. Tel. (93) 315-1709. Cash Only.*

While far from fancy or exotic in any way, this highly respected low budget regional restaurant in the Barri Gothic is another great choice for those looking for a special meal in the low price category. After waiting half an hour to get inside, I was delighted to find a menu that included three course lunch and dinner specials with huge portions of well prepared local fish, chicken, and meat dishes that almost never cost more than 2,175 *ptas* and were even better tasting than I had ever imagined or expected. You can try to make a reservation, but the people waiting to get in at the front doorare well worth conversing with.

TELEPIZZA, *Carrer de Gran Via de Gràcia, 35. Tel. (93) 415-0778. Cash only.*

Whether you're in the mood for a quick bite in the small dining room, or prefer to have them deliver a hot snack to your hotel, this is about the best pizza in town. The price is just 675 *ptas* for individual pizzas, 975 *ptas* for medium pizzas, or 1500 *ptas* for family sized pizzas, plus about 125 *ptas* for each additional topping. The most amazing part of the deal is that there is a 2 for 1 offer on weekdays, so that you get double for the same price if you ask at no additional cost. A great place when you just don't feel like leaving the hotel, but don't want to pay hotel prices to eat informally. Several other central locations within town might be closer to your hotel.

MANGO, *Platja Nova Icária, Vila Olímpica. Telephone unlisted. Cash only.*

A simple takeout and dine-in restaurant a few minutes walk down from the Port Olímpic that is half the price of the port's other establishments. The menu offers pizza, empenadillas at 55 *ptas*, half roasted chickens for 500 *ptas*, chicken plates with french fries and a glass of *Cava* at 595 *ptas*, black rice with seafood and vegetables for 975 *ptas*.

THE BARCELONA CARD

*The new **Barcelona Card** is a great way to see all the major attractions of the city for 10% to 50% off the regular price. Available from any **Oficina de Turisme** tourist information area in Barcelona, the card is accepted at over 70 different museums, amusuement parks, restuarants, bars, clubs, boutiques and the public transport system. The card costs 2,500 ptas per person for 24 hours, 3,000 ptas per person for 48 hours, and 3,500 ptas per person for 72 hours. For more details call their offices at Tel. (93) 394-3135.*

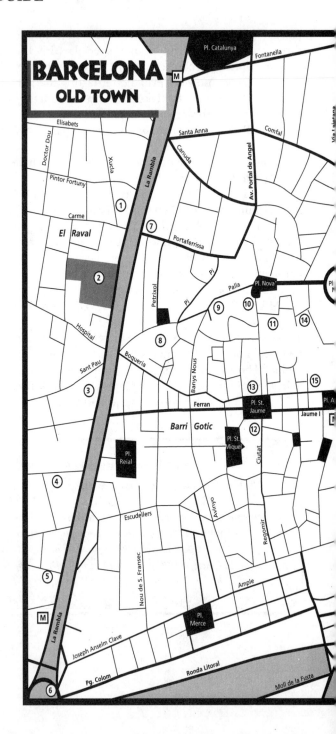

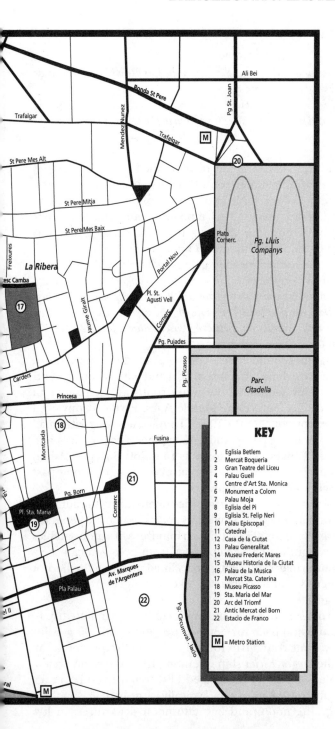

Ali Bei

Ronda St Pere

Pg. St. Joan

Trafalgar

Mendez Nunez

Trafalgar

M

St Pere Mes Alt

20

St Pere Mitja

St Pere Mes Baix

Freixures

La Ribera

esc Camba

Portal Nou

Plata Comerc.

Pg. Lluis Companys

17

Jaume Giralt

Pl. St. Agusti Vell

Comerc

Pg. Pujades

Carders

Pg. Picasso

Parc Citadella

Princesa

18

Montcada

Fusina

KEY

1   Eglisia Betlem
2   Mercat Boqueria
3   Gran Teatre del Liceu
4   Palau Guell
5   Centre d'Art Sta. Monica
6   Monument a Colom
7   Palau Moja
8   Eglisia del Pi
9   Eglisia St. Felip Neri
10 Palau Episcopal
11 Catedral
12 Casa de la Ciutat
13 Palau Generalitat
14 Museu Frederic Mares
15 Museu Historia de la Ciutat
16 Palau de la Musica
17 Mercat Sta. Caterina
18 Museu Picasso
19 Sta. Maria del Mar
20 Arc del Triomf
21 Antic Mercat del Born
22 Estacio de Franco

M = Metro Station

21

Pg. Born

Comerc

Pl. Sta. Maria

19

Av. Marques de l'Argentera

Pla Palau

22

Pg. Circumval. lacio

el II

ral

M

SEEING THE SIGHTS
TOUR 1

The Port de Barcelona waterfront, the Port Vell, Las Ramblas & Plaça de Catalunya, & the Avinguda Diagonal.

Approximate duration (by foot) is about 6.5 hours, including church, museum, monument and side street visits. Start from the Drassanes metro station.

The Port Area

To begin this tour, walk all the way down to the end of *Las Ramblas* towards the city's charming waterfront. The first stop is over at the towering **Monument a Colom** statue in the center of the **Plaça Portal de la Pau** square and traffic circle. This nine story monument depicts Christopher Columbus pointing the way towards America and was constructed as part of the 1888 **Universal Expo**. Visitors can take a short elevator ride up to the domed viewing gallery, where you'll see exceptional panoramic views over the city. *The monument is open Tuesday through Saturday from 10am until 2pm and again from 3:30pm to 7:00pm, and Sundays and holidays from 10am until at least 7pm. During the summer months, it often opens on Mondays as well. Admission including the elevator ride is 225 ptas for adults and 125 ptas for children and senior citizens.*

After returning to ground level, continue another block down towards the **Port de Barcelona**, an unusual port and harbor zone just off the Mediterranean. This section of the waterfront has been active in maritime commerce since before the Middle Ages. Partially converted into a pleasant recreation zone for the 1992 Olympics, it is rung with small parks, outdoor cafés, walking paths, and fishing piers. The popular palm tree-lined **Moll de la Fausta** (also known as the **Moll Bosch i Alsina**) promenade adjacent to the harbor is a great place to stroll along past moored naval vessels and small restaurants.

In addition to a small *Turismo* tourist office open during the summer months, the area contains plenty of small bars and cafés that are generally packed with locals and tourists alike sitting on hundreds of outdoor tables during the warmer months. A few steps away from here you can see a series of small **Golondrinas** sightseeing boats lined up along the harbor front. These inexpensive mini-cruises can take passengers from here to nearby seafront sights.

The most affordable of these excursions includes a 30 minute trip to the nearby lighthouse and back for 380 *ptas* per adult and 200 *ptas* for children. A full two hour round-trip tour to the **Vila Olímpica** area can be taken aboard the larger *Escua* ship operating from the same area at 1,210 *ptas* per adult, 830 *ptas* for those aged 11 through 13 and over 65, or 505 *ptas* for kids up to 10 years of age. Typically in the high season there are daily morning, afternoon, and late afternoon departures; in low season they tend only to be in service on weekends. *Stop in or call the reservation offices at Tel. (93) 442-3106 to confirm a space and double check the schedule.*

Another unique form of transportation can also be caught from the harbor front. The **Transbordador Aeri** cable car station a few steps. The cable car will take you just across the harbor to Barceloneta or inland up to Montjuïc Mountain's castle area. *With daytime operating hours between Tuesday and Sunday, the round-trip fare is 1,100 ptas per person.*

Recently, a new walkway called **La Rambla del Mar** has been added to allow pedestrians to cross over the harbor to other attractions. The walkway ends at the **Moll de Espanya** pier and entertainment complex that is home to the luxurious **Reial Club Marítim de Barcelona** yacht club and restaurant. Alongside this exclusive yacht basin is a brand new tourist mall known as the **Port Vell** that now boasts a multiplex cinema, a huge shopping arcade, several restaurants and bars, and a state of the art **Imax** movie theater with a heart pounding 6000 watt digital sound system and huge semi-circular screen.

The center of attraction here is the new **L'Aquarium** aquarium buidling. This is Europe's largest aquarium and features 21 tanks filled with 8000 different examples of marine life from all over the world. The main tank has over 80,000 gallons of sea water and you can actually pass through it via an underwater walking tunnel. You can view everything from sharks to sea turtles and see multimedia presentations about life under the waves. *The aquarium is open daily from 9:30am until at least 9pm, and costs 1,400 ptas per adult and 950 ptas per child under 12.*

The Rambla del Mar may be closed to pedestrians periodically for up to 30 minutes at a time, while its swivel draw bridges allow for boats to pass into the sea from the yacht club.

When you're finished wandering around the port area, return to the Plaça Portal de la Pau square and traffic circle with the statue of Columbus, and bear slightly to the left onto the Avinguda de las Drassanes. A few steps later you can't help but notice the triangular shaped roofs that cover the remains of the 13th century **Reials Drassanes** royal shipyards. It was from buildings once located on this site that many medieval boats were built for their long range voyages of trade and defense. During an ongoing archaeological restoration project a section of the city's original **murallas** (medieval defensive wall) was uncovered and refurbished, and the southwestern edge of the building can now be viewed for free.

Inside the shipyard there is a wonderful **Museu Marítim** boat museum. As you enter the museum beneath a coat of arms belonging to Peter the Ceremonious, you are lead into a series of Gothic wings that have been beautifully preserved. Inside these structures is a fantastic collection of historical naval paintings, miniature ships, navigational instruments, wooden figureheads, charts and documents belonging to famous sailors. The most impressive part of the museum is the vaulted **Royal Gallery** that contains full size original and replica vessels, including a wooden submarine and a reproduction of an opulent 16th century oar powered galleon in the process of being painstakingly built by a team of artisans and experts. Large picture windows alongside this gallery provide visitors with a great chance to watch the teams of craftsmen building new models and restoring the original ones.

Another great section of the museum is housed in an original 13th century defensive tower, where intricately carved wooden furnishings and leather-bound books are displayed alongside other antiques. A small gift shop is the perfect place to buy unique anchor shaped key rings and ships in crystal bottles for those friends of yours with nautical interests.

The museum is open Tuesday through Saturday from 9:30am until 1pm and again from 4pm until 7pm, Sundays and holidays from 10am until 2pm. Admission is 800 pta.s per adult, 450 ptas on Wednesdays, 450 ptas for students with International student ID cards and Senior Citizens, and is free on the first Sunday of each month.

Around Rambla Santa Monica

Upon exiting the museum, return to the **Plaça Portal de la Pau**, this time bearing left to head straight up the world famous **Las Ramblas**. Without doubt, the enchanting pedestrian-only promenade in the center of this main drag is one of the most enjoyable places to stroll in the whole city. The word *rambla* means a small river that dries up in the hot weather, and this actually was a dry riverbed just outside the city's medieval defensive walls. Although its name changes frequently as it passes several zones while heading northwest through the heart of the city, the entire boulevard is commonly referred to as Las Ramblas.

This lower section is officially called the **Rambla Santa Monica** and leads past several sights and attractions. On the first block above the statue of Columbus there is a wonderful weekend outdoor **handicraft market**. The walkway is surrounded by a narrow street on each side, and alongside the street are some of the city's most beautiful antique and modern facades. Be careful – there are numerous pick-pockets.

Off to the right side of the street there is a small lane called the Passatge de la Banca that leads a few dozen steps down towards the amusing **Museu de Cera** wax museum. Housed in a turn of the century former bank building, the museum offers an array of over 300 wax figures depicting some of history's most famous and infamous personalities in realistic settings. *The museum is open daily from 10am until 2pm and again from 4pm until 8pm. The entrance fee is currently 800 ptas for adults and 500 ptas for kids under 11 and Senior Citizens.*

The museum's adjacent annex is free to enter and is home to the surprisingly affordable **Bosc de les Fades** café and restaurant. The interior of the café is designed to resemble a haunted cave, and also displays some wax figures for those who might prefer to avoid paying the museum's steep admission charges.

Once you've returned back to Las Ramblas, cut across to the left side of the street and continue heading up. The next important attraction on this block is the **Centre d'Art Santa Monica** arts center that is located in the remains of a 17th century convent. Here you can enjoy a series of temporary seasonal art exhibitions that are usually free. *The hours here are sporadic, but when an exhibition is being shown the doors are usually open Tuesday through Saturday from 11am until 2pm and again from 5pm until 8pm, Sundays and holidays from 11am until 3pm.*

As you continue up the boulevard, the area becomes packed with cheap souvenir shops, cafés, and tacky sex shops for a short while before becoming somewhat more exclusive, with a vast assortment of international newsstands and street artists filling up much of the pedestrian central walkway. On the left side at #27, just off the small Plaça del Teatre, you can see the antique facade of the **Teatre Principal** theater. This structure started out as an opera house, was then converted to a cinema, and now hosts the rehearsals for large stage productions held at other venues. You really can't enter the structure, but it's worth looking at from a distance.

Around Rambla dels Caputixins

At this point the street officially changes its name to the **Rambla dels Caputixins** as it keeps heading in the same direction. If you stay on the left side of the boulevard there is a small lane called the **Carrer Nou de la Rambla**. Make a left turn to head just a little bit into the adjoining **Raval** district. Halfway up the lane at #3 is the fantastic **Palau Güell** mansion. Built in the late 19th century by Barcelona's famed **Antoni Gaudí** to serve as a private residence for Count Eusebio Güell, this opulently designed structure features innovative exterior elements including enclosed balconies, Gothic spires, mosaic-covered abstract chimneys, and a truly unique entrance.

The interior is also strikingly original and features a mosaic fireplace, strangely shaped columns, and oddly vaulted ceilings. The structure belongs to the private Institut del Teatre; they've installed a **Museu del Teatre** museum of theatrical arts. *The mansion and museum are open Monday through Saturday from 10am until 1:30pm and again from 4pm until 7:30pm. Admission is 300 ptas per person.*

Now return to the Ramblas and cross over to the right side of the street. A few steps further up is a small archway and lane called the Carrer de Colom that leads to the border of the charming **Ciutat Vella** (Old Town) district that is marked by the massive 18th century **Plaça Reial** square. This large plaza is lined by balconied four-story period buildings that have several restaurants and bars on their ground floor. The central fountain and unique lamp posts were designed by Antoni Gaudí. On warm summer nights, the square becomes a popular meeting place for people to sit at outdoor tables and talk over a gourmet meal, a falafel sandwich, or an ice cold beer. On Sunday mornings an interesting outdoor coin and numismatic market can be viewed here as well.

BARRIO XINES

*Care to take a walk on the wild side? The old **Barrio Xines** (Chinese neighborhood) of the **Raval** district lies just to the left of this part of the Ramblas. Although few Chinese people still live here, the area now consists mainly of beautiful but crumbling old buildings. There are numerous sights of interest here, but remember that the zone is by far the favorite haunt of junkies and prostitutes after dark, so be careful.*

*To get here, turn left onto the **Carrer de Sant Pau** just next to the Gran Teatre del Liceu. After walking about four blocks, you will find the foot of the small Plaça de Salvador Segui plaza; make a right turn onto the ever-interesting **Carrer d'en Robador** street. The sleaze just oozes out of this block, and I do not suggest being here after dark. At the end of this street, turn right onto the much safer **Carrer de L'Hospital**, where a few doors down on the left side will be the Gothic stone block **Antic Hospital de la Santa Creu**. Built over time from the 15th through 18th centuries, the hospital that once occupied this site was moved to uptown Direta de L'Exiample district. Now what stands here is the **Biblioteca de Catalunya** library, and the **Academia de Medicina** medical school, both of which can be visited for free during business hours to see unusual ceramics and a beautiful inner garden.*

*Almost next door at #9 is the hospital's **Sala D'Exposicions Capilla** that exhibits fine art, open Tuesday to Sunday from 10am until 8pm with no admission fee. Now continue down the street until once again reaching the Ramblas. Turn right to head down a few blocks to the Gran Teatre del Liceu, and turn around to continue the tour below.*

One of the most bizarre streets in this part of town is located just one block below the Plaça Reial. Known officially as the Carrer dels Escudellers, at night this street is packed with punk rockers, biker gangs, prostitutes, drug dealers, and plenty of slime ball bars. Although not on the sightseeing list for all but the most adventurous visitors, this is a great street for younger visitors to people watch. One thing to note is that the street is not at all as dangerous as it may sound, but it is quite strange.

Return once again to the Ramblas and cross over to the left side to look for the magnificent **Gran Teatre del Liceu** opera house at #63. Originally constructed in the mid-19th century, this acoustically perfect theater has burnt down twice, and was bombed by anarchists once since its founding. The golden and red velvet classic interior is frantically being restored, hopefully in time for the 1997 season premier of the opera Carmen. If you ask politely, perhaps the front office staff will open the doors for you to get a quick peek at the work in progress. Heading back up the central pedestrian walkway, visitors will be surprised to see plenty of people stepping all over the colorful circular mosaic called the **Pla de l'Os**, just off the central Plaça de la Boqueria, created by none other than the artist, Juan de Miró.

Around Rambla de Sant Josep

At about this point, flower kiosks start to crop up on the walkway, and the street once again changes its name to the **Rambla de Sant Josep**. The most exciting attraction on this part of the boulevard is near #91 at the 18th century **Mercat de la Boqueria** (also known locally as **Mercat de San Josep**), a produce market on the left side of the street. Beneath its glass and iron structure you can find smiling women in hand-embroidered aprons selling some of the freshest cheeses, fruits, vegetables, fish, and meats to the general public from 8am until 7:45pm from Monday through Saturday. This is the place to stock up for a picnic. The most interesting time to visit is during lunchtime, when the local office workers haggle with the vendors trying to get a leaner cut of meat or a better price.

A few steps further up on the left at #99 is the 18th century **Palau de la Virreina**, whose humble Baroque exterior does little to attract tourists inside. If you do visit, you will find the city's Department of Culture offices as well as a handful of municipal galleries and a museum. One of the free galleries here is called the **Gabinet Numismatic de Catalunya** and offers a vast collection of regional gold and silver coins, some of them dating as far back as four centuries before Christ. *These coins can be viewed by appointment only from 9am until 2pm Monday through Friday by calling Tel. (93) 301-7775.*

A bit further inside the building is a museum of local art, where you pay from 300 to 500 *ptas* to view seasonal displays, and a good bookshop. *The culture offices and museum are open Tuesday through Friday from 10am until 2pm and again from 4:30pm until 9pm, Sundays and holidays from 10am until 2pm.* The ticket and cultural events office will be glad to give you a free copy of *La Revista del Mercat*, a monthly cultural guide to Barcelona.

RENT A TAPE CASSETTE
& LEARN ABOUT BARCELONA

*The bookshop of the **Palau de la Virreina** rents cassettes with narrated city tours for tourists. The cassettes cover the downtown sections of town and are available in several languages. If you want detailed information on all the buildings of historic and architectural interest around the Ramblas, this is a lot cheaper than hiring a private guide or taking an organized city tour. Just walk into the bookshop and ask about the "Barcelona Plus" cassette rentals. The price for this service at press time was 450 ptas per day, plus a deposit of 2,000 ptas You might also be able to rent a walkman to use if you don't have your own. The bookshop is open Monday through Saturday from 10am until 2pm and again from 4:30pm until 8:30pm. This is a great way to discover little known facts about this great city.*

Around Rambla dels Estudis

This time when you continue up the Ramblas you will find that its name changes yet again, this time to **Rambla dels Estudis**, and you will also begin to see small kiosks selling cages full of singing birds, hamsters, and fish. As you walk up the left side of the boulevard for another block or so you will soon come to a small lane on the left called the Carrer del Carme. If you turn down this lane and walk a few paces, you will see the twisted Baroque columns that mark the entrance to the 17th century **Iglesia de Betlem** church.

Although fairly simple and lacking in any dramatic interior elements, the church is still worth a quick peek inside during its constant daily masses. After seeing the church, return to the Ramblas and keep walking up the left side of the boulevard. A few steps further is the unusual facade of the **Compania de Tobacos de Filipinas** building that has graced this sight since the late 19th century. The building is in private hands, and is not presently open to the public.

Around Rambla de Canaletes

As you rejoin the journey northwest up the pedestrian walkway in the center of the *Ramblas*, its name once again changes to the **Rambla de Canaletes**. At this point the boutiques and restaurants that surround the boulevard become somewhat more deluxe and expensive. If you walk on the right side of the street, keep a look out for a small lane called the Carrer de la Canuda; take a right turn here.

A block or so down this street is a small square known as the **Plaça Vila de Madrid**. In the middle of the plaza near a fountain with fish spouting water, there is a set of stairs leading down into a sunken garden. Here you can see a series of Roman tombs *(open Tuesday through Saturday from 10am until about 6pm, no admission)*. During all other hours, visitors can still take a peek through the iron gates and see them from a bit further away.

Now return to the Rambla de Canaletes where there are few specific sights worthy of note in this small section, with the possible exception of the **Font de Canaletes**. This grey iron fountain on the left side of the central pedestrian walkway has been a famous source for potable water since the 19th century. Legend has it that if you drink water from one of its four spigots, you will fall in love with Barcelona (or someone living here) and never wish to leave.

The Plaça de Catalunya

Just above the fountain, the Ramblas gets interrupted by a large commercial square called the **Plaça de Catalunya**. This is by far the busiest and most famous plaza in the downtown area. This square is the primary point of access for the Aerobus airport bus, the Tomb Bus downtown shuttle van, the #100 Bus Turistic sightseeing express bus, major Renfe and local commuter train stations, the TMB bus stops with their information kiosks and of course a giant metro station with connections to almost every other subway line. Because of all these transportation options the square is often packed with local students and office workers on their way to and from downtown. During lunch and late afternoon hours, many people just come here to sit on the grassy areas and take a short break before moving along.

Several fountains, monuments, benches, and trees line the circular mosaic in the center of the square. The major avenues that radiate from here are full of large office buildings and some of the city's best retail shops. The huge **El Corte Inglés** department store rings the right side of the plaza, and contains restaurants, currency exchange booths, and a full service travel agency.

On the opposite side of the plaza is the famed **Café Zurich** where tourists sit at its outdoor tables, rubbing shoulders with locals while basking in the sun. Besides a few banks and corporate headquarters, the rest of the plaza holds few other attractions.

Around Rambla de Catalunya

At the far left edge of the plaza, the Ramblas once again appears, but this time its name is altered to the **Rambla de Catalunya**. This is where the most pricey shops and eateries of this zone begin to appear. There are a few amazing museums and galleries in this area, including the **Fundació Arqueológico Clos** Egyptian art museum, which should not be missed. It's a few blocks up on the left side at #57. The non-profit foundation was organized by the brilliant local businessman, Jordi Clos, who owns the magnificent Hotel Claris, among other holdings. His love for ancient Egyptian artifacts has lead to the creation of this learning institute and museum to display his priceless collections. A small annex to this museum may also be viewed.

There are three floors with items on display which include mummies, funerary objects, as well as golden jewelry and scarabs previously owned by Rudolf Valentino and Yoko Ono. Since the institute sponsors archaeological digs and student grants, there is a fantastic research library with computerized hieroglyphic translation programs and thousands of rare volumes including etchings commissioned by Napoleon during his travels through the Arab world. This is quite an interesting and dramatic museum. *The museum is open Monday through Saturday from 10am until 2pm and again from 4pm until 7pm. Admission is well worth the 700 ptas per adult, and 350 ptas for students. Guided tours in English can be hosted upon request by calling the curator (Sr. Luna) in advance at Tel. (93) 488-0188.*

The boulevard continues ahead for another few tree-lined blocks until it ends abruptly at the intersection of Avinguda Diagonal. The final sight at the Ramblas lies right here, at the early 20th century **Casa Serra** municipal building. Built by Josep Puig i Cadafalch, this former mansion contains a vast array of architectural styles that all seem to complement each other rather well. Most noteworthy is the castle-like tower in its center, and its multicolored Spanish tile roof with geometric patterns. The building is not really open to the public, but a quick look at the exterior is worth a few minutes.

TOUR 2

The Plaça de Catalunya, the Passeig de Gràcia and Avinguda Diagonal, and the Quadrat d'Or section of the Eixample district.

Approximate duration (by foot) is about 6 hours, including buildings, museum, monument, and side street visits. Start from the Catalunya metro station.

The Lower Section of the Passeig de Gràcia

Pass through the Plaça de Catalunya until you reach its far right border, and follow the **Passeig de Gràcia** northwest as it heads towards the rising mountains off in the distance. Now you have arrived at the beginning of the zone known locally as the **Quadrat d'Or** (Golden Square) in the heart of the **Eixample** district.

This part of town became the center of bourgeois Barcelona after the city's downtown had expanded above the Plaça de Catalunya after 1860, when the city's medieval defensive walls were torn down. The principal designer of this newly expanded part of town was Ildefons Cerda, a civil engineer who was responsible for the grid street layout. This pattern of symmetrical blocks made the zone much more logical than the older Gothic quarter's irregularly shaped lanes.

With the construction of several magnificent structures built by Spain's most famous Modernist architects, this gridded extension of the business district became one of the most fashionable parts of town to conduct commerce. The streets and avenues in the area are still home to super-expensive designer boutiques, impressive art museums, excellent restaurants, buildings of national importance and the head offices of Europe's best known banks and multinational corporations.

If you start the journey on the right side of the avenue, keep your eyes out for the **Cases Rocamora** at #10, built in 1913 by Joaquim Dassegoda i Amigo and boasting bold stone balconies fronting the street. Although not open to the public, a quick look at the exterior is worth a few seconds in passing. Continue up the block, and cross over to the left side of the avenue after passing the Gran Via de les Cortes Catalanes. Another block up the left side of the Passeig de Gràcia at #21 is the **Edificio la Unión y El Fenix Español**. Built in 1932 by Eusebi Bona i Puig and featuring a wonderful winged angel upon its top floor dome, this building houses business offices. If you walk quickly you should be able to get past the security desk to view its impressive interior.

The Manzana de la Discordia

Further up this side of the avenue are three important buildings on the same block that have been built by perhaps the most important architects of 20th century Barcelona. Known together as the **Manzana de la Discordia** ("the block of discord") due to the stylistic competition between its important structures, this may be the most famous single block in the whole city.

The first of these buildings is the striking **Casa Lleó-Morera** at #35 that was erected in 1906 by Lluís Doménech i Montaner. The facade is emblazoned with unusual floral designs carved around many fine balconies, spires surrounding its rooftop garden, and a pinnacled tower reaching up towards the heavens. This five story Modernist mansion also has an interior rich with stained glass windows, mosaics, and grand stairways. The ground floor of the building is occupied by a boutique, so you can usually enter part of the building free of charge during normal retail business hours.

A few doors down at #41 you will find the **Casa Amatller** that was built in 1900 by Josep Puig i Cadafalch and restored in 1985. This house has an exterior that boasts beautiful wrought-iron balconies, columned windows, and creative ceramic bordering. The building is privately owned, and the general public may be barred from entering.

Just next door at #43 is the most dramatic of all these buildings, the **Casa Batlló**. The house was completely redesigned from an older existing structure as a private mansion for a local industrialist in 1904 by Antoni Gaudí. The first aspect that people notice from street level are the seemingly psychedelic balconies and turret-topped undulating roof line. Many people come away from this house with the feeling that it represents a dragon, and this is possibly what Gaudí had in mind. The mansion is unfortunately not open to the general public, but that doesn't stop hundreds of people taking photos of its exterior each day.

Also on the same block is a small museum that is all but ignored by the vast number of tourists flocking to the above mentioned landmarks. The small **Museu del Perfum** (Perfume Museum) located at #39 has an unusual collection of cosmetic containers, scents, and glass perfume bottles that date as far back as Roman times. *The museum is open Monday through Friday from 10:30am until 1:30pm and again from 4:30pm until 8pm, and admission is free.*

Around the Passeig de Gràcia

At the next corner, turn left onto the Carrer de Aragó where you will find the **Editorial Montaner i Simo** building at #255. This truly bizarre structure was built by famed architect Lluís Domènech i Montaner in 1880 to house a major publishing company and serves as a wonderful example of modernist Catalonian design. These days the building houses the **Museu Fundació Tàpies** with a unique collection of modern art by artist Antoni Tàpies and others. *The museum is open Tuesday through Sunday from 11am until 9pm. Admission is 400 ptas per adult and 200 ptas for students.*

Now return to the Passeig de Gràcia and follow the right side of the avenue until you reach the corner of Carrer de Provenca. You can't help but notice the **La Pedrera** (also known as the **Casa Milà**) apartment and office building. This is one of the most important sights in Barcelona. Built in 1905 during the heyday of Gaudí's fame, the strange facade is made of large blocks of stone that have been joined together to create a wave-like pattern used to cover a series of odd balconies. There are thousands of Art Nouveau reliefs, mouldings, iron railings, wooden panels and doorknobs that were all manufactured specifically for this project and are found nowhere else on earth. Even the rooftop is a delightful example of a unique sense of rhythm, and is strewn with mosaic-covered chimneys and turrets.

The structure was first commissioned by a local couple who were dissatisfied that the building went 100% over budget, and had an interior lacking in practicality. Since almost every surface is either curved or non-symmetrical, furnishing the owner's private apartment turned out to be a real nightmare. Try buying a sofa for a living room that has no straight walls! Another problem was that the then-innovative elevators, all but unheard of in those days, that connected the upper floors were prone to constant electrical outages. In any case, the building was eventually sold to a large banking company who now use the lower floors for office space. Seven families still occupy the upper floor apartments, including several descendants of original tenants whose rent contract remains fixed at only about 2,000 *ptas* per month. The building is open to the public by appointment only. *You should either stop by or call Tel. (93) 487-3613 at least two business days in advance in order to reserve a place on a mandatory guided tour.*

If you happen to be in the area and have not made an advance appointment, try asking to be put on the wait list, and if there is a no show, you may be allowed on that day's tour. These free tours are generally given on Tuesday through Saturday at 10am, 11am, 12noon, and 1pm, only and are limited to two groups per time slot, one in English or French and one in Spanish. Each tour takes about 15 people. The tour lasts 40 minutes or so and covers a walking tour up the stairs to limited parts of the interior and the bizarrely ornamented roof with its famous 26 chimneys. You must get here 15 minutes before each tour or you will lose your place. The office is located just off the corner on Carrer de Provenca and also contains a great bookshop loaded with Gaudí-related gift items.

Along the Avinguda Diagonal
When you're finished here, return to the Passeig de Gràcia and stroll up its left side until reaching the intersection of Avinguda Diagonal. At this corner is the **Palau Robert** palace that has been converted into a fine arts exhibition hall. The hall displays some of the city's most sought after retrospectives on a seasonal basis. Depending on when you arrive here, there may be exhibits from such artists as Dalí or Picasso. *When open, the palace's exhibits run Tuesday through Saturday from 10am until 8pm, Sundays and holidays from 10am until 3pm. Admission varies but the average ticket price is 300 ptas per person.*

After popping into the exhibition hall, turn right alongside the Plaça de Joan Carlos I and then bear sharply to the right onto the heavily trafficked **Avinguda Diagonal**. The first building of interest along the right side of this major thoroughfare is the **Casa Vidal-Quadras** at #373. This Gothic structure was converted from a pre-existing house in 1904 by Josep Puig i Cadafalch to serve as the residence for Baron Vidal-Quadras. The lovely facade is filled with highly decorative arches and stonework. Inside you can visit the **Museu de la Música** museum of 16th through 20th century musical instruments. *Although the museum is scheduled to relocate, if it is still here the hours are Tuesday through Sunday from 10am until 2pm, with* *special Wednesday hours from 5pm until 8pm. Admission is 300 ptas per adult, 150 ptas for students with International student ID and Senior Citizens, 150 ptas on non-holiday Wednesdays, and free on the 1st Sunday of each month.*

One block further along the left side of this avenue at #416 is the **Casa de les Punxes** (also known as the **Casa Terrades**), which looks like a castle. Built in 1905 by Josep Puig i Cadafalch, this three winged apartment building is topped with tower-like spires. I was fortunate enough to find an open door that revealed the richly decorative inner spaces, but generally you have to know a resident to get past the locked entrance.

The Quadrat d'Or
Now cross the Avinguda Diagonal and turn right onto Carrer Pau Claris. After about three blocks turn left onto the Carrer de Mallorca, where you can visit the **Casa Montaner** on the right side of the street at #278, built by Lluís Doménech i Montaner in the late 19th century. *It's free from Tuesday through Saturday from 9am until 1pm.*

From here, cross the street and take a peek at the beautiful facade of the 19th century **Palau Casades** at #283, a small mansion that houses part of a law school. This beautiful structure is not open to the general public. Another block down on the left side of the same street is the turn of the century **Casa Thomas** at #291 that was built by Lluís Doménech i Montaner and now contains a furniture store that is open during normal retail business hours.

At the next corner, turn right onto the Carrer del Bruc and follow it for two blocks until bearing right onto the Carrer de Valencia. About a half a block down on the left is an entrance to the 19th century iron and glass-roofed **Mercado e Iglesia de la Concepcio** (market) – *open Monday through Saturday from 8am until 1pm and again from 4pm until about 8pm.* The adjacent Gothic church and cloister dates back to the 15th century, though it actually was moved here from the lower part of town in the latter part of last century.

Now you can continue along the Carrer de Valencia in the same direction until once again meeting up with the Carrer de Pau Claris where you will bear left. Keep your eyes open for the facade of the former 19th century **Palau Vedruna** at #150, now the home of the absolutely fantastic **Hotel Claris** which contains fine restaurants, a great bar, and the **Museu Claris**. The museum features dozens of priceless Egyptian pieces that belong to the founder of the nearby Fundació Arqueológico Clos.

The museum is one of those almost unknown sights in town, and admission is free. The hours of operation depend on the exact day you wish to view the collection, so pop into to this luxurious oasis *or call Tel. (93) 487-6262.* Ask at the front desk if someone can take you up to this great little exhibit.

TOUR 3

The Plaça de Catalunya to the old Barri Gòtic district.

Approximate duration (by foot) is about 5 hours, including buildings, museum, cathedral, monument, palace, Roman ruin, and side street visits. Start from the Catalunya metro station.

Around the Via Laietana

From the far right edge of the Plaça de Catalunya take a right turn onto the Ronda de Sant Pere. Follow it another block or so and bear right onto the wide **Via Laietana**. This wide avenue has remained one of the main routes from the heart of town towards the seafront since its construction at the turn of the century.

After walking down the avenue's left side for two blocks or so, turn left onto a small street known as the Carrer de Sant Pere Mes Alt where a few dozen steps up the left side is the fantastic **Palau de la Música Catalana**. This music hall was built in the Modernist style in 1908 by Lluís Doménech i Montaner and continues to serve as one of the principal venues for live music in the city. Its main red brick facade features highly ornate columns lined with ceramics, bold window arches, and a remarkable statue of Saint George by Miquel Blay i Fabregas.

The building's interior is even more dramatic, and contains a beautiful oval theater adorned with a Tiffany style sky light, thematic sculptures, hand-carved wooden panels, red velvet seating, a central rack of organ pipes and a number of ceramic pieces. The music hall is best enjoyed during one of its many jazz and classical music concerts, but can also be toured during official visiting hours. To view the interior when a concert is not being held here, *call Tel. (93) 268-1000 at least two days in advance and reserve a space on the guided tours that cost 200 ptas and are held Tuesdays and Thursdays at 3pm, and Saturdays at 10am and 11am. The tours are not held during the month of August.*

After seeing the exterior (and interior if you get a chance) of the music hall, return to the Via Laietana and turn left on it to continue heading down in the direction of the sea. If for any reason you're in the mood for a great capucchino, take a short break over at **Il Café di Roma** a couple of blocks down on the left side at #44, where in my opinion you can get the best coffee in all of Barcelona for only 165 *ptas*. When you are finished with your short coffee break, cross over to continue down the right side of Via Laietana for another block or so until reaching the **Plaça Antoni Maura**.

Around the La Seu Cathedral

At the plaza, turn right onto the delightful Avinguda de la Catedral. Alive with cafés, this avenue hosts an outdoor **antique market** on

Thursdays. From here it leads across to a couple of impressive plazas including the **Plaça de la Seu**, one of the city's most popular meeting places, especially during Sundays at about 12 noon when local folklore enthusiasts practice the *Sardana*, a traditional Catalan circle dance.

In front of this famous square is the main entrance to the Gothic **Catedral** known locally as the **La Seu** cathedral. Construction of this massive cathedral, dedicated to the city's martyred patron saint (Santa Eulalia), began in 1298 when the first stones were laid atop the sight of former Paleo-Christian and Romanesque churches that date back to the 4th century. By the mid-15th century most of the structure was completed, with the exception of this main entrance and spire that were actually finished only about 100 years ago. Whether you see its magnificent spire-topped facade during sunlight hours, or during the night when it is imaginatively flood lit, you are in for a real treat. Once inside the cathedral you can wander down its aisles to pass alongside more than two dozen side chapels lined with religious art and crypts dating back to the 11th century.

Beneath the column-supported vaulted ceiling is also a fine **Coro** with hand-carved choir stalls displaying golden royal coats of arms and miniature spires just like the ones above the building. The simple main altar itself is fronted by a table whose supports are actually made of pieces from original Romanesque columns. Also worthy of noting is the alabaster crypt of Santa Eulalia that can be found behind the high altar. Don't miss the 14th century side cloister that can be entered just to the right of the altar area. The **claustro** (cloister) has a wonderful fountain called the Font de Sant Jordi with an equestrian statue, colonnaded arches, and a pond stocked with live geese. From here you can enter the small **Museu de la Catedral** in the cloister's original chapter house where you can view a collection of paintings and religious objects. *The museum, choir area, and cloister are open daily from 8am until 1pm and again from 4pm to 7:30pm. The museum is open weekdays from 11am until 1pm. Admission is free for the cathedral and cloister, 40 ptas for the choir area, and 50 ptas for the museum.*

From the La Seu Cathedral to the Plaça del Rei

Depart the main entrance of the cathedral and turn right to head back into the **Plaça de la Seu**. A few steps later you will immediately pass the 15th century **Casa de la Pia Almoina** and the adjacent **Museo Diocesá de Barcelona** at #7, with a vast collection of sculptures, drawings, gold, silver and religious vestments from the 12th through 20th centuries. Much of the museum is presently closed for renovations, but you may be able to enter the small temporary exhibition space until the rest of the museum reopens sometime in 1997 or so. *When fully operational, the museum is open Tuesday through Saturday from 10:30am until 1:30pm and again from 5pm until 8pm, Sundays from 11am until 3pm. Admission is 200 ptas.*

After departing this museum, turn down the adjacent lane called the Carrer dels Comtes for about a block until reaching the **Plaça de Sant Lu**, where at #5 you can find the **Museo Frederic Marés**. This museum, housed in a former palace, contains several sections including both ancient and modern sculpture, works by the famed artist whose name the museum bears, and a sentimental area with reconstructions of daily life in the 15th through 19th centuries. *The museum is open Tuesday through Saturday from 10am until 5pm, Sundays from 10am until 2pm. Admission is 300 ptas per adult, 150 ptas for students with International student ID and Senior Citizens, 150 ptas on non-holiday Wednesdays, and free on the first Sunday of each month.*

After leaving the museum, bear left onto the Carrer dels Comtes until it ends and you are forced to turn left onto the Carrer de Santa Clara. This small lane leads past several medieval palaces that are closed to the public, and then ends at the foot of the remarkable Gothic **Plaça del Rei** square. This charming square, located just beyond the side of the cathedral, contains a heavy concentration of historic buildings. and really worth a look.

Two sides of the square are flanked by wings of the **Palau Reial Major**, the former palace of the Catalan royal family and was first built in the 11th century and extended even more until the dramatic Mirador del Rei Marti watchtower was added onto the top of the palace some 500 years later. To enter the palace, walk up the curved stairway and enter into the part of the structure known as the **Saló de Tinell** that dates back to the 14th century. This rectangular vaulted royal hall was designed by Guillem Carbonell in the 14th century and contains a rich wooden ceiling supported by massive stone arches. When Christopher Columbus returned in 1493 from his discovery of the Americas, this is where he was greeted by King Ferdinand and Queen Isabella. Also part of the palace complex is the narrow Gothic 14th century **Capilla de Santa Ágata** chapel with its fine stained glass, handcrafted medieval wooden ceiling, original wrought-iron chandeliers (unfortunately converted to hold flood lights) and a fantastic altarpiece painted by Jaume Huguet. *The palace is open Monday through Saturday from 10am until 8pm, Sunday from 10am until 2pm. Admission is 300 ptas.*

On the opposite side of the plaza is the Renaissance facade 15th century **Palau del Lloctinent** designed by Antoni Carbonell to serve as an official residence for visiting bureaucrats and royal guests. Now this structure contains the region's original medieval archives, but is strictly off limits to the general public. A few steps below the plaza on the Carrer del Veguer is the 15th century **Casa Clariana Padellas**. Moved to this location from a nearby street earlier this century, this beautiful structure is now home to the interesting **Museu d'Historia de la Ciutat** (City

HISTORICAL WALKING TOURS

*The Museu d'Historia de la Ciutat is headquarters for the exhibitions and information offices of the **Institut Municipal d'Historia**. This organization has created a self-guided walking tour through more than two dozen sights within the Barri Gòtic, where Roman relics and standing ruins of the 1.3 kilometers (0.8 mile) circular Roman defensive walls once stood. If you happen to be near the museum, make sure to stop in and grab one of the free yellow colored **Barcino-Barcelona** maps that detail (in Spanish only) these historic points of interest. If you happen to be wandering down a street and you notice a blue banner with an illustration of a woman playing a harp and the words "Barcino-Barcelona" hanging from above, this indicates that a Roman ruin is in the immediate vicinity. These banners usually point out the exact location of the sight, and give a small description in both Spanish and Catalon.*

Historical Museum). The museum offers collections of artifacts, documents, and exhibits relating to Barcelona's colorful history. During excavation of the site, workers uncovered Roman ruins that can be visited here. *This museum is open Tuesday through Saturday from 10am until 2pm and again from 4pm until 8pm, Sundays and holidays from 10am until 2pm. Admission is 500 ptas per adult, 300 ptas for students with International student ID cards and Senior Citizens, 300 ptas on non-holiday Wednesdays, and free on the 1st Sunday of each month.*

The Plaça de Sant Jaume

From the bottom of the Plaça del Rei, take the Carrer del Veguer down for a few blocks (although its name officially changes to Carrer de Trompetes de Jaume I) until bearing right onto the wide Carrer de Jaume I. A few blocks later the street ends up in the center of the spectacular **Plaça de Sant Jaume** square. This sight is steeped in history as this is where the city's original Roman forum once stood. The plaza continues to be the heart of Barcelona's political scene.

On most Sunday afternoons at about 6:30pm, a group of local folklore enthusiasts practice the **Sardana** traditional regional circle dance here.

On one side of the plaza is the main entrance to the old **Ajuntament** (also known as the **Casa de la Ciutat**) city hall building. Originally built in the 14th century by Pere Llobet, the present Neo-Classical facade was added in 1822 by Josep Mas i Vila when the plaza itself was redesigned. Another more dramatic 14th century Gothic side entrance by Arnau

Bargues can still be seen around the corner off the Carrer de la Ciutat. *While much of the building remains off limits to visitors, call Tel. (93) 402-7262 in advance and ask if and when it is possible to tour the interior.*

Once inside, make sure you take a look at the outstanding inner gallery laden with Gothic columned arches and marble geometric tiles. Also worth a visit are the 14th and 15th century salons like the **Saló de Cronicas** filled with exquisite period paintings by Josep María Sert, and the famed **Saló de Cent** council chamber whose regal interior boasts fine wooden furnishings, stained glass, and chandeliers. Two additional modern wings of the city hall have been built just behind this older part.

Across the square from the city hall is another fine example of municipal architecture at the **Palau de la Generalit** palace. Built in the 15th century on the sight of a former chapel, it is still in use today by the autonomous regional government of Catalunya. The structure's main Renaissance entrance to the plaza was designed by Pere Blay. Several sights including a spire-topped open air courtyard filled with orange trees, and the magnificent **Saló de Sant Jordi** chapel can be viewed by the general public only on the 23rd of April during the Sant Jordi day festivities in the plaza.

BARCELONA'S TOP SHOPPING ZONE

*For some great window shopping, wander over to the fantastic **Carrer del Ferran** before the day is over. This wide commercial street runs between the Plaça de Sant Jaume and cuts through part of the Barri Gòtic until reaching the Ramblas. Here you can find some of the city's best designer boutiques, jewelers, bakeries, reasonably priced clothing stores, antique shops, and all sorts of other retail outlets. During weekends the street is packed with well dressed locals and tourists alike.*

Around the Carrer del Bisbe Irurita

From the right side of the Palau de la Generalit, head up the medieval **Carrer del Bisbe Irurita** with its overhanging Gothic bridge that is connected to the 15th century **Casa dels Canonges**. This house and its amazing bridge are closed to the public, but can be admired from street level. A couple of blocks further up on the left side will be a small lane called the Carrer de Montjuïc del Bisbe that leads into the lovely **Plaça Sant Felip Neri** square. This tranquil plaza is surrounded by several fine buildings. The Baroque **Església Sant Felip Neri** church and monastery dates back to the 17th century and can be entered during its frequent masses, while the adjacent **Palau Episcopal** (Episcopal Palace) is some 500 years older but is currently not open to the public.

Also in the square is the **Museu d'Historia del Calcat** museum of antique footwear, where you can view over one hundred examples of shoes worn by famous people from medieval through modern times. Housed in the former Shoemakers' Guild of Barcelona building, *it is open Tuesday through Sunday from 11am until 2pm, and costs 200 ptas.*

Now retrace your steps back to the Carrer del Bisbe Irurita and turn left to continue heading back towards the La Seu. Across on the right side of the street (just after passing the front of the cathedral) is the 15th century deacon's house known as the **Casa de L'Ardiaca** with a spouting fountain in its ceramic panel- lined inner courtyard. The interior of this fine building is not open to the general public but it still can be enjoyed from the outside. Another block or so up the Carrer del Bisbe Irurita are two fine Roman towers and a draw bridge (actually rebuilt around the 14th century) called the **Portal del Bisbe** that once marked the boundaries of the old walled city.

The Plaça Nova & the Plaça Sant Josep Oriol

After crossing the drawbridge you will end up alongside the cathedral and in the **Plaça Nova** just off the Avinguda Catedral. On the other side of the plaza you should take a look at the Pablo Picasso mural on the facade of the 1960's **Colligi d'Arquitects** architects college building. From your position in the plaza facing the Picasso, turn left onto the Carrer de la Parra.

A few blocks down the street intercepts with the **Plaça Sant Josep Oriol** and the smaller **Plaça del Pi**. It is alongside these squares that you will notice the huge octagonal bell tower and buttress supports of the 14th century **Església de Santa María del Pi**. The church's giant rose window, stained glass, Gothic interior elements and fine altars are all worth a look.

The small plazas surrounding the church become packed with street artists, scenic painters, flamenco guitarists, Dixieland bands, and vendors selling organically produced cookies and cheese during the outdoor markets held here on weekends.

TOUR 4

The Carrer de Montcada, the historic La Ribera district, the massive Parc de la Ciutadella, & the Arc del Triomf.

Approximate duration (by foot) is about 4 hours, including museum, church, palace, park, zoo, and side street visits. Start from the Juame I metro station.

Around the La Ribera district

After exiting the subway station, walk a few steps up the Via Laietana until you are able to turn right onto the Carrer de la Princesa. This cute little street marks your entrance into the **La Ribera** district, once the commercial center of Barcelona during medieval times. Keep your eyes open for several imaginative shops here, including the unique **El Rey de la Magia**, a wonderful magic and joke store founded way back in 1881.

After walking a few blocks further down Carrer de la Princesa you will turn right onto the Carrer de Montcada. This dramatic narrow lane was once home to Barcelona's most powerful noble families, and their many fine Gothic and Renaissance mansions can still be found here. A block or so up on the right side of the street at #15 through #19 is the **Museu Picasso**, located within the interiors of three fantastic 15th century mansions known as the Palau Berenguer Aguilar, Palau Meca, and Palau Baro de Castellet.

First opened in the 1960's, the museum offers a good insight into the early and later works of Spanish modern artist Pablo Picasso who spent several years in this city as a teenager and young man. Inside you will find several floors displaying a large collection of the artist's lesser known paintings, engravings, sketches and ceramics. Since this is the single most popular museum in town, get here as early as possible to get an unobstructed view of the works. *Opening hours are Tuesday through Saturday from 10am until 8pm, and Sundays from 10am until 3pm. Admission is 600 ptas for the permanent collection, 800 ptas for the temporary exhibits, or 1000 ptas for a combination ticket. Senior citizens and students with International student ID cards get half-price admission on the above rates. On non-holiday Wednesdays there is a discounted entrance fee. You can enter the museum on the first Sunday of each month for free, but expect long lines.*

Return to the Carrer de Montcada and a couple of steps further down on the right side at #12 is the entrance to the **Museu Téxtil i d'Indumentaria** clothing and textile museum. Housed in another two beautiful 14th century mansions called the Palau de Llio and the Palau de Nadal, the building also contains one of the city's best schools of textile design. The museum features a collection of textiles and garments from the 14th through 20th centuries. There is a nice gift shop featuring one-of-a-kind accessories and crafted jewelry, and the design school's budget **Téxtil Café** where students serve up tasty meals and snacks at bargain prices. *The museum is open Tuesday through Saturday from 10am until 5pm, Sundays and holidays from 10am until 2pm. Admission is 300 ptas per adult, 150 ptas for students with International student ID cards and Senior Citizens, 150 ptas on non-holiday Wednesdays, and free on the first Sunday of each month.*

Continuing down the same street there are a series of art galleries including the **Galeria Maeght**, located at #25 inside the 15th century Casa Cervello Guidice mansion. Unlike some of its more uptight neighbors, this fine arts gallery encourages visitors to browse through its huge assortment of at books, affordable posters, prints, and more pricey original paintings. There are also several intriguing exhibition spaces on its upstairs floors that feature high quality original works by internationally renowned local artists such as **Miró**. *The gallery is open Tuesday through Saturday from 10am until 2pm and again from 4pm until 8pm. Since the gallery is actually a retail store, admission is free.*

This exciting street ends a couple of blocks down at the base of the Plaça de Santa María that is all but dominated by the towering **Església de Santa María del Mar**. Considered one of the finest examples of Catalan Gothic architecture, this huge church was designed in the 14th century by Ramon Despuig and Bereguer de Montagud. Above the main entrance's Gothic portico is a beautiful rose window surrounded by two octagonal bell towers that were each added during subsequent centuries. Inside the church you will find a seemingly barren vaulted interior supported by long octagonal columns. The church can be entered during its several daily masses or during one of its many regal weddings.

After leaving the church's main entrance, follow the adjacent Carrer de Santa María for a block until reaching the café and pub-lined Passeig del Born past the rear of the church. From here the street ends at the Carrer del Comerc where you will turn right. One block after passing the 19th century **Antic Mercat del Born**, a former market that now holds seasonal cultural events, turn left onto the wide Avinguda Marqués de L'Argentera.

The Parc de la Ciutadella

The avenue ends directly across from the side entrance to the city's second largest park, the attraction-filled **Parc de la Ciutadella**. This large green space was redesigned by Josep Fontsere for use during the **Universal Exhibition** of 1888 on the site of a former 18th century Ciutadella (citadel).

There are some great attractions here. In the upper section of the park you can stroll along its border with the Passeig de Picasso where you can see the **Umbracle**, a wood and brick structure that was built for the exhibition and is now used as a green house. Further along Passeig de Picasso in this section of the park is the **Museu Geologia** geology museum with a varied collection of mineralogical and geological specimens and exhibits. Enthusiasts may find it worthwhile. *The museum is open Tuesday through Sunday from 10am until 2pm. Admission is 300 ptas per adult, 150 ptas for students with International student ID cards and Senior Citizens, 150 ptas on non-holiday Wednesdays, and free on the 1st Sunday of each month.*

Still ahead is the beautiful **Hivernacle** glass and iron greenhouse built in the late 19th century by Josep Amargos where special events are now held. A little bit beyond you will find the wonderful **Castell dels Tres Dragons** originally built by Lluís Doménech i Montaner to serve as the exhibition's official restaurant. This majestic castle-like brick structure was later converted to house the **Museu de Zoologia** (Zoology Museum) where you can find a large but uninspired assortment of entomological and other zoological exhibits. *The Zoology Museum is open from Tuesday through Sunday from 10am until 2pm. Admission is 300 ptas per adult, 150 ptas for students with International student ID cards and Senior Citizens, 150 ptas on non-holiday Wednesdays, and free on the first Sunday of each month.*

If you now turn right at the corner of the Passeig de Pujades on the upper border of the park, a few steps later on the right you can follow the romantic Avinguda dels Til. Lers as it connects to various tree-lined paths leading towards the other attractions inside. I would suggest starting all the way at the bottom of the park over at the giant **Parc Zoològic** zoo. The zoo features many unusual creatures, including *Floquet de Neu* ("Snow-flake"), the world's only albino gorilla in captivity, as well as live lions, tigers, exotic birds, dolphins, snakes, lizards and over 400 more animal species. The zoo area also offers a children's farm and animal petting park, snack shops, a gift shop and public restrooms. *The zoo is open daily from 10:00am until 5pm during the winter, and 9:30am until 7:30pm during the summer. Admission is 900 ptas for adults, 450 ptas for Senior Citizens, and free for children under 3 years of age.*

From the zoo, you can stroll along one of the walkways leading towards the middle section of the park where you can find the central **Plaça de les Armes** oval plaza. The plaza's focal point is a pond surrounding a magnificent sculpture by Josep Llimona known as El Desconsol ("Despair"). The large structure adjacent to the plaza has been converted from the remains of the old citadel's arsenal. Inside this building is the **Parlament de Catalunya** parliament offices that are generally closed to the public. Also inside the building is a wing of the **Museu d'Art Modern de Catalunya** (**MNAC**) where you can view 19th and 20th century works by local modern artists such as Mir, Fortuny, Casas, Rusinol, Canais, and Gagallo. Although often overshadowed by other museums in town that are dedicated to more famous artists from the same era, it still is a pleasant enough museum to merit at least a quick visit. *This museum is open Wednesday through Monday from 9am until 9pm. Entrance fees are 300 ptas for adults and 200 ptas for Senior Citizens.*

After wandering around the Plaça de les Armes, head towards the upper section of the park. While passing the gardens and statues keep our eyes open for a large lake. Here you can rent peddle boats, row boats, and bicycles from about 450 *ptas* per hour while enjoying a bit of sun. Just above the lake is a bandstand that sits beside the Baroque **Font de la Cascada** fountain, designed by Josep Fontsere and his then assistant, Antoni Gaudí.

The Arc del Triomf

Depart the park via the exit on its upper border with the Passeig de Pujades where you will turn left. A block or so later turn right onto the **Passeig Lluís Companys**. This quaint café-lined lane has a pedestrian-only central walkway and recreation zone with highly decorative lamp posts where you can find people relaxing and feeding the numerous pigeons. During Sunday afternoons, a small outdoor market specializing in the sale and trade of small pins (yes, small pins) is held here.

On the right side of the lane at #18 is the turn of the century **Palau de la Justícia** tower-topped court building that is currently not open to the public. The street ends at the bold **Arc del Triomf** gateway built by Josep Vilaseca i Casanovas as the official entrance leading to the 1888 Universal Exhibition. This red brick structure features unusual domes, winged angels, and coats of arms above its inner arch.

TOUR 5

Parc Güell, the Direta de L'Exiample district, & the Plaça de Toros Monumental bullring.

Approximate duration (by foot) is about 4.5 hours, including park, museum, hospital, and side street visits. Start from the Vallcara metro station.

The Parc Güell

After leaving the subway station, follow the Avinguda de Hospital Militar down a few blocks while following the many well-marked signs leading to the park. The signposts will direct you to then turn left onto the **Baixada de la Gloria** stairway and escalator banks that run up the side of a steep hill. The helpful electric stairs operate from 5am until about at least 11pm, and there is no charge to use them. The top of this hill marks the side entrance of the impressive **Parc Güell**.

The park was created by Antoni Gaudí in the early 1900's for Count Eusebio Güell, who had already commissioned Gaudí to create other masterpieces such as the Palau Güell just off the Ramblas. The original idea was to construct a small English garden-style private housing development atop Mount Carmel. The sight was to have plenty of green spaces, a central market, tree-lined pathways, common recreation areas, architecturally amusing structures, and enough room to comfortably situate 60 single family middle class houses.

After enlisting the help of architects Josep María Jujol and Francesc Berenguer to assist in this project, Gaudí became obsessed with finishing the massive Sagrada Familia church and never completed this development. As a result, only two houses were built here, one of which Gaudí ended up living in, and the development was eventually turned into a public park.

At this juncture, there are several paths that lead to various points around the park. If you turn right onto the main access road and then follow the first major turn-off towards the left you can proceed uphill past the cacti to reach the top of Mount Carmel. Here, there is a fortress-like cluster of sculptured boulders topped off by three crosses, where you can sit down to enjoy a picnic or just stare out over the great panoramic view of downtown Barcelona. After a short rest, backtrack to the main but unmarked Carretera de Carmel road where you will turn left and head towards the heart of the park. Soon the dirt road becomes lined on both sides by large round stones and you will see some fine examples of Gaudí's bizarre architecture.

The main circular terrace style plaza that now confronts you is surrounded by outrageous curved benches created by Josep María Jujol. Covered on both sides by little pieces of ceramics that have been formed into mosaics, these benches are about the most pleasant place to sit down and enjoy a nice view of the city. Behind this central terrace are a series of caves whose entrances are decorated by rock columns, some sculptured with figurines. Off to the side of the terrace is the turn of the century house designed by Francesc Berenguer, where Gaudí lived from 1906 until 1926.

The house has been converted into the **Casa Museu Gaudí** museum. The first floor contains several furnishings designed by Gaudí for other houses he created in the city, like the hall taken from the Casa Calvet, and the original dining room set of the Casa Batalló. After walking up a small flight of stairs the exhibits include furnishings from the La Pedrera and Palau Güell, reproductions of Gaudí-designed doorknobs, chairs, fireplace mantels, tables, wrought-iron pieces by Francesc Berenguer, sculptures by Charles Mani, and drawings from Josep María Jujol.

Other highlights include Gaudí's private study and bedroom that are still full of his personal belongings, and various other pieces of religious and decorative arts by his contemporaries. *The museum is open Sunday through Friday from 10am until 2pm and again from 4pm until 6pm. Admission is 300 ptas per person. Those who are interested in Gaudí can call Tel. (93) 284-6446 in advance to arrange a visit to the private library on Modernist architecture in the museum.*

When you're done with the museum, head back downhill to view the great hall of columns that lie below the terrace. The hall was originally built to serve as the local marketplace, but was never occupied. There are 86 angled Doric columns that support a strange mosaic-covered bubbled ceiling. From the hall of columns follow the road towards the main entrance of the park, where you will find a double staircase leading down past the famous mosaic Dragon fountain and sculpture. There's a painting and sculpure market here on weekends. *The park itself is open from*

10am until 6pm during winter, 10am until at least 8pm during summer, and admission is free to all.

The Hospital Santa Creu i Sant Pau

At the bottom of the park's stairs you turn right onto the Carrer d'Olot and then turn left to walk downhill via the Carrer de Larrard. This street ends several blocks away at the major **Travessa de Dalt** highway, where you will carefully turn left on its adjacent service road. A few blocks later you will find an overpass; cross over to the other side of the highway and continue following it in the same direction. When the highway soon meets a large intersection and forks, bear right onto the Ronda Guinardo and follow it as it passes the Parc Aigues where its name officially changes to the Ronda del Mig. A couple of streets later, this road comes to an abrupt end, and you will now bear right onto the Carrer de Cartegena that leads into the upper section of the **Direta de L'Exiample** district.

Another two blocks down this street you will find the **Hospital Santa Creu i Sant Pau**. Designed in 1901 by Lluís Doménech i Montaner, this fantastically ornate hospital is a masterpiece of his Catalan Modernist architectural style. The best way to get inside this medical complex is to make the next left turn onto the Carrer de Sant Antoni María Claret. Since the hospital is not really open to the general public, walk quickly though its main entrance doors beneath the clock tower and make sure you look like you know where you are going. If you hesitate or ask any questions at the door, the guards will most likely ask you to leave the building.

Once inside you can wander past the gardens that are dotted with dozens of small red brick pavilions, many of which are connected by underground tunnels and decorated with domes, spires, and ceramics. Since the architect did not approve of the boring symmetrical block design typified in the Eixample district by architect Ildefons Cerda, he built these structures to diametrically oppose the neighboring buildings. The city has recently been discussing the possibility of demolishing the complex to create an uglier, but much larger modern hospital on this sight. *The official hospital visiting hours are from 8am until 5pm Monday through Thursday, and 8am until 2pm on Friday.*

From the Avinguda de Gaudí to the Sagrada Família church

After exiting the hospital, cross over the plaza adjacent to Carrer de Sant Antoni María Claret and follow the **Avinguda de Gaudí**. This delightfully wide avenue has a pedestrian-only center that is lined on both sides by many fine bakeries, candy shops, boutiques, and cafés. About six blocks down the avenue you will reach the massive facade of the not-to-be-missed **Temple Expiatori de la Sagrada Família** (Church of the Holy Family). Construction of this bizarre church began in 1881 under the direction of Francesc de Paula Villar. A couple of years later the project was reassigned to Antoni Gaudí who later completely altered the plans to better suit his own concepts.

Gaudí had become so obsessed with the creation of this truly monumental house of worship that he in fact began to live in a small apartment on the construction site itself, and dedicated his final years to no other projects. The church's new design was to have three separate facades, each with a series of four huge towers reaching towards the heavens. By the time that Gaudí was run over by a tram and died in 1926, less than 40% of the project was completed. Although work on the church was soon continued by the architect's contemporaries, all work once again ceased during Spanish Civil War and was not taken up again until several years later.

The structure that now stands is still decades away from completion, but teams of dedicated craftsmen and engineers still labour each day to try and finish the job. Although originally conceived with three facades, each with four surrealistic pinnacles, a lack of available space has led to the current two facade and eight pinnacle design.

As you approach the church from the avenue, the first glimpses you will have of the structure are of the massive construction cranes rising up behind the eerie "Nativity Facade" and its four crosses atop the convex bell towers. This particular ingress is not open, and you must round the corner to reach the church's public entrance near the *Passion and Death Facade* along the Carrer de Mallorca. Once inside the building visitors can first enter the crypt that now houses the **Museu de la Sagrada Família** museum. Here you can view some of the remaining original sketches, scale models, slide shows, photographs, examples of the interior iron work, and plaster of Paris molds of the towers. From the museum you will pass through a gift shop and enter into the central parts of the church that do not as of yet have a roof above them. Access is somewhat limited, but there are several sections that can be viewed if the construction crews are not working in them.

If you have some spare coins, its worth the extra 200 *ptas* to rent an audio machine that will guide you through most of the major parts of the church. You can also walk up the hundreds of stairs, or better yet pay the 150 *ptas* for the elevator to reach the top of one of the already completed towers to admire the painstaking detail that has gone into the creation of this masterpiece. *The church and its museum are open from 9am until 6pm daily during winter, and 9am until at least 8pm during the summer. Admission to both the church and its museum costs a whopping 700 ptas for both.*

Towards the Plaça de Toros Monumental

After exiting the church, turn left onto the Carrer de Mallorca and make the first right turn to head along the Carrer de Marina. After about two blocks you will cross over the wide Avinguda Diagonal and continue straight ahead as the street's name changes to the Passeig de Carles I. Another few blocks down off the corner of the Gran Via de les Cortes Catalanes and you should notice the circular **Plaça de Toros Monumental** on your left side. This bullring was designed in the Modernist style by Domènech Sugranyes and Ignasi Mas i Morell at the turn of the century. Its ceramic arch-lined walls are topped by Moorish looking blue and white ceramic egg shaped domes.

Bullfights are held here during the April through September bullfighting season. Inside the bulling you can visit the **Museu Tauri** (Bullfighting Museum). Displays include antique bullfight posters, matador's costumes, and the heads of famous bulls killed during events held here. *The museum is open daily from 10:30am until 2pm and again from 4pm until 7pm during the bullfighting season only. Admission is 300 ptas per adult, and 200 ptas for kids under 14 years of age.*

TOUR 6

The Plaça d'Espanya, the Les Arenes bullring, the Parc Joan Miró, Olympic pavilions, and the gardens of Montjuïc mountain.

Approximate duration (by foot) is about 5.5 hours, including park, bullring, museum, garden, and castle visits. Start from the Espanya metro station.

Note: There are several ways to reach Montjuïc's more popular sights without following the long (but enjoyable) walk suggested via the Plaça d'Espanya. I have listed these at the end of this section. Keep in mind that many of the other forms of transportation do not run daily, especially during the low season.

From the Plaça d'Espanya to the Les Arenes bullring and Parc Joan Miró

After exiting the subway, turn right onto the Carrer de Tarragona. Just off the corner is the round **Plaça de Toros Les Arenes** bullring that was designed in the 1880's by August Font. A couple of blocks behind the bullring the Carrer de Tarragona is the lovely **Parc Joan Miró** park, the former site of the city's largest slaughter house. These days an oddly shaped modern sculpture called **Dona i Ocell** (Woman and Bird) by Miró towers above a large pool of water.

From the Plaça d'Espanya to the Palau Nacional

Return to the **Plaça d'Espanya** and cross the street until you're able to pass between the large pyramid-topped **Torres de la Exposición** towers that mark the entrance to the Avinguda Reina María Cristina. Follow this avenue up as it passes along the numerous modern exhibition halls of the **Fira de Barcelona** convention center. At the end of the avenue a series of three escalator banks (in operation daily from sunrise to sunset) leads up the side of the hill.

Along the way, energy saving automatic start/stop escalators pass by the **Plaça de Carles Buígas**, in whose center lies the beautiful circular **Font Magica** (magic fountain). Beyond this are various smaller fountains also designed by Carles Buígas that lead the way past the **Plaça de les Cascades**. In past years there was a spectacular free sound and light show held here at about 9pm each weekend during the summer; the whole area including the fountains were brilliantly illuminated. A recent project has been undertaken to renovate these fountains, so the show may not be in operation during your visit.

At the end of the final set of escalators you can't help but notice the dome and tower-topped facade of the **Palau Nacional**. Situated on the rising slope of **Montjuïc** (the Mountain of the Jews) close to the sight of a former Jewish cemetery, the palace was originally built to house exhibitions during the **Expo** of 1929. Soon after the Expo ended the building became home to the wonderful **Museu d'Art de Catalunya** (**MNAC**) art museum. The museum is currently closed to the public during its massive renovation program that was supposed to be finished by now.

The last time I visited the palace (in early 1995), a worker told me that it might not be finished for a few more years. If you're lucky enough to find it open once again, see its dozens of rooms filled to the brim with wonderful medieval art. Among the fine works on display here are Spanish masterpieces of religious oriented frescoes, altarpieces, and paintings taken from churches decorated during the Gothic and Romanesque periods. *If open, the museum hours are Wednesday through Monday from 9am until 9pm. Admission was most recently 700 ptas per adult, and 350 ptas for Senior Citizens and students with International student ID cards.*

The Poble Espanyol Theme Park

After visiting the Palau Nacional and its nearby gardens, take the escalators back down to the foot of the magic fountain in the Plaça de Carles Buígas. From here, turn left onto the Avinguda del Marqués de Comillas. The avenue twists and turns for a few minutes before passing the entrance to the **Poble Espanyol** (Spanish Village). This small village recreation contains reproductions of famous traditional structures and old world monuments that can be found in cities and towns all over the country. Now redesigned to be enjoyed by the whole family as a charming theme park, this fun little place is packed with adults and kids during the weekends and holidays.

As you pass through its Avila inspired medieval tower entrance, visitors are led though a series of stone lanes and plazas lined with replica stone and whitewash houses where they can now enjoy regional cuisine, handicraft shops, costumed street performers, and recreations of typical rural fiestas. There is also a 25 minute multimedia extravaganza called *The Barcelona Experience* where tourists can learn a little about the city's history and culture via one of seven different languages, including English.

A few hours after sunset, the ambiance here changes dramatically as singles and couples flock to several restaurants, *tapas* bars, jazz clubs, an expensive flamenco hall called **Tablao de Carmen**, the incredibly enchanting **Torres de Avila** disco with its rooftop bar, or the adult oriented **Erotic Restaurante 69**. *The theme park is open Monday from 9am until 8pm, Tuesday through Thursday between 9am and 3am, Friday and Saturday from 9am until 4am, and Sunday between 9am and 12 midnight. Daytime admission costs 650 ptas per adult, 325 for kids under 15, free for children under 7 years old. After 8pm the door admits adults only and charges 300 ptas.*

Expect to pay high prices to eat, drink, or enter any of the clubs and discos here.

The Anella Olímpic zone

After exiting the Poble Espanyol, turn left back on to the Avinguda del Marqués de Comillas and keep following it as it curves through the Plaça de Sant Jordi and officially changes its name to the Avinguda de l'Estadi. Soon the avenue passes by the **Anella Olímpic** (Olympic Ring), a special zone designed by Alfons Mila and F. Correa to encompass many of the buildings used to host sporting events during the 1992 Olympics. The first attraction along this section are the **Piscines Bernat Picornell** swimming pools. *Open to the public daily from 9am until 8pm for a fee of 500 ptas (bring a passport to enter).* These are Olympic-sized facilities are and are among the best I've visited in Spain.

Just to the right of the roadside is the huge open air **Estadi Olímpic** stadium. Built in 1929, this impressive sports venue was renovated for the 1992 games and can hold up to 55,000 spectators. *The stadium can be visited free of charge daily from 10am until 6pm.* Also inside the building, near the south gate, is the **Galeria Olímpica** section where you can view Olympic memorabilia, videos, and still photos of the events, as well as buy gifts. *Although its hours may vary slightly from those of the stadium, entrance to the gallery costs 300 ptas per adult and 100 ptas for kids under 12.* Just across the way is the **Palau Sant Jordi** domed arena designed by Japanese architect Arata Isozaki for the Olympics. This award winning ultra-modern 17,000 seat complex can be visited for free on non-event weekends between 10am and 6pm.

The Etnológic, Arquelógic, and Fundació Joan Miró museums

When finished with the Olympic section, continue along the Avinguda de l'Estadi for another couple of minutes and bear left onto the Passeig de Santa Madrona until it reaches a hairpin curve (be careful) in front of the **Museu Etnológic** (Ethnological Museum). Here interested visitors can wander along three floors filled with exhibits on early Latin American art, West African religion, Japanese ceramics, ancient Nepalese masks, Indian jewelry and aboriginal Australian paintings. The museum also has a fine research library and bookshop.

The hours here are Tuesday through Sunday from 10am until 2pm during winter, with extended summer hours on Tuesday and Thursday until 7pm. Admission for adults is 300 ptas for the museum, 300 ptas for temporary exhibits, or 450 ptas for both. Special prices include 50% discounts for Senior Citizens and students with International student ID cards, 50% off full admission on non-holiday Wednesdays, and free entrance to all on the first Sunday of each month.

From this museum, the Passeig de Santa Madrona curves up, to the right, and then left until passing a fork in the road where you will bear to the left to then find the **Museu Arquelógic** (Archaeology Museum). Inside there are exhibits on the early history and colonization of Catalunya including relics from the Paleolithic era, Carthaginian art, Greek sculptures and Roman tombs. *This museum is open Tuesday through Saturday from 9:30am until 1:30pm and again from 3:30pm until 7pm, Sundays from 10am until 2pm. Admission is 200 ptas for adults, free for students with International student ID cards, and free to all on Sundays.*

After visiting the relics, return to the last fork in the road, and this time bear right onto the Passeig de l'Exposició. A minute's walk up on the right hand side and you'll come to a path leading to the **Teatre Grec**. This semicircular replica of an ancient Greek amphitheater was built for the **1929 Expo**. These days the structure is used mainly during July when the city's Greek cultural festival presents concerts, plays, and ballets here with up to 2000 spectators in attendance. Even if the gates leading to the theater are closed, you can still get a good look at it for free from the roadside.

Now it's time to retrace your steps back along the Passeig de Santa Madrona until it intersects with the main Avinguda de l'Estadi and turn left. Soon the modern white facade of the **Fundació Joan Miró** can be found on the left side of the road. Designed by Josep Lluís Sert and Jaume Freixa in 1973, the building serves as the headquarters for a foundation created by Miró himself when he donated 5000 of his paintings, drawings, tapestries and sculptures. Once inside the museum you can enjoy hundreds of the bold and colorful works by this Barcelona born master.

Also within the building is a special section called *To Joan Miró*, a series of paintings by other internationally known artists such as **Matisse** who wanted to show their respect and admiration for the museum's namesake. Other inspirational exhibits include the *Mercury Fountain* by

Calder, and a peaceful sculpture garden. There is also a wonderful art library, bookshop, caféteria, and coat check area within the complex. *The foundation is open Tuesday through Saturday from 11am until 7pm, Sundays and holidays from 10:30am until 2:20pm, and special extended hours on Thursday until 9:30pm. Admission costs 600 ptas per adult, and 300 ptas for students with proper ID.*

The Parc d'Atracciós amusement park and the Castell de Montjuïc

From the foundation, continue following the Avinguda de l'Estadi as it becomes renamed the Avinguda del Miramar. A few minutes later on the right hand side of the road are the **Jardins de Mossen Jacint Verdaguer** gardens boasting delightful walking paths with small creeks and an abundance of well-manicured floral-lined grounds. *The gardens are open daily from sunrise until sunset and there is no fee to enter.* Nearby are the stations for both the **Funicular** railway tram and the **Teleféric** cable car (see sidebar on next page).

If you wish instead to walk to the additional sights further up the mountain, keep following the same road until bearing right at Plaça de Torreforte onto the **Carretera de Montjuïc**. As this road heads uphill it will soon pass the entrance to the **Parc d'Atracciós** amusement park. Set on hundreds of acres of mountainside with nice city views, this busy family-oriented attraction has more than 40 rides to thrill the living daylights out of you. Among the many rides available are roller coasters, Ferris wheels, bumper cars, a house of horrors, gravity defying spin machines, and a selection of less dangerous kiddie activities. There are also restaurants, bars, snack shops, gift stores and a concert bowl.

During the summer the park is open Monday through Thursday from 6pm until 12 midnight, Friday and Saturday from 6pm until 1am, and Sundays and holidays from 12 noon until 11pm. During the other seasons the park is only open on Weekends and holidays from 11:30am until about 10:30pm. Admission costs 600 ptas per person, and an unlimited ride ticket is 1,800 ptas.

After the amusement park, continue along the Carretera de Montjuïc as it winds to the top of this part of the mountain until reaching the **Castell de Montjuïc**. This fantastic star-shaped castle was built in the 18th century on the site of a ruined fortification on the highest point of Montjuïc. Formerly occupied by Napoleon's troops, it was later converted into a high security prison. The castle now hosts the **Museum Militar** (Military Museum) where visitors can enjoy exhibitions of model castles, toy soldiers, a collection of military uniforms, and antique weapons. Best of all are the incredible views from the castle walls out onto the city and its seafront. *The castle and its museum are open Tuesday through Sunday from 9:30am until 1:30pm and again from 3:30pm until 7:30pm. Admission is 150 ptas per person.*

ALTERNATIVE TRANSPORTATION TO & AROUND MONTJUÏC

For a dramatic aerial cable car ride from the downtown seafront to Montjuïc, check out the **Transbordador Aeri**. This cable car can take you between the city's Barceloneta or Moll de Barceloneta seafront area to its station in the Plaça de Armada just below the amusement park for 1,100 ptas round-trip. It is open year round on Tuesday through Friday from 12 noon until about 6pm.

For those wishing to avoid walking to most of the sights listed in Tour 6, the year round **#61 bus** covers almost every museum and attraction listed below from its base at the Plaça d'Espanya for 120 ptas each stop. There is the special high season only **#100 Bus Turistic** express bus that offers unlimited stops all over town, including several of the above tour's most impressive sights. Its circular route begins at the Plaça de Catalunya and its use also entitles passengers to discounts at some of the above attractions. The fare is only 1,000 ptas per day or 1,500 ptas for two days.

The **Funicular** railway tram runs back and forth between the Parallel metro station and its base near the Miró foundation for 165 ptas one way or 275 ptas round-trip. During the summer it operates Monday through Thursday from 11am until 10pm, Friday and Saturday from 11am until 12 midnight, and Sundays and holidays from 11am until 11:30pm. During the winter it only runs on weekends and holidays from 11am until 8pm.

Finally, the **Teleféric** cable car transports people between the above funicular railway tram's upper base near the Miró foundation, and onto the castle grounds. It costs 325 ptas one way or 525 ptas round-trip for adults, and 225 ptas one way or 375 ptas round-trip for kids under 12. During the summer it operates daily from 11:30am until 9:30pm. During the winter it only runs on weekends and holidays from 11am until 2:45pm.

Below the western slope of the hill are the beautiful **Jardins Mossen Costa i Llobera** gardens, with exotic trees and plants and a great view of the harbor. *The park is open daily from sunrise to sunset, and admission is free.*

TOUR 7

The Plaça de Pau Vila square, Barceloneta, the waterfront, & the Vila Olímpica village and port.

Approximate duration (by foot) is about 4.5 hours, including beach, museum, monument, and side street visits. Start from the Barceloneta metro station.

The Barceloneta district

Once you have surfaced from the subway, walk a block down to reach the **Plaça de Pau Vila** square. This plaza is flanked by the **Port Vell** marina where some of the largest cabin cruisers in town can be found. Among the fine buildings located along the seafront is the 19th century **Palau del Mar**, a former warehouse complex that was recently converted to offices and some excellent seafood restaurants. From here, the wide Passeig de Don Joan de Borbó (also known as the Passeig Nacional) curves along past several other marinas and dry docks until reaching the **Torre de San Sebastiá** tower. It is from this point that the **Transbordador Aeri** cable car station can take visitors on a fun aerial adventure. With daytime operating hours between Tuesday and Sunday, its final destinations are either just across the harbor to the Moll de Barcelona pier, or inland up to Montjuïc mountain's castle area. The round-trip fare is 1,100 *ptas* per person.

Those looking for a less exciting excursion should consider bearing right from the tower onto the Passeig de Escullera that leads down a long thin jetty towards the open sea. At night this is a favorite makeout spot for young couples who park their cars on the edge of the piers facing the water. At the end of this strip is a cheap self-service snack shop and caféteria called the **Bar Porta Coeli** that has wonderful views over both the city and the sea.

After checking out the seafront, return to the Passeig de Don Joan de Borbó, and cross over to the other side of the street (locally known as the Carrer del Mar) just across from the marina. This harbor-view street is lined with inexpensive seafood restaurants, and is the principal road of the enchanting **Barceloneta** area. This small triangle shaped district was once just a swamp, but became dry land in the late 17th century after the enlargement of the nearby commercial port and harbor zones led to a massive accumulation of sand on this side of the new ocean break walls. The development of Barceloneta began in 1755 under the direction of army engineer Juan Martin Cermeno. It was designed to relocate the local residents, sailors, and fishermen who were displaced from their homes close to where the Parc de la Ciutadella park was to be built.

Still full of craggy old seamen, this fun part of town is a real treat to visit. Several of the small lanes that head deeper inland into the heart of Barceloneta are unique. One of the best places to wander through is the Carrer de Sant Cadres. This small side street cuts back from the main drag and heads into the delightful **Plaça de la Poeta Boscán** square where you can pop into the daily fish and produce market. Past the plaza, the same street continues through the center of this district until ending at the Passeig Marítim.

The beach directly in front of you is the famed **Platja Barceloneta**, and its access area is undergoing a massive modernization project.

Hopefully by the time you read this book, there will be a new boardwalk and recreation area just above the beach. In the days before this zone became a major tourist attraction, lots of inexpensive seafood joints along this street set up candle-lit tables on the beach itself. Those times have vanished, but the many restaurants have moved back a block or two and still serve up some wonderful meals.

The Poblenou district & Vila Olímpica

After wandering the back streets of Barceloneta until reaching its beaches, turn left to follow the oceanfront **Passeig Marítim Esplanade**. Now complete with wheelchair accessible ramps, small informal restaurants, and changing rooms, the esplanade leads along the water while passing the lovely but often crowded **Platja de Passeig Marítimo** cove beach. Either relax for a while in the beach's rental lounge chairs and sun umbrellas, sip on a cold beverage at the beach side bars, or continue walking.

After a few minutes you'll pass the large modern Hospital de Nuestra Senora del Mar. The esplanade leads to another zone specially designed by a team of international architects for use during the 1992 Olympics called the **Vila Olímpica** (Olympic Village), also known as the **Area Parc de Mar**. The entrance to this zone is marked by the towering five-star **Hotel Arts**. Designed by Bruce Graham of America for the Ritz Carlton hotel group, at 44 storys it's the tallest building in all of Spain.

Just next door is the neighboring **Mapfre** insurance building whose equally tall structure was designed by Enrique León and Inigo Ortiz. Just in front of these two skyscrapers is a newly opened **Sogo** department store on the Moll Marina pier. From the hotel, continue heading along the waterfront as the street name changes to the Passeig Marítimo Port Olímpic. The first sights you will encounter are the many restaurants and boutiques that line the **Port Olímpic** sheltered harbor and recreation zone. This trendy attraction was designed to be utilized for the games, and then converted into a super expensive retail shopping, nightlife and fine dining center. Packed on weekends, the port is still attempting to fill many of its **Moda Shopping** center's still vacant storefronts. Don't expect to find any bargains here, but a good meal on the outdoor tables of the port's 30 or so dining establishments is a lof of fun.

There is also a series of adjoining piers where you can admire the various yachts and motor boats docked here. In the far corner of the port area on the Moll Gregal pier is a small pavilion where you can rent ten-speed bicycles for 500 *ptas* per hour. On the other end of the pier visitors can take advantage of sailing lessons given at the nearby **Centre Municipal de Vela Port Olímpic** sail boat and water sports rental center.

After finishing with the port, continue heading away from town along the sea front **Passeig Marítim Nova Icária**. The modern buildings beside and behind the seafront were originally sporting venues and housing for the 16,500 athletes during the '92 games. Now transformed into expensive condos and apartments, this is where many of Barcelona's yuppies live. This esplanade then passes several more seafood restaurants on its way towards the beautiful **Platja Nova Icária**, **Platja Bogatell**, **Platja Mar Bella**, and **Platja Nova Mar Bella** beaches.

TOUR 8

The museums of the Palau de Pedralbes, the Zona Universitaria, the Camp Nou football stadium, the Plaça de Pius XII square, & the Monestir de Pedralbes museum.

Approximate duration (by foot) is about 3 hours, including monastery, museums, stadium, and side street visits. Start from the Palau Reial metro station.

The Palau de Pedralbes & the Zona Universitaria

After leaving the subway you arrive on the major Avinguda Diagonal avenue in the heart of the city's upper middle class **Sarriá** district. A few steps from here, at #686, is the main entrance point to the park before the ornate **Palau de Pedralbes**. This 4 story yellow palace was built in 1921 by Francesc de Paula Nebot as a royal residence of King Alfonso XII. Unfortunately, by the time this structure was completed, the revolution had made it impossible for the king to move in, and Franco later began to use it. About 24 years ago, the city decided to convert its fine interior, complete with a former throne room and music room, into a new home for several museums.

Here you can visit the **Museu de Ceramicá** (Ceramics Museum) that boasts a magnificent collection of Spanish ceramics from the 12th through 20th centuries, including pieces by Picasso and Miró. The adjacent **Museu d'Atres Decoratives** (Decorative Arts Museum) can be entered with the same ticket and shows off a great assortment of antique pocket watches and historic glassware.

These two museums are open Tuesday through Sunday from 10am until 2pm. Admission to both costs 300 ptas per adult, 150 ptas for students with International student ID cards and Senior Citizens, 150 ptas on non-holiday Wednesdays, and is free on the first Sunday of each month. Also in the same building is the **Gabinet Postal** antique stamp and postal exhibit, recently closed for a while. *If once again open, hours are the same as the above museums, but admission is free.*

After viewing the palace's museums, return to the Avinguda Diagonal and cross over to wander up the left side of the avenue that now runs alongside the campus of the **Zona Universitaria**. The university was built here about 40 years ago and is now among the largest in the city. Its dozens of modern buildings are dedicated to the study of the arts and sciences. As you continue along the avenue, bear left onto the Avinguda de Doctor Maranon to follow the southern border of the university campus.

The Nou Camp football stadium

The Avinguda de Doctor Maranon now curves further to the left, and soon intersects with the Avinguda de Joan XIII, on which you will bear left. Several paces along the right hand side of this avenue is the giant **Nou Camp** football stadium. Built in the 1950's to seat well over 115,000 spectators during sporting events and occasional concerts, this is the venue where the city's excellent **Futball Clube de Barcelona** professional soccer team (known locally as the **Barca**) can be found during the season.

Inside the stadium is the **Museu del Futball** (Soccer Museum) that is filled with memorabilia and video clips from the team's infamous past seasons. *The museum is open between November to March on Tuesdays through Fridays from 10am until 1pm and again from 3pm until 5pm, weekends and holidays from 10am until 2pm. Between April and October the hours here change to Monday through Saturday from 10am until 1pm and again from 3pm until 8pm. Admission is 300 ptas per person, and 150 ptas for students.* There are also other facilities in the complex including a gift shop, a mini-stadium, and ice skating rink.

After dark, the ring road around the stadium's parking lot is the sight of a strange procession. Dozens of cars continuously circle the area to catch a glimpse (or sometimes more) of the half-naked prostitutes that use this area as a base of operations!

The Plaça de Pius XII to the Monestir de Pedralbes

The Avinguda de Joan XIII now curves to the left after passing the stadium and leads directly into the **Plaça de Pius XII**. Now cross through the plaza until continuing straight ahead along the Avinguda de Pedralbes. Almost immediately on the left side of this avenue is the dramatic dragon-style gateway designed by Gaudí to mark the entrance to the **Finca Güell**, a ruined private estate that is not open to the public.

Continue up the avenue for about another 18 blocks as it cuts through the center of the high end **Pedralbes** residential district and then ends at the foot of a stone lane leading up the **Monestir de Pedralbes**. This former Gothic-style royal monastery was founded in 1326 by Queen Elisendra de Montcada, who later occupied a now ruined part of the complex. Visitors to this amazing stone block structure can wander through its simple nun's dormitories, kitchens, gardens, towering walls, and enchanting courtyard cloisters.

Also worthy of special attention is the **Cappilla de Sant Miquel** chapel with medieval murals by Ferrer Bassa, the bold octagonal bell tower, and a small single nave church where several tombs including the final resting place of Queen Elisendra can be found. *The monastery is open Tuesday through Friday from 10am until 2pm, Saturdays from 10am until 5pm, and Sundays from 10am until 2pm. Admission is 300 ptas per adult, 150 ptas for students with International student ID cards and Senior Citizens, 150 ptas on non-holiday Wednesdays, and is free on the first Sunday of each month. A great 50 minute guided tour is given at no additional charge on Wednesdays at 11am.*

Also inside the building is the **Fundació Colección Thyssen Bornemisza** art museum. Here you can view over six dozen masterpieces of 13th through 18th century paintings and sculpture by such masters as **Rubens** and **Tintoretto**. *The museum is open the same hours as the monastery, and admission is 300 ptas per adult, and 175 ptas for students with International student ID cards and Senior Citizens.*

TOUR 9

The Plaça John F. Kennedy, the Museu de la Ciéncia science museum, & Tibidabo mountain.

Approximate duration (by foot, tram, and cable car) is about 4 hours, including observation tower, museum, amusement park, and side street visits. Start from the Av. Tibidabo FF.CC. Generalitat commuter rail line station.

Up to Tibidabo Mountain

After departing the commuter rail station, walk up through the **Plaça John F. Kennedy**. Just on the other side of the plaza is the beginning of the Avinguda del Tibidabo avenue and an adjacent waiting platform for the **Tramvia Blau** trolley. This blue colored trolley has been running up the lower portion of this mountain since the turn of the century, and makes for a pleasant ride.

The tram operates every half hour in each direction daily during the summer, and only during weekends and holidays during other times of the year from 7:15am until 11:30pm. On days when the trolley is not running, a well-marked bus is provided instead. The price is 120 ptas each way on weekdays, or 165 ptas each way (275 ptas round-trip) on weekends and holidays.

The tram now travels along the Avinguda del Tibidabo for about ten minutes before the line ends at the lush Parc de la Font del Raco gardens. From here you're just steps away from the **Plaça del Doctor Andreu**, where you will then connect to the Swiss designed **Funicular** railway (the oldest in Spain) leading much further up the mountain's slopes. *The railway operates regularly in both directions daily from 7:15am until at least 9:45pm. The ride costs 300 ptas one way and 400 ptas round-trip, with a 50% reduction for Senior Citizens.*

After reaching the upper station of the cable car, you have ascended to the summit area of **Tibidabo** mountain, the highest point in the **Serra de Collserola** hills that create the city's northwestern border. From here there are a series of well-indicated roads that continue to the various sights and attractions of this recreational zone. Start your visit by bearing right for a couple of minutes until reaching the odd Neo-Gothic facade of the **Temple Expiatori de la Sagrat Cor** church. Built in 1902 by Enric Sagnier, this towering church is topped off by a statue of Jesus with his open arms facing across the panoramic view of the city below. An elevator will take you up to the statue's lookout point for 90 *ptas* round- trip. *The church is open daily, and admission is free.*

Just across from the church is one of the entrances to the **Parc d'Atraccións Tibidabo** amusement park. Although lacking luster when compared to its competition on Montjuïc, this smaller family fun center was first erected in 1901 and still packs the crowds in. Among the dozen or so rides available here are a tunnel of terror, a roller coaster, a so-called museum of automated devices, a carousel, and other diversions. *The park is open during the summer from Monday through Saturday from 5:30pm until 2:30am, Sundays from 12 noon until 11pm. During the rest of the year it opens on weekends and holidays from 11:30am until 8pm. Admission is 975 ptas per person, or 1,800 ptas per person including free use of the rides.*

If you now return to the cable car station and bear left, signs will indicate the road towards the **Torre de Collserola** telecommunications tower. This giant steel supported spike towers 288 meters into the sky. Built in 1990 by British architect Norman Foster, this is currently the tallest such structure in Spain – until the planned nearby microwave tower scheduled for completion in 1999 eclipses this one to become the largest tower in the world. Visitors pay 500 *ptas* each to enter and can take an exterior glass enclosed elevator up to the 10th floor observation gallery, with superb 360 degree views of the whole region. A restaurant and gift shop can be enjoyed on the subterranean first floor of the tower.

Also of note on the mountain is the tranquil **Parc de Collserola** public park, with its pretty walking paths, green spaces, and, if you need a break, plenty of inviting benches.

The Museu de la Ciéncia

After enjoying the sights of Tibidabo, take the **Funicular** railway back down to its base station at the **Plaça del Doctor Andreu**. Now you can take a small side trip before hopping on to the tram by following the **Carretera de Tibidabo** along the western edge of the Parc de la Font del Raco gardens. When the road makes its second curve to the left and comes to a fork, take a soft right onto the Carrer de Teodor Roviralta. A bit further down this street at #55 is the marvelous **Museu de la Ciéncia**, an interactive science museum.

Here you can enjoy multimedia presentations, and easy to follow computerized scientific exhibits designed for people of all ages. There is also a large planetarium that offers 35 minute shows on a regular basis. *The museum is open Tuesday through Sunday from 10am until 8pm. Admission is 500 ptas per adult for the museum and 250 ptas per adult for the planetarium. For students with International student ID cards and Senior Citizens the entrance fee is 300 ptas for the museum and another 200 ptas for the planetarium.*

After the museum you can return to the **Plaça del Doctor Andreu** and take the Tramvia Blau back to the commuter rail station to finish the tour.

ALTERNATIVE TRANSPORTATION TO & AROUND TIBIDABO

*A special express bus called the **Tibibus** offers service between Plaça de Catalunya and the mountain's amusement park with a dozen stops along the way. Summer hours are Monday through Friday from 5pm until 3am, and weekends and holidays from 10:30am until 8:30pm. During the rest of the year it runs on weekends and holidays only from 10:30am until 8:30pm. The price is 225 ptas per person each way.*

*The special high season only **#100 Bus Turistic** express bus offers unlimited stops all over town, including several of Tour 9's most impressive sights. Its circular route begins at the Plaça de Catalunya and its use also entitles passengers to discounts at some of the above attractions. The fare is only 1,000 ptas per day or 1,500 ptas for 2 days.*

*For those wishing to avoid walking to some of above sights, a free year-round **shuttle bus** covers the short route between the summits cable car station and the Collserola tower.*

GUIDED CITY TOURS

Most Barcelona city tours are offered by major excursion operators via large air conditioned buses and either a live guide (in the language of your choice) or a multilingual tape recorded guide. Expect to be offered a variety of half and full day trips that generally cost between 4,000 *ptas* and 5,500 *ptas* per half day, and between 7,000 *ptas* and 8,500 *ptas* per full day without meals. Special interest excursions that include specific history, art, nightlife, or cultural events may cost upwards of 11,000 *ptas* including dinner and drinks.

The companies listed below offer a wide range of these trips, and may actually be able to pick you up directly from your hotel lobby with advance notification. Tickets for city tours can be purchased from the following operators directly, or from most hotels and travel agencies. Call in advance to determine the exact times and days of the week for your preferred excursion, what language the tour will be narrated in, and where the pick up location nearest to you will be.

• **Pullmantour,** *Gran Via de les Cortes Catalenes, 635, Tel. (93) 317-1297*
• **Julia Tour,** *Ronda Universitat, 5, Tel. (93) 317-6454*

NIGHTLIFE & ENTERTAINMENT
Downtown

    L'OVELLA NEGRA, *Carrer de les Sitges, 5. Tel. (93) 317-1087.*

    Of all the student bars in town, this is the best place to visit. Situated a block off the Ramblas near the Barrio Xines, this highly charged whitewashed and stone wall cavern gets totally packed by 1am. You can listen to loud rock music while sitting down at long tables surrounded by the under 20 crowd. Beers cost only 275 *ptas,* there is no entry fee, and the scene is really happening.

    EL QUATRE GATS, *Carrer de Montsió, 3. Telephone unlisted.*

    Housed in a fine Modernist building on a small side street off the Via Laietana (designed by Josep Puig i Cadafalch), this famed café once served the likes of artists such as Pablo Picasso. It still has an artsy feeling, and now even offers good food as well. Grab a beer for about 375 *ptas* here before heading off to the more aggressive nightspots elsewhere. A real gem!

    BAR MARSELLA, *Carrer de Sant Pau, 65. Telephone unlisted.*

    I was not ready for what I found when I passed through the old world facade of this *Barrio Xines* tavern. Inside there was a crowd of local artists and musicians having their tarot cards read while discussing politics and love. The bar is unusually classy, with the 30 to 45 year old patrons dressed in everything from jeans to Armani haute couture. The music ranges from soul on weekdays to live jazz and soft rock bands on weekend nights. There is no cover charge, the drinks are strong and cheap, and the interior is turn-of-the-century. A great place to sit back and unwind.

    LES GENS QUE J'AIME, *Carrer de Valencia, 286 (Basement level). Tel. (93) 215-6879.*

    Of the many bars and clubs in Barcelona, this one really stands out. This is a small speakeasy-style pub off the Passeig de Gràcia that only seats about 80 people in its plush sofas and sitting chairs. The pub gets an eclectic crowd of all ages, who sit and converse or have their fortunes read while sipping imported beers in an antique-filled hideaway. The interior is tranquil, full of odd art collections and turn of the century curiosities, and provides the best place in town to spend a quiet night with a special friend. There is no cover charge, and drinks start at 450 *ptas.*

NICK HAVANA, *Carrer del Rossello, 208. Tel. (93) 215-6591.*

Once upon a time this ultra-modern Eixample area dance club was the talk of the town. These days it has become much less selective, and a bit more down to earth. There are several rooms with different music and ambiance, and the crowd is a good mix of people in the 25 to 35 year old range.

CHIC STUDIO, *Avinguda Parallel, 64. Tel. (93) 329-5454.*

When you're looking for the typical one-liner pickup disco, this is a good bet. This huge disco is located near the old Drassanes boatyards off the Ramblas and gets a 16-22 year old crowd of one night standers. Expect to pay about 1,600 *ptas* to get in, including one drink. Nothing special, but it's quite a trip.

GLACIAR, *Plaça Reial. Telephone unlisted.*

This unpretentious café-style beer hall is decidedly low key. Most people at the long bar and adjacent small tables just stay for a couple of beers and talk before moving on. The music is either blues or soft rock, and the ambiance is rather welcoming. If you're in the mood for a laid-back drinking session with the locals, come here by about 10pm and grab one of the outdoor tables. There is no cover charge, and the drinks are cheap.

TARANTOS, *Plaça Reial, 17. Tel. (93) 212-2661.*

When you're looking for a good venue for live jazz and ethnic music from around the world, this is one of the city's best spots. On my last visit I caught a great Brazilian band on one night, and some great flamenco on the next. One thing to keep in mind is that the performances don't start until about midnight. This intimate establishment has seating for a couple of hundred music lovers who generally range from 30 to 45 years of age. The cover charge ranges from 1,500 *ptas* to 2,000 *ptas* per show and usually includes one cocktail.

LA BOITE, *Avinguda Diagonal, 477. Tel. (93) 419-5950.*

I had a great night of live jazz at this medium-sized concert venue in the Eixample district. The booking agent gets the best American and European jazz, blues, and soul artists to play here, and you can get tickets starting at just 1,200 *ptas* per show. Call in advance and get their schedule.

The Port Olímpica area

TALAIA DREAMS, *Carrer de Marina, 16. Tel. (93) 221-9090.*

Located on top of the Talaia restaurant in front of the Olympic port, this circular disco gets the suited 35+ set in at about 11pm on weekends. Its arched bars, plush red sofas, stainless steel walls, and pounding house mix music make it the best place to dance the night away while in this part of town. Admission starts at 1,800 *ptas*, with drink prices averaging at 900 *ptas* each.

KLIBDIS BAR, *Moll del Mistral. Telephone unlisted.*

A small super-modern bar with a small dance floor that gets packed on weekend nights by about 11:30pm with a mixed crowd. Besides offering strange concoctions and imported beers at good prices, you can also indulge in a game of darts. One of the better small clubs in this area.

OH TEQUILA, *Moll de Mistral, 3. Tel. (93) 221-3768.*

This little Mexican bar and restaurant is a great place to down a few in the Olympic Port. After a couple of tacos, I had a few tequila shots that took my mind off the hard work necessary to research this book. The people who frequent this establishment come from all walks of life and are rather open to conversation with foreigners. Nothing special, but still a good stop while in the neighborhood.

Uptown

TORRES DE ÁVILA, *Carrer Marqués de Comillas, Poble Espanyol. Tel. (93) 424-9309.*

Situated alongside the dramatic gateway into the Poble Espanyol theme park on Montjuïc, the Torres is by far the most luxurious bar and disco in the city. The multi-story ultra-modern interior is packed by midnight with the well dressed yuppie set, and contains several backlit side rooms, stainless steel sculpture furnishings, old stone walls, rock tables, circular bars, star gazing domes, a nice dance floor and an unforgettable rooftop lounge. Admission is about 2000 *ptas*, and drinks start at 800 *ptas* each and up.

UP AND DOWN, *Carrer de Numancia, 179. Tel. (93) 280-2922.*

Now popular among singles in all age ranges, this exclusive Sarria district restaurant and nightclub has a strongly enforced dress code and selective doormen. The disco gets hot after midnight, and you can find some of the city's best dressed night crawlers here. Expect to pay 2000 *ptas* or more to get in, and upwards of 900 *ptas* per drink. There are also special dance shows and other events throughout the week. This place is for the richer and more sophisticated 30 something and up set.

OTTO ZUTZ, *Carrer de Lincoln, 15. Tel. (93) 238-0722.*

Still busy after several years of operation in the uptown Sant Gervasi district, this three floor mega-disco likes to bill itself as a "New York Style" club. Although it doesn't remind me of the Big Apple, it certainly tends to attract so-called beautiful people of all ages to its many dance rooms, each with its own bar. Admission starts at 2000 *ptas*, and drinks cost at least 750 *ptas* each. The doormen are tough about picking just the best dressed or prettiest 20 to 40 year old patrons, and on weekends after 2am it is often impossible to get in.

TABLAO DE CARMEN, *Carrer de Arcs, Poble Espanyol. Tel. (93) 425-4616.*

As far as watching Flamenco in this city is concerned, this is your best bet. This authentic looking Andalucian building offers two live shows nightly (except Mondays) on a central stage surrounded by small tables. Meals are served here. Call in advance to book your tickets. Expect to pay well over 1,250 *ptas* for the show, and about 750 *ptas* and up per cocktail.

SPORTS & RECREATION

Amusement, Water, & Theme Parks
- **Parque d'Atracciôns**, *Montjuïc, Tel. (93) 441-7012*
- **Poble Espanyol**, *Montjuïc, Tel. (93) 325-7866*
- **Parc d'Atracciôns**, *Tibidabo, Tel. (93) 211-7942*
- **Port Adventura**, *Solou, Costa Dorada, Tel. (902) 202-220*
- **Catalunya Miniatura**, *(Torrelles de Lobregat), Tel. (93) 689-0960*
- **Isla Fantasia Aquaparc**, *(Vilasar de Dalt), Tel. (93) 751-4553*
- **Aquatic Paradis**, *(Sitges), Costa Dorada, Tel. (93) 894-0369*
- **Marineland**, *(Palafollos), Costa Brava, Tel. (93) 765-4802*
- **Water World**, *(Lloret de Mar), Costa Brava, Tel. (972) 368-613*

Bicycle Rentals & Excursions
- **Bicitram**, *Av. Marqués de l'Argentera, 15, Tel. (93) 792-2841*
- **Los Filicletos**, *Passeig de Picasso, 38, Tel. (93) 319-7885*
- **Icará Sports**, *Av. Icária, 180, Tel. (93) 221-1778*
- **Sun Bikes**, *Carrer de Navata, 8, Tel. (93) 434-0824*
- **Port Olímpic**, *Villa Olímpica*

Bowling
- **AMF Bowling**, *Carrer Sabino de Arana, Tel. (93) 330-5048*
- **Bolera Pedralbes**, *Av. Doctor Mananon, 11, Tel. (93) 333-0352*

Bullfights
- **Plaça de Toros Monumental**, *Gran Via de C. C., 749, Tel. (93) 245-5804*

Boat Rentals
- **Centre Municipal de Port Vell Olímpic**, *Port Olímpic, Tel. (93) 221-1499*
- **Club Marítimo de Barcelona**, *Moll de Espanya, Tel. (93) 315-0059*
- **Parc de la Ciutadella**, *Barceloneta*

Casinos
- **Gran Casino**, *(Sant Pere de Ribes), Costa Dorada, Tel. (93) 893-3666*
- **Casino de Lloret**, *(Lloret de Mar), Costa Brava, Tel. (972) 366-512*
- **Casino Castell**, *(Peralada), Girona, Tel. (972) 538-125*

Golf

- **Real Club de Golf,** *(El Prat de Llobregat),* Tel. *(93) 379-0278, 18 holes x 2, par 72*
- **Club de Golf San Cugat,** *(San Cugat de Valles),* Tel. *(93) 674-3908, 18 holes + 9 holes, par 70*
- **Club de Golf Vallromanas,** *(Vallromanas),* Tel. *(93) 572-9064, 18 holes, par 72*
- **Caldes Golf,** *(Caldes de Montbui),* Tel. *(93) 865-3828, 9 holes, par 68*
- **Club Golf Llavarnes,** *(San Andreu de Llavarnes),* Tel. *(93) 792-6050, 18 holes, par 68*
- **Club de Golf Terramar,** *(Sitges),* Costa Dorada, Tel. *(93) 894-0580, 18 holes, par 72*
- **Club de Golf Costa Brava,** *(La Masia),* Costa Brava. Tel. *(972) 837-152, 18 holes, par 70*

Gyms & Health Clubs

- **Gimnasio Numancia,** *Carrer de Numancia, 118,* Tel. *(93) 439-3534*
- **Club Vall Parc,** *Carretera de Ambassada, 97,* Tel. *(93) 212-6789*

Horseback Riding

- **Escola Hipica Fuxarda,** *Av. Muntanya, 1,* Tel. *(93) 426-1066*
- **Equitour Trail Tours,** *Carrer de Juan Güell, 163,* Tel. *(93) 490-4437*
- **Catalunya Caballo Viajes Treks,** *Carrer Ballester, 3,* Tel. *(93) 221-8448*

Outdoor Markets

- **Sunday Art and Organic Produce Market,** *Plaça Sant Josep Oriol*
- **Weekend Handicraft Market,** *Rambla Santa Monica*
- **Thursday Antique Market,** *Avinguda de la Catedral*
- **Sunday Stamp Market,** *Plaça Reial*
- **Weekend Painting and Sculpture Market,** *Parc Güell*

Pro Soccer Teams & Stadiums

- **Futball Club de Barcelona,** *Estadio Nou Camp, Av. Aristides Mailloi, 12.,* Tel. *(93) 330-9411*
- **Reial Club,** *Estadio Sarria, Carrer Ricardo Villa, 3,* Tel. *(93) 203-4800*

Swimming Pools

- **Piscinas Bernat Picornell,** *Montjuïc,* Tel. *(93) 423-4041*
- **Piscina Municipal Les Corts,** *Travessa de les Corts,* Tel. *(93) 490-8333*
- **Piscina Municipal Marítim,** *Passeig de Marítim,* Tel. *(93) 221-0010*
- **Piscina Municipal Perill,** *Carrer de Perill, 22,* Tel. *(93) 459-4430*
- **Piscina Municipal Trinitat Vella,** *Carrer Via Barcino,* Tel. *(93) 311-3701*

Squash
• **Squash Barcelona**, *Av. Dr. Maranon, 17, Tel. (93) 334-0258*
• **Squash 2000**, *Carrer Sant Antoni María Claret, 84, Tel. (93) 458-2202*
• **Sport Dyr**, *Carrer de Castillejos, 388, Tel. (93) 347-6644*

Tennis
• **Polideportivo Can Caralleu**, *Carrer de Esports, Tel. (93) 203-7874*
• **Tenis Muntjuic**, *Carrer La Fuxarda, Tel. (93) 424-7926*
• **Club Vall Parc**, *Carretera de Ambassada, 97, Tel. (93) 212-6789*
• **Centre Municipal de Tenis**, *Passeig Vall d'Hebron, Tel. (93) 427-6500*
• **Zona Franca Tenis**, *Consorci Zona Franca, Tel. (93) 335-9106*

Zoos & Aquariums
• **Parc Zoològic**, *Parc de la Ciutadella, Tel. (93) 221-2506*
• **Oceanarium**, *Moll d'Espanya*, still under construction at press time

EXCURSIONS & DAY TRIPS

These are just a few of the sidetrips you can take outside Barcelona. You'll need at least six hours and in most cases the sightseeing and excursion companies listed below provide guided tours to these destinations on a set schedule. Hotel pickups can be arranged with advance notice. More independent travelers may wish to save money and follow the directions via train, bus, or car.
• **Pullmantour**, *Gran Via de les Cortes Catalanes, 635, Tel. (93) 317-1297*
• **Julia Tour**, *Ronda Universitat, 5, Tel. (93) 317-6454*

MONTSERRAT

Situated 53 km (33 miles) northwest of Barcelona within the craggy **Serra de Montserrat** mountain range, the mountaintop Benedictine **Monestir de Montserrat** monastery and its adjacent walking trails are among the top half-day excursions. Legend has it that Saint Peter himself left the now famous icon of the Black Virgin (known as *La Moreneta*) atop this mountain. By the 11th century a monastery had been built here to enshrine this highly revered symbol of Catalunya's patron saint after visions of the Virgin Mary were reported around the mountain by locals. Almost all of the original structure was rebuilt in the 19th century, and what is now standing here is of minimal architectural interest.

Since there are still a few hundred or so monks who live and work at the monastery, its dramatic Renaissance **Basilica** containing the icon is about the only part of the complex currently open to the general public. Each day at 1pm and again at 6:45pm (except for July and Christmas) the **Escolania de Montserrat** boys choir give an impressive concert for free inside. The adjacent Plaça de Santa María square is also home to the **Museu de Montserrat** religious art and ancient artifact museum. The museum has two separate wings that contain everything from prehistoric tools and artifacts to beautiful art from masters like **El Greco** and **Caravaggio**.

The Basilica is open daily from 6am until 8pm, and admission is free. The icon can be viewed in its shrine daily from 8am until 10:30pm, 12noon until 1:30pm, and 3pm until 5:30pm. The museum's antique section is open daily from 10:30am until 2pm, while the modern section is open daily from 3pm until 5pm. The entry fee for the museums is 300 ptas for adults, 150 ptas for senior citizens.

There are a couple of **Funicular** railways that continue up the mountain from the Plaça de Creu area near the monastery to a couple of additional sights. One possibility is to hop on the **Funicular de St. Joan** that runs every 20 minutes daily from 10am until at least 5:30pm. This route offers rides to the hermitage of **St. Joan** for 730 *ptas* round-trip and leads to several walking paths nearby. Another worthwhile ride is on the **Funicular de Santa Cova** that operates daily during the same hours, and for 295 *ptas* round-trip goes to the 17th century **Santa Cova** chapel where the famed icon was first discovered. Over a dozen other hermitages and excellent view points can be enjoyed via one or two hour walks on well-marked paths in these zones.

Major Local Festivals

Contact the local Turismo office, *Tel. (93) 835-0251*, for more details. The vast majority of visitors arrive here on the pilgrimage days of the April 27 and September 8 when countless thousands of religious people flock to this site to pay their respects to the icon.

Directions

To get here by car, take the A-2 highway northwest from Barcelona and exit at Martorell. From this town, follow the little C-1410 road north in the direction of Manresa until soon passing signs leading to Montserrat.

The Montserrat-Aeri train station is just below the mountain, and is serviced from Barcelona's FF.CC.-Generalitat commuter train station in Plaça d' Espanya four or five times per day from about 9am until at least 3pm for about 1500 *ptas* round-trip including the cable car ride below. If arriving by train, you will need to take the Teleféric cable car that runs in both directions every 20 minutes daily from 10am until 6pm. This enjoyable seven minute ride will take you from the station at the base of the mountain to the Plaça de la Creu square near the monastery.

Bus service here is provided by the Coaches Julia bus company via the Sants Viriat bus station on Carrer Viriat and runs at least once per day in each direction with a round-trip cost of some 1,000 *ptas*.

The excursion companies listed above run bus tours here throughout the year for approximately 4,850 *ptas* per person, for a half-day trip with guide and admission included.

THE SANT SADURNÍ D'ANOIA WINE CAVES

Located 44 km (27 miles) to the south of Barcelona, the sparkling wine producing town of **Sant Sadurní d'Anoia** is a great place to spend a rainy day. Several wine producing companies are scattered throughout the area, and over a dozen of them offer free or inexpensive tours and tastings of the famed **Cava** champagne-style wines. The best way to enjoy the area is to select a couple of wineries and call them in advance to reserve a date and time for the visit.

A few of the more commercial wine companies in town such as **Cordorniu** and **Freixenet** receive hundreds of visitors each day and make it easy to join a tour and tasting. For those of you with more intense interest in these products, I suggest contacting one of the smaller and more specialized companies who may or may not be open to providing much more than a walk-through tour of the facilities.

The following is a brief listing of companies that have been known to open their doors (not always in some cases) to the public if contacted in advance. Most of the tour guides are actually multilingual wine makers or top company executives that have had many years of hands-on experience in the production of Cava. Several of the factories also offer great deals on direct purchases of specific vintages.

Keep in mind that some vineyards are constantly changing their hours, so don't just show up without calling first.

Larger Wineries
• **Cavas Cordorniu**, *Carrer Afueras, Tel. (93) 818-3232 or (93) 891-0125.* Open 8am until 1pm and 3pm until 7pm on most weekdays.
• **Cavas Freixenet**, *Carrer Joan Sala, Tel. (93) 818-3200 or (93) 891-0700.* Open 9am until 11:30am and 4pm until 6pm on most weekdays.
• **Cavas Castellblanch**, *Casetas Mir, Tel. (93) 818-3001 or (93) 891-0000.* Open 9am until 11:45am and 3pm until 5pm weekdays.

Smaller Wineries
• **Cavas Antonio Mestres Sagues**, *Plaça de Ayuntamiento, 8, Tel. (93) 891-0043.* Open 8am until 1pm and 3pm until 7pm daily. Call Sr. Remei Mateu.
• **Cavas Canals & Casanovas**, *Carrer de Masia Canals, Tel. (93) 899-3202.* Open 8am until 1pm and 3pm until 9pm daily. Call Sr. Canals i Casanovas.

- **Cavas Canals & Munne**, *Plaça Pau Casals, 6, Tel. (93) 891-0318.* Open 8am until 1pm and 3pm until 7pm daily. Call Sr. Jose María Canals
- **Cavas Sola Raventos**, *Carrer Industrial, 40, Tel. (93) 891-0837.* Call Sra. Montserrat Tina Gil for an appointment.
- **Cavas Colomer Bernat**, *Carrer Diputacion, 58, Tel. (93) 891-0804.* Open 8am until 1pm and 3pm until 7pm weekdays.

Another good stop if you're interested in *Cava* is just a few minutes' ride away at the town of **Vilafranca del Penedes**. Besides being home to even more wineries, the town also features the interesting **Museo del Vino** wine museum on its **Plaça Jaume I** square. The museum gives visitors a great opportunity to see both antique and modern implements of wine production and trade, and also includes a wine tasting and souvenir glass in its admission charge. A great way to start your visits to Cava country. *The museum is open Tuesday through Saturday from 10am until 2pm and again from 4pm until 9pm, Sunday from 10am until 2pm, and during the summer its hours are extended. Admission including a tasting costs 250 ptas per person.*

Directions

To get here by car, take the A-2 highway southwest from Barcelona and follow the exit for Sant Sadurní d'Anoia.

The Sant Sadurni d'Anoia train station is within walking distance to some of the wineries, and is serviced by Renfe from Barcelona's Sants train station at least twice a day for about 1,100 *ptas* round-trip.

Bus service here is provided by the Coaches Hispano Llacunense bus company at *Tel.* (92) 891-2561 via their bus depot on Carrer Ugell and runs at least once a day in each direction with a round-trip cost of some 1,400 *ptas.*

The above-listed excursion companies run bus tours here during the summer months in conjunction with afternoon tours of Montserrat for approximately 6,050 *ptas* per person, for a half-day trip with guide and admission included.

PRACTICAL INFORMATION

- **Main City Tourist Office**, *Turismo, Gran Via C. Catalanes, 668, Tel. (93) 301-7443*
- **Airport Tourist Office**, *Aeropuerto de Barcelona, Tel. (93) 474-4704*
- **Barcelona Airport**, *El Plat de Llobregat, Tel. (93) 478-5000*
- **Airport Lost and Found Office**, *El Plat de Llobregat, Tel. (93) 478-5000 ext. 2051*
- **Spanish Customs Offices**, *El Plat de Llobregat, Tel. (93) 370-5155*
- **Iberia Airlines at the Airport**, *El Plat de Llobregat, Tel. (93) 412-5667*
- **Iberia Airlines Reservations**, *Passeig de Gràcia, 30, Tel. (93) 412-4748*

- **Airport Bus Information**, *Tel. (93) 415-6020*
- **Regional Train Info**, *Renfe, Tel. (93) 490-0222*
- **Franca Train Station**, *Avinguda Marqués de l'Argentera, Tel. (93) 319-6416*
- **Sants Train Station**, *Plaça Paisos Catalans, Tel. (93) 490-0222*
- **Regional Bus Info**, *ESTACIÓ NORD, Carrer Ali-Bei, 80, Tel. (93) 265-6508*
- **Regional Bus Info**, *ESTACIÓ SANTS, Carrer Viriat, Tel. (93) 490-4000*
- **Barcelona Municipal Bus and Metro Info**, *TMB, Tel. (93) 412-0000*
- **Public Transportation Info Headquarters**, *Tel. (93) 336-0000*
- **Barcelona Commuter Train Info**, *Ferrocarrils de la Generalitat, Tel. (93) 205-1515*
- **Highway Condition Hotline**, *Tel. (93) 204-2247*
- **Barcelona Radio Taxi Companies**, *Tel. (93) 357-7755 or (3) 490-2222*
- **Central Post Office**, *Plaça Antoni Lopez, Tel. (93) 318-3831*
- **Municipal Lost and Found Office**, *Ajuntament de Barcelona, Tel. (93) 317-3879*
- **Pre-recorded Weather Forecast**, *Tel. 094*
- **Regional Directory Assistance**, *Tel. 1003*
- **National Directory Assistance**, *Tel. 1009*
- **Medical Emergencies Hot Line**, *Tel. 061*
- **Late Night Pharmacy Listings**, *Tel. 098*
- **Hospital Clinic**, *Carrer de Cassanovas, 143, Tel. (93) 454-6000*
- **Red Cross (Ambulances)**, *Tel. (93) 433-1551*
- **Tourist Police**, *La Rambla, 43, Tel. (93) 301-9060*
- **National Police**, *Tel. 091*
- **Municipal Police**, *Tel. 092*

THE COSTA BRAVA

If you have at least one full day to spend outside of Barcelona, or if you intend to enjoy part of your vacation along a sandy beach resort, join hundreds of thousands of fellow travelers and head straight over to the nearby **Costa Brava**. This long stretch of Mediterranean beachfront coastline starts from the town of **Calella**, about 47 km (33 miles) northeast of Barcelona. From here it continues northward along the coast for some 110 km (68 miles) through the pretty coastal communities of **S'agaro** and **Cadaques** until reaching the town of **Portbou**, just below the French border.

Each summer day thousands of young attractive single boys and girls (average age of 18) from all over Germany, Holland, France, Norway, Sweden, England and even Russia have been showing up in the massively developed coastal beach resorts of **Lloret de Mar** and **Platja de Aro** for decades now. But even in these cement jungles there are still a few hidden old neighborhoods and seclude suburban beach areas that are unknown to all but locals and the most savvy travelers. Also along this stretch of coast there are several smaller and quite charming former fishing villages including **San Feliu de Guixols** and **Tossa de Mar** that are just a short drive north.

What most visitors never realize is that the wide inland section of the Costa Brava is rung by a series of small medieval walled or castle-topped white villages, such as **Pals** and **Begur**, which are just 10 minutes drive or less from a beach. These cute old world villages are home to some of the region's best values in both lodging and dining, and are home to both awesome monumental structures and boutiques full of unique local antiques. Most visitors to this region are single Europeans that arrive here by the busload during the summer and fill up the larger resort towns' beaches, towering condos, aparthotels, fast food restaurants, and tacky discotechs. During the winter many hotels close down for the season and much of the area is nice and peaceful.

While my first package vacation to the Costa Brava back in 1987 left me unimpressed, several years of further casual exploration has made this one of my favorite places to relax in all of Spain, especially during June and September when everything here is much cheaper and not totally packed.

ARRIVALS & DEPARTURES/GETTING AROUND

By car, the cheapest way to get to the Costa Brava resorts and cities from Barcelona is to take the N-II highway north and exit at Malgrat de Mar and then follow one of the well marked coastal roads to the north. The fastest but most expensive method to reach the Costa Brava resorts and towns from Barcelona is to follow the high-speed A-7 toll motorway towards Girona. From here follow one of several different winding (but well-indicated) small roads that lead eastward towards the exact destination you desire.

Renfe trains run multiple daily routes from Barcelona via both the Estació Sants and Passeig de Gràcia rail stations in each direction (even more during the summer), to the Figueres station on the Plaça de Estació, the Blanes station, and onward to the Girona station on Plaça d'Espanya with one way fares from 870 *ptas*. From here you must transfer to a local bus for many of the regional destinations listed below.

Buses from Barcelona on the Safra line, *Tel. (92) 265-1168*, drive back and forth between city's Estació d'Autobuses Barcelona Nord bus depot and the resorts of Lloret de Mar, Tossa de Mar, L'Escala and Empúries and cost upwards of 970 ptas each direction. The Barcelona Bus company,

Tel. (92) 232-0459, has frequent express coaches between the Estació d'Autobuses Barcelona Nord station and Girona and Figueres from 1,125 ptas and up. The best and most frequent service between the resorts, villages, and beaches of the Costa Brava is offered by the Pujol bus line, *Tel. (972) 364-074,* and they charge about 12 ptas per kilometer of travel.

Water taxis service the route between the beaches of Blanes, Platja de Boadella, Fenals, Lloret de Mar, Tossa de Mar, and San Feliu several times daily for around 100 ptas per kilometer per person. The best companies running this service are Cruceros, *Tel. (972) 364-499,* and Viajes Maritimos, *Tel. (972) 369-095,* for full schedules and destinations.

WHERE TO STAY
CALELLA
Moderate

HOTEL GARBI, *Passeig de les Roques, 3, Calella. Tel. (937) 690-858, Fax (937) 660-474. Internet: www.hotelgarbi@publintor.es. Low season rack rates from 7,750 ptas per double room per night (B.P.) . High season rack rates from 9,000 ptas per double room per night (B.P.). All major credit cards accepted.*

While far from fancy, this good beach-front three-star hotel is a good value for the money. Although popular with screaming teenagers at times, this 1980's style modern tower hotel on the best part of the beach offers some 150 rooms (not air conditioned!) with private bathrooms, simple hardwood furnishings, direct dial telephone, cable television, and for an extra 1,500 *ptas* per room they also offer a seaview terrace. The hotel has an outdoor pool and patio, a bar, a restaurant, nearby parking, and not much else. It's a good value for the money.

PINEDA DE MAR
Moderate

PROMINADE PARK HOTEL, *Passeig Maritim, 7, Pineda de Mar. Tel. (937) 670-003, Fax (937) 671-906. Low season rack rates from 6,000 ptas per double room per night (B.P.) . High season rack rates from 13,800 ptas per double room per night (B.P.). All major credit cards accepted.*

This is a really good brand new family oriented beach-front hotel along the most enjoyable section of the main town beach. Modern, sophisticated, and totally casual, the Prominade Park is proof that a new large modern hotel can be quite a good place to stay. This sparkling new property offers some 172 large rooms, studios, and duplex 1 bedroom apartments that are all nicely furnished and have air conditioning, remote control cable television, direct dial telephone, hair dryers, great windows looking out over the sea or the inner courtyard, and in the case of the apartments there is also a modern and clean kitchenette. The property also features several swimming pools, a game room, high season kids programs, a dance club, a sauna, a health club, a buffet restaurant, garage parking, safe deposit boxes, a great multi-lingual staff, currency exchange and much more. Though a bit noisy due to the number of kids here, it is the best value for the money anywhere within a 30 kilometer radius of here.

LLORET DE MAR
Expensive
RIGAT PARK HOTEL, *Platja de Fenals, Lloret de Mar, Costa Brava. Tel. (972) 365-200, Fax (972) 370-411. US & Canada bookings (UTELL), Tel. 800/44-UTELL. Low season rack rates from 15,000 ptas per double room per night (E.P.). High season rack rates from 19,800 ptas per double room per night (E.P.). Closed from November through March. All major credit cards accepted.*

This superb five-star deluxe hotel is beautifully situated right above the Platja de Fenals beach. Favored by celebrities, rock stars, politicians and wealthy international businessmen, the Rigat Park is fully booked during most nights in the summer. The good news is that during the months of April, May, September and October (when the weather is still usually great) there is plenty of availability at reduced rates. While many of the hotel's 105 spacious and beautiful rooms and suites (decorated in several different classical styles including Elizabethan, Victorian and Louis XIV) boast huge sun terraces with spectacular views out to the beach, air conditioning, antique furnishings, marble-lined private bathrooms, remote control satellite television, mini-bar, executive style desk, mini-safe, direct dial telephone, hair dryer, original local art work and lots of natural sunlight.

The hotel also offers facilities such as direct beach access, a large swimming pool with underwater music and a pool bar, three different restaurants with open air terraces, plenty of business meeting rooms for up to 700 people, boutiques, billiards, ping-pong, a tennis court, a solarium, secure parking and some wonderful sitting rooms with fine oil paintings and fireplaces. The service here is world class, with a great front desk staff that will be glad to help arrange rounds of golf at several nearby courses, horseback riding, yacht and boat rentals and all sorts of exciting excursions. Their main sea-view semi-formal dining room offers wonderful regional cuisine with white linen and silver service. This is a great place to go when you want to be near Barcelona and enjoy all the unforgettable features of the Costa Brava. Selected as one of my "Best Places to Stay" (see Chapter 13).

HOTEL SANTA MARTA, *Platja de Santa Cristina, Lloret de Mar, Costa Brava. Tel. (972) 364-904, Fax (972) 369-280. US & Canada bookings (Relais*

& Chateaux), Tel. 212/856-0115. Low season rack rates from 17,000 ptas per double room per night (E.P.). High season rack rates from 20,000 ptas per double room per night (E.P.). All major credit cards accepted.

The four-star Santa Marta is an exclusive seaview hotel situated just five minutes drive away from the center of Lloret de Mar just above the pristine sandy cove *Praia de Santa Cristina* beach. Comprised of a five floor modern main hilltop building and a separate garden annex (recommended for those seeking additional peace and quite), this nice deluxe beach hotel is full during most of the summer. The property offers 70 nice, casually furnished single, double, and family rooms that all have air conditioning, satellite television, private bathrooms, hardwood furnishings, and great terraces with views of either the beach or gardens. The hotel also offers a good restaurant, an outdoor swimming pool, two tennis courts, relaxing lounges, a bar, room service and plenty of free parking.

Moderate

HOTEL ROSAMAR MARITIM, *Passeig Maritim, Lloret de Mar, Costa Brava. Tel. (972) 364-066, Fax (972) 370-911. Low season rack rates from 8,000 ptas per double room per night (E.P.). High season rack rates from 12,600 ptas per double room per night (E.P.). Half board meal plan available from 1,000 ptas per person per day. All major credit cards accepted.*

Located just steps away from the main beach in Lloret, this is my favorite moderately priced three-star seaside property in the center of town. The Rosamar Maritim offers 90 beautiful double rooms (about half are seaview) that feature air conditioning, private bathrooms, nice modern furnishings, satellite color television and plenty of charm. Since it caters to families and couples, there are high season kids programs and game rooms, as well as huge outdoor swimming pools, plenty of parking, several bars, restaurants and great service. For a seaview room expect to pay around 3,000 *ptas* or so extra per room.

TOSSA DE MAR
Moderate

HOTEL DIANA, *Placa de Espana, Tossa de Mar, Costa Brava. Tel. (972) 341-886, Fax (972) 341-886. Low season rack rates from 6,500 ptas per double room per night (E.P.). High season rack rates from 10,100 ptas per double room per night (E.P.). Closed from November through March. Most major credit cards accepted.*

Situated just a few steps away from the main beach area, this cozy little two-star Victorian styled inn offers 28 pretty little rooms. While you can expect to pay about 1,200 *ptas* extra for a seaview accommodation, all rooms feature antique furnishings, telephone, cable television and plenty of charm. The building reminds me of a Victorian English bed and breakfast, and the staff are both helpful and nice. It's a great little place to get away from it all.

SAN FELIU
Expensive
   HOSTAL DE LA GAVINA, *Platja de S'Agaro, San Feliu de Guixols. Tel. (972) 321-100, Fax (972) 321-573. US & Canada bookings (Relaix & Chateaux) (212) 856-0115. Low season rack rates from 23,000 ptas per double room per night (E.P.). High season rack rates from 35,000 ptas per double room per night (E.P.). Closed from November through March. All major credit cards accepted.*

This magnificent five-star hotel, originally built back in 1932 as a small inn for the friends of wealthy local homeowners, has grown to its present capacity of 56 fabulous rooms and 16 regal suites. Set amidst several acres of semi-tropical gardens which terminate at an elegant outdoor swimming pool on the edge of the Mediterranean, the Hostal is a place of elegance, comfort, and hospitality. The three story structure itself is an architectural delight in its own right with convent- style ceilings, Romanesque mosaic floors, limestone columns, huge terraces, opulent fireside salons, and an endless array of museum quality objects d'art from the 16th through 20th century.

All accommodations here feature large dual basin marble covered private bathrooms, rare antique walnut and mahogany furnishings with mother of pearl inlays, remote control air conditioning/heating systems, ceiling fans, remote control satellite television, Murano glass lamps, big picture windows with views out over either the dramatic seaside of the pristine gardens, mini-safe, mini-bar, plenty of closet space, executive style desks, direct dial telephones, freshly cut flowers, beautiful works of art, and either wood parquet or Spanish tile floorings. Many of the accommodations here also offer huge ocean-view terraces, while a limited number boast a wonderful Louis XV decor complete with Italian silk wall coverings and hand carved wooden moldings.

The hotel offers five excellent Catalan restaurants, and even the breakfast here is a gourmet delight with both a fine continental buffet and cooked to order omelets and pastries. Other facilities include a health club with both sauna and Jacuzzi, two tennis courts, free outdoor parking, a garage, currency exchange, available health and beauty treatments including invigorating massages, a nearby semi-private beach and a large inner courtyards dotted with fantastic fountains. The well staffed concierge desk will help you arrange rounds of golf or suggest a variety of day trips and excursions around this unspoiled sector of the Costa Brava. Perfect for couples, honeymooners, or stressed out executives that need to get away from it all, this is one of the finest deluxe hotels in Europe. Selected as one of my "Best Places to Stay" (see Chapter 13).

Moderate
HOTEL PLAÇA, *Plaça de Mercat, 22, San Feliu de Guixols. Tel. (972) 325-155, Fax (972) 821-321. Low season rack rates from 9,000 ptas per double room per night (E.P.). High season rack rates from 11,000 ptas per double room per night (E.P.).Most major credit cards accepted.*

Situated in the heart of the market square, just two short blocks from the main town beach, this nice simple and very clean hotel is a good value for the money. This modern three-star hotel offers 16 bright and airy rooms that all have private bathrooms, cable television, mini-bar and telephone. They also have a swimming pool and sundeck on the roof, a solarium, and for a small surcharge you can also get air conditioning. The only problem I found was the attitude of the front desk staff who were far from friendly or helpful during my last visit here.

PLATJA D'ARO
Expensive
PARK HOTEL SAN JORGE, *Carrer de Palamos, Platja d'Aro. Tel. (972) 652-311, Fax (972) 652-576. Low season rack rates from 15,500 ptas per double room per night (B.P.). High season rack rates from 23,800 ptas per double room per night (B.P.). All major credit cards accepted.*

Located on a cliff above two adjacent semi-private cove beaches on the northern border of town, this deluxe four-star hotel is the best place to stay in the area. The hotel has several adjacent low rise wings which boast 104 beautifully decorated single and double rooms (the majority of which have seaview balconies) that all feature deluxe dual basin marble bathrooms, air conditioning, remote control satellite television, direct dial telephones and really nice modern furnishings. The hotel also offers a health club, a sauna, free parking, seaside outdoor swimming pool, beach chairs, well manicured gardens with walking paths, two restaurants, boutiques, a snack bar, business meeting rooms, seaview luncheon terraces, and extremely comfortable public lounges and lots of charm.

Moderate
APARTHOTEL COMTAT SANT JORDI, *Carrer de Palamos, Platja d'Aro. Tel. (972) 816-061, Fax (972) 816-717. Low season rack rates from 9,000 ptas per 1 bedroom apartment per night (E.P.). High season rack rates from 13,500 ptas per 1 bedroom apartment per night (E.P.). Closed from November through March. All major credit cards accepted.*

For families that are looking for modern, large, and clean self-catering apartments within five minutes walking distance to the main town beach, the Comtat Sant Jordi is the best place to stay. The three-star complex features four modern cement garden apartments consistinf of three floors each. Each surrounds an oversized outdoor swimming pool and garden. The 160 one and two bedroom terraced apartments feature well stocked kitchens, double bedrooms, a living room with sofa bed, nice simple pine furnishings, modern art and lots of sunlight. A great deal for the money, but can be a bit noisy if there are kids at the pool.

BEGUR
Expensive

MAS DE TORRENT, *Estrada de Torrent, Torrent. Tel. (972) 303-292. Fax (972) 303-293. US and Canada Bookings (Relais & Chateaux) Tel. (212) 856-0115. Low season rack rates from 29,000 ptas per double room per night (C.P.). High season rack rates from 35,000 ptas per double room per night (C.P.). Half Board meal plan available from 6,500 ptas per person per night. All major credit cards accepted.*

This exclusive five-star hotel is based around a beautiful converted 18th century mansion surrounded by sumptuous gardens. The hotel is located just about six kilometers southwest of the medieval town of Begur, just a few minutes drive away from both fine sandy beaches and lush valleys. Mas de Torrent has 26 suites and four double rooms in both its level main building and a series of adjacent connecting bungalows. Each accommodation is beautifully decorated with antique rural furnishings, with air conditioning, private marble bathrooms, remote control satellite television, mini-bar, direct dial telephone, electronic mini-safe and large windows which look out onto pristine gardens and countryside. The hotel is also home to a superb semi-formal restaurant which is set amidst huge picture windows and a sloped ceiling of exposed hardwood beams. Hanging on the main dining room's walls are a series of priceless sketches drawn on lace panels which were created by Catalan artists such as Miro and Tapies to celebrate the 90th birthday of Pablo Picasso in 1991. During the warmer months the garden-side al fresco dining patio opens as well.

The overall ambiance here is unusually relaxed yet somewhat sophisticated, with an affluent international clientele that tend to enjoy socializing with each other over cocktails and dinner. Additional facilities here include an outdoor swimming pool with sundeck, a tennis court, a snooker room, mountain bicycles, a game room, business meeting rooms, opulent chandelier lit salons, fine antiques and rare works of art. Nearby there are several golf courses, horseback riding stables, fine sandy beaches and quaint little towns where local ceramics can be purchased. The service here is quite good, and the overall experience is best enjoyed by those seeking a private and sophisticated place to stay while visiting this precious coastal section of Catalunya. Listed in the "Best Places to Stay" chapter (Chapter 13).

Moderate

HOTEL AIGUA BLAVA, *Platja de Fornells, Aiguablava, Costa Brava. Tel. (972) 622-058, Fax (972) 622-112. Low season rack rates from 10,800 ptas per double room per night (E.P.). High season rack rates from 13,000 ptas per double room per night (E.P.).Half board meal plans available from 2,100 ptas per person per day. Closed from December through February. All major credit cards accepted.*

After just one minute of sitting in the lobby and hearing the comments of departing guests, I knew this was a special place. Owned and managed by four generations of the same family since it started out as a small restaurant and cozy inn back in 1932, these days it is looked after by the exceedingly charming Sr. Juan Gispert Lapedra, several family members, and a superb multilingual staff.

The friendly Hotel Aigua Blava has 89 rooms and suites that in most cases have seaview terraces and are drenched in warm Spanish sunlight. Each room is uniquely and beautifully decorated in casual yet elegant style and features deluxe marble or tile lined private bathrooms, large double or king size bedding (and extra sofa beds in some cases), hand carved hardwood furnishings, direct dial telephones, mini-safe, mini-bar, original artwork, and air conditioning. There are also a family suites complete with a separate children's bedroom and sitting room.

Within the small "pueblo" styled property there are peaceful inner courtyards, an Olympic sized swimming pool and sun-deck, private reception and meeting rooms, a bar with live entertainment in the summer evenings, and a cute and clean little cove beach. There are also three restaurants serving wonderful gourmet cuisine on outdoor terraces as well as in casual seaside dining areas and a formal candlelit dining room. No wonder that clients from all over the globe have been coming back year after year for as many as 45 straight seasons. In some cases the children of these repeat clients have met each other and fell in love while on holiday here, and are now returning with their own kids. Selected as one of my Best Places to Stay (see Chapter 13).

PARADOR DE AIGUABLAVA, *Platja de Aiguablava. Tel. (972) 622-162, Fax (972) 622-166. US and Canada Bookings (Marketing Ahead) Tel. 800/223-1356. Low season rack rates from 13,500 ptas per double room per night (E.P.). High season rack rates from 15,000 ptas per double room per night (E.P.). All major credit cards accepted*

This nice modern four floor hotel on a cliff above beautiful Aiguablava beach is another good choice in the area. The sun drenched government owned *parador* has 87 large and beautifully decorated and air conditioned rooms and suites, all with deluxe marble private bathrooms, heating, tile and hardwood flooring, hair dryers, satellite color television, mini-bar, modern hardwood furnishings, direct dial telephones, windows with views out over the sea. Facilities here include a huge outdoor swimming pool at the edge of the cliff, a seaside restaurant and beach club, an excellent regional restaurant, bar, fireside lounges, meeting and convention rooms, gardens, plenty of free parking, foreign currency exchange, and an indoor garage. Service here is prompt and efficient, and the people working are really nice.

Inexpensive

HOSTAL ROSA, *Carrer Pi i Rallo 11, Begur. Tel. (972) 623-015. Fax (972) 622-938. Low season rack rates from 6,690 ptas per double room per night (B.P.). Low season rack rates from 9,730 ptas per double room per night (B.P.). Most major credit cards accepted.*

Of all the hotels up in the old section of downtown Begur, this is certainly the best. This simple yet charming two-star hotel is housed in a pair of old stone buildings that share a tranquil inner courtyard, just steps away from the main square. The hotel has 23 nicely furnished single and double rooms that all feature private tile bathrooms, satellite color television, direct dial telephone, hand hammered wrought iron fixtures, small reading tables, nice hand-stenciled hardwood furnishings, and great big windows with views out onto the medieval lanes of the town. The hotel also has a nice bar complete with a cave style ancient ceiling, laundry machines, nearby parking, a sun terrace, a library, small meeting rooms, safe deposit boxes, and a hearty continental breakfast buffet included in the price. The staff here are very nice, and the overall ambiance in both the rooms and the public spaces is simply delightful.

HOSTAL SA TUNA, *Platja de Sa Tuna, Begur. Tel. (972) 622-198. Fax (972) 622-198. Low season rack rates from 8,000 ptas per double room per night (C.P.). High season rack rates from 9,000 ptas per double room per night (C.P.). Closed on Weekdays between October and late March. Most major credit cards accepted.*

This family owned and operated restaurant and pensione offers four basic and very simple sea-view double rooms with large patios and one interior view double room that all have clean modern tile private bathrooms, twin double beds, plenty of closet space and simple hardwood furnishings. There is no television, radio, or telephone to distract you from enjoying the peace and quiet available here. From your own private terrace you can take some sun while watching the local fisherman haul in their daily catch, and later in the day see a hundred or so Spanish visitors sunbathing nearby. Or you could just stroll along the rocky cove beach. All rooms come with breakfast made to order, and if desired it will be sent up to your room. While there are few facilities in the pensione itself, those with a car can take an endless array of short drives to busier beaches, mountain trails, nearby fishing villages, the ceramic factories and antique shops in the nearby town of Bisbal and the large cities or coastal resorts such as Girona and Lloret de Mar. This is the perfect little getaway for those that want to be right on the seaside, yet away from the maddening crowds that fill up most of the beaches along the Costa Brava. While far from deluxe, it does have a special quality to it that makes its guests feel right at home from the moment they arrive.

CADAQUÉS
Moderate

HOTEL PORT LLIGAT, *Carrer de Port Lligat, Cadaques. Tel. (972) 258-162, Fax (972) 258-643. Low season rack rates from 6,800 ptas per double room per night (E.P.). High season rack rates from 9,700 ptas per double room per night (E.P.). Most major credit cards accepted.*

Located just in front of Port Lligat's Dali museum four kilometers away from the downtown core, this delightful and affordable little three-star hotel is about the only real bargain in Cadaques. There are 29 simple but nice single and double rooms that have private bathrooms nice pine furnishings, and windows or terraces with either sea, village, or mountain views. For a little supplement you can get a cable television, mini-bar, bay-view patios, kitchenettes, and a lot more space. Facilities include an outdoor swimming pool, nearby tennis facilities, free parking, an art gallery, a restaurant, and a nearby pebble beach area. The service here is friendly, and while far from luxurious, it is a great place to stay while visiting Cadaques if you have a car and really want to explore the area.

WHERE TO EAT
TOSSA DE MAR
Moderate

TAVERNA DE L'ABAT RAMON, *Placa Pintor Vila Longa, 1, Tossa de Mar. Tel. (972) 340-708. Most major credit cards accepted.*

Located at the base of the Vila Vela old town quarter, this great traditional Catalan restaurant is worth spending a bit extra for. Housed in a medieval mansion just behind a defensive wall, either the restaurant's stone and exposed beam interior dining room or its more relaxed al fresco patio will definitely get you in the mood for a hearty delicious meal. Their extensive menu includes a more traditional sampling of classic Catalan dishes such as coastal fish soup, huge mixed salads, grilled shrimp, filet of sole, sirloin steak, grilled turbot, cannelloni with truffles and good home made desserts. The typical three course al la carte dinner here will cost about 3,950 *ptas* per person plus drinks.

SAN FELIU
Expensive
CANDLELIGHT RESTAURANT (*at the Hostal de la Gavina*), *Platja de S'agaro, San Feliu de Guixols. Tel. (972) 321-100. All major credit cards accepted.*

This romantic little a la carte restaurant in the beautiful Hostal de la Gavina is far more comfortable and innovative than any other dining room in the area. Set amidst dark wooden panels and fine oil paintings, the dozen or so tables here are expertly serviced by a team of white gloved waiters that really know how to treat their guests well. Somewhat formal yet light and welcoming, the Candlelight offers a season menu of delicious French influenced gourmet Catalan specialties such as cream of squash soup with Sevruga caviar, smoked salmon bilinis, fresh bean salad with shrimp and mint leaves, hearty paella, basked fillet of local turbot, sea bass grilled in olive oil, roast saddle of rabbit, rack of lamb for two, filet of sole, hot chocolate soufflé and fresh tropical fruits with homemade sorbet. They also offer a superb wine list and excellent coffee.

For a special night out, dress nicely and make sure you call ahead for a reservation and expect a wonderful four course a la carte dinner. The cost is about 8,750 *ptas* and upwards per person plus wine.

Moderate
VILA MAS, *Platja de Santa Pol, San Feliu de Guixols. Tel. (972) 822-526. All major credit cards accepted.*

Housed in a beautiful Modernist villa right in front of the beach, this well known restaurant and bar is a good place to enjoy an al fresco lunch. The restaurant has a small indoor section, but I suggest sitting at one of the wicker tables with a sea view and watching the action on the beach while dining. Although far from gourmet, the cuisine here is light and tasty and their menu includes huge tropical and mixed salads, sandwiches, entrecote, rice with mixed seafood in saffron sauce, grilled fresh catch of the day, burgers and great desserts. The service here is good but the clientele can be a bit on the snobby side, yet I still enjoyed the place. Expect to pay around 3,300 *ptas* a person plus drinks for a fairly good three course lunch or dinner here.

PLATJA D'ARO
Expensive
JOAN PIQUE, *Barrio de Castell, 3, Castell d'Aro. Tel. (972) 817-925. All major credit cards accepted.*

Situated in a medieval castle tower three kilometers outside of Platja d'Aro in the quaint old village of Castell d'Aro, this superb semi-formal gourmet restaurant is a true bastion of culinary delights. The French influenced Catalan cuisine here presented on beautiful bone china is served in a rustic interior dining room or on a wonderful al fresco dining terrace. The menu here changes seasonally, but during my last visit here it featured oysters with black caviar, home made foie gras, ravioli stuffed with squid, grilled filet of sole, duck carpaccio, entrecote, lobster with truffles and roasted rabbit. The desserts and wine list are both exceptional, and the service is top quality. A three course a la carte menu here will cost about 5,750 *ptas* per person plus wine.

BEGUR
Expensive
RESTAURANTE MAS DE TORRENT, *Estrada de Torrent, Torrent. Tel. (972) 303-292. All major credit cards accepted.*

Situated on a a peaceful garden estate six kilometers southwest of Begur, this delightful restaurant with an outdoor dining terrace is well worth the short drive from anywhere along the Costa Brava. The main indoor dining room features huge picture windows looking out onto tranquil gardens, a chapel style sloped ceiling with exposed wood beams, and a collection of original sketches drawn on lace panels by Catalan artists such as Miro and Tapies to pay homage to Pablo Picasso.

Although their menu changes seasonally, during a recent visit it featured bay scallop salad with asparagus and artichokes, ravioli of shrimp and eel, rock fish soup, crab and lobster lasagna, veal sirloin in mustard butter, squab served with braised vegetables and sausage, gilthead baked in a sea salt crust, tangerine sherbet with mini chocolates and tiramisu. The wine list here is excellent, and the service is great. A typical course gastronomic menu here will cost around 6,500 *ptas* per person plus wine.

Moderate
RESTAURANTE SA RASCASSA, *Platja de Aiguafreda, Begur. Tel. (972) 622-845. Most major credit cards accepted.*

Located just 25 meters away from the tiny beach of Aiguafreda, this beautiful little seafood restaurant is one of the most pleasant establishments along the Costa Brava to enjoy a simple lunch or a more complicated dinner. There is a nice outdoor dining patio and the Sa Rascassa's interior dining room is housed in a Moorish styled villa complete with Arabesque windows, Romanesque columns, and exposed stone walls. Inside you will find bright pastel yellow walls adorned with modern art and some dozen or so blue stained pine tables. The color combinations and the way the natural sunlight hits the building itself create a wonderful effect, and the antique clocks inside make for an amusing detail. The menu here features sandwiches and light snacks at lunch time, as well as a more traditional sampling of classic Catalan dishes such as coastal fish soup, huge mixed salads, chicken salad, calamari Romano, grilled shrimp, filet of sole, veal steak Provincial, and good home made cakes. The average three course al la carte dinner here will cost about 3,350 *ptas* per person plus drinks.

RESTAURANTE SA TUNA, *Platja de Tuna, Begur. Tel. (972) 622-198. Most major credit cards accepted.*

This restaurant in the hostal of the same name (see listing under *Places to Stay*) is the best place around here to enjoy wonderfully presented rice and seafood specialties. They have a huge outdoor dining terrace, a rock-faced inner dining area, and a glass enclosed seaside dining room that all offer the same menu. Among the house specialties are vichyssoise, rockfish and rice soup, peppers stuffed with cod, goats cheese salad with wild mushrooms, paella, spinach and cheese cannelloni, leg of lamb in mint sauce, grilled prawns, fresh grilled tuna with ratatouille, salmon in cava, plums in armanac and cava sherbet. The ambiance here is casual and relaxed, and the staff are both multilingual and extremely friendly. The average price of a three course al la carte meal may cost around 2,850 *ptas* per person plus drinks.

RESTAURANTE FONDA CANER, *Carrer Pi i Rallo 14, Begur. Tel. (972) 622-391. Most major credit cards accepted.*

Owned by the same people as the Hotel Rosa, this delightful inexpensive dining establishment is also located on an old town street just steps away from Begur's main town square. Fonda Caner has three beautiful separate dining rooms that all contain medieval architectural elements including exposed wood beam or curved cave style tiled ceilings, original rock-faced walls, and deep cut windows. There are also 17th century documents and a collection of unusual artwork covering the walls. The menu here includes a good selection of typical local cuisine prepared to high standards such as vegetable soup, wild mushroom salad with cured ham, cannelloni au gratin, black paella, roasted rabbit, baked local fish, grilled lamb chops, duck liver pate in port wine, pigeon stuffed with pork and vegetables, and fresh pasta with salmon and parmesan cheese. A special daily three course menu is offered for just 1,300 *ptas* per person including wine and water, while the average three course a la carte meal will cost somewhere around 2,550 *ptas* per person plus drinks.

SEEING THE SIGHTS
COSTA BRAVA HIGHLIGHTS

Heading northward along the coast, and returning southward via the inland cities.

Calella

As the closest real coastal resort to Barcelona along the Costa Brava, Calella has become popular with both Spanish and German visitors up from the city for a day. There are dozens of giant unimpressive hotels here, but the town relies on daytrippers anywhere from 17 to 35 year old, that tend to head home after they are done with either the beach or one of the 30 different discos.

Heavily developed in the 1980's, Calella is a modern and cheerful resort town with a reasonably nice kilometer-long beach front. The sea front and town center are separated from each other first by an electric train track that is part of a new rapid rail service from Barcelona, and a few blocks behind by the wide N-2 highway. To hit the beach you must always walk through one of several tunnels below the electric train tracks.

The beach at Calella itself has plenty of space to set down a towel, but the real fun here is to spend your time at one of several inexpensive fenced-in beach clubs that offer tasty snacks and strong cocktails. Each club is free to enter, and they play different types of music ranging from reggae to disco, and feature semi-private sunning areas with windscreen and chair rentals for about 500 *ptas* each. The promenade just in front of the sand (often packed with bicyclists and roller-bladers) is lined by ugly big hotels, fast food joints, and kiosks offering glass bottom boat trips for around 850 *ptas* a head.

The center of the town center begins along a street called the **Riera de Capaspre** and extends for a dozen or so streets along which you can park your car inexpensively at metered spots. One block behind this Riera along the **Carrer de Jovara** there are plenty of bars, money exchange kiosks, and leather shops next to small English style pubs. From here you can wander along the old stone lanes and search for good seafood restaurants and bargains at the boutiques. The north edge of town is primarily residential and is flanked by converted old fisherman's houses on a grid of several interesting old lanes. There is not much else of importance here, but for a beach resort only 45 minutes away from the big city it isn't bad at all.

Pineda de Mar

If you are not interested in singles action and want to enjoy time along the beach in the southern Costa Brava, Pineda is the place for you. While there is little of historic or tourist interest, the beach here is just a bit smaller than the one at nearby Calella, but the occupants are generally Spanish and Northern European families and couples averaging 35 years old and up. Located just a few kilometers north of Calella along the electric train line from Barcelona, the main beach-front esplanade here is called the **Passeig Maritim** and is full of laid back cafes and good family-style hotels. The town itself is less than half the size of Calella, and offers a few nice restaurants and boutiques, but not much else except for charm.

Santa Susana

Santa Susana is just a few more kilometers northeast along the coast from Pineda, is also along the electric train line, and basically offers the same ambiance with mainly Spanish retirees and families as typical guests. About the only real difference here is that the main **Platja Dorada** beach has somewhat calmer waters that are better for children and beginning swimmers. The seaside esplanade here is also known as the **Passeig Maritim** and, as can be expected, is once again lined with pubs and pizza & burger joints. Just one block behind is the more interesting **Avenguda del Mar**.

Blanes

Blanes is a pleasant medium sized working class city about five kilometers northeast of Santa Susana. The city also happens to boast a popular coastal beach resort area. The two kilometer long crescent shaped main town beach is divided into two distinct sections by a small rocky peninsula with a nice panoramic walkway. The younger sun worshippers head for the south section of the division, while families and the more mature 30+ year old jeans and sunglasses crowd head for the north beach and its cafes. Its a nice enough place, but specific points of interest other than the beach itself are few and far between.

Lloret de Mar

Located six kilometers northeast of Blanes, the first world class tourist resort city you will pass while heading up the Costa Brava is Lloret de Mar, population 15,438. Since it was "discovered" by Northern Europeans in the 1970's, most of Lloret de Mar has been tastelessly transformed into one of Spain's most densely inhabited summer vacation resorts. Towering concrete hotels and condo complexes line most of the downtown core. The **Avenguda Just Marles i Vila Rodona** (known by locals as the **Riera**) is the main avenue that runs from the commercial district towards the beach-front and is jam-packed with fast food joints and mega-discos blasting out techno music until sunrise each night.

The main attraction here is the long sandy **Platja de Lloret** beach which is invaded by countless teenage Dutch, German, Scandinavian, Russian and English tourists during July and August each year. The adjacent suburb of **Fenals** is better suited for those over 21 years old who are seeking a more upscale and less crowded vacation destination.

Most visitors here will be astonished to see the giant cement hotels and condos that surround the main streets in and around the city center. There are well over 50,000 hotel and boarding rooms here, making Lloret one of the country's largest vacation destinations. The main attraction: the giant stretch of white sand known as the **Platja de Lloret** beach.

Mansion-topped cliffs border both the north and south edges of the beach.

Since the sand here is cleaned each evening by municipal tractors, the beach is usually rather clean. The oceanfront is located within walking distance of almost any part of town, and is well over a kilometer long. Here you can choose to either just bring a big beach towel and hang out with throngs of horny Northern European teenagers, or spend the 450 ptas or so to rent a reclining beach chair and socialize with their parents instead. Just be careful in the water since the undertow is very strong at times, and the sea bottom gets deep quite quickly!

The entire beach is lined by an esplanade known simply as the **Passeig** which is lined by plenty of inexpensive or free car parking spots, but don't park illegally in this town or they definitely will tow your car away. The Passeig is also home to dozens of fast food restaurants, beach bars, over-priced souvenir shops, expensive seaview condo buildings, and a few medium quality yet high priced hotels. The beach-front itself has several kiosks selling cold drinks and ice cream, a few jet ski rental stations, and several water taxi boats that pull right up to the sand to shuttle passengers to and from other nearby beaches such as Tossa de Mar and Blanes (tickets are sold at the beach-front water taxi kiosks).

As the afternoon sets in and the beach crowds get their fair share of darkened skin, they head off through the maze of stone lanes just behind the sea. To get a good feeling for the heart of Lloret, I suggest stopping in at a few sights of historical and cultural interest. Along the Passeig itself is a peaceful seaview square called the **Plaça de la Casa de la Vila** that is lined with benches, outdoor cafes, palm trees, and a bandstand that hosts free evening concerts sometimes. Here in the antiquated town hall building at the southern edge of the plaza you will find an extremely helpful **Oficina de Turisme** tourist office that will be glad to give you free maps and great advice on nearby sights and excursions.

From the tourist office you can head into town along the Carrer de Cervantes and after a block or you will be lead directly into the bustling **Plaça de la Església** plaza. The plaza is lined by several boutiques and jewelry shops, but is most famous for being home to the stunning Modernist mosaic covered side chapel of the 16th century **Església de San Roma** church. Open to the public for free daily from 10am until 12noon and again from 5:30pm until 7:30pm, the front door to the church is bordered by old Arabic inscriptions. From the church you can walk along the Carrer de la Vila as it cuts through the old part of this former fishing village and pop into some of the countless boutiques and clothing shops along all of the intersecting side streets.

For an interesting hour long walk, try heading towards the cliffs at the south edge of the main beach. From the very end of the Platja de Lloret you can climb up a series of stairways and zigzag along small roads and paths atop a massive cliff while passing by the tiny 10th century **Castell de Sant Joan** castle before finally reaching the impressive **Platja de Fenals** beach area. Although this area has also been heavily developed, it has somehow managed to retain a more subdued ambiance.

Half the size of Lloret's main beach, the people at Fenals tend to be a more friendly and relaxed mixture of local families, foreigners 18 years of age and up, and romantic couples looking for a bit of space and privacy (something they would never find at Lloret's big beach). The water here is calmer, there is almost no undertow, and the sea bottom drops off gradually. On the sand itself are buildings belonging to the **Clube Maritim Fenals** sailing school and the **Clube Motonautica Fenals** jetski and parasailing school which are both open to the public for inexpensive scheduled lessons during the summer. The streets behind the beach have plenty of free or inexpensive parking spots, English pubs, and reasonably priced restaurants around this zone.

Just a a kilometer away from Platja de Fenals begins a string of some of the coast's most beautiful secluded beaches. While the local government fortunately has yet to signpost or even pave the access roads to the following beaches (known only to locals until recently), unfortunately by the time you read this that may no longer be the case. By car or taxi you will head one kilometer south of Fenals along route GI-682 to then turn left just after the McDonalds to follow a dirt road access road for about 175 meters. On the left side of the street you will find small paths leading to the amazing little crescent shaped sandy beach known as the **Platja de Sa Boadella**. This is one of the country's most beautiful and romantic little silky white sand cove beaches, and is completely natural and undeveloped (other than a thatched hut snack shop).

Further south along the same route are the marked and paved access roads to the nice but larger white sandy beaches of **Platja de Santa Cristina** and the adjacent **Platja de Truemel**. These remote beach areas are all more quaint, secluded, and charming than anything in Lloret, but have little in the way of services. One all to often overlooked attraction around this area rests peacefully on a cliff just above at the Platja de Santa Cristina. The quaint little **Jardim Tropical Botanico Pinya de Rosa** (Tropical Botanical Gardens) are well worth the effort to visit while beach hunting. This beautiful hilly little garden area is complete with 10,000 different species of exotic plants and trees that in many cases are posted with their Latin names and countries of origin. In the heart of the small botanical garden is the 17th century **Ermita de Santa Cristina** (Chapel of Saint Christina) which features a fine Neoclassical altar, antique model sailing vessels, and wonderful stained glass windows. If you get hungry or thirsty there is a cozy shady oceanview promenade with a cute seafood restaurant and an outdoor cafe just behind the chapel. *The botanical gardens and chapel are usually open from sunrise to sunset daily, there is no entrance fee, but parking near here will cost 600 ptas.*

If you are more interested in longer hikes of two to four hours each, ask the tourist office for a free copy of *"Camins de Lloret."* This combination map and sightseeing brochure has been made for those hikers that wish to view several secluded beaches while on the way to historical sights such as the 3rd century B.C. Iberian ruins at the **Puig Castellet Montbarbat**; a few Roman era structures, Gothic churches, and some fine buildings designed by famed Catalan architect J. Puig i Cadafalch. All of these sights are just on the outskirts of town and are well worth a visit for those with strong legs.

Those looking for a bit of refreshing summertime fun might also wish to consider heading some two kilometers north of the main town beach via route GI-680 (also known as the Carretera de Vidreres) to the 80,000 square meter **Water World** Parc Aquatic (water park). Here kids and teens will love the Black Night water slide, the huge tropical style freeform swimming pools with wave machines, crazy rapid rides, Jacuzzis, kiddie pools and burger restaurants. Besides free parking, Water World also offers free scheduled round-trip bus service from various points in Calella, Pineda, Sta. Susana, Malgrat, Blanes, Tossa and downtown Lloret. *The park can be reached at Tel. (972) 368-613 and is open daily from mid June through late August from 10am until at least 8pm and costs 1,975 ptas per adult and 1,150 ptas per child under 12.*

Some nine kilometers south of Lloret in the town of **Palafolls** is the **Marineland** sealife and water park. Besides offering 40,000 square meters of water flumes, a great Canyon River rapid ride, several tropical heated swimming pools, and kiddie tire tube rides, this park has an amphitheater with multiple daily scheduled performances of trained dolphins, sea lions, and parrots. *The park can be reached at Tel. (972) 795-4802 and is open daily from mid June through August from 10am until at least 7pm and costs 1,800 ptas per adult and 1,225 ptas per child under 12.*

As the day turns into night the focus of activity shifts away from the beach and over towards the **Avinguda Just Marles i Vila Rodona**. This is the wide main avenue (known to many locals as the **Riera**) that leads from the beach towards the heart of the new part of town. The avenue is lined by over two dozen mega-discos and pubs which get packed with the 16 to 24 year old singles set every summer night from 11pm until the sun rises. The streets that intersect this main avenue are also loaded with pubs and restaurants serving the various ethnic foods and beers of many European nations. Lloret is also home to a nice but small **casino** over by the bus station in the Grand Hotel Casino Royale that costs about 600 ptas to enter and requires the presentation of a valid passport. The casino is open to those over 18 years old from 9pm until 3am nightly, and proper attire is expected.

Tossa de Mar

Resting at the foot of the Mediterranean ocean between two lush green mountains, the quaint little former fishing village of Tossa de Mar, a mere 11 kilometers northeast from crowded Lloret de Mar, is a real gem. With a population of only 3,403 year round residents, Tossa has managed to remain a low-key beach village and to preserve several elements of its Greek, Roman, and Medieval origins. While tourism is the major industry here, Tossa continues to ban the construction of any towering cement complexes along its beach-front, thus maintaining its charm and avoiding the overdevelopment problems that plague much of the Costa Brava. Since the area first gained notoriety during the 1930's when it became a summer hangout of famous artists and intellectuals, it has become an upscale yet casual vacation getaway for discriminating travelers that enjoy off the beaten path destinations.

Tossa still contains a magnificent 800 year old walled medieval quarter on a cliff above the beach that is complete with a castle and several old villas. In fact, the entire downtown has an authentic small village ambiance which is really lovely. No matter where you plan to stay in this region, this town is well worth the effort to visit for the day. Perhaps after a few hours of wandering around the town's old stone lanes and its medieval quarter, you may have the urge to cancel your hotel reservation elsewhere and take a room here for a few nights instead!

The town starts at the beach and continues back through a small valley for a few small blocks. The main sheltered crescent shaped **Platja Gran** beach is a mere 400 meters long and besides having a few interesting rock formations and islets, it is generally blessed with both calm waters and a shallow sandy sea bottom. Just to the north of the main beach is a smaller 140 meter long stretch of sand that is more popular with families. Just about the only convenient parking in town is limited to a seaside lot that charges a whopping 300 ptas for the first hour and another 175 ptas for each additional hour. Bordering the beach and its parking lot is a charming little esplanade known as the **Passeig del Mar** which is a good starting point to wander around town. Most of the three and four story whitewashed buildings that line the Passeig are home to cozy little moderately priced inns and seafood restaurants, and at night the town's residents and visitors stroll and converse along here.

From the south edge of the beach there is a paved walking path that reaches a 225 step stairway. This ascends past several crenellated circular watch towers that form an oval defensive wall originally designed to ward off pirate attacks eight centuries ago. You'll pass some coin operated telescopes (which magnify the impressive coastal views), and then cross under an archway cut into the walls. Once you reach the lighthouse, proceed a bit further and you will reach the famous cliff-top 12th century **Vila Vela** old town quarter. In this charming quarter, certified as a national historic landmark, visitors can stroll past a few dozen quaint old villas that are covered in bougainvillea, several of which are now small cafes and galleries. At the edge of the old quarter you will find a small square called the **Plaça Roig y Soler** where the former governor's mansion has been transformed into the **Museu Municipal** museum. The museum displays several interesting archaeological exhibits, Roman mosaics, and paintings from some of the most famous artists that came here in the 1930's. Just behind the museum is a tiny little cove beach.

The museum is open during Monday through Saturday from 10am until 1pm and again from 3pm until 5pm, Sundays from 10am until 1pm, and has extended hours during the summer on most nights until 8pm. Admission is just 175 ptas for adults and half price for students and senior citizens.

One other interesting adventure to be considered if you're here in the summertime is to take a water taxi ride. Lasting 30 minutes to one hour, the water taxi pulls up to the beach and then heads along the coast towards Lloret and Blanes as it passes several small villages, caves, and almost virgin beaches. Tickets can be found at the kiosks along the main beach for around 750 *ptas* per person each way.

San Feliu de Guíxols

San Feliu is a friendly and relaxed little coastal city that boasts several worthwhile historical sights, a compact old commercial center, and of course a fine strip of long sandy white beach. Situated along two small yet active Mediterranean bays some nine kilometers northeast of Tossa de Mar, San Feliu is mostly frequented by wealthy Spanish families with nearby vacation homes and apartments. The old town lanes are full of old churches, small market squares, and local taverns that are all great to peek into.

Most first time visitors head straight for the closer of town's two main town beaches, the bustling **Platja de San Feliu**. This well maintained cove beach is seldom visited by foreigners, and the locals here are unusually friendly. This first beach extends for around 600 meters and offers a few beach kiosks, sunchair rentals, watersports facilities, and plenty of space to stretch out on. The northern end of this beach rests a nice pleasure-craft marina with some awesome yachts. Above the Platja de San Feliu is a palm shaded esplanade called **Le Pesseig del Mar** which is rung by a few fine Modernist mansions. Structures such as the **Nou Casino la Constantia** (built in 1869) and the **Casa Patxot** (built in 1917) have bold facades in even bolder colors. The esplanade is also home a few outdoor cafes next to the **Jardins de Juli Garreta** gardens. Every week on Sunday a nice outdoor market is held here and the whole city comes out to greet each other.

Another great place to stroll around is just a couple of blocks behind the Passeig esplanade at the cafe lined **Placa de Mercat** square. This is the point of confluence for almost all of the tiny stone lanes that zigzag through the old quarter of San Feliu. The plaza is home to several old buildings including the 1929 **Casa de la Villa** (town hall) who's yellow facade is embellished by carved stone lions holding up the city's coat of arms. Near the fountain in the center of the plaza is a daily (except Sunday) general products open air market. Just a few steps away is the **Mercat Cobert**, an enclosed fruit and vegetable market which is also worth visiting for great picnic supplies.

After you have seen the beach and the old town center, I suggest taking a five minute walk over to the superb local **Oficina Municipal de Turisme** (tourist office) located at the **Placa de Monestir**. This is the best tourist information office anywhere on the coast and they give out a vast selection of maps and brochures of all the municipality's historic sights, natural wonders, excursions, nightlife possibilities and museums. *The tourist office is open Monday through Saturday from 10am until 1pm and again from 5pm until 7pm, Sundays from 10am until 5pm.*

Just steps away from the tourist office is the Benedictine **Monestir** (monastery). Although the majority of the monastery complex dates back to the 18th century, there are remnants of older structures such as Romanesque towers and portals (some dating back to the 10th century) integrated into the facade. The highlight of the monastery is the somber Romanesque **Esglesia** (Church) which was first constructed over a millennium ago but has since been rebuilt adding Gothic styling. Make sure to take a look at church's adjacent the Porta Ferrada wall who's exact purpose within the monastery has baffled historians for decades.

In a separate section of the complex is the **Museo d'historia de la Ciutat** (municipal history museum) where you can inspect a vast collection of prehistoric megaliths, Roman amphorae, 500 year old Catalan ceramics, stained glass windows, and of course a sampling of the churches religious statuary, silver, and paintings. Also in the complex is a special **Arxiu Historic** (historical document library where some of the regions oldest maps and land deeds (some over 500 years old) are expertly restored and preserved.

When you're done with the main sights in town, its time to take a shady twenty minute hike northward past the marina and continue along San Feliu's huge rocky seacliff to reach the serene **Platja de Sant Pol** beach-front. Cut off from the rest of town by the sea cliff itself, this 700 meter long strand of pure white silky sand is fronted by huge Victorian and Modernist villas that belong to rich bankers and famous Barcelona based business tycoons. This part of San Feliu exudes a casually elegant ambiance and feels much like a sleepy coastal village in a permanent state of Siesta. A good percentage of those sitting at the tropical seaview bars and cafes such as **Vila Mas** spend the afternoon sipping cool drinks and checking out each other's tiny Chanel swimsuits and massive Gucci sunglasses. For sail boat, jet ski, and wind surfing rentals, this is also the place to go. Just to the north of this beach area is the fantastic hotel called the **Hostal de la Gavina**, and behind it lies a super exclusive private residential area and beach called **S'Agaro** which keeps its gateway closed to non-residents.

Platja d'Aro

The increasingly popular beachside resort town of Platja d'Aro is situated some three kilometers northeast of San Feliu. Although the town and its seemingly endless beach front tend to attract a somewhat more mature, better dressed, and wealthier crowd than the larger Costa Brava resorts, in many ways it tries rather hard to model itself as a little sister to Lloret de Mar. Frequented mainly by upper middle class Spanish, German, Dutch, and Russian families (whose teenage kids love to party all night at the many discos and pubs around town), the downtown boasts some of the Costa Brava's most expensive designer boutiques scattered amidst souvenir shops and family fun amusement centers.

Besides shopping and sun worshipping, visitors to Platja d'Aro can also find a picturesque little medieval village just three kilometers inland at Castell d'Aro. Golf enthusiasts will enjoy their proximity to the fine 18 hole championship Club Golf d'Aro just a few minutes drive away in the suburb of Mas Nou.

Although much smaller and more exclusive than Lloret, in many ways Platja d'Aro has tried to duplicate its success in marketing itself to tourists. The 1.7 kilometer long **Platja d'Aro** sandy white main town beach is bordered by an esplanade flanked by many high rise apartments and hotels which contain beach bars and restaurants on the ground level. Packed with mostly affluent Spanish and German families that spend their July and August vacation weeks sun bathing all day long, the entire beach area caters to young, middle aged, and older visitors alike.

The southernmost point of the town's seafront is home to the **Puerto de Platja d'Aro** sheltered boat marina. This small harbor is the home away from home for dozens of expensive cabin cruisers and yachts, several of which can be rented by the day, week, or the entire summer. The port is also the sight of a private yacht club that has a good seafood restaurant that is open to the public at meal times. Nearby you will also find a summer only sailing school and several beach bars, and a nice walkway.

Just three short blocks behind the beach-front is town's main commercial avenue called the **Avinguda St. Feliu de Guixols**. This long avenue cuts through the entirety of the town and is divided up into separate sections by means of a few traffic circles. The southern section of the avenue is lined by several dozen fast food restaurants, expensive designer boutiques, cafes, bars and pubs, discos, amusement centers, 24-hour ATM machines, realtors, supermarkets and cheap souvenir kiosks. Among the larger department stores is the massive **Vall Magatzems** and **Mar Franc** shops where you can by designer haut-couture. This area is also the best place to find a metered parking space for your car, and is where much of the evening action takes place. The northern section of the main avenue is quieter and flanked by hotels, a few discos, and some better restaurants. Behind the main avenue are several more blocks full of smaller shops selling everything from jewelry to sunglasses and beachwear.

The Platja d'Aro area is also home to a few family fun amusement parks and other activities that become popular from June through August. On the southern part of the main avenue through town is the small **Magic Park** amusement park and recreation zone. Here there are sections featuring bumper car rides, a bowling alley, a ferris wheel, a disco roller rink, a haunted house, go karts, carousel rides, slot machines, and fast food restaurants. *The amusement center is open daily from 9am until 9pm and costs nothing to enter, but rides start at 400 ptas and up per person.*

Just under two kilometers north of town on the Carretera de Circumvalacio is the 60,000 square meter **Aquadiver** parc aquatic (water park). Here kids and teens can enjoy zigzag water toboggans, simulated river rapid rides, the Adventure Lake children's activities area, giant tire tube rides, a huge tropical style freeform swimming pool with wave machines, Jacuzzis, kiddie pools and fast food restaurants. Besides free parking, Aquadiver also offers free scheduled round-trip bus service from downtown Platja d'Aro. *The park can be reached at Tel. (972) 818-732 and is open daily from mid June through late August from 9am until at least 8pm and costs 1,750 ptas per adult and 1,025 ptas per child under 12.*

For more adventurous adults and families seeking thrilling daytime excursions there a a few other places to contact around Platja d'Aro. The well managed **Santa Cristina Horse Club** located a few minutes drive away along the Carretera de Girona in the suburb of Santa Cristina d'Aro offers an excellent array of guided horseback rides on nearby beaches and mountain valleys for riders of all experience levels. Call them at *Tel. (972) 835-212* and reserve at least a day in advance. Another exciting possibility is to head over to the Puerto de Platja d'Aro main town port and pop into the **IOE Marina**. This facility can arrange sail boat and motorboat rentals starting from just 15,000 *ptas* per half day. Call them at *Tel. (970) 564-544* and ask about their special off season and multiple day rentals. Those more interested in underwater activities should contact **DAN Europe** in the Hotel Columbus, *Tel. (909) 712-711,* for details about their scuba lessons and ocean dives for beginning through certified level divers.

A possibility for a relaxing self guided short excursion is to head four kilometers west on the Carrertera a Santa Cristina by car or municipal bus to the cute little neighboring village up **Castell d'Aro**. Here you can visit the old lanes and simple stone villas of the charming and rather authentic little **Barrio de Castell** district that still really seems stuck in the 15th century. Also worthy of note is the **Castell** (a medieval castle) which is open for free guided tours on Saturdays at 6pm and Sundays at 11am.

Begur

The small town of Begur rests on the top of a sea-view hill 19 kilometers northeast of Platja d'Aro. The town itself is dominated by a large circular medieval tower known as the **Castell de Begur** below which are several streets that make up the medieval quarter. Just a few minutes drive down the hill leads to some of the coast's nicest little beach areas.

The most obvious starting point for a walk around town is by the **Castell de Begur** tower. Built atop a boulder on the highest point of town 200 meters (305 feet) above sea level, the tower is only accessible by foot via an old street known as the **Pujada al Castell**. It is certainly worth a short hike to see the great panoramic view out over the sea and several nearby towns. While all the lanes in the old part of town are interesting, the main **Placa de la Esglesía** square is where you'll find the local **Oficina de Turisme** (tourist office) where you can get free area walking maps and all sorts of good advice about nearby beaches and historic sights. Also in the same square is the dramatic 18th century gothic **Esglesía de St. Pere** church which can be visited for free daily between sunrise and sunset (a coin operated system that illuminates the church's interior costs 100 ptas to activate). Besides those sights, Begur's old town center is full of 400 year old stone houses and quaint cobblestone lanes that contain several art galleries, bars, and good restaurants. The town also boasts a summertime open air movie theater, and several fine medieval mansions.

Another attractive aspect to Begur are the beaches that rest four kilometers or so below the town at the edge of the sea. Among the nicest is the romantic **Platja de Sa Tuna**, a tiny little pastel colored Mediterranean village. Here 35 or so private houses (including an exact replica of a Medieval castle tower) dot the gently sloping northern edge of a cove that features an 80 meter long rocky sheltered beach-front. The beach itself is home to a few fisherman who haul in their daily catch for the two sea front restaurants which are very good and popular with people from Barcelona who have their summer homes around here. There are also a few German and English tourists that come to avoid the craziness of the larger coastal resorts such as Blanes and Lloret de Mar. Considering the high level of over-development along the Costa Brava, this village is truly precious, and it is well worth a look around. Municipal bus service to and from the quaint beaches is offered about four times daily, for around 175 *ptas* each way.

Just north of Sa Tuna is the minuscule 40 meter long **Platja de Aiguafreda** beach (accessible by either coastal footpath or by car) which has no sand but does offer a good restaurant and P.A.D.I. scuba diving facility called the Sa Rascassa Diving Center, *Tel. (972) 624-247*. They also rent a variety of boats and offer all sorts of water based excursions.

A few kilometers south of Begur is the small beach community of **Aiguablava** which has a fine sandy bay beach surrounded by cliffs, a few good seaside grill restaurants, a good modern **Parador** and the amazing **Hotel Aiguablava**.

Pals

Four kilometers northwest of Begur is the captivating walled **Vila Velha** (old town) section of Pals. Although the municipality of Pals has a population of 1,823 residents, most of them don't inhabit the old quarter, preferring instead to buy modern condos and homes a few kilometers away in the modern suburbs of Masos de Pals and Platja de Pals. Even if you come up to the Costa Brava just for a few days in the sun, make sure to hop a bus or rent a car to spend a few hours wandering around all the dozen or so lanes dissecting the fortified old quarter of Pals. This dramatic part of town rests atop a hilltop called **Mont Aspre** and is comprised of a hundred or so stone block castle towers, villas, houses and other buildings of historical interest that were all totally restored after being ruined in the Spanish Civil War. Since then, most of the finest Gothic villas have been bought as vacation homes by wealthy Barcelonians.

Before you reach the old quarter I suggest popping into the excellent **Oficina de Turisme** tourist offices located just off the main traffic circle dividing the old quarter from the beach and suburban sections of town. They have a fantastic free map of Pals with multilingual information that will help you to navigate through the narrow lanes of the old quarter. Once you finally arrive in the center of the old quarter, look for one of the many free parking spots and proceed directly to the 10th century Romanesque **Esglesía de St. Pere** church which is open daily from sunrise till sunset with no entrance fee. If you insert a 100 *ptas* coin in a small machine off to the side the entire interior lights up for you inspection. From the church it is a two minute walk up the Carrer de la Torre to the round 11th century Romanesque **Torre de les Horres** watchtower which is topped by a 15th century gothic belfry. This is just one of four towers remaining from the old town's defensive walls.

From the tower make a right turn down a set of stone stairs and then turn left onto the Carrer Mayor. All along this route several visigothic graves were found during the post Civil War restoration of the city. After passing beneath a few archways and popping into a few handicraft shops, make sure to peek inside a small alleyway on the left side known as the **Pasatje Casa Rufina**. This alley is home of a beautiful courtyard full of stone archways and an ancient wooden bridge. Keep heading down the Carrer Mayor until you finally reach the **Plaça Mayor** which is the old quarter's main square and is also home to the town hall.

From the beginning of the main town square, make a left turn to head along the Carrer de L'Hospital until you pass an old square watchtower, and turn right. As you descend the hill, turn right at the next intersection and follow the Carrer de la Raval until it ends. Then, turn right onto the Carrer del Abeurador, make the next left turn onto the Carrer de la Creu, and a few seconds later make a right turn onto the Carrer Paul Companyo. Along this street you will find the 15th century **Casa de Cultura Ca La Pruna** museum and cultural center which is home to temporary exhibitions as well as the new **Museu d'Arquelogia Submarina** museum of underwater archaeology. *The museum is open Tuesday through Saturday from 10:30am until 1:30pm and again from 4pm until 6pm and costs 200 ptas a person to enter.*

From the museum you can take a right turn, walk a few paces, and then turn left to follow the Carrer Joaquim Pi until it brings you right back to the old church where you began your tour through the city. A block or so behind the church is the **Mirador Josep Pla** lookout point from which you can have a superb panoramic view out over the land and sea. The old town has no hotels, but there are several great boutiques selling locally produced art and handicrafts, and a few decent restaurants to be found along the old cobblestone lanes.

Although the city does have a long sandy beach area known as the **Platja de Pals**, it is rung by telecommunications towers and is far from charming. The only points of interest around the beach area is a fine championship golf course, a few expensive seaside hotels, and lots of cheap camp sites full of Germans and their caravans.

L'Estartit & Les Illes Medes

Located 11 kilometers north of Begur, the small coastal town of L'Estartit is a pleasant resort community visited mainly by vacationing French families. The town itself boasts a nice 800 meter long sandy beach area, a palm shaded seafront esplanade called the **Passeig Maritim** that is lined with several quaint boutiques and cafes, and a picturesque sheltered harbor and port area known as **El Moll**. Although I was not all that impressed with L'Estartit as a primary vacation destination, it makes for a pleasant enough daytrip, and as the point of departure for several sea based excursions and activities which are well worth the effort to participate in.

The major reason that most tourists come here is for the access to the off-shore archipelago known as **Les Illes Medes**. This series of seven islets and their corresponding reefs are just off the coast and have become the government protected **Reserva Natural de Les Illes Medes** nature preserve. Well known as a prime sight for scuba divers and snorkelers from all over Europe, the preserve is home to over 1,300 different species of native marine creatures and plants, as well as lizards and migrating birds. The area is accessible only by boats but you'll need special permits which are issued by the local government's **Departamento d'Agricultura, Ramaderia, i Pesca** (department of fish and wildlife) offices just off the harbor along the Passeig Maritim. The office will be glad to give you a free copy in English of an excellent brochure entitled *Illes Medees* that features great detailed information on the islets and their topography, history, flora, and fauna.

Those wishing to partake in a wonderful scuba or snorkeling trip to the island preserve should contact the **Medaqua** offices on the Passeig Maritim, 13, *Tel. (972) 752-043*. With a few hours advance notice they can arrange for you to be part of a daily (high season only!) snorkeling trip to the reefs for around 1,500 *ptas* a head., a beginner's scuba class with open water dive for around 3,000 *ptas* a person, a variety of official P.A.D.I. certification courses, and private scuba trips. They also can arrange parasailing, sailing, kayaking, and boat rentals.

There are also hour-long glass bottom boat rides around the islands on small boats such as the **Triton**, as well as a floating "submarine" boat with a glass bottom known as the **Nautilus Star**, which take off from the harbor. Whether you decide to get wet or stay dry, expect to see many varieties of marine life such as coral reefs, star fish, sea urchin, and schools of colorful bream and wrasse. These boat based excursions coast around 1.550 *ptas* a person, last about one and a half hours, and are scheduled several times daily from June through August.

L'Escala, Empúries, and Sant Martí d'Empúries

Although several other beach towns can be found a bit further up along the coast, the next impressive location is L'Escala, some 10 kilometers northwest of L'Estartit. The town itself is quite enchanting, with a population of 2,210, and Spanish weekend and summer vacationers come here to soak up the sun on the couple of nice adjacent 400 meter beaches. Although far from tranquil the town is bordered by a nice marina, and there are several seaside plazas with nice cafes and seafood restaurants all over the old quarter at the north edge of town.

The main attraction in the area is two kilometers north at **Empúries**, where there is a wonderful archaeological site. The site was originally settled as a trading post by the Greeks in the 6th century B.C., and a hamlet was soon built here. A few centuries later the Romans took over, followed by the Visigoths, each adding their own structures. What now stands on the grounds of the so-called **Museu D'Arqueologia de Cataluna en Empúrias** archaeological museum are excavated ruins from both of these civilizations, including remains of Greek temples, a Roman market and mosaic-lined villas, a paelo-Christian basilica and an acropolis on the highest part of the site. A large museum in the center of the complex offers a multimedia presentation about the items dug up here and the ancient peoples that once inhabited the area. There is also a nice sandy beach area just a minutes walk from the parking lot. *The museum and its grounds are open daily during the winter from 10am until 1pm and again from 3pm until 6pm. During the summer it is open daily from 10am until 7pm. Admission is now 400 ptas per person, and includes free secure parking. The multimedia presentation costs another 300 ptas a person to view.*

A few kilometers north from the ruins along route GI-623 is the charming medieval village of **Sant Martí d'Empúries**. This tiny walled hamlet has a half dozen cobblestone streets filled with well preserved medieval villas, a few of which have been converted into art galleries and restaurants. After parking your car you will walk up a set of stairways and head up past the Plaça Petita via the Carrer Major until reaching the central Plaça Mayor where you can visit the Gothic 10th century **Esglesia de San Marti** church which is open for mass at 12 noon daily. Just next door to the church are art galleries and restaurants. Behind the church is a picturesque seafront esplanade and a great little sandy white beach. From here you can follow any of the old lanes as they pass next to old medieval wells and castle ruins. The village is well worth a look around, but just about the only available parking costs 100 *ptas* per hour.

Empúria-Brava

Located 19 kilometers north of L'Escala, the ever-expanding seaside resort of Empúria-Brava is known as the "Venice" of Spain due to the many intercoastal canal waterways that surround its downtown core. Heavily developed by mainly German apart-hotel companies that cater to a mainly German clientele, the town is not all that charming. The one remarkable feature here is the magnificent central pleasure-craft marina that looks just like the one in Fort Lauderdale, Florida, complete with a string of deluxe marina-front condos and restaurants. The two kilometer long beach here is long and sandy, but is not as nice as others just a few kilometers north or south of town. There are also plenty of family-fun amusements such as go-karts, mini-golf, cinemas, snorkeling excursions, and canal boat tours. Basically there is not much else here to do or see, unless you want to try out your German for a day.

Cadaqués

Situated between lush green mountains and a series of peaceful fishing bays 11 kilometers northeast of Empúria-Brava, the enchanting city of Cadaqués is a real gem. Well known as a hideaway for world famous artists and intellectuals such as Dali and Picasso, it is easy to see why the beauty of this town inspired so many famous paintings. Favored by well dressed French and Spanish couples on honeymoons and romantic interludes, this is a truly special place to spend a couple of days just wandering around old stone lanes, soaking up some sun, view fine works of art and enjoying the cool breezes at quaint cafes full of friendly local ambiance.

After a slowly traveling uphill along the dangerous and curvaceous route GI-614 to reach town, the first thing you will want to do is park you car (not an easy task here!) and stretch your legs. This white-washed Mediterranean fishing village offers plenty of charm, but little in the way of historical sights besides a nice Baroque church on the highest point in town, and several charming waterfront villas. The best advice I can give you is if you enjoy art you can spend days wandering around the dozens of trendy galleries, and if you prefer natural scenery you should explore the nearby rocky coastline of the **Cap de Crues** peninsula.

Within the center of town's old quarter itself the major highlight is the seaside **Passeig** promenade. This is the sight for a great outdoor antique market on the last Sunday of each month. From here you can walk a few blocks back through the center of town to reach the **Museu de Arte Municipal** art museum on the Carrer Narcis Monturiol, and retrace your steps to peek inside several fine boutiques and art galleries. Afterwards I would suggest that you head over to the nearby **Plaça de Doctor Tremols** and sip a nice cool beverage before heading off down one of the many small lanes cutting through the old town. The tourist office on the Carrer Cotxe # 2 will be glad to give you a free walking map of town, but the text will most likely be available only in French or Spanish.

While you can spend your mornings walking up and down the old quarter's lanes while window shopping, after lunch you might try some short afternoon getaway trips. Try heading north about 1.5 kilometers along the coast from the north edge of town, and within 25 minutes by foot (or 5 minutes by car) you come to, **Platja de Confitera**, the first of several picturesque fishing hamlets. This secluded little bay-cove has a small pebble beach, and just 20 meters away there is a romantic little rock islet. Scenes like this one were the inspiration for paintings by many of the famed artists that moved here in the 1930's.

Another three kilometers further up along the **Cap de Crues** peninsula the coastal roads and hiking paths reach the settlement of **Port Lligat**. This small cluster of converted fishing huts and seamen's homes just steps from the sea was until this year a quiet and sleepy village. Fast becoming a major attraction, one of these old houses is the sight of the **Casa-Museu Salvador Dalí**, a museum built inside of the surrealist artist's home from 1930 to 1974. Inside the museum you will see Dali frescos along the ceilings, exhibits detailing Dali's studio, a reconstruction of his library, and personal effects, although almost none of his original paintings are not currently exhibited here. *The museum is open from mid March through October and has low season hours on Tuesday through Sunday from 10:30am until 6pm, and high season hours every day from 10:30am until 8pm. Entrance is a steep 1,200 ptas per person, or 700 ptas for students and seniors.*

About the only other activity worth mentioning is the fact that boat rentals, snorkeling, kayaking, windsurfing, and scuba diving are easily arranged from sporting excursion operators in and around town. For more details about underwater activities please contact either Sotamar Diving, *Tel. (972) 258-876,* or Radical Diving, *Tel. (972) 159-361.* For details about several above water sporting possibilities you should instead give a call to either Nautica Cadaques, *Tel. (972) 258-750,* or Motonautica Manel, *Tel. (972) 258-429.*

Figueres

There are a few more seaside towns to see, but from here, I suggest heading inland. The first inland city worth a side trip is about 28 kilometers west of Cadaques at Figueres (also known as Figueras), population 33,520. About the only reason to come here is to pop inside the strangely designed **Teatre-Museu Dalí** on the Plaça Gala y Salvador Dalí. Designed and built by famous Figueres-born painter Salvador Dalí (1904-1989) and his wife Gala back in 1974 to exhibit a private collection of his own surrealist works, this is the most interesting of the three museums that the Gala Dali foundation has developed along the Costa Brava (Figueres, Cadaques, and Púbol).

Once inside the dome-topped main building there are dozens of several lesser known surrealistic paintings and sculptures by Dalí, and his personal collection of works by old masters and a few of his contemporaries. *The museum is open daily during the summer from 9am until 7:15pm, and during the rest of the year from Tuesday through Sunday from 10:30am until 5:15pm. Admission is a whopping 1,200 ptas per person.*

Girona

The beautiful walled city of Girona, population 69,800, lies some 37 kilometers south of Figueres. Divided into two sections by the wide **Onyar** river, the most dramatic sights can be found in the old quarter on the north side of the river.

A good one hour walking tour of this ancient city would be best started from the central **Plaça de la Catedral** square, where you can walk up the adjacent stairway to first see the Gothic **Catedral** (Cathedral). Beside containing the original 11th century **Torre de Carlomagno** tower, the building is filled with fine 15th century art and hand-carved reredos. Just off the tranquil cloisters, lined with columns carved in the Romanesque style, is the **Museu-Tesoro Catedralico** museum that exhibits beautiful tapestries and religious artwork that dates back as far as the 9th century. The cathedral can be entered for free daily from 10am until 6pm. The museum costs 400 ptas to visit and is open from 10am until 2pm and again from 4pm until at least 6pm. Closed on Tuesday and Sunday afternoons.

Just around the corner from the cathedral on the Carrer de Subida de la Catedral is another museum called the **Museu de Arte**. Based in a converted Episcopal palace, this museum offers a good assortment of 11th through 19th century art, furnishings, sculpture, gold, silver, glass, and textiles. *This museum costs 175 ptas to enter and is open Tuesday through Saturday from 10am until 6pm, and Sundays from 10am until 2pm.*

From the Plaça de la Catedral, head down the picturesque Carrer de la Força a short distance until passing the **Museu d'Historia de la Ciutat** local history museum. This small museum housed in a former convent displays a collection of antique devices and photos, as well as an old mortuary. This museum costs nothing to enter, and is open Tuesday through Saturday from 10am until 2pm and again from 5pm until 7pm, Sundays from 10am until 2pm. The same street heads down into the fascinating **El Call Jeue**, the medieval Jewish ghetto. The small side streets that run off this street were home to hundreds of Jewish residents (many of whom were prominent mystics in their day) and merchants until the 14th and 15th centuries, when they were first massacred by jealous locals, and later expelled from Spain during the Inquisition.

To get some idea of what life like for these persecuted residents, pop into the **Centre de Issac el Cec**. This rebuilt series of medieval buildings includes a Jewish temple (now sort of a museum), baths, and a butcher shop just off the Carrer de la Força on a tiny lane called the Carrer de Sant Llorenç. The complex is open Tuesday through Saturday from 10am until 2pm and again from 5pm until 7pm, Sundays from 10am until 2pm. Admission is free to all visitors.

After wandering around the Jewish quarter, return back up through the Plaça de la Catedral, this time passing under an old arch and bearing right onto the Carrer de Ferran el Catolic to find the **Banys Árabes**. Back in the 13th century, descendants of the Moors who had once controlled the area for several centuries built a four chamber public bath house here with both hot and cold rooms. Still mostly intact, the baths are lined with columns that support a lovely vaulted ceiling. *Visiting hours are from Tuesday through Saturday from 10am until 1pm and again from 3pm until 7pm, Sundays from 10am until 2pm. Admission is 175 ptas per person.*

Just across the small **Galligans** river in the upper part of the old town is yet another good museum. If you leave the baths and turn left to head down the stairs and the Plaça de Jurats, a small bridge will soon come into view. Cross over the bridge and head into the Plaça de Sant Llucia to enter the **Museu Arqueológico** museum of archaeology. Housed in the former 12th century Església de Sant Pere de Galligans church, this intriguing building is full of rare artifacts from Paleolithic, Greek, Roman, Moorish, and Jewish settlers from the region. *This museum opens Tuesday through Saturday from 10am until 1pm and again from 4:30pm until 7pm, Sundays from 10am until 1pm. Admission is 175 ptas per person.*

The final attraction in town is the **Passeig de Arquelógic** esplanade walkway that passes alongside the old walls and towers as it curves around the old town. Entrances onto this scenic promenade can be found across the river from the Museu Arqueológico, as well as near the Arab baths, and at several other old quarter locations.

NIGHTLIFE & ENTERTAINMENT
CALELLA
While the beach-front and intersecting side streets are full of pubs serving cold German beer all afternoon and evening, the discos that are most fun here. You can start on the beach after 11:30pm at **Menfis** and later head over to the nearby **High** club. On the north edge of town is the **Red Planet** disco that gets packed by 1am.

LLORET DE MAR
Unlike most cities and towns, the nightlife in Lloret is rather active every night of the week (during the high season). More mature visitors may prefer to head over to the streets just behind the Platja de Fenals where several fun English pubs such as the **Duke of Wellington**, **Robin Hood**, and **Popeyes** can be loads of fun.

Most young, attractive, and single visitors start off by having cheap beers with their friends in one of the bars on or near off the main Avinguda Just Marles i Vila Rodona avenue such as the great **Moby's** pub where 2 for 1 drinks are often offered before 11pm. Since parking along this zone is strictly regulated, I suggest that if driving here you should spend the 200 ptas per hour and put your car inside the avenue's large secure 24-hour underground parking lot. Just a block or two away on the

Carrer de Santa Catarina there are another 15 different pubs such as **Highwayman** and the **Hard Rock Bar**.

By midnight the vast majority of younger party animals head over to the discos on **Avinguda Just Marles i Vila Rodona**. This is the wide main avenue (known to many locals as the **Riera**) is home to dozens of pubs, late night fast food joints, and discos. On this street there are usually several commissioned hawkers passing out free entrance invitations (although a 2,000 *ptas* per person minimum consumption charge is typical) for most of the discos mentioned below. The hottest discos these days are **Tropics**, **The Londoner**, **Flamingo**, **Colossos**, and **XTRA**. A few blocks away you can pop into **Hollywood** where the fun really begins after 2am.

Romantic couples seeking a fun night out without being blasted by techno music can take a car or a taxi over to the magnificent **Cala Banys** seacliff fireside bar near Fenals. Located at water's edge, this rustic lodge's indoor area has cozy sofas and plays funk and soul music while bar tenders serve up great cocktails. The more interesting outdoor section has dozens of candlelit tables for two that are so close to the water they get hit with occasional sea-spray. Ask your hotel for exact directions because it is a hard place to find, but is well worth the effort.

SAN FELIU DE GUÍXOLS

This town doesn't really bother with heavy nightlife until Thursday, Friday, and Saturday come around. The best places to begin your night out at around 11pm are over at the chic **Vila Mas** restaurant and bar over in a cute mansion on the waterfront at Platja de Sant Pol, or a few hundred steps away at the **Taberna del Mar** tavern and beach cabana club. Near the Platja de San Feliu a few good pubs include the unusual **El Corsari** cave bar next to Las Vegas, and **Lawyers** on the Carrer St. Domenic. The majority of the disco action here takes place after 1am at the **Palm Beach Club** on the south edge of Platja de San Feliu and at **Las Vegas** over at the north edge.

PLATJA D'ARO

The summer evening nightlife here starts off in the pubs such as **Charlie's** located on the smaller streets off the beach. By about 2am most singles head for the big discos along the Avinguda St. Feliu de Guixols itself such as **Costa Azul**, **Kamel**, **Joy**, and **Pascha**.

PRACTICAL INFORMATION
LLORET DE MAR
• **Main City Tourist Office**, *Praca de la Vila, Tel. (972) 364-735*
• **Bus Station**, *Carretera de Blanes, Tel. (972) 365-776*

- **Sarfa Bus Lines**, *Tel. (972) 364-142*
- **Pujol Bus Lines**, *Tel. (972) 364-476*
- **Euroline Buses**, *Tel. (972) 365-789*
- **Train Station**, *(Located in the town of Blanes), Tel. (972) 331-827*
- **Taxis**, *Tel. (972) 364-803*
- **Municipal Police**, *Carrer Verge de Loreto1, Tel. (972) 364-344*

Major Local Festivals
   Contact the local Turismo, *Tel. (972) 364-735*, for more details.
- **Festa Sta. Cristina**, *Late July, Marine Processions*
- **Festa Major**, *Late August, Processions, Fireworks, and Parties*
- **Las Alegrias**, *8 September, Folk Dancing*
- **Festa San Roman**, *18 November, Folk Dancing*
- **Car Rally**, *Early May, Car Race*

TOSSA DE MAR
Major Local Festivals
   Contact the local Turismo, *Tel. (972) 340-108*, for more details.
- **Pelegri de Tossa**, *20 January, Pilgrimage*
- **Festa San Pedro**, *29 June, Processions and Parties*
- **Fast Painting Contest**, *mid August, International Painting Competition.*

PLATJA D'ARO
- **Main City Tourist Office**, *Carrer de Verdaguer, Tel. (972) 817-179*
- **Bus Station**, *Avinguda St. Feliu de Guixols, Tel. (972) 826-787*
- **Sarfa Bus Lines**, *Tel. (972) 600-250*
- **Pujol Bus Lines**, *Tel. (972) 364-476*
- **Euroline Buses**, *Tel. (972) 365-789*
- **Municipal Police**, *Tel. (972) 825-777*

PALS
- **Main City Tourist Office**, *Carrer a la Platja, Tel. (972) 636-161*
- **Municipal Police**, *Tel. (972) 667-777*

L'ESCALA, EMPÚRIES, & SANT MARTÍ D'EMPÚRIES
Major Local Festivals
   Contact the local Turismo, *Tel. (972) 770-603*, for more details.
- **Festa Major**, *Early September, Processions, Fireworks, and Parties*
- **Festa del Virgin**, *16 July, Processions*
- **Festa San Martin**, *Mid-November, Processions and Parties*

CADAQUÉS
- **Main City Tourist Office**, *Carrer de Cotxe,2, Tel. (972) 258-315*
- **Bus Station**, *Tel. (972) 258-713*
- **Municipal Police**, *Carrer Vigilant,2, Tel. (972) 159-343*

Major Local Festivals
Contact the local Turismo, *Tel. (972) 258-315,* for more details.
- **Festa Sol-Ixent**, *New Years Day at 7am, Dancing, Music, and Parties*
- **Canaval**, *February, Processions, Music, Street Parties*
- **Semana Cultural**, *mid April, Cultural Week, Folk Dancing, Music*
- **Fesival de Cadaques**, *August, Street Fair, Processions, Folk Dancing, Music*
- **Festa Mayor**, *December, Street Fair, Processions, Folk Dancing, Music*

FIGUERES
Major Local Festivals
Contact the local Turismo, *Tel. (972) 503-155,* for more details.
- **Festa Santa Creu**, *Late May, Processions, Music, and Parties*
- **Festa Sant Pere**, *28 June, Processions, Folk Dancing, Music*

GIRONA
Major Local Festivals
Contact the local Turismo, *Tel. (972) 216-296,* for more details.
- **Festa San Jaime**, *Late October, Processions, Folk Dancing & Parties*

THE COSTA DORADA

For those who can take at least a full day away from their time in Barcelona, there are good destinations nearby that await you to the south of the city along the **Costa Dorada** (also called the **Costa Daurada**). This coastal zone stretches down from Barcelona and continues southward along the Mediterranean for 145 km (90 miles).

While packed with beach-goers and Sunday drivers during July and August, some of the more interesting towns and resorts have managed to escape the overdevelopment that plagues much of the other resort areas in northeastern Spain. High-rise hotels and condos still line much of the beach front, but with a little effort you can find great historic, artistic, and sandy places to enjoy here.

ARRIVALS & DEPARTURES

To drive to **Sitges** from Barcelona, take the small C-256 south. To get to Tarragona or Salou, follow the fast A-7 south.

Buses run to **Sitges** multiple times daily in each direction from Barcelona via the Hillsa bus depot, *Tel. (92) 891-2561* on Plaça de Universitat for about 700 *ptas* each way. Buses to **Tarragona** and **Salou** operate multiple times daily in each direction from Barcelona via **Bacoma** bus lines, *Tel. (92) 231-3801* from the Estació d'Autobuses Barcelona Nord station for about 1,250 *ptas* each way.

Trains to **Sitges**, **Tarragona**, and **Salou** run via Barcelona's Renfe Estació Sants and Passeig de Gràcia train stations several times daily each way for around 775 *ptas* and up in each direction.

SEEING THE SIGHTS
COSTA DORADA HIGHLIGHTS
Sitges

On the ocean 38 km (23 miles) southeast of Barcelona, the amusing city of Sitges (population 11,855) is among the most visited areas in this zone. Way back in the 1880's, the area was gaining popularity as a summer retreat for artists and poets, attracting an unusual mix of people with alternative lifestyles that still frequent this area today. By the 1920's, the local bureaucrats began to plan its future as an upscale beach resort area.

A good place to start your visit is over by the enchanting **Passeig Marítim** promenade that runs alongside the sea for 2.5 km (1.5 miles). It is along this hotel, restaurant, and bar-lined walkway heading southwest that you will pass the nice crescent shaped **Platja de la Fragata** and **Platja del Ribera** beaches. Much further down the coast there are numerous other beaches, including a few that are dedicated to the gay and nudist communities that flock here in large numbers in the summer.

Besides beaches, there are a few noteworthy sights to be enjoyed in the heart of this former fishing village. The center of the old town can be found on a small hill rising just above the seacoast. The charming Carrer de Fonollar is at the hill's edge and is lined with attractions. Here you can find the Baroque **Església** parish church with its simple stone exterior and beautiful octagonal tower. A few steps down the same seafront street you will find the **Museu del Cau Ferrat** art museum. Housed inside the former house and studio of local artist Santiago Rusiñol (1861-1931), the artist donated his collection to the city upon his death. Inside this ornate structure there are paintings by **Rusiñol, Casas, El Greco, Picasso,** and **Soler**, as well as sculptures, sketches, and a huge assortment of wrought-iron objects. *The museum is open Tuesday through Saturday from 10am until 1pm and again from 4pm until at least 6pm, Sundays from 10am until 2pm. Admission is 225 ptas per person, and is free on Sundays.*

Just next door is a building that looks like a castle, now home to the **Museu Maricel de Mar,** that displays a collection of sculpture, ceramic tiles, and paintings from various eras that were donated by local resident

Jesus Perez Rosales. *This museum is open Tuesday through Saturday from 10am until 1pm and again from 4pm until at least 6pm, Sundays from 10am until 2pm. Admission is 225 ptas per person, and is free on Sunday.*

After leaving the museum, continue along the same street passing beneath the small overhead arch. Now you'll make the first possible left turn onto the small Carrer de Bosc. From here, turn left again, this time onto the charming Carrer de Davallada with its old whitewashed houses. This part of town was first laid out in medieval times and contains plenty of narrow winding lanes that are all worth strolling along.

Further uptown, on the Carrer de Sant Gaudenci, is the **Museo Romántico Provincial** museum that is housed in an elegant 19th century mansion. Here you can see a series of 18th through 19th century handmade dolls, furnishings, decorative arts, and other possessions that belonged to rich families from Sitges. *The museum is open Tuesday through Saturday from 10am until 1pm and again from 4pm until at least 6pm, Sundays from 10am until 2pm. Admission is 225 ptas per person, and is free on Sunday.*

Tarragona

The historical port city of Tarragona, population 112,760, sits on a hilltop above the sea 98 km (61 miles) southwest of Barcelona. This welcoming ancient city is a wonderful place to spend a full day just walking around. It has been strategically important since it was first settled by the Phoenicians and later controlled by Cathaginians, Greeks, and Romans. Tarragona's heyday came as the Roman empire's regional capitol (then called **Tarraco**) and was a major base of operations during its conquest of the Iberian peninsula. Tarragona then became a rather cultured and elegant city. Although it has recently declined and become an industrial center, the artifacts and ruins from its more glorified past still provide a wealth of historical richness and delight.

There are several possible ways to see all of the ancient ruins, old world districts, and museums in town, but to simplify matters start at the **Parc del Miracle** just above the unimpressive **Platja de Miracle** beach. Besides having lots of benches and nice summertime floral areas, the park is strewn with restored ruins left from the Roman occupation. Among the highlights are the **Amfiteatre** (amphitheater) and nearby **Balcon del Mediterráneo** lookout. A short walk up from the park on the main Rambla Vella is the **Circ Romá** circus where locals watched chariot races and other spectator events in Roman times. *All of these are open Tuesday through Saturday from 10am until at least 6pm, and Sunday from 10am until 2:30pm. The admission is included in a special 575 ptas entry pass that allows access to most of the ancient ruins in town.*

From the circus, continue up the wide Rambla Vella for several blocks until turning right onto the Via del Imperi Roma. At the next major intersection there is an old town gateway called the **Portal del Roma**. From this point visitors can enter the wonderful **Passeig Arquelógic** promenade that curves along the upper edge of the old town, along the old Roman walls that were later fortified with Moorish and Christian defensive towers, and after that 18th century English cannons. These walls once encircled the whole town until half of them were demolished in 1854 to make the city's expansion possible. Now what remains has become sort of an open air museum with local artifacts being displayed along the walk. *The promenade is open Tuesday through Saturday from 10am until at least 6pm, and Sunday from 10am until 2:30pm. The admission is included in the above mentioned special 575 ptas entry pass that allows access to most of the ancient ruins in town.*

The promenade ends at the other side of the old town on the **Passeig de Torroja** that in turn intersects with the **Passeig de Sant Antoni**, where you will bear right. At the end of this street is the back side of the **Plaça del Rei** square. The plaza is home to the huge **Museu Nacional Arquelógic** archaeology museum. Exhibits here include artifacts such as mosaics, medieval paintings, and local antique ceramics and explanations and facts about Roman history. *The museum is open Tuesday through Saturday from 10am until 1:30pm and again from 4pm until 7pm during the winter, Tuesday through Saturday from 10am until 8pm during the summer, and Sunday from 10am until 2pm all year. The admission is 200 ptas and is also valid for entering the Museu i Necropolis Paleocristian (see below).*

Around the corner is another good stop at the **Pretori Romá**, a 2000 year old former Roman government building with dungeons and tunnels that now houses the **Museu d'Historia de Tarragona** regional historical museum. This tower-like building contains a collection of historical details and charts explaining the origins of the city. *The museum is open Tuesday through Saturday from 10am until 1:30pm and again from 4pm until 7pm during the winter, Tuesday through Saturday from 10am until 8pm during the summer, and Sunday from 10am until 2pm all year. Admission is included in the above mentioned special 575 ptas entry pass that allows access to most of the ancient ruins in town.*

From the plaza, turn right onto the Carrer de Santa Anna for a couple of blocks and soon you will enter the former **Judería** or Jewish quarter. No specific sights still remain here, but its narrow lanes are a good place to get a feel for what life was like for Spanish Jews before they were expelled during the Inquisition.

Now return to the far edge of the **Plaça del Rei**, turn right onto the Carrer Nau, and walk a few blocks until bearing right onto the old town's central Carrer Major. Before going on to the next sight, its time to pop into the *Turismo* tourist office at #39 to pick up a free walking map. Now keep going along the same street until finding the 12th century **La Seu**

Catedral. This fine cathedral is a good example of Gothic and Renaissance styles and has a beautiful rose window, an ornate handcrafted altar, memorable *reredos*, and several unique side chapels. While inside visitors can enter a series of stunning Gothic cloisters, and visit the chapter house that encloses the **Museu Diocesá** museum full of wonderful tapestries, ancient artifacts, and art. *The cathedral is open Monday through Saturday from 10am until 1pm and sometimes again from 3:30pm until 6pm during the winter, Monday through Saturday from 10am until 7pm during the summer. Admission is 400 ptas for the cloisters and museum.*

Besides a couple of decent beaches, the last sight I suggest seeing is the **Museu i Necropolis Paleocristian** museum and Necropolis that is a long walk west from the old town off the Paseo Independencia. Here it is possible to see tombs, sculptures, mosaics, and the ruins of a Visigothic burial ground and mausoleum. The museum displays even more artifacts in good condition that were taken from the sight. *Open Tuesday through Saturday from 10am until 1:30pm and again from 4pm until 7pm during the winter, Tuesday through Saturday from 10am until 8pm during the summer, and Sunday from 10am until 2pm all year. Admission is 200 ptas and is also valid to see the Museu Nacional Arqueológic.*

Salou

Located 22 kilometers (17 miles) southwest of Tarragona, the heavily developed coastal tourist resort town of Salou is a favored destination for Northern Europeans on cheap summer package holiday vacations. Filled with high rise timeshare and aparthotel structures, this place is far from an ideal destination to spend a relaxing vacation abroad, but hundreds of thousands of Dutch, German, and English visitors (mainly a mix of families and party animal type singles) seem to have a different opinion. Besides the beach and dozens of popular pick-up bars, about the only other real attraction here is the brand new **Port Aventura** theme park, about a ten minute train, bus, or car ride away from the town in a suberb known as Vila-Seca. The park contains reproductions of villages from exotic locales such as Mexico, China, the Wild West, and Polynesia.

The amusements include water rides, roller coasters, oriental dances, spinning wheels, Mariachi musicians, can-can girls that break-up gunfights, and plenty of international foods as well as souvenirs. Families can easily spend a whole day wandering around from village to village in search of new rides and attractions. *For the latest details about special prices and events, call their information line, Tel. (902) 202-220. Port Aventura is open from mid-March through late October from 10am until 8pm (with extended opening hours until midnight only during the Summer). Day Tickets cost 4,000 ptas per adults, 3,100 ptas for kids from 5 to 11 years old, and is free for children under 5. Reduced price "Night Tickets" for entrance after 7:30pm are available in the Summer for 2,500 ptas per adults, 1,900 ptas for kids from 5 to 11 years old, and is free for children under 5.*

PRACTICAL INFORMATION
SITGES
Major Local Festivals
Contact the local Turismo office, *Tel. (93) 894-4700*, for more details.
• **Carnival**, *Late February, Masked Balls and Processions*
• **Festa Major**, *Late August, Processions, Fireworks, and Parties*
• **Corpus Cristi**, *May, Streets are Carpet with Flowers*
• **Car Rally**, *March, Vintage Cars*

TARRAGONA
Major Local Festivals
Contact the local Turismo office, *Tel. (977) 232-143*, for more details.
• **Festa San Magin**, *Late August, Processions and Human Towers*
• **Festa San Tecla**, *23 September, Processions*

VALENCIA

Although first inhabited by the **Greeks** and **Carthaginians**, it wasn't until after the Second Punic War that the **Romans** settled in here in 139 BC and founded a colony that was then known as **Valentia**. By the 6th century the **Visigoths** had taken control of the area, followed by the invasion of the **Moors** under the direction of Musa ibn Nusayr in the 8th century.

The Arabs then made the region a part of their kingdom of **Al-Andalus**, and went to great lengths to improve the systems of irrigation and industrial production first started by the Romans. Soon the city began to flourish in agriculture and the production of silk, metals, ceramics, and crafts.

El Cid (Rodrigo Diaz de Vivar) then conquered the city in 1094, and upon his death some six years later, the **Almoravids** took control. In 1238, the powerful King of Aragón, **Jaime l**, triumphantly battled his way into town, and stability graced the region for several centuries. It was during this period that the varied religious and cultural communities of Valencia, comprised of Jews, Arabs, and Christians, lived and worked together to make it an economically and artistically rich city. Scores of ornate buildings were built, universities were founded, and the area became a haven for the arts and sciences.

After the Jews and Arabs were expelled, the city fell into deep economic and moral decay. The 19th century brought renewed success to the region's economy, but it was not until the 1960's that Valencia would once again succeed in becoming a world class city that could support both itself and the rest of Spain.

Valencia is one of the most enjoyable cities to visit in all of Spain. Full of beautiful palaces, gardens, ancient ruins, fantastic museums, and impeccably maintained gardens, the best way to get around by foot. The city may seem rather small at first, but with every corner you turn, there are countless historic treasures and amusing activities.

The temperature here is pleasant throughout the year, and the people seem to enjoy life to the fullest. For those looking for a bit of sun and a taste of the *paella* which Valencia is famous for, try heading out to the beach at Playa **de la Malvarrosa**. Don't rush through your stay in this enchanting and historic city, as there is something for everyone in Valencia, and no trip through Spain would be complete without spending at least a few days here.

ARRIVALS & DEPARTURES

By Air

Valencia's small international airport is called the Aeropuerto de Valencia-Manises, located 8 km (5 miles) west of Valencia off the N-III highway near the town of Manises.

Although several flights do arrive here from large European cities outside of Spain, it primarilly services domestic flights.

Buses between the Airport & Downtown

Bus service via the CVT line operates in both directions between the airport's arrival area and the Valencia Estación de Autobuses bus depot on the other side of the garden-filled old river bed at the Avenida de Menedez Pidal, 13, about one kilometer (.6 of a mile) northwest of the city center. The price is 175 *ptas* each way, and it runs every 80 minutes Monday through Friday from 6am until 7pm, and much less fequently on Saturdays.

There is in fact no service on Sundays and most holidays. From this station, a municipal bus can take you to the heart of town for about 120 *ptas*, or a taxi can be hired for about 595 *ptas*.

Taxis from the Airport to Downtown

Taxis are generally yellow and black sedans marked with the *Taxi* sign, and can be found in abundant supply at well-indicated taxi stands at the airport. Please note that almost all of the taxis here are fairly small sized four door cars.

Normally, a taxi's trunk can hold about two large suitcases, but those with roof racks can secure two more medium pieces of luggage, and perhaps a couple of carry-on bags inside as well. Expect to pay between 1,550 and 2,400 *ptas* per ride from the airport to most downtown locations.

By Bus
Most of the bus lines between Valencia and other parts of Spain, as well as the rest of Europe, pull into the Valencia Estación d'Autobuses bus station arcoss the dry river bed, on the Avenida de Menedez Pidal, 13 about one kilometer northwest of the city center.

From this station, a municipal bus can take you to the heart of town for about 120 *ptas*, or a taxi can be hired for about 875 *ptas*.

By Car
From Madrid, the best way here is to take the fast N-III Autovia east for 352 km (218 miles) until reaching Valencia. From Barcelona, head southwest along the rapid A-7 toll motorway for 349 km (216 miles) before exiting at Valencia. Once inside the city you may have to drive around quite a bit before finding free street-side parking.

Many private garages can be found throughout the city, but you can expect to pay somewhere around 1,950 *ptas* and up per day.

By Ferry
Since Valenica is situated on the Sea, ferries to and from the Balearic Islands of Palma de Mallorca, Ibiza, and Mahón call in over at the Puerto de Valencia ferry landing in El Grao about 4 km (2.5 miles) southeast of town. From the port's Estación Marítimo, a municipal bus can take you to the heart of town for 85 *ptas*, or a taxi can be hired for about 1,250 *ptas*.

By Train
Valencia is connected to the rest of Spain and Europe by extensive rail service via Renfe. The main Estación del Norte (also called the Estación del Nord) rail station is located at the Calle de Xátiva, 15, just three blocks from the center of downtown.

From here municipal bus #8 goes downtown and stops right in front of the main train station near the core of the downtown zone at about 120 *ptas* per ride. Taxis can also be found just in front of the station, and the average charge is about 845 *ptas* to most downtown hotels and sights.

ORIENTATION
Valencia, the capital city of the Valencia region (population approximately 750,000) lies just off the Mediterranean Sea on the east coast of Spain. It is located 352 km (218 miles) southeast of Madrid, and roughly 349 km (216 miles) south-southwest of Barcelona.

GETTING AROUND TOWN

By Bus

Valencia's municipal bus company, known officially as Empresa Municipal de Transportes, or EMT, has several Autobuses (buses) that criss-cross almost every neighborhood. With over a dozen different numbered bus lines and hundreds of well-marked bus stops, each with its posted corresponding route map, getting around above ground is fairly easy. I was unable to locate a public transportation system map or timetable anywhere except for the out of the way EMT main offices on Calle Sanz, 4. Perhaps the *Turismo* tourist offices might photocopy one of their limited copies if asked politely.

The operating hours for most buses are around every 12 minutes from about 6am until about 10:30pm daily, and special nightowl buses with a much more limited schedule that continues between 11pm and 2am or in some cases later. The fare is about 120 *ptas* per ride, and tickets can be paid for on the bus, or bought in advance from newsstands. The main municipal bus stop is over at the Plaza del Ayuntamiento.

By Subway – Metro

Although a few lines currently exist on the Ferrocarils Generalitat de Valencia, or FGV commuter railroad, these are mostly used by suburban workers to reach downtown. A massive project is now being completed to have a full service *metro* system in this city within five years. For now, stick with the municipal buses, taxis, or your feet.

By Taxi

There are more than 11,000 licensed taxis that roam the streets and major passenger arrival points during all hours of the day and night. Drivers are here are generally polite, humorous, and great sources of inside information. To find a taxi, either hail an unoccupied taxi (when empty they will illuminate a small *Taxi* light above the car) that is driving by, go to one of the dozens of obvious taxi stands throughout the city, or call Valencia Radio Taxi Companies *at Tel. (96) 370-3333 or Tel. (96) 357-1313* for a radio response pickup on demand. During rainy days, festivals, trade fairs, or weekday morning and evening rush hours (6am until 10am and 6pm until 9pm) it may be quite a wait until you get lucky.

Taxis charge customers using the zone system, but tend to cost somewhere around 750 *ptas* per ride (not per person) between most downtown locations in the central zone, or over 1,200 *ptas* to locations further in the suburbs, depending on how many zones you pass through and traffic conditions. Legally chargeable supplements are posted on a sticker in the taxi's interior.

VALENCIA'S MAJOR FESTIVALS

Contact the local Turismo office at Tel. (96) 394-2222 for more details.
- *Carnival, late February, Processions, All Night Parties*
- *Las Fallas, mid-March, Fireworks, Burning of Figurines Semana Santa*
  - *Prior to Easter, Processions*
- *Desamparadas Fiesta, mid-May, huge feast to the patron saint Corpus Christi*
  - *June, antique carraige parade*
- *July Fair, late July, Music and Theater in the streets*
- *San Dionis Fiesta, early October, Processions and Parties*

WHERE TO STAY

Expensive

HOTEL VALENCIA PALACE, *Paseo Alameda, 32. Tel. (96) 337-5037, Fax (96) 337-5532. Year round rack rates from 30,800 ptas per double room per night (E.P.). All major credit cards accepted.*

The Valencia Palace is a modern five-star deluxe hotel, and is the most prestigious place to stay in the downtown sector. The hotel has 200 deluxe air conditioned rooms and luxurious suites, each with huge private bathrooms, direct dial telephones, mini-safes, designer furnishings, satellite television and sound proofed windows. The hotel also offers a wide variety of business and convention services, meeting rooms, restaurant and lounge areas, a full service excursion desk, boutiques, a great sun deck and swimming pool, a fully equipped health club with sauna, private parking, room service, available secretarial services, and all the amenities you would expect from a five-star hotel.

Service here is top-notch, and guests are often corporate types who have chauffeur-driven sedans waiting for them in front of the building. This is a serious place for serious people, and may be perfect for those who demand only the best that money can buy.

HOTEL SIDI SALER, *Playa de El Salér, El Salér (Valencia). Tel. (96) 161-0411, Fax (96) 161-0838. US & Canada Bookings: (UTELL), Tel. 800/ 44-UTELL. Low season rack rates from 21,500 ptas per double room per night (E.P.). High season rack rates from 27,000 ptas per double room per night (E.P.). All major credit cards accepted.*

Situated about ten minutes south of the city along the beautiful beach at El Salér, this modern five star hotel is my favorite deluxe place to stay while in the area. The hotel features 276 air conditioned seaview rooms and suites that all have private terraces, deluxe bathrooms, mini-bar, direct dial telephone, satellite television, mini-safe, extremely comfortable furnishings, and electronic keypass locks. There is also a full service conference and business center, beauty salon, several good restaurants and bars, a heated indoor pool, a huge outdoor pool and sun deck, available child day care, free parking, room service, tennis and squash facilities, sauna, a tour and car rental desk, boutiques and a golf putting green.

Service here is prompt and professional, with the hotel catering to a rather demanding clientele of German, Spanish, and British businessmen and leisure travelers that know what five star quality means. Here guests can arrange a round of golf in one of three nearby courses, enjoy a massage or therapeutic treatments in their full "Beauty Farm" health spa, use the handy free round-trip mini-bus shuttle service into the heart of the city, or just sit back and relax on the picture perfect beach area. This is a great place to base yourself while touring Valencia.

HOTEL REINA VICTORIA, *Calle de Barcas, 4. Tel. (96) 352-0487, Fax (96) 352-0487. Year round rack rates from 20,800 ptas per double room per night (E.P.). Most major credit cards accepted.*

This Old world, four-star downtown hotel is a good choice for businessmen and travelers who want to be within walking distance to all the major sights and attractions in town. The historic hotel was built back in 1913 and completely renovated in 1989, and now features 97 small but comfortable air conditioned rooms that all have private bathrooms, wall to wall carpeting, color television, in-room music systems, mini-bars, floral prints, direct dial telephones, mini-safes, and simple furnishings. The rooms without a view tend to be much quieter than those facing the adjacent streets.

The hotel also has a restaurant serving three meals daily, a bar and lounge area, nearby parking, meeting rooms, room service, and a front desk that can help booking excursions and car rentals. Service here is pretty good, and the hotel is packed during much of the festival season, so book well in advance.

Moderate

AD HOC HOTEL, *Calle Boix, 4. Tel. (96) 391-9140, Fax (96) 391-3667. Low season rack rates from 12,900 ptas per double room per night (E.P.). High season rack rates from 18,500 ptas per double room per night (E.P.). All major credit cards accepted.*

This brand new boutique hotel is housed in a beautifully renovated 19th century historic building near the old city wall. The Ad Hoc has easily become one of the best little places to stay in the downtown sector of the city. The hotel features 28 beautiful and rather large air conditioned rooms and super deluxe suites with cute private bathrooms, custom made ultra-modern wooden furnishings, terraces, color televisions with satellite channels and direct dial telephones. There is a restaurant, nearby parking, small meeting rooms, and unusual public rooms. Service here is great, and the staff is really friendly.

NH HOTEL CIUDAD DE VALENCIA, *Avenida del Puerto, 214. Tel. (96) 330-7500, Fax (96) 330-9864. US & Canada Bookings: (UTELL), Tel. 800/44-UTELL. Year round rack rates from 18,500 ptas per double room per night (E.P.). Special weekend rates from 9,750 ptas per double room per night (B.P.). All major credit cards accepted.*

This great modern executive-style hotel is a great bargain in its price range (especially during weekends). Located a few minutes away from the historic part of town, the Ciudad de Valencia offers 149 superbly decorated air conditioned rooms and suites that all have deluxe private bathrooms with hair dryers, remote control satellite televisions with movie channels, electronic key pass locks, a deluxe assortment of ecologically sensitive skin and hair care products, direct dial telephones, minibars and comfortable furnishings and beds.

The hotel features an indoor parking lot, a good restaurant, a nice little bar, room service, ultra-modern public rooms full of plush seating, and some of the nicest staff in this part of the country. A favorite among visiting executives in town for trade shows, this is also a great place for tourists with cars to save some money and get four-star service and quality at three-star prices.

HOTEL LLAR, *Avenida Colon, 46. Tel. (96) 352-8460, Fax (96) 351-9000. Year round rack rates from 12,600 ptas per double room per night (E.P.). Most major credit cards accepted.*

Located a handful of blocks away from the main train station in town, this small three-star hotel is a reasonably good selection in the moderate price range (with one caveat listed below). All of the 50 interior and exterior view rooms are air conditioned, have small private bathrooms, color television, carpeting or polished stone floors and simple basic furnishings. Facilities here include nearby parking, meeting rooms, a decent restaurant. The staff, however, is a bit moody and less than friendly.

Inexpensive

HOSTAL EL RINCON, *Calle el Carda, 11. Tel. (96) 331-6083, Fax None. Year round rack ractes from 2,800 ptas per double room per night (E.P.). Cash Only.*

This is about the best safe choice for bright, clean, and spacious basic accomodations near the heart of the old town. The *hostal* has about 44 private rooms, most of which have shared bathrooms but little in the way of facilities.

WHERE TO EAT

Expensive

EL ANGEL AZUL, *Calle Conde Altea, 33. Tel. (96) 374-5656. Most major credit cards accepted.*

Owned and operated by German-born master chef Bernd Knoller, this fantastic gourmet dining establishment is among the best in this region of Spain. His innovative creations using the freshest seasonal ingredients has made this charming yet elegant 45 seat restaurant a favorite among the most prominent residents and businessmen in Valencia.

Specialties include Mediterranean-influenced dishes from a large menu that changes each month, featuring beautifully prepared salads , cold lettuce soup with smoked salmon and gelatin, duck liver pate with armagnac, mousse of eggplant with tomato, fresh tuna with red wine sauce, monkfish with sun dried tomatoes, sting ray wings served with smoked garlic and shitake mushrooms, Barbarie duck, ragout of rabbit, and fantastic desserts. Special *prix-fixe* menus, a selection of daily specials and a huge wine list with well over 200 different selections. Advance reservations are recommended. A superb three course gourmet meal here will cost around 4,950 *ptas* per person plus wine.

MARISQUERIA CASA RAMON, *Calle de Dr. Peset Cervera, 3. Tel. (96) 392-2436. All major credit cards accepted.*

If you're looking for the freshest seafood and meats that money can buy, check out this great local landmark. Chef and owner Mercedes Gutierrez Romero takes pride in using his own fishing boats to provide a vast daily selection of regional seafood to this cozy restaurant.

Here you can feast on wonderfully prepared Spanish dishes such as Gazpacho, seafood soup, crispy salads, smoked salmon, Iberian ham, roasted partridge, Beluga caviar, and your choice of dozens of the day's catch of fish and shellfish like sole, hake, monkfish, prawns, lobster, oysters and clams served by the kilo. They also offer a full range of affordable and delicious *tapas* throughout the day. Also available are a great dessert menu, a full wine list, and a giant four course 6,500 *ptas menu de la casa* featuring the best of their offerings.

Moderate

RESTAURANTE LA SAL, *Calle Conde Altea, 40. Tel. (96) 395-2011. Most major credit cards accepted.*

If you're in the mood for a cozy regional restaurant where you don't have to get too dressed up for a fine meal, try La Sal. It is a small modern establishment where the prices are surprisingly reasonable for the high quality of their unforgettable dishes, all served with piping hot home-made breads.

The restaurant's constantly changing two page menu featured cold cream of clam soup, sautéed spinach with pine nuts, a great salad with lentils and rockfish, salad with quail bits, fantastic shrimp croquettes with onion, home made duck liver pate, the day's fresh catch with lemon infused oil, half a dozen different rice based dishes with assorted vegetables and seafood, monkfish and saffron sauce, turbot with duck liver vinaigrette, roasted lamb chops and plenty of other fish and meat specialties. This is a special little place. A hearty three course meal here will set you back around 3,975 *ptas* a person plus wine.

RESTAURANTE EL GOURMET, *Calle Taquigrafe Marti, 3. Tel. (96) 395-2509. Most major credit cards accepted.*

This is a small, formal downtown restaurant where the crowd seems to come back repeatedly. The menu is huge, and offers some fine selections including consommé with sherry, endive and anchovy salad, York ham salad, crudities with salmon, asparagus from Navarra with two sauces, codfish carpaccio, smoked Norwegian salmon, assorted seafood in garlic sauce, scrambled eggs with asparagus and shrimp, eggplant and shrimp pastries, rice with lobster, sautéed eel, scallops au gratin, hake with clams in green sauce, filet of sole with prawns and almonds, roast beef, steak tartar, entrecote with green peppers and veal scallopini with camembert cheese sauce. This is a nice place so make reservations in advance. Expect to spend around 3,550 *ptas* for a three course meal here.

Inexpensive

RESTARANTE NATURISTA LA LLUNA, *Calle San Ramon, 33. Tel. (96) 392-2146. Cash Only.*

I stumbled upon this quirky little restaurant while getting lost wandering around the city. What I found were unusually good vegetarian dishes at really low prices. Selections include fresh squeezed juices at 250 *ptas* each, half a dozen great salads from 300 *ptas* each, vegetable soup for 275 *ptas*, cream of mushroom soup at 350 *ptas*, Gazpacho for 350 *ptas*, rice with mixed vegetables at 450 *ptas*, green lasagna for 525 *ptas*, oven roasted artichokes at 400 *ptas*, eggplant parmigana for 400 *ptas*, veggi croquettes at 450 *ptas*, stuffed pimentos for 525 *ptas*, omelets starting at 375 *ptas*, and a four course menu of the day at only just 800 *ptas* They also offer herbal teas, great pastries, and good cheap wine and sangria. Nothing fancy, but a great, healthy place to eat on a budget.

SEEING THE SIGHTS

Approximate duration (by foot) is about 7.5 hours, including church, museum, monument, and side street visits. Start from the Estación del Norte train station on the Calle de Xátiva.

Ciutat Vella (Old Town)

To begin this tour, walk into the **Estación del Norte** itself and have a good look around. This Modernist train station is actually located on the south part of the downtown zone. Built in 1917, the ornate lobby of this hangar-like structure is a delightful place to view unique architectural and decorative motifs. Look for the stained glass and mosaic covered wooden ceilings, bold columns topped with hand-carved orange designs, the small ceramic plaques near the turn of the century ticket booths that display the words "Have a Pleasant Journey" in several languages and the former caféteria whose walls are lined with impressive tile murals.

This is one of the nicest train stations in Europe, but unfortunately is rumored to be demolished by the year 2001 to make way for a municipal garden and new underground *metro*. *The building is open daily from 6am until 11pm and is free to enter.*

After leaving the station, turn right onto the Calle de Xátiva and a few steps later you will find the circular brick 18th century **Plaza de Toros** bullring. Designed in the Neoclassical style, this four story venue is the sight of many bullfights between March and July. Tickets are unusally easy to find for these events at the front box office without much advance notice, and cost less if seats are still available in the sundrenched part of the ring. Just behind the bullring on the small Pasaje de Doctor Serra is the **Museo Taurino** museum, with a good collection of bullfighting memorabilia including old posters, the heads of bulls that have died in the ring, and displays of famed bull fighters. *This museum is open from Monday through Friday from 10:30am until 1:30pm and is free to enter.*

Now return to the Calle de Xátiva and immediately cross the street to continue straight ahead on the large pedestrian-only boulevard called the **Calle de Ribera**. Lined with small outdoor cafés and boutiques, this is a great place to pop in for a quick coffee or ice cold drink before moving on with this tour. This street ends a couple of blocks up at the beautiful **Plaza del Ayuntamiento** square. The plaza was once occupied by a now demolished monastery, and is now one of the busiest areas in the city due to its many historic governmental buildings, kiosks selling flowers, and the main municipal bus stop.

On the right hand side of this square is the **Placio de Correos y Telegrafos** post office, built in 1922. If you happen to be here during business hours, step inside this Classical structure to admire its huge stained glass domed circular lobby. Just across the plaza is the turn of the century **Ayuntamiento** (City Hall), with its fine facade that features a fine bell tower, the city's coat of arms (the only one in Europe that contains a bat), and four statues of women that represent the themes of freedom, justice, temporance, and prudence. Inside this building you can take a quick peek into the **Museo Historico Municipal** museum that has a series

VALENCIA

KEY

1 Monumento El Cid
2 Santa Lucia
3 Iglesia Del Pilar
4 Antiguo Hospital
5 Monumento a Cervantes
6 Iglesia San Austin
7 Ayuntamiento
8 Museo Paleontologico
9 Correos
10 Plaza de Torinos
11 Iglesia San Juan De La Cruz
12 Museo Nacional Ceramica
        Gonzalez Marti
13 Colegio Del Patriarca
14 Palacio Marques Dos Aguas
15 Monumento a Jaime I
16 Palacio de Justica
17 Puerta Del Mar
18 Antiguo Convento Sto. Domingo
19 Monumentoe a Jose Ribera
20 Iglesia S. Esteban
21 Palacio Marques De Campo
22 Palacio Arzobispal
23 Catedral
24 El Micalet
25 Mercado Central

of historical exhibits pertaining to Valencia. *The museum is open Monday through Friday from 9am until 2pm and has no entrance charge.*

Another good place to visit in the building is the *Turismo* office where you can get free maps and information on special events and museums. This plaza is the sight for most of the important events during the **Fallas de San José** festival in mid-March.

After departing the City Hall, turn left into the square and then after a block and a half bear left onto the Calle En Llop. After about a block, this street more or less merges straight onto the Calle del Miestro Clave that you will follow up to the next intersection before turning right onto the Calle de Musico Peydro. This cute pedestrian-only side street is a great place to show up on weekdays when small handicraft vendors sell their wares. A few more blocks along this street and you will find yourself in the **Plaza del Mercado** square.

The El Mercat (Market) district

Once you have entered the **Plaza del Mercado** square, the most obvious sight to begin with is the blue and white tile covered Modernist facade of the **Mercado Central** covered produce market. Designed in 1914 by Francisco Guardia and Alejandro Soler, the vendors set up shop beneath the domed interior to sell excellent fresh fruits, cheeses, vegetables, and meats that are often amusingly displayed such as a chicken dressed up like Santa Claus! The market is the best place in town to purchase picnic supplies. *Open daily (except some Sundays) from 8am until 2pm.*

Just outside the market are small lunchtime-only food kiosks that supply local office workers with tasty seafood *tapas* at reasonable prices. Take a seat and point to what looks best, but I suggest having a few garlic-laced shrimp. Further along the opposite side of the square is a weekend morning stamp, coin, and antique pocket watch market.

The unmistakable Gothic building that comes next on the right hand side of the square is **La Lonja**. Built in the 15th century by Pere Compte, this dramatically fortified structure was build to house the old Silk Exchange. Later the building was converted and expanded to become a commodity exchange and maritime consulate. Its delightful facade features unusual columned porticos and window ledges that have been carved with small figurines (including some showing people having sex). Upon entering the building you will find a fantastic vaulted ceiling, twisted columns, and Latin inscriptions advising the merchants not to cheat each other. A small door in the middle of the exchange leads up to a tower that was once used to imprison dishonest merchants working here that didn't abide by the advice.

LAS FALLAS DE SAN JOSÉ FESTIVAL

Valencia is host to one of the world's most unusual and exciting festivals. The **Las Fallas de San José** festival takes place between March 9th and 19th every year. Although the whole town has parades and festivities, it is around the **Plaza del Ayuntamiento** that the most spectactular events take place. Up to half a million people from around the globe come here to witness a series of bizarre processions, pyrotechnic explosions, cooking contests, and sporting events that have become the city's single most popular attractions. For several months before the Las Fallas, community organizations raise the funds necessary to sponsor local artisans in designing figurines (called **ninots**) used in the creation of huge papier mache sculptures that are four stories high. These bizarre effigies (each known as a **Falla**) are completely different in each neighborhood, and portray local and international celebrities in highly satirical poses. Among the handmade Fallas are images of Michael Jackson and Elvis Presley, portrayed nude with giant sex organs! European politicians are depicted taking bribes from large multinational corporations, ther are old men looking up woman's dresses, and local civic leaders are shown in compromising positions with their secretaries.

With the whole of Valencia in attendance, the party begins on or about the 9th of March when the daily 2pm explosive fireworks shows called **mascletas** kick off at the Plaza del Ayuntamiento. Dozens of special events are scheduled throughout the old town on the next ten days, including soccer games, bullfights, paella cooking contests, parades and outdoor fairs. There is also an exhibition of the **ninots** at the **La Lonja,** so that people can vote for their favorite Falla in this year's festival. On the night of the 15th, the secret Fallas are completly assembled, and then displayed to the public in and around the Plaza del Ayuntamiento creating a huge traffic jam that makes it all but impossible to park or drive in the old town zone for a few days.

At 4pm on the 17th and 18th a procession of traditionally costumed participants parade through the streets to the **Plaza de La Virgen** and place flowers at the foot of the statue of the Virgin there. The whole event climaxes on the evening of the 19th of March when at about 11pm the Fallas are all ceremoniously set on fire in the Plaza del Ayuntamiento, creating a huge bonfire that lights up the whole city. A fireworks display follows at 1am, after which the whole town goes out to the clubs and discos to dance until at least dawn. Don't miss this incredible event, even if you are hours away. Please keep in mind that all of the town's hotels, trains, buses, and restaurants are fully booked at least 7 months in advance for the dates of this festival.

During the Fallas festivities, the interior is adorned with *ninots* (see sidebar) and visitors are ask to fill out a ballot to vote for their selections as the best of that year. At the end of the festival, the figurine that wins the most votes is spared from the flames and kept in a special museum. At other times of the year, La Lonja is sometimes filled with temporary art exhibits.

The building is open Tuesday through Friday from 9am until 2pm and agin from 4pm until 6pm, weekends from 9am until 1:30pm. Admission is usually free, but maybe as much as 400 ptas for special events such as the Fallas.

Across from the Lonja is the Baroque 18th century **Iglesia de los Santos Juanes** church that was erected here on the site of an old Arab mosque. *The church is open during masses and there is no admission fee.* When the Catholic King Don Jaime of Aragón liberated Valencia from Arab control in 1238 and was about to expell the Moors from this region, he leveled all of the city's mosques and replaced them with new churches. The King was surprised that the Moorish population did not rebel against him after this event, and thus they were not forced to leave town. This act was most likely responsible for the ability of the Arab, Jewish, and Christian populations to live together in harmony for several more centuries.

As the city became both tolerant and rather secure, many artists, merchants, and craftsmen flocked to Valencia in order to persue a life that included protection of their artistic and political freedom. This is one of the reasons that so much wealth, fine art, and architecture can be found here. After the Inquisition, when all non-Christians were expelled, the local economy immediately plummeted.

The La Seu (Cathedral) district

From the church, turn right, pass in front of the market once again, and at the bottom of the **Plaza del Mercado** turn left onto the small Calle del Trench. Head a couple of blocks up along this small side street until reaching the **Plaza Lope de Vega** square where during weekdays a small outdoor market is set up where vendors can be found selling leather belts and handicrafts. Just off the upper edge of the plaza is the Gothic 15th century **Iglesia de Santa Catalina** church. Heavily damaged by Franco's bombing raids during the Spanish Civil War, its once beautiful collections of priceless artwork were lost forever.

A small achway on the corner of this plaza leads into the circular **Plaza de Redonda** that is actually a ring of curved buildings dating back to the mid-19th century surrounding a lovely fountain. This plaza is home to a weekday textile and clothing market, but on weekends it becomes a lively handicrafts market. Now return back through the same archway back into the **Plaza Lope de Vega.**

FROM MULBERRY TREES TO WORLD FAMOUS ORANGES!

If you are wondering why there was a need to build a silk exchange on this spot, I have the answer. Back in the late 15th century, Valencia was the major European center of production for raw silk. The city was once surrounded by mulberry trees that had plenty of hard working silk worms in them. A hundred or so years later a blight destroyed these trees, and from that time onward, orange trees were planted instead. Since then the production of silk for the European market shifted to the far east, and Valencia became synonymous with the cultivation of its famed oranges.

From the square, immediately make a right onto Calle de la Sombreria whose name dates to the time when hat makers once lined this street. Nowadays this busy commercial block is lined with bakeries, and the famous **Horchateria El Siglo** and **Horchateria Santa Catalina** that has been serving up *horchata* (the town's famed cold beverage made from ice, sugar, milk, and the juice of chufa nuts) since the 1800's. Make sure to pop into one of these establishments to try some.

From here, the road passes the octangonal 17th century Baroque **Torre de Santa Catalina** bell tower that marks the entrance to the **Plaza de la Reina** (also known as **Plaza de Zaragoza**) square. Although I will have you come back to this plaza in a few minutes to experience the awesome sights located on its opposite side, for now just cut straight through the square and head onto the Calle de la Paz. After a handful of blocks, turn right onto the small Calle de la Cruz Nueva that leads into the **Plaza de Colegio del Patriarca** square. Surrounded by antique buildings that are part of the former universities that have been relocated to the modern sections of town, this plaza still offers a few good sights.

Besides looking at the exteriors of the fine buildings, make sure to visit the square's 17th century Italian inspired **Colegio del Patriarca** seminary school to view their memorable **Museo del Patriarca** fine arts museum. Here a small gallery exhibits the works of famed artists like **El Greco, Ribalta, Joanes**, and **Morales**. *This musuem is open daily from 11am until 1:30pm and costs 200 ptas to enter.*

Now backtrack to return to the **Plaza de la Reina** and turn right into the plaza to walk towards the massive domed facade of the **Catedral**. The cathedral dates back to the 13th century when it replaced the city's main Arab Mosque, that in turn was built where a Roman temple previously stood. Since the building was built over the course of 500 years, it has elements that display the characteristics of several different styles and time periods. The main entrance of the cathedral is called the **Puerta de los Hierros** and shows the influence of later Baroque modifications.

Once inside the building, visitors have several sights to see. Formerly covered comteply by 17th and 18th century Neoclassical additions, the once masked parts of the original Gothic interior (including the beautiful vaulted ceiling) were discovered after damage to the building as a result of bombing raids during the Spanish Civil War. The enchanting alabaster domed main altar is a fine example of Rococo design and features Baroque columns and gold leaf cupids and angels. Just behind this altar is a silver display case that contains the embalmed arm of martyred Saint Vincent and a haunting image of the Madonna with child. This is the spot where local pregnant women come to bless their unborn child by praying to the image, and then walking around the cathedral once each month. Also inside are colorful stained glass windows, hand carved wooden confessional booths, and several ornate chapels including two from the 16th century deigned by Pere Compte.

Alongside the cathedral is the octagonal Gothic **El Micalet** (also known as **El Miguelete**) spired tower that was built in 1381. From the inside of the cathedral, a series of spiral stairways can take visitors up the 207 steps to the top of the tower and its fine panoramic lookout point. *The cathedral is open daily from 8am until 8pm and admission is free. The tower is open daily from 10am until 1pm and again from 4:30pm until 7pm and entrance costs 200 ptas.*

The most famous attraction in this building is undoubtedly the **Museo de la Catedral** museum that can be entered from its front right corner. The most impressive place to start a visit to the museum is in the **Capilla de Santo Caliz** (Chapel of the Holy Chalice). This chapel was once a separate 14th century building, but was incorporated into the cathedral complex as it grew in size. Inside this chapel is a fine Gothic altar whose centerpiece is a gold and agate chalice said to be the true **Holy Grail** used by Jesus during the last supper. Other rooms of the museum contain two huge paintings by **Goya**, statues by **Cano** and **Cellini**, and a massive golden tabernacle encrusted with jewels. *The museum is open year round Monday through Saturday from 10am until 1pm, and between March and December it opens again from 4:30pm until 6pm. Admission is 200 ptas.*

After inspecting the interior of the cathedral, depart from the main entrance and turn left towards the back of the building. Along the way you can stop to view the 15th century Romanesque portico with busts of the 14 people that the King of Aragón brought with him to Valencia in 1238 in order to repopulate the city. He did this after he mistakinly assumed its Moorish residents would leave after he had their mosques destroyed. Almost immediately behind this section of the cathedral just off of the Calle del Palau are a series of archaeological excavations of the old Roman city. Since the excavation work is not finished, a gate will stop people from getting too close.

As you now continue alongside the cathedral to its other side, you will pass its final portico. The Gothic **Puerta de los Apostoles** entrance has been recently fitted with an ultrasonic sound system that scares all the pigeons away. Perhaps the reason for selecting only this part of the building to test this device is that it happens to be the meeting point of the black robed **Tribunal de las Aguas** water court each week. In a tradition that dates back to Moorish times, local farmers meet here on Thursdsays at noon to debate the solutions to the many irrigation problems that affect Valencian farmers. Just in front of the portico is the large **Plaza de la Virgen** square, with several beautiful buildings that surround its lovely fountain and and nearby embedded plaque with a cornucopia and the history (in Latin) of the city's founding.

On the side of the square closest to the cathedral is the Baroque 17th century **Basilica de la Virgen de los Desamparados** church, with an ornate elliptical interior that has been frescoed by Palomino. *This church is open daily during masses, and has no admission charge.*

The Barrio del Carme district

Now cut through the the **Plaza de la Virgen** square and head up the Calle de Caballeros. This street marks the beginning of what may just be the most dramatic neighborhood in town. Besides being the stomping grounds for most of the all-night bar and club enthusiasts, there are countless fine buildings on almost all of its charming streets and winding lanes. This becomes obvious within seconds of walking down the Calle de Caballeros, when you pass in front of the Gothic 15th century **Palau de la Generalitat** palace. This structure is home to the regional parliament of Valencia, *and with advance notice can be visited weekdays from 9am until 2pm by calling the office at Tel. (96) 386-3461.* Inside there are great frescoes and period furnishings.

A quick side trip around the corner to the back of the palace leads into the impressive **Plaza de Manises** square. Here visitors can view the inner courtyards and bold exteriors of such fine mansions as the 14th century **Palau de Baylia** (now a municipal building), and the 16th century **Palacio del Marquis de la Scalla** (with occasional free art exhibitions).

Now return to the Calle de Caballeros and continue to head up the street in the same direction you were headed before. You'll pass the bars which were formerly noblemen's palaces. The most impressive of these is called **Hanax** and is located at #36. Make sure to stop inside this amazing multi-story disco during its afternoon or evening opening hours to enjoy a cool drink, and be enchanted by the ancient walls that were uncovered during its construction.

A few blocks up on the left side is the fantastic Calle de Calatrava that is the sight of even more great cafés and bars that are packed almost every night. The Calle de Caballeros keeps heading up, and changes its name to the Calle de Quart. A few block further up this street is the magnificent 15th century **Torres de Quart** towers.

This is one of the only two surviving medieval gateways that once led through Valencia's now demolished defensive walls. Cross under the arch in the middle of the towers and take a good look at its interesting facade, marked with bullet holes caused by Franco's troops during the Spanish Civil War. In the 19th century, the interior of the towers were used to imprision female criminals. At this point visitors are not allowed inside.

The Turia River Bed

From the towers, continue up along the Calle de Quart for a few more blocks until reaching Plaza de Sant Seybastian, and just across the street you will find the tranquil **Jardín Botánic** botanical gardens. First created in the early 19th century, these large and lovely gardens showcase over 2,500 varieties of flora in the greenhouse and along shady walking paths. There is even a small aquarium and a pavilion containing collections of rare butterflys on the premises. *The gardens are open Tuesday through Sunday from 10am until 8pm, and admission is just 50 ptas. The aquarium is open daily from 10:30 am until sunset and costs 225 ptas to enter.*

After viewing the gardens, turn right along its border with the Calle de Beato Gaspar Bono and again turn right onto the **Paseo de la Pechina**. Follow this busy road at the edge of the old city for several blocks as it curves its way alongside the dry river bed that once was the sight of the **Rio Turia** river before it was diverted to irrigate the region's many orange groves. There are well over a dozen bridges of both medieval and 20th century origin that cut across this small basin and connect to the more modern zones of Valencia. The city is continuing to do a fantastic job of filling in the river bed with beautiful parks and gardens.

After walking along the basin for about four blocks, make a right turn onto Calle de Guillem de Casto where at #118 you'll find the strikingly modern building that houses the **Instituto Valenciano de Arte Moderno (ITVA)** (modern art museum). This excellant new museum features eight galleries on two seperate floors displaying fine 20th century paintings and sculptures by nationally revered modern artists such as the **Gonzalez** brothers, **Tàpies**, **Pinazo**, **Arroyo**, **Chillida**, and **Saura**. There are temporary and permanent exhibits, an archive section, a book and gift shop, a great snack shop, and a small video screenng room. In the basement of the building are some of the relocated exhibitions from the city's famed **Museo de Cerámica Gonzalez Marti** ancient ceramics museum. Since the normal location of the cermics museum (at the Baroque Palacio del

Marqués de Dos Aguas) will be closed until at least 1997 for restoration, this basement offers many of its best treasures for public inspection in the interim.

Situated in a darkened basement chamber complete with excavated medieval defensive wall fragments, exhibits include 11th century Arab water jars, beautiful 13th century ceramics made in the nearby village of Paterna, 15th century tile panels, medieval gold painted plates, 18th century *azulelos* tiles, porcelain figurines, a room full of ceramic pieces made by Picasso and of course the relics from the old towers and defensive wallls that once rung the city. Another ITVA exhibition building a few blocks away at Calle del Museo, 2 (ask the polite English speaking museum employees for directions) called the **Centre del Carme** has a wonderful assortment of related pieces that change seasonally.

The ITVA museum is open Tuesday through Sunday from 11am until 8pm. Admission is 450 ptas for adults, 225 ptas for students with International student ID cards, and is free all Sundays. The ceramics section is open more or less on the same schedule as above, and entrance is free. The nearby wing on Calle del Museo is open Tuesday through Sunday from 12noon until 2:30pm and again from 4:30pm until 8pm, and it costs nothing to visit.

Once you have finished with all of the ITVA wings, return to the river bed and turn right. A few blocks later you can't help but be drawn to the dramatic 14th century **Torres de Serranos** towers. This three story fortified structure was designed by Pere Belaguer as a main defensive entranceway through the now demolished medieval defensive walls that encircled the city. The steps lead inside to an eerie interior, *which is free on Tuesdays through Friday from 9am until 1:30pm and again from 4pm until 6pm.* After taking a good look at the tower, turn right along the river bed and walk a couple of blocks. Now you should cross over the Gothic 14th century **Puente de la Trinidad** ten arched bridge.

On the other side of the bridge, turn immediately right onto the Calle de San Pio V and a few steps later enter into the Baroque **Palacio de San Pio V** which is now home to the **Museo de Bellas Artes** fine arts museum. Inside there is an impressive collection of Spainsh art by such masters as **Goya**, **Murillo**, **Velasquez**, **Juanes**, and members of the Valencian primitive school. *This museum is open Tuesday through Saturday from 10am until 2pm and again (except during August) from 4pm until 6pm, Sundays from 10am until 2pm. Admission is free every day.*

Just next door are the tranquil **Jardins el Real** gardens, **Viveros Municipal** park, and **Parque Zoològico** zoo. The gardens have been here since Moorish times. This is the most delightful place in town to have a picnic or just walk along its relaxing sculpture-lined paths. *Park and gardens are open each day from 6am until 8pm, no charge, while the zoo is open from 10:30am until 6pm or so with a 250 ptas per person entrance fee.*

Playa de la Malvarrosa

Once the gathering spot for most young people during the summer months, the crescent shaped beach called **Playa de la Malvarrosa** has had its fair share of pollution and overcrowding. A recent project has been completed to restore the elegant seaside promenade and dredge the sand back along the beach, and this may give new life to the beachfront.

At this point there are still dozens of small seafood restaurants serving countless different varieties of rice dishes, including the famed *paella* that this town has become synonymous with. A few discos and about 20 or so terrace bars also line the beach, and are busy on most summer evenings.

GUIDED CITY TOURS

Unlike the larger cities and tourist resorts in Spain, Valencia offers a much smaller range of companies offering daily scheduled city tours. The *Turismo* offices can provide some details about who may be offering bus excursions in and around town, but I strongly suggest using a smaller company to experience this unique city's sights and attractions.

NIGHTLIFE & ENTERTAINMENT

Valencia has the most abundant and exhilarating nightlife in all of Spain. There are so many places to go that many people here seem to go straight from the clubs to work each morning. There is something for everyone here, and nightlife is a major aspect of appreciating the soul of this incredible city. Residents and visitors of all ages can be seen dancing and flirting their way through the various zones of town until the wee hours of the morning.

Ask around and get names of this month's current hot spots, but this small sampling of clubs and bars should get you headed in the right direction.

Downtown's Best

JOHANN SEBASTIAN BACH, *Calle del Mar, 31. Tel. (96) 392-0402.*

Situated in the heart of the historic La Xerea district, this converted nobleman's palace is a must-see. Once you pay the 1,000-1,500 *ptas* cover charge to enter (including one cocktail) you are led to a table in one of several elegent candle-lit baroque rooms loaded with antique art; you almost feel as if you have been invited inside a haunted castle. The atmosphere is enhanced even more by the addition of strange medieval music and black suited waiters. The crowd here is comprised of well-dressed couples and small groups of all ages who spend hours here chatting and then can be found wandering through the palace's small salons, glass domed inner courtyard, upper floors or main bar area with two caged live lions. They are open during most afternoons and evenings, and this is this is certainly one of the more unique bars you'll find!

HAÑAX, *Calle de Caballeros, 36. Tel. (96) 391-8101.*

This amazing multistory disco has been converted from a beautiful knight's palace, complete with old stone walls and arches that date back to at least the 11th century. The club can hold well over 1,000 people in its many side rooms, packed dance floors, open air patio lined by palm trees, and rooftop patio. There is even a great tranquil lounge upstairs that features special coffees and live piano music, as well as art exhibitions by local painters, live concerts by internationally known bands, and many special events including theater and dance performances.

The café section is open daily from 3pm to 3am, and the club is open 7pm until 3pm from Wednesday to Sunday. The crowd here ranges from under 20's in mini skirts and jeans, to middle aged lawyers and VIP's who are looking for a great place to meet people. The club has no cover charge, and is one of the most enjoyable places to spend several hours.

JOHNNY MARACAS, *Calle de Caballeros, 39. Tel. (96) 391-526.6*

Well known to locals for several years as the place to listen and dance to the hottest Latin beats, Johnny Maracas is busy every night of the week. As one of the loudest places to hang out on this active street full of bars and clubs, casually dressed people wander in and out all night as they search for a companion to groove to the sounds of Salsa, Cuban jazz, Merengue, and Brazilian music.

There is only one huge floor divided into several smaller sections, and on weekends it is impossible to walk through the crowd without spilling a drink or two in the process. A 1,000 *ptas* cover charge may be imposed on some nights.

FOX CONGO, *Calle de Caballeros, 35. Tel. (96) 392-1764.*

This brand new ultra-modern club and bar is the current hot spot for the young yuppie singles crowd who loves to party until early in the morning. The music here ranges from house to funk, and there is usually no cover charge to get in. By about 2am on weekends there are over 750 rather friendly people dresed in everything from jeans to suits, dancing and drinking away at a furious pace.

Other Good Bars Downtown

Also in the **El Carme** district and its surroundings are hundreds of small bars and cafés, many of which are worth serious exploration. A good number of my favorites are on the on the Calle de Caballeros, where the heart of Valencian nightlife beats. On this street there are several huge clubs (some are listed above), as well as smaller joints like the brick-lined **Solera** bar or the **Café Cavallers** where they play music from the 50's and 60's. A couple of streets away is the Calle de Calatrava where you can check out the **Café Bar Negrito** where they play blues music, or grab a cold drink or some Tex-Mex snacks at the **Sin Pardon** bar. Nearby on Calle de Corregera you can pop into the artsy **Café El Bar** with its Brazilian music and cheap beers.

A much younger bar scene that caters to the 16 through 20 year olds can be found in the **L'Eixampla** district of downtown. If you walk or take a taxi along the Gran Via de Marqués del Turia until reaching the bustling **Plaza de Canovas del Castillo** plaza, and head down the Calle de Salamanca for a block or so, you will find dozens of teenagers dressed to kill and hanging around (after 10pm or so) in front of small clubs and disco playing extremely loud *makina* or machine-style dance music. These clubs have names like **Muchi Tanga**, the **Panic Bar**, the small **Birra 7** club, the **Aforo** disco, the packed **Trago** dance club, and a handful of more laidback places like the **Cerveceria Brube**.

On the other side of the **Plaza de Canovas del Castillo**, there are a few more bars that cater to a more couples oriented crowd, most of which can be seen along the plaza itself and a small street called the Calle de Serrano Morales. Among the better places to sit down and have a relaxing nightcap are the mozaic lined **Antiguo Café**, the **Plaza** bar and café, **Embarcadero**, the **Color Pub** karaoke bar, the more relaxed **Spinello**, the **Giralda** with its occasional Flamenco dances, **Vanity's** terrace pub, the often crowded **Estación**, the **Decada Loca** club and **Bar Buss**.

During the warmer months of July and August, a fair number of open terraces and discos welcome the suntanned beach-goers who hang out along the city's famed **Playa de Malvarrosa** beach. Here I suggest looking for the bright signs that direct you toward the **Tropical** disco, or sample a few of the countless small bars until you find the one that's right for you.

Bars Across the Turia River
DISTRITO 10, *Calle General Elio, 10. Telephone unlisted.*

Located just across the Puente del Real bridge, Distrito 10 is probably the largest of the mega-discos in the city. If you get here after 11pm on weekends you will find the place filled to the brim with almost two thousand 20 to 30 year old locals dancing to loud and often obnoxious house and techno music until at least 4am. This is the place for the most serious dancers and clubbies to meet and try to impress each other. The cover charge can be well over 1,000 *ptas*, and the wait at the bar to be served can be more than a bit frustrating at times.

JARDINES DEL REAL, *Plaza Legion Espanola. Tel. (96) 361-5667.*

Although no longer the hottest place in the nightlife scene, this subterranean disco just a few steps from Distrito 10 still can be fun for those looking for a good non-aggressive club to dance in. The interior looks kind of like an old caberet from the 1920's. Several comfortable crecent-shaped sofas line the dance floor and stage areas. The music here can range from 70's disco to more modern US and English rap, and there is generally no line up to pay your 1,200 *ptas* or so cover (or a two drink minumum on other nights).

BLACK NOTE CAFÉ, *Calle de Polo y Peyrolon, 15. Tel. (96) 393-3663* Every city in Europe seems to have its premier spot for live jazz and blues concerts, and in Valencia, the Black Note fits the bill. There are shows almost nightly with acts from around the world, including well known jazz quartets, R & B bands, Flamenco shows, and others. The cover ranges from free to 1,200 *ptas*, depending on how famous the act is. There may also be a one drink minimum. Call in advance to get the schedule.

Other Good Bars Across the Turia River

Just northwest of the old part of town, across the dry *Rio Turia* riverbed, are several good bars and clubs for the 25 to 40 year old single set. Among the most exciting areas in this part of town for clubbing is along the Avenida Aragón and its adjacent side streets. Located about three blocks past the **Puente de Aragón** bridge, a series of hotspots start to come into view.

Among the better ones are the **Opera** disco-bar with a mixed crowd of young and middle aged people, the down-to-earth **Lupulo** bar and pub, the small and more dressy **Diagonal 30** dance club, the ultra-modern and somewhat trendy **Zero Bar**, the **NY** club, the hot and heavy **Panal** disco, the intimate **Gasoil** pub, **30 Minutes**, and several others worth a good look at once you've had your share of the packed downtown zones.

Out-of-town Clubs and the infamous "Ruta de Bacalao"

After about 3:30am, most of the bars and clubs in town start emptying out and the crowds move on to the beach-lined suburbs like **El Salér** and **El Perelló** about 10 minutes and 2,400 *ptas* away by taxi. Here you can ask around to get directions to clubs and big discos like **Barraca**, **Puzzles**, **Chocolate**, **Spook**, and **Canal**. At these places you can expect to pay around 1,350 *ptas* to enter, and try to keep up with the youthful crowd that stays here trying to pick each other up until the sun rises.

I would like to mention the treacherous *"Ruta de Bacalao"*, the expression used to describe the series of huge clubs and discos that stretch along the coastal area from Valencia to below Alicante. Univeristy students have created a route that can allow them to start drinking Friday afternoon, and often times with the help of Ecstasy and amphetamines, many people keep dancing from club to club until Monday morning when they return to work or school. The club set has arranged to make sure that when one disco closes, another one opens a bit further down the coast. There are several accidents each weekend, but for those who like to rave the night away, its a unique experience in Europe. I tried to participate in part of the route, but by 3pm Saturday, I had no more energy! To get details about this infamous route, ask a few students in Valencia. They might even invite you along with them.

SPORTS & RECREATION

Amusement, Water, & Theme Parks
• **Aquasol**, *N-332 (Cullera), Tel. (96) 172-4949*. Call about free summertime bus transfers from downtown Valencia.
• **Devesa Gardens**, *(El Salér), Tel. (96) 362-0676*

Bullfights
• **Plaza de Toros**, *Calle de Xátiva (Valencia), Telephone unlisted.*

Boat Rentals
• **CIAS Activities Center**, *Calle Sagunto, 129 (Valencia), Tel. (96) 365-8914*
• **Club Nautico Valencia**, *Camino de Canal (Valencia), Tel. (96) 367-9011*

Casino
• **Casino de Monte Picayo** *(Puzol), Tel. (96) 142-1211*

Golf
• **Club de Golf** *(El Salér), Tel. (96) 161-1186. 18 holes, par 72*
• **Club de Golf** *(Manises), Tel. (96) 153-1261. 18 holes, par 36*
• **El Bosque Club de Golf** *(Chiva), Tel. (96) 180-4142. 18 holes, par 72*
• **Club de Golf Escorpion** *(Betera), Tel. (96) 160-1211. 18 holes, par 72*

Horseback Riding
• **Sociedad Hipica**, *Calle de Comedias (Valencia), Tel. (96) 362-6323*

Major Outdoor Markets
• **Daily leather and craft market**, *Plaza Lope de Vega*
• **Weekend Stamp and Coin Market**, *Plaza del Mercado*

TAKE THE TRAM TO THE BEACH

The city has a great public tram system that runs from the **FEVE** *funicular and commuter train station off the* **Plaza de Santa Monica** *across the dry river bed and down the street from the Museo de Bellas Artes, and continues to the sandy* **Playa de la Malvarrosa** *beach zone. This short ride operates during the summertime from sunrise to sunset daily and costs 125 ptas each way.*

- **Weekday Textile and Clothing Market,** *Plaza de Redonda*
- **Weekend Crafts Market,** *Plaza de Redonda*

Tennis
- **Club de Tenis,** *Calle Botanico Cavanilles, (Valencia), Tel. (96) 369-5170*

Zoos & Aquariums
- **Parque Zoològico,** *Viveros Municiapl (Valencia), Tel. (96) 369-1944*
- **Jardín Botánico,** *Acuario (Valencia), Tel. (96) 331-1657*

PRACTICAL INFORMATION
- **Regional Tourist Office,** *Turism, Calle Paz, 48, Tel. (96) 394-2222*
- **Municipal Tourist Office,** *PMTV, Plaza del Ayuntamiento, 1, Tel. (96) 351-0417*
- **Airport Tourist Office,** *Aeropuerto de Valencia-Manises, Tel. (96) 152-1452*
- **Valencia Airport,** *Manises, Tel. (96) 370-9500*
- **Iberia Airlines at the Airport,** *Manises, Tel. (96) 152-0065 or (6) 351-9737*
- **Airport Bus Information,** *CVT, Tel. (96) 347-1898 or (6) 391-6022*
- **Regional Train Info,** *Renfe , Estación del Norte, Tel. (96) 352-0202*
- **Commuter Rail Info,** *FGV, Tel. (96) 380-1819*
- **Municipal Tourist Office,** *Estación del Norte, Tel. (96) 352-8573*
- **Municipal Bus Info,** *EMT, Calle Sanz, 4, Tel. (96) 352-8399*
- **Regional Bus Info,** *Estación de Autobuses, Tel. (96) 349-7222*
- **Ferry Info,** *Transmediterranea Lines, Tel. (96) 367-6512*
- **Traffic Condition Hotline,** *Tel. (96) 362-6250*
- **Highway Condition Hotline,** *Tel. (96) 353-5522*
- **Municipal Garage and Tow Lot,** *Tel. (96) 369-9034*
- **Valencia Radio Taxi Companies,** *Tel. (96) 370-3333 or (6) 357-1313*
- **Central Post Office,** *Plaza del Ayuntamiento, 24, Tel. (96) 351-6750*
- **Municipal Lost and Found Office,** *Ajuntament de Barcelona, Tel. (96) 317-3879*
- **Pre-recorded Weather Forecast,** *Tel. 094*
- **Regional Directory Assistance,** *Tel. 1003*
- **National Directory Assistance,** *Tel. 1009*
- **Medical Emergencies Hot Line,** *Tel. 085*
- **La Fe Hospital Clinic,** *Av. Campanar, 21, Tel. (96) 386-2700*
- **Ambulances,** *Tel. (96) 352-2322*
- **National Police,** *Tel. 091*
- **Municipal Police,** *Tel. 092*

EXCURSIONS & DAY TRIPS

If you have seen all the major sights in Valencia and want to spend at least five hours visiting the area outside of the city, here a few of the best day trips. Since few excursions are offered by major companies, you may need to take a bus, train, rent a car, or hire a private guide with a sedan to get to the following destinations.

NORTHWARD ALONG THE COSTA DEL AZAHAR

The city of Valencia is located in the heart of a coastal area along the Mediterranean Sea called the **Costa del Azahar**. If you head northeast up and along the seafront from the city, this sector continues for 140 km (87 miles) before intersecting with the Costa Dorada. While known for its dramatic sundrenched beaches and coastline (especially towards its northernmost limits), other densly populated parts of the northern Costa del Azahar such as **Castellón de la Plana** and **Benicassim** are now home to heavy industry.

Directions to the Northern Costa del Azahar

To drive to **Sagunto** from Valencia, take the small N-340 north, or the larger A-7 motorway north. For **Peñiscola**, continue up the coast along the N-340 north. For **Morella**, continue on the N-340 north until reaching Vinaros about 12 km past Peñiscola, and turn west onto the winding route N-232.

Bus service into this region is fairly limited, but available via connections in Valencia and Castellón de la Plana. Please check with either area's tourist office for more information.

Trains to and from most of the above coastal areas can be boarded on a daily basis year round at the Estación del Norte train station in Valencia and cost somewhere around 950 ptas or less to reach any point serviced on the Costa del Azahar. Call Renfe, *Tel. (96) 352-0202,* for exact schedules during peak (summer) and off peak (winter) times.

Sagunto

One of the first remarkable cities that you will pass about 24 km (15 miles) into this zone from Valencia is the historic city of Sagunto, population 57,500. Situated on a fertile plain, below a hill topped by an old castle, this ancient Roman seaport city was besieged by Hannibal's Carthaginian troops for over 9 months in 218 B.C. to mark the beginning of the Second Punic War. After the Romans returned to retake the city, they built several glorious structures that can still be seen today. Later Moorish inhabitants built the massive hilltop fortifications, while the Jewish and Christian residents from the 12th through 17th centuries added even more interesting buildings.

Upon arriving in town, head straight to the 12th century Gothic Romanesque **Iglesia de El Salvador** church on the Calle Mayor. The same street will take you straight into the palace-lined **Plaza Mayor**, with its bold 14th century Gothic **Iglesia de Santa María** church. From here follow the signs uphill through the small stone arch-lined lanes of the former **Jewish quarter** until reaching the path towards the restored 2nd century **Roman amphitheater** and adjacent **Museu de la Muralla de Sagunto** archeaological museum, displaying a good collection of artifacts from Roman through Moorish periods. *The museum and ampitheater are open Monday through Saturday from 10am until 2pm and again from 4pm until 6pm, Sundays and holidays from 10am until 2pm only, and admission to both is 300 ptas.*

A bit further uphill are more striking ruins of the huge Moorish fortress with its lookout points affording beautiful panoramic vistas. After visiting the old town, there are a couple of good beaches you can visit over by **Alamarda** and **Canet de Bereguer**.

Major Local Festivals
Contact the local Turismo office, *Tel. (96) 266-2213*, for more details.
• **Semana Santa**, *April, Religious Processions*
• **Fiesta San Abdon**, *late July, Processions and Feasts*
• **Fiesta Virgen María**, *early August, Bullfights*

Peñiscola
As you head further north past the less exotic large cities of Castellón de la Plana and Benicassim, much of the coastline is brimming with development and industrial areas. Continue past these unattractive places until the dramatic village of Peñiscola, about 112 km (69 miles) northeast of Sagunto. This intriguing walled village rests on a peninsula surrounded by the 14th century Templar fortress known as the **Castillo El Macho** that was rebuilt for deposed Pope Luna (Benedict XIII).

Within the old hamlet of whitewashed houses and medieval churches, you can wander down centuries-old Calle de la Castillo and get a good feel for what life was like here in the old days. The castle itself contains a small museum of relics, a vaulted basilica, and the deposed pope's study. *The castle is open daily from 9am until 1pm and again from 4pm until 7pm, but in the past the castle has been known to close for long periods of time during the low season. Admission is currently free, but a 250 ptas charge may be in effect by now.*

Although many restaurants and souvenir shops have started to change the ambiance somewhat, this is still a beautiful place to walk around and photograph. A series of small beaches on either side of the rocky promontory, and much better ones just over in the newer mainland part of town, can also be enjoyed during the more busy summer months.

Major Local Festivals

Contact the local Turismo office, *Tel. (964) 480-208,* for more details.
• **Fiesta Virgen María**, *September, Dances and Moorish Costume Parade*

INLAND FROM THE NORTHERN COSTA DEL AZAHAR

Directions to the Southern Costa del Azahar

To drive to **El Salér** and **La Albufera** from Valencia, take the N-340 south. For **Gandia** and **Denia**, continue down the coast along the N-332 south. For **Xátiva**, turn off to the west at the road from Gandia.

Daily bus service to and from Valencia to **El Salér** and the towns around **La Albufera** costs around 650 ptas each way via the city's bus depot along the Puerta del Mar. Buses between **Valencia** and **Gandia**, **Denia**, and **Xátiva** leave at least six times each day via the main station on Av. M. Pidal and cost upwards of 1,100 *ptas* each way. Check with the area's tourist office for more information.

Trains to and from most of the above coastal areas can be boarded on a daily basis year round at the Estación del Norte train station in Valencia and cost somewhere around 950 ptas or less to reach any point serviced on the Costa del Azahar. Call Renfe, *Tel. (96) 352-0202,* for exact schedules during peak (summer) and off-peak (winter) times.

Morella

The tiny walled town of Morella, population 3,458, is located on the slopes of a castle-topped hill 58 km (36 miles) northwest of Peñiscola. With its massive ring of defensive walls and commanding view out over the rugged countryside, it isn't hard to guess that ancient warriors had a tough time trying to conquer this village. As you enter through one of the several well preserved gates, make your way towards the Calle Blasco de Alagon to view the arcades around the **Mercado** Sunday marketplace and nearby wooden balcony-fronted mansions. Continue along the Cuesta de San Juan to take a peek at other ornate 14th through 16th century buildings like the **Casa de Ciurana de Quadres**, and along the Calle Carcel with its Gothic **Ayuntamiento** town hall.

The most famous sights here include the charming **Plaza Arciprestal** that surrounds the Gothic 14th century **Iglesia Arciprestal de Santa María la Mayor** basilica with its fantastic porticos, rose windows, handcrafted organ, spiral choir's staircase, altar, and **Museo Arciprestal** ecclesiastical museum, *open daily from June through September from 11am until 1:30pm and again from 4pm to 6pm with an admission charge of 200 ptas* Nearby in the **Plaza de San Francisco** you can visit the **Real Convento de San Francisco** convent to walk through its elaborate Gothic cloisters. Here you can visit the **Museo Etnológico de Morella y Maestrazgo** ethnographic museum, where displays of handcrafted artifacts and local art are on display. *Open daily from 10am until 2pm and again from 4pm until 6pm for 125 ptas.* After you've hit the lower portions of town, hike uphill to the massive 13th century **Castillo** fortress and treat yourself to a wonderful panorama and perhaps a picnic.

If you have a car and a few extra hours to kill, ask a local to give you directions to the remarkable village of **Ares del Maestre**, a tough winding 37 km (23 miles) to the south. This traditional village sits under the crest of a huge boulder, and is among the most authentic rural villages in Spain. While there are not many specific sights besides a Gothic church, the town seems like a place where time has stood still for 500 years. It is not uncommon to see herds of sheep or stray pigs wandering down the rock paths that lead past the ruined castle. This is a great place that until recently remained unknown to tourists.

Major Local Festivals
Contact the local Turismo office, *Tel. (964) 173-032,* for more details.
• **Fiesta San Julian**, *early January, Religious Processions*
• **Fiesta Antoni**, *mid-January, Processions and Parties*
• **Corpus Christi**, *June, Religious Processions*
• **Sexeni**, *every six years, Dances and Parades in August*
• **Baroque Festival**, *August, Concerts in the Basilica*

SOUTHWARD ALONG THE COSTA DEL AZAHAR
The sector that stretches southwest from Valencia to Denia for about 92 km (57 miles) is actually the southern part of the **Costa del Azahar**, but is also locally known as the **Ribera Baja**. While large chunks of this area near the **La Albufera lagoon**, such as **El Salér** and **El Perelló**, feature beautiful dune beaches and protected wildlife areas, other large cities such as **Gandía** and **Denia** have unfortunately become a bit overdeveloped.

Here are a few of the nicest places to enjoy a peaceful day trip and perhaps a dip in the ocean.

El Salér
Situated 14 km (9 miles) southeast of Valencia along the coastline, the picture perfect sand dune beaches of El Salér, population 3,478, are certainly worth a side trip. Although some excellent hotels and restaurants have been built along the seashore, a ban on all new construction imposed about 20 years ago has allowed the area to maintain its natural beauty.

This is the most popular summertime hangout for sun worshipping singles and families who are looking for a pristine beach not too far from Valencia. Here you can enjoy miles and miles of long sandy stretches, great waves, a scattering of good *paella* restaurants, and an assortment of huge discos in town that get packed on weekend nights after 2am or so. Public restrooms are also available.

Major Local Festivals
• **Fiesta El Palmar**, *early August, Processions on Boats in the Lake*

Parque Natural de La Albufera
Located about 5 km (3 miles) south of El Salér, this tranquil protected wildlife refuge and park is based along the marshes, waterways, and beaches of the largest lagoon in Spain, known as **La Albufera**. Home to countless migratory birds and small animals, the park's wetlands have historically been used for the cultivation of rice.

These days the area is still used for the hunting of fowl (allowed only by special permission), traditional fishing, and limited pleasure boating on its large lake. All in all this is a good place to hike around and watch the birds in their natural habitat. A couple of old fishing villages such as **El Palmar** and **El Perelló** now have converted their whitewashed fishing huts into fun seafood restaurants that are worth a try. There are also a few small beaches that can be enjoyed via entrances at the perimeter of the park.

Gandía
This once peaceful seaside port village, population 52,640, down the coast about 65 km (40 miles) from Valencia has been subjected to the construction of too many condos and hotels over the past 25 years. Although it still has a great beach called the **Playa de Gandía**, and a tranquil old quarter with a couple of historic sights, the interesting sections of the city will only take an hour or two to see.

The main attraction here is undoubtedly the 15th century **Palacio Ducal** palace on Calle de Sant Duc. The structure was originally a mansion belonging to the powerful Duke of Borja, later to be canonized as Saint Francis of Borja. It was later connverted by the saint into a Jesuit college, and visitors can tour the structure to view its fine Gothic courtyard, Moorish tile walls, marble and fresco covered rooms and fantastically ornate coffered ceilings. *The palace is open daily in the summer months from 10am until 12noon and again from 5pm until 7pm, and during other times of the year from 11am until 12noon and again from 4:30pm until 5:30pm. Admssion including a guided tour costs about 200 ptas per person.*

Also worth a quick look is the **Museo Arqueológico Comarcal** regional archeaology musuem just three blocks away on the Plaza de Rei Jaume. Here you can see a great selection of local relics and artwork that date back to before the Arabs came here. *The museum is open on weekdays* *from 10am until 1pm and again from 3pm until 6pm, and on weekends and holidays from 10am until 1pm. There is no charge to enter.*

Major Local Festivals
Contact the local Turismo office, *Tel. (96) 284-2407,* for more details.
- **Fiesta Del Mar**, *mid-July, Blessing of the Boats and Races*
- **Dia San Francisco**, *October, Outdoor Festivals*

Denia
The port city of Denia, population 24,270, lies 98 km (61 miles) below Valencia on the edge of the sea. While used primarily as a point of departure for ferry passengers going to northern Africa, the city offers a few interesting sights. One of these is the 17th century **Castillo** (castle) that now houses the **Museo Arqueológico Municipal** museum with a collection of local art and relics from medieval through modern times. *The museum is open Monday through Saturday from 10am until 2pm and again from 4pm until 8pm, and on Sunday from 10am until 2pm. Admisson is just 100 ptas per person.*

Also worth a quick peek is the 17th century **Casa Consistorial** town hall building, and the 18th century **Iglesia de Santa María** church. Otherwise, there is not much else to do here.

Major Local Festivals
Contact the local Turismo office,*Tel. (96) 578-0957,* for more details.
- **Palm Sunday**, Procession of Palms
- **Fiesta Elche**, mid-August, Miracle Play
- **Fiesta Virgen**, late December, Processions

INLAND FROM THE SOUTHERN COSTA DEL AZAHAR: XÁTIVA
The historic town of Xátiva, population 24,236 (also known as Játiva), can be found on the base of a mountain 11 km (7 miles) west of Gandía. Filled with mansions and the ruins of castles that date back several centuries, this is a great place to spend at least five or six hours wandering around.

Where to Stay – Moderate
HOSTERIA DE MONT SANT, *Subida al Castillo, Xativa. Tel. (96) 227-5081, Fax (96) 228-1905. US and Canada bookings (Marketing Ahead) at Tel. 800/223-1356. Yea-r round rack rates from 17,500 ptas per double room per night (B.P.). All major credit cards accepted.*

Dramatically situated on a dramatic mountaintop below an awesome 13th century Arab palace, just a 25 minute ride from the pristine beaches of the Mediterranean coast, Hosteria de Mont Sant is a wonderfully charming and welcoming little hotel. This delightful place features seven beautifully decorated rooms with a carefully selected assortment of regional antiques, central heating and air conditioning, deluxe private bathrooms stocked with the finest quality imported hair and skin care products, direct dial telephone, remote control satellite television, executive style desks, mini-bar, mini-safe, hand-made ceramic floors, and French doors leading out to some of the most incredible views imaginable.

Guests enjoy one of the country's finest regional restaurants, complete with age old decorative arts and an unusually pleasant relaxed ambiance, live weekend jazz and classical music concerts, an outdoor swimming pool, one of fantastic complimentary breakfasts daily, plenty of free parking, and over 15,000 square meters of impeccably maintained gardens. The highest levels of service are flawlessly provided by the inn's talented young multilingual staff who are extremely friendly and hardworking. I guarantee that you will never forget the time you spent at this one of a kind establishment. See also *Best Places to Stay*, Chapter 13.

Seeing the Sights

The best way to get a good feel for the village is to follow the signs pointing to the uphill path that leads to the massive **Castillo**, a castle that has elements dating back to the Moorish and Roman periods. Once inside the castle complex you can see the old prison, several tombs and chapels, and a great lookout point. *The castle is open Tuesday through Sunday from 10am until 2pm and again from 5pm until 8pm, and there is no entrance fee.*

After departing make sure to pop into the **Hosteria de Mont Sant** for some of the best paella in Spain. A bit further down from the castle heading downhill, you will soon pass by the entrance to the 13th century **Iglesia de Sant Feliu** church, the oldest house of worship in town. This church contains a wonderful atrium with pink marble columns, a fine Romanesque portico, and several antique paintings. *The church is open daily from 10am until 12:30pm and again from 3pm until 6pm with no admission fee.*

Continue back into the heart of town and head over to the Calle de la Corretgeria from which you can pop into the **Museu de L'Almodi** municipal museum housed in a 16th century mansion that contains such exhibits as a rare Islamic fountain, rooms full of archeological artifacts, Gothic sculptures, gold and silver pieces, and a collection of Baroque period art includng works by Goya, Giordano, Lopez, Mazo, and locally born master Ribera. *The museum is open to the public daily (except Monday) from 10am until 1pm, and again on Tuesday through Friday from 4pm until 6pm. The entrance fee is only 125 ptas per person.*

The rest of the old quarter is filled with dozens of churches, palaces, mansions, and fountains from as far back as the 14th century, as well as several peaceful parks and caves. Visit the charming *Turismo* office at Calle Noguera, 10, and ask for an extremely helpful step by step walking guide to the town's various sights.

This is a great town to visit, filled with friendly townspeople, great food and beautiful sights to see.

Major Local Festivals
Contact the local Turismo office, *Tel. (96) 227-3346,* for more details.
• **Fiesta Jesus Nazareno**, *late April, Processions*
• **Fiesta San Juan**, *late June, Bonfires and Parades*
• **Fira de Xátiva**, *mid-August, Music, Fairs, Bullfights*

ALICANTE

Alicante is the largest city along the seafront **Costa Blanca** section of the Valencia region. It is a pleasant city with lots of things to see and do, and an active population that takes full advantage of the superb year round climate.

ARRIVALS & DEPARTURES
By Air
Alicante's small international airport is called the Aeropuerto de Alicante–Altet, located 10 km (6 miles) southwest of Alicante off route N-332 on the outskirts of the town of El Altet. Although some flights do arrive here from major European cities outside of Spain, it primarily services domestic flights.

Buses between the Airport & Downtown
Bus service via the Alcoyana line operates in both directions between the airport's arrival area and dozens of stops within the city center. The price is about 600 *ptas* each way, and it runs almost hourly Monday through Friday from 7am until 9pm, and much less fequently on weekends and holidays.

Taxis from the Airport to Downtown
Taxis are usually marked with the *Taxi* sign, and can be found in abundant supply at well-indicated taxi stands at the airport. Note that almost all of the taxis here are fairly small sized four door cars. Normally, a taxi's trunk can hold about two large suitcases, but those with roof racks can secure two more medium pieces of luggage, and perhaps a couple of

carry-on bags inside as well. Expect to pay somewhere between 1,700 and 2,300 *ptas* per ride from the airport to most downtown locations.

By Bus

Most of the bus lines between Alicante and other parts of Spain arrive at the Alicante Estación de Autobuses bus station at Calle de Portugal, 17. From here you can easily walk the six blocks to the Paseo Explanada de España esplanade, or to several other points in the city center. From this station, municipal bus lines A, B, F, or G can take you to other locations in the heart of town for about 120 *ptas*, or a taxi can be hired for about 675 *ptas*.

By Car

From Valencia, the best way here is to take the wide A-7 toll highway south for 166 km (103 miles) until reaching the well-marked exits for Alicante. Once inside the city you may have to drive to the waterfont to find metered parking, or use one of the well-indicated private garages that charge about 1,600 *ptas* per day.

By Ferry

Since Alicante is situated on the Sea, ferries to and from **Tangiers** and the **Balearic Islands** of Palma de Mallorca, Ibiza, and Mahon call in at the Puerto de Alicante ferry landing at the city's main waterfront. From the port's Estación Marítimo, a municipal bus can take you to the heart of town for 80 *ptas*, or a taxi can be hired for about 610 *ptas*.

By Train

Alicante is connected to the rest of Spain and Europe by extensive rail service via **Renfe**. While coastal and commuter trains may pull into smaller stations around town, the larger main Estación Ferrocarril train station is located on the intersection of Avenida de Salamanca and the Avenida de la Estacion, just four blocks from the Plaza de los Luceros in the center of the downtown zone. From here the municipal bus lines E, F, and M each go through various points downtown at about 120 *ptas* per ride. Taxis can also be found just in front of the station, and the average charge is about 655 *ptas* to most downtown hotels and sights.

ORIENTATION

With a population of 264,562, Alicante lies at the edge of the Mediterranean Sea on the southeast coast of Spain. It is 422 km (262 miles) southeast of Madrid, and 166 km (103 miles) south of Valencia.

GETTING AROUND TOWN

By Taxi

There are hundreds of licensed taxis that roam the streets and major passenger arrival points during all hours of the day and night. To find a taxi, either hail an unoccupied taxi (when empty they will illuminate a small *Taxi* light above the car) that is driving by, go to one of the dozens of obvious taxi stands throughout the city, or call Alicante Radio Taxi Companies, *Tel. (96) 510-1611 or Tel. (96) 525-2511* for a radio response pickup on demand. Taxis charge customers using meters and the fare usually will cost somewhere around 650 *ptas* per ride (not per person) between most downtown areas. Legally chargeable supplements are posted on a sticker in the taxi's interior.

By Bus

Alicante's municipal bus company, known as **Masatusa**, has several **Autobuses** (buses) that criss-cross almost every neighborhood. With over a dozen different bus lines, each lettered and color-coded, and hundreds of well-marked bus stops each with its posted corresponding route map, getting around above ground is fairly easy.

Ask at one of the friendly *Turismo* tourist offices for a copy of the free *Guia de Itinerarios Autobuses Urbanos*. Most buses operate every 10 to 30 minutes in both directions from about 6:15am until 10:15pm daily, with less frequent service on weekends and holidays. The fare is about 120 *ptas* per ride, and tickets can be paid for on the bus.

WHERE TO STAY

Expensive

MELIA ALICANTE HOTEL, *Playa Postiguet. Tel. (96) 520-5000, Fax (96) 516-3346. US & Canada Bookings: (UTELL), Tel. 800/44-UTELL. Low season rack rates from 19,500 ptas per double room per night (E.P.). High season rack rates from 23,500 ptas per double room per night (E.P.). All major credit cards accepted.*

For my money, this is the best centrally located hotel in town. Situated on a pier between the beach and the famed esplanade, the new Melia offers 545 rooms and apartments with private bathrooms, seaview terraces, air conditioning, mini-bar, satellite televisions, in-room music, am-fm radios, direct dial telephones, and comfortable furnishings.

The hotel also has valet and garage parking, boutiques, a nice pool, two restaurants, business and conference facilities, baby sitting, a hair salon, game room, a piano bar and one of the town's best discos. With its prime location and large rooms, this is a good seletion for deluxe travelers and businessmen.

HOTEL SIDI SAN JUAN, *Playa de San Juan, San Juan (Alicante). Tel. (96) 516-1300, Fax (96) 516-3346. Low season rack rates from 17,900 ptas per double room per night (B.P.). High season rack rates from 20,600 ptas per double room per night (B.P.). All major credit cards accepted.*

Located about eight minutes north of the city center along the beach at San Juan de Alicante, this modern five-star hotel is one of the best resort hotels in the area. Five stories high, the Sidi San Juan features 176 air conditioned seaview rooms and suites each with private terraces, deluxe marble bathrooms, mini-bar, direct dial telephone, satellite television, mini-safe, extremely wood and wicker comfortable furnishings, huge closets and electronic keypass locks. There is also a full service conference and business center, beauty salon, several excellant restaurants and bars, a heated Olympic size indoor pool, a huge outdoor pool and sun deck, six tennis courts, summertime child day care, free parking, room service, tennis and squash facilities, sauna, a tour and car rental desk and boutiques.

Service here is prompt and professional, with a demanding clientele of well dressed European businessmen and leisure travelers. You can have a round of golf arranged for you in one of three nearby courses, choose special dietetic menus at the restaurants, learn how to improve your tennis skills, enjoy a massage or therapeutic treatments in their newly expanded "Beauty Farm" health spa pavilion, utilize the complimentary round-trip mini-bus shuttle service into the heart of the city, or just sit back and relax in the large private gardens or beach area.

Moderate

NH HOTEL CRISTAL, *Calle de Tomas Lopez Torregrosa, 11. Tel. (96) 514-3659, Fax (96) 520-6696. US & Canada Bookings: (UTELL), Tel. 800/44-UTELL. Year- round rack rates from 13,000 ptas per double room per night (E.P.). All major credit cards accepted.*

The Cristal is a nice modern three-star full service hotel located just a two minute walk from attractions in the old quarter of town. The hotel features 53 ultra-modern air conditioned rooms that each have deluxe private bathrooms packed with amenities, color satelite television, direct dial telephones, modern artwork, in-room music, direct dial television, mini-bar, room service and laundry service. The hotel also offers nearby parking, a breakfast room, business meeting rooms, and a nice staff of true professionals.

Inexpensive

HOTEL PALAS, *Plaza del Mar. Tel. (96) 520-9309, Fax (96) 514-0120. Low season rack rates from 8,700 ptas per double room per night (E.P.). High* *season rack rates from 9,700 ptas per double room per night (E.P.). All major credit cards accepted.*

The Hotel Palas is a great deal for accommodations in Alicante. Located just one block from both the water and the old quarter, this charming three-star hotel and restaurant is housed in a beautiful old mansion full of antiques and old world charm. Their 39 rooms have nice private bathrooms, tile flooring, antique bedding, color remote control televisions, turn of the century furnishings, direct dial telephones, and either interior or seaviews (with balconies).

The hotel also has a beautiful marble lobby, a full service restaurant featuring great menus of regional specialties and an extremely friendly staff. This is a great choice if you want to save some money and not give up quality.

WHERE TO EAT
Expensive
RESTAURANTE CURRICAN, *Calle Canalejas, 1. Tel. (96) 514-0818. All major credit cards accepted.*

This formal yet intimate little restaurant near the waterfront offers a superb selecion of constantly changing regional meat and freshly caught seafood selections. The menu is always different, so ask Sr. Lopez, the head chef, for his suggestions, and expect to spend somewhere in the range of 4,250 *ptas* per person for a multiple course meal with a good bottle of Spanish wine.

Since they only seat about 70 or so well-dressed patrons each night, make sure to call ahead for reservations. The service, cuisine, and ambiance here is superb. If you want a special meal in an elegant environment, this is certainly the place to go.

Moderate
TROPISCAFO, *Muelle de Levante, 7 . Tel. (96) 520-5945. Most major credit cards accepted. .*

Located on the heart of the new Puerto de Alicante entertainment area just in front of downtown, this great casual restaurant, bar, and café offers an extensive menu of tapas and cocktails for a great little meal. Their menu includes such favorites as toasted sandwiches with smoked salmon, tuna with pimentos, assorted clams by the bowl, regional sausage, croquettes, fried chicken, several tropical salads and great desserts. Average price per person here for a few great late night snack items is around 1,550 *ptas* plus drinks.

Inexpensive
GRACIA, *Calle Mayor, 22. Tel. (96) 520-7981. Cash Only*.

Although far from fancy, this small cafeteria-style restaurant offers a large menu of nicely prepared lunch and dinner items, including Russian salad for 200 *ptas*, seafood salad at 225 *ptas*, grilled sardines for 250 *ptas*, grilled calamari at 400 *ptas*, shrimp in garlic for 475 *ptas*, tuna sandwiches at 275 *ptas*, chicken club sandwiches for 450 *ptas*, and plenty more choices for a simple meal.

SEEING THE SIGHTS

Approximate duration (by foot) is about 4.5 hours, including church, castle, waterfront, museum, monument, and side street visits.

The best place to begin exploring the lively city of **Alicante** is to start along the seafront **Paseo Marítimo** prominade. Here you can wander past the small harbor from which glass bottom boat rides and charter fishing trips depart. If scuba diving is your thing, there is also a summertime ferry service from this part of the waterfront to the nearby **Isla de Tabarca** island (18 kilometers southeast of the harbor), with its 13th century fortifications, an old walled village, and cute beaches. The promenade is also lined by a series of small parks with plenty of benches, and a nice walkway where parents take romantic afternoon strolls while their kids race ahead on roller skates. This also happens to be just about the best (and safest) place in the whole town to find 24-hour metered car parking.

While looking to your left facing the sea, you'll notice a long pier (actually part of the renovated **Puerto de Alicante** port area) lined with modern condos and a large hotel jetting out towards the sea. This pier itself is called the **Muelle de Levante** and has recently been expanded into a bustling new harbor-side entertainment area with well over 50 different bars, discos, restaurants and other entertainment venues that are packed starting midnight on weekend nights. Walk towards and then past the pier where you will come to the town's narrow **Playa Postiguet** beach. Besides being a nice place to get a good tan in the summer, a special tunnel and elevator ride just across above the beach can take you up through the hill to visit the 16th century **Castillo de Santa Bárbara** castle. The castle is well-preserved with great panoramic lookouts over the whole coast, dramatic defensive walls, several period rooms including a chapel, and a small **Museo de las Hogueras** museum of floats that have been salvaged from the giant bonfires of the San Juan festival. *The elevator/tunnel ride operates from 9am until 7:30pm on weekdays and from 9am until 1pm on Saturdays, and costs about 300 ptas each way.*

After the castle, retrace your steps (once again passing the pier) back onto the Paseo Marítimo, and cross over the avenue to reach the lovely

Explanada de España. This famous palm-lined esplanade is paved by a multicolored mosaic made up of over over six million marble tiles, and is packed with outdoor cafés and small fast food joints that thousands of commuters visit while on their way to and from work each day. Continue along the espalande until reaching the well- marked *Turismo* at #2, where a staff of helpful young tourist advisors can give you some great maps and pamplets and answer any questions you might have.

After the tourist office, turn left at the next corner onto the Calle Cervantes and start your walk through the colorful **El Barrio** old town quarter. A couple of blocks further up you will intersect with the **Plaza de la Ayuntamiento**, where the beautiful Baroque style 18th century **Ayuntamiento** town hall awaits your visit, *on weekdays between 9am and 3pm for free if you ask politely at the door or call Tel. (96) 520-5100 during weekday working hours*. Inside you can view its highly decorated chapel and "Blue Room" that feature fine art and massive chandeliers.

After taking a peek at the city hall, pass beneath the adjacent **Portico Consistorial II** archway, and take a right turn at the next street known as Calle Mayor and follow for it a few blocks as its name changes to the Calle de Villavieja. At this point you will find the **Plaza de Santa María** where you'll find two of the old town's most impressive attractions.

First, on the right hand side of the plaza you can see the Baroque facade of the 16th century **Iglesia de Santa María** church. Built atop a former Arabic mosque destroyed after the Moors were expelled, the church has a fantastically ornate portico and a beautiful Rococo high altar. *The church is open during several daily mass hours and admission is free.* The second sight is just across the street from the church, the awe-inspiring **Colección de Arte del Siglo XX–Museu de la Asegurada** Spanish modern art museum. Housed in a spectacular 17th century mansion and former prison known as the **Casa de la Asegurada**, this wonderful museum contains the paintings of **Alfaro**, **Miró**, **Tàpies**, **Picasso**, **Chillida**, **Dalí**, **Gris**, and others that were owned by local artist Eusebio Sempere who donated his private collections to the city. *The musuem is open Tuesday through Saturday from 10:30am until 1:30pm and again from 6pm until 9pm during the summer, from 10am until 1pm and again from 5pm until 8pm during the winter, and on Sunday Year round from 10:30am until 1pm. There is no admission fee.*

After passing through the museum, turn around and retrace your steps back down the Calle Mayor until passing the city hall, turn right onto the Calle de San Nicolas and then left at the next corner onto the Calle de Miguel Soler. Here you will pass next to the fine Renaissance 18th century **Concatedral de San Nicolas de Bari** cathedral. This house of worship is almost always open and contains a unique Baroque communion chapel and an intricately adorned cloister. In front of the cathedral is a small street called the Calle de San Jose where much of the city's best nightlife action takes place. Here you can walk down the street and its adjacent blocks as you pass turn of the century cafés, modern dance clubs, and live music venues where blues and jazz shows take place almost nightly.

At the end of the street you will turn right at the intersection of the wide Rambla de Méndez Núñez, one of the city's most commercial shopping zones. As you continue up the Rambla for about a half dozen blocks you will cross over the Avenida Alfonso X El Sabio and turn left for a couple of blocks. Soon you will be directly in front of the **Mercado Central**. This red brick covered market was built in 1922 and is the best palce to pick up supplies for picnics while in town. Keep walking down this wide avenue until intersecting with the **Plaza de los Luceros** with its traffic circle and large statue. At this point turn right onto the Avenida de General Marva and walk up about five blocks until the avenue ends at a park below the mountain.

If you want to take an invigorating steep uphill walk, take the path behind the benches at the end of the avenue and follow it up to through the park and on to the less than dramatic tree-filled ruins of the unfinished 19th century **Castillo de San Fernando**. In any case, walk back down the Avenida de General Marva, this time turning right onto the Avenida de la Estación. On this block you will find the **Diputation** building that house both city council offices and an interesting **Museo Provincial** provincial archeology museum that displays exhibits on prehistoric, Iberian, Greek, Roman and Phoenician relics. *The museum is open Tuesday through Saturday from 9:30am until 1:30pm and on sundays and holidays from 11am until 1:30pm. There is no admission charge.*

NIGHTLIFE & ENTERTAINMENT

One of the best areas for people of any age is over in the old quarter of town around the *Calle de San Jose* just in front of the cathedral. On this small fun street you can find the **Vanguard Café**, **Arte Jazz Bar**, and the **Jamboree** blues bar with live music. Around the corner on the Calle Labradores you can also check out the **La Naya Bar**, the **Potato** Jazz bar, and **Celestrial Copas**, while steps away on the Calle de San Isidro you can hit the **Café Epoca** with its candlelit outdoor tables. All the dozen or so stone lanes (such as the Calle Virgen de Belen) surrounding the cathedral are filled with over 50 different small pubs and dance clubs of every imaginable type, which are normally packed on Thursday (local students' night) through Saturday nights between 11:30pm and 4:00am. Many of these clubs have small cover charges of around 400 *ptas,* and tend to attract a good looking crowd of single people between 17 and 24 years of age.

As I mentioned above, the newest zone for nightlife is the harbor-front **Muelle de Levante** along the city's **Puerto de Alicante** pier area where you can find 50 different bars, clubs, discos, and restaurants along a strip of two story modern buildings. Among the best places to party here during the weekend are over at the **Puerto di Roma**, the **Cora di Gallo**, the **Tropiscafo** and the **Directo Café**, all of which are café-bars with dancing and usually no cover charge.

Discos can be found on the edge of town and in various other areas and include the **Pacha Disco** on Avenida Aguilera, the flashy **Nodo Discoteca** at the Melia Hotel on the waterfront, the **Underground Club** on Calle de San Francisco, and the **Texaco Pub and dance club** on the beach in San Juan de Alicante.

SPORTS & RECREATION
Amusement, Water, & Theme Parks
• **Octopus Parque Acuatico** (San Juan de Alicante), Tel. (96) 594-0300
• **Rio Safari y Delfinario** (Elche), Tel. (96) 545-2288

Bullfights
• **Plaza de Toros** (Alicante), Telephone unlisted.

Casino
• **Casino Costa Blanca** (Villajoyosa-Benidorm), Tel. (96) 589-0700
• **Casino de Alicante** (Alicante), Tel. (96) 521-3829
Golf
• **Club de Golf Don Cayo** (Altea), Tel. (96) 584-8046. 9 holes, par 36
• **Club de Golf Ifach** (Calpe), Tel. (96) 649-714. 9 holes, par 36
• **Campo de Golf Villamartin** (Torrevieja), Tel. (96) 676-0350. 18 holes x 2, par 72

Major Outdoor Markets
• **Thursday & Saturday Morning Outdoor Market**, Plaza de Toros

Zoos & Aquariums
• **Museo Municipal y Acuario** (Santa Pola), Tel. (96) 541-1100

EXCURSIONS & DAY TRIPS
Once you have visited all of the best attractions in the city of *Alicante*, the following is a partial listing of some of the most interesting half and full day trips in the nearby areas. Since few excursions are offered around *Alicante* by major companies, you may need to take a bus, train, rent a car, or hire a private guide with a sedan to get to the following destinations.

NORTHWARD ALONG THE COSTA BLANCA

The city of Alicante is located roughly in the middle of a coastal area along the Mediterranean called the **Costa Blanca**. If you head northeast up and along the seafront from the city, this sector continues for 86 km (53 miles) before intersecting with the Costa del Azahar.

Known primarily for its large resort communities such as **Benidorm**, it also contains long stretches of pristine sandy beaches and quaint little villages. Some of the most popular, as well as a few of the least developed traditional towns, are listed below.

Directions to the Northern Costa Blanca

To drive to all of the coastal sights listed below from Alicante, take the small and winding N-332 north or the high speed A-7 toll highway.

Buses to Altea, Benidorm, Calp, Denia, and Javea from either Alicante or Valencia are offered several times each day by the Enatcar bus company, *Tel. (96) 359-2611*. Bus service to **San Juan de Alicante** can be accessed via **Alcoyana** and **Auplasa** bus service from stops in front of Alicante's waterfront esplanade. Other cities further up the coast can be reached by private bus lines operating via Alicante's main bus station. Check with either area's tourist office for more information.

Trains to and from most of the above coastal areas can be boarded on a daily basis year round at one of Alicante's three regional and commuter train stations and cost somewhere around 975 *ptas* or less to reach any point serviced along the Costa Blanca. Call Renfe, *Tel. (96) 592-0202*, for specific station departure locations and exact schedules during peak (summer) and off-peak (winter) times.

San Juan de Alicante

The town of San Juan de Alicante, population 13,986, is situated just about eight km (5 miles) above Alicante's waterfront. This suburban coastal area marks the beginning of a long stretch of beachfront resort communities. Although very little of historical and artistic value can be found here, its countless hotels and condos have become a major summertime draw for upper middle class residents from Spain's largest cities.

The wide commercial Avenida de Niza cuts right next to the large and turbulent **Playa de San Juan** beach, where thousands of people gather to suntan, swim, and windsurf. At night, the many seafood and international restaurants get packed during the high season, and afterwards the younger set hits one of several beach area discos and live music venues.

Since there really is nothing of great interest to see here other than the beach itself, this city is a good place to visit when you want to relax and enjoy the sea. If you have a car, you can also follow the coastline further up and find a much more secluded beach.

Benidorm

This long strip of prime sundrenched beachfront, 39 km (24 miles) northeast of Alicante, has grown into a mega-resort area. Each year, well over 2.5 million visitors from all over Europe can be found on its huge beaches and overpriced shopping arcades. Now that the city, population 41,198, has become one of the top destinations for low to medium budget package tour travelers, much of its once glorious mountain backdrop has been obstructed by the construction of countless skyscraper apartment and hotel buildings. Despite the overdevelopment, there are still a few good things to see and do if you end up here.

The main focal points of the city are the famed crystal clear, crescent shaped beaches that stretch out for over five km (3 miles) and have almost no undertow. Separated from each other by a dramatic rocky cliff topped by the terraced lookout point of the ruined **El Castillo** castle, the sandy **Playa de Levante** and **Playa de Poniente** beaches are where much of the action takes place during the day. The much more interesting secluded cove beach known as the **Playa Mal Pas** can be found immediately below the ruined castle itself.

Although busy throughout the year due to the consistently warm climate, these beaches get totally packed during July and August when every inch of sand is covered by skimpily-clad bodies of all ages and nationalities. Watersports rental facilities, umbrella-topped chairs, and snack shops can be found everywhere. Scuba diving can also be arranged in the area surrounding the small **Isla de Benidorm** island just a short boat ride into the bay.

Besides the seafront, the other interesting part of town is over by the old fishermen's quarter. Here you can stroll down a series of narrow streets and age-old alleys that surround the **Plaza de la Constitución**. At night, most people find themselves inside the hundreds of English-owned pubs, aggressive mega-discos, and smaller dance clubs both along the beachfront and in the old town. There are also well over 1,000 boutiques scattered around the city selling souvenirs and clothing.

Major Local Festivals

Contact the local *Turismo* office *at Tel. (96) 585-1311* for more details.
• **Carnival**, *February, Processions and All Night Parties*
• **Fallas de San Jose**, *March, Processions and Bonfires*
• **Fiesta San Juan**, *late June, Processions and Bonfires*
• **Fiesta del Virgen**, *November, Parades*

A MOORISH CASTLE IN A CLIFF!

*If you're looking for an exciting side trip from town to enjoy a breathtaking mountain village, try taking a car or bus about 16 km (10 miles) inland to the northwest, to the Moorish village of **Guadelest**. Here you can visit the **Castello de Guadelest** castle, built into the top of a cliff, once inhabited by Arabs. Also in this charming village is a museum of miniatures and several quaint alleys and gateways worth checking out.*

Altea

The pleasant resort town and artist colony of Altea, population 12,400, rests on the slopes of a church-topped hill surrounded by both mountains and the sea nine km (6 miles) above Benidorm. In the old days when the area was primarily a traditional fishing village, local residents built hundreds of charming whitewash and iron grill fronted cottages on the cobblestone alleyways that wind their way up through the old **Barrio Vellaguarda** district. It is within this part of town that you can walk around the **Plaza de la Cantareria** and nearby **Plaza de la Iglesia** to visit the magnificent blue domed **Iglesia de la Virgen del Consuelo** church on the hilltop, with its beautiful interior and adjacent watchtower.

The more modern seafront section of town features a nice, quiet (but small) man-made beach that is lined on the inland side by a commercial esplanade featuring shops and restaurants. A few minutes walk south you can find all sorts of watersports near the sheltered marina, check out the local fish market, enjoy a **Tuesday craft market**, or relax and sip on a cool drink in a simple outdoor café.

For those looking for more substantial beaches, try heading south by foot or car to the more impressive **La Roda** and **Cap Blanch** beach areas near the lighthouse. Altea is a nice spot to get away from the more famous nearby resort towns, and enjoy a laid-back afternoon full of peaceful walks and charming residents.

Major Local Festivals

Contact the local *Turismo* office at *Tel. (96) 584-4114*, for more details.
- **Cristo de la Salud**, *February, Processions*
- **Fiesta San Juan**, *late June, Bonfires*
- **Fiesta de Virgen**, *mid-July, Marine Processions*
- **Fiesta Castell L'Olla**, *August, Fireworks*

Calpe (Calp)

Located about another 7 km (4 miles) up from Altea, on a hill above the sea, the former ancient fishing village of Calpe (population 11,482) has been transformed into a family oriented restful town. The main sight here is the famed **Peñón de Ilfach**, a huge monolithic rocky outcrop that rises sharply for over 300 meters (1000 feet) up from the sea front towards the sky. Just below the outcrop is the town's fishing harbor and adjacent beach areas, where you can still see the remains of old Roman baths. The town also has a lovely old quarter with a Gothic-Mudéjar church and 16th century fortress ruins.

TRAIN & FERRY RIDES TO THE ISLAND OF TABARCA

*During the summer months, a company called Cruceros Kontiki and the regional train company offer special full day excursions to **Tabarca**. This cute island is 18 kilometers southeast of Alicante and has a nice old walled village with lots of historic sights and great beaches. A ticket including train transfers to the ferry from Calp, Altea, and Benidorm, and the ferry ride itself costs only 2,150 ptas per adult and there are discounts for kids available. For more details about this great trip call Ferrocarrils de la Generalitat Valenciana, Tel. (96) 526-2233.*

Major Local Festivals

Contact the local Turismo office, *Tel. (96) 583-1250*, for more details.
· **Fiesta de Virgen**, mid-July, Marine Processions
· **Dia de Virgen María**, August, Carriage Parade & Folk Dances

The Cabo de la Nao

From Calpe the coastline continues along a mountainous cape known as the Cabo de la Nao that features hillsides dotted with pine trees, expensive villas, and caves. The picturesque towns of **Tuedela-Moraira** and **Javea** can be visited along the cape, where you'll find tiny beaches and community farming areas.

INLAND FROM THE SOUTHERN COSTA BLANCA
Directions to the Southern Costa Blanca

To drive to all of the southern Costa Blanca coastal sights from Alicante, take the winding route N-332 south. To reach **Elche** and **Orihuela**, instead head south on the inland N-340 south.

All towns and cities listed along the southern Costa Blanca and its nearby inland sections can be reached by private bus lines operating via

Alicante's main bus station. Please check with either area's tourist office for more information.

Trains to and from the southern Costa Blanca areas and nearby inland cities can be boarded on a daily basis year round at one of Alicante's three regional and commuter train stations and cost somewhere around 975 *ptas* or less. Call Renfe, *Tel. (96) 592-0202*, for specific station departure locations and exact schedules during peak (summer) and off-peak (winter) times.

Elche

Located 22 km (14 miles) inland and southwest from Alicante, the major city of Elche (also known as Elx) is best known for the **El Palmeral**, a huge forest of palm tree groves planted on the edge of the city well over 2,000 years ago. Now a successful industrial city, population 180,250, there is still an old quarter in the center where visitors can stroll around to see such sights as the 17th century **Basilica de Santa María**, beneath whose dome the city's world famous medieval *Misteri de Elx*, a play about the Virgin Mary performed by a cast of local volunteers to packed-in crowds numbering in the thousands for two days during mid-August of each year.

Also in the center are the Moorish era **Torre de Calahorra** watch-tower, and the 15th century **Palacio Altamira** palace. Nearby is the striking **Museo de Arte Contemporaneo** modern art museum off of the central **Plaza del Raval**, where a collection of modern paintings, ceramics, and tapestries are on display. *The museum is open Tuesday through Saturday from 10am until 1pm and again from 5pm until 8pm, with an entrance fee of 125 ptas.*

Within the palm groves alongside the city is the town's **Parque Municipal** park, with its **Museo Arqueológico** featuring exhibits of prehistoric and medieval artifacts. *The museum is open Tuesday through Saturday from 9am until 1pm and again from 4pm until 7pm for 225 ptas.* Over at the **Huerto del Cura** are lovely gardens that are planted below palm trees, including a 160 year old palm with seven arms. *The gardens are open daily from sunrise to sunset, and cost 275 ptas to view.*

The last major sight is the ancient Iberian settlement of **La Alcudia**, about two km (1 mile) south of town. This was where the famed **Dama de Elche**, a magnificent ancient Iberian carved stone head, was excavated and formerly displayed before being moved to the Museo Arqueológico museum in Madrid. The settlement sight now is housed inside a complex called the **Museo Monografico de la Alcudia**, *open daily from sunrise to sunset for 175 ptas.*

Major Local Festivals
 Contact the local *Turismo* office, *Tel. (96) 545-2747*, for more details.
• **Palm Sunday**, *Processions*
• **Misteri de Elx**, *mid-August, Medieval Mystery Play*
• **Fiesta de Virgen**, *Late December, Parades and Processions*

Orihuela
 Situated below a hillside on the banks of the Segura river 32 km (20 miles) further inland and southwest from Elche, the historic city of Orihuela (population 47,000) deserves several hours of your attention. Not only was this city home to **King Ferdinand** and **Queen Isabella** in 1488, but was also a respected regional capitol, Episcopal See, and major university town from the 15th through 18th centuries. During those days, many fine palaces, mansions, and government buildings were erected that still can be seen today.
 The best place to start your journey is over by the 14th century **Catedral de El Salvador** cathedral off of the Calle Ramon y Cajal in the heart of the old quarter. *Open daily from 11am until 1:30pm and again from 3:45pm until 6pm*, the fantastically vaulted cathedral contains the **Museo Diocesáno Catdralico de Arte Sacro** sacred arts museum where you can see religious gold and silver pieces and several beautiful paintings by **Ribera**, **Velázquez**, and **Morales**. *The museum is open from 11am until 1pm daily, and is free to enter.* Also worth a look is the 15th century Gothic **Iglesia de Santiago** parish church in the **Plaza de Santiago** that was built for King Ferdinand and Queen Isabella, and has its own **Museo Tesoro** treasury museum full of ornate sculptures and golden religious articles. *This museum is open daily from 11am until 2pm, and again from 5pm until 8pm, and has no admission fee.*
 From the Iglesia de Santiago church , walk to the nearby *Turismo* office on Calle Francisco Diez to ask for a free walking tour map. This will allow you to find a half dozen other elaborate mansions scattered throughout town, and also get you to the road that leads to the Baroque **Colegio de Santo Domingo** at the north edge of town. Although not well preserved, you can still get inside this university building to see the church's frescoed nave and tiled cloisters.

SOUTHWARD ALONG THE COSTA BLANCA
 From Alicante, the **Costa Blanca** continues southwest for 95 km (59 miles) as it passes by countless small resort communities and excellent beach areas. Within the space of about seven hours, it is possible to see most of this area's best sights, and venture inland for a short excursion to one of the larger old cities. Below are a few ideas to point you in the right direction.

Santa Pola

Located 29 km below Alicante, the small resort town of Santa Pola, population 12,440, has always been a major fishing port. This is where much of the region's fresh fish is caught and sold to wholesalers, but the restaurants in town always seem to have the first pick.

Besides having a small sheltered beach area, the town also has a few interesting sights, including the 16th century **Castillo** castle off of the **Plaza de Castillo** that is now home to the **Museo Municipal Arqueológico, Pesquero y Acuario** museum with sections relating to local artifacts, old and new methods of fishing, and a small aquarium. *The museum is open daily from 11:30am until 1:30pm and again from 4pm until 6pm in the winter and 6pm until 8pm in the summer. The price to get in is only 225 ptas.* Just above the town is a nice small cape with a functioning lighthouse and a ferry port with summertime service to the **Isla de Tabarca**.

Major Local Festivals

Contact the local Turismo office, *Tel. (96) 541-5911,* for more details.
• **Fiesta de Virgen**, *mid-July, Marine Processions*
• **Dia de Virgen María**, *September, Processions*

Torrevieja

Like so many of the nearby coastal towns, Torrevieja (population 17,150) was subjected to pirate raids and pillages during the 16th through 18th centuries. While hotels have cropped up along its beachfront, much of the town's economy is still derived from the production of salt from its lagoons and a large fishing fleet.

There are no real sights in town, but the nearby 18th century watchtowers at **Cabo de la Mata** and **Cabo Cervera**, once used to warn inhabitants of approaching pirate raiding ships, are worth a quick look. A short drive up the coast from here will reveal some of the more quiet and pristine beaches in the region.

Major Local Festivals

Contact the local *Turismo* office at *Tel. (96) 571-0722*, for more details.
• **Semana Santa**, *Processions*
• **Fiesta Habaneras**, *August, Processions*

PRACTICAL INFORMATION

• **Regional Tourist Office**, *Tourist Info, Explanada de España, Tel. (96) 521-2285*
• **Municipal Tourist Office**, *Turismo, Plaza del Ayuntamiento, 1, Tel. (96) 521-7835*

- **Alicante Airport**, *El Altet, Tel. (96) 528-5011 or (6) 520-6000*
- **Airport Bus Info**, *Alcoyana, Tel. (96) 526-7911*
- **Iberia Airlines**, *Tel. (96) 521-8510*
- **Regional Train Info**, *Renfe, Tel. (96) 522-6840 or (6) 592-0202*
- **Commuter Rail Info**, *FGV, Tel. (96) 526-2943*
- **Municipal Bus Info**, *Masatusa, Tel. (96) 520-6547*
- **Regional Bus Info**, *Estación de Autobuses, Tel. (96) 513-0143*
- **Morocco Ferry Info**, *Transmediterranea Lines, Tel. (96) 520-6011*
- **Morocco Ferry Info**, *Romeu Y Cia, Tel. (96) 514-1509*
- **Tabarca Ferry Info**, *Kontiki, (908) 762-118*
- **Alicante Radio Taxi Companies**, *Tel. (96) 510-1611 or (6) 525-2511*
- **Central Post Office**, *Plaza Gabriel Miró, Tel. (96) 520-2193*
- **Regional Directory Assistance**, *Tel. 1003*
- **National Directory Assistance**, *Tel. 1009*
- **Medical Emergencies Hot Line**, *Tel. 085*
- **National Police**, *Tel. (96) 522-1100*
- **Municipal Police**, *Tel. (96) 510-4711*

Alicante's Major Festivals

Contact the local Turismo office *at Tel. (96) 521-7853,* for more details.

- **Fiesta San Juan**, *late June, Parade of Floats and Bonfires*
- **Fiesta San Pedro**, *late June, Fireworks*

JÁVEA

(Xábia)

Jávea, situated about 29 kilometers (19 miles) northeast of Calpe, is one of my favorite beachfront resort areas in the Costa Blanca due to the fact that the development of seaside hotels and related tourism industries was carried out in a rather tasteful way. Jávea is a small city bordered by 24 kilometers (15 miles) of picture perfect crescent-shaped beaches.

ARRIVALS & DEPARTURES

Jávea is located 10 kilometers (6 miles) southeast of Denia along the infamous winding N-332 coastal road. The city itself rests in a valley surrounded on either side by rocky cliffs that in turn end at the sea where they become the dramatic Cabo Nao and the Cabo de San Antonio capes. Your approach into the city takes you down a softly sloping valley, backed by the towering 753 meter (2470 foot) Montgo peak behind it, through a maze of small lanes that end up a few kilometers later in front of the beautiful Platja del Arenal beach.

WHERE TO STAY

Expensive

HOTEL VILLA MEDITERRÁNEA, *Calle Leon, 5. Jávea. Tel. (96) 579-5233, Fax (96) 579-4581. Low season rack rates from 25,000 ptas per double room per night (B.P.). High season rack rates from 39,000 ptas per double room per night (B.P.). All major credit cards accepted.*

For several months before my most recent trip to Spain I had been hearing rumors that Jávea finally had a unique little five-star luxury hotel, but nothing prepared me for the opulence and beauty of this simply amazing small luxury hotel and gourmet restaurant. The hotel, hundreds of years ago, was a mansion, but was recently redesigned by a charming jazz singer from Germany named Ursula Rockstedt, who along with her husband, built their dreams into a reality. The Villa Mediterranea is dramatically situated in the hills, facing the seashore, just above town, resting below the huge Montgo mountain. It's about a five minute drive away from Jávea's main beach area. The wonderfully converted mansion is full of fine antiques and stunning original works of art, and the entire property is surrounded by lush semi-tropical gardens full of singing birds, fruit bearing plants, and towering cypress trees.

The hotel offers seven exquisite rooms and suites that all feature deluxe dual basin private marble bathrooms, remote control satellite television with video machines and movie channels, air conditioning and heating systems, mini-bar, mini-safe, local *azulejos* tiles and tapestries, direct dial telephone, comfortable custom designed beds and furnishings, and in a few cases even a private Jacuzzi or a working wood burning fireplace. Every aspect of these superb accommodations has been lovingly created to make sure that you will feel at home from the instant that you arrive, and that you will want to stay here forever.

Besides offering a truly spectacular restaurant (see separate review below) and delicious 24-hour room service, this amazing little hotel also features an outdoor swimming pool with a tranquil sun-deck and luncheon terrace, a glass enclosed indoor swimming pool, a sauna, a health club, optional massages, a brand new jazz club with scheduled live entertainment, plenty of free parking, and a breakfast that will start your day off on the right foot. Service here is top notch, with a multinational staff that will be glad to offer their advice on local outings and nearby sights. This is one of the better new hotels in the country, and although it's quite refined, it is also friendly and casual. See review under "Best Places to Stay" (Chapter 13).

PARADOR DE JÁVEA, *Playa del Arenal, Jávea. Tel. (96) 579-0200, Fax (96) 579-0308. US & Canada bookings (Marketing Ahead), Tel. 800/223-1356. Low season rack rates from 12,000 ptas per double room per night (E.P.).*

High season rack rates from 19,500 ptas per double room per night (E.P.). All major credit cards accepted.

This modern four-star parador is one of the best affordable beachfront hotel in all of Jávea. The six floor structure is sold out for months in advance during the highest season, and is the home away from home for hundreds of repeat guests from Spain, Germany, England, France and America. This relaxing property features 130 large Mediterranean style rooms (almost all have great sea view terraces) which contain private bathrooms, Mexican tile floors, remote control satellite television, mini-bar, hair dryer, direct dial telephone, whitewashed walls, air conditioning and bleached pine furnishings. Facilities here include direct access to a great beach, huge palm tree gardens with walking paths out on the seaside break-wall, plenty of sun chairs, a fully equipped business meeting room, a nice outdoor swimming pool, free parking, and a very good regional restaurant. The service here is good, and the guests are treated particularly well.

Moderate

HOTEL VILLA NARANJOS, *Carretera del Montanar, Jávea. Tel. (96) 579-0050, Fax (96) 646-0661. Low season rack rates from 5,750 ptas per double room per night (B.P.). High season rack rates from 11,500 ptas per double room per night (B.P.). All major credit cards accepted.*

Situated only 100 meters from the main town beach, this reasonably good three-star hotel has 147 simply furnished rooms (some with sea-view) that all have patios, air conditioning, color television, and telephone. Mostly used by families that stay on their heavily discounted week long full board packages, this hotel also has a large outdoor pool, free parking, and a restaurant.

WHERE TO EAT

Expensive

RESTAURANTE VILLA MEDITERRÁNEA, *Calle Leon, 5. Jávea. Tel. (96) 579-5233. All major credit cards accepted.*

Nestled in the hills just above Javea and its great beaches, this fine inn features a spectacular restaurant that is well worth the effort to dine in, even if you are staying a hour's drive away.

Chef Javier Azpitarte and his kitchen staff have worked hard to create a fusion of local Spanish and international cuisine and present their dishes with both class and innovation. While seated at large white linen covered tables in the sea-view dining room, patrons here are presented with an outstanding menu featuring wonderfully prepared delicacies as local fish soup with saffron for 1,750 *ptas*, lobster bisque at 1,950 *ptas*, warm partridge on a bed of salad for 2,160 *ptas*, home made foie gras with truffles at 2,850 *ptas*, monkfish and scampi in red currant vinaigrette for 2,750 *ptas*, ostrich medallions in port wine at 2,750 *ptas*, duck breast in sherry for 2,700 *ptas* and an full range of freshly baked breads and desserts. They also have a superb wine list featuring over 100 Spanish wines from all the great regions and vintages. The service here is truly impressive, with a young and helpful staff that smile and say hello in whatever language you prefer. A great place for a casual lunch by the pool terrace, or a more dressy evening out with friends or family.

Moderate
     RESTAURANTE CLUB NAUTICO, *Club Nautico de Jávea, Puerto de Jávea, Jávea. Tel. (96) 646-0614. Most major credit cards accepted.*
     If you want to try some of the Costa Blanca's most fresh and delicious seafood at lunch or dinner time, head for the marina and stop by this friendly little water-side restaurant. Popular with international yachtsmen and local businessmen alike, this is a great place to enjoy a great reasonably priced meal and get a serious sun tan at the same time. The restaurant has about 12 indoor tables and about 16 outdoor al fresco tables complete with white linen tablecloths that are embroidered with maritime symbols.
     Specialties of the house include gazpacho, a rich fish soup, mixed salads, asparagus in spiced mayonnaise, grilled sardines, dried hake in spicy pil-pil sauce, assorted paellas, grilled whole sole with sautéed garlic, local shrimp in garlic oil, and grilled entrecote of beef with red peppers and Roquefort cheese . After one meal here I can all but guarantee that you will want to buy a boat and become a yachtsman yourself. A great location and good service make this a must for anyone in Javea on a sunny day. They also offer breakfasts. You'll pay around 4,150 *ptas* per person for a giant four course seafood based meal here, plus drinks.

SEEING THE SIGHTS
     Start at the beautiful **Platja del Arenal** beach. The 800 meter (1/2 mile) stretch of soft white sand is bordered by a cozy array of low rise restaurants and cafes to its back, and by a rocky outcrop and a wonderful palm lined breakwater on either side. Fairly quiet until either Easter or Summer comes along, this beach is used in the low season mainly by Spanish tourists that have been coming here for years, and in the high season by different people of all ages from around the globe.
     Just behind the cafes and restaurants at the sand's edge are a series of quaint boutiques that sell beachwear, designer suits, jewelry and souvenirs. Make sure to walk along the northern border of the beach and cross over a small canal to pass by the wonderful **Parador de Jávea** hotel and restaurant. Here you can access its walking paths that take you past

the palm tree gardens lining the beach until you reach the breakwater. There is a great view of the nearby capes from this spot.

From the beach, continue another 2 kilometers (1.5 miles) north along the coast until you reach the **Puerto de Jávea** marina area. This area features the new **Ofradia de Pescadores** wholesale fish market where daily fresh seafood auctions are held daily, but unfortunately not open to the public. The **Paseo Maritimo** walkway is also here though, where you can find the **Club Nautico de Jávea,** home to hundreds of fine sail and power boats. You'll also see the local fishing fleet, and a superb sailing school where you can learn to sail in almost no time at all. The port area has a tourist information kiosk, a nice marina-view restaurant that serves freshly caught fish and seafood, a few pubs, and a huge breakwater that has a walking path above it with an excellent panoramic view.

From the port, visitors should take the effort to stroll through the **Casco Historico** (old city center) which contains countless Gothic porticos, cast iron railings, antique ceramic murals and fine old mansions converted into boutiques and art galleries. The best place to begin your walking journey is to head off to the central **Placa de L'Esglesia** square which is surrounded by centuries old buildings and mansions. I suggest your first stop should be at the **Turismo** tourist information center on the side entrance of the old city hall building to pick up one of several free walking tour maps. Just steps away in the center of the same square is the Gothic-Isabeline 14th-16th century **Iglesia-Forteleza de San Bartolome** church/fortress that is open free daily during normal mass hours.

Adjacent to the church tower is a fine Gothic oval portal that once was the sight of the entrance to an old marketplace known as the **Mercado de Abastos**. A block or so away from the plaza is the extremely interesting **Museo Arquelogico i Etnografic Solar Blasco** which is housed in an ornate 17th century former nobleman's mansion on the Calle Primicies #1. The museum contains artifacts from prehistoric, Roman, Medieval , Moorish, and Christian periods which were excavated near here including a famous collection of jewelry that was stashed away inside a clay pot that was unearthed nearby. *The museum is open daily from 10:00am until 1:00pm and in the summer it opens again from about 5:00pm until 9:00pm with no entrance fee.*

Other interesting buildings in the same general zone include the 16th century **Capella de Santa Anna** church whose facade can be found off the nearby Calle d'Avall, and several gothic homes which are still in private hands but can be appreciated from the outside along streets such as the Calle de Sor Maria Gallart and the Calle de Sor Catalina Bas. Besides all of the above sights there are several more great beaches if you want a swim, such as the Platja de la Barraca, Platja de la Granadella, and the Platja d'Ambolo (used by nudists). The city center also has plenty of bustling side streets full of great boutiques, small restaurants, discotechs, and art galleries to explore. There is also a great outdoor **Mercado** marketplace on the edge of the downtown core in the Plaza de Constitutiorial each Thursday from 7am until 2pm or so. Short drives up and down the coast will also lead to lovely lookout points and the chance to see all sorts of natural scenery.

NIGHTLIFE & ENTERTAINMENT

Most of the better bars and pubs are found just behind the **Platja del Arenal** beach shopping zone. Here you can pop into the classy **Champagne** cocktail bar, the **Octopus** pub, the **Surf Bar** club, and several other small disco-pubs. Just outside of the center is a large mega-disco called **Rico's**.

SPORTS & RECREATION

- **Club Nautico Sailing School**, *Tel. (96) 579-1025*
- **Amigos del Mar Scuba Center**, *Tel. (96) 579-1845*
- **Jávea Golf Club**, *Tel. (96) 579-2584*
- **Centro Hipico Horseback Riding**, *Tel. (96) 597-4021*
- **Euro Charter Yacht Rentals**, *Tel. (96) 579-4420*

PRACTICAL INFORMATION

- **Tourist Information**, *Tel. (96) 579-4356*
- **Police**, *Tel. (96) 579-0081*
- **Ambulance**, *Tel. (96) 579-1961*
- **Renfe Trains**, *Tel. (96) 578-0445*
- **Ubesa Buses**, *Tel. (96) 579-0845*
- **Taxi**, *Tel. (96) 579-1060*

Major Local Festivals

Contact the local Turismo office, *Tel. (96) 579-4356,* for more details.
- **Semana Santa**, *Easter Week, Parades and Parties*
- **Fiesta de San Juan**, *Late June, Dancing, Parades, Bull Runs*
- **Fiesta del Viegen Loreto**, *Early September, Fireworks, Floral Parades*
- **Santo Lucia**, *Mid-December, Processions*

LA MANGA (DE LA MAR MENOR)

The resort area of **La Manga** is located on the **Murcia** region's southeastern coast, some 468 kilometers southeast of Madrid, and just about 92 kilometers (54 miles) south of Alicante. If you arrive in La Manga during any time other than the summer, you might think that you're in a ghost town. During high season, this small piece of land dividing the Mediterranean Sea from a small semi-enclosed saltwater lake is packed beyond belief with singles, couples, and families from all over Spain and Europe. There are several nice beaches on both coasts, as well as a good variety of small local fishing villages and seaside resort complexes.

ARRIVALS & DEPARTURES

By Air

Although Murcia's small regional airport at San Javier can be used for those flying in on either charter flights or regional Spanish airliners, most passengers arriving from North America will find themselves flying into the further away international airports at Alicante or Almeria. From these more distant airports, taxis can cost upwards of 11,750 *ptas* (or more) to get here, so I suggest either renting a car, taking a municipal bus from these city's centers, or arranging a private transfer from the hotel that you intend to stay in while in La Manga.

By Car

From Madrid you can follow the N-IV highway south for some 40 kilometers (25 miles), and just after the city of Aranjuez exit on to the smaller route N-301 south for about 413 kilometers (256 miles) until it ends near Cartagena, where you will merge onto the coastal route N-332 north for about 16 kilometers (10 miles) before reaching the La Manga area. If instead you are coming from Alicante you can take the coastal route N-332 south for about 111 kilometers (69 miles) until reaching La Manga.

By Train

The closest major Renfe train stations to La Manga are located in Cartagena and Murcia. From these stations it is best to either rent a car or to arrange transfers by sedan in advance from the hotel you will be checking into. You can also take a regional bus for between 800 and 1750 *ptas* (see below), or a taxi which can cost upwards of 4,500 *ptas* from Cartagena or perhaps as much as 9,750 *ptas* or more from Murcia. Please check with your nearest Renfe station or ticket office for this season's specific price and schedule information.

By Bus

Private bus lines such as Egea, Entacar, and Garcia operate on a daily basis via either connections or direct service from Madrid, Barcelona, Murcia, Cartagena, Alicante, and Almeria. Check with the closest major bus station in the area you wish to depart from for specific details.

ORIENTATION

To avoid confusion, please keep in mind that the super posh **La Manga Club** resort with its world class golf and tennis clubs is actually located in a lavish a self contained resort area some 7 kilometers west of the La Manga strip. Busy all year round, the La Manga Club resort is a deluxe vacation zone and as such has a much, much higher standard of accommodations, sports facilities, and restaurants.

WHERE TO STAY

Expensive

HYATT REGENCY LA MANGA, *La Manga Club Resort. Tel. (968) 331-234, Fax (968) 331-235. US & Canada Bookings: (Hyatt) 800/233-1234. Low season rack rates from 36,000 ptas per double room per night (E.P.). High season rack rates from 38,000 ptas per double room per night (E.P.). Special sports & leisure packages are available upon request. All major credit cards accepted.*

Located just a few minutes drive away from the popular beach area of La Manga, this superb world class golf, tennis, and casino resort is an excellent five-star hotel and sporting center. The Hyatt Regency is situated in the heart of the world famous La Manga Club Resort which is bordered by both the sea and a peaceful mountain valley on over 1,400 acres of beautifully landscaped gardens planted with olive trees, bougain-villea, and palms. This outstanding oasis of true luxury and hospitality is one of my favorite places to stay when I really want to get away from all the stress and strains of city living.

The hotel itself is contained in a beautiful pastel colored, three story, Mediterranean style building that is embellished with a seemingly endless array of fine marbles, Moorish style stone carvings, regional ceramic tiles, Romanesque archways, cast iron chandeliers, a collection of original Spanish works of art, and comfortable public rooms. The property boasts 192 stunningly decorated rooms and suites (including some specially designed for the physically challenged) which all contain private marble bathrooms, golf course or pool view balconies, individually controlled air conditioning systems, remote control satellite television with multilingual movie channels and pay per view feature films (and a new internet access system), a well stocked mini-bar, electronic mini-safe, executive style desks, direct dial telephones, 24-hour room service and fine double or king-sized beds.

Within the general area of the main hotel building itself there is a new 2,500 square meter casino, a wonderful free form heated outdoor swimming pool with sun deck, four separate, casual gourmet dining establishments, a tranquil library and game room with a working fireplace, a bar and grill that doubles as a live music venue and dance club (a great spot to party on weekend nights), a beauty salon, several high-end boutiques and logo shops, a concierge where you can easily book excursions and various scheduled (high season) daily activities, car rental services, plenty of free parking, express laundry and dry cleaning services, an international newsstand and tobacconist and elegant and well equipped business meeting or private reception rooms (with a combined total capacity of over 400 occupants).

The reason many guests choose the Hyatt Regency is for its outstanding range of specialized sports and recreation facilities. Accessible by foot, car, or complimentary shuttle service, the property's world class sport and recreation areas include three of Spain's best championship 18 hole golf courses where golf clinics and private pro training at all skill levels are offered all year round, the La Manga Club Tennis Center where you can play a few matches on one of 18 courts and even improve your game with the help of a professionally staffed tennis academy, a private cove beach with complimentary beach chairs and a romantic tropical al fresco dining patio. There are also five different outdoor European football pitches, a large health club with computerized workout gear as well as sauna and Jacuzzi (and a full range of available therapeutic massages), a pitch and putt course, mini golf, a year-round children's activity club, two more beautiful swimming pools, pro shops, optional mountain bike rentals and affiliated nearby horse back riding and water-sports centers.

Public rooms here include an opulent marble lobby with plush designer sofas and fabulous tapestries, and a tranquil library with a working fireplace. During meal times, guests can choose to dine in one of several restaurants including the romantic and more formal Amapola dining room, the Bar 37 golf course snack-bar, the Andale Mexican restaurant, the romantic seaside La Cala open air restaurant, a nice little Deli and snack shop, Luigi's pasta and pizza restaurant, the Sol y Sombra pool side dining terrace, the richly decorated yet casual Lorca lounge and piano bar, the top floor terrace which is home to a weekly (high season) buffet barbecue with live entertainment, the Biblioteca library and cigar bar, and the lively Spike's bar and grill where good live music draws in lively crowds on weekend nights.

Service here is top rate, with an internationally trained multilingual staff who goes well out of its way to assure that every guest can't wait to return. If you are looking for a truly deluxe resort with more than enough facilities and luxury to keep anyone more than busy for over a week, this is the place to go. Selected as one of my "Best Places to Stay" (see Chapter 13).

Moderate

LAS LOMAS APARTAMENTOS, *La Manga Club Resort. Tel. (968) 137-234, Fax (968) 137-272. US & Canada Bookings (Hyatt) 800/233-1234. Low season rack rates from 16,500 ptas per studio apartment per night (E.P.). High season rack rates from 18,200 ptas per studio apartment per night (E.P.). Special Weekend rates from 12,000 ptas per studio apartment per night (E.P.). All major credit cards accepted.*

Las Lomas is an extremely attractive four-star Mediterranean-style mini-village that contains some 60 oversized deluxe studio,one, two, and three bedroom apartments. Located just a few minutes ride from the sea on the edge of the La Manga Club resort, this great family oriented property is operated by Hyatt although several units are also sold as timeshare apartments. Here you can rent nicely furnished apartments with full kitchens including dishwashers and laundry machines, remote control satellite televisions with video cassette players, marble lined private bathrooms, individually controlled air conditioning and heating systems, heated towel racks, direct dial telephones, a selection of bedding and sofa beds, and private patios with charcoal fired barbecues that overlook the Hyatt Regency's PGA golf courses as well as the distant seaside.

There is plenty of free parking, a huge outdoor heated swimming pool, video rental facilities, a good international mini-market and delicatessen, a Chinese restaurant, and an Italian dining room, as well as a poolside snack-bar. Guests here have complete access to all of the facilities of the Hyatt La Manga Club Resort including golf, tennis and health club privileges. If you want plenty of space, a mplace for your kids to have as much fun as the adults, twice weekly maid service, and the ability to do some of your own cooking, this is a great choice.

HOTEL LOS DELFINES, *Plaza Europa, La Manga del Mar Menor. Tel. (968) 145-300, Fax (968) 145-415. Low season rack rates from 9,000 ptas per double room per night (A.I.). High season rack rates from 17,000 ptas per double room per night (A.I.). All major credit cards accepted.*

This three-star, pastel-colored apart-hotel is shaped like a pyramid and situated just off the Gran Via in a small plaza just a minute's walk away from a shallow beach area. This is one of Spain's only "all inclusive" resorts and as such includes three decent buffet style meals per day and unlimited cocktails in their room prices. The 160 rooms come in different styles, but most have small hideaway kitchenettes, balconies with city or limited sea views, simple wooden furnishings, remote control cable television, direct dial telephone, ceiling fans, mini-safe, and private bathrooms. While the food here is far from gourmet, it is still a good value for the money, and in some cases you may be able to persuade the front desk to rent you a room with either breakfast only or with half board at lower prices than listed above. The hotel also has a small swimming pool, outdoor parking, a garage, business meeting rooms, scheduled daily activities, a cafe bar, a nice marble lobby area with lounges and a nice staff. The hotel is favored by English and German package vacation guests.

HOTEL CAVANNA, *Gran Via, La Manga del Mar Menor. Tel. (968) 563-600, Fax (968) 654-431. Low season rack rates from 5,400 ptas per double room per night (E.P.). High season rack rates from 12,000 ptas per double room per night (E.P.). All major credit cards accepted.*

The Cavanna is a massive 10 floor modern waterside hotel that is among the busiest places to stay in the area. While far from deluxe, it has a dedicate clientele from all over Europe that come here for the views and the large number of in- house facilities. This four-star hotel features 408 good sized rooms that all have private bathroom, air conditioning, cable television, direct dial telephone, mini-safe and balconies with either city or sea views. The hotel also offers a windsurfing and sailing schools, two swimming pools, a beach club with sun chair rentals, a kids play area, three tennis courts, an English pub, a buffet restaurant, daily scheduled activities in the high season, health club, sauna, free parking, optional spa services, business meeting rooms and several boutiques. The hotel is mostly used by large bus tours.

HOTEL DOBLEMAR, *Gran Via, La Manga del Mar Menor. Tel. (968) 563-910, Fax (968) 563-833. US & Canada bookings: (UTELL), Tel. 800/44-UTELL. Low season rack rates from 8,250 ptas per double room per night (E.P.). High season rack rates from 11,800 ptas per double room per night (E.P.). All major credit cards accepted.*

As the largest hotel along the La Manga strip, the Husa Hotel Doblemar gets rather busy with both groups and individuals during the high season. This giant four-star seafront property has 484 large rooms and suites, each with private bathroom, cable television, direct dial telephone, mini-safe and balconies with either city or sea views. The hotel also offers a casino, a nice outdoor swimming pool, a dark sandy beach area with sun chair rentals, a buffet restaurant, daily scheduled activities in the high season, health club, sauna, free parking, business meeting rooms and several boutiques.

Inexpensive

SOL ELITE GALUA HOTEL, *Hacienda dos Mares, La Manga. Tel. (968) 563-200, Fax (968) 140-630. US & Canada bookings: (Melia), Tel. 800/ 33-MELIA. Internet: www. sol.elite.galua@solmelia.es. Low season rack rates from 3,725 ptas per double room per night (B.P.). High season rack rates from 10,700 ptas per double room per night (B.P.). All major credit cards accepted.*

The modern nine floor Sol Galua sea front hotel is a decent place to spend your time while in this area. The whitewahed concrete four-star hotel is located near the *Plaza Bohemia* and features some 177 air conditioned sea view rooms (most with patios) that all have private bathrooms, simple furnishings, satellite color televisions, and direct dial telephones. There is also a restaurant, adult and children's outdoor swimming pools, boutiques, beauty salon, car rental and excursion desk, supervised children's programs in the high season, free outdoor parking, nearby windsurfing rentals and lessons, and available tennis and golf club access. While not quite deluxe, this is a reasonably good buy for it's price range and location.

HOTEL DOS MARES, *Plaza Bohemia, La Manga del Mar Menor. Tel. (968) 140-093, Fax (968) 104-455. Low season rack rates from 5,750 ptas per double room per night (E.P.). High season rack rates from 8,750 ptas per double room per night (E.P.). Most major credit cards accepted.*

Located close to the sea and just off this central urban plaza, this small two-star hotel offers 28 rooms with private bathroom, air conditioning, direct dial telephone, and simple but comfortable furnishings. Although nothing special, it's a good choice for those on tight budgets.

WHERE TO EAT

Expensive

RESTAURANT AMAPOLA (HYATT REGENCY LA MANGA), *Los Belones, La Manga. Tel. (968) 331-234. All major credit cards accepted.*

The Hyatt Regency's most opulent and highly regarded dining establishment is the beautiful La Amapola restaurant located just above the resort's south golf course in the main hotel building. This impressive gourmet establishment is among the best restaurants along the *Costa Calida* and features a talented team of Murcian chefs that really know how to prepare delicious regional specialties.

The menu here changes each season, but during my last dinner here the kitchen staff prepared several amazing dishes including a roasted vegetable salad, cream of asparagus soup with morsels of crab, a magnificent lobster paella, chicken breast marinated in local fresh herbs and then grilled with lemon and peppers , seared red mullet filets with pine nuts, pan fried Spanish beef tenderloin, and a dessert trolley that will knock you right off your diet with just one look. They have popular Saturday and Sunday buffet lunches, an extensive wine list, and a great affordable weekday lunch menu packed with local specialties. Expect to pay around 5,950 *ptas* a person for a giant four-course seafood based meal here, plus drinks.

Moderate

RESTAURANTE ALBATROS, *Cabo de Palos, La Manga. Tel. (968) 564-897. All major credit cards accepted.*

This quaint converted farmhouse in the fishing village of Cabo de Palos near the beginning of the La Manga strip is home to the one of the best casual restaurants in the region. It has a traditional Spanish white-washed interior complete with exposed wooden beams, a working fire-place, and a dozen or so cozy candlelit tables. The Albatros has been owned and operated by a pair of charming Belgians for over 15 years and they really know how to run a welcoming place in which to enjoy a special meal. Their wonderful menu of local and continental specialties are delicious, proving once again that the Belgians are among Europe's best chefs!

A seasonal menu might feature gazpacho, seafood soup, tropical salad with fresh fruits, melon with cured ham, home made pate, salmon and spinach crepes, prawns in garlic oil, paella, filet of sole meuniere, grilled swordfish, breast of duck in orange sauce, lamb chops and a wonderful selection of desserts and regional wines. The outdoor summer terrace is the place to go on hot nights. A typical four course meal will cost about 4,650 *ptas* a person plus drinks.

SEEING THE SIGHTS

Approximate duration (by car) is about 4.5 hours including beach, fishing village, and side street visits.

The La Manga area itself is a thriving, if way too overdeveloped, resort community comprized of several adjoining towns. These adjacent towns are located along both sides of a wide avenue known as the **Gran Via** which runs roughly alongside a sandy 26 kilometer (16 mile) strip of land that divides the shallow protected waters of the **Mar Menor** saltwater lake from the crashing waves of the Mediterranean sea. Since it is surrounded on both sides by fine beaches fronted by hundreds of high rise hotel and condo complexes offering a vast assortment of water sports, this is one of the most busy resorts in the whole Murcia region during Easter as well as the entire summer season. It is during these times that upper-middle class residents from Madrid and other major Spanish cities return to their summer homes and apartments around here, while other European tourists fill up most available hotel rooms and rental apartments. Local bus service from the Mar Menor Bus company can get you from point to point via well marked bus shelters along the entire strip, but at night a taxi will be your only option to get back to your hotel.

Make sure to pop into the local *Turismo* office on the main road in the Castillo del Mar condo complex. They will be glad to assist in creating an itinerary to follow, or suggest activities to suit your needs. The majority of the action here during summer and the crazed Easter week known as Semana Santa which takes place along the beach front esplanades and their adjoining plazas on either side of this thin strip of land. At night, dozens of restaurants, discos, and the Hotel Doblemar's **Casino** just off the Gran Via are hopping, while there are smaller bars and cafés centered around the appropriately named **Plaza Bohemia** and the amusing entertainment complex known as the **Zoco**.

For those interested in experiencing the more luxurious side of this general area, head west from the strip for 7 kilometers (4.2 miles) to reach the super elegant **La Manga Club** resort. This seperate and completely different self-contained resort community is home to villas belonging to the rich and famous, some of the country's finest golf, tennis, football, and horseback riding facilities, superb gourmet restaurants, as well as the beautiful Hyatt Regency hotel.

During the slow low season here, the weather is quite warm but the only other people you are bound to run into at this time are the fishermen that live and work along the Paseo la Barra walkway in the rustic harbor of **Cabo de Palos**. This is still a quaint traditional fishing village and a Sunday market town just on La Manga's southern tip.

NIGHTLIFE & ENTERTAINMENT

Most of the better bars and pubs are found just in a small low rise complex of shops and restaurants called the *Zoco* just a few kilometers up from the beginning of the La Manga strip. Here you will find the **Pub Planta Baja**, the **C$** dsico, the **Y Punto**, the **Precinto Playa** disco pub, the **Zeppelin** rock club, and the **Barra de Baron** dance club, and plenty of ethnic food restaurants. Another late night dancing club called the **Cayo Coco** can be found just off the **Plaza Cavanna** square. Those interested in gambling can pop inside the **Casino de Mar Menor** located in the Hotel Doblemar where for a 600 *ptas* entrance fee which includes one free cocktail (you must bring a passport to enter) and will allow you to access blackjack, poker, roulette, and slots from 8:00pm until 3:00am or so daily.

SPORTS & RECREATION
- **La Manga Resort Golf Club**, *Tel. (968) 175-000*
- **La Manga Resort Tennis Club**, *Tel. (968) 175-000*
- **Aquasport Watersports**, *Tel. (968) 145-193*
- **Vela International Sailing School**, *Tel. (968) 437-059*
- **Nautic Center Sailing School**, *Tel. (968) 141-787*
- **Centro de Buceo Scuba Center**, *Tel. (968) 145-475*
- **Isla Hormigas Scuba School**, *Tel. (968) 145-530*
- **Centro Hipico Horseback Riding**, *Tel. (968) 137-305*
- **Cavana WIndsurfing**, *Tel. (968) 563-600*
- **Manga Surf WIndsurf Rentals**, *Tel. (968) 145-331*
- **Pedruchillo Watersports**, *Tel. (968) 140-002*

VISIT THE PLAYA DE CALBLANQUE

From the beginning of the La Manga strip follow the MU-312 highway west for a bit more than 5 kilometers. Exit at "Los Belones", and go all the way around the traffic circle to re-enter the MU-312 highway east (back towards La Manga). At the next exit # 13 marked "Calblanque" get off the road and about 50 meters later make a right turn down the dirt road signposted towards "Calblanque."

Upon turning down this unpaved road (go slow!) you will enter the **Espacio Natural Protegido Calblanque** *nature reserve. A small house another hundred meters down the road is home to the park's visitor information office which is a good place to get a local map with details about several nature walks and local wildlife. After visiting the information center, continue along the same dirt road for another kilometer or so until the road forks. Take the right fork marked "Playas" and keep going until you reach yet another fork in the road where this time you will bear left. Watch out for slow moving rabbits and lizards as you proceed down this bumpy road for another one and a half kilometers until you finally reach a parking area where you will leave your car and walk down the pathway to the* **Playa Larga de Calblanque** *beach.*

This beach is a wonderful spot that is known only by locals, therefore only a handful of people usually can be found along its one kilometer long, straight stretch of fine white sand. Sometimes visited by topless and nude bathers (illegal here but nobody will notice), the only thing that may disturb you are the occasional F-14 air force fighter jets that zip by at supersonic speed every so often. There are other beaches such as the **Playa de las Canas** *to the right of this larger one, and plenty of adjacent walking trails where you can see all kinds of granite mountains, cacti, wildlife, and various wild plants. Make sure to bring plenty of water, and don't expect any cafes, bars, or bathrooms within walking distance since the area is devoid of all development. For those interested, a pair of local brothers offer great horseback rides through this enchanted park (ask for details at either the visitor information center or from the conceirge at the Hyatt Regency La Manga). If the visitor information center is closed you can get some general park information by calling the regional parks department in Murcia, Tel. (968) 362-512.*

EXCURSIONS & DAY TRIPS

From La Manga, the coastal area known as the **Costa Calida** decends southwest for 105 km (65 miles) as it passes by the city of **Cartagena** and several fishing villages, small resort communities, and enjoyable beach areas such as **Mojácar**. Inland there are a few more historic cities, such as

Murcia and **Lorca**, that are also worth a visit if you have the time. Each of these towns is treated below as a separate destination in their own right.

PRACTICAL INFORMATION
- **Tourist Information**, *Tel. (968) 141-812*
- **Police**, *Tel. (968) 563-114*
- **Ambulance**, *Tel. (968) 142-060*
- **Renfe Trains**, *Tel. (968) 502-214*
- **Egea Buses**, *Tel. (968) 502-018*
- **Garcia Buses**, *Tel. (968) 291-911*
- **Enatcar Buses**, *Tel. (968) 564-811*
- **Taxi**, *Tel. (968) 563-039*

Major Local Festivals
Contact the local Turismo office, *Tel. (968) 141-812*, for more exact details.
- **Semana Santa**, *Easter Week, Parties*

CARTAGENA

An easy 21 kilometer (13 mile) trip southwest from La Manga, the port city of **Cartagena** (population 173,790) is a great place to see historic sights and enjoy a variety of *tapas*.

Originally founded by the Carthaginians in the 3rd century B.C, there are still some traces of it's later Roman occupation scattered all around town. Since the city is home to a naval academy and a few military establishments including a huge antique armory, there are usually hundreds of polite off-duty sailors wandering around the streets on any given day. There are many fine Roman and Byzantine- era sights located on various side streets and near some of the major plazas throughout the city. Many of these dramatic historical landmarks just look like partially excavated plots surrounded by chain link fences with absolutely no indications as to what they really are.

ARRIVALS & DEPARTURES
To drive to Cartagena from La Manga, take route MU-312 west for about 8 kilometers until merging onto route N-332 south.

Bus service to all the above points can be accessed from the La Manga area via transfers at Cartagena's two main bus stations. Please check with your destination's tourist office for more information. Daily scheduled buses between Lorca, Murcia, Almeria, Cartagena, Valencia, Alicante, and other points are serviced by either the Enatcar bus company, *Tel. (968) 441-107,* or the Alsina Graells bus company, *Tel. (968) 441-961.*

Trains to and from most of the above coastal areas can be boarded on a daily basis year-round at Cartagena's Renfe train station on the Avenida de America and cost somewhere around 650 *ptas* or less to reach any point listed above. Lorca's main rail station, *Tel. (968) 466-998,* services many cities throughout Spain such as Barcelona, Alicante, and Valencia, and is located just two blocks below the central Avenida Juan Carlos. Call Renfe's central information line, *Tel. (968) 501-796,* for specific station departure locations and exact schedules during peak (summer) and off peak (winter) times.

WHERE TO STAY
Moderate
   HOTEL CARTAGENOVA, *Calle Marcos Redondo 3, Cartagena. Tel. (968) 504-200, Fax (968) 505-966. Year round rack rates from 12,100 ptas per double room per night (E.P.).*

This is one of the few accepteble modern hotels in the city center. This towering business style hotel has some 126 rooms with private bathrooms, direct dial telephones, color televisions, mini-safe and simple modern furnishings. Just steps away from the Navy barracks and the heart of the old section of downtown. They also offer an optional buffet breakfast, indoor garage, and several business related services. Nothing special but not a bad place to spend the night while visiting town.

SEEING THE SIGHTS
   The best place to start off a walking tour of town is over by the **Puerto** port area where there is plenty of parking for those of you that arrived by car. The sheltered bay port has been active since Roman times and is still the sight of many large commercial and military ships. The entire port area is fronted by the relics of a centuries old defensive wall known as the **Muralla de Alfonso XII** which have recently been converted into a wonderful palm tree lined prominade walkway. In an effort to attract mid-size cruise ships to Cartagena as a new European port of call for luxury liners, the local and regional governments are starting to spend serious money to beautify the city's entire downtown area starting from this port zone.

   At the far end of the port, a huge plaza called the **Plaza de la Ayuntamiento** (City Hall square) comes into view on your left side. This plaza is a great place to enter the older section of the city which is officially known as the **Casco Antigo**. As you enter the square you will immediately see the dramatic domed stone block facade of the old city hall called the **Palacio Consistorial** which is large enough to take up half the square itself. From the city hall building a wide pedestrian only commercial street called the **Calle Mayor** leads visitors directly through the heart of the city. Along the Calle Mayor you should keep your eyes open for several good restaurants, boutiques, and pubs, as well as a few historic structures. The most impressive buildings along the street are the art noveau **Palacio del Marques de Casatilly** palace on the left side at #13 that is now home to the members only Casino de Cartagena club.

Further into **Casco Antigo** section of the city there are plenty of other interesting sights to see including the **Restos Romana**, the remains of an old Roman street located just off the atmospheric Plaza de los Tres Reyes. Also worth a good look are the remains of the **Teatro Romano** Roman Theater just adjacent to the burnt out shell of the 15th century **Iglesia de la Santa María la Vieja** church off of Calle de la Baronessa. Don't forget to pop by the **Muralla Bizantina,** the remnants of Roman and Byzantine era walls located just off of the Calle de Soledad. The **Castillo** castle ruins are at the very top of the small mountain in the heart of the old town and are accessible from dozens of points within the old section of town. This hike requires a good deal of steep uphill walking to enter. Since renovations are ongoing at the Castle, there are no specific opening hours for this sight.

The town is full of hard to find relics, but take a half hour or so to peek inside one of the town's history museums. The **Museo Arqueológico Municipal** on the Calle Ramon y Cajal in the northwest corner of town several blocks above the major Plaza de España traffic circle is an interesting place, offering a comprehensive collection of locally found prehistoric, Roman, and medieval artifacts. *This museum is open Tuesday through Friday from 10am until 1pm and again from 4pm until 6pm, Weekends from 10am until 1pm only.*

From the museum, you can walk over to the unispiring modern **Plaza de España** and peek inside the turn of the century architectural masterpiece known as the **Casa Zapata** which has a fantastic Arabesque inner arcade. *This can be entered on weekdays from 10am until 1pm and again from 4pm until 6pm.*

From here, you can head back into the center of the downtown **Casco Antigo** and look for the central **Plaza de San Francisco** where there are several turn of the century mansions including the ornate **Casa Maestre**. From here, a series of small lanes, lined with cafés and boutiques spoke out through the downtown section. Several fine churches can be entered during mass hours including the 18th century **Iglesia de Santa María de Gracia** off the Calle San Miguel, which contains a fine carving of the four saints by Francisco Salzillo. If you can stand a good long walk, the **Parque Torres** park on the easternmost section of town is a good place to head. Within the park itself are the ruins of the 14th century **Castillo de la**

Concepcion, a castle with excellent views out over the old town and it's surroundings.

NIGHTLIFE & ENTERTAINMENT

The best bars and pubs are found at the edge of the *Casco Antigo* old town area along an old street called the *Calle de Cuatro Santos* and include the **Moger** bar, the **Ruta** pub, and disco bars such as **Ventana** and **Julias.**

PRACTICAL INFORMATION

- **Tourist Information,** *Tel. (968) 506-483*
- **Police,** *Tel. (968) 128-877*
- **Ambulance,** *Tel. (968) 502-750*
- **Renfe Trains,** *Tel. (968) 502-214*
- **Bus Station,** *Tel. (968) 505-656*
- **San Javier Airport,** *Tel. (956) 172-000*
- **Enatcar Buses,** *Tel. (968) 564-811*
- **Taxi,** *Tel. (968) 510-023*

Major Local Festivals

Contact the local Turismo office, *Tel. (9968) 506-483,* for more details.
- **Semana Santa,** *Easter Week, Processions*
- **Dia de Virgen,** *Mid-July, Processions*
- **Naval Cinema Week,** *November, Movie Screenings*

MURCIA

Located 46 kilometers (29 miles) northwest from Cartagena, the huge city of **Murcia** (population 305,340) is the capital of the Murcia province and region.

ARRIVALS & DEPARTURES

To drive here from Cartagena, take the fast N-301 highway north. From Murcia to Lorca, follow the N-340 road south. From Cartagena to Mojacar take the high speed E-15 highway south.

Bus service can be accessed from the La Manga area via transfers at Cartagena's two main bus stations. Check with your destination's tourist office for more information. Daily scheduled buses between Lorca, Murcia, Almeria, Cartagena, Valencia, Alicante and other points are serviced by either the Enatcar bus company, *Tel. (968) 441-107,* or the Alsina Graells bus company, *Tel. (968) 441-961.*

Trains to and from most of the coastal areas can be boarded on a daily basis year round at Cartagena's Renfe train station on the Avenida de America and cost somewhere around 650 *ptas* or less to reach any point listed above. Lorca's main rail station, *Tel. (968) 466-998*, services many cities throughout Spain such as Barcelona, Alicante, and Valencia, and is located two blocks below the central Avenida Juan Carlos. Call Renfe's central information line, *Tel. (968) 501-796*, for specific station departure locations and exact schedules during peak (summer) and off peak (winter) times.

SEEING THE SIGHTS

The best place to start your visit through town is at the massive **Catedral** off the Calle de Escultor Francisco Salzillo. Built between the 14th and 18th centuries, this impressive house of worship is world famous for it's Baroque main facade, huge adjacent bell and lantern tower, and fantastically vaulted ceilings of the 15th century Capilla de los Velez chapel. In the cathedral's chapter house and side chapels you can visit the **Museo Catedralicio** religious arts museum to see a number of handcrafted gold and silver pieces, including an enormous monstrance, antique tapestries, fine medieval paintings, and sculptures by locally born Francisco Sazillo. *The museum is open daily from 10am until 1pm and again from 5pm until 8pm, and admission is 125 ptas per person.*

From the cathedral, walk up for two blocks through the old part of town along the pedestrian only **Calle de la Traperia** until passing alongside the 19th century **Casino** which was later transfromed into an exclusive men's only social club. Make sure to get inside to see it's frescoed ballroom and ornate salons. Further up and into town you should make a point to enter the **Museo Salzillo** on the Calle de San Andres. This is the single largest collection of etchings and sculptures created by renown local artist Francisco Salzillo, and well over 750 items are on display. *This museum is open Tuesday through Sunday from 9:30am until 1pm, and again from 2:30pm until 6:30pm, and admission is 175 ptas.*

PRACTICAL INFORMATION

Major Local Festivals

Contact the Turismo office, *Tel. (968) 362-000*, for more details.
• **Semana Santa**, *Easter Week, Parades with Sazillo Sculptures*
• **Fiesta de Murcia**, *Early September, Folklore and Fairs*
• **Spanish Cinema Week**, *October, Movie Screenings*
• **Fiesta Musica**, *December, Concerts*

LORCA

The friendly medium-sized city of **Lorca** (population 68,280) can be found some 62 kilometers (38 miles) southwest from Murcia. There are a number of 16th through 19th century monumental buildings, surrounded by countless ten story modern apartment buildings in the city center. There are many cute little cafe-pubs and majestic old mansions. The only drawback for some, is that there is a limited choice of restaurants in town.

Make sure to keep you eyes out for shops that sell Lorca's beautiful silk and gold embroidery and wool carpets, of which the most famous creators are at **Tresiervos**, Calle de Rio Guadalentin 9.

ARRIVALS & DEPARTURES

To drive here from Murcia, follow the **N-340** road south.

Bus service can be accessed from the La Manga area via transfers at Cartagena's two main bus stations. Check with your destination's tourist office for more information. Daily scheduled buses between Lorca, Murcia, Almeria, Cartagena, Valencia, Alicante, and other points are serviced by either the Enatcar bus company, *Tel. (968) 441-107*, or the Alsina Graells bus company, *Tel. (968) 441-961.*

Trains to and from most of the coastal areas can be boarded on a daily basis year round at Cartagena's Renfe train station on the Avenida de America and cost somewhere around 650 *ptas* or less to reach any point listed above. Lorca's main rail station, *Tel. (968) 466-998*, services many cities throughout Spain such as Barcelona, Alicante, and Valencia, and is located two blocks below the central Avenida Juan Carlos. Call Renfe's central information line, *Tel. (968) 501-796*, for specific station departure locations and exact schedules during peak (summer) and off peak (winter) times.

WHERE TO STAY

Moderate

HOTEL AMALTEA, *Carretera de Granada. Tel. (968) 406-565, Fax (968) 406-989. Web Site: www.softly.es\turismo\sercoTel. Low season rack rates from 11,500 per double room per night (E.P.). High season rack rates from 15,100 per double room per night (E.P.).Special weekend rates from 9,800 per double room per night (E.P.). All major credit cards accepted.*

The brand new Amaltea is the city's most modern executive-class hotel. Situated about a three minute drive from the center of town, this great four-star hotel boasts 58 ultra modern and seriously comfortable rooms and suites that have private bathrooms, air conditioning, remote control satellite television, extremely comfortable bedding, mini-bar, electronic key pass locks, executive desks, hair dryer and mini-safe. The hotel offers a good restaurant, a relaxing café and lounge, plenty of business meeting rooms and conference facilities, a huge garden with three mini-lakes and a giant swimming pool with Jacuzzi, free parking, a nice friendly staff and the great weekend rates.

WHERE TO EAT

Moderate

RESTAURANTE TEATRO, *Plaza de Colon. Tel. (968) 469-909. Most major credit cards accepted.*

On most nights one of the chefs actually serves the guests at this nice, little place. The interior here, dotted by ceramic tiles and oil paintings, is reminiscent of an old world tavern, and there are only enough tables for about 35 patrons to dine at one time. The chefs prepare simple, delicious homemade Spanish/French cuisine, offered at extremely low prices for the quality of the food. Situated just steps away from the Teatro Guerra, this nicely decorated dining establishment is casual, quiet, and relaxing.

Their extensive menu features a wonderful vegetable soup, hearts of palm salad, garlic soup, York ham and Manchego cheese, delicious vegetarian paella, assorted pizzas, pork chops, steak tartare, pepper steak with potatoes, lamb cutlets and all sorts of seasonal fish dishes. The cost is around 3,250 *ptas* per person for a large three course meal here, plus drinks.

Inexpensive

TELEPIZZA, *Plaza de Oval 4. Tel. (968) 444-411. Cash only–no credit cards accepted.*

Whether your in the mood for a quick bite in the small dining room, or prefer to have them deliver a hot snack to your hotel, this is about the best pizza in town. The price is just 675 *ptas* for individual pizzas, 975 *ptas* for medium pizzas, or 1600 *ptas* for family sized pizzas, plus about 155 *ptas* for extra toppings. There is a 2 for 1 offer every day so that you get 2 of the above (excluding the smallest size) for the same price if you ask for it, at no additional cost.

SEEING THE SIGHTS

All the roads entering town pass the central traffic circle known as the **Plaza de Ovalo**, so it makes sense to use this small round plaza as a starting base to explore downtown . From the circle (with your back to the Telepizza restaurant), turn left down the main commercial avenue here called the **Avenida de Juan Carlos I**. Lined on both sides by towering office buildings and apartment buildings from the 1970's with shops of all types on the ground floor, the avenue is a good place to hunt for bargains. A couple of blocks up on the right side of the avenue you'll find a wide public square called the **Alemeda de la Constitución** with a baroque fountain. The square is lined on one side by antique mansions, while on the other side there are a series of ultra-modern condominium and townhouse complexes. This odd combination of old and new is a perfect example of the city's unusual mix of architectural styles in the same small zone.

At the next corner along the avenue you should make a left turn up the quaint street called the Calle de Musso Valiene. At the very next corner turn left onto a street known as the **Calle Lope Gisbert**. The first structure on the left side, flanked by a tiny little garden plaza, is the awesome 17th century **Casa de Las Columnas** (House of the Columns). Originally built for Sr. Guevara Garcia de Alcaraz who was a knight in the Order of St. James in the 1680's, the mansion's front portal is made of steel and is surrounded by a pair of bold baroque columns and ornately carved cherubs. This structure is now home to a local art institute, *open for visits during the several yearly free art and photo exhibition.* At its far end, there is the main office of the Lorca **Oficina de Turismo** (tourist information center) where a friendly multilingual staff can provide you with plenty of free maps and advice about the city. Also on the left side of the same street and adjacent to the tourist office is the center for regional art, and next door you can't help but notice the facade of the 18th century **Iglesia de San Mateo** which is open for visits during its regular posted mass hours. Further along the same side of the street is the enchanting 17th century **Casa Condes de San Julian** with its unusual stone facade and royal crests.

A few steps further along the Calle Lope Gisbert you will make a brief detour by taking a right turn a few steps up along the Calle de Pio XII and the second building on the right side is worth a quick peek inside. Known as the **Casino de Artistico y Literario**, this beautiful three story 19th century Casino (open only to private members) has a wonderful Art Nouveau foyer which is topped by a glass ceiling and has a fine staircase bordered by a pair of unusual Egyptian styled lamp statuettes. While the Casino itself is not open to the general public, they will usually let visitors inside the front door to look at the foyer during normal afternoon business hours.

Return back to the Calle Lope Gisbert and continue walking in the same direction as you were before detouring towards the casino. Another block and a half later you will find the tranquil **Plaza de Colon** square which centers around an old fountain depicting fish spraying water from their mouths. Also in this square is the 19th century **Teatro Guerra** theater where plays are still produced with average ticket prices at around 4,000 *ptas* a person.

To avoid getting totally lost in the maze of twisting lanes in the adjacent old quarter of town, just simply turn around and retrace your steps back down the Calle Lope Gisbert until you once again reach the tourist information center. At the next corner make a left turn up on the enchanting **Calle del Alamo**. This street seems to be a quiet little lane surrounded by aging 18th century merchant's homes, but at night it turns into the center for night-life in Lorca.

The Calle del Alamo is also the easiest and most interesting way to reach the oldest section of the city which is known locally as the **Barrio Antigua**. The first building on the right side of the street has recently been rebuilt, but is still embedded with an amazing royal crest of stone called the **Escudo de Garcia de Alcaraz** (the crest of the man who owned the Casa de Columnas discussed above) which has marked the entrance to the old quarter since 1545. About a block or so later along the same street, you should glance off to the left where you can see the rear side of several old homes which still have original elements and give you a feel of what this whole city looked like back in the 16th century.

The street soon ends as it merges into the magnificent **Plaza de España** square. Visited by the King Juan Carlos and Queen Dona Sofia back in 1994 after intensive renovations, visitors here are confronted with one dramatic structure after another. The fine 17th century **Casas Consistoriales** town hall, the massive 16th through 18th century **Colegiata de San Patricio** church (open for free from 11am until 2pm and again from 4:30pm until 6:30pm daily) where choral concerts are held every now and then, and several private mansions line the square. As you head straight through towards the rear of the plaza you will proceed uphill along the Calle Corregidor.

A few steps up this block on the left side you can see the royal crests carved in 1750 by Juan de Uzeta on the front of the **Casa del Corregidor** building (the old town court building). Continue up the same street for a block or so, and just after passing a small square which centers around a statue of the **Angel de La Fama** you will turn right upon the Calle de Barandillas. The street winds its way uphill past several more 16th century houses and at the fork in the road bear left onto the Calle Mayor de Santa Maria. This lane proceeds steeply uphill towards one of several towers remaining from the giant 13th century **Castillo** castle.

When you reach the tower, look out for a small adjacent archway under which you can pass through. Turn left to wander along one of two roads that pass by wonderful panoramic lookout points over the city and several other ruins of old castles. After visiting the castle you can either retrace your steps back down to the center of the city via the same roads you just used to get here, or for the more adventurous, take a zigzag route via the strange Calle de Pedro Montiel, where a few of towns less fortunate (and rather shy) residents live in crumbling 500 year-old houses that were formerly barns.

NIGHTLIFE & ENTERTAINMENT

The best area to head for entertainment is over on the Calle de Alamo with all sorts of small pubs and clubs. It only gets busy on weekend nights after 10pm or so. On this street look for the **Bohemio, Don Baco, Preludo, Fraguel,** and the **Cafe Acaurio.** The only real disco around is called **Tivoli** and it is located on the small service road towards Almeria.

PRACTICAL INFORMATION

- **Tourist Information,** *Tel. (968) 466-157*
- **Police,** *Tel. (968) 443-392*
- **Medical Emergencies,** *Tel. (968) 445-500*
- **Taxis,** *Tel. (968) 467-096*

Major Local Festivals

Contact theTurismo office, *Tel. (968) 466-157,* for more details.
- **Romeria de la Salud,** *Early February, Songs and Dances*
- **Semana Santa,** *Easter, Plays and Processions*
- **Fiera Lorca,** *Late September, Folk Dances and Fairs*
- **Fiesta San Clemente,** *Late November, Cultural Activities*

MOJÁCAR

Mojácar is situated just off the Costa de Almeria shoreline about 59 kilometers (26 miles) south of Lorca. The former Moorish hilltop of Pueblo Blanco, set in the foothills of the Sierra Cabrera mountains, and its more touristy section just under 1.5 kilometers (about 1 mile) away along a wide strip of sandy beach, have become a popular tourist destination. Much smaller and more tranquil than the other large holiday resorts, Mojácar and its growing population of around 4,245 people has recently attracted a fair number of English and German ex-patriots and tourists to an ever-growing number of low-rise condominiums, hotels, apartments and villa developments.

Blessed with plenty of warm sunny days throughout the year (but not crowded until either summer or the Easter break), Mojácar is a nice place to stay for a while before heading up the coast to Alicante, or down to the Costa del Sol. In the high season this is a prime destination for holiday makers and wind-surfing beach bums alike. Make sure to pop into the town's outdoor produce market on Wednesday and the antique market on Sundays.

Originally settled around 2100 BC, the area was later inhabited by Celtics, Phoenicians, Greeks, Romans and Visigoths before the Moors absorbed this area into their empire and started a small but lively silk production industry here sometime in the 6th century. In 1488, the Reconquest reached the Mojácar and the Moors were expelled (even though many of the old Islamic customs and traditions still live on today). In the 1930's a group of eccentric bohemian Spanish artists and writers (later to be known as members of the Indaliano Movement) came to live here and Mojácar soon became a well-known center for abstract art and liberal intellectualism.

ARRIVALS & DEPARTURES

To drive here from Cartagena, take the high speed E-15 highway south.

Bus service can be accessed from the La Manga area via transfers at Cartagena's two main bus stations. Check with your destination's tourist office for more information. Daily scheduled buses between Lorca, Murcia, Almeria, Cartagena, Valencia, Alicante, and other points are serviced by either the Enatcar bus company, *Tel. (968) 441-107*, or the Alsina Graells bus company, *Tel. (968) 441-961.*

There are also at least four buses each day in both directions from Almeria to Mojácar, two each day via Murcia, and one each day via Barcelona. For more details, check with your nearest tourist information office or bus station.

Trains to and from most of the coastal areas can be boarded on a daily basis year round at Cartagena's Renfe train station on the Avenida de America and cost somewhere around 650 *ptas* or less to reach any point listed above. Lorca's main rail station, *Tel. (968) 466-998*, services many cities throughout Spain such as Barcelona, Alicante, and Valencia, and is located two blocks below the central Avenida Juan Carlos. Call Renfe's central information line, *Tel. (968) 501-796*, for specific station departure locations and exact schedules during peak (summer) and off peak (winter) times.

WHERE TO STAY

Moderate

PARADOR DE MOJÁCAR, *Playa de Mojácar. Tel. (950) 478-250, Fax (950) 478-183. US & Canada bookings (Marketing Ahead), Tel. 800/223-1356. Low season rack rates from 13,000 ptas per double room per night (E.P.). High season rack rates from 15,000 ptas per double room per night (E.P.). All major credit cards accepted.*

This unusual three-star resort parador faces a nice windswept beach on the coastal section of town. This is a good choice for international travelers wishing to enjoy this delightful town and it features some 108 Mediterranean style single and double sea-view rooms which all contain private bathrooms, Mexican tile floors, remote control satellite television, mini-bar, hair dryer, direct dial telephone, whitewashed walls, exposed beam ceilings, huge sea-view terraces and rustic wooden furnishings.

Facilities include a huge front lawn with views over the sea and plenty of sun chairs, a fully equipped business meeting and convention center, an outdoor swimming pool, tennis, free parking and a very good regional restaurant. The service here is good, and the guests are an interesting mixture of European nationalities.

HOTEL EL MORESCO, *Avenida de en Camp. Tel. (950) 478-025, Fax (950) 478-262. Low season rack rates from 14 000 ptas per double room per night (E.P.). High season rack rates from 18,500 ptas per double room per night (E.P.). All major credit cards accepted.*

Located on the road from the center of the *Pueblo* to the top of the hill, this fairly good three-star business style hotel is good for those looking to have full service accommodations within walking distance to the Barrrio Vieja. The modern 1970's style El Moresco offers 147 rooms that each have private bathrooms, television, direct dial telephones and nice terraces with views of the countryside. Facilities here include a high season beach shuttle bus, a restaurant, a game room, a pub and safe deposit boxes at the front desk.

HOTEL INDALO, *Paseo del Mediterraneo 1. Tel. (950) 478-001, Fax (950) 478-176. Internet: www.besth@tinet.fut.es. Low season rack rates from 5,600 ptas per double room per night (E.P.). High season rack rates from 13,800 ptas per double room per night (E.P.). All major credit cards accepted.*

The Indalo is a typical three-star sea front hotel that is favored primarily by older German tourists arriving by the busload on package holidays. While far from charming, this is a reasonably good place to stay if you are looking for a full service hotel in this area. Here there are 308 terraced rooms with private bathrooms and simple furnishings. The hotel also has a television room, restaurant, outdoor swimming pool, free parking and that's about it.

Inexpensive

PENSION EL TORREON, *Calle de Jazmin 4. Tel. (950) 475-259, Fax (950) 475-259. Low season rack rates from 5,000 ptas per double room per night (E.P.). High season rack rates from 6,000 ptas per double room per night (E.P.). Cash only - no credit cards accepted.*

Of all the hotels in Mojácar, the El Torreon is by far the most memorable place to stay. Located in the *Barrio Vieja* district of the hilltop, this simple yet extremely charming one-star inn is adorable. Set within the walls of an antique Moorish style mini-mansion resting on the mountain's edge, the El Torreon boasts some of the best views you could ever imagine. The owner and manager (a wonderfully friendly local woman named Charro) offers five beautifully decorated traditional bedrooms that contain antiques and curiosities, old tiles, and in some, a view you will never forget. The bathrooms are shared. The inn also has a stunning sun terrace that is covered by bougainvillea vines, and looks right out over the sea. There is optional continental breakfast, nearby free parking, and access to outside telephone lines if necessary. The owner also rents out a cozy casita (small house) with a kitchen and space for either three adults or two adults with two small children, as well as a nearby one bedroom fully equipped apartment (both for similar prices as the rooms at the pension but long stay rates can be negotiated). For a one-star hotel this place is very romantic and I highly recommend it to any couple visiting Mojácar. Selected as one of my Best Places to Stay (see Chapter 13).

HOTEL PUNTAZO, *Paseo del Mediterraneo. Tel. (950) 478-265 Fax (950) 478-285. Low season rack rates from 5,650 ptas per double room per night (E.P.). High season rack rates from 6,730 ptas per double room per night (E.P.). All major credit cards accepted.*

For a simple one-star seaview hotel and apart-hotel this is a good value. The Puntazo is a Moorish style low rise hotel across the street from the beach that has 39 nicely decorated modern rooms and apartments. All units here feature private bathrooms, color television, and direct dial telephones, while others also have terraces, fully equipped kitchenettes, mini-safes and up to two separate bedrooms. The staff here are nice, and the property is within walking distance to everything that the beach area has to offer.

WHERE TO EAT

Moderate

RESTAURANTE ANTONELLA, *Playa de Mojácar. No telephone. Most major credit cards accepted.*

This is a great place to eat along the beach, offering fresh home-made pastas and other good Italian fusion fare. Situated just steps away from the crashing waves, this nicely decorated dining establishment is casual and relaxing. Their extensive menu features mixed salads, lasagna, over a dozen varieties of pizza, black tagliatelli with prawns, gnocchi in cheese sauce, pasta with mushroom Alfredo sauce, pork loin in duck sauce, grilled prawns, deer with apple sauce and several good desserts. A hearty three course meal here will cost around 2,950 *ptas* a person plus wine.

RESTAURANTE VIRGEN DEL MAR, *Playa de Mojácar. Tel. (950) 478-230. Most major credit cards accepted.*

For fresh seafood items this is a great place to go. This sea-front restaurant with huge picture windows overlooking the town beach is a bit more expensive than its competition, but the Virgen del Mar is simply much better. Here you can feast on such delicious specialties as seafood soup, garlic soup, mixed salad with tuna, seafood paella, grilled filet of sole, grilled prawns, grilled chicken, steak Cordon Bleu, salmon in cream sauce, fresh swordfish steak, entrecote of beef with Roquefort and for dessert, fresh strawberries in cream. A three course meal here will cost around 3,150 *ptas* a person plus drinks.

BISTROT BRETON, *Avenida del Mediterraneo. No telephone. Most major credit cards accepted.*

Located on the second floor of a simple structure across the avenue form the beach (next to Snoppy's) is this quaint French restaurant. This is a nice romantic spot for couples that want to enjoy good cuisine in a casual yet warm and welcoming environment. Their menu includes French onion soup, fish soup, bistro salad, entrecote in Chateaubriand sauce, sting ray with capers, grilled salmon and over a dozen varieties of delicious crepes. A good a la carte three course meal here will cost around 2,750 *ptas* a person plus wine.

SEEING THE SIGHTS

A Quick Tour of The Barrio Vieja

The best place to start off a short tour through the **Barrio Vieja** or old town (the historic part of Mojácar situated on the hilltop) is to park your car or to take the bus up to **Plaza Nueva**. This small cozy square contains several bars, shops, and the simple white 18th century Neoclassical facade of the former **Ermita de Nuestra Senora de Los Dolores** church. The church is now a boutique but may still be admired from the outside.

From the side of the church you can take a small stone lane called the **Calle Cuesta de la Castillo** which winds it way, up past bougainvillea covered old houses and on to the **Plaza del Castillo** square. This plaza was once the site of a massive 13th century castle which no longer stands here but still has a wonderful panoramic lookout area where you can see many local towns and beaches from a distance. Nowadays this spot is occupied by the residence of famous South American pianist Enrique Arias who has built a music theater on the site as well and hosts occasional concerts here. From the top of the hill you can wander along any of the old lanes to see such sights as the tranquil **Plaza del Sol** square, the 16th century **Puerta del Ciudad** town gateway, a tiny district of old Moorish style homes known to locals as the **Arribal** and the recently restored 14th century **Iglesia de Santa Maria** church.

Beaches

From the center of Mojácar Pueblo, it is just an easy 1.6 kilometer (1 mile) ride to the center of a series of wide dark sand beaches that stretch for over 16 kilometers (10 miles) along the Mediterranean Sea. The main beach area is known locally as the **Playa Mojácar** and is flanked by a narrow main road known as the **Avenida del Mediterraneo**. Parking is generally free and safe along the beach area. Although a few beach bars have been built along the sea-front itself, most hotels and restaurants around here have been placed directly across the avenue to reduce the environmental impact on sea-life. There are over 10 hotels, 24 restaurants, 16 boutiques, two supermarkets, and about 20 bars found on the opposite side of the avenue from the beach.

Further along the coast (south) near the sub-division known as **Indalo** you can find five different nude beaches for those looking to get an even tan. A project is well under way to complete a seaside walkway to be known as the **Paseo Maritimo** that will most likely have lots of palm trees and benches. During most of the year, this is a quiet area where you may be the only person on the beach for miles, while during Easter and the summer months you will find thousands of tourists and water-sport enthusiasts competing for space along the sand. There are several places along the coast that offer beach chair rentals for around 500 *ptas* each, and those interested in wind-surfing and scuba diving can check with the front desk of their hotel about the various equipment rental facilities in and around Mojácar.

If you are looking for peace and quite with a great deal of sunshine and almost no rain, may I suggest arriving here in the last two weeks of March or first two weeks of September when the hotels are charging low season prices, and there are only a handful of visitors on the beaches. The temperatures at this time average about 26 degrees celsius (81 degree farenheit) temperatures. There is a modern two floor shopping center just across the street from the beach known as the **Parque Commercial de Mojácar**, and a great new public bus system known as the **Mojácar Bus** is in service from about 9:30am until 7pm daily and has 25 stops along the beach and up to the old part of the Pueblo. (Price is about 150 *ptas* per person each way).

NIGHTLIFE & ENTERTAINMENT

All along the beachfront and the avenue you will find several good places to go depending on what mood you are in. During the summer the best discos in the area (built right on the edge of the sea) are **Pascha** and **Aku-Aku** but expect to get hit with a cover charge. For a more pub-like atmosphere you can try the places across the avenue from the beach such as **Los Amigos**, **The Cave Bar**, **Snoppy's**, or the **Zig Zag Rock** bar. There is also a dinner theater called **Music Musica** that has weekly variety shows including a buffet dinner for just 1,600 *ptas* a head.

In the Pueblo, a few good place include the **La Taberna** tapas bar, the **El Castillo** bar, and the **Neon Club**.

SPORTS & RECREATION
- **Caving Adventures**: Natur Sport, *Tel. (950) 364-481*
- **Golf**: Cortijo Grande, *Tel. (950) 479-176*
- **Horseback Riding**: Rutas Cuvea del Lobo, *Tel. (950) 478-991*; Cortijo Kupando, *Tel. (950) 479-314*; Molino de la Higuera, *Tel. (950) 528-882*
- **Mountain Bikes**: Moto Rent Magu, *Tel. (950) 132-941*
- **Mountain Hiking**: Professor Manzano, *Tel. (950) 270-812*
- **Scuba Diving**: Manuel Manzanares, *Tel. (950) 240-898;* Buceo Mojacar, *Tel. (950) 472-760*
- **Tennis**: La Mata, *Tel. (950) 475-001*
- **Ultralight Flying**: Juan Martinez, *Tel. (950) 475-230*
- **Windsurfing**: Samoa Surf, *Tel.* (950) 478-376; Windsurf Hotel Vera, *Tel. (950) 467-475*

PRACTICAL INFORMATION
- **Tourist Information**, *Tel. (950) 475-162*
- **Police**, *Tel. (950) 475-129*
- **Medical Emergencies**, *Tel.* (950) 475-113
- **Taxis**, *Tel. (950) 478-184*

Major Local Festivals
- **Moors & Christians**, *June*
- **San Isidro Pilgrammage**, *15 May*

CABO DE GATA NATURAL PARQUE

Located about 32 kilometers (18 miles) southeast of Mojacar, the **Cabo de Gata** is a truly spectacular and enchanting destination. This is a huge area of almost entirely undeveloped beauty, set aside by the Spanish government as a nature preserve and conservation program. Dotted with a population of 3,426 who live along all but uncharted beaches, in quaint salt flats, and small fishing villages, some 28,500 hectares of unspoiled inactive volcanic mountain valleys full of wildlife and tropical vegetation makes this park a must for nature enthusiasts as well as those seeking the most secluded and tranquil destination.

Situated in the extreme southeastern cornern of Spain, about a 45-minute drive from Almeria, the Parque Natural de Cabo de Gata-Nijar rests within a hot and sunny micro-climate with an average daily tempera-

ture of over 20 degrees celsius that is technically classified as a Mediterranean sub-desert. Originally used by the Romans as a silver mining area,
throughout the ages it has been mostly populated by hard working
farmers that have fought hard to keep away tourist industry development.

While a few hotels and restaurants are found in the small towns along
the coast, most visitors here take day trips into the park in order to trek
along dozens of superb nature paths to see the flaura and birds, or those
interested in snorkeling along the long coastline. In summer, a small
number of sun worshippers arrive to find their way via rough dirt roads
(purposely rough to dissuade the majority of tourists from finding their
way here) to over a dozen gorgeous cresent-shaped beaches including
those at Playa de Monsul, Playa de los Genoveses, Playa Playazo, Playa
Plomo, and Playa Torregarcia. Take at least a couple of liters of drinking
water with you, just in case you get lost or have a car breakdown.

ARRIVALS & DEPARTURES

The best access to the park is via Almeria. From Almeria you can take
the E-15 highway north for about 19 kilometers (12 miles) until exiting
onto route N-344. From here you will take a series of small roads, all
signposted to San Jose, for another 25 kilometers towards San Jose.

WHERE TO STAY

Expensive

HOTEL DE SAN JOSE, *San Jose. Tel. (950) 380-116, Fax (950) 380-
002. Low season rack rates from 18,400 ptas per double room per night (H.B.),
High season rack rates from 21,400 ptas per double room per night (H.B) Visa
and Mastercards accepted.*

This pricey and somewhat snobby little boutique hotel lies on a cliff
near the sea, some 350 meters from the center of town. Although
charmingly beautiful, some of the front desk staff here can have a quite
an attitude, and their hefty prices include two mandatory meals for all
guests. The hotel offers eight nicely designed rooms in a Spanish country
style, with nice furnsihings and some have sea views. The hotel has a good
restaurant, parking, television, but not much else for these prices.

Moderate

APARTHOTEL TRES PINOS, *Camino de la Escuela, San Jose. Tel.
(950) 380-212, Fax (950) 380-213. Low season rack rates from 5,000 ptas per
studio apartment per night (E.P.), High season rack rates from 9,000 ptas per
studio apartment per night (E.P.). 1 bedroom apartments (up to 4 guests) from
10,000 ptas per room per night. Visa and Mastercards accepted.*

Located on a hill just a few minutes walk or ride away from the heart
of the town of San Jose, this amazingly friendly and beautifully designed

sea view apart-hotel is a greatplace to stay in the park. The Tres Pinos is a traditional yet modern styled three floor structure that offers a half dozen or so nicely designed studio and one bedroom apartments (several have great sea views) which have fully- stocked kitchens, television, comfortable bedding including extra sofa beds in some, daily housekeeping and nice rattan furnishings.

The hotel has free parking, a nice outdoor swimming pool, a sun deck and the staff is really nice. It's a great deal at these prices, but book well in advance. See also the "Best Places to Stay" chapter (Chapter 13).

HOSTAL LAS GAVIOTAS, *Camino de San Jose, San Jose. Tel. (950) 380-010. Fax (950) 380-013. Low season rack rates from 5,000 ptas per double room per night (E.P.), High season rack rates from 8,000 ptas per double room per night (E.P). Visa and Mastercards accepted.*

This is a nice two story modern hotel and is located just a minute or so up from the center of San Jose. It has a dozen or so pleasantly decorated air conditioned rooms that feature private bathrooms, private terraces, color television, direct dial telephone, and are very spacious. The staff here are friendly, and there is free parking and loads of tourist brochures.

HOTEL CASA EMILIO, *Camino de Los Escullos, Los Escullos. Tel. (950) 389-76. Low season rack rates from 5,000 ptas per double room per night (E.P.), High season rack rates from 6,500 ptas per double room per night (E.P). Cash only - no credit cards accepted.*

Situated near a beachside cliff at the edge of this tiny fishing village, the Casa Emilio has a dozen or so simple rooms with private bathrooms, basic facilities, and simple furnishings. They also have a full service restaurant, a disco, and plenty of free parking. It's nothing special, but it's not bad.

WHERE TO EAT
Moderate

MESON TEMPRANILLO, *Puerto de San Jose, San Jose. Tel. (950) 380-206. Visa and Mastercard accepted.*

Situated along San Jose's tiny port, this is an upscale yet casual international restaurant with a great outdoor terrace and indoor dining room. You can eat like a king on delicious dishes such as paella, swordfish, omlettes, burgers, mixed salads, an amazing fish soup, fried sardines, shrimp in garlic, fresh asparagus in mayonaisse, and pepper steak in Roquefort sauce. The average al la carte dinner price per person is 2,250 *ptas* plus drinks.

Inexpensive
  TABERNA DE LA PUERTA, *Puerto de San Jose, San Jose. No telephone. Visa cards accepted.*
  This restaurant is also situated alongside of the town of San Jose's little port. It is a tiny, informal seafood restaruant and a favorite among local fisherman. With only a handful of indoor tables and a about a dozen outdoor tables, this place serves up amazingly fresh fish and typical tapas at cheap prices. Among my favorites here are the calamari, chicken in garlic, fresh grilled tuna, prawns with garlic and the salads. The average al la carte lunch price per person is 1,750 *ptas* plus drinks.

SEEING THE SIGHTS
From Las Amoladeras to the
Torre de Vigia Watchtower via San Miguel
  After exiting the highway and reaching route N-344, follow the signs towards San Jose. About 2 kilometers later, as you pass through the outskirts of an industrial town called Las Amoladeras, look out on the right side of the road for the **Las Amoladeras Centro de Visitantes** park information center. Here you should pick up a 300 *ptas* map of the Cabo de Gata and ask for all the information that they have about the area and its natural wonders. *The information center should be open daily from 10am until 6pm and their exhibition about the history and wildlife in the area is free of charge to visit.*
  Continue along the N-344 for another kilometer or so, until making a right turn at the indications for Cabo de Gata. Pass through the village of Pujaire and a few minutes later you will find the town of **San Miguel de Cabo de Gato**. This sleepy town is home to a narrow stretch of beach that is favored by wind surfers, but has little in the way of attractions besides a few bars, restaurants, cheap hostals, and a disco. At San Miguel's main traffic circle, follow the turn off marked towards **La Almadarabe de Monteleva**, a small seaside community a few minutes down the road that is home to a giant salt flat.
  About three kilometers up from the San Miguel traffic circle turn off, on the left side of the road, you will see the old **Las Salinas church**, and a lookout point where you can spot many migrating birds resting on the salt flats. Continue along the same road (be careful, it narrows considerably!) for a few minutes after passing the town of La Almadarbe, and follow the road as it heads up through the mountains. About 5 kilometers later the road ends at a fork where you will turn to the right towards the **Faro de Cabo de Gato** lighthouse. Built in 1861 over the ruins of an old castle, the lighthouse itself is usually closed to the public, but parking your car near here and walking around will lead you to some dramatic lookout points over the mountains and sea. After visiting the lighhouse, turn you

car around, and at the next fork in the road take a right turn onto a small road. This follows the coastline northward (be very careful on this road as herds of sheep are known to wander across it). The road continues for a few minutes until it ends at the 17th century **Torre Vigia de la Vela Blanca** watchtower. The best panoramic views of the sea and cliffs can be seen from here. When you are done at the watchtower area, just retrace your route for some 13 kilometers back to the main traffic circle in San Miguel.

From San Miguel to the Playa de los Genoveses via San Jose

From the traffic circle in San Miguel, follow the turn off marked towards San Jose. After some five kilometers during which you will pass through Pujaire, make a right turn onto the road signposted to San Jose. After passing by the green houses full of tomatoes and the village of Ruescas, you will again turn right to follow the signs towards San Jose. Another fourkilometers later the road forks and you will follow it to the right to as it passes through the hamlet of Pozo de los Frailes and about three kilometers later you shall finally reach the village of San Jose.

Now that you have entered **San Jose**, make a left turn to follow the signs marked to the Playa de San Jose town beach and its adjacent **Puerto de San Jose** harbor. The beach itself is not to special, but the tiny sheltered harbor is a great place to wander around and have a fresh al fresco seafood meal. Park you car for free at the harbor, and after lunch you should walk a few blocks away to the town center where locals and tourists alike can be seen playing dominos and relaxing at the outdoor tables at the cafes. The town has little of historic or cultural interest besides a few handicraft shops, but it is the point of departure for several high season excursions by boat and horseback into the natural park area that can be booked at the so-called the **Centro de Informacion de San Jose**, a private enterprise disguised as a Turismo, on the main street.

Once you have walked around all eight of the city's major streets, go get your car and drive to the main road. Here you will bear left and follow the road as it loops around and then heads uphill along the seashore. Less than one kilometer later the road forks and you follow a small dirt road signposted to the Playa de los Genoveses less than another two kilometers away. When you arrive at the parking area on the left, don't leave anything valuable in plain sight in your car. Walk down the pathway through the brush to the amazing cresent shaped the **Playa de los Genoveses** beach, one of Spains most beautiful places to get a suntan. Hidden between two small mountains to either side, the gentle bay has almost no undertow , and is visited by local families, adventurous tourists, and a few nudists. This beach has no real facilities, since there is absoutely no develoment allowed in this zone. Just inland from here there is also a charming old windmill called the **Molino de Las Genoveses,** a nice place to visit on a hike in this area. The same dirt road can be taken for another three kilometers or so, to reach the equally impressive **Playa Monsul** beach, but recent floods have made it all but impossible to continue down southward past there. The Cabo de Gato, is also a spectacular place to see the sunset.

From San Jose to Las Negras via Los Escullos

After leaving San Jose and its fine beaches, retrace your steps back out of San Jose and head four kilometers or so towards the hamlet of **Pozo de las Frailes**. On the left side of the road as you pass through the hamlet is an interesting old water well and windmill that can be seen. A few hundred meters later make a right turn to follow the signposted road towards Los Escullos. Head up through the mountains, pass by a towering volcanic crater known as the **Cerro del Fraile** (height of 493 meters), and in about five kilometers you will reach the right side exit to the small town of **Los Escullos**. Just to the right of town, as small dirt road heads 250 meters south of here to the beachfront **Cuartel de San Felipe** and the adjacent **Cuartel de la Guardia**, two lovely castle-like forts that have guarded the coastline here since the 18th century. Just across the street from here is an unusual Moorish-styled discotech, a great place to party in the area, called **Chaman** that is open on summer weekend nights.

Even more interesting is the charming fishing village of **La Isleta (del Moro)** at the edge of a miniature peninsula, less than another two kilometers up the road. Hardly touched by tourism, this small cluster of two dozen fisherman's houses has plenty of old world ambiance. Rugged old men and women can usually be seen hauling in fish from small boats, or just sitting around, taking long siestas in the shade. Although a few cafes and restaurants have popped up, this is truly an authentic fishing town and should not be missed. There is even a small cheap hostel above a restaurant at the edge of the sea that offers cheap accommodations with plenty of charm but no real services or facilities. Just beyond town is a fairly nice beach called the Playa del Penon Blanco.

After wandering around Las Isleta, return to the same coastal road and continue to follow it for another 2.5 kilometers or so until you pass the lookout point off to the right called the **Mirador de la Amatista.** Stop for a moment and take advantage of the coin-operated telescope to look out onto some incredible seashore views. After the lookout point, return to the main road. Thirteen kilometers later, after turning off on two forks (follow signs), you will enter the town of **Las Negras**. Once a cute fishing village, heavy condo development has spoiled all the charm here, but the beaches are still acceptable and it makes for a good place to stretch your legs.

Interestingly, a small community of anarchistic hippies have taken control of some castle ruins just above a cove beach at Cala de San Pedro, which is down a walking path on the other side of a mountain just a few kilometers north of town. After walking about 25 minutes to reach this place, I found an unusual little free-zone commune that was quite interesting. Those interested in seeing this strange remnant of the 1960's, should ask for directions in Las Negras.

From town, go back to the main road and follow the signs for 16 kilometers until reaching Campo Hermoso where a traffic circle will lead you to the park exit towards either Murcia or Almeria.

SPORTS & RECREATION
• **Centro de Informacion de San Jose**: *San Jose, Tel. (950) 380-299*
• **Boat Rides**: Ociomar, *San Jose, Tel. (908) 056-477*
• **Boat Rentals**: Alpha, *San Jose, Tel. (950) 270-050*
• **Horseback Riding**: La Noria Hipico, *Los Escullos, Tel (950) 525-213*
• **Jeep Safaris**: Groupo J, *San Jose, Tel. (950) 380-299*
• **Taxi Tours**: Auto Taxi, *San Jose, Tel. (950) 389-737*

18. SOUTHERN SPAIN

Including the region of Andalucía

SEVILLA

The outlying area of what is now the city and suburbs of **Sevilla** (known to North Americans as **Seville**) were originally home to Iberian and Phoenician settlement of Hispalis. By the 3rd century BC, the Romans had taken control of the city, and by 45 BC it became an important walled city in Julius Caesar's Baetica region. The area prospered, as the ruins of the nearby Roman regional capital city of Italica clearly indicate. By the 5th century AD, the Roman Empire began its steady decline, and the Visigoths then took control and made Hispalis their kingdom's capital for a few hundred years.

In 712, the Moors conquered the city, changed its name to Izvilla, and placed it under the control of the Caliphate of Córdoba. When Moorish leader Banu Abbad emerged as the ruler of the city in 1023, independence was won from the Caliphate. As power changed hands first to other Arabic Berber factions, like the Almoravids and Almohads, the city's rulers began to order the construction of monumental buildings such as the La Giralda and Torre del Oro towers and some parts of the Los Reales Alcázares that can still be seen today.

In 1248, King Fernando III and his Christian forces from the north defeated the Moors. The King converted mosques into churches and changed the city's name to Sevilla, a corruption of its former Moorish name. Although the Arab community was allowed to stay, at least for a while, the city took on a much different character. Sevilla surged in population, built massive shipyards to secure a position in international trade, erected one of the world's largest and most stunning cathedrals, and became a center for the exploration and exploitation of the new world. Businessmen, artists, craftsmen and intellectuals found their way here from all over Europe, and in the process helped create an unparalleled city, full of palatial structures and artistic masterpieces.

Sevilla is still growing, greatly assisted by both the 1929 and 1992 Expositions, which brought the world to its doors. There is no other city in Spain that can boast a more powerfully romantic and compelling atmosphere than Sevilla. Maybe it's the intoxicating smell of the abundant orange blossoms, or the incomparable beauty of its residents, or just the vast magnificence of its old buildings and neighborhoods, but there is something undeniably unique about this city that charms visitors into never wanting to leave!

Every street in town offers countless sights to be further investigated. As the sun goes down, you'll find yourself drawn by some strange power into the small bars and taverns in the plazas, where the crowds spill out onto the streets and mingle all night long. For such a big city, Sevilla soon begins to feel like a small medieval village of friendly people that really know how to enjoy life.

While some people think they can see the sights in just a day or two, this is really not enough time. In the space of about four days, it is possible to familiarize yourself with a fraction of the most charming districts and unforgettable attractions. I have listed a series of tours that will take you through the most important sights and streets, but with a little intuition and further exploration, there is much more to be seen and experienced here.

The only word of caution I urge you to keep in mind, is that there are pickpockets and gypsies from out of town that occasionally come here to depart with your wallet and the contents of your parked car. Just like anywhere else in the world, use common sense while wandering around town. Otherwise, relax, keep your mind open, and expect to be over-whelmed by this city's special ambiance.

Sevilla's Incredible Festivals!

The most spectacular times to visit the city are in March and/or April during the yearly **Semana Santa** and **Feria de Abril** festivities. These world-class events attract hundreds of thousands of visitors who plan their trips as much as two years in advance and still end up paying 40%-60% surcharges over the normal high season rates. You won't find a hotel room within 75 km of the city during these time periods, so expect to leave the city late each night and return before 7am each morning, before all the parking spaces, or bus and train seats, are already taken.

The bizarre **Semana Santa** celebrations held for a week just before Easter are much more dramatic here than in any other city in Spain. Since the 16th century, Sevilla has prided itself on presenting the largest processions of penitents from local religious brotherhood associations known as *cofradías*. Each church group's members are often dressed in capes with pointed hats or Roman military costumes as they march through the old town plazas and streets each day and night from 2pm on Palm Sunday until after midnight on Good Friday. Above the shoulders of marching cofradías are elaborate floats called **pasos** containing priceless medieval monstrance and holy altar pieces. Throughout the parades, the strong smell of a specially made incense thickens the air all over the city. As the processions wind their way from each of Sevilla's churches to the official parade route down the Calle de las Sierpes and onward to the Archbishop's palace adjacent to the cathedral, the thousands of cheering spectators break out into Flamenco-like hymns that have a truly haunting quality.

The last major procession begins at midnight on Good Friday when the pace picks up and the noise level becomes maddening. The entranced residents and visitors will spend each day and night partying up a storm in the bars of the **Barrio Santa Cruz** and at hundreds of private gatherings. A special free schedule of all the processions is printed in the local newspapers, and may also be obtained at the Turismo office. This is a magnificent display of religious respect, and despite all the problems and crowds associated with the holiday season and festival itself, make an attempt to see at least part of the ceremonies if possible.

On the other hand, several weeks later the **Feria de Abril** (April Festival) rolls into town. This week-long series of bullfights and circuses, Flamenco dancing and music, and all-around amusement is celebrated on the opposite side of the **Guadalquivir** river at the nearby **Real Campo de la Feria fairgrounds**. After spending a long time building and then decorating over 1,000 multicolored canvas and wood framed cabana tents (known here as **casetas**), local groups and families gather inside to drink wine while singing and dancing *Flamenco*. Hundreds of women put on their most provocative gypsy-style ruffled dresses, while many men wear equestrian outfits, and each night they just go totally nuts while flirting in the most obvious ways. Starting at about 1pm, horse-drawn carriages parade through the fairgrounds, after which, a series of excellent bullfights takes place over at the bullring, followed by long nights of music, dance, heavy drinking, and romance. This is a light-hearted cultural event where everyone is in the best possible mood. For more details and exact scheduling, contact the Turismo offices.

ARRIVALS & DEPARTURES
By Air

Sevilla's main international airport is the Aeropuerto de San Pablo. Located 11 km (7 miles) north of the city center just off of the N-IV highway, this newly enlarged facility has separate domestic (*terminal nacional*) and international (*terminal internacional*) wings.

Among the many services offered in the airport are free luggage carts, wheelchairs for the physically challenged, 24-hour currency exchange desks, banks with ATM machines, a tourist (*Turismo*) office, luggage storage at 550 *ptas* per bag each day, restaurants and cafés, a beauty salon, boutiques featuring designer goods, a pharmacy, a newsstand and cigarette shop, soda machines, dozens of pay phones that accept coins and credit cards, a full service post office, a multilingual information desk, a hotel booking kiosk, duty free shops, car rental offices, tour operator and excursion desks, and VIP lounges for business and first class passengers.

For those who need to pick up or drop off passengers at the airport, parking is available at 175 *ptas* per hour and 1,150 *ptas* per day. If you want to leave your rental car at the airport while you explore Sevilla for a few hours or days, ask your rental company's kiosk in the airport. Most major car rental companies will let you park in their officially assigned airport parking areas for free.

Buses between the Airport & Downtown

A well-marked airport shuttle bus can be found right in front of the arrivals terminal and is marked Especial Aeropuerto (EA) on its front. The route continues each half hour or so daily in both directions from 7am until 10pm, and takes passengers between the airport and the Puerta de Jerez or the area near the Santa Justa rail station for 450 *ptas* each way. From the Puerta de Jerez you can easily walk to most of the major plazas and sights downtown, or you can take a taxi for about 485 *ptas* to just about any hotel downtown.

Taxis from the Airport to Downtown

Taxis can be found in abundant supply at well-indicated taxi stands at the airport. Almost all of the taxis here are fairly small sized four-door sedans. Normally, a taxi's trunk can hold about two large suitcases, but those with roof racks can secure two more medium pieces of luggage, and perhaps a couple of carry-on bags inside as well. Unfortunately, there are no station wagon or van style taxis available in Sevilla.

Expect to pay somewhere between 1,880 and 2,450 *ptas* per ride from the airport to most downtown locations, but rip-offs do occasionally occur. If you think you are being overcharged, ask for an official receipt (*recibo oficial*), write down the license number of the taxi usually posted near the meter, and call the local police to file a complaint.

By Bus

Most, but not all, of the bus lines between Sevilla and other parts of Spain as well as the rest of Europe tend to stop at the Estación Plaza das Armas, just off the river about one kilometer from the heart of town. From here you can either walk to your hotel, take municipal bus #C1 or #C2 to several stops downtown, or hire a taxi for about 535 *ptas* to reach just about any hotel or sight in the city.

There is also the older Estación d'Autobuses on the Prado de San Sebastián near the Plaza de España. From here you can either walk into the older parts of town, take municipal bus # 5 into downtown, or hire a taxi for about 545 *ptas* or so to reach most major sights.

By Car

From Madrid, the fastest way here is to follow the high speed N-IV highway south and then west for 541 km (335 miles). If coming from Málaga, take the winding route N-321 north for 43 km (27 miles) before reaching Antequera, where you will then merge onto the somewhat faster route N-334 west for another 176 km (109 miles) before reaching the city.

By Train

Sevilla is linked to the rest of Spain and Europe by an extensive series of rail lines. This city's main Renfe rail station is called the Estación de Santa Justa and is located on the Avenida Kansas City about 1.5 km north of downtown. From here you can either take municipal bus #70 for 125 *ptas* to reach the Prado de San Sebastián near the bus station and the Plaza de España, or take a taxi for roughly 850 *ptas* or so, depending on how much luggage you have and where you are going.

ORIENTATION

Sevilla, capital city of the giant **Andalucía** region (population 708,706), lies in the southwestern corner of Spain, 541 km southeast of Madrid.

GETTING AROUND TOWN

By Bus

Sevilla's municipal bus company, known officially as Transportes Urbanos de Sevila (TUSSAM) offers an abundant supply of large Autobuses (buses) that criss-cross almost every neighborhood. During rush hours, you may find yourself packed in like a sardine.

With dozens of different, numbered bus lines and hundreds of well-marked bus stops each with its posted corresponding route map, getting around above ground is fairly easy. The first thing I would suggest, is picking up a free pocket *Guía del Transporte Urbano de Sevilla*, which is a multilingual public transportation system map and timetable. These can be found, for free, during business hours at the TUSSAM bus information kiosks at the Plaza Nueva, Plaza Encarnación, Gran Plaza, and Prado de San Sebastián, or at any local or regional *Turismo* tourist office in town.

The operating hours for most buses is from 7:30am until about 9:30pm daily. Just in case you're out late at night, several special (*Servicio Nocturno*) nightowl buses whose number is preceded by the letter "N" run from the Plaza Nueva to several other major bus stops in town at 12 midnight, 1am, and 2am. There are also four bus lines that run in a circle all day that provide the town's cheapest and shortest sightseeing trip, all of which are marked with the letter "C." The price for a single use normal bus ticket is currently 125 *ptas* each way, and can be bought directly from the bus driver who will be glad to make change for small bills. Additional ten trip *Bonobonus* tickets and monthly *Tarjeta Mensual* monthly passes can be prepaid at the above mentioned kiosks at a good discount.

By Taxi

There are several hundred licensed taxis that roam the streets and major passenger arrival points day and night. Drivers are here are generally polite, quiet, and great sources of inside information if you can manage to get them talking. To find a taxi, either hail an unoccupied taxi (when empty they will illuminate a small *Taxi* light above the car), go to one of the dozens of obvious taxi stands throughout the city, or call Sevilla Radio Taxi Companies, *Tel. (95) 496-000 or (95) 458-000 or (95) 462-2222,* for a radio response pickup on demand. During rainy days, festivals, trade fairs or weekday morning and evening rush hours (6am until 10am and 6pm until 9pm) it may be quite a wait until you get lucky.

Taxis charge somewhere around 490 to 900 *ptas* per ride (not per person) between most downtown locations depending on exact distance and traffic conditions. All licensed taxis have electronic meters that click away at different rates depending on the time and day it is occupied. Normally this works out to somewhere around 15 *ptas* per city block during non-rush hour city rides. Legally chargeable supplements (most typically 25% more for service after 10pm and on Sundays) that are posted on a sticker in the taxi's interior and are reflected in the meter rate. These extra charges can be combined, but are occasionally are illegally utilized, so pay attention.

If for any reason you think you are being overcharged, ask for an official receipt (*recibo oficial*), write down the license number of the taxi (posted near the meter), and call the police to register your complaint. Over 500 taxis in Sevilla are equipped to accept credit cards for their tariffs.

WHERE TO STAY

Expensive

HOTEL ALFONSO XIII, *Calle de San Fernando, 2. Tel. (95) 422-2850, Fax (95) 421-6033. US & Canada bookings: (The Luxury Collection), Tel. 800/ 325-3589. Low Season rack rates from 40,000 per double room per night (E.P.).High Season rack rates from 48,000 per double room per night (E.P.). All major credit cards accepted.*

Without doubt, the Hotel Alfonso XIII is the city's best luxury hotel. This majestic place was built under the express desire of King Alfonso XIII to serve as a deluxe hotel to serve the V.I.P. crowd for the famed 1929 Ibero-American exhibition. Teams of the country's most talented artisans hand crafted hundreds of opulent Mudéjar and Baroque style public and private rooms in this palatial structure using the finest materials available such as rich marble, stunningly carved alabaster, hand painted *azulejos* tiles, and rare hardwoods. Every corner boasts unique tapestries, carpets, chandeliers, and custom made furnishings. The property went through a major restoration and upgrade process (just in time for the 1992 World Expo) while still under the ownership of the billionaire Aga Khan and since has hosted an endless stream of celebrities and royalty (including the entire Spanish royal family who stayed here during the wedding of their princess a few years ago) from every corner of the globe.

Located just steps away from the most important historical sights in the city, this super deluxe hotel caters to a well dressed clientele of top executives and high end travelers. The property features 149 amazingly beautiful air conditioned rooms and suites in either the Moorish or Baroque style. All of the accommodations feature exquisite furnishings, huge private bathrooms, remote control satellite television, mini-bars, direct dial telephones, impressive carpets, top quality European hair and skin care products, comfortable bedding and fine art. The list of facilities is endless, including a fantastic inner courtyard serving lunches during the summer, a tranquil piano lounge, an excellent formal restaurant, 24-hour room service, a garden-lined outdoor swimming pool, art galleries, boutiques, an in-house medical doctor, state-of-the-art conference and business meeting facilities, regal banquet rooms, valet parking, excursion and car rental desks, foreign currency exchange, beauty salon and full concierge service. The staff here work hard to make each guest feel like a King. Selected as one of my Best Places to Stay (see Chapter 13).

HOTEL CASA IMPERIAL, *Calle Imperial, 29. Tel. (95) 450-0300, Fax (95) 450-0330. Internet: www.casaimperial.es. Low Season rack rates from 22,500 per double room per night (B.P.).High Season rack rates from 28,000 per double room per night (B.P.). All major credit cards accepted.*

A few months ago I received two letters from readers, who told me to be sure and head over to this amazing little gem before finishing this new second edition of the Spain Guide. After seeing this wonderful hotel, I knew what they both were so excited about. The Hotel Casa Imperial is a completely unique hotel that takes the standards of deluxe accommodation to a new high for Sevilla.

Just a couple of years ago, a well respected German businessman named Jochen Knie and his wife purchased the ornate 16th century house that was built for the butler of Don Alonso de Villafranca who lived next door at the Casa de Pilatos. He then converted this former mansion, designed by the same architect as the adjacent national monument (the Casa de Pilatos) into what I firmly believe is the best deluxe boutique hotel in all of Spain. Situated in one of the oldest and most quaint sections of downtown Sevilla, this fantastic little gem of a hotel is simply breathtaking in every aspect.

The property features less than a dozen individually designed and decorated duplex suites and large super-deluxe rooms that all feature Moorish-style tiled bathrooms with unusual antique fixtures and huge bathtubs, an enormous array of fine marbles and granites, hand painted azulejos tiles and ancient artwork, a fully equipped kitchenette (although the guests never seem to use it!), electronic mini-safe, mini-bar, direct dial telephone, air conditioning and heating systems, opulent custom designed furnishings covered by beautiful imported and local fabrics, remote control satellite televisions (with audio/video systems in some cases), direct dial telephones, one of a kind hardwood trimming and Andalusian tapestries, and in several cases either spiral staircases or huge terraces leading out to either one of the 16th century inner courtyard patios or fine views over the historic heart of Sevilla.

Each part of the mansion is covered by yet another ancient object d'art or rare artifact. The hotel has several Mexican tile covered inner patio-gardens that are lined by galleries bordered by Roman era columns topped by Corinthian capitals. The stairways are covered by Pisan tiles that date back to the structure's origins, and the woodwork throughout the hotel is truly a masterpiece. Besides numerous fountains and sitting rooms scattered around this ideal oasis from the noise and bustle of town, there are unforgettable roof-top sun decks, a cafe, and a fantastic antique breakfast room that you will certainly never forget.

Favored by discreet movie stars and well to do travelers from all over the world, this new and enchanting five-star hotel (technically listed as an Apart-Hotel) specializes in the highest levels of personalized service and hospitality, two items that have long been missing from the hotel business in Sevilla. If you are looking for a small, casual, yet elegant getaway in the heart of this special city, the Hotel Casa Imperial is definitely the place to stay. Selected as one of my Best Places to Stay (see Chapter 13).

HOTEL LOS SEISES, *Calle de Segovias. Tel. (95) 422-9495, Fax (95) 422-4334. Low Season rack rates from 16,000 per double room per night (E.P.). High Season rack rates from 25,000 per double room per night (E.P.). All major credit cards accepted.*

This charming four-star deluxe hotel is a great bargain. Located just around the corner from the cathedral, this is a truly incredibly beautiful 16th century palace in the best part of the Barrio Santa Cruz. Upon the restoration of the building, it's owners have uncovered fantastic Roman mosaics, Mudéjar tile work, medieval frescoes, and ancient arches that can be seen in their original locations throughout the structure. All of the hotels 43 huge and uniquely designed rooms and suites feature powerful air conditioning, deluxe bathrooms, remote control satellite television, mini-bar, am-fm clock radio, mini-safe, direct dial telephones, handcrafted furnishings, delightful artwork and the vast majority look out onto unforgettable views of the Giralda tower and cathedral.

The facilities here include posh sitting rooms, a great inner garden courtyard, the city's finest rooftop panoramic sun deck and swimming pool, a fine gourmet restaurant surrounded by Roman mosaics and Moorish arches, business meeting rooms, banquet facilities, excursion and rental car reservation desk, a quaint café and a very helpful staff. If you are looking for a truly memorable experience for a price much lower than one would expect, this is definitely the place to go.

HOTEL DOÑA MARÍA, *Calle de Don Remondo, 19. Tel. (95) 422-4990, Fax (95) 421-9546. Low Season rack rates from 14,500 per double room per night (E.P.). High Season rack rates from 19,500 per double room per night (E.P.). All major credit cards accepted.*

This nice old world style four-star hotel just steps away from the cathedral offers 61 large air conditioned double rooms with private bathrooms, satellite television, direct dial telephone, am-fm radio, antiques and/or canopy bedding and either exterior or interior views. The hotel also has a rooftop swimming pool, nice antique laden public rooms, a good restaurant, meeting rooms and a very nice staff. A good value for the money and a great location.

Moderate

HOTEL TABERNA DEL ALABARDERO, *Calle de Zaragoza, 20. Tel. (95) 456-0637, Fax (95) 456-3666. Low Season rack rates from 13,000 per double room per night (E.P.). High Season rack rates from 15,500 per double room per night (E.P.). Most major credit cards accepted.*

Owned by a wealthy local priest, this surprisingly quaint and luxurious boutique style hotel (now part of the city's Hotel Collage) is located in a dramatically restored 19th century poet's mansion near the Torre del Oro, just a couple of minutes walk to the major tourist sights. A series of some 10 lavishly appointed rooms and huge suites can be found above the fine inner courtyard, all of which feature air conditioning, deluxe private bathrooms with Jacuzzi, remote control satellite television, fax machine, direct dial telephone, mini-bar, beautiful local paintings, and impressive furnishings. The hotel also is home to a fantastic little restaurant, opulent banquet facilities, a 24 hour caféteria, and a staff that truly understand the meaning of personalized service.

HOTEL ALVAREZ QUINTERO, *Calle Alverez Quintero, 9. Tel. (95) 422-1298. Fax (95) 456-4141. Low Season rack rates from 10,000 per double room per night (E.P.). High Season rack rates from 13,500 per double room per night (E.P.). Most major credit cards accepted.*

This delightful little converted 17th century mansion near the *Ayuntamiento* has some incredibly comfortable rooms. This cozy establishment offers 40 air conditioned rooms with private tiled modern bathrooms, satellite television, direct dial telephone, wall to wall carpeting, and in some, a great balcony overlooking the old town. The facilities here include are a great Moorish style marble and column lined lobby and sitting area, modern caféteria, room service, rooftop panoramic sun deck, a full service restaurant, and a garage. The service here is also quite impressive.

N.H. HOTEL PLAZA DAS ARMAS, *Calle Marqués de Paradas. Tel. (95) 490-1992, Fax (95) 490-1232. US & Canada bookings: (UTELL) 800/44-UTELL. Year round rack rates from 12,900 per double room per night (E.P.). Special weekend rates from 9,100 per double room per night (E.P.). All major credit cards accepted.*

The Plaza das Armas is a modern full-facility executive class hotel, situated near the Plaza das Armas and it's main bus station. This great three-star property boasts 262 ultra modern and seriously comfortable rooms and suites that all have private bathrooms, air conditioning, remote control satellite television, mini-bar, and more. The hotel offers a good restaurant, a relaxing café and lounge, plenty of business meeting rooms and conference facilities, a rooftop sun deck and swimming pool, a garage, a friendly staff, and some of great weekend rates.

Inexpensive

HOTEL ABRIL, *Calle de Jerónimo Hernandez, 20. Tel. (95) 422-9046. Fax (95) 456-3938. Low Season rack rates from 7,500 per double room per night (E.P.). High Season rack rates from 9,500 per double room per night (E.P.). Most major credit cards accepted.*

When I was looking around the charming neighborhood just above Calle Sierpes I stumbled upon this little gem of an affordable hotel. The two-star property is located in a former mansion on a quiet residential side street just a four minute walk from the cathedral. The hotel's 20 perfectly maintained rooms with modern private bathrooms, beautiful furnishings, marble floors, satellite television, telephone, and in many cases a great balcony make this place a real bargain.

HOSTAL CÓRDOBA, *Calle de Farnesio, 12. Tel. (95) 422-7498. Fax (95) 421-0450. Year round rack rates from 4,850 per double room per night (E.P.). Cash only - no credit cards accepted.*

This small nine room hostel near the heart of the Barrio Santa Cruz is far from fancy, but offers good value for clean, safe accommodations with private and shared bathrooms.

WHERE TO EAT

Expensive

RESTAURANTE LA GALERIA *(Hotel Alfonso XIII), Calle de San Fernando, 2. Tel. (95) 422-2850. All major credit cards accepted.*

The opulent Hotel Alfonso XIII has transformed its lavish restaurant into a superb gourmet affair. La Galeria's unforgettable interior design, complete with a huge Moorish-style, al fresco dining patio, is enough in itself to warrant a stop here. The ambiance and fine level of service here are in perfect harmony with a great team of experienced chefs. During my last visit, the kitchen served outrageously well prepared Gazpacho, sautéed mussels, Carpaccio of beef and arrugola , giant shrimp with lemon sauce and pistachios, scallop and crab salad with peppercorns, asparagus au gratin, pasta puttanesca, baked turbot with seaweed, grilled swordfish, duck with orange sauce, sirloin steak with almonds, grilled lamb cutlets with rosemary, and some fantastic desserts. An excellent three course meal here will cost around 5,750 *ptas* per person plus wine.

TABERNA DEL ALABARDERO. *Calle de Zaragoza, 20. Tel. (95) 456-0637. Most major credit cards accepted.*

This amazing semi-formal restaurant in the heart of town is among my favorite places for a serious dressy night out. Award-winning, executive chef Juan Manuel Marcos and his staff of students from Sevilla's new School of Hotels create a fantastic seasonally changing menu that will cost somewhere in the area of 3,950 *ptas* per person for a 4 course dinner that is sure to include the region's finest steak, game, shellfish, and garden fresh vegetables. Service here is world class, and the setting of the main and side dining rooms is something you will never forget. Call in advance for reservations, as they tend to get full.

Moderate

RESTAURANTE HANG ZHOU, *Calle de Mateos Gago, 5. Tel. (95) 456-0197. Most major credit cards accepted.*

This large and nicely decorated Chinese restaurant is on the most active street at night in the Barrio Santa Cruz. It has a huge two page menu full of surprisingly good, classic Chinese fare. A spicy and filling three course meal here will cost each person around 2,300 *ptas* plus beverages.

MESON SERRANITO, *Calle de Alfonso XII, 9. Tel. (95) 421-8299. Most major credit cards accepted.*

Whether you sit at the counter, patio, or dining room area, the giant menu of *tapas*, and complete meals is well worth the money. Here you can feast on oversized portions (the *tapas* here are the size of most other restaurant's full orders) of roasted meats, grilled chicken, swordfish, Serrano ham, Manchego cheese, shrimp with garlic, pork and tomatoes, chicken cutlets, Roquefort cheese sandwiches for 175 *ptas*, and a wide variety of freshly mixed salads. A hearty snack here will set you back around 1,450 *ptas* per person.

Inexpensive

BODEGA DE LA ANDANA, *Calle de Argote de Molino, 12. No telephone. Cash Only- No credit cards accepted.*

This highly atmospheric tavern and *tapas* bar in the best part of the *Barrio Santa Cruz* offers fantastic snacks at great prices and is open until 2:30am. Among the items available here are spicy potato salad at 200 *ptas*, tuna with tomato paste for 225 *ptas*, pork cutlet sandwiches at 225 *ptas*, toasted shrimp pepito sandwiches for 200 *ptas*, sausage with bacon at 200 *ptas*, Spanish omelet sandwiches for 275 *ptas*, clams with red or white sauce at 250 *ptas*, house salad for 200 *ptas*, wine fermented with oranges at 175 *ptas*, Sangria at 175 *ptas* per glass, and beer at 150 *ptas* per glass.

BAR AJOBLANCO. *Calle de Alhondiga, 19. Tel. (95) 229-320. Cash only- no credit cards accepted.*

This small neighborhood bar specializes in really good Mexican tapas. Open late during weekends, they also play superb jazz and blues music until 1am and serve the coldest beer in town. The food here served at both lunch and dinner time includes nachos with guacamole, beef quesadillas, chicken tacos, vegetarian enchiladas, huge burritos, pork strips with whisky sauce, grilled vegatables with Roquefort cheese, and cheap Corona beer. A great little place to relax, eat, and meet nice people. A filling three course Tex-Mex meal here will cost around 2,350 *ptas* per person plus wine.

SEEING THE SIGHTS
TOUR 1

The Catedral, the Universidad, the Plaza de España, & Parque de María Luisa.

Approximate duration (by foot) is about 6 hours, including church, museum, park, monument, and side street visits. Start from the side of the Catedral overlooking the Avenida de la Constitución.

The Catedral & Giralda tower

To begin this first intensive walking tour of the most obvious sights in the heart of the city, start over by the city's wide Avenida de la Constitución in front of the massive **Catedral** (Cathedral). When the city's cathedral chapter leveled most of the Almohad mosque that rested upon this sight prior to 1401, they declared "Let us build a church so great that those who see it completed may take us for madmen". Anyone who visits the city should try to imagine how difficult it must have been to construct this magnificent five nave structure in less than 100 years . This amazingly beautiful Gothic cathedral dates back to the 15th century when architect Alonso Martinez was commissioned to build it on a floor plan that measures of 116 meters (380 feet) long by 76 meters (249 feet) wide. it soon became largest cathedral in all of Spain (and now the forth largest in the world). The Late Gothic exterior is adorned by fantastic portals, flying buttresses, spires, stained glass, rose windows, and intricate stone carvings.

To find the main entrance of this vaulted structure, go just around the corner until you pass the near edge of the Plaza de la Virgen de los Reyes square with it's old lantern topped stone pillory. Once through the door, you will notice the Platteresque **Capilla Real** royal chapel in the apse just to your left as you enter. First, stare up at the beautifully decorated Renaissance dome above, before lowering your eyes down to the fine altar topped off by a 13th century wooden statue of Sevilla's patron saint, the **Virgen de los Reyes**. The statue is said to have been given to King Fernando III by his cousin King Louis IX of France. Near the base of the altar is a shrine that contains the remains of the later canonized King Fernando III in a silver urn. On the sides of the chapel rest the tombs of King Alfonso X and his mother, while stairs behind the chapel's fine 18th century grill lead down to the tombs of King Pedro the Cruel and his mistress.

Further inside the cathedral you will be drawn towards the center of it's towering central nave, where the **Capilla Mayor** main chapel is guarded by a wonderful Plateresque grill. Inside this section stands the famous Gothic wooden and gold leaf altarpiece, created by Flemish artisan Pierre Dancart to become the world's largest at a high of 20 meters (65 feet). The altar's carvings depict the 45 scenes of Jesus and Mary's lives, and are topped off by the images of the 12 apostles. Across from the chapel is the **Coro** choir with it's outrageously elaborate Baroque marble screen and organ pipe clusters. Inside you will find 117 delicately carved 16th century wooden choir stalls surrounding a lectern with beautiful old hand painted codices. Off in the corner you will find the oval **Sala Capitular** chapter house with it's fine frescoed dome, marble floors, and a dramatic painting of the Immaculate Conception by Murillo. Adjacent to the chapter house stands the **Sacristía Mayor** (sacristy) and the adjacent **Sacristía de los Cálices** where after viewing impressive paintings by masters such as Zubarán, Valdes Leal, and Goya you can enter the **Tesoro** treasury collections. The collection contains fine works of art, a fantastic 16th century gold and silver candelabra monstrance by Enrique de Arfe, as well as a number of plates with religious-motifs. There is also a set of keys to the city presented by the local Jewish and Moorish communities to King Fernando III as a gesture of good faith after he conquered the city.

A bit further along this side of the building is the **Tumba de Colón**, a tomb carved by Arturo Melinda, holding the coffin of discoverer Christopher Columbus. It is raised by the statues of four crowned noblemen. Before departing the main body of the cathedral, make sure to walk along it's sides to view all of the richly decorated smaller chapels that are lined with sculptural and painting masterpieces.

Now head back through the cathedral, and walk a bit past the main entrance where you will find the access door to the 12th century Moorish **Giralda** minaret. Originally part of the former mosque located on this sight, this fantastic 98 meter (321 foot) tall brick tower can be seen from miles around. Saved from destruction by King Alfonso X after he threatened to kill anyone who removed even one brick, the four huge golden globes which once adorned the top were a world famous symbol of Sevilla, but fell off during an earthquake. The globes were subsequently replaced in the 16th century with a bell tower designed by Henando Ruiz. It was then that the 25 bells now perched on its top were added, as well as a weathervane topped with a bronze statue representing faith. For those of you in good shape, a series of narrow inclined ramps lead up the 670 or so paces to the top where the best views out over the city can be seen. The way down is much easier! Once you have reached the ground level again, make sure to walk around the adjacent **Patio de los Naranjos** inner courtyard, that was also part of the old mosque complex. Now planted with orange trees and a small garden with fountains, the Puerta de Perdón doorway that connects the patio with the inside of the cathedral is also from the Moorish era. In the corner of the courtyard you can pop into the small gift and book shop where posters and cards are available seven days a week.

The cathedral and it's treasury are open Monday through Saturday from 10:30am until 6pm, Sundays and Holidays from 2pm until 4pm. The Giralda is open Monday through Saturday from 11:00am until about 6pm, Sundays and Holidays from 10:30am until 1:30pm and again from 2pm until 4pm. Although small sections of the cathedral can be entered for free (for those that wish to pray), a combined ticket with access to all of its art and treasury laden rooms, as well as access to the Giralda tower and Patio de los Naranjos courtyard costs 700 ptas per adult and 200 ptas per child. On Sunday mornings, a ticket valid for just the

Giralda and the Patio de los Naranjos can be purchased for only 400 ptas Ask about special rates for those with student ID cards.

Throughout most of the year, there are horse-drawn carriages parked in front of the Cathedral. The drivers will be glad to take you and up to three friends or family member on a 40 minute tour of the old Jewish quarter for a mere 4,000 *ptas.*

The Los Reales Alcázares Royal Palace

After exiting the cathedral, turn right and follow the exterior of the building around the corner into the Plaza del Triunfo square. Here you will find the old crenellated walls which defended the stunning 12th to 14th century **Los Reales Alcázares** buildings of the Royal Palace. A series of regal structures have existed on this sight since Muslims controlled the city, but a vast majority of the buildings that occupy the area date back to the days when they were home to a string of successive Catholic rulers starting with King Pedro the Cruel. It was this King who hired Moorish laborers from Granada and Toledo to create the outstanding Mudéjar structures and decorations for his royal residence. Extensive alterations and expansion by later rulers left their mark on the complex, but the older sections still remain the most impressive to visitors and historians alike. In the 19th century, the Los Reales Alcázares was restored to it's current condition. The palace has been the sight of many famous events including the marriage of King Carlos V and the festivities of the internationally telecast 1995 marriage of King Juan Carlos's daughter, Princess Elena.

The main entrance can be reached by passing under the **Puerta de León** doorway, named for the lion painted on the ceramic tiles above the portal. Once inside you can either wait in line, or use the new automated ticket dispensers to pay your admission fee and continue into the compound. The excellent **Audio Guide** is a wireless multilingual audio-narration system, which enables visitors to hear experts discussing the various historical and artistic aspects of all the sections of the Alcázares as you walk through. These can be rented for a mere 400 ptas per person.

After paying your entrance fee and renting an Audio Guide, you will walk directly through the **Patio de la Montería** patio and it's adjacent **Patio de León** stone paved courtyard that are separated by old sections of the original Moorish wall. On your right side is the 16th century **Cuarto del Almirante** admiral's quarters where the powerful royally appointed Casa de Contratación (a sort of national chamber of commerce) planned the financing of major expeditions to the new world. The building also displays a fine altar by Alejo Fernandez as well as several antique Flemish tapestries. On the opposite side of the courtyard is the 14th century **Sala de Justicia** justice room, where King Pedro the Cruel would pronounce sentences upon accused people.

At the back end of these courtyards lies the fantastic Mudéjar **Palacio del Rey Don Pedro** palace. Built for King Pedro the Cruel in 1361, the original structure consisted of several fine Mudéjar rooms centered around the inner courtyard with fine arches and tiles known as the **Patio de las Doncellas**. Although almost all of these older rooms (and in fact the patio itself) had been altered by later rulers when the building was enlarged, they still contain interesting original as well as more recent elements. Make sure to pay special attention to the stunning **Salón de Embajadores** ambassadors hall where you can see fine tile work, horseshoe arches, iron balconies, and a cedar cupola.

As you walk around the upper and lower floors, keep your eyes out for the **Salón de Carlos V**, the ornate apartments of María de Padilla (King Pedro the Cruel's mistress), the main dining room, the 16th century chapel with it's fine coffered ceiling and tile covered altar by Francisco Niculoso Pisano, the **Patio de las Muñecas** patio where several guests were murdered by King Pedro the Cruel, and the so called **Salón de Reyes Moros** royal quarters. Just next door to the left of the palace is the less enchanting 16th century **Palacio de Carlos V** wing where you can quickly pass through while looking at some interesting tapestries and lavishly decorated apartments. Behind the palace buildings are beautifully manicured English style box gardens full of semi-tropical plants, Myrtle trees, towering palms, vaulted baths, and a small domed Moorish style pavilion.

The Los Reales Alcázares royal palace buildings are open during the Winter from Tuesday through Saturday from 9:30am until 5pm, Sunday from 10am until 1:30pm, and during the Summer from Tuesday to Saturday from 10am until 1:30pm and again from 5pm until 7pm, Sunday from 10am until 1:30pm. The entrance fee is now 600 ptas per adult, and is free for both students with International Student ID Cards and for children under 12 years old. Audio Guides cost 400 ptas per person.

Towards the Plaza de España

After exiting the palace complex, return to the **Plaza del Triunfo** square where horse-drawn carriages can be hired to take you around the fascinating side streets in this area. From the plaza, bear left and head down the Calle Santo Tomas for a few steps until passing alongside the rectangular 16th century **Archivo General de Indias** (locally known as the **Lonja**) archive building on your right hand side.

Originally designed by Juan de Herrera as a commercial exchange, King Carlos III decided in 1785 to convert the structure's second level into the official archives of the New World expeditions, including more than 35,000 rare documents and maps displayed in large wooden cases, some from the voyages of Columbus and Magellan. *The archives can be visited by the public on weekdays from 10am until about 1pm and is free to enter.*

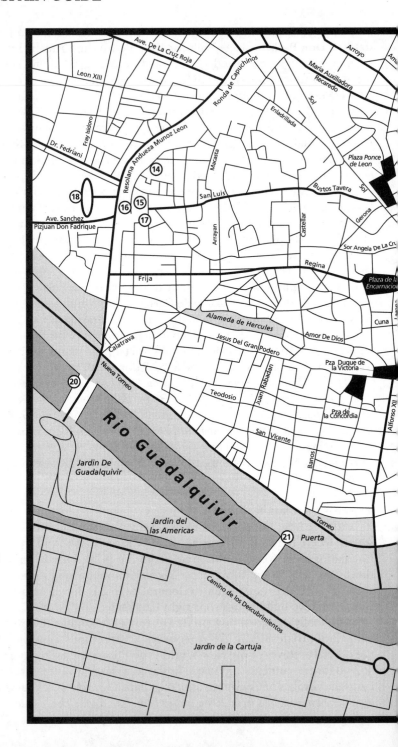

SEVILLE

KEY

1 Cathedral and Giralda
2 Archbishop's Palace
3 Convent of La Encarcion
4 Church of Santa Cruz
5 Monument to Columbus
6 Royal Alcazar
7 Archive of the Indies
8 Hospital of La Caridad
9 Maestranza Theater
10 Maestranza Bullring
11 Gold Tower
12 Plaza de Espana
13 Pilate's House
14 Walls
15 Church of San Gill
16 Gateway of La Maracena
17 Basilica of La Maracena
18 Hospital of the Five Wounds
19 University
20 Barqueta Bridge
21 "Pasorela La Cartuja"
22 Cachorro Bridge
23 Isbell II Bridge
24 San Telmo Bridge

Almost directly across the Calle de Santo Tomas is the 18th century former chapel building of the cathedral chapter house that was designed by Pedro de Silva. Inside this structure you will find the **Museo de Arte Contemporáneo** modern art museum with its fine collections of 20th century paintings, sculpture, ceramics, tapestries, glass, and woodwork. This is the sight of several seasonal thematic temporary exhibits, so ask at the museum's front desk for a copy of the free monthly *El Giraldillo* arts and entertainment guide for Sevilla to find out what's happening here and throughout town. *The museum is open during the winter on Tuesday through Friday from 10am until 8pm, Weekends from 10am until 2pm, and during the summer on Tuesday through Sunday from 10am until 2pm (except for August when it closes all weekend). There is currently no fee to enter this museum.*

At the next corner, turn left onto the busy Avenida de la Constitución and follow it down for a couple of short blocks until you reach the major intersection at the **Puerta de Jerez** plaza with its large central fountain. Cross the plaza and turn left to walk down the far side of Calle de San Fernando. After a few steps you should find the gateway on your right leading up to the absolutely fantastic **Hotel Alfonso XIII**. Although it is a private property, you should still walk inside the lobby to see the fantastic interior spaces, inner courtyard, and turn of the century furnishings. This is the most prominent place to stay in town (see *Where to Stay*) and its excellent semi-formal restaurant is the scene of some serious power lunches. The hotel was actually built to accommodate the most important guests of the 1929 Ibero-American exhibition, and was officially opened up by King Alfonso XIII himself. These days it is still the home away from home for visiting royalty, owing to the palatial decor of both its public and private rooms.

After having a look inside the spectacular hotel, walk back out the gates and turn right to continue along the Calle de San Fernando. At the next corner, make a right turn onto the small Calle de Doña María de Padilla and follow it on the left side until finding the obvious entrance to the huge two floor **Antigua Fábrica de Tabacos**. This wonderfully decorated Baroque former cigar factory was built by Dutch architect Sebastián van der Borcht in the mid-18th century. The building once employed thousands of young women in the production of hand rolled cigars, including **Carmen**, the namesake of Bizet's famous opera.

In 1954, the building became home to the main campus of the **Universidad de Sevilla**. The general public can follow the steady stream of students in through the building each day and walk around to view its fine inner courtyards, packed classrooms, tile paved floors, domed marble staircases, a fantastic chapel and billboards full of notes advertising American foreign exchange students who are willing to tutor students in English. Make sure to pop into the bookshop where you can buy great sweaters with the university's renowned crest and name on it – a perfect gift to bring home.

Depart through the same door you that you entered the university, and turn left to continue along the Calle de Doña María de Padilla until reaching the corner. Turn right onto the Calle Palos de la Frontera and walk down for half a block to see the Baroque 18th century **Palacio de San Telmo** on your left hand side. This former college of navigation and one-time royal palace of the Duke and Duchess of Montpensier now houses regional governmental offices. Although it is not open to the public. You can see sculptures of the discoverers of the New World atop its dramatically carved three story main facade by Leonardo de Figueroa, and the ceramic urn adorned gates and walls that enclose its fine private gardens.

Now turn around and walk back up the Calle Palos de la Frontera passing alongside the university. A half a block or so later on your right side will be the highly adorned beige and yellow **Teatro Lope de Vega**. This unusual 765 seat theater with its tile covered walls and dome was built especially for the 1929 Ibero-American Exposition and is surrounded by a peaceful park. You can't enter the theater unless there is a special event going on, bit it's a nice place to relax.

The Plaza de España & Parque de María Luisa

At the next corner you will carefully cross the Avenida de El Cid and pass by the statue in the central plaza before bearing slightly to the right to head up along the Avenida de Isabel la Católica. A block or so up on the left side is the enchanting **Plaza de España**. Built as the Spanish pavilion of industry for the 1929 Exposition, the majestic semicircular building with fine tile trimmings, occupying most of the plaza, has an interesting first floor lined with arches. From one tower- topped side of the facade to the other, a series of hand-painted tile murals depicting scenes, poems, and royal crests from each major city in Spain (arranged in alphabetical order) can be found lining the alcoves below the arches. In front of the building are geometric stone mosaic pavements, separated by a canal with small bridges where you can rent paddle boats for 350 *ptas* per hour or take a horse-drawn carriage ride for around 3,000 *ptas*.

Now cross over to the other side of the Avenida de Isabel la Católica where you will find the large but still somewhat tranquil **Parque de María Luisa** public park and recreation area, open daily from 8am to 10pm when its gates close. Founded by the Duchess of Montpensier, María Luisa de Orleans, who, in 1893 donated much of the grounds that surround the nearby Palacio de San Telmo to the city. The park was later transformed into its present design for the 1929 Exposition. Several wide promenades cut through the park and lead past gardens, bench-lined fountains, statues, children's pay areas and former pavilion buildings.

If you turn left into the park and head towards the back, you will eventually come to the large **Plaza de America** square with a large pool and fountain in its center. On one side of the fountain you will find the **Pabellón Mudéjar** that was designed by Anibal González in 1914 to house exhibits for the Expo. These days the structure is home to the **Museo de Artes y Costumbres Populares** popular arts and costume museum. Inside you will find an assortment of 18th through 20th paintings, horse-drawn carriages, jewelry, clothing, musical instruments, farm instruments, saddles, bullfighting suits, hand embroidered religious vestments, ceramics, replica houses, furnishings, crafts and the costumes and posters used during the famed Feria de Abril festival.

Much more compelling is the **Museo Arqueológico** archeology museum just across the square. Also designed by Anibal González for the Expo, inside this Neo-Renaissance building you can find dozens of rooms arranged in chronological order. The **Salas Prehistoría** prehistoric rooms downstairs contain ancient items found throughout the region and elsewhere in Spain, including fossils, arrow heads, stone tools, pottery, skeletons, burial urns and megaliths.

On the ground floor are the temporary and semi-permanent exhibitions that may feature Phoenician statues, a Corinthian statue of Trajan, Roman ruins from nearby excavations like Italica, gold and silver coins, highly detailed jewelry from nearby Carambolo, mosaic pavements, tombs, Arabic ceramics, Mudéjar columns, and local artifacts. *Both museums are open Tuesday through Sunday from 9am until 2:30pm and cost 250 ptas to enter.*

TOUR 2

The Plaza de San Francisco, the Calle de Sierpes, the Plaza del Salvador, & the Museo de Bellas Artes art museum.

Approximate duration (by foot) is about 4.5 hours, including church, museum, plaza, monument, and side street visits. Start from the side of the Catedral overlooking the Avenida de la Constitución.

For this tour, you will once again start off at the side of the Cathedral that faces onto the Avenida de la Constitución. From your position facing the cathedral, turn left to walk up the right side of the street for a couple of blocks. Soon the street ends at a sort of fork in the road where you are faced with a simple choice, either bear left and walk into the bustling **Plaza Nueva** square (home to dozens of municipal bus stops), or better yet, turn right and walk into the more tranquil and pretty **Plaza de San Francisco**.

The building that separates these two very different plazas is the awesome 16th century **Ayuntamiento** city hall building. Designed by Diego de Riaño, this very beautiful structure was built just after the wedding of King Carlos V. The Neo-classical facade on the other side of the building was greatly altered during the mid-19th century when the formerly adjacent Convento de San Francisco convent was demolished and the city hall was enlarged. Inside the building (entered via Plaza Nueva) you can ask if it's possible to peek inside the stunningly decorated council chambers, library, and meeting rooms that contain ceilings with golden carvings of rosettes, images of Spanish Kings, antique furnishings, old town archives, Flemish tapestries, massive chandeliers, a 15th century banner of Sevilla, rare leather bound books, and paintings by some of the country's most famous masters. *The city hall is only open to the general public on most Tuesdays and Thursdays between mid-July and mid-September from 6pm until 7:30pm, but you can call them at 459-0101 to make sure there are no official functions that will stop you from being allowed in.*

After passing in front of the city hall, walk through the plaza to reach the beginning of the Calle de las Sierpes street. Near the start of this extremely busy boutique-lined street is a plaque and bust that notes where the old town **Carcel** (jail) once stood. It was inside the former jail that the writer Cervantes started his work on *Don Quixote*. While strolling along this amusing street you can't help but notice the great bargains on leather goods, ceramics, and jewelry. Keep in mind most of the shops in town close for lunch between 2pm and 5pm from Monday through Saturday, and are not open on Sunday. Also try your best to avoid getting caught up in the street-side three card monte and shell games. These are scams run by local gypsies, and they are impossible to win.

Another block or so up, make a right turn onto the Calle Gallegos (or Calle Sagasta) and follow it for half a block until you reach the **Plaza del Salvador**. The obvious highlight of this plaza is its 17th century Baroque **Iglesia del Salvador** church. Built on the sight of a former mosque, the red colored facade incorporates an original Moorish minaret that has been converted into the church's bell tower. Inside there are several beautiful chapels and fine works of art, including the famed carving of Jesús de la Pasión by Martinez Montañés that is carried through town during part of the fabulous Semana Santa Easter processions.

The church can be entered year round for free, Monday through Saturday from 8:30am until 10:30am and again from 5pm until at least 8pm, Sundays from 10:30am until 2pm and again from 7:30pm until 9pm during winter months.

After visiting the church, walk across the plaza where you can pop inside any of the inexpensive café/bars. These places are standing room only each night after 8pm, when working class locals hang out here after the day's work is done. From the front of the bars, turn left and head out of the square via the Calle de Cuna street. Here you can window shop at the stores selling traditional, colorful Flamenco dresses. Make a left a block down on the Calle de Cerrajería and then turn right to end up back on the Calle de las Sierpes. Another couple of blocks further up, this shop-lined street ends, and you will turn left onto the Calle de Martin Villa that passes in front of the commercialized **Plaza del Duque de la Victoria**.

This plaza is flanked by the huge **El Cortes Ingles** department store and several municipal bus stops. In the middle of the plaza there are usually kiosks and tables set up to sell crafts and handmade leather goods. Continue walking past the square and along the Calle de Martin Villa as it merges first with the Calle Campana and then the major Calle de Alfonso XII.

Now follow this wide street for several blocks until you reach the peaceful little **Plaza del Museo** on the left hand side. This plaza is home to one of the city's top attractions, the incredible 19th century **Museo de Bellas Artes** fine arts museum. Housed within the red and yellow facade of the former Convento de la Merced Calzada convent, and surrounded by a series of cannon balls, this magnificent museum is among the best places in Spain to see 15th through 19th century paintings in an ornate setting. Upon entering the building you will first pass through the Libería with its tile murals of religious and scenic hunting scenes. Further inside is the colonnaded courtyard with an old well in its center and many more beautiful *azulejos* tile pieces.

After dropping a coin in the well for good luck, a doorway leads visitors through to the two floors of permanent exhibition spaces. These are organized in more or less of a chronological order. Among the works usually on display, all with descriptive plaques, are religious icons, sculptures, murals, and oil paintings by masters like **Millan**, **Pacheco**, **Martorell**, **Vasquez**, **Castellano**, **Castillo**, **Uceda**, **Roelas**, **Murillo**, **Velazquez**, **Zurbarán**, **Carpio**, **Ribera**, **Barrera**, **Gutierrez**, **Valdes Leal**, **Perez**, **Valdes**, **Martinez**, **Cano**, **Senet**, **Villegas**, **Esquivel**, and hundreds of other anonymous works from churches scattered around the city. *The hours are Tuesday through Sunday from 9am until 3pm, and admission is only 250 ptas per person.*

From the museum, return to the Calle Alfonso XII and turn left to continue down for a few blocks as it cuts through the **Plaza de San Laureano**. Now turn left at this square and follow the Calle Marqués de Paradas as it passes the back side of the bus station and at the end of this street, turn right onto the Calle de Reyes Católicos. The tour will end as this street leads in front of the **Guadaquivir** riverfront where you can sit down in one of the adjacent promenade's outdoor cafés and relax.

TOUR 3

The Hospital de la Caridad, the Waterfront, the Triana district, & Cartuja park.

Approximate duration (by foot) is about 6 hours, including church, museum, park, monument, and side street visits. Start from the side of the Catedral overlooking the Avenida de la Constitución.

Towards the Hospital de la Caridad

From the large portal of the cathedral, cross the Avenida de la Constitución and turn left. A few steps down at the next corner, turn right onto the tiny Calle de Almirantazgo for half a block until it ends. Now take the next right turn onto the small Passaje de Los Seises that then curves immediately to the left, and passes beneath the old **Arco del Postigo** archway to merge with the large Calle Dos de Mayo. The arch is connected to a dramatic two story towered building that houses the **El Postigo Mercado de Artesania** craft market that sells locally produced handmade jewelry, leather goods, paintings, and wood crafts. *The artisan shops in this building are open Monday through Friday from 10am until 2pm and 5pm until 7pm.*

From the front of the market, continue to walk down the Calle Dos de Mayo. About a block later, turn left onto the Calle Temprado and on your left hand side will be the Baroque 17th century **Hospital de la Caridad**. Inside the hospital is a sumptuous inner courtyard and nearby church that contains haunting paintings by Murillo and Valdes Leal, including a fantastic frescoed dome. Beneath the church's altar lie the remains of the hospital's founder, Don Miguel de Mañara, an infamous hedonist before later becoming deeply committed to the church. On his crypt are written the words, "Here lie the bones of the wickedest man that ever lived on earth." Some legends persist in the notion that he was the role model for the Don Juan character in the famous book *El Burlador de Sevilla* by the great Spanish writer Tirso de Molino. *The church is open Monday through Saturday from 9:30am until 1pm and again from 3:30pm until 6pm with an entrance fee of 250 ptas per person.*

Down to the Riverfront & the Torre del Oro

From the church, continue walking along the Calle de Temprado until it ends in front of the centuries-old **Torre de Menagem** watchtower, next to where a small archway leads a few steps into the excavations of ancient defensive walls that once surrounded the old town. From your position facing the front of the tower, take a right turn onto the Calle de Santander and follow it for a block or so until it intersects with the riverfront **Paseo de Colón**.

Cross over to the other side of the street and turn left. Walk a few steps towards the towering 13th century **Torre del Oro**. Once completely covered in golden tiles, this crenellated 12 sided tower was originally used by the Almohads to protect the city from any hostile boats with the help of a huge chain that spanned the river to its twin tower that once stood at the opposite bank. Its thinner upper sections were added sometime during the 18th century. These days it is home to the small **Museo Marítimo de Torre del Oro** naval museum that features depictions of the old port and other maritime themes. *The museum is open Tuesday through Friday from 10am until 2pm (closed all August) and costs 125 ptas to enter.*

The area immediately in front of the tower is the main departure point for a series of river cruise excursions (and even bus trips) run by companies like Cruceros Turistica Torre de Oro, *Tel. 456-1692,* that charge about 1100 *ptas* per person for a guided hour-long sightseeing trip.

Across the Bridge to the Triana district

After exiting the tower, take a few steps to the roadside walkway and turn left to head up alongside the Paseo de Colón highway. A series of great benches and tourist-packed outdoor cafés can be found off to your left on the riverfront **Paseo Alcalde Marqués del Contadero** promenade. On the other side of the street you will first find the modern **Teatro de Maestranza** theater where concerts and operas take place seasonally, and then the **Plaza de Toros de la Maestranza** bullring.

When you reach the **Puente de Isabel II** bridge, cross over it and head into the former gypsy quarter of **Triana** district. To the left of the bridge, the Calle Betis straddles the riverfront, offering lots of bars and discos. Since there are no real sights on this street (except at night when tons of kids come out to party), continue straight and walk along the Calle de San Jacinto for a block or so, until bearing right onto the quaint Calle de San Jorge. After another block or so you'll come across some of the city's oldest and most respected ceramic workshops, where you can custom order one of a kind handmade tile murals and plaques at great prices in shops like **Cermica Santa Ana**, **Ceramica Ruis**, and **Ceramica Rodriguez Dias.** This street now ends at the triangular **Plaza de Callao** where you will bear right and then curve to the left in order to follow the Calle de Castilla.

This main street has plenty of nice taverns and restaurants and now continues for a few blocks before reaching the **Plaza de Chapina**, were you will turn right to access the **Puente del Cachoro** bridge to get back across the river.

The Isla de la Cartuja

If you look over to your left just before crossing the bridge, you can see the walled complex of both modern and antique buildings that mark the **Isla de la Cartuja** island complex. Originally the sight of the Expo 1992 pavilions, the complex has recently been converted into a sort of theme park were visitors can see the highlights and odd looking structures remaining from the year long festival. The main international pavilions were built adjacent to the 15th century **Monasterio de Santa María de las Cuevas** monastery where Christopher Columbus was a frequent guest.

Around the monastery are bizarre ultra-modern structures that housed exhibits from all over the world during the Expo '92 opening. Now that the Expo is over, the city has finally begun to attract commercial development in the until vacant **Parque de los Descubrimientos** exposition grounds. This area is now the home to over two dozen giant bars, discotechs, and live conncert venues. Combined, these places attract up to 85,000 young, single party animals on warm weekend nights.

About the only other point of interest, especially for those traveling with small children, is the *Isla Magica* amusement park. Where you can spend a few hours on carnival style rides that are almost the same as at home. *You can enter the amusement park for 600 ptas a person daily between June and September from 10:30am until at least 7:30pm, and special events may add extended hours.* Check with the *Turismo* office for more details about what is currently being offered.

TOUR 4

The picturesque Barrio Santa Cruz (Old Jewish quarter). Approximate duration (by foot) is several hours, depending on your energy and interest level, including church, museum, park, monument, plaza, café, and side street visits. Start from the side of the Catedral overlooking the Plaza del Virgen de los Reyes.

This is a very charming district of old whitewashed houses embellished with hanging plants and fine inner patios, exquisite little historic plazas, and plenty of charming cafés, bars and restaurants. The zone forms a sort of elongated triangle who's apex starts just behind the Los Reales Alcázares and widens to form it's western-most border at the wide Avenida de Menendez y Pelayo, it's eastern-most border more or less at the major Avenida de la Constitución, and it's north border along the Calle de Imagen (the continuation of Calle Alfonso XII).

There is no possible way to guide you on a street by street walking tour through this district as there are no straight roads. The names of each lane remain unposted for the most part, and each road may change it's name several times as it curves around numerous times. The best I can do is to give you addresses and basic location information for the most charming sights, and let you get totally lost for a while before finally stumbling on to the correct place by chance and metaphysical navigation. I apologize for this method, but numerous attempts to explain the route to each of the following sights has proven to be more than a little frustrating. The easiest approach into the district is to walk to the entrance of the cathedral, and walk across to the far side of the Plaza del Virgen de los Reyes from where you should start your journey by heading up the memorable boutique and bar laden **Calle de Mateos Gago**, the commercial center of the old Jewish quarter.

Among the most impressive sights just blocks from this part of the Barrio Santa Cruz are the peaceful **Plaza Doña Elvira** square where plays were once performed, and the nearby 17th century **Hospital de los Venerables Secredotes** priest's hospital off of the Plaza de Venerables with it's fine Baroque courtyard and paintings by Valdes Leal. *The hospital is usually open to the public daily from 10am until 2pm and again from 4pm until 8pm with an admission charge of 600 ptas per person, and guided tours in Spanish are given at about 15 minutes past almost every open hour.*

A couple of blocks further, inside the district, rests the **Plaza de Santa Cruz.** Lined with mansions, the plaza itself surrounds a beautiful 17th century iron cross which marks the grave of Baroque painter Murillo. The artist once lived in what is now the **Casa Murillo** house and museum steps away on the Calle de Santa Teresa. The museum contains a good collection of Baroque paintings by Murillo and some of his personal belongings. *It is open from Tuesday through Friday from 10am until 2pm and again from 4pm util 7pm, Saturdays from 10am until 2pm, and admission is 300 ptas.*

Much farther away in the northern reaches of this district is the **Casa de Pilatos** off the Plaza de Pilatos and not too far from the Plaza del Salvador. This 16th century nobleman's mansion contains some of the city's finest Mudéjar and Renaissance elements including fantastically ornate tile work through it's interior and superb colonnaded courtyard, elaborate ceilings, ancient Greek and Roman sculptures, countless antique furnishings, and a staircase that you will never forget. Also just off the same square are several 16th through 18th century churches and convents that can be visited during daily mass hours for free. *The mansion which today is still owned by a Duke, can be visited daily from 10am until 2pm and again from 4pm until 7pm, and costs 500 ptas per person to enter each floor (a total of 2 floors may be visited). Guided tours are given in Spanish on most Thursdays at 1pm and 5pm.*

At night the Barrio Santa Cruz takes on a unique ambiance as the hundreds of wine and beer drinking crowds spill out on to the street from remarkable ancient taverns on lanes like the Calle de Mateos Gago, Calle Alemanes, Calle Argote de Molina, and many more. Your best chances of finding cheap and excellent tapas and drinks and to hear gypsy Flamenco guitarists are in this area. You might also find the unusual sounds of strolling *Tunas* (see side bar below). Overall, the whole area is dotted with hundreds of delightful sights that have an amazingly romantic air about them. Thehe Barrio Santa Cruz neighborhood, is the perfect place to rekindle or start off a love affair, it's that romantic.

TRADITIONAL "TUNAS" IN SEVILLA

*While rambling along the wonderful Barrio Santa Cruz, keep your eyes and ears open for the sight of roving groups of young men dressed in medieval costumes. These interesting people are known as **Tunas**, university students that are continuing a tradition that dates back several hundred years. They are practicing the art of serenading beautiful young women during the evening in order to either show their secret affection, or to just extol the virtues of their beauty. In the old days they were called **Sopistas** (the soup men), because in medieval times they were poor students who played music and sang in the streets in exchange for a badly needed bowl of nourishing soup which they could ill afford while still in school. These days most of the boys involved in this unique fraternity-like tradition are from richer families and are studying to become doctors, engineers, and lawyers.*

If you happen to be in a bar or on the streets while they are in the process of doing their thing, and they pass around the hat, consider giving a small donation which will be put to some sort of charitable or scholastic cause. If you can pull one of them aside, they all have a few good stories to tell. One Tuna told me about the time his band of Tunas was standing on a sidewalk serenading a stunning young lady standing on the balcony above (while at the same time they were looking up her dress) when her irate husband came outside and threatened them. In general they just want to flatter people with their attention and enchanting songs of love. Any trip to Sevilla is not complete without seeing these guys in action! Look out for them, especially on weekend nights.

GUIDED CITY TOURS

The typical city tour of Sevilla is provided by large tour operators who have big air conditioned buses and either a live guide (in the language of your choice) or a multilingual tape recorded guide. Expect to be offered a variety of half and full day trips that generally cost between 2,950 *ptas* and 5,650 *ptas* per half day, and between 6,500 *ptas* and 9,750 *ptas* per full day without meals.

Special interest excursions that include specific history, art, nightlife, or cultural events may cost upwards of 11,250 *ptas* including dinner and drinks. If you walk down towards the Torre del Oro on the riverfront, you can choose between several hour long boat and bus tours that are much less expensive. The companies listed below offer a wide range of the above trips, and may actually be able to pick you up directly from your hotel lobby with advance notification. Contact them directly or ask a travel agent to make reservations for you:

- **Pullmantur**, *Paseo de Colón, 11, Tel. (95) 421-3142*
- **Trapsatour**, *Avenida Luis de Morales, Tel. (95) 457-4590*
- **Cruceros Torre del Oro**, *Torre del Oro, Tel. (95) 456-1692*
- **Cruceros del Sur**, *Paseo de Colón, 11, Tel. (95) 456-1672*

NIGHTLIFE & ENTERTAINMENT

Although a bit too staged for my tastes, most tourists arriving in Sevilla head for one of the few good **Flamenco** clubs that specialize in traditional song and dance showcases. While the admission fee may be as high as 4,000 *ptas* per person, and dinner might also be part of the deal, this is the best way to see year round performances of this unique cultural activity.

The most popular Flamenco clubs are **El Arenal** at Calle de Rodo, 7 *(Tel. 421-6492)*, **Los Gallos** at the Plaza de Santa Cruz, 11 *(Tel. 422-8522)*, **Puerto del Triana** on Calle Castillo, 137 *(Tel. 437-2507)*, and **Patio Sevillano** over on the Paseo de Colón, 11 *(Tel. 421-4120)*. Show times generally start at 9:30pm or later. Smaller and more authentic Flamenco bars with little or no cover charge include the **El Pianillo** just of the Plaza Arenal and on some evenings at the **Quita Pesares** off the Plaza Jerónimo de Córdoba.

People aged 18 to 30 head straight for the **Barrio Santa Cruz** around the cathedral to hit the pubs and taverns like the **Bodega Santa Cruz** on Calle Rodrigo Caro, the **La Andaluz Bar** on Calle Garcia de Vinuesa, the **Carbonería** on the Calle Levies, the **Bodega La Andana** and nearby

FREE FLAMENCO PERFORMANCES

*For great free Flamenco on Wednesday and Thursday nights, you should wander along the riverfront promenade called the **Paseo de la O** in the **Triana** district. Located just a two minute walk away from the Giralda, this narrow esplanade is home to a dozen medium sized bars, some of which have a unique feature. During the quiet nights of mid-week they hire Sevilla based musicians to provide superb entertainment. In several of these bars you might hear the unmistakable sounds of two live guitars and soulful female vocals blasting out from the windows. These watering holes have no cover charge and don't even seem to care whether or not you buy a drink. Don't miss your chance to see the real thing.*

Antiguedades bars on the Calle Argote de Molina, and the **P. Flaherty** Irish pub just across the street from the Cathedral over on the Calle Alemanes.

The younger 15 to 19 year old set heads across the river and along the Calle Betis in the **Triana** district. Here on weekend nights the kids hang out in places like the **SVQ Disco**, the **Alhambrique Club, Rrio**, and **B60**. Among the better clubs in this area for somewhat more mature people is the **Sol y Sombra** disco on the nearby Calle de Castilla. After 11pm or so, the strip of bars along the side of the bullring on Calle Adriano such as **A3** and **Ddue** start to really happen.

More interesting, especially during warm weekend nights, is the movement towards outdoor establishments near the river. The most popular among the 17 to 30 year old crowd is called **Capote** which is located next to the Plaza das Armas bus terminal on the Sevilla side of the Chapina bridge. This place is a giant outdoor patio bar with no cover charge and has thousands of young singles checking each other out until the wee hours of the night.

Across the other side of the same bridge is the world famous **Puerta de Triana** nightlife section of the **Isla de la Cartuxa** island, where **Expo '92** was held. Here you will find a dozen or so huge dance clubs with up to 3,500 people in each, that are all open until 6am (most have no cover charge). Among these open air dance clubs are the **Salsadromo** salsa club, the **Ebano** disco, the **Sala Rociera** flamenco dance club (with great live live Flamenco on weekends), and several others. Be warned that the lines for both your initial entry, as well as for the bathrooms, get extremely long here after 1am when the majority of Sevilla's attractive young singles arrive for a night of flirtatious dancing and drinking. Parking is totally impossible, so either walk for 20 minutes to get here, or spend the 650 *ptas* or so for a taxi ride to reach this area from downtown.

Other mega-discos scattered throughout the city include the **Hipodromo** and **La Aduana** near the Avenida de Bonanza, the **Aire Club** off of Avenida de Andalucía, **Atenas** on Avenida Garcia Morato, the **Pacha** on Calle María Auxiliadora.

SPORTS & RECREATION
Amusement Parks
• **Acuatico Guadalpark**, *Poligono Aeropuerto, Tel. (95) 440-6622*

Bicycle Rentals
• **El Ciclismo**, *Paseo Catalina de Ribera, 2, Tel. (95) 441-1959*

Bullfights
• **La Maestranza Bullring**, *Paseo de Colón, Tel. (95) 422-3152*

Boat Rentals
• **Plaza de España**

Golf
• **Club Pineda de Sevilla**, *Carretera de Cádiz-Km.3, Tel. (95) 461-1400. 18 holes, par 72*
• **Real Club de Golf**, *(Montequinto), Tel. (95) 412-4301. 18 holes, par 71*
• **Sevilla Golf**, *(Aznalcázar), Tel. (95) 575-0414. 18 holes, par 72*

Horseback Riding
• **Hipica Puerta Principe**, *Carretera de Utrera-Km.11, Tel. (95) 486-0815*
• **Club Pineda de Sevilla**, *Carretera de Cádiz-Km.3, Tel. (95) 461-1400*

Outdoor Markets
• **Thursday Market**, *Calle Feria*
• **Sunday Market**, *Alameda de Hercules*
• **Sunday Pet Market**, *Plaza de la Alfalfa*
• **Sunday Stamp and Coin Market**, *Plaza del Cabildo*

Pro Soccer Teams
• **BETIS**, *Estadio Benito Villamarin*
• **SEVILLA F.C.**, *Estadio Sanchez Pizjuan, Calle Luis de Morales*

Public Swimming Pools
• **Piscinas Sevilla**, *Avenida Ciudad de Jardin*
• **Piscina Municipal Virgen de los Reyes**, *Avenida Doctor Fedriani*

EXCURSIONS & DAY TRIPS

If you have a minimum of six hours to spare, consider visiting **Italica** or the **Costa de la Luz** (covered below in its own section). In most cases the sightseeing and excursion companies listed below provide guided tours on a seasonally changing schedule. There are also additional half and full day guided tours to such destinations as Jerez, Cádiz, Córdoba, Carmona, Granada, and Ronda, as well as multiple day tours to further destinations in both Spain and Portugal.

Prices start at about 5000 *ptas* for a short local bus tour, and go up to over 9,750 *ptas* for full day tours with lunch, and well over 185,000 *ptas* per person for a 12 night tour with meals and hotels included. More independent travelers may wish to save money and follow the directions listed here via train, bus, or rental car. If you intend to visit Portugal, make sure to purchase a copy of my Portugal Guide (Open Road Publishing) for more detailed sightseeing information and money saving tips.

Bus Excursions

Tickets for the dozens of guided tours operated daily by the following operators can be purchased from most hotels, travel agencies, or directly from the companies listed below.

Call in advance to determine the exact times and days of the week for your preferred excursion, which language the tour will be given in, and where the pickup location nearest to you will be for that specific outing.

• **Pullmantur,** *Paseo de Colón, 11, Tel. (95) 421-3142*
• **Trapsatour,** *Avenida Luis de Morales, Tel. (95) 457-4590*

ITALICA

Located about 10 km (6 miles) northwest Sevilla, just above the town of Santiponce, the fantastic ruins of **Italica** are a must-see. The community was originally founded in 206 B.C. by Roman General Scipio Africanus as a retreat for his soldiers wounded during battles with the Carthaginians. This once great city of over 10,000 inhabitants was the birthplace of the Roman emperor Trajan, and was the seat of regional power until the empire's decline during the 4th and 5th centuries A.D. After the Visigoths took over as rulers of what is now Andalucía, most of the residents moved into nearby Sevilla, and by the time the Moors arrived, the city was all but deserted.

What remains of the Roman era are a series of dramatic ruins that form the **Conjunto Arqueológico de Italica** archaeological site. The complex has two separate sections, with the vast majority of excavations from the 2nd through 4th century A.D. of the so called **Nova Urbs** (new sections). These contain the town's defensive walls, the ground floors of villas complete with gymnasiums, colonnaded gardens, courtyards with cross shaped pillars, cisterns, Roman baths, old town lanes, an amazing 25,000 seat amphitheater, and mosaic floors that rival those found anywhere else on earth. In Santiponce itself are the remains of the **Vetrus Urbs** (old sections), with Roman theater and other less important ruins. Many of the objects found here have since been moved into the **Museo Arqueológico** archaeology museum, but the remaining items are still awesome.

Hours

The complex is open from Tuesday through Saturday from 9am until at least 6:30pm, Sundays from 10am until at least 3pm, and costs 375 ptas per person.

Directions

To get here by car, take route N-630 northwest from Sevilla for about 9.5 km (6 miles), until reaching the town of Santiponce where you will find signs directing you just a bit further to Italica.

Bus service here is provided by the **Empresa Casal** bus company via their station at Calle Marqués de Parades, 53, and runs about a dozen times a day in each direction with a round-trip cost of some 380 *ptas*.

The excursion companies listed above run bus tours here throughout the year for approximately 3,600 *ptas* per person for a half day trip, with guide and museum or monument admissions included.

PRACTICAL INFORMATION

- **Main City Tourist Office**, *Turismo, Ave de Constitución, 21, Tel. (95) 422-1404*
- **Municipal Tourist Office**, *Turismo, Paseo de las Delicias, 9, Tel. (95) 423-4465*
- **Airport Tourist Office**, *Aeropuerto de San Pablo, Tel. (95) 425-5046*
- **Sevilla Airport**, *San Pablo, Tel. (95) 451-0677*
- **Iberia Airlines Reservations**, *Tel. (95) 422-8901*
- **Regional Train Info**, *Renfe, Tel. (95) 441-4111*
- **Santa Justa Train Station**, *Tel. (95) 442-1562*
- **Regional Bus Info**, *Estación Plaza das Armas, Tel. (95) 490-7737*
- **Regional Bus Info**, *Estación Prado de San Sebastián Tel. (95) 441-7111*
- **Sevilla Municipal Bus Info**, *TUSSAM, Tel. (95) 442-0011*
- **Public Transportation Info Headquarters**, *Tel. (95) 441-1152*
- **Sevilla Commuter Train Info**, *Regionales Renfe, Tel. (95) 454-0202*
- **Sevilla Radio Taxi Companies**, *Tel. (95) 496-000 or (95) 458-000*
- **Central Post Office**, *Ave. de Constitución, 32, Tel. (95) 421-9585*
- **American Consulate in Sevilla**, *Paseo de las Delicias, Tel. (95) 423-1884*
- **Canadian Consulate in Sevilla**, *Ave. de Constitución, 30, Tel. (95) 422-9413*
- **Municipal Lost and Found Office**, *Tel. (95) 421-5694*
- **Regional Directory Assistance**, *Tel. 1003*
- **National Directory Assistance**, *Tel. 1009*
- **Medical Emergencies Hot Line**, *Tel. (95) 422-2222*
- **Red Cross (Ambulances)**, *Tel. (95) 435-0135*
- **Municipal Police**, *Tel. (95) 428-9300*

THE COSTA DE LA LUZ

If you have at least one full day to spend outside Sevilla and want to hit the beach or do some sherry tasting, one of the best choices is to head over to the **Costa de la Luz**. This beautiful stretch of Atlantic Ocean coastline is less developed, with peaceful wine producing villages, and livestock ranches starting from the quaint but extremely windy seaside resort town of **Tarifa**. This is where the Atlantic merges with the

Mediterranean about 175 km (109 miles) south of Sevilla, and curves northwestward towards its end at the Portuguese border.

In the summer, tens of thousands of tourists from all over Spain and northern Europe fill up its relatively inexpensive hotels, condos, and pub-lined old town lanes. This part of Spain is a great place to enjoy windsurfing, affordable seaside restaurants, wineries offering free sherry tastings and equestrian events. Although the whole coast and its adjacent rural inland villages and major cities all have something special to offer, I have listed a few places of interest here that are among the better possibilities for a good long day trip from Sevilla.

ARRIVALS & DEPARTURES

By car, the best method to get to the inland city of Jerez de la Frontera or the coastal city of Cádiz from Sevilla is to take the A-IV highway south until reaching the exits for these cities. From here to Tarifa, take the coastal route N-340 south.

Renfe trains run multiple daily routes from Sevilla via the Estación Santa Justa rail station in each direction (even more during the summer), to the Cádiz station on the Plaza de Sevilla, and the Jerez station on Plaza de Estación with one way fares from 395 *ptas.*

Buses from Sevilla run to these and more destinations along the coast and interior areas. Call Sevilla's Estación Plaza das Armas, *Tel. (95) 490-7737,* and the Estación Prado de San Sebastián, *Tel. (95) 441-7111,* for exact fare and scheduling information in both directions.

Pullmantur, *Tel. (95) 421-3142,* and Trapsatour, *Tel. (95) 457-4590,* offer full day summertime bus tours from major hotels and other points in Sevilla to coastal attractions and cities such as Jerez and Cádiz and others for about 7,500 *ptas* without meals.

WHERE TO STAY
CADIZ
Moderate

PARADOR-HOTEL ATLANTICO, *Avenida Duque de Najera, 9. Tel. (956) 226-905, Fax (956) 214-582. US and Canada Bookings (Marketing Ahead) Tel. 800/223-1356. Year round rack rates from 18,500 ptas per double room per night (E.P.). All major credit cards accepted.*

This government owned modern sea front hotel has some of the best services and facilities in the area. This modern and charming resort *parador* has 149 large and beautifully decorated rooms (and deluxe suites with Jacuzzis), all with private bathrooms, air conditioning, tile and hardwood flooring, hair dryers, satellite color television, mini-bar, mod-ern hardwood furnishings, direct dial telephones, windows or private terraces with views out over either the sea or the old streets of the Casco Historico zone, executive styled desks, and plenty of natural sunlight.

Facilities here include an excellent regional restaurant, a bar with live music on weekends, large sitting rooms, a game room for kids, a nice outdoor swimming pool, meeting and convention rooms, gardens, plenty of free parking, foreign currency exchange, room service and an indoor garage. The beach at La Caleta, the old town center, and several beautiful gardens walkways are just a minute or two away by foot from the parador's front door. The service here is very good.

SEEING THE SIGHTS
TARIFA

The traditional fishing and maritime trade city of Tarifa, population 14,623, has become one of Spain's premier windsurfing destinations. Originally founded by Romans as a port for departure for their conquests to Africa – the town lies just 16 km (10 miles) across the adjacent straights of Gibraltar – it wasn't until the 8th century when a city developed here under the control of caliph Tarif ben Malluk. The city is full of beautiful cobblestone streets and small café-lined plazas where young sunburnt tourists (mostly Germans) sit around and drink beer all day.

The main highlights include the quiet **Playa Chica** beach on the Mediterranean and its neighboring huge **Playa de los Lances** beach that marks the start of the Atlantic. This is where some of the windsurfing and fishing takes place, and over at the seafront **Club Nautico de Tarifa** you can sip cheap drinks, eat good meals, and rent water sports equipment. The town's nearby commercial port is also the sight of ferry service to and from Tangiers.

Just across from the beach and its newly renovated promenade you can take a look at the dramatic 13th century fortified **Torre de Santa Catalina** watchtower. A bit further inside the city center, you can tour the city's main **Plaza de San Mateo**, with its exquisite 15th century Baroque church and the nearby remains of the 8th century **Castillo de Guzmán el Bueno** castle. This is the spot where, during a siege in 1292, Christian military leader Alonso Perez de Guzmán told the invading Moors who had kidnapped his young son that he would never surrender the castle. Sensitive guy that he was, he then threw his own dagger to the ground and suggested they use it to execute his child.

Also worth the effort are strolls along the **Plaza de Santa María** old town square. There's a cute municipal museum and city hall buildings surrounding a fine box garden with an unusual fountain. You might also want to walk along the pedestrian only **Paseo de Alameda** promenade, with its tall palm trees and fine restaurants, or around the seaside along the old **Murallas Árabes** Moorish era defensive walls. If you continue, you'll eventually come to the wonderful **Plazuela del Viento** square and the adjacent **Mirador Estrecho de Gibraltar** park and lookout point, complete with antique ceramic lined benches and numerous cacti.

The most serious windsurfers and sun worshippers head at least another six km (four miles) or more up the coast to the west to the more barren windswept **Playa de Tarifa** and the amazingly beautiful **Playa de Valdevaqueros** sand dune beaches, where Germans camp out in tents and VW campers just off the sand. There are numerous windsurf shops and schools alongside cheap hotels and restaurants.

A few kilometers further west, off the N-340 near the crescent shaped **Playa de Bolonia**, there is a turnoff to the left marked with a sign for Monumento Baelo. This leads, seven kilometers (4 miles), to the **Monumento Historico Artistico Baelo Claudio**. These are ruins of temples, baths, a market, and civic buildings from the 1st century A.D., the abandoned and recently excavated Roman town of **Bolonia**. *The site can be toured for 250 ptas per person on Tuesday through Saturday at approximately 10am, 11am, 12noon, 1pm, 5pm and 6pm starting from the small office compound.* Even if there is nobody in the office, you can see right through the chain link fence and stare at the huge piles of yet to be rebuilt columns and statues surrounding the remains of the former structures.

Those looking for some regional Flamenco music and Andalucían horseback riding shows can pop into the **Cortijo el Valle** stables and clubhouse, just a bit further west along the N-340.

Major Local Festivals
Contact the local Turismo office, *Tel. (956) 684-186,* for more details.
• **Fiesta de Folklorica**, *August, Folk Music*
• **Fiesta del Santa**, *September, Processions, Fireworks*

CADIZ
For great beaches and a quaint old town center within easy walking distance of a large port city, Cádiz might be a good choice.

Cadiz, population 156,886, is located about 90 km (56 miles) further northwest from Tarifa, or 115 km (72 miles) south of Sevilla, this diverse city is located on a rocky peninsula and was first settled about 3,000 years ago. Originally a Phoenician trading post, Cádiz passed through the hands of the Carthaginians, Romans, Moors, and finally the Christian Kings, becoming one of the wealthiest ports in all of Europe. It was from this harbor that explorer ships heading to the New World set sail, as did the Spanish Armada in 1588. Since the area was so strategic, it suffered several blockades including the attack by Sir Francis Drake and his British ships during which the naval ships anchored here were set ablaze and much of the city was sacked.

Although your first view of the city will be its unimpressive new section of towering condos and huge commercial avenues, the walled **Casco Historico** (old part of town) is a real treasure. Just be advised that during the summer, the entire population of the city heads for the seaside. Those living in the old town bring huge bags full of chairs and sunscreens to the shallow cove beach called **Playa La Caleta** which is surrounded by old fortresses. The folks from the newer part of town head over to the much longer white sandy beaches such as the **Playa de la Victoria** which are located just off the wide Avenida de Andalucia.

Among the most interesting sights to visit are the sea front walkways and parks that border the north and eastern sides of the peninsula. These include the tranquil **Alameda Marqués de Comillas**, the **Alameda de Apodaca**, and the peaceful **Parque de Genoves** waterfront park. Further into the town itself you can pop into the **Museo de Cádiz-Bellas Artes y Arqueológico** (fine arts and archeology museum) located in the same building off the main Plaza de Mina square, near the *Turismo* tourist office. In the fine arts section you can view paintings by **Zubarán**, **Ribera**, **Rubens**, and **Murillo**, while the separate archaeology section features Roman statues, gold and silver coins, pre-Colombian relics and ancient pottery and jewelry. *The museum is open Tuesday through Sunday from 9:30am until 2pm and costs 275 ptas to enter both sections.*

There is also a good **Museo Historico de Cádiz** history museum off of the Calle de Santa Ines where you can see a wood and ivory scale model of the town circa 1780, among other local history related exhibits. *This museum is open Tuesday through Friday from 9am until 1pm and again from 4pm until at least 7pm, weekends from 9am until 1pm, and costs 275 ptas to enter.*

Besides some historic old lanes and a wonderful selection of great boutiques around the heart of town, the only other worthwhile sights are the few interesting houses of worship that are scattered throughout town. The 18th century **Oratorio de la San Felipe Neri** church near the history museum on the Calle de San José has a fine painting on its altar by Murillo, and can be visited for free during its daily morning mass. This was the sight of the first Cortes meetings where the Republic of Spain was proclaimed in 1812.

The impressive 18th century Baroque and Neoclassical **Catedral** (cathedral) just off Calle Arquitecto Acero features a fairly dramatic interior, but the main highlight is its **Museo Catedralicio** religious arts museum that displays gold and silver plates, a massive monstrance, and some fine paintings. *The museum is open Monday through Saturday from 10am until 1:30pm and costs 125 ptas to enter.*

Last but not least, is the 17th century **Capilla de la Santa Cueva** church off the Calle de Rosario, where there are beautiful frescoes by Goya, *Monday through Saturday from 10am until 1pm for 100 ptas.*

Also worth a look at in the old town area are several palaces, churches, fortresses and mansions that can be found on the free map from the tourist offices and hotels. Among these sights is the 45 meter high 17th century **Torre Tavira** tower off the Calle Marques del Real Tesoro which, within the roof, has a great camera obscura, a moving mirror image system first invented by Leonardo Da Vinci. This interesting observation system gives amazing 360 degree views of the city. The tower also has a multimedia exhibition of the city and its history. *The Torre Tavira is open from 10am until 8pm daily during the summer, and 10am until 6pm daily during the winter and costs 400 ptas per person to enter.*

For more excellent beaches and great local seafood, head across the bay into the neighboring city of **Puerto de Santa María**. You'll find nice sandy beaches like **Playa Vista Hermosa**, **Playa La Puntilla**, and **Playa de Valdelagrana** where some small-scale development is just starting to kick in. In the town itself there are a few sherry *bodegas* where you can enjoy free wine tastings on weekday mornings.

Major Local Festivals

Contact the local Turismo office, *Tel. (956) 253-254,* for more details.
• **Carnaval**, *February, Festivals and Parades*
• **Semana Santa**, *Before Easter, Processions*

JEREZ DE LA FRONTERA

Locally known simply as Jerez, this peaceful inland village with a sizable population of just over 200,000, lies 36 km (22 miles) northeast of Cádiz. Jerez is respected throughout the world as the major center for the production of the highest quality sherry and for its famed horses.

There are a few historic and cultural sights to see here, especially the Moorish 11th century **Alcázar** fortress that lies in ruins in the gardens just below the **Plaza del Arenal**. Also, the 13th century Mudéjar **Iglesia de San Dionisio** church off the **Plaza de Asuncion**, and the **Real Escuela Andaluza de Atre Ecuestre** horse training school on the edge of town on the Avenida Duque de Abrantes with its amazing equestrian events held for spectators each Thursday at noontime make Jerez an interesting stop.

But the main reason to visit this area is the sherry. You can enjoy a free and informative sherry tasting session at any of the several *bodegas* in the city limits. Although open to the public at various times each day, it is always best to call and reserve a place on the tour and tasting that most interests you. Typically a small group of visitors will be led through the various fermentation and storage rooms while a multilingual guide explains the fermentation, fortification, storage, and blending processes used in the creation of these sweet wines. After the tour, an informal tasting of several varieties of *Fino* will follow, and usually you can purchase specific vintages straight from the factory at good prices.

See the sidebar below for sherry tastings:

SHERRY BODEGAS

Try the following historic cellars:

Pedro Domecq, *Calle de San Ildefonso, 3, Tel. (956) 331-800. Open 10am until 12:30pm on most days. Closed in late July and August.*

Gonzáez Byass, *Calle María González, 12, Tel. (956) 340-000. Open 11am until 1pm on most weekdays. Closed in July and August.*

John Harvey & Sons, *Calle de Arcos, 53, Tel. (956) 346-000. Open 9am until 2pm on most weekdays. Closed during August.*

Sandeman Coprimar, *Calle de Pizzaro, 10, Tel. (956) 301-100. Open 9am until 1pm on most weekdays. Closed in late July and August.*

Williams & Humbert, *Calle Nuno de Canas, 1, Tel. (956) 331-300. Open 11am until 2pm on most weekdays. Closed mid-July to mid August.*

Major Local Festivals

Contact the local Turismo office, *Tel. (956) 331-150,* for more details.

• **Rodeo de Abril**, *April 24, Horseraces and rodeos*
• **Fiesta Ecuestre**, *May, Equestrian shows and parades*
• **Fiesta de Vino**, *September, Grape Harvest Festival*

CARMONA

When you have the urge to leave the noise and action of Sevilla behind for an afternoon, or even a couple of days, **Carmona** is the perfect diversion. The old city itself is surrounded by spectacular defensive walls that give a unique ambiance to what is really a small town (population 22,779) with countless historical sights.

As the evidence in the nearby necropolis and at other accidental discoveries at construction locations in and around town suggest, the roots of this city date back at least 5000 years. The city is so fortified that it has never been captured. On every street there are fantastic old buidings and churches. The sophisticated townsfolk here will go out of their way to direct lost foreigners to the best spots to visit.

I love Carmona, and I strongly suggest you see it for yourself while in the region. It's a place you'll always remember.

ARRIVALS & DEPARTURES

By Bus

The Empresa Casal, Empresa Bacoma, and Servibus bus companies each offer several scheduled buses in both directions daily between their depots in Sevilla and Carmona's depot on Calle de San Pedro, for about 375 *ptas* each way.

By Car

From Sevilla, take the N-IV highway northeast. Once inside the city you will find plenty of free and metered parking on the streets if you spend a few minutes looking around.

ORIENTATION

The walled city of Carmona rests on a hilltop overlooking the southeastern portion of southern Spain's **Andalucía** region, a 29 km (18 mile) drive east from Sevilla.

GETTING AROUND TOWN

Once inside Carmona, you can walk anywhere. If you need a taxi, you can walk over to the central taxi stand on the Paseo del Estatuto.

WHERE TO STAY

Expensive

PARADOR DE CARMONA, *Alcázar de Arriba. Tel. (95) 414-1010. Fax (95) 414-1712. US & Canada bookings (Marketing Ahead) 800/223-1356. Low season rack rates from 18,500 ptas per double room per night (E.P.). High season rack rates from 18,500 ptas per double room per night (E.P.). All major credit cards accepted.*

Finally reopened after a massive two year refurbishment project, this fantastically managed and extremely friendly deluxe hotel is a wonderful place to stay. Situated in the reconstructed royal palace of a Spanish King, this enchanting, small luxury hotel offers some of Europe's most memorable accommodations and public rooms.

Their 63 beautifully furnished rooms and suites come equipped with air conditioning, deluxe private marble bathrooms, satellite television, mini-bar, direct dial telephone, fantastic picture widows or terraces with serious views, comfortable bedding, Spanish tile flooring, tapestries, designer fabrics, and impressive hardwood furnishings. Facilities include plenty of free secure parking, private guest lounges with large screen televisions and plush sofas, an picture perfect ceramic tile lined patio and sun deck, beautiful gardens, a huge outdoor swimming pool, a superb gourmet restaurant and a peaceful bar. The service is absolutely top class. Selected as one of my Best Places to Stay (see Chapter 13).

HOTEL CASA DE CARMONA, *Centro de Ronda. Tel. (95) 414-3300, Fax (95) 414-3752. Year round rack rates from 22,000 ptas per double room per night (E.P.). Most major credit cards accepted.*

What a shame that this opulent 16th century mansion behind the Casa de Cultura in the heart of the old town, now converted into a luxury hotel, has continued to go through more management changes than Elizabeth Taylor has had husbands. If they ever get their act together and find a better staff, it would certainly be a good choice for upscale travelers. They offer 30 or so accommodations that range from deluxe suites to tiny rooms, so make sure to reserve a larger unit. All of the beautifully decorated rooms and suites come with air conditioning, satellite color television, antique furnishings, mini-bar, mini-safe and fine original artwork.

Facilities include a swimming pool, luscious lounges, laundry and dry cleaning services, a library with rare volumes, beauty salon, business meeting rooms, a beautiful courtyard, open bar, work out room with sauna, free parking, and room service. Pop inside during your visit to Carmona and see if things have gotten any better there; if so let me know.

Moderate

HACIENDA DE LOS GRANEROS, *Carretera de Sevilla. Tel. (95) 595-3020, Fax (95) 595-3020. Year round rack rates from 7,500 ptas per double room per night (E.P.). Year round rack rates from 47,000 ptas per double apartment per week (E.P.). Cash only - no credit cards accepted.*

This wonderful, converted traditional farmhouse is not well known, but it is one of Carmona's real gems. Run by a charming Spanish-German family, this delightful property is situated only 10 minutes away from the center of town. Unlike most hotels in this area, the owners have spent all of their lifelong savings to create a unique and welcoming environment for day tripping visitors, and more demanding long stay clients. The apartments have been beautifully decorated with modern furnishings and antique trimmings, featuring private bathrooms, nice bedrooms, great views out over the surrounding fertile plain and nice modern kitchens.

Facilities here include the highest quality of personalized service, a great swimming pool, available breakfast, an antique salon for business meetings and groups, available nearby horseback riding, a wonderful rooftop and courtyard sunning area. Make sure to first call the multilingual owners to get specific directions as it is located on an old farm road that is not so easy to find at first. I guarantee that no other guide book will even tell you about this place, but it really deserves all the praise I can give it. Selected as one of my Best Places to Stay (see Chapter 13).

Inexpensive

HOSTAL CASA CARMELO, *Calle de San Pedro, 15. Tel. (95) 414-0572, Fax (95) NONE. Low season rack rates from 4,500 ptas per double room per night (E.P.). High season rack rates from 5,250 ptas per double room per night (E.P.). Cash Only - No credit cards accepted.*

This clean and friendly little hostel near the main gate into town has several rooms either both private and shared bathrooms and basic no frills furnishings. Nothing special, but a good deal in this limited budget category.

WHERE TO EAT

Expensive

PARADOR DE CARMONA, *Alcázar de Arriba. Tel. (95) 414-1010. All major credit cards accepted.*

All I can say is wow! This fine *parador* is also home to an equally impressive yet not too formal restaurant that serves up some of the best regional and traditional Spanish cuisine for miles around. They have two separate menus available during lunch and dinner. Set in a remarkably pretty dining room, the restaurant features a prix-fixe menu for about 3,750 *ptas* per person, and you can choose from a seasonally changing list of delicious items.

Specialties include lettuce and anchovy salad, terrine of halibut, Andalucían soup, grilled swordfish with garlic sauce, lamb cutlets with red peppers, salmon with vermouth, veal entrecote with blue cheese and a serious diet-busting selection of desserts. Their special regional menu offers seasonal al la carte selections such as stewed ox tail, roasted lamb with rosemary, creamed spinach cooked in a secret sauce, codfish with dried tomato, red cabbage stuffed with apples and bacon, pickled venison. stewed local partridge fillet of sole, prawn and fish brochettes, duck in tangerine sauce, and many more delicious items including great desserts and fine wines. This is the best place in town to eat and their superb threecourse prix-fixe menu is only 3,750 *ptas* per person plus drinks.

Inexpensive

RESTAURANTE GAMERO, *Calle de San Pedro, 10. Tel. (95) 414-1171. Cash Only.*

Located on the main road into the old town, this nice and simple local eating establishment is about the best place to grab a quick snack during your visit to Carmona. Although far from fancy, they offer a large menu of typical foods including *tapas* like shrimp with garlic, grilled tuna, fried hake, Russian salad, ham croquette, calamari, fresh gazpacho, assorted omelets, shrimp with Jerez sauce, grilled swordfish., and lots of simple puddings and cakes. A good snack here will cost around 1,450 *ptas* per person.

SEEING THE SIGHTS

Approximate duration (by foot) is about 4.5 hours, including church, museum, rampart, plaza, and side street visits.

The Old Part of Town

No matter how you choose to get here, the point of arrival into the old city is via the **Plaza de Blas Infante**, where there are several boutiques, cafés, and banks across the street from the majestic 15th century **Iglesia de San Pedro** church with its splendid Giraldillo bell tower. Just in front of this nice little square is the dramatic 1st century **Puerta de Sevilla** gateway and its attached **Alcázar** castle that leads through the old town walls.

The structure was built by the Carthaginians during the 2nd Punic War and later modified by the Romans, Moors, and Christians until reaching its present size and shape. Restored after centuries of neglect and the occasional earthquake damage, the gateway's fortress contains vestiges of an old Roman temple, a prison, Moorish horseshoe arches, two great watchtowers, and a former water tank on its roof. Besides having to pass beneath its archway to gain entrance into town, you can view the interior and roof (with excellent photo opportunities out over the whole city!) of the fortress *on Fridays and Saturdays from 11am until 1pm, for a fee of 200 ptas per person.*

After passing through the gateway you will be entering the Plaza del Palenque, the former heart of the old Jewish quarter. From here you will bear slightly to the left to head onto the main Calle Prim. On the right hand side a half block or so up is the enchanting 15th century **Iglesia de San Bartolome** that can be entered for free on Sundays from 12noon until 1pm to see its fine chapels and sacristy where a beautiful sculpture by Francisco de Ocampo and other antique works of art can be found. After about another block, the street now ends in the picturesque **Plaza de San Fernando** (also known as Plaza de Arriba or even Plaza Mayor) that is surrounded by a series of fine 17th and 18th century municipal office buildings with iron balconies, and centers around a fantastic circular garden park of tall palms.

From the far right corner of the square, head straight up the Calle de El Salvador a few steps as you pass the 16th century **Ayuntamiento** city hall building on your right side. This structure was originally a Jesuit monastery before being converted into city governmental offices, so its fine inner courtyard with Roman mosaics is not really open to public inspection. (I was able to persuade the doorman to let me in anyway). Continue walking along the Calle de El Salvador as it passes by the now closed Iglesia de el Salvador church until the street ends a block or so later.

From here take a left turn onto the Calle de Carlota Quintanilla and on your right side is the bold facade of the Gothic 15th century **Iglesia de Santa María** church. Built atop the town's former main mosque, which in turn was built amid the ruins of a Visigothic church, this vaulted house of worship can be visited on most days *from 10am until 12noon and again from 6:30pm until 8pm.* Inside is the Patio de los Naranjos courtyard and its *Mudéjar* tower that both contain remnants from its earlier Visigothic and Moorish roots. Just across from the main facade of the church is the massive 17th century **Casa Palacio de los Rueda** mansion that is not open to the public. You may want to ask the *Turismo* offices at the Casa de Cultura if there is any way possible to be allowed to see its amazing marble colonnaded courtyard and elegant period furnishings.

After leaving the church, turn right to continue to the end of the block where you will turn right onto the Calle de Santa María de Grácia and a few steps later turn left into the **Plaza Descalzas**. The most important structure here is the 18th century **Casa de las Descalzas** (now known locally as the **Casa de Cultura**), a former college building that now houses city governmental offices including the *Turismo* office. Here you can pick up comprehensive maps with multilingual historical summaries of every old building around town. *The tourist office is open weekdays from 10am until 1:30pm and again from about 4:30pm until at least 7pm.*

After popping into the tourist office, retrace your steps back a block or so until you can turn left onto the Calle de Santa María de Grácia. Just as you start walking up this street, you will find yourself surrounded by several 17th and 18th century buildings along the **Plazuela del Marqués de las Torres**.

On the right side of the street is the 15th through 18th century *Mudéjar* **Convento de Santa Clara,** a Franciscan convent that you can enter for free during the daily morning masses. Here you'll see, along the nave, a selection of interesting 17th century portraits of women. Directly across the plaza is the Baroque 17th century **Convento de las Descalzas** convent whose awesome interior can be visited for free during morning mass hours. Proceed a bit further up the street and on the right side you will find the 16th century **Hospital de la Misericordia y de la Caridad** hospital and chapel building, with its wonderful old art and carvings, *open daily at 8:30 during its services.*

Now from here continue to the end of the road where you will turn right onto the Calle de Dolores Quintanilla. Follow it as it then curves around to the right and passes just in front of the 1st century **Puerta de Córdoba** gateway through the old Roman era walls. Surrounded by two magnificent fortified octagonal towers, this one of a kind gateway was rebuilt in the 17th century and now boasts a painting of the city's patron saint in its central portal. The top of the gate has a balcony that continues along the top of the adjoining towers and is supported by two sets of stone block columns. *There is no fee to look around this structure, and it is always open.*

After seeing the gateway and its fine panoramic perspectives, turn left on to the Calle de Calatrava and in about a block and a half on your right side will be the lovely **Plaza de Santiago** square with its 14th century **Iglesia de Santiago** church. Look at the beautiful main altar crafted by Bernardo Simon de Pineda, peek into the 15th century Capilla de Jesus Nazareno chapel, and get a good look at the antique organ. *Visitors can go inside on Sundays from 10am until 12:30pm.*

From the church, the Calle de Calatrava now merges with the Calle de María Auxilladora that you will follow until bearing left at the fork in the road and continuing onto the Calle de General Freire. At the end of this street on your left side is the hard-to-miss 9th century **Alcázar de Arriba del Rey Don Pedro I** fortress. Originally built as a Moorish fortress, King Pedro the Cruel decided to convert this massive castle into a lavishly decorated royal palace during the 14th century.

Used by the Catholic monarchs for a couple of centuries, the building was later seriously damaged by the 1755 earthquake that destroyed Lisbon, Portugal, and severely shook all of the Iberian peninsula. After a giant renovation project was completed earlier this century, it was beautifully transformed into Spain's single best *parador* (government-owned hotel), the **Parador de Carmona**. Even if you're not lucky enough to have chosen this establishment as the place you will be staying, at least go inside and walk around its ornate interior and awesome exterior, or relax and enjoy a cool drink. *Visitors are more than welcome to tour the premises for free during daylight and early evening hours.*

After visiting the fortress/hotel, cross the street and turn left onto the Calle de Puerta Machena, which changes its name to the Calle de Pedro I as it passes the inspiring 14th century **Iglesia de San Filipe** church. As one of the region's most impressive monuments to *Mudéjar* craftsmanship, the church is unfortunately not usually open to the public, but its facade and tower are well worth the effort to see.

The Conjunto Arqueológico Necropolis

Just about 1.5 km (1 mile) east of the city center off the Avenida de Jorge Bonsor is the recently excavated Roman era necropolis, known here as the **Conjunto Arqueológico** complex. Close to 1,000 tombs dot this fenced-in area where you can guide yourself through a series of marked paths.

As you walk around the complex, several ladders and stairways descend into column-lined subterranean chambers that hold the stone funerary urns and stone vaults filled with the remains of 2nd and 3rd century residents. Among the highlights are the **Tumba de Elefante** tomb with its statue of an elephant, the **Tumba de Servilla** with its carved dome, and the small adjacent museum containing 8th B.C. through 6th century A.D. pottery, glass jars, ceramics and jewelry. Across the street there are the ruins of an old Roman amphitheater that cannot yet be visited.

The complex is open Tuesday through Friday from 10am until 2pm; during the winter it opens again from 4pm until 6pm, and weekends from 10am until 2pm. Admission is 250 ptas per person.

PRACTICAL INFORMATION
- **Tourist Office**, *Casa de Cultura, Plaza de la Descalzes, Tel. (95) 414-2200*
- **Carmona Radio Taxi Companies**, *Tel. (95) 414-1359*
- **Central Post Office**, *Calle Prim, 29, Tel. (95) 414-1024*
- **Regional Directory Assistance**, *Tel. 1003*
- **National Directory Assistance**, *Tel. 1009*
- **Medical Emergencies Hot Line**, *Tel. (95) 414-0997*
- **Red Cross**, *Tel. (95) 414-0751*
- **Municipal Police**, *Tel. (95) 414-0008*

Major Local Festivals
Contact the local Turismo office, *Tel. (95) 414-2200*, for more details.
- **Carnaval**, *late February, Parades and Parties*
- **Semana Santa**, *prior to Easter, Strange Processions*
- **Las Mayas**, *May, Children's Parades*
- **Feria de Mayo**, *May, Outdoor Festivities*
- **Corpus Cristi**, *June, Processions*
- **Romeria de la Virgen**, *early September, Religious Ceremonies*

CÓRDOBA

Córdoba is one of this region's most dramatic and compelling cities. Controlled by the Romans, Moors, and Catholic Kings during different periods of its heyday, the entire old quarter of town is packed with countless historical sights, museums, peaceful plazas, centuries-old castles, religious buildings, and medieval whitewashed mansions featuring some of Europe's finest patios.

Since Jews, Arabs, and Christians lived together in peace and prosperity for several centuries before the Inquisition, outstanding relics from each group can be visited and fully appreciated here more than in almost any other place in Spain. It may take a couple of days to fully see the sights here, so I have created a tour that will help you find the true heart and soul of this magnificent destination. Keep in mind that Córdoba is not an inexpensive place, and that bargains are few and far between, with the possible exception of locally made silver filigreed jewelry.

ARRIVALS & DEPARTURES

By Air

Córdoba's small regional airport is called the Aeropuerto de Córdoba-San Jerónimo and is located just off route N-431, 9 km (6 miles) west of town.

Buses between the Airport & Downtown

Scheduled bus service between the airport and downtown is currently under revision. Check with the Turismo for up-to-date information and prices.

Taxis from the Airport to Downtown

Taxis can be found in abundant supply at well-indicated taxi stands at the airport. Almost all of the taxis here are fairly small sized 4 door sedans. Normally, a taxi's trunk can hold about two large suitcases, but those with roof racks can secure two more medium pieces of luggage, and perhaps a couple of carry-on bags inside as well. Expect to pay between 1,250 and 1,650 *ptas* from the airport to most downtown locations.

By Bus

The dozen of more bus companies that offer service between Córdoba and all other parts of Spain arrive at several different depots and stations scattered throughout the city. To make things simple, these are the three most common companies and their station locations: Alsina Graells buses *(Tel. 236-474)* to and from Sevilla, Granada, and Málaga pull into Avenida Medina Azahara, 29. Priego buses *(Tel. 290-158)* to and from Madrid and Barcelona stop at Paseo de la Victoria, 29. Urena buses *(Tel. 472-352)* to and from Madrid, Valencia, Barcelona, and Jaen have a station over at Avenida de Cervantes, 22.

For other unlisted companies, call the tourist office or check with any local travel agency.

By Car

From Madrid, the best way here is to take the high speed N-IV highway as it heads south and then west for 401 km (249 miles) until reaching Córdoba. The route from Sevilla to here is via N-IV highway northeast for 138 km (94 miles). From Granada you can take the winding route N-432 northwest for 166 km (103 miles) to get here. From Málaga, you will follow the slow N-331 north for about 189 km (117 miles) before reaching the exits for downtown.

Once inside the city you will find it almost impossible to locate street side or metered parking, so ask your hotel or look for one of several parking lots that charge approximately 1,950 *ptas* per day.

By Train
Córdoba is connected to the rest of Spain and Europe by extensive rail service via Renfe. The large Estación de Renfe Ave. is located about one kilometer north of the old quarter on the Avenida de America. From here you can take bus #12 for 90 *ptas* into the old part of town, or hire a taxi that will cost about 520 *ptas*.

ORIENTATION
Córdoba, population 284,737, is located in the north-central reaches of the **Andalucía** region along the banks of the **Guadalquivir River**.

GETTING AROUND TOWN
By Taxi
Hundreds of licensed taxis roam the streets, plaza side taxi stands, and major passenger arrival points day and night. To find a taxi, either hail an unoccupied taxi (when empty they will illuminate a small *Taxi* light above the car), go to one of the dozens of obvious taxi stands throughout the city, or call Córdoba Radio Taxi Companies, *Tel. (957) 450-000,* for a radio response pick-up on demand.

Taxis charge customers using meters and the fare usually will cost somewhere around 550 *ptas* per ride (not per person) between most downtown areas. Legally chargeable supplements are posted on a sticker in the taxi's interior.

WHERE TO STAY
Expensive
OCCIDENTAL CÓRDOBA, *Calle Poeta Alonso Bonilla, 7. Tel. (957) 400-440, Fax (957) 400-439. US & Canada Bookings: (UTELL), Tel. 800/44-UTELL. Year round rack rates from 16,250 ptas per double room per night (E.P.). All major credit cards accepted.*

Although a few minutes away from the city center in a high end residential neighborhood, this is my first choice for deluxe accommodations in the area. This ultra-modern four-star executive class hotel is situated on several dozen acres of prime landscaped grounds just on the outskirts of town. They offer 154 beautifully decorated rooms and suites with air conditioning, remote control satellite television, huge private marble bathrooms, direct dial telephones, mini-bar, garden views and mini-safes.

The hotel also features two tennis courts, a large outdoor swimming pool, plenty of free parking, a complementary shuttle bus to downtown, two good restaurants, business meeting and conference facilities, 24-hour room service, foreign currency exchange, tranquil public lobbies, and a nice staff of helpful professionals.

N.H. HOTEL AMISTAD, *Plaza de Maimonides, 3. Tel. (957) 420-335, Fax (957) 420-365. US & Canada Bookings: (UTELL), Tel. 800/44-UTELL. Year round rack rates from 15,000 ptas per double room per night (E.P.). Special weekend rates from 9,800 ptas per double room per night (E.P.). All major credit cards accepted.*

The Hotel Amistad is a beautifully converted nobleman's mansion just off the Plaza de Maimonides in the heart of the Jewish quarter. The structure dates back to the 18th century, and has a wonderful *Mudéjar* courtyard, beautiful public rooms, and a tranquil refined environment. Here you can choose from 69 deluxe rooms and suites each offering air conditioning, marble bathrooms stocked with fine European amenities, remote control satellite television with VCR, mini-bar, fine designer furnishings, am-fm clock radios, direct dial telephones, and beautiful art.

The hotel also offers fantastic lounges, a good regional restaurant, an inner patio and bar, business meeting rooms, private dining facilities, complimentary video tape rental service, laundry and dry cleaning services, and room service. Service here is pretty good, and the price is well below what might be expected, but the absence of a currency exchange and parking facilities are drawbacks.

Moderate

HOTEL MAIMÓNIDES, *Calle de Torrijos, 4. Tel. (957) 471-500, Fax (957) 483-803. Low season rack rates from 11,600 ptas per double room per night (E.P.). High season rack rates from 14,300 ptas per double room per night (E.P.). Most major credit cards accepted.*

You couldn't ask for a better location, just across from the Mezquita-Catedral in the best part of downtown. This charming three- star hotel features 83 nice mid-sized rooms with private bathrooms, air conditioning, satellite television, direct dial phones, comfortable furnishings, and either interior or more expensive exterior views. Facilities here include nearby parking, breakfast room, bar, meeting rooms and a great staff.

HOTEL AL MIHRAB, *Avenida del Brillante, km. 5. Tel. (957) 272-188, Fax (957) 272-198. Year round rack rates from 12,500 ptas per double room per night (E.P.). Most major credit cards accepted.*

Perfect for those who have a car while touring this area, the Al Mirhab hotel is a unique Old World three-star hotel just a few minutes from downtown. Here you will find rooms housed in a series of 19th century mansions at the foothills of the mountains that surround the city. Each of the 29 uniquely decorated rooms and suites have period style furnishings, air conditioning, private bathrooms, satellite television, telephone, in-room music systems and great views of the nearby countryside and city center. The people who run this B&B inn have made this among a most welcoming and lovely place to stay.

Inexpensive

ALBERGUE JUVENIL DE CÓRDOBA, *Plaza de Juda Levi. Tel. (957) 290-0166, Fax None. Year round rack rates from 2,200 ptas per double room per night (E.P.). Most major credit cards accepted.*

This is one of Europe's most luxurious youth hostels and is perfect for people of any age who are looking for a fun, safe, and perfectly located inexpensive place to stay. This modern marble floored structure offers 44 private and shared double rooms, each with surprisingly comfortable furnishings, shared or private bathrooms, air conditioning and large windows. Facilities here include a television room, a good inexpensive restaurant, and absolutely no curfew.

Packed year round with both students and adults from all over the world, you have to do is present a valid Hostelling International card (see hostel details in Chapter 8, *Types of Accommodations*) or purchase one here for about 3,000 *ptas*. Those over 26 who wish to stay here will be asked to pay a 20% surcharge. Selected as one of my Best Places to Stay (see Chapter 13).

WHERE TO EAT

Expensive

EL BLASON, *Calle de José Zorrilla, 11. Tel. (957) 480-625. All major credit cards accepted.*

The El Blason is the most luxurious formal gourmet dining establishment in all of Córdoba. Located near the Gran Teatro theater in a converted 19th century tavern, this beautifully decorated restaurant serves a constantly changing selection of nouveau style international cuisine. They always have fresh shellfish, local and imported game, and the finest cuts of steak, all served with sauces that are made to perfection. Since the menu changes based on the availability of the highest quality ingredients, I can't list specifics, but you can expect to pay around 4,250 *ptas* per person for a multiple course dinner that will take your breath away. Make sure to reserve early, and ask for a table in the old part of the building.

Moderate

MESON LA MURALLA, *Calleja de La Luna. Tel. (957) 298-076. All major credit cards accepted.*

Located inside the old town wall's La Luna gateway into the old Jewish Quarter, this delightful restaurant has a huge multilingual menu with something for just about everyone, and a great charming dining room. Among the many tasty items available here are chilled gazpacho, shellfish soup, garlic soup, stuffed peppers, mushrooms with garlic, assorted omelettes, fresh salmon, grilled prawns, sirloin steak with Roquefort cheese and roasted suckling pig. Expect a three-course dinner to cost about 2,675 *ptas* per person plus drinks.

CAFE BAR JUDA LEVI, *Plaza Juda Levi. No telephone. Mastercard accepted.*

When you have been walking around the old quarter all day and just want to sit down and enjoy a few *tapas* and an ice cold beer, this modern restaurant is about the best casual choice in the area. Although a bit overpriced, they still offer a great variety of filling local specialties including chicken and ham croquettes, gazpacho, Russian salad, codfish balls with tomato sauce, mushroom and shrimp, chef salads, burgers with French fries and decent desserts. Nothing fancy, but a good place to snack in a central location. A good lunchtime snack here is about 1,800 *ptas* per person.

Inexpensive

EL GALLO DE ORO, *Plaza de Abades. Tel. (957) 475-204. Cash Only.*

Just a block and a half northeast from the Mezquita Catedral, this cute little takeout place is known almost exclusively to local families. Here you can get huge portions of snack foods such as burgers for 140 *ptas*, club sandwiches at 120 *ptas*, calamari for 370 *ptas*, pizzas at 375 *ptas*, assorted croquettes for 300 *ptas*, filet of hake at 550 *ptas*, chicken empanadas for 80 *ptas*, and lots of other well prepared fast food items that you can eat on the benches of nearby squares.

SEEING THE SIGHTS

Approximate duration (by foot) is about 7.5 hours, including mosque, synagogue, museum, monument, and side street visits.

The Mezquita Catedral

The most logical place to start your exploration of this magnificent city is at the **Mezquita Catedral** mosque and cathedral in the old part of town. This fantastically elaborate structure was originally built around the year 785 A.D., when Moorish Emir Abd al-Rahman reused the land and materials from an older Visigothic church on this site that he had bought and then leveled. The first phase of construction was completed in only one year, but over the the next two centuries it was further enlarged by successive Muslim rulers until it reached its present size.

Although there are several entrances to pass through its thick defensive walls, the best way to approach this truly awesome house of worship is by following the building's north side along the Calle del Cardenal Herro and entering the gateway known as the **Puerta del Perdón** (The Doorway of Forgiveness). This entrance was somewhat altered in the 14th century, but still boasts a fine *Mudéjar* door embellished with Arabic inscriptions.

Upon entering the complex you will first walk through the peaceful arcaded **Patio de los Naranjos** (Courtyard of the Orange Trees), added during the 10th century. Originally used for perfoming Muslim purification rituals, the patio later was planted with the orange and palm trees that surround its Baroque era fountain. At the courtyard's corner you can climb up the stairs of the striking **Torre** minaret that dates back to 951 A.D. but was later encased in a 17th century Baroque shell, topped by a sculpture of Saint Raphael carved by Pedro Paz.

From the courtyard, you will first walk up to the box office kiosk, pay the admission fee, and walk through the Platteresque **Puerta de las Palmas** (Doorway of the Palms) to enter the mosque. The first section that you pass through is the oldest part of the complex and is known as the **Mezquita Primitiva** area. Here you will find the original rectangular mosque's first 110 marble and granite columns (most of which were remnants of the Visigothic church that once stood here and nearby ruined Roman temples) that support the double arches (striped with alternaing layers of red brick and beige limestone) and divide the 12 oldest aisles. As you move further into the building, the next section you pass contains parts of the expansion by Emir Abd ar-Rahman II that moved the mosque further back another 25 meters (about 25 yards) in 848.

Another expansion was ordered by Emir al-Hakam II, who in 976 pushed the rear wall back another 32 meters (about 32 yards) or so, as far as the building could be pushed to the south. The last major Moorish expansion of the mosque came in 990 when Emir al-Mansor greatly widened the struture by adding several more aisles on the east side of the building. At the end of this 215 year enlargement process, well over 1,000 additional columns were added to finally create what became a much larger 19 nave mosque.

Among the most dramatic and artistic elements from the Moorish era to be found here (besides the columned double arches) is the unequalled 10th century Byzantine mosaic covered domes above the marble sculpted **Mihrab** (sacred prayer niche) and adjacent **Maksura** (caliph's prayer enclosure), along the southern holy wall facing east toward Mecca. Also keep your eyes open for the old Roman capitals and intricate wooden ceilings atop many of the columns throughout the building.

Once the Christians led by King Fernando III had captured the city from the Moors in 1236, things at the mosque stayed pretty much as they were until the Inquisition took its toll on Spain's Muslim population. In 1523, the powerful local Bishop Alonso Manrique commisioned the construction of a Catholic **Catedral** (Cathedral) within the walls of this revered building. Most of the city's residents were greatly opposed to any such project, but with the support of King Carlos V the works proceeded anyway and was completed in the 18th century.

Within the middle of the Mezquita a large transept was built that necessitated the roof being rebuilt to accommodate higher vaulting. Several styles ranging from Gothic to Baroque were used to create this new (and totally out of place) house of worship. Upon seeing the devastating damage done to the mosque's interior during the early stages of its conversion, King Carlos V stated: "You have destroyed something unique to build something rather commonplace." The few sections of the cathedral that are worth taking in is the *Mudéjar* **Capilla de Villaviciosa** and **Capilla Real** chapels, the **Capilla Mayor** main altar, the fine **Coro** with its Italianate stucco dome and 18th century Baroque mahogany choirstalls, and the half dozen or so other chapels that hold the tombs of local noblemen and clergy.

In the basement of the cathedral you can wander through several rooms of the sacrisity and chapterhouse to view the **Museo Tesoro de la Catedral** treasury museum, displaying a good collection of 15th through 20th century religious art including a 16th century huge silver monstrance, a wonderful ivory crucifix by Alonso Cano, processional crosses, chalices, rare manuscripts, medallions and a few beautiful Baroque chapels filled with antique paintings.

The Mezquita Catedral mosque and cathedral is open daily from 10am until 5:30pm October through March, and daily from 10am until 7pm April through September. On Sundays they may only open several parts of the interior from 3:30pm until the normal season's closing time. The admission price is 700 ptas for adults, and 350 ptas for children.

The museum is open daily from 10:30am until 1:30pm and again from 3:30pm until 5:30pm October through March, and daily from 10:30am until 1:30pm and again from 4pm until 7pm April through September. While it currently does not cost anything additional to enter, this may change in the near future.

Around the Old Quarter

After exiting the old mosque via the orange tree patio, make a left onto the Calle del Cardenal Herro. At the next corner, turn left onto the

Calle de Torrijos to follow the mosque's exterior wall for a few steps before crossing over to the other side of the street. Stop by the regional *Turismo* desk at the Palacio de Congressos building at #10 for a free map.

A few steps further down the same side of the street is the excellent **Museo Diocesáno de Bellas Artes** art museum. Housed in a 13th century **Palacio Episcopal** (Episcopal Palace) that was built within the ruins of the Moorish Emir's palace, this fairly interesting museum is a good place to spend an hour or two on a rainy day when you have little else to do. Upon entering the building you are led through a patio laden with citrus trees that surround an pig statue left from the iron age, a symbol of fertility in ancient times. Across from the patio is an entrance into the 18th century **Capilla de La Nosa Señora del Pilar** chapel with its golden altars. A set of stairs leads past stained glass windows and into the exhibition areas of the museum. Among the items on display are more than 500 well preserved 13th through 18th century icons, crucifixes, processional crosses, tapestries, portraits, *retable* doors, and other religious items.

Open from Monday through Friday from 9:30am until 1:30pm and again from 3:30pm until 5:30pm, Saturdays from 9:30am until 1:30pm, and during the summer they have been known to extend the opening hours. The admission is either 150 ptas per person, or free with a recent ticket stub from the mosque.

Continue down the same street until it ends at the next corner where you will turn left and head a few steps down into the **Plaza de del Truinfo**. For those interested, this is where, for 4,500 *ptas* per hour, you and three friends can hire a horse-drawn carriage to ride through the old parts of town. From the plaza, walk through the large **Puerta del Puente** archway and across the **Guadalquivir** river via the **Puente Romano** old Roman era bridge.

Once on the other side of the bridge you can't help but notice the 13th century *Mudéjar* **Torre de la Calahorra** defensive tower, now home to the fantastic privately run **Museo de la Torre de la Calahorra** cultural museum featuring great historical exhibitions. The best way to enjoy the museum is to spand a little extra and see one of the several scheduled 55 minute multimedia presentations. Included in the general admission price is a rental set of infrared headphones that guide you through each of the many rooms with superbly narrated explanations in the language of your choice.

Among the exhibits on display here are discriptions and scale models of 10th century life. These include mock-ups of the original Mezquita, the Zoco silk market, the synagogue, the cathedral, old palaces, the Arabic university, Moorish surgical instruments, and much, much more. It is possible to learn more about this city's history in one hour here than by reading two or three thick books. After enjoying the exhibition, make sure to climb the stairs to the tower's top where you can get an incredible view out over the entire old quarter. *The museum is open from 10am until 6pm daily between October and April, and 10am until 2pm and again from 5:30pm until 8:30pm between May and September. The price to enter is 350 ptas per person, or 550 ptas for a ticket that included the multimedia presentation.*

From the tower and museum, go back across the old Roman bridge and turn left onto the near side of the Ronda de Isasa to follow the riverbank. If you look down below at the riverside, you will notice the **Albolafia** water well that was rebuilt to resemble the 10th century original that once brough fresh water into the Moorish Emir's palace. Now carefully cross the street and walk up Calle Santa Teresa de Journet and at the end of this lane make a left turn onto the Calle Amador de los Rios to enter the Gothic **Alcázar de los Reyes Cristanos** (Fortress of the Christian Kings).

Built in 1328 under orders of King Alfonso XI, this enourmous rectangualar fortress was later converted into a royal palace with picturesque formal gardens. Later it was briefly used as a prison during the Inquisition, and then once again restored to house visiting nobility. Inside you can climb up the **Torre de los Leónes** and **Torre del Homenaje** watchtowers, view Roman mosaic pavings in the **Salón de los Mosaicos**, walk through the **Baños Reales** Moorish style baths with star-shaped dome windows, and wander amidst the well-manicured gardens behind the main structure.

The fortress and its grounds are open from Monday through Saturday from 9:30am until 1:30pm and again from 4pm until 7pm, and Saturdays from 9:30am until 1:30pm. Admission is currently 400 ptas per person, and free on Tuesdays.

Nearby Gardens & Beautiful Patios

After visiting the fortress, walk directly across the way and into the **Jardines de Campo Santo de los Martires** gardens, where the old ruins of a Moorish palace can be seen under excavation. From the bottom of the gardens, you can walk along the Calle Caballerizas, and at the next intersection take a right turn onto the Calle Martin Roa.

Buildings #7 and #9 on this cute street, as well as buildings #17, #22, and #50 of the intersecting Calle San Basilio, are mostly 16th through 18th century whitewashed houses that are fronted by serene courtyards that are used as open air living rooms. Privately maintained by local families, they compete yearly for prizes given for the most delightful patios in the city. Common throughout Andalucía, Córdoba's courtyards are especially well maintained and decorated with flowers, wrought-iron railings, fountains, and antique arches. During the day the patios may be gated off, but you can still get a good look through the wide bars and into these delightful spaces. It is common for the gates to be opened up for the general public to see these spectacular courtyards throughout the summer, and during the winter months between 6pm and 8pm daily.

Another beautiful garden can be reached by walking back to the edge of the Jardines de Campo Santo de los Martires gardens and bearing left onto the wide Avenida de Doctor Fleming. At the end of this major avenue, bear right onto the central **Paseo de la Victoria** and walk a block or so until you get to the **Jardines de la Victoria** gardens on the park to your left.

The Barrio de la Judería Jewish Quarter

Return once again to the bottom edge of the **Jardines de Campo Santo de los Martires** gardens and take Calle Cairuan up for a block or two as it passes along the old walls of the city. Turn right at the next gateway through the walls known as the **Puerta La Luna**. This gateway leads onto a small lane called the Calleja La Luna; from here you will make a left turn onto the Calle Tomas Conde and follow it for about a block until you reach the quaint **Plazuela de Maimónides**. Situated in the heart of the old Jewish quarter, this square is home to several beautiful buildings, including the 18th century mansion that has been converted in the deluxe **Hotel Amistad**, and the 13th century *Mudéjar* Capilla de San Bartolome church that can be visited only during public masses.

Just next door to the church is the impressive 16th century **Antiqua Casa de las Bulas** (Old Papal Bull Mansion) that is now home to the **Museo Municipal de Taurino** bullfighting museum. Here you can see two floors of exhibition rooms surrounding a tranquil old patio. Among the items displayed here are old bullfighting posters, lithographs, photographs, matador costumes, assorted bull heads and skins, and the personal objects of famed bullfighters such as Manolete. *The museum is open Tuesday through Saturday from 9:30am until 1:30pm and again from about 4pm until about 6:30pm or later, Sundays from 9:30am until 1:30pm only. Admission is 400 ptas per person, and is free on Tuesdays.*

After departing the museum, turn right into the square and bear immediately right onto the **Calle de los Judios** (Street of the Jews). Walk up this street for a half block or so until reaching the tiny **Plaza de Tiberiades** where you will find a bronze statue of **Dr. Maimónides**, a 12th century Jewish scholar and philosopher who lived in this area and is well known for greatly advancing the medical sciences of medieval Europe. Keep walking up the Calle de los Judios for another half a block or so, and turn right at the archways that lead into a peaceful patio where the old **Zoco** (Arab Marketplace) once stood. These days it is home to the **Zoco Municipal de Artesania** crafts market with artisans demonstrating the process of hand crafting silver, bronze, wood, ceramics, and leather goods that can be purchased in a series of small boutiques surrounding a lovely fountain. *The shops are open almost every day from about 10am until 5pm.*

Once you have window shopped at the market, return to the Calle de los Judios and keep walking up the street for another half a block or so until passing in front of building #20 on the left hand side that houses the 14th century **Sinagoga de Córdoba**. This small, wonderfully ornate Jewish house of worship was the center of spiritual life for many members of the city's once huge Jewish community. In the days before they were expelled by order of the Inquisition, the local Jewish, Moorish, and Christian residents lived in peace with each other, even though they mostly lived in separate neighborhoods. Inside the synagogue are fine Hebrew inscriptions, murals, stucco *Mudéjar* decorations and a women's prayer hall.

The temple is open (you may have to ring the bell at #20 to be let in) Tuesday through Saturday from 10am until 2pm and again from 3:30pm until 5:30pm, Sundays from 10am until 1:30pm, with admission at 50 ptas.

From the synagogue, retrace your steps back down to the Plaza de Maimonides and cut through to the opposite side of the square, where you will continue heading in the same direction along the Calle de Tomas Conde. After about a block or so, bear left onto the winding little Calle de Albucasis that merges with the Calle Manriques which in turn leads straight into the side of the bustling **Plaza Juda Levi**. Here you can pop into the helpful Turismo tourist information center at the right hand corner.

On the other side of the square, stroll along the boutique-lined Calle de Deanes to shop for some gifts such as silver jewelry and leather goods at affordable prices. Now return to the edge of the Plaza Juda Levi and take a rather sharp left onto a small street called the Calle Judería, which splits off this side of the plaza and will take you right back in front of the northern facade of **Mezquita Catedral** mosque and cathedral. From here, follow the left side of Calle del Cardenal Herro for about a block until turning left down a small lane called the Calle de Velasquez Bosco.

Now make your first right turn onto the **Calleja de las Flores**, a small alley full of whitewashed houses whose facades are decorated in colorful potted plants. Also on this street at building #2 is the **Meryan** leather shop, world famous for its fine custom leather crafting. Now retrace your steps back down to the mosque.

Other Old Quarter Sights

After once again ending up in front of the **Mezquita Catedral** mosque and cathedral, continue following the left side of Calle del Cardenal Herro until it ends at the corner of the Calle de Encarnación, where you will bear left. The long structure that you will pass on the left side of this street is the 16th century **Convento de la Encarnación**, which can be entered during Sunday mass hours to see its fine Baroque church. At the next intersection, make a right turn onto the Calle de Rey Heredia, and then a few steps later bear left onto the Calle Horno del Cristo that leads almost directly into the heart of the **Plaza de Julio Jerónimo Paez**. This peaceful plaza contains an assortment of beautiful old structures, including the 16th century Renaissance **Palacio de los Paez Quijano**, a nobleman's mansion lovingly converted into the **Museo Arqueológico Provincial** archaeology museum.

This excellent museum boasts one of the country's best collections of Neolithic, Celtiberian, Roman, Visigothic, Moorish, and more recent relics. Its 13 separate exhibition rooms are full of one-of-a-kind objects such as columns, weapons, tombs, mosaics, statues, jewelry, coins and ceramics. The museum has also excavated an original Roman mosaic patio on the grounds. *The museum is open Tuesday through Saturday from 10am until 1:30pm and again from 5pm until 7pm, Sundays from 10am until 1:30pm, and costs 250 ptas to enter.*

From the museum, walk back and turn left on the Calle de Rey Heredia. Keep following it as it curves to the left and merges with the Calle Caldereros and then the Calle de Lucano, where just about a block up on the left hand side is the stunning **Plaza del Potro**. Surrounding its centuries-old equestrian fountain are some of the most attractive sights in town. On the left side of the square is the 14th century **Posada del Potro**, a wonderful whitewashed old tavern and inn that is mentioned in Cervantes' book *Don Quixote*. The ground floor of this building now houses a cultural exhibition space that sometimes features special concerts and art displays. If you walk inside you will find one of the city's most delightful inner courtyards.

Adjacent to the former inn is the **Museo Romero de Torres** art museum with room after room of somber nudes and religious paintings by intuitive turn of the century local master Julio Romero de Torres. *This museum is open Tuesday through Saturday from 9:30am until 1:30pm and again from 4pm until 7pm, Sundays from 9:30am until 1:30pm, and costs 400 ptas to enter.*

Across the square is the Platteresque facade of the **Hospital de la Caridad**, now home to the popular **Museo de Bellas Artes** fine arts museum. Inside you will find hundreds of paintings and sculptures from the 13th through 19th centuries including works by **Castillo**, **Valdes Leal**, **Ribera**, **Palomino**, **Zubarán**, **Zuloaga**, **Goya** and many other mostly Spanish artists. *This museum is open from Tuesday through Saturday from 10am until 1:30pm and again from 5pm until at least 7pm, Sundays from 10am until 1:30pm, and costs 250 ptas to enter.*

After departing the plaza, take a left turn to continue along the Calle Lucano whose name changes to Calle Lineros. Make sure to pop into building #32, the home of the quaint old **Bodegas Campos** wine bar that dates back to 1908.

NIGHTLIFE & ENTERTAINMENT

A good area to hit after 11:30pm or so are the streets that converge into the **Plaza Costa del Sol**, where the university kids hang out in large numbers in places like the **Cervecería Pal-Cual II**, the sophisticated champagne and wine bar called **Café Becquer**, and the **Big Ben** pub.

Over by the Gran Teatro, you can head for later nightlife near the **Plaza San Hipolito**. Try the **Pub KZ**, the **Pataya** café bar, the **Arigo Dance Club**, the young **Quorum** club, and the **El Poluorim** bar.

EXCURSIONS & DAY TRIPS

MADINAT AL-ZAHARA

A few minutes drive northwest of the city lies the relics of an extraordinary Moorish palace town. Known as **Madinat al-Zahara** (also called **Medina Azahara**), these 10th century ruins formerly housed the family, staff, and close associates of Emir Abd ar-Rahman. During its heyday, the palace and its adjacent complex contained massive gardens, giant army barracks, a fine mosque, a zoo, countless houses, and several courtyards lined with fantastic mosaics.

Built with over 3,500 columns imported from all over the Arab world, it must have been among the most dramatic structures of its time. Unfortunately, the structures here were completely destroyed in the early 11th century by invading Berbers, who also executed the hundreds of remaining inhabitants. The whole area was excavated earlier this century, and plenty of money has been spent to reconstruct various buildings to their former glory.

Highlights include the former **Alcázar** building that now contains a small historical museum, the **Dal al-Muk** royal house with its halls lined with ornate Arabic arched and decorative stucco wall panels where visiting leaders were entertained, and other less complete sections and artwork that are still awaiting additional funds to be put back together. This is a great place to spend a few hours at most, especially if you have already visited the city and would enjoy some peace and quiet in a wonderful ancient sight.

The palace city and its grounds are open during the winter on Tuesday through Saturday from 10am until 1pm and again from 4pm until 6pm, Sundays from 10am until 1pm; during the summer on Tuesday through Saturday from 10am until 2pm and again from 6pm until 8:30pm, Sundays from 10am until 1pm. Admission is 300 ptas per person.

Directions

By car, you should hop on the tiny local route C-431 northwest from Córdoba for some 8 km (6 miles) before following the signs to the palace.

Bus service is available to the access road (about a 15 minute walk away) several times daily in both directions via Córdoba's Calle de Bodega bus station for about 175 *ptas* in each direction.

PRACTICAL INFORMATION

- **Regional Tourist Office**, *OTCJA, Calle de Torrijos, 10, Tel. (957) 471-235*
- **Municipal Tourist Office**, *Turismo, Plaza Juda Levi, Tel. (957) 200-522*
- **Córdoba Airport**, *San Jerónimo, Tel. (957) 239-200*
- **Iberia Airlines**, *Ronda de los Tejares, 3, Tel. (957) 478-928 or (957) 472-695*
- **Regional Train Info**, *Renfe, Tel. (957) 490-202 or (957) 475-884*
- **Córdoba Radio Taxi Companies**, *Tel. (957) 450-000*
- **Central Post Office**, *Calle de Cruz Conde, 15, Tel. (957) 478-267*
- **Regional Directory Assistance**, *Tel. 1003*
- **National Directory Assistance**, *Tel. 1009*
- **Red Cross**, *Tel. (957) 293-411*
- **Ambulance**, *Tel. (957) 275-600*
- **National Police**, *Tel. (957) 257-050*
- **Municipal Police**, *Tel. 092*

GRANADA

Although sometimes overshadowed by the larger and more heavily promoted Andalucían cities, **Granada** itself is simply a fantastic spot to spend a few days while in Spain. With its bold treasures like the awesome Moorish palace of **Alhambra**, the dramatic royal **Capilla Real** chapel, and such striking ancient neighborhoods like the **Albaicín** and **Sacromonte**, this is one of the most compelling destinations in all of Europe.

The residents here are delightfully friendly and have a strong sense of their cultural roots. At night, for example, some of the city's huge population of university students may be found practicing the art of *flamenco* dancing in small taverns and workshops.

Another attractive aspect to staying here is the abundance of great, affordable gourmet cuisine, plenty of first-rate accommodations, locally produced handicrafts, excellent shopping possibilities, and absolutely unique nightlife possibilities that add even more to the rich cultural landscape of Granada. Since it's so close to the massive **Sierra Nevada** mountain range, and only about an hour's drive from the sea, Granada makes a good base for day trips to several of the region's most interesting attractions and traditional villages.

ARRIVALS & DEPARTURES

By Air

If you are arriving by air, the city offers one small regional airport located 18 km (10.5 miles) west of town. There are one or two flights scheduled each day to and from Madrid. If you take a taxi from the airport to the center of town, expect to pay about 2,275 *ptas*. Buses can also be found just outside the terminal that are scheduled to coincide with arriving and departing flights. The airport bus, in either direction, costs 300 *ptas* each way to get to and from Plaza Isabel la Cathólica in the heart of the city.

By Bus

There is a vast selection of bus routes offering inexpensive daily service to Granada from a huge variety of nearby cities, towns, and mountain resort areas. Many of these routes are serviced by a company called Alsina Graells, *Tel. (958) 251-258,* that runs to and from the city's main bus station off the Camino de Ronda (although a few terminals do exist elsewhere) on the city's southwest edge. The #11 bus line stops on this avenue, and will also take you as far as the Gran Vía de Colón for 95 *ptas*. Expect a taxi to cost about 490 *ptas* to almost any hotel or sight in town.

By Car

The most common driving routes to Granada include the 460 km (286 mile) trek from Madrid via the fast N-IV highway south, and connecting at the Bailén exit onto the scenic N-323 south. Other common approaches include the mountainous 169 km (114 mile) ride from Córdoba along the newly widened N-432 southeast that cuts through a pretty landscape rich in olive groves, flocks of sheep, traditional "white" villages, and a treacherous mountain pass (do not attempt this route at night).

From the coastal city of Málaga, there is a nice 131 km (82 mile) road trip east along N-340 to merge onto the adrenalin pumping N-323 north, passing by the majestic Sierra Nevada mountains. Once inside the city you will find an extremely limited amount of parking spaces on the streets (usually free of charge), but there are several municipal and hotel lots that cost about 1,750 *ptas* per day.

By Train

Granada's main rail station is 2 km (1.4 miles) west of the city center on Avenida de Adaluces, just off Avenida de la Constitución. There are multiple daily arrivals and departures between this city and dozens of other locations throughout the country via the extensive national rail system. From the station, a taxi to just about anywhere in town is about 430 *ptas*, while the #11 bus can take you all the way up to the Gran Vía de Colón for 110 *ptas*.

ORIENTATION

Granada, population 262,183, lies near the center of southern Spain's region of **Andalucía**, about a 360 km (223 mile) drive south of Madrid.

GETTING AROUND TOWN

Once inside Granada, you really can walk to just about anywhere you may want to go.

By Bus

If you prefer to reduce your time on foot, I suggest taking advantage of the dozen or so bus lines (known as *Rober)* that offers single-use fares for 110 *ptas*, or 24 hour unlimited use tickets for 375 *ptas*, available from any bus driver. Maps and other information are available on bus stop signs, in each bus, or from the tourist information offices.

By Taxi

Taxis are also easily found at dozens of taxi stands or roaming the streets. Just look for any cab that is exposing the *Libre* (unoccupied) sign in its front window and wave to the driver. The drivers here are unusually helpful, and can sometimes provide good tips on nightlife and local restaurants if you try to speak to them in even the least polished Spanish. Typical taxi rides rarely cost more than 550 *ptas* within city limits.

WHERE TO STAY

Expensive

HOTEL LA BOBADILLA, *Finca la Bobadilla (Loja). Tel. (958) 221-440. Fax (958) 222-264. Low Season rack rates from 26,200 ptas per double room per night (E.P.). High Season rack rates from 30,400 ptas per double room per night (E.P.). All major credit cards accepted.*

This sprawling country estate turned five-star hotel and conference center is located a little over half an hour's drive northwest from the center of Granada. The palatial Andalucian style resort features 50 uniquely designed super-deluxe air conditioned rooms and apartments that all have luxurious private bathrooms stocked with the finest quality hair and skin care products, traditional tile flooring, direct dial telephones, remote control satellite television, lavish furnishings, patios0 and great picture windows overlooking the nearby mountains and dramatic rural scenery.

The hotel offers its international guests an assortment of special facilities, including two superb restaurants, beautiful *Mudejar* styled tranquil public rooms and lounges, a 16th century private chapel, hundreds of acres of breathtaking grounds and gardens, 24-hour room service, tennis courts, a giant swimming pool, a fitness and health club with sauna and Jacuzzi, available horseback riding, nearby fishing, excursions and optional jeep safaris, a beauty clinic, business meeting rooms, free parking, and a great staff.

PARADOR SAN FRANCISCO, *Alhambra. Tel. (958) 221-440, Fax (958) 222-264. US & Canada bookings (MARKETING AHEAD) 800/223-1356. Low season rack rates from 29,500 ptas per double room per night (E.P.). High season rack rates from 33,000 ptas per double room per night (E.P.). All major credit cards accepted.*

This is certainly one of the best *paradores* in Spain, offering 36 double rooms in a dramatically converted 15th century historic convent (Queen Isabella was once buried here) just behind the Alhambra. The inn has been designed to provide complete tranquility to its fortunate guests, who travel from all ends of the earth to stay here.

The rooms, some with a private balcony, contain beautiful furnishings, large closets, countryside views, air conditioning, television and telephones. The *parador* also boasts an excellent restaurant, tranquil gardens, and a peaceful inner courtyard. The service here is first-rate, and the front desk manager will be more than happy to help you pick an excursion or walking tour to enjoy during your stay. This is a great place for those who are seeking a quiet retreat with minimal distractions.

HOTEL ALHAMBRA PALACE, *Peña Partida, 2. Tel. (958) 221-468, Fax (958) 226-404. Year round rack rates from 19,500 ptas per double room per night (E.P.). All major credit cards accepted.*

With its fantastic views over the oldest parts of Granada, this inviting four-star castle hotel features the best full service accommodations in town. The palace actually dates back to 1910 when a local Duke decided to build a grand hotel to host the most deluxe visitors to his city. The result is a classy, ornate luxury hotel that now caters to some of Europe's most demanding travelers.

After several renovations, the property boasts impressive public lounges, outdoor terraces, a fantastic bar, designer boutiques, and 144 large double rooms and suites each with air conditioning, marble bathrooms, mini-bars, local artwork, mini-safes, direct dial phones and satellite televisions. The palace's location couldn't be better for those wishing to sightsee in Granada, since it's only a five minute walk to either the Alhambra or the center of town from the front door.

Services here include a 24-hour concierge desk offering advice and tickets for local excursions and events, free parking, room service, business meeting rooms, a foreign currency exchange desk with excellent conversion rates (especially for a hotel), friendly staff and a good restaurant.

Moderate

N.H. HOTEL INGLATERRA, *Calle Cettei Meriem, 4. Tel. (958) 221-559, Fax (958) 227-100. US & Canada Bookings: (UTELL), Tel. 800/44-UTELL.. Year-round rack rates from 14,000 ptas per double room per night (E.P.). Special weekend rates from 9,000 ptas per double room per night (E.P.). All major credit cards accepted.*

Located on a small side street just steps away from the Cathedral and old silk market, this fantastic little three-star hotel is the best bargain in town. The Inglaterra has been creatively converted from a gorgeous antique four story Andalucían townhouse, and maintains many of its original architectural elements, including a glass covered inner court-yard. There are 36 mid-sized air conditioned rooms that all feature deluxe private bathrooms with hair dryers and ecologically friendly hair and skin care products, mini-bars, remote control satellite color televisions, comfortable furnishings, in-room music systems, and direct dial telephones and laundry service. There is also a good restaurant.

Ask for one of the top floor attic rooms (although the elevator doesn't reach this level) with breathtaking views out over the old town and Alhambra. Highly recommended for those who are looking for great accommodations at affordable prices.

HOTEL SARAY, *Paseo Tierno Galvan. Tel. (958) 130-009. Fax (958) 129-161. Year round rack rates from 18,000 ptas per double room per night (E.P.). All major credit cards accepted.*

Located in the new part of the city in front of the convention center, this towering modern four-star executive class hotel has more facilities than any other hotel in town. All 214 air conditioned rooms and suites have large private bathrooms, remote control satellite television, direct dial telephone, mini-bar, mini-safe, extremely comfortable modern furnishings, small balconies, and large windows looking out over the newer districts of Granada. Additional features include a large swimming pool, adjacent shopping center, 24-hour room service, business meeting and convention rooms, restaurant and snack bar, lounges, express laundry and dry cleaning, available child care, fax machine and computer rental, private parking, gardens, and wheelchair accessible accommodations.

HOTEL GRANADA CENTER, *Avenida Fuentenueva. Tel. (958) 205-000. Fax (958) 289-696. Year round rack rates from 19,600 ptas per double room per night (E.P.). All major credit cards accepted.*

Situated near the university district, and only a 5 minute walk to the old part of town, this new four-star modern hotel is another good choice for visitors looking for a full service property. Here there are 172 exterior view air conditioned rooms with private bathrooms, soundproofed windows, remote control satellite television, mini-bar, mini-safe, and great bedding. Facilities include wheelchair accessible rooms, business meeting and convention salons, boutiques, restaurants, hair salon, glass enclosed elevators, room service, and private garage.

Inexpensive

HOTEL LA PERLA, *Calle de los Reyes Católicas, 2. Tel. (958) 223-415, No Fax. Year round rack rates from 3,750 ptas per double room per night (E.P.). Visa and Mastercard accepted.*

This simple two-star hotel in the heart of town offers 59 rooms with either shared or private bathrooms, elevator service, direct dial phones, and simple but comfortable furnishings. Although not particularly impressive, the service and value for the money is about as good as it gets in this price range. Good for budget travelers who are looking to save some money while staying in a clean and safe place.

PENSION LISBOA, *Plaza del Carmen. Tel. (958) 221-413, No Fax. Year round rack rates from 5,250 ptas per double room per night (E.P.). Most major credit cards accepted.*

A basic budget inn located in the old part of town with 28 medium-sized clean single and double room with private or shared bathrooms and not much else. Nothing special, but a good selection for those on tight budgets looking for a good location.

WHERE TO EAT

Moderate

PILLAR DEL TORO, *Calle de Hospital Santa Ana, 12. Tel. (958) - 223-847 or (958) 225-470. Most major credit cards accepted.*

This beautiful converted 17th century convent just off the Plaza Santa Ana is a remarkable dining establishment. There's a large front bar area, a plush inner courtyard that serves drinks and *tapas*, and two antique-filled floors with several intimate little exposed beam dining rooms facing into the courtyard. There is no dress code to speak of, and the loyal clientele socialize together downstairs before heading up to enjoy a sumptuous culinary delight. Among the most impressive dishes served here are crispy leek salads, endive and anchovies in sherry vinegar, garlic soup, French onion soup gratinee with goat cheese, filets of veal with quail eggs, pickled duck with rosemary, barbecued ox sirloin, angler fish with saffron, sauteed red cabbage with duck and desserts such as homemade ice cream with truffles. Expect a great three course meal to cost about 3,350 *ptas* pere person plus wine.

RESTAURANTE VELASQUEZ, *Calle de Profesor Emilio Orozco, 1. Tel. (957) 280-901. Most major credit cards accepted.*

When you're in the mood for a serious steak, this beautiful university district restaurant fits the bill perfectly. Inside its rich wooden and interior you can sit beside beautiful tiled walls with nice paintings, and enjoy a superb gastronomic meal for around 3,950 *ptas* per person plus wine. The menu also offers many seafood and meat dishes, but the filet mignon is the star attraction here! Reservations suggested and a jacket is preferred.

ALCHACENA DE LAS MONJAS, *Plaza del Padre Suarez, 5. Tel. (957) 224-028. Most major credit cards accepted.*

Chef Jose Luis Paviar has done a great job in creating a typical Andlucian menu at reasonable prices in this old 16th century church building in the city center. His seasonal menu may feature such specialties as swordfish filled empanadas, perfectly grilled chicken, roasted meats, and huge salads. Expect to spend about 3,600 *ptas* for a filling three course meal in this good local establishment.

Inexpensive

MESON YANQUE, *Plaza de San Miguel Bajo. Unlisted telephone. Cash Only.*

This simple local restaurant in the Albaicin serves up an assortment of cheap tapas and daily specials that are the first choice of student and local lunch breaking office workers. My last full meal here cost me only 1,250 *ptas* and was quite good.

SEEING THE SIGHTS
TOUR 1

The Plaza de Isabel Católica, downtown attractions, through the Albaicin, & the gypsy section of Sacromonte.

Approximate duration (by foot) is about 4.5 hours, including museum visits.

Central Granada & the Cathedral Quarter

Two of the city's busiest commercial avenues intersect in front of the **Plaza de Isabel Católica** square, the heart of Granada. From here turn left onto Calle de Reyes Católicas, and about half a block later you can again turn left onto a small lane marked with arrows leading a few steps away into the **Corral del Carbón**. This small open courtyard and well is surrounded by a 14th century structure that was once a Moorish inn.

These days, the building houses an excellent *Turismo* office where you can pick up bags full of maps, brochures, entertainment listings, and receive expert advice from a friendly multilingual staff. Make sure to pick up a free walking map of Granada here. *Their hours are from 9am until 8pm on weekdays and 10am until 8pm on Saturdays, closed Sundays.*

Also in the same historic building is the **Artesania** regional furniture and handicrafts shop that offers two floors full of local wooden boxes and crafts inlaid with Arab-inspired geometric designs, hand-carved furnishings, replicas of old world compasses with sundials, tapestries and other highly priced items. *The shop is open from 10am until 2pm and again from 4:30pm until 8pm, closed Saturday afternoon and Sunday.*

You might wish to window shop up and down the Calle de Reyes Católicas, but when you're finished, return to the **Plaza de Isabel Católica**. This time cross the street and head up along the left side of the **Gran Vía de Colón**, Granada's main commercial avenue. After walking about half a block, you will find a large iron gate with a doorway cut through it. Turn left and pass through the iron gateway onto the small stone lane called Calle de los Oficios that leads into the heart of Granada's medieval cathedral quarter. Just as you enter this pedestrian-only lane, on the right hand side is the entrance to the city's 16th century **Catedral** that was designed by Diego de Siloé. Although its somber and less than impressive interior is open to the public, this cathedral is not particularly notable, and is best enjoyed from the outside.

The first building of real interest on this lane, reached after descending a series of ten rock studded steps, is the bizarre, faux tile facade of the **Palacio de la Madraza** on your left. This structure was first built in the 14th century to house the Islamic Universidad de Yusuf 1 university. After the expulsion of the Moors, it was later transformed into Granada's city hall building for a time, but curiously enough its original octagonal domed Muslim prayer room was left virtually intact. To enter this sight, it will be necessary to walk through the massive spike covered outer doorway, bang loudly on the inner door, and wait for somebody to let you inside. *When cultural exhibits are hosted here, they are open to the public from about 10am until 2pm and again from 4:30pm until 8pm on weekdays, and admission is free, closed Saturday and Sunday.*

Across the lane is the imposing spire topped and royal crest emblazoned facade of the beautiful 16th century **Capilla Real** (Royal Chapel) that was designed by Enrique Egas. The chancel of this Gothic masterpiece contains the intricately sculpted marble crypts of King Ferdinand and his Queen Isabella (as well as their daughter and son-in-law), who finally consolidated what is now Spain by liberating Granada from the Moors in 1492. The vaulted chapel contains an elaborate 40 foot tall sculpted iron grill leading to the mausoleum, and several glass cases packed with religious prayer gowns, 17th century gold and silver ceremonial chalices, an opulent antique bible, fine 18th century coffers, and other historic religious items. The chapel's sacristy has been converted into a museum featuring the royal scepter, Gothic era gold altarpieces, and a fine exhibition of 15th century European paintings from masters like De Bouts, Memling, and Botticelli that were once part of the Queen's private collection. *Both the cathedral and royal chapel are open from 10:30am until 1:30pm and again from 3:30pm until 6:30pm on weekdays, and weekends and holidays from 11am until 1pm. Admission is 200 ptas each, per person.*

The Alcaicería

After visiting the royal chapel, continue down along the Calle de los Oficios until it intersects with a small pedestrian-only lane called the **Alcaicería** where you will turn left and pass beneath the sign marked *Mercado de Artesania*. During Moorish times, this area was the old silk market, and now contains dozens of small shops selling locally crafted silver filigree jewelry, inlaid wooden chess sets and music boxes, authentic flamenco dresses, old coins, antique pistols, Arabic coffee sets, ceramics and post cards. It is key to bargain with the merchants, since the selection is vast but the prices are somewhat high. Most of this street's shops will be open on weekdays, but tend to close during lunch hours, on Saturday afternoons, and most Sundays.

After bargaining your way to the arch marking the end of the Alcaicera, turn right onto Calle Zacatin with its designer shoe stores and clothing boutiques, and continue straight for another block or so until winding up at the edge of **Plaza Bib-Ramblas**. This delightful square contains several flower kiosks and is surrounded with cafés, candy shops, and small gift shops.

Walk across the width of the plaza, past the fountain, until reaching the Calle de Colegio Catalino that you will follow for one block before turning right up the Carcel that is adjacent to the side of the cathedral. During the day, a few vendors set up tables here to hawk a variety of unusual exotic spices and herbs. At the next corner, turn left onto Calle de San Jerónimo, and after another block turn right onto Calle de San Agustin. On weekdays during the late morning and early afternoons, this narrow road is home to an outdoor market that specializes in fresh produce and even live birds. Follow the road up for a couple of blocks until it intersects with the Gran Vía de Colón where you will cross the street and bear right.

The Old Town

Follow the Gran Vía de Colón for one block until turning left up the tiny Carcel Baja. Continue straight ahead as the street changes its name to the Calle de Calderería Nueva. As you stroll up this colorful road, keep your eyes out for the many Arabic tea houses (*teterías*) that are delightfully inexpensive and serve over 80 different types of exotic teas with sweets. There are also over a dozen casual couscous, shish kebab, and vegetarian restaurants to sit down and enjoy a quick snack.

Keep walking up the mosaic-lined stairs on this road until reaching a small plaza called the **Placeta de San Gregorio**. Here you can try to pop inside the Gothic **Iglesia de San Gregorio** to see its unique ceiling frescoes and beautiful golden altar. *The church may only be open during public masses, and admission is free.* As you face the front of the church, bear right onto Calle de San Juan de Los Reyes and make the first right turn onto the Carcel Alta that leads past the Escuela Flamenca flamenco school and then into the heart of town's main plaza.

After entering this square known as **Plaza Nueva**, turn left and continue into the **Plaza Santa Ana**. During the summer, this square is filled with outdoor terrace cafés that are packed with locals and visitors socializing with each other. The southwest side of this plaza is dominated by the three story clock tower-topped facade of the 17th century **Real Chancillería** (Royal Chancellery), now home to municipal offices and not open to the public. The northeast edge of the plaza is flanked by the main entrance to the lovely 16th century **Iglesia de Santa Ana** church and its tile covered bell tower.

From the front of the church, turn to the right up a small set of stairs, and then make the first right turn to head south on the Calle de Hospital de Santa Ana that boasts several beautiful terraced mansions, a well-known law school, and the absolutely fantastic **Pillar del Toro** restaurant and cocktail lounge. The restaurant has been beautifully converted from a 17th century convent, and has a peaceful inner open air courtyard.

The Albaicín

After a well deserved lunch or drink at the restaurant, return to the front of the church, and this time bear left to head up on the romantic little **Carrera del Darro** that follows the left bank of the **Darro** river. You will pass by several ancient stone arch bridges before reaching the vaulted remains of the 11th century Moorish **El Bañuelo Termas Árabes** bath-house at #31. *The baths and their decorative columns and sunlight pierced ceilings can be visited from 10am until 2pm and again from 4pm until 6pm from Tuesday through Saturday, and admission is free.*

A few steps further up this street you will find the 16th century **Casa de Castril** mansion that now is home to Granada's fine **Museo Arqueológico** (Archaeology Museum) containing a large collection of Greek and Roman sculptures, prehistoric artifacts from nearby caves, and old coins. *The museum is open from 10am until 2pm Tuesday through Sunday, and admission is 200 ptas, closed on Mondays and all afternoons.*

As you continue up along this riverside street you will find several more churches, including the massive 16th century **Convento de Santa Catalina de Zafra** convent and 16th century **Iglesia de San Pedro** church that are both open for free to the general public during masses.

At this point, the Carrera de Darro decends slightly and becomes renamed first as the Paseo del Pedre Manjon and then as the Paseo de los Tristes. This wider street now leads past the outdoor cafés and scenic promenade of the **Plaza San Nicolás**, offering superb views up to the Moorish Alhambra palace complex. Continue up this larger street until it ends, and turn left at this intersection onto the Cuesta del Chapiz. As you walk up the somewhat steep hill, you will next find the 15th century **Casa del Chapiz** which is currently not open to the public.

The Sacromonte area

After passing the Casa del Chapiz, make the next right turn onto the winding **Camino de Sacromonte** that will take you up past several gypsy's houses that have been here for ages. The sounds of *flamenco* guitars can often be heard pouring out the windows of these unique whitewashed residences. Bars, pubs, taverns, restaurants and cavern-like disco clubs are found all over this area, as are several small caves that can be visited.

On summer nights, the local gypsy community sometimes hosts live *flamenco* shows in the larger caves, but be careful about their notorious overpricing and hidden cover and minimum charges, and ask your hotel's front desk to suggest a fairly reputable show. Otherwise you better have some serious hiking boots and a powerful flashlight to even think about exploring these caves. Beware of strangers offering their services as cave guides – you may lose your wallet, only to discover it several hours later.

TOUR 2

The Alhambra.

Approximate duration (by foot) is about 3.5 hours, including museum, palace, garden, and fortress visits.

The Alhambra

No matter where you stand in Granada, you can't help but notice the massive fortified complex of walls and towers rising above the city on the nearby Asabica hillside. The **Alhambra** is one of the world's great Moorish monuments, and is also undoubtedly Spain's most popular tourist attraction.

A series of defensive fortresses has stood on this strategic location since at least the 9th century. With the 11th century additions by the Ziridians, and massive improvements ordered by the Arabic Nasrids during the 13th century reign of King Mohammed I (Ibn el Ahmar), this hill was transformed into an awesome compound of unprecedented civic, royal, and military importance. With every step you take there are countless examples of fine artistic craftsmanship, lush gardens, and examples of dramatic architecture that remain unrivaled in all of Europe.

Getting to The Alhambra

The best way to reach the Alhambra is to walk over to the city's main **Plaza Nueva**, and walk up a steep road called the Cuesta de Gomérez. After a few minutes, you will reach the Renaissance **Puerta de las Granadas** archway with its fine sculpted pomegranates and angles. After passing through the arch, the road splits into a few different directions, so be sure to continue on the left side lane.

A few more minutes of passing thick shrubbery and the road will lead past a large fountain. This road takes you through the zigzags of the 13th century **Puerta de la Justica** gateway with its carved symbols taken from the Muslim Koran. At this point you have entered the complex, and can purchase your tickets at the nearby information center and head office building.

If you're driving, cars can also access the sight via a complicated route through the back end of the city. Just follow the signs found all over the downtown area, and lock up tight as you park in the massive lots at the top of the hill.

The city has recently added a special minibus that operates from the Plaza Nueva during the high season to take visitors to and from the Alhambra without the need for the long walk. The service costs about 150 *ptas*, and tickets can be purchased at the well-marked kiosk in the plaza.

Starting Out

The best way to start viewing the Alhambra is to turn left at the ticket booth and head towards the trapezoidal **Alcazaba** fortress. This is the most ancient part of the complex and dates back to at least the 9th century, but was later rebuilt and extended by both the Ziridians and the Nasrids. The highlight of this defensive structure is the 13th century **Torre de la Vella** watchtower, from where a staircase leads to a bell-topped platform with views over the whole compound, the old parts of Granada, and the more distant Sierra Nevada mountains that are outstanding. It was on the tower's highest point that the **Cross of the Reconquest** was placed for all to see after the victorious Christian troops of Fernando and Isabella defeated the Moors here in 1492.

From the fortress, walk back past the other ruined towers of the Alcazaba until reaching the **Plaza de los Aljibes**. This was originally a ravine during the Arab occupation, but was later converted by the Christians into a series of cisterns. The cisterns are occasionally open to public inspection during limited hours. From the plaza, exit through the Moorish **Puerta del Vino** gateway where wines were once sold to the Alhambra's residents. Take special note of the upper floor's arched windows and fine decorative carving. From the archway, turn left to reach the next series of structures.

ALHAMBRA INFO

The Alhambra is open year round, although it changes its hours of operation during different seasons. From April to September you can visit from 9am until 7:45pm on Mondays through Saturdays, 9am until 6pm on Sundays, with special nighttime visits on Tuesday, Thursday, and Saturday evenings from 8pm until 10pm. From October to March you can visit 9am until 5:45pm daily, with special nighttime visits on Saturday evenings from 8pm until 10pm. The art and archaeological museums in the Palacio Carlos V are open from Tuesday through Sunday from 10am until 3pm, but often are closed for renovation on other days, check with the ticket office for more details.

The Alhambra's admission price is 650 ptas per person to enter all segments of the complex, except for the two art museums in the Palacio Carlos V that cost 250 ptas additional to enter if open. On most Sundays, the general public is invited to enter for free after 3pm or so. I strongly suggest asking for a copy of the free sight map (if they have any left) since unfortunately nothing here is marked or indicated in any language. If no maps are available, buy one at the small shops near the entrance. Keep in mind that each ticket has three small boxes on its edge that will be punched as you enter the various sections of the compound.

Due to the heavy volume of tourists here, you're given a specific 30 minute time slot to visit the Alcázar (Palacios Nazaries) palace sections. If you do not reach the Palaces by the time your ticket states, you will not be allowed to enter them.

Now you will head towards the 14th century **Alcázar** (also called the **Casas Real** or **Palacios Nazaries**) palace sections. This part of the complex was originally built by the Moors out of simple materials like clay and wood. You will pass by some towers and adjacent gardens to enter the first of three palace buildings with their spectacular inner courtyards. The first of these structures you will enter is called the **Mexuar** and was used by the King and his royal council to hear complaints by local residents and discuss administrative solutions to a wide variety of problems.

The most impressive parts of this structure is the **Main Hall** that was later converted into a Christian chapel, the column supported ivory inlaid ceilings of the **Golden Room**, and the small **Oratory** that is positioned to face in the direction of Mecca.

From here you will enter the tiled **Patio de los Arrayanes** courtyard with its peaceful pool and fountain, bordered by a pleasant myrtle hedge.

On either end of the patio are delicately sculpted Arabesque colonnades that are among the best I have ever seen anywhere. The northern archways lead to the **Torre de Comares** tower with impressive rooms in another section of the palace called the **Serallo**, where visiting emissaries were welcomed.

Make sure to wander through the remarkable **Hall of the Boat**, whose painted ceiling has been recreated after being destroyed in a fire in 1890, and the **Hall of the Ambassadors** that was once the sultan's throne room and is opulently decorated with fine carved cedar ceilings, elaborate tile work, panoramic windows, Arabic inscriptions and lots of stucco. From here you can exit right into the final part of the palace.

The final section of the palace is the **Harem**, where the sultan enjoyed much of his free time in the company of his vast assortment of female companions. This part is entered via the world famous **Patio de los Leones** courtyard. This is among the most spectacular parts of the Alcázar and is named for the 12 marble lions that support the fountain in the middle of the patio. Although slightly altered from its original version, the courtyard still displays some of the most enchanting ornamental crafts-manship found anywhere. Many people, including myself, have spend countless hours by the patio's fountain just staring at every square inch of the arched columns.

A series of rooms leads from the patio, including the **Hall of the Kings** with its unique leather paintings and the **Hall of the Abencerrajes** where many heads literally rolled beneath an amazing çeiling. From here, walk to the southeast corner of the courtyard and wander into the **Mocarbes Gallery** with its stalactite-like ceiling, the ruined **Royal Mausoleum**, and **The Hall of the Two Sisters** that has an intricate honeycomb ceiling.

From here, small paths lead to various royal apartments, including the one where famed American writer Washington Irving penned his book called *Tales of the Alhambra*. Additional signs point the way towards the mosaic-covered **Baños Reales** baths that featured running hot and cold water and luxurious fixtures. Another route will take visitors to the fantastic **Jardines del Lindjara** gardens that were added after the Christians arrived, or up to the Queen's **Peinador de la Reina** tower.

Now it's time to backtrack a bit, below the patio with the lion fountain and head to the massive 16th century **Palacio de Carlos V** palace. This classically inspired two story marble and stone block royal residence was designed by Pedro Machuca, a student of Michelangelo. It's not all that impressive, except for an archaeological museum and a small art museum. There are also special events and concerts held here during the summer months. A better idea would instead be to walk towards the eastern part of the complex, past dozens of well-manicured gardens, towards the 14th century **Generalife** summer palace.

Here you can peek into several vacant rooms, walk around the huge courtyard surrounded with pools, and enjoy a fine vista from its lookout point. Another good stop is over at the adjacent **Parador San Francisco**, an inn converted from the old convent where Queen Isabella was once buried. The best part of your visit to the Alhambra is just wandering around and appreciating the dramatic combination of Moorish and Christian architecture, while resting in some of the best gardens in the country.

NIGHTLIFE & ENTERTAINMENT

Although there are several bars, pubs, and discos throughout the city, the best area for nightlife is the **ghetto** district near the university. The major street in this section for nightlife is Calle de Pedro António de Alarcón that gets packed with university students and young professionals on Thursday through Saturday nights starting at 11pm.

Most of the bars in the **Sacromonte** and **Albaicin** also offer great nightlife on the weekends, but they often have cover charges and stiff drink prices.

EXCURSIONS & DAY TRIPS

If you have seen all the major sights in Granada and want to spend at least five hours visiting the area outside of the city, the best day trip you can take is to the traditional villages southeast of town. Since no guided excursions are offered here by major companies inside Granada, you may need to take a bus, or better yet rent a car or private guide with a sedan to get to the following destinations.

There is limited bus service from Granada on the Alsina Graellas bus company, *Tel. (958) 251-358,* to the destinations listed below.

DRIVING TOUR THROUGH LAS ALPUJARRAS

Among the most impressive traditional villages in all of Spain are those located within the **Las Alpujarras** section of **Andalucía**. This is a superb area if you appreciate the great outdoors, and is easily accessible between February and October when snow doesn't block the majority of the curvy roads.

Situated just below the often snow-capped peaks of the Sierra Nevada mountain range, this highly picturesque series of hilltop villages and adjacent wildlife reserves has historically been the secret hiding place for many persecuted peoples through Spain's turbulent past. Way back when the Christians conquered Granada, Moors came to this area to avoid the wrath of their enemies. More recently it has been home to military officers from the losing side of the Spanish Civil War who quietly slipped off into small huts here for decades before surrendering. Even now, a growing contingent of artistic people from all over Europe come to be left alone or to get away from the urban environments some felt had stifled their creativity.

Many of the towns and villages in the **Alpujarras** area near Granada are traditional by nature, and preserve the old way of live. As night falls, shepherds walk their flocks of sheep through the middle of small villages and herd them into ancient corrals located in the basements of their Moorish era houses. In the smaller hamlets, the townsfolk don't wear wristwatches and rely solely on the ringing of the church bells to know what time it is. In some cases, the water they drink comes from centuries-old fountains, and the food they eat comes from their own small farms.

As artists and tourists began to find their way here, other small towns and tourist infrastrcuture developed. Small rural hotels and incredibly beautiful wood and stone walled mountain chalets can be rented by the week. Old walking trails have been widened for casual walking trips through the hillside, horseback riding excursions were created to allow foreigners to experience overnight equestrian trips, electricity and paved roads now connect most of the scenic zones to each other, and local artists now have small galleries to exhibit and sell their fine hand crafted ceramics, Moorish style carpets, and folk art.

The best approach to the area from Granada is to take the high speed **N-323 highway south** for 45 km (28 miles), until exiting at **C-333 east**, a winding road. The first place of interest that you will pass by along this route is the famed spa city of **Lanjarón** where older Spaniards go in the summer to bathe in the thermal mineral waters that are also bottled here and marketed around the nation. The city's quaint **Barrio Hondilla** quarter is a good place to wander around, after whcih you should proceed to the ruins of the Moorish era **Castillo** castle. For hikers, a seven hour hike (moderate skill level) from the city's bridge goes down through the **Rio Lanjarón** and heads through the pines and dry valley area to reach impressive views out to the **Pico del Caballo** mountain peak before returning back into town. Also of interest here is the yearly **Fiesta del Agua y Jamon** festival on the 24th of June, when the whole town engages in water fights between complimentary snacks of cured ham!

From here, continue along the **C-333 east** until it ends at the valley town of **Orgiva**. This is a good place to stock up on groceries, gasoline, and other supplies that will be either hard to find, or much more expensive further along the way up into the mountains. The town has a couple of sights to visit, including the 16th century **Palacio de los Condes de Saastago** castle that is now home to boutiques, and the unnamed 16th century parish church. About two weeks before Easter the city is filled with the sound of exploding gunpowder explosions: it's the **Cristo de la Expiration** festivities!

After passing through town, bear left onto the difficult curves (don't try this road during snow season) on route **GR-421 east** that leads into up the higher elevation areas of the **Alpujarra Alta**. The narrow road twists and turns several times before reaching the turnoff to the charming town of **Pampaneira**. With its charming side streets displaying locally made crafts and leather goods, this is a good place to get out and walk. If you take a good look around, you can find the centuries-old **Fuentes** fountains, and a pretty main plaza. For hikers, there is a series of two to six hour walks (beginners skill level), depending on how far you wish to travel. They start from the city's edge and can take visitors along the cliffs, valleys, brooks, and old stone lanes of the nearby villages mentioned below.

Just a bit further along the main road, a fairly well marked turnoff to the left then leads around the cliffs above the **Barranco de Poqueira** canyon to the world famous village and artists colony of **Bubión**. This town has become the major attraction of the area, and thus has the largest concentration of shops, art galleries, excursion operators, hotels, restaurants, and bars. All of this has still not affected the lower part of town, where small lanes look out over impressive views of the valleys and adjacent villages. The town also offers a few fine sights including its dramatically situated 16th century whitewashed parish church, and plenty of old stone and wooden houses for rent along dirt roads that don't show up on most maps.

This is the best place to get local tourist information, and run into other travelers who may wish to join you for a horseback ride or local trek. For those looking for affordable yet comfortable accommodations with great views, check over at the extremely friendly **Apartmentos Las Terrazas** for the best deal in town. A bit further up this same side road is the town of **Capileira**, where recent condo construction projects have begun to take their toll on the scenery. There are a few good reasons to visit this town, though, including its interesting **Museo de Costumbres y Artes Populares** (museum of folk art). The museum also houses the writings and personal effects of famed 19th century writer Pedro António de Alarcon who spent some time here. The 15th of August is the town's main festival and is plenty of fun.

Return to the **GR-421** and continue east until the infamous **Barranco de la Sangre** canyon, where through the centuries countless people on the wrong side politically of major disputes have been thrown to their deaths. Soon after you'll come to the delightfully traditional mountain village of **Portugos**. This town has not been altered to suit the needs of tourism, and still retains much of its cultural heritage. Each evening shepherds come back through the old lanes escorted by their sheep. The tiny main square leads to small streets lined with old houses, some of which were built right into caves and date back hundreds of years.

There is also the ancient **Fuente Agría** fountain that spews out red colored ferrous water. This is the most friendly of the Alpujarras villages, and must be seen before leaving the area. While here make sure to pop inside the wonderful **Hotel Nuevo Malagueno** for a great room or a terrific meal of excellently prepared local specialties.

After this town, the road soon winds sharply around the **Rio Trevélez** and its perilous gorge to meet with the town of **Trevélez**. Known as the highest village in Spain at an altitude of 1,476 meters (4,841 feet) above sea level, and contains a series of interesting terraced houses. This is where you can buy or just sample the country's best cured ham, especially during their **Dia de Jamón** celebrations on the 15th of August. For hikers, there's a five hour hike (beginner's skill level) from the riverside up towards the mountain passes. At this point the route continues for quite a while, but you have already passed the most dramatic sights.

PRACTICAL INFORMATION

- **Main City Tourist Office**, *Turismo, Corral de Carbón, Tel. (958) 225-990*
- **Regional Tourist Office**, *P.P.T.G., Plaza Mariana Pineda, 10, Tel. (958) 223-528*
- **Granada Regional Airport**, *Ctra. de Málaga, Tel. (958) 447-081*
- **Iberia Airlines Offices**, *Plaza Isabel la Cathólica, Tel. (958) 227-592*
- **Regional Bus Info**, *Alsina Graells, Camino de Ronda, Tel. (958) 251-258*
- **City Bus Info**, *Rober, Granada, Tel. (958) 813-711*
- **Regional Train Info**, *Renfe, Calle de los Reyes Católicos, 63, Tel. (958) 227-170*
- **Municipal Police**, *Tel. 092*

Major Local Festivals
Contact the local Turismo office, *Tel. (958) 225-990,* for more details.
- **Reconquest Festival**, *early January, Parades*
- **Carnival**, *late February, Processions, All Night Parties*
- **Semana Santa**, *prior to Easter, Strange Processions*
- **Fiesta Musica**, *June, Music and Dance Shows*
- **Jazz Festival**, *November, Outdoor and Indoor Concerts*

THE COSTA DEL SOL RESORTS

The **Costa del Sol**, a series of some of the world's most famous beach resorts, stretches across 160 km (99 miles) of Spain's southern coast on the Mediterranean Sea. This area boasts dozens of completely different seaside towns and cities that each attract its own type of visitors. The eastern reaches of this region contain the vacation condos and apartments of upper middle class Spaniards who are only in evidence here during Easter and the summer months.

Among the prettiest of these smaller resort areas is the beautiful town of **Nerja**, whose cove beaches have become increasingly popular with English tourists. As you move west to the more commercial city of **Málaga**, you pass the medium priced and highly overdeveloped resorts of **Torremolinos**, **Benalmádena Costa**, and **Fuengirola**. These beach areas attract a year round mixture of vacationing retired and working class Europeans and North Americans. During the summer season, thousands of English, German, English, Dutch, Scandinavian, and an increasing number of North American singles seem to take over these same beaches in the pursuit of each other and a good tan.

Further to the west, an entirely opposite selection of high-end vacation destinations like **Marbella** and **Puerto Banús** successfully marketed themselves to a much more deluxe European crowd. In the lower season, Dutch, English, German, and English ex-patriots and tourists can be seen socializing in a somewhat more refined setting. In the summer, the children of rich families, and aging millionaires from around the globe may be found enjoying the expensive hotels, beaches, bars and yacht clubs lining the coastline.

Depending on your budget, and the type of ambiance you're looking for, almost any of these cities can be enjoyable. But if you're expecting to find superb natural beauty and unspoiled stretches of white sand beach, this is not the place to come. Since the 1960's, almost every square inch of available seafront in the region has been developed to its maximum revenue-making potential. The glut of massive hotel and apartment complexes has left the Costa del Sol with scars that will never heal, a constant low supply of potable water, and skylines that often resemble Miami Beach. There are still, however, safe and clean beaches, plenty of bargains (especially in the off-season), and lots of people to meet all year.

In the following pages you'll find listings and details on the best resort areas and villages in this large region.

NERJA

Of all the seaside towns along the eastern part of the Costa del Sol, **Nerja** is without a doubt the most charming. This small historic town of both traditional whitewashed houses and newer tourist villas is sandwiched between the blue waters of the **Atlantic Ocean** and the dramatic **Sierra Almijara** mountains. This unique location has blessed the area with a year round warm micro-climate that is perfect for visitors and the nearby cultivation of sub-tropical fruits.

Although its history can be traced back through Neolithic, Roman, and Moorish times, this former fishing village began to grow in both size and importance after the Christians reclaimed the area from the Arabs in the late 15th century. By the 17th century, there were more than 500 residents who lived on the newly built residential streets in the town's center such as Calle de Granada and Calle del Carmen.

It was also about this time that the town began construction of the **Iglesia El Salvador** parish church and the **Balcón de Europa** defensive post. It was not until the 1960's that English and German tourists began to spend their summers here, and small hotels and condo complexes sprung up along the shoreline and nearby orchid covered plain. Tourists and locals alike seem to love the tremendously scenic **Paseo de los Carabineros** pathway.

Nearby at the **Cuevas de Nerja** caves you can visit enchanting caverns that were inhabited by prehistoric men who left crude but beautiful cave paintings. Now with a strong local economy based on both tourism and agriculture, Nerja has grown in size to become a delightful small city rich in beauty and activities.

ARRIVALS & DEPARTURES

By Bus

Several private bus companies offer daily motorcoach services to this city from Málaga, Granada (via Torre del Mar), Córdoba, Almería, Cádiz, and Sevilla. The price varies between 475 *ptas* each way to Málaga, and up to 2,625 *ptas* each way to Sevilla. Local bus service between the town's bus station and the Cuevas de Nerja caves run about every hour in each direction and cost 90 *ptas* each way. From the bus stop at the caves, you can connect to a weekday only bus that runs up and down to most of the resorts on the Costa del Sol.

The city's small bus station is situated on the Calle de San Miguel, just off Plaza Cantarero in the north part of town. Expect a taxi from here to cost 370 *ptas* to almost any hotel or beach in town.

By Car

The easiest way to drive to Nerja is to take the winding N-323 south from Granada for 57 km (35 miles) before merging onto the extension of the N-340 Autovia de Mediterraneo highway west for 29 km (18 miles) from Salobreña. Another possible route is to follow the N-340 Autovia de Mediterraneo highway east for 51 km (32 miles) from Málaga. There are precious few free parking spaces along the side streets of town, but parking lots can be found all over town for about 950 *ptas* per day.

By Train

There is no good train service to this area. Your best bet is to take a train to Málaga and reach this city via connecting regional bus service.

ORIENTATION

Nerja, population 12,750, lies on the seaside in the eastern **Costa del Sol** section of the **Andalucía** region. The trip here is about 521 km (322 miles) south from Madrid, 86 km (53 miles) southwest from Granada, and only about 51 km (32 miles) east from Málaga.

WHERE TO STAY

Expensive

PARADOR DE NERJA, *Calle de Parador. Tel. (95) 252-0050, Fax (95) 252-1997. US & Canada bookings (Marketing Ahead), Tel. 800/223-1356. Low season rack rates from 15,000 ptas per double room per night (E.P.). High season rack rates from 19,000 ptas per double room per night (E.P.). All major credit cards accepted.*

This modern four-star sea-view parador, situated on three acres of panoramic gardens on a tranquil promenade resting just above the beach on downtown Nerja's east end, is a good value for the money. While the facade is far from impressive, one glimpse of the sun rise over the ocean from each room's large terrace will make you want to stay forever.

This is a good choice for the more deluxe travelers who wish to enjoy this delightful town. It has 73 Mediterranean style double sea-view rooms which contain private bathrooms, large private bathrooms, Mexican tile floors, remote control satellite television, mini-bar, hair dryer, direct dial telephone, and rustic wooden furnishings. Facilities here include a beautiful sea-view garden with plenty of sun chairs, a tennis court, an outdoor swimming pool, free parking and a good regional restaurant. The service here is good, and the guests are a mixture of nationalities of all ages.

HOTEL RIU MONICA, *Playa de la Torrecilla. Tel. (95) 252-1100, Fax (95) 252-1162. Low season rack rates from 18,000 ptas per double room per night (E.P.). High season rack rates from 24,000 ptas per double room per night (E.P.). All major credit cards accepted.*

The Riu Monica is a massive, fancy, and overpriced four-star hotel located off the main town beach on a nice breezy spot about a five minute walk away from the heart of Nerja. All of the 234 air conditioned rooms have private bathrooms, terraces, satellite television, mini-safe, direct dial phones, and in-room music systems. The hotel also offers paddle-boat rentals, children's activity program, outdoor swimming pool with lounge chairs, billiard, tennis courts, boutiques, parking, business meeting rooms, excursions, car rental desk, beauty salon, live evening entertainment, massage therapy and a good assortment of restaurants and bars. For those of you who enjoy large full service beach front resorts, this is your only option. Make sure to ask for a sea view room.

Moderate

HOTEL PERLA MARINA, *Calle Merida 7. Tel. (95) 252-3350, Fax (95) 252-4083. Low season rack rates from 9,500 ptas per double room per night (E.P.). High season rack rates from 14,000 ptas per double room per night (E.P.). All major credit cards accepted.*

I like this friendly and well equipped three-star sea front hotel situated directly off the beach in a good part of town. The Perla was built just eight years ago and features 106 nicely furnished beachview rooms with private bathrooms, small terraces, air conditioning, direct dial telephones, and televisions. The property also features a tour desk, business meeting rooms, indoor garage, outdoor café, safe deposit boxes, restaurant, bar, snack bar, available beach chairs, nearby boat rentals and a helpful staff. They also rent out 20 nice and cozy two and three bedroom seafront townhouses located next to the hotel for about 50% more than the double room prices listed above, which are a real bargain if they are not totally sold out.

HOTEL BALCON DE EUROPA, *Paseo Balcon de Europa, 1. Tel. (95) 252-0800, Fax (95) 252-4490. Low season rack rates from 11,200 ptas per double room per night (E.P.). High season rack rates from 16,100 ptas per double room per night (E.P.). All major credit cards accepted.*

This fairly nice three-star sea view hotel is located atop a small beach on the historic *Balcon de Europa* promenade in the heart of *Nerja*. As the most famous hotel in town for over two decades, it becomes heavily booked up in advance with groups and individuals from all over Europe. The property features some 105 air conditioned guestrooms (most with beach view balconies) that have a large private bathroom, mini-bar, satellite television, mini-safe, direct dial telephone and nice furnishings. Other facilities include a tour desk, business meeting rooms, indoor garage, outdoor café, restaurant, bar, snack bar, semi-private beach with lounge chairs, sauna, boat rentals, game room and ping pong. Service here is not great, but the hotel represents a good value for the money, especially if you request a sea view room.

HOTEL PLAZA CAVANA, *Plaza Cavana, 10. Tel. (95) 252-4000, Fax (95) 252-2008. Low season rack rates from 8,900 ptas per double room per night (E.P.). High season rack rates from 13,900 ptas per double room per night (E.P.). All major credit cards accepted.*

If you prefer small hotels with lots of ambiance and personalized service, this is a great place to stay while in town. Situated just a one minute walk to the beach, this charming new three-star hotel is one of my favorite small hotels in this part of the *Costa del Sol*. All of it's 34 bright and airy rooms have air conditioning, satellite television, private bathrooms, am-fm clock radios, mini-safes, hair dryers, direct dial telephones, and beautiful new furnishings. The hotel has a marble covered restaurant and caféteria, indoor parking, a rooftop swimming pool (a new indoor heated pool and sauna are scheduled to by the time you read this), meeting rooms, an outdoor café and a nice front desk staff.

MARINAS DE NERJA, *Playazo. Tel. (95) 252-2300, Fax (95) 252-1153. Low season rack rates from 5,500 ptas per dbl studio apartment per night (E.P.).*

High season rack rates from 18,750 ptas per dbl studio apartment per night (E.P.). All major credit cards accepted.

This nice family-oriented apart-hotel is a modern five story complex on the extreme western edge of town. It offers some 108 studio, one and two bedroom, apartments with kitchen facilities. With it's good location just off *Playazo* beach, this is the perfect place for those who prefer to do some of their own cooking during their vacation. All of the apartments contain private bathrooms, pine furnishings, seaview terraces, direct dial telephones, marble floors, and televisions with optional movie channels.

Facilities in the complex include a summer barbecue buffet, restaurant, snack bar, beach bar, tennis courts, volleyball, health club, outdoor swimming pool, wind surfing gear and boat rentals, business meeting rooms, game room, live music during the evenings, a shuttle bus to and from downtown, and inexpensive beach chair rentals. The one catch here is that even though they advertise in-room satellite color television, the front desk has the nerve to charge guests up to 1000 *ptas* per day to use it.

HOTEL VILLA FLAMENCA, *Calle Andalucía, 1. Tel. (95) 252-3200, Fax (95) 252-2196. Low season rack rates from 9,200 ptas per double room per night (E.P.). High season rack rates from 11,800 ptas per double room per night (E.P.). All major credit cards accepted.*

If you have a car, or don't mind walking a few quick minutes to get to good beaches or the heart of town, this is a decent and almost affordable two star hotel. They offer 88 acceptable rooms with private terraces, heating, private bathrooms, and direct dial telephones. Facilities include a large outdoor pool, a TV room, children's play area, restaurant, bar, meeting rooms, gardens and sauna.

Inexpensive

HOTEL CALA BELA, *Calle Puerta del Mar, 10. Tel. (95) 252-0700. Low season rack rates from 4,750 ptas per double room per night (E.P.). High season rack rates from 8,900 ptas per double room per night (E.P.). Some credit cards accepted.*

Although far from fancy, this small nine room hotel and restaurant offers guests an affordable alternative to the more luxurious accommodations in town, Situated down the block from the tourist office, the Cala Bela has nine guestrooms with private bathrooms, heating, direct dial telephones and simple but comfortable furnishings. There is also a good restaurant, TV room, nearby parking and nice people working here.

WHERE TO EAT
Moderate

RESTAURANTE CASA LUQUE, *Plaza Cavana 2. Tel. (95) 282-1004. All major credit cards accepted.*

You certainly couldn't ask for a better medium priced seafood and meat restaurant than this! Located just of the main town square in an attractive Moorish style building complete with a beautiful glass roof, antique ceramic tiles, Arabesque arches, and one of the best sea-view terraces anywhere, this wonderful and relaxed restaurant serves wonderful meals in a lovely setting. The Casa Luque offers its patrons a huge multilingual menu that includes such delicious items as homemade pate with hazelnut dressing, prawn cocktails, cream of lobster soup, grilled salmon in mustard sauce, chicken stroganoff, sherry laced beef stew, red peppers stuffed with codfish and rice, partridge salad, wild boar served with mango, filet of sole wrapped around scampi and sumptuous desserts. Expect a relaxing three course dinner to cost around 2,450 *ptas* per person plus wine per person. Ask in advance for a sea view terrace table.

MERENDERO MONTEMAR, *Playa de Burriano. No telephone. Visa credit cards accepted.*

Open for breakfast, lunch, and dinner for most of the year, this simple beach-side dining terrace is also a good choice. Located just off a large beach on the east end of town, the Montemar has several simply set tables resting under a bamboo awning. Their reasonably priced menu includes fresh grilled sardines on a stick, paella, gazpacho, mixed salad, rabbit in garlic sauce, roasted chicken and grilled giant shrimp. Far from fancy but great for a 1,650 *ptas* per person lunch while you take a break from tanning on the beach.

Inxpensive

RESTAURANTE & CAFE LA PLAZA, *Avenida de Castilla Perez. Tel. (95) 252-0287. Some major credit cards accepted.*

If you want a great little informal spot to enjoy a hearty home cooked lunch or dinner, this is a really nice spot to head to. The Plaza is a casual cafe and restaurant that is located on a quaint sea-view plaza just a few blocks away from the heart of downtown Nerja and its main city beach. They offer both indoor and outdoor open air seating with a clean dining room, bathrooms, and bar. Their menu includes traditional local favorites such as shrimp in garlic, salad nicoise, chicken salad sandwiches, burgers, grilled sausages, chicken breast, Spanish omelets, sautéed red perch, and a fantastic grilled filet of sole topped with roasted garlic. Expect a good three course lunch or dinner to cost around 2,450 *ptas* per person plus wine. At only 1,300 *ptas*. This is a friendly place with good food and fast service at reasonable prices.

SEEING THE SIGHTS

Approximate duration (by foot) is about 4.5 hours, including church and beach visits.

The best place to start your exploration of town is at the **Balcón de Europa**. This seaside plaza and lookout point was originally the sight of a 9th century Arab castle, but was rebuilt as a defensive fort by royal decree in 1660. Although the fortress is all but gone, the balcony still serves as a wonderful place to sit on a bench or outdoor café table and stare out onto both the sea and the **Playa la Caletilla** beach just below. There are even pay telescopes here that can be used to enjoy views over the 16 kilometers (10 miles) of adjacent rocky cove beaches. The balcony is always open, and you don't have to pay anything to access the area.

From the balcony, turn left onto **Calle de Carmen**. This pub and restaurant lined street dates back to 1655 when the town began to develop in it's present form. A few steps down this street you will find the quaint **Iglesia El Salvador** parish church with it's checker board marble flooring and bold golden altar. This whitewashed church and bell tower dates back to the late 17th century, and is a perfect example of Baroque design with Mudéjar elements. The church is only open during daily masses, and admission is free. After seeing the church, keep heading down the same road until reaching the delightful **Plaza Cavana** where you will bear left onto Calle El Barrio. A few steps later, I suggest turning left down the Calle de Málaga, which is the best access point for the wide and sandy **Playa del Salón** beach. Further ahead and just off of this street is the more developed **Playa de la Torrecilla** beach area where there are several new hotel developments as well as a tennis club. From this point you can continue down the shoreline until reaching the busy **Playazo** beach area.

After visiting these less than tranquil beaches, return into town via the Calle de Málaga until ending up at the Plaza Cavana once again. Here you will bear left onto the atmospheric **Calle Granada** and take it for a few blocks before turning right onto Calle de San Miguel. A few steps up this street is the **Plaza Ermita**. This great little square is home to the 17th century **La Ermita de Nuestra Señora de las Angustias** sanctuary. The chapel was built by Don Tomas de Castro and Luis Lopez de Alcantara to pay homage to the town's patron saint.

Inside there are wonderful paintings and a memorable dome which was frescoed by Alonso Cano. The church is open daily for masses, and admission is free. Nearby is also town's **Mercado** market where you can stock up on picnic items before heading for the most magnificent beaches imaginable on the west end of town. I should also mention that throughout most of the year there are horse drawn carraiges parked in front of the Plaza. Friendly Sr. Miguel Narvaez, *Tel. 909-565-529,* will be glad to take you and up to four friends or family member on a 25 minute tour of the old quarter of Nerja for a mere 2,500 *ptas*.

After seeing the plaza and it's sights, turn right onto Calle Angustias and follow it for about two blocks before turning right onto Calle Pintada. This street then merges with the shopping lane known as the **Calle Puerta del Mar** where at #2 you can pop into the helpful **Turismo** tourist office to pick up some free maps and advice. After leaving the tourist office, make a right turn onto Calle Hernando de Carabeo. It is off this road that you can access some of the world's most dramatic beaches. Keep your eyes out (or ask for directions at the Turismo) for a small lane descending downhill to the right that leads to the beautiful **Playa de Calahonda** beach.

From about this point there is also a fantastic tile-lined path known locally as the **Paseo de los Carabineros**. This winding path cuts through some hedge and wild orchid gardens, and leads down to several tiny romantic rock cove beaches like **Playa del Chorrillo**, **Playa de Carabeo**, and **Playa de Carabeillo** where you can be totally alone during most of the year (except for August). Additional beach areas can be found further along the Calle Hernando de Carabeo and past the **Jardines Urbano de Capistrano Playa** gardens including the more crowded **Playa de Burriana** beach.

NIGHTLIFE & ENTERTAINMENT

Almost all of the night life in town centers around the English-style pubs which line the **Plaza Cavana** and **Balcon de Europa**. Among my favorites are the **Chexogonos Pub** and the **Green Parrot**.

EXCURSIONS & DAY TRIPS
THE CUEVAS DE NERJA CAVES

One of the most famous excursions from Nerja are the famous **Cuevas de Nerja** caves, which are only about 3.5 km (2 miles) northeast of town. These gigantic underground limestone caves were first discovered in 1959 and are divided into a series of hauntingly floodlit caverns, some of which were inhabited (or at least visited) by prehistoric families about 24,000 years ago.

There is a vast assortment of huge stalagmites and stalactites, as well as cave paintings of fish and other animals that date back to the Paleolithic, Neolithic, and Bronze Ages. There are also archaeological exhibits set up in glass cases that show primitive tools and artifacts, as well as basic information about life during these times. Unfortunately, things have gotten overly commercialized here, with silly music being piped in to the Colomillo, Belen, Cascada, and Fantasmas caverns to create a tacky tourist trap ambiance here. As you wander around the caves there is also a team of annoying photographers who blind you with their flashes before attempting to sell a photo of your visit upon exit.

Near the entrance to the caves there are souvenir shops, a snack bar, and a nice garden and picnic area. Each July the caves host the **Festivales de la Cuevas de Nerja**, where internationally acclaimed musicians and ballet dancers perform in this fantastic acoustical environment.

The caves are open daily from 10:30am until 6pm, and admission is 450 ptas for adults and 250 ptas for kids under 12.

Directions

By car, you should hop on the N-340 east from Nerja for 3.5 km (2 miles) before following the exit signs to the left that lead to the caves. Municipal bus service is available 11 times daily in both directions, via the Nerja bus station on Calle de San Miguel for 90 *ptas* each way.

PRACTICAL INFORMATION

- **Main City Tourist Office**, *Turismo, Calle Puerta del Mar, 2, Tel. (95) 252-1531*
- **Bus Station**, *Calle de San Miguel, Tel. (95) 252-1504*
- **Taxi Stand**, *Plaza Ermita, Tel. (95) 252-0537*
- **Red Cross**, *Tel. (95) 252-2450*
- **Municipal Police**, *Tel. (95) 252-1545*

Major Local Festivals

Contact the local Turismo office, *Tel. (95) 252-1531,* for more details.

- **Bando Pancho**, *mid-May, Processions*
- **Fiesta Marítimo**, *16 July, Seafront Boat Parade, Fireworks*
- **Festivales de la Cuevas**, *August, Concerts, Theater in Nerja Caves*
- **Fiesta N.S. Angustias**, *early October, Processions*

MÁLAGA

Most tourists only see **Málaga** for a few minutes before being transferred to one of the famous nearby coastal resorts from this city's newly expanded international airport. While Málaga might not be the most dramatic of the southern cities, there are plenty of reasons to spend a day or so walking around this large seafront city. Within the space of a few hours you can visit most if not all of the best sights.

The city has a few poor and seedy districts, but if you stick to the central downtown zones, you will find plenty of charm and culture waiting around each and every corner.

ARRIVALS & DEPARTURES

By Air

Málaga's newly expanded Aeropuerto Pablo Picasso international airport is located about 5 km (3 miles) west of the center of town. There are dozens of scheduled flights daily to and from Madrid, and scores of other major cities in Europe, Africa, Asia and the Americas.

Among the many services offered in the airport are free luggage carts, wheelchairs for the physically challenged, 24-hour currency exchange desks, banks with ATM machines, a tourist (*Turismo*) office, luggage storage at 490 *ptas* per bag each day, restaurants and cafés, a beauty salon, boutiques featuring designer goods, a pharmacy, a newsstand and cigarette shop, soda machines, dozens of pay phones that accept coins and credit cards, a full service post office, a multilingual information desk, a hotel booking kiosk, duty free shops, car rental offices, tour operator and excursion desks, and VIP lounges for business and first class passengers.

For pick up or drop off of passengers at the airport, parking is available at 275 *ptas* per hour and 1,850 *ptas* per day. If you want to leave your rental car at the airport while you explore the coast for a few hours or days, ask your rental company's kiosk in the airport. Most major car rental companies will let you park in their officially assigned airport parking areas for free!

If you take a taxi from the airport to the center of town, expect to pay about 1,390 *ptas*. Buses and trains can also be found just outside the arrivals terminal bound for the city center, and both cost under 350 *ptas* each way.

By Bus

There are dozens of bus routes offering inexpensive daily service to Málaga from a huge variety of nearby cities, towns, and mountain resort areas. The city's main bus station is situated on Paseo de las Tilos, about a block and a half north of the train station on the city's western side, although there are other smaller terminals and regional bus stops elsewhere.

The #3 municiplal bus line stops near the station, and for about 100 *ptas* it will bring you into the city center. Expect a taxi to cost about 470 *ptas* to almost any hotel or sight in town.

By Car

From Madrid, the fastest way here is to follow the high speed N-IV Autovia de Andalucía south, connecting to the twisting route N-323 south at Bailén, and then turning west onto coastal route N-340 near Motril to complete this 548 km journey.

From Granada via the fast N-342 highway west and then transferring to the equally rapid N-321 expressway south from Antequera to finish this 139 km (87 mile) drive. From Sevilla, take the N-334 east until merging into the fast N-321 expressway south from Antequera to finish this 231 km (143 mile) trip.

Once inside the city you will find plenty of parking on the streets near the Paseo del Parque and other major sights. Even though these spaces are usually free of charge, local "attendants" will stronly suggest a 100 *ptas* "donation" to look after the car.

By Ferry & Sea

Since Málaga is situated along the sea, there is ferry service between the city's ferry landing and the Spanish city of Melilla on the northern tip of Africa. Contact Trasmediterranea, *Tel. (95) 222-4391,* for up-to-the-minute details and prices.

By Train

Málaga's main rail station is 2 km (1.4 miles) west of the city's historical center on the Explanada de la Estación, just off Avenida Héroes de Sostoa Cuarteles. There are multiple daily arrivals and departures between this city and dozens of other locations throughout the country via the extensive national rail system.

From the station, a taxi to just about anywhere in town is about 480 *ptas*, while the #3 bus can take you from here to the heart of town for about 100 *ptas*.

ORIENTATION

Málaga, population about 575,000, is the second largest city in the region of **Andalucía**. Located in the **Costa del Sol** area, just off the Mediterranean Sea, the ride here is 569 km (353 miles) south-southwest from Madrid.

GETTING AROUND TOWN

Within Málaga, most of the major tourist attractions and historical sights are well within wlking distance from each other. If necessary you can take advantage of a comprehensive municipal bus system that offers single-use tickets for about 100 *ptas* that are available from any bus driver. Maps and other infomation are available on bus stop signs or from the tourist information offices.

Taxis are also easily found at dozens of taxi stands, or roaming the streets. Just look for any cab that is exposing the *Libre* (unoccupied) sign in its front window and wave to the driver. Typical taxi rides rarely cost more than 480 *ptas* within city limits.

WHERE TO STAY

Expensive

PARADOR DE MALAGA-GIBRALFARO, *Barrio de Cstillo Gibralfaro. Tel. (95) 238-1255, Fax (95) 238-2141. US & Canada bookings (Marketing Ahead), Tel. 800/223-1356. Low season rack rates from 15,000 ptas per double room per night (E.P.), High season rack rates from 18,500 ptas per double room per night (E.P.). All major credit cards accepted.*

Rising up next to a fine castle just above a cliff overlooking the beaches of Malaga, this amazing parador is a superb place to stay. This classic and romantic hotel has a dramatic mixture of modern designer furnishings, classic Spanish fabrics, as well as plenty of exotic hardwoods and marbles.

Most of the parador's 60 deluxe rooms and giant suites feature marbled tiled private bathrooms stocked with soaps and shampoos, hard wood flooring, cast iron lighting fixtures, Andalucian carpets, mini-bar, electronic mini-safe, executive style desks, direct dial telephones, remote control cable television, hair dryers, extremely comfortable double bedding, an additional sofa bed and plenty of closet space. The rooms either have a fantastic oversized private balcony or a huge picture window overlooking incredible views over the city and the nearby saeside.

The property also offers a great Adalucian style gourmet restaurant with fine cuisine, free parking, complete elevator access, international currency exchange services, elaborate lounge and sitting areas with giant panoramic windrows, a small yet relaxing outdoor swimming pool and sun deck, lots of business meeting and reception rooms, a cafe, available baby-sitting, a tour desk that can help arrange all sorts of private excursions including boat rides to delightful nearby coastal areas and a friendly staff.

HOTEL MÁLAGA PALACIO, *Cortina del Muelle, 1. Tel. (95) 221-5181, Fax (95) 221-5185. Year round rack rates from 16,500 ptas per double room per night (E.P.). All major credit cards accepted.*

The Palacio is the city's most famous address for visiting executives, who are looking for excellant four-star accommodations in the heart of the business district. The modern bayview hotel offers 220 superior air conditioned rooms with private bathroom, satellite television, mini-bar, terraces, and in-room music systems.

The facilities here are equally serious and include business meeting rooms, rooftop swimming pool, boutiques, newsstand, restaurant, bar and a beauty salon. If you need a great hotel in the center of everything, this is a good choice.

HOTEL GUADALMAR, *Carretera de Cádiz-Km. 238.9. Tel. (95) 223-1703, Fax (95) 224-0385. Low season rack rates from 18,950 ptas per double* *room per night (E.P.). High season rack rates from 27,562 ptas per double room per night (E.P.). All major credit cards accepted.*

Although this great four-star resort hotel is about a ten minute drive from the heart of town, its beachfront location makes it well worth the extra drive. This eight story modern resort is set among gardens in a quiet residential zone. The hotel offers 185 beautiful rooms, each with air conditioning, private bathrooms, seaview patios, mini-safe, satellite televisions, wall-to-wall carpeting, direct dial telephones and extremely comfortable furnishings.

Facilities at the Guadalmar are impressive and consist of three swimming pools, tennis, health club, beachfront snack bar, two restaurants, billiards, game room, sun deck, disco, bar, live piano music, entertainment nightly, available baby-sitting, gardens, boutiques, drugstore, newsstand, room service, beauty salon, nearby golf, business meeting rooms and plenty more. This is a very good full service hotel.

Moderate

HOTEL LOS NARANJOS, *Paseode Sancha, 35. Tel. (95) 222-4316, Fax (95) 222-5975. Year round rack rates from 14,800 ptas per double room per night (E.P.). All major credit cards accepted.*

Situated just off the Paseo Marítimo beach area, this small and charming hotel is on a residential street about a five minute walk from most of the major attractions in Málaga. The typically Andalucían styled hotel has just 41 rooms with air conditioning, marble bathrooms, mini-bar, satellite television, mini-safe, direct dial telephones, beautiful furnishings and private terraces. With the added convienience of parking and a great front desk staff, this is a fabulous little place.

Inexpensive

HOTEL LIS, *Calle Córdoba, 7. Tel. (95) 222-7300, Fax (95) 222-7309. Low season rack rates from 5,400 ptas per double room per night (E.P.). High season rack rates from 6,300 ptas per double room per night (E.P.). All major credit cards accepted.*

When looking for a good budget hotel in this city, I suggest trying the Lis. Unlike other inexpensive hotels in the city center, this is a fairly nice and well maintained property. All of the 53 city view guestrooms and apartments have private bathrooms, telephones, and reasonably comfortable furnishings. As long as you don't expect luxury, this is about the best budget choice in town.

WHERE TO EAT

Other than wandering the city and exploring, your best bet is with the hotel restaurants listed above.

SEEING THE SIGHTS

Approximate duration (by foot) is about 4.5 hours, including castle, church, museum, and seafront visits.

The Paseo del Parque & Its Castles

After arriving in town, make your way to the promenade known as the **Paseo del Parque**, with its lovely trees and benches. On weekends, this tranquil little park is beseiged by thousands of locals who stroll its paths and socialize. After walking around the park, head directly north and cross the street onto the parallel Avenida del Cervantes.

It is on this smaller road that you can stop to have a quick glimpse at the unusual **Ayuntamiento** (City Hall) with its unusual facade and adjacent box gardens. While facing the front of the city hall, turn left and follow this avenue up to the next corner where you will make a sharp right turn to head down Cortina de Muelle. After about a block, you will be led straight into the front access area of the fantastic **Alcazaba** castle and palace.

This massive structure was built in the 8th through 11th centuries by local Moorish leaders to serve as their opulent palace, and further excavation has even unearthed a Roman era ampitheater near the palace walls. As you climb the winding path leading past the ramparts and into the palace area, you will pass some fine gardens that have great panoramic views over the city.

Once inside the main palace area, you will soon discover that it has been converted into the fantastic **Museo Arqueológico** museum. The museum features 12 rooms full of local and regional artifacts, including Phoenician statues, artifactss from the Roman ampitheater, Roman era statues, 11th century Moorish ceramics, geometrical mosaics from the palace's original flooring, 14th century Hispanic-Muslim glass jars, medieval pottery and many more ancient objects (signs are in Spanish only). The rooms are divided into seperate time periods indicating the Prehistoric, Roman, Moorish, and Medieval eras.

After visiting the museum, walk back down to street level, and if you have the energy, walk up the small road to the right of the front access area of the palace grounds and head up to the 14th century **Castillo Gibralfaro** castle looming high above the city. The castle has retained much of its original defensve walls and towers, and is a great place to spend a relaxing afternoon. The castle also houses a nice government owned *parador* with a good restaurant.

During the weekends, Spanish families come here to be together and rediscover their cultural roots, while several young romantic couples can be seen dissapearing to the more secluded spots on the grounds. *The Alcazaba and its museum are open Tuesday through Friday from 9:30am until*

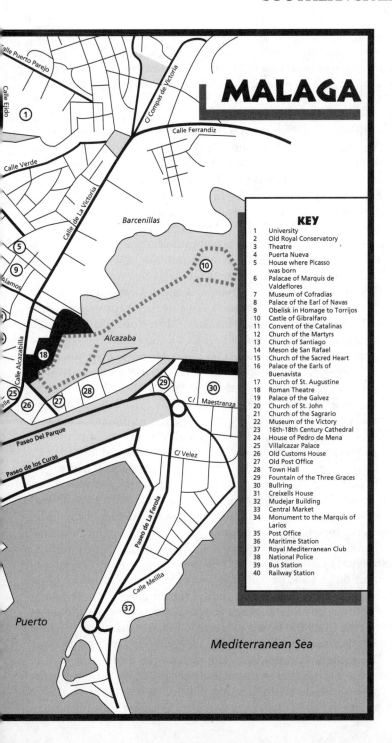

MALAGA

KEY

1 University
2 Old Royal Conservatory
3 Theatre
4 Puerta Nueva
5 House where Picasso was born
6 Palacae of Marquis de Valdeflores
7 Museum of Cofradias
8 Palace of the Earl of Navas
9 Obelisk in Homage to Torrijos
10 Castle of Gibralfaro
11 Convent of the Catalinas
12 Church of the Martyrs
13 Church of Santiago
14 Meson de San Rafael
15 Church of the Sacred Heart
16 Palace of the Earls of Buenavista
17 Church of St. Augustine
18 Roman Theatre
19 Palace of the Galvez
20 Church of St. John
21 Church of the Sagrario
22 Museum of the Victory
23 16th-18th Century Cathedral
24 House of Pedro de Mena
25 Villalcazar Palace
26 Old Customs House
27 Old Post Office
28 Town Hall
29 Fountain of the Three Graces
30 Bullring
31 Creixells House
32 Mudejar Building
33 Central Market
34 Monument to the Marquis of Larios
35 Post Office
36 Maritime Station
37 Royal Mediterranean Club
38 National Police
39 Bus Station
40 Railway Station

1:30pm and again from 4pm to 7pm in the winter or again from 5pm until 8pm in the summer, Saturdays from 10am until 1pm, Sundays and holidays from 10am until 2pm, and admission to both is only 20 ptas per person. The castle grounds are almost always open, and there is currently no entry fee to get in.

The Old Town

After finishing with the palace and perhaps the castle, turn right onto Calle de Alcazabilla and walk about a block before reaching the **Plaza de la Merced** just off to the left. This plaza was the birthplace of Pablo Picasso, and is still surrounded by small indoor and outdoor cafés and many of the oldest streets remaining in town. At the southwest corner of the park is the old Calle de Granada. Walk along this street and the first sight on your agenda should be the **Iglesia Santiago**, featuring a nice domed ceiling, delightful stained glass windows, unique confessional booths and an unusually bright and lively interior. *The church is open throughout the day for masses, and admission is free.*

After seeing the church, keep going up Calle de Granada for another block and a half until bearing left onto Calle de San Agustin. Just a few steps down this street, at #6, is the remarkable **Museo de Bellas Artes** fine arts museum. Inside the museum you will find a good collection of classic and contemporary paintings by **Murillo**, **Cano**, **Morales**, **Zubáran**, and a rare exhibit of some early **Picasso** works. There are also a few small rooms containing Roman and Moorish artistic artifacts.

The museum is open Tuesday through Friday from 10am until 1:30pm and again 3pm to 7pm, Saturdays, Sundays, and holidays from 10am until 1:30pm, and admission is 250 ptas. Also in the general vicinity are a couple of unusual tea houses (*teterías*) serving superb exotic teas and desserts.

About a block after the church there is a tiny side street off to the right called Calle de Echegaray where the most sophisticated bars for the over-25 set are located. Among the most curious of these is the **Café Teatro Toulouse Lautrec** at #9, that boasts a scaled-down version of the Eiffel Tower piercing through its two floors.

The Santa Iglesia Cathedral

Continue down Calle de San Agustin until it intersects with Calle de Santa María. Here, you can't help but be drawn into Diego de Siloe's elaborate 16th century **Santa Iglesia Catedral**. One of my favorite sights in this town, the cathedral boasts elegantly sculpted Corinthian columns that support dozens of intricate domes, extending from a breathtaking ceiling. The cathedral's awesome vaulted Baroque interior should be visited to view its fine altar, painstakingly carved cedar and mohagany choirstalls and sculptures, golden grandfather clocks, massive antique bible, paintings by Cano, Ortiz, and Guevara, a massive tube pipe organ from the 18th century, and a small museum containing religious items of gold and silver among other things.

The church and its museum are open from 10am until 1pm and again from 4pm to 6pm Tuesday through Saturday, and Sundays the church is open for several masses. Admission to both is only 200 ptas.

The Seafront

Facing the front of the church, turn left onto Calle de Santa María, then left past the clocktower following Calle Molino Lairo down the hill, where you will once again meet up with the **Paseo del Parque**. Stroll northeast along the paseo until it ends at the **Plaza Hospital Noble**, with its large fountain and major traffic circle. Walk counter-clockwise around this circle, taking the second exit to the right that leads to the seaview **Paseo de la Farola**.

From here you can walk around the little peninsula to see the lighthouse, and people-watch your way back up the **Paseo Marítimo,** lined with cafes and restaurants. It runs the lenghth of the city's famous **Playa La Malagueta** beach. During both winter and summer weekends this area is full with some of the city's most sociable people. After a cool drink on the promenade, turn left at Avenida Cánovas del Castillo, and you will shortly see the traffic circle again. Follow the circle counter-clockwise to the third right exit leading back to the Passeo del Parque.

NIGHTLIFE & ENTERTAINMENT

The prime downtown areas for bars, pubs, and discos is centered on the side streets leading off the **Plaza de la Merced**, such as Calle de Granada. Try the **Bodega Bar El Pimpi** at #62, where you can sit with wine barrels in full view and enjoy great local wines and beer – but don't arrive until after 11pm when the teenagers leave.

Nearby, at #9 Calle Echegaray, the more worldly over 30 crowd can be found at the unique two floor **Café Teatro Toulouse Lautrec** where drinks cost a bit more, but the upper floor really jumps on weekend nights after 1am. For those with more down to earth tastes, try the casual little **Café Bar La Moncola** at #1, where the mixture of local and foreign nightcrawlers stop in for good rock music and cheap drinks after 10pm.

The other major hotspot for evening activities is around the sea front. Here in the vicinity of the lighthouse, dozens of cafés and discos line the **Paseo Marítimo**. Try **Bar Malacca**, **Pub el Navegante**, and the **Bar Bora-Bora**. After about 1am, the heart of the town's nightlfe beats in the many huge discos in the **La Malagueta** and **Pedregalejo** sea front districts on the eastern edge of the city, where hefty admission charges and drink prices are the norm. The most famous of these clubs are **La Chancla**, **Krystal**, **Zona Málaga**, and **Indigo**.

PRACTICAL INFORMATION

- **Main City Tourist Office**, *Turismo, Pasaje de Chinitas, Tel (95) 229-421*
- **Regional Tourist Office**, *Turismo, Marqués de Larios, 5, Tel. (95) 221-3445*
- **Málaga International Airport**, *Tel. (95) 224-0000*
- **Iberia Airlines Offices**, *Calle de Molina Lario, 13, Tel. (95) 227-600*
- **Regional Bus Station**, *Paseo de las Tilos, Tel. (95) 235-0061*
- **Regional Train Info**, *Renfe, Calle de Strachan, 2, Tel. (95) 221-3122*
- **Roadside Emergencies**, *Guarda Civil, Tel. (95) 239-1900*
- **Carlos Hata Hospital**, *Camino de Antiquera, Tel. (95) 239-0400*
- **Municipal Police**, *Tel. 092*

Major Local Festivals
    Contact the local Turismo office, *Tel. (95) 213-445*, for more details.
- **Tres Magi**, *January, Processions*
- **Semana Santa**, *April, Strange Processions*
- **Summer Fair**, *late August, Feasts, Parades, Culture*
- **Fiesta Santos Inocentes**, *28 December, Spanish April Fool's Day*

TORREMOLINOS

Of all the moderately priced and heavily populated seaside resorts along the sundrenched Costa del Sol, **Torremolinos** is perhaps the most interesting and enjoyable. In addition to a wildly popular wide sandy beach called **Playa del Banjondillo**, the city boasts a bustling commercial district surrounding the **Plaza de Costa del Sol** that provides excellent shopping and dining possibilities, especially on the pedestrian only Calle de San Miguel.

Although the town's beach front has been crammed full of mostly uninspiring hotels and giant apartment complexes along the main **Paseo Marítimo**, a five minute walk west reveals some of the old world charm of **La Carihuela**, a former fishermen's village. Considering that this place has so many wonderful hidden sights, a fine beach, dozens of nearby attractions, one of the region's widest range of dining and nightlife possibilities, and a full range of accommodations in all price ranges, Torremolinos makes a perfect place to spend some time in the sun.

ARRIVALS & DEPARTURES

By Bus
There is a circular bus route run by Portillo offering inexpensive daily service to Torremolinos from several Costa del Sol resort areas and nearby cities, including Málaga, Marbella, Córdoba, Granada, Jerez de la

Frontera, and Ronda. The city's main bus station is situated on the Calle de Hoya just off Plaza Costa del Sol in the center of town. Expect a taxi to cost about 360 *ptas* to almost any hotel or sight in the area.

By Car

The best way to drive to Torremolinos is to take the major N-340 Autovia de Mediterraneo highway west for 14 km (9 miles) from Málaga. There are hundreds of free parking spaces along the beachfront and side streets of town, but in the high season finding an open space will be difficult after 8am.

By Train

Daily scheduled train service connects Torremolinos with other points along the Costa del Sol between Málaga and Fuengirola. Expect to pay about 540 *ptas* for each local rail ride. The station is located in the middle of town near La Nogelera. If you don't want to walk, taxis should cost no more than 430 *ptas* to the beach or any hotel in town.

ORIENTATION

Torremolinos, population 25,000, is located on the seaside **Costa del Sol** section of the **Andalucía** region. The trip here is about 572 km (355 miles) south-southwest from Madrid, and is only about 13 km (8 miles) southwest from Málaga.

WHERE TO STAY

Expensive

MELIA COSTA DEL SOL, *Paseo Marítimo. Tel. (95) 238-6677, Fax (95) 238-6417. US & Canada Bookings: (UTELL), Tel. 800/44UTELL. Low season rack rates from 10,300 ptas per double room per night (E.P.). High season rack rates from 15,500 ptas per double room per night (E.P.). All major credit cards accepted.*

Besides having a great staff of multilingual professionals, the hotel has a great assortment of unique services. All 540 of the spacious and comfortable guestrooms (and suites) have fantastic seaviews. Each room is exceedingly well maintained, nicely decorated, and has large private terraces, air conditioning, huge bathrooms with hair dryers, cable television, am-fm radios, direct dial phones, and electronic safes. A special executive floor contains rooms with all these amenities plus small refrigerators, fluffy bathrobes, an electric trouser press and a private check in area for V.I.P. clients.

Among the many services offered on premises is a full health and beauty spa offering the latest European treatments, free indoor parking, room service, laundry and dry cleaning, a large swimming pool, several business meeting rooms, a hair salon and a game room for kids. Its full service concierge desk offers valuable assistance and reservation services for local excursions, restaurants, and transportation. There is live entertainment at least once a week, featuring *Flamenco* artists or a fine pianist. These shows areoffered free of charge to all guests. The hotel has just completed even more renovations in its lobby and public rooms, making the place even more impressive than before.

HOTEL CERVANTES, *Calle de Las Mercedes. Tel. (95) 238-4033, Fax (95) 238-4857. Low season rack rates from 10,400 ptas per double room per night (E.P.). High season rack rates from 13,500 ptas per double room per night (E.P.). All major credit cards accepted.*

Situated in the middle of town near the bus and train stations, this nine floor modern hotel offers nice accommodations just a five minute walk from the beach. This four-star hotel has 400 rooms (mostly with seaviews), each with air conditioning, private bathrooms, in-room music systems, mini-safes, direct dial telephones, satellite television, terraces and comfortable furnishings. The facilities here include an outdoor heated swimming pool, an indoor pool, two restaurants, bar, billiards, solarium, gardens, boutiques, gift shop, snack bar, baby-sitting services, health club with optional massages, game room, beauty salon and several business meeting rooms.

Moderate

HOTEL BELPLAYA, *Paseo Marítimo. Tel. (95) 238-3266, Fax (95) 238-3194. Low season rack rates from 7,500 ptas per double room per night (E.P.). High season rack rates from 12,000 ptas per double room per night (E.P.). All major credit cards accepted.*

A favorite among English and German tour operators, this beach front three-star hotel is actually made up of two separate wings that rise to four and nine floors respectively. Here you can choose between 244 single and double rooms (almost all with beach view balconies) that all have air conditioning, private bathrooms, telephones, mini-safe, and comfortable furnishings. Hotel facilities include a snack bar, outdoor swimming pool, restaurant and tour desk. It's a nice place for this price range.

Inexpensive

APARTMENTOS BOCA CHICA, *Primero Linea de Playa, Torremolinos. Tel. (95) 238-7855, Fax (95) 237-3660. Low season rack rates from 3,800 ptas per dbl studio apartment per night (E.P.). High season ack rates from 7,000 ptas per dbl studio apartment per night (E.P.). All major credit cards accepted.*

These are basic but comfortable small studio and one bedroom terraced sea view apartments. The six story building is at the very edge of

Playa del Bajondillo and each unit has a small kitchenette, linoleum flooring, comfortable bedding, and formica furnishings that retain the cool air during the summer. The more spacious (and more expensive) apartments offer balconies with nice sea views and a lot more space. While services here are limited, it's a good budget choice for independent travelers looking for nice but still affordable accommodations on the beach.

WHERE TO EAT

Expensive

EL ROQUERO, *Calle de Carmen, La Carihuela, Torremolinos. Tel. (95) 238-4946. Most major credit cards accepted.*

This is the most famous restaurant in this fishing hamlet, and its pretty interior may be the perfect place for an upscale yet informal dinner, either indoor or on an *al fresco* patio. Their extensive menu features such house specialties as seafood soup, gazpacho, mixed salads, baby cockles, sauteed clams, fillet of sole, fresh swordfish and lobster. A good three course dinner here will cost around 2,575 *ptas* per person plus wine.

Moderate

LA LAGOSTA, *Calle Bulto, La Carihuela, Torremolinos. Tel. (95) 238-4381. Visa and Mastercard accepted.*

With its spacious inner dining areas and huge, multilingual, photo enhanced menus, this good restaurant attracts lots of tourists and locals alike. The best items served here include chilled gazpacho, anchovies in vinegar, baked potato with shrimp salad, smoked salmon, lasagne, half chicken with fries, prawns in whiskey, paella, Entrecote with pepper, and roast beef. Expect a three course dinner to cost around 2,650 *ptas* per person plus drinks.

EL LEBECHE, *Calle de Carmen, La Carihuela, Torremolinos, Tel. (95) 238-2533. Most major credit cards accepted.*

Another good choice in the La Carihuela zone is this moderately priced steak and seafood restaurant with the best service in town. Their menu offers classic dishes like vegetable soup, seafood stew, mixed salads, shrimp omelettes, chicken, and an assortment of pork and steak dishes starting at 850 *ptas*.

Inexpensive

LA CIGALA III, *Paseo Marítimo de La Carihuela, Torremolinos. Tel. (95) 238-0478. Visa and Mastercard Accepted.*

If you're looking for a great inexpensive restaurant to enjoy a down-to-earth meal at a reasonable cost, this informal little establishment wins my vote. The interior is standard, with paintings of rural scenes, but the menu is what gets my attention. Try a complete meal with gazpacho, salad, potatoes, and your choice for only 775 *ptas* They offer tender pork cutlets, filet of fish, chicken and daily specials. Also of note are the shrimp with garlic for 300 *ptas*, grilled sardines at 300 *ptas*, pimiento salad for 300 *ptas*, excellent gazpacho for 350 *ptas*.

SEEING THE SIGHTS

Approximate duration (by foot) is about 6.5 hours, including town, fishing village, and beach visits.

The most logical place to start your tour of town is at the **Playa Del Bajondillo** beach which, along with its adjacent (and less congested) **Playa de Playamar**, have made this resort so popular. This wide and sandy beach has cool waters and a constant breeze that attracts up to 24,000 sunbathers from all over the world each day during the height of summer.

Separating the beach from a long string of resort hotels, unimaginative condo buildings, family fun centers, miniature golf courses, tourist trap gift shops, moderately priced restaurants and nightclubs, is the **Paseo Marítimo**. Here you can enjoy a swim, or just sit at on a terrace at any of the many restaurants and cafés on the beach and people watch all day. After walking around the beach, continue to the southwest end of the beach.

After passing the building marked Apartmentos Roca Chica, follow the sea front stone walkway around the breakers and you're in the **La Carihuela** section. It's hard to believe that this wonderful relaxed hideaway is only a few minutes walk from the heart of Torremolinos, and I'm glad to report that it still hasn't become trendy or expensive. Originally an ancient fishing village, most of the town's old fishing cottages and merchant's houses have been tastefully converted into inexpensive seafood restaurants, pubs, and handicraft shops.

Unlike many tacky reproductions of old villages recreated to attract tourists into expensive boutiques, this authentic old hamlet still has a life and history of its own. Handcrafted wooden fishing boats continue to line the area's small and somewhat peaceful beach, and in fact there are even a few fishermen who continue to live here. Fortunately there are no structures over three stories high to distract your attentions from the whitewashed houses, some flecked with blue and other colors, where pet canaries sing from their windowbox cages.

If you are visiting or staying in Torremolinos, the restaurants along La Carihuela's beachfront offer four course meals with freshly caught fish for less than 800 *ptas*. Make sure to pop into the humble **Perroquia de la Carihuela Nuestra Senhora del Carmen** church on Calle de Carmen, which has a great chandelier made from old boat anchors. Also in the area, mostly around **Plaza del Remo**, is a *Turismo* office, a public telephone calling center that even takes credit cards, and a selection of foreign currency exchange kiosks that post exceptional rates with no deducted commission.

After wandering around the 14 or so streets of the old fishing area, you should make your way towards the heart of town. By far, the most convenient way of reaching the city center is to walk back to the nearest edge of Torremolinos' **Playa del Bajondilla**. From here take the elevator from around the corner of the Melia Costa del Sol Hotel that for about 75 *ptas,* will take you to the central **La Nogalera** shopping area. You can also walk up Calle de Carmen Morales and bear right onto the noisy Avenida Carlota Alessandri, and then left onto the more pleasant Avenida de Palma de Mallorca to reach the same general area.

Either way, the best place to start this part of your tour is at the **Plaza Costa del Sol**. Besides the eyesore of a newly added McDonald's restaurant, this elongated plaza is surrounded by dozens of shops and newsstands. On the southwestern corner of the plaza is Calle San Miguel, the town's most impressive shopping street. While wandering along this wide pedestrian-only road, there are countless small shops selling regional filigree jewelry, finely crafted leather goods, discounted perfumes, and of course, tasteless souvenirs. Cafés, aromatic bakeries, and pricey restaurants packed with Dutch, German, and English tourists also line the plazas that this street bisects.

If you take a right turn at the first intersection, the **La Nogalera** shopping area will come into sight. Turn right at the second intersection and the famous Calle Casablanca confronts you with a vast assortment of pubs and clubs for evening entertainment. From the end of Calle San Miguel follow the signs leading down the hill back to the Calle Cuesta del Tajo, with its many stairways, and you'll end up back at the beach.

NIGHTLIFE & ENTERTAINMENT

Around the **Playa del Bajondillo** and its less busy neighbor, the **Playa de Playamar**, there are scores of pubs, bars, live music clubs, and flashy discos. On the **Primero Linea de Playa** or on the beach itself, you might want to try the **Los Gallegos Bar**, **Caprice Discoteca**, **Bar Las Bahamas**, **Disco Ali Baba**, and **Bar Playa de Naranjita**.

Around **La Carihuela**, keep an eye out for **Winston's** and **The Wonky Donkey**. In the heart of town, the bars with no cover charge off Calle Casablanca like **Iguana**, **Bodega El Colmao**, **El Tren**, especially the more locals-oriented **Catastophe Pub**. This will fill to capacity by 11pm on summer nights, and by 12:30am on low season weekends. The best discos are **Pipers Macrodisco** in the Plaza Costa del Sol, the **Palladium** on Avenida de Palma de Mallorca, and **Discoteca Gatsby** off Avenida

Montemar. These discos may charge up to 3,000 *ptas* to get in, and drinks can be expensive as well.

Look around for complimentary or reduced rate invitations at your hotel's front desk. The nightlife scene here is aggressive and fast paced, with many people looking for the same thing. If you don't have any luck, the exclusive **Club Selecta** on Calle Decano Juan de Hoyos can provide a selection of European hostesses who will accompany men in opulent suits for about 21,000 *ptas* per hour.

PRACTICAL INFORMATION

- **Main City Tourist Office**, *Turismo, Calle Casablanca, 27, Tel. (95) 237-1159*
- **Regional Tourist Office**, *O.T.J.A., Guetaria-La Nogalera, Tel. (95) 238-1578*
- **Bus Station**, *Portillo, Calle de Hoya, Tel. (95) 238-0964*
- **Municipal Police**, *Tel. (95) 238-1422*

Major Local Festivals

Contact the local Turismo office, *Tel. (95) 237-1125,* for more details.
- **Carnaval**, *February, Processions, All Night Parties*
- **Fiesta N.S. Carmen**, *mid-July, Processions*
- **Festivales San Miguel**, *September, Parades and Outdoor Fair*

BENALMÁDENA COSTA

As you move southwest along the Costa del Sol from Torremolinos, the overdevelopment of the seaside towns becomes even more apparent. Among the larger, and perhaps less attractive of these massive tourist developments lies along the beach front at **Benalmádena Costa** (also known simply as Benalmádena). The only purpose of this community is to serve as a giant magnet for long stay couples and families on a low to medium budget. These tourists hail from England, Holland, and Germany during the busy summer season, and a few thousand retired Canadian sun birds come during the slow and less enchanting winter.

ARRIVALS & DEPARTURES

By Bus

Portillo schedules daily bus service to Benalmádena from several Costa del Sol resort areas and nearby cities such as Málaga, Marbella, Córdoba, Granada, Jerez de la Frontera, and Ronda. The city's main bus station is situated in the center of town. Expect a taxi to cost about 510 *ptas* to almost any hotel or sight in the area.

By Car

The best way to drive to Benalmádena Costa is to take the major N-340 Autovia de Mediterraneo highway west for 15 km (9 miles) from Málaga. There are some free parking spaces along the Puerto Deportivo and some side streets of town, but finding one will be difficult on weekends and in the summer. Additional private and municipal lots offer beach area and marina section parking spaces at about 150 *ptas* per hour.

By Ferry & Sea

Since Benalmádena Costa is located on the sea, there is ferry service between the city's ferry landing and Tangiers on the northern tip of Africa. Contact Yasmin-Line, *Tel. (95) 244-5576,* for current information.

By Train

There is no good train service to this area. Your best bet is to take a Renfe train to Málaga and then a connecting regional bus.

ORIENTATION

Benalmádena Costa is located in the Costa del Sol section of **Andalucía**, about a 585 kilometer (363 mile) ride south-southwest from Madrid, 3 kilometers (2 miles) southwest from Torremolinos, or only about 16 kilometers (10 miles) southwest from Málaga.

WHERE TO STAY

Expensive

HOTEL TORREQUEBRADA, *Carretera de Cádiz-Km.220. Tel. (95) 244-6000, Fax (95) 244-5702. US & Canada bookings: (UTELL) 800/ 44UTELL. Low season rack rates from 19,500 ptas per double room per night (E.P.). High season rack rates from 25,725 ptas per double room per night (E.P.). All major credit cards accepted.*

This gigantic resort complex sits above the beach in a new commercial and residential zone at the edge of town. This impressive five-star hotel and resort offers 350 modern Mediterranean style rooms and suites which are all air conditioned and contain private bathrooms, beach view patios, satellite television, mini-safe, am-fm clock radio, electronic key pass locks, mini-bar, comfortable furnishings, and direct dial telephone. The complex offers plenty of sporting facilities including tennis, health club, squash, sauna, jacuzzi, massage, two large swimming pools, a sun deck full of lounge chairs, and a nearby private 18 hole golf club. The hotel also features several restaurants and bars that cover the price spectrum, great front desk staff, room service, lots of parking, newsstands, boutiques, beauty salon, tour desk, rental cars, babysitting, business meeting rooms and the area's only real casino.

Although favored by higher priced package tour companies and huge corporate groups, this hotel is still a good selection for individuals that want all the facilities of a five star hotel with a sea front location.

HOTEL TRITON, *Avenida António Machado,29. Tel. (95) 244-3240, Fax (95) 244-2649. US & Canada Bookings: (UTELL), Tel. 800/44UTELL. Low season rack rates from 18,500 ptas per double room per night (E.P.). High season rack rates from 20,500 ptas per double room per night (E.P.). All major credit cards accepted.*

The Triton is a pleasant modern hotel housed in two adjoining five-story buildings just off the town's main beach. This 4 star property offers 190 air conditioned rooms and suites that have been beautifully designed and feature huge private bathrooms, satellite televisions, mini-safe, seaview balconies, direct dial telephones, and nice furnishings. As with other resort hotels in this upper price range, facilities are abundant and consist of several swimming pools, two tennis courts, surprisingly good restaurants, bars with live entertainment, plenty of trees and well-manicured grounds, garage, health club, available babysitting, mini-market, boutiques, excursion desk, rental cars, business meeting rooms and nearby golf club access. An excellent choice for this area, and be sure to ask about special package rates when reserving.

Moderate

SUNSET BEACH CLUB, *Carretera de Cádiz-Km.220. Tel. (95) 244-5840, Fax (95) 244-2918. Low season rack rates from 16,500 ptas per dbl apartment per night (E.P.). High season rack rates from 19,500 ptas per dbl apartment per night (E.P.). Most major credit cards accepted.*

Although there are several *aparthotels* in this town, the Sunset Club is about my favorite. It's just a one minute walk to the beach and a good selection if you intend to do some of your own cooking. There are 400 air conditioned one bedroom apartments with fully equipped kitchens, private bathrooms, spacious bedrooms, satellite television, direct dial telephone, comfortable interiors, nice but simple furnishings, and private patios. There are numerous hotel-style facilities here such as three swimming pools, laundry room, health club, mini-market, boutiques, beauty salons, supervised children's activities and lots of parking.

Inexpensive

HOTEL BALI, *Avenida de Telfonica, 7. Tel. (95) 244-1940, Fax (95) 244-5915. Low season rack rates from 5,500 ptas per double room per night (E.P.). High season rack rates from 8,500 ptas per double room per night (E.P.). Most major credit cards accepted.*

This large, pyramid shaped two-star hotel complex is just a three minute walk to the town's beach. Here you can choose from 374 simple but nice double rooms, each with private bathrooms, direct dial telephones, mini-safe, and patios. There are also a fair amount of facilities for a hotel of this price, including indoor and outdoor swimming pools, squash, a restaurant, snack bar, lounge, boutiques, game room, TV room, parking, beauty salon, and evening activities during the high season. This is a good budget choice.

HOTEL BALMORAL, *Carretera de Cádiz-Km. 227. Tel. (95) 244-3641, Fax (95) 244-3642. Low season rack rates from 5,500 ptas per double room per night (E.P.). High season rack rates from 7,200 ptas per double room per night (E.P.). Most major credit cards accepted.*

This two-star hotel is a seven minute walk to the beach, and offers 210 basic rooms with private bathroom and patio. There is also a restaurant, bar, mini-golf course, game room, billiards, tour desk, rental cars, two outdoor pools, tennis, parking, and nearby activities such as an amusement park, golf and horseback riding. It's far from deluxe, but still worth considering, especially when air conditioning is not needed.

WHERE TO EAT
Moderate

EL BAHIA DEL PUERTO, *Puerto Deportivo. Tel. (95) 244-6460. Visa and Mastercard accepted.*

You can sit indoors or on an open-air patio overlooking the harbor and enjoy huge portions of great steak and seafood dishes in a casual setting. The best items include delicately seasoned gazpacho, mixed salads, crispy fried calamari, grilled swordfish, pork chops, perfectly cooked sirloin steaks and fantastic seafood paella.. Expect a three course dinner to cost around 2,800 *ptas* per person plus drinks.

PINOCCHIO PIZZERIA, *Puerto Marina, Puerto Deportivo. Tel. (95) 244-0892. All major credit cards accepted.*

The outdoor patio of this good Italian restaurant is packed with a combination of well-dressed locals, and casually attired northern European tourists trying to catch a few rays during lunchtime. The extensive menu features typical courses like minestrone soup, simple salads, shrimp cocktails, spaghetti with marinara sauce, fettucini carbonara, a vast selection of pizzas, veal scallopini, entrecote with Gorganzola cheese and mushrooms, and beef carpacchio. A good three course lunch or dinner will cost around 2,750 *ptas* per person plus drinks.

SEEING THE SIGHTS

One of the major points interest here include the family fun amusement park known as **Tivoli World**. Located on the main approach road to town, the park contains bumper cars, small roller coasters, an large amphitheater with daily live shows, a house of horrors, and dozens of other forms of entertainment. *During the high season, the park charges 650 ptas per person, no charge for kids under 5, and is open daily from 6pm until at least 1am. When the low season kicks in, hours are from 1pm until 11pm on weekends and holidays only, admission is just 200 ptas for adults, free for children under 5. The price of each ride ranges from 200 ptas to 550 ptas each, but you can also buy a ride-inclusive pass for between 1,100 ptas and 1,400 ptas.*

Although seemingly deserted until mid March, the town's sandy beach front is about the only other major sight or attraction worth mentioning here. The beaches such as **Playa de Carvajal** and **Playa La Perla** have long stretches of dark tinted sand, and a wide avenue separating a seemingly endless chain of glitzy bars, souvenir shops, and giant aparthotel and timeshare apartment buildings. The more interesting **Puerto Deportivo** recreational marina and yacht club and recreational zone is only about 1.5 kilometers (1 mile) northeast of here. A unique complex of balconied buildings with ancient Arab-Hispanic architectural elements, surround the yacht club, and contain the city's finest condo's, restaurants, outdoor terrace cafés, and nightclubs.

A couple of small plazas like the **Puerto Marina** spoke out from the sea front where you'll find more outdoor cafés and restaurants. Although not it may not be everyone's cup of tea, a small miniature train called the Moncho Tren Turistico can take up to 80 tourists at a time on a spin through the marina with departures all day for about 300 *ptas* per person. Another major attraction is the mid-sized **Casino** complex and nearby golf center that are both at the edge of town in the Torrequebrada hotel and resort.

NIGHTLIFE & ENTERTAINMENT

The heaviest action in town can be found around the 'Puerto Deportivo district. To enjoy the scene, start off after 10pm, and wind your way to places like the purple **Swan Club**, the open air **O'Clock bar**, the tropical **Cacatua Club**, the large **Modina Discoteca** and the more sophisticated **El Desyn** lounge. The dozen or so other clubs and discos located below ground level in the center of the port area range from the tacky **Hard Rock Café** to several 70's style discos for the under 20 year old set. Most of the clubs here are for young locals and UK or Scandinavian tourists who like loud music.

The place to hang out after 11pm is in the packed **Plaza Sol y Mar** square just alongside the town's main drag. Besides a few fast food restaurants, this plaza is home to several busy discos and bars such as the **KIU** disco, the **Dutch Inn** pub, the **Pub Genesis** and **Jules** disco. Cover charges range from zero to 1,500 *ptas* per person and the average age is often 17. The town's beachfront has a few other good spots to party including **Bananas Disco**. If you want to try your luck at gambling, the

Casino just outside of town at the Torrequebrada Hotel offers typical gaming rooms with a 600 *ptas* entrance fee (open 8pm until 5am). Their **La Fortuna** dinner theater has a three hour show featuring Flamenco and topless dancers. It costs 7,900 *ptas* per person including three courses and house wine. Please remember that a passport, and nice clothes are both mandatory for admission to the casino complex.

PRACTICAL INFORMATION
· **Main City Tourist Office**, *Turismo, Carretera de Cádiz-Km. 222, Tel. (95) 244-2494*
· **Municipal Police**, *Tel. 092*

Major Local Festivals
· **Fiesta Virgin de la Cruz**, *mid-August, Outdoor Festivals*

FUENGIROLA
Packed in the summer with hundreds of thousands of Europeans of all ages, **Fuengirola** is yet another unattractive coastal resort. Don't be fooled by the occasional Rolls-Royce driving by; this is a low to medium budget destination, and its hundreds of giant cement apartment buildings and hotels have been built one right next to the other with absolutely no regard for aesthetics.

Fortunately, the area does offer a few interesting sights and attractions that can help kill some time between trips to the beach. These include the nearby inland village of **Mijas**, well worth a half day excursion to view its traditional whitewashed houses, churches, and markets. There are also many golf courses within a 15 minute ride from town.

ARRIVALS & DEPARTURES
By Bus
Portillo has daily scheduled service to Fuengirola from several Costa del Sol resort areas and nearby cities such as Torremolinos, Málaga, Marbella, and Benalmádena. The city's main bus station is situated almost directly across from the train station. Expect a taxi to cost about 380 *ptas* to just about any point within town.

By Car
The fastest drive to Fuengirola is to take the major N-340 Autovia de Mediterraneo highway west for 28 km (27 miles) from Málaga. There is a fair amount of free parking spaces along the waterfront, but it might be necessary to circle the area a few times to catch an open spot.

By Train

Daily scheduled train service connects Fuengirola with other points along the Costa del Sol all the way east to Málaga. Expect to pay about 580 *ptas* for each local rail ride. The train station is located only 250 meters (250 yards) from the marina, and taxis should cost no more than 380 *ptas* to any local hotel or beach area you may wish to visit.

ORIENTATION

Fuengirola, population 46,506, can be found along the southern coast of Spain in the center of the **Costa del Sol** zone of **Andalucía**, and is about a 597 km (371 mile) ride south-southwest from Madrid, a 12 km (7.5 mile) ride southwest from Benalmádena-Costa, and about a 28 km (17 mile) trip southwest from Málaga.

WHERE TO STAY

Expensive

HOTEL BYBLOS ANDALUZ, *Urbanization Mijas-Golf, Mijas. Tel. (95) 247-3050, Fax (95) 247-6783. US & Canada Bookings: (Leading Hotels), Tel. 800/223-6800. Year round rack rates from 44,000 ptas per double room per night (E.P.). All major credit cards accepted.*

Located about a ten minute drive from Fuengirola, this super deluxe and expensive five star hotel is well known for both its fine accommodations and plentiful sporting activities. This traditional Andalucían style low-rise complex features 144 beautiful rooms and suites each with air conditioning, marble bathrooms, mini-safe, direct dial telephone, remote control satellite television with video, mini-safe and designer furnishings throughout.

The hard working staff here will be happy to direct the guests to the many facilities here, including two 18 hole golf courses, three swimming pools, a famous spa offering special treatments, health club, five tennis courts, 24-hour room service, optional child care, and garage. The cuisine here is exceptional and is offered in an assortment of venues, from opulent restaurants to a special low calorie dining room. This is the place for deluxe travelers to relax, unwind, and get in a few rounds of serious golf.

Moderate

HOTEL PYR FUENGIROLA, *Lamo de Espinosa, 6. Tel. (95) 247-1700, Fax (95) 247-3604. Low season rack rates from 10,000 ptas per double studio apartment per night (E.P.). High season rack rates from 16,000 ptas per double studio apartment per night (E.P.). All major credit cards accepted.*

This is a great *aparthotel* is located just in front of the town's marina and beach area. The Pyr has 400 studio and one bedroom apartments each with air conditioning, modern private bathroom, cityview or seaview terraces, satellite televisions, and nice furnishings. There is also a mid-priced restaurant serving three meals a day, snack bar, outdoor swimming pool, boutiques, excursion desk, beauty salon, lots of parking, and top floor deluxe apartments that have their own private plunge pools. A great choice for those looking for rather comfortable apartments with good views.

HOTEL LAS PALMERAS, *Paseo Marítimo. Tel. (95) 247-2700, Fax (95) 247-2908. Low season rack rates from 9,500 ptas per double room per night (E.P.). High season rack rates from 16,000 ptas per double room per night (E.P.). All major credit cards accepted.*

The massive fourstar Las Palmeras is situated on Fuengirola's marina, within walking distance to all the major attractions in town. There are just under 400 rooms, suites, and apartments that all offer air conditioning, private bathroom, and terraces. Facilities consist of three swimming pools, a bowling alley and supervised children's activities. The hotel can help to arrange excursions, horseback riding, golf reservations, rental cars and daily membership at local health clubs.

Inexpensive

HOTEL STELLA MARIS, *Paseo Marítimo. Tel. (95) 247-5450, Fax (95) 247-5759. Low season rack rates from 7,000 ptas per double room per night (E.P.). High season rack rates from 10,300 ptas per double room per night (E.P.). All major credit cards accepted.*

A towering modern three star hotel on the beach. The hotel has 196 rooms and suites with private bathrooms, direct dial telephones, mini-refrigerators, direct dial telephones, and seaview balconies. Facilities consist of outdoor swimming pool, a nice beach area, game room, available baby-sitting, safe deposit boxes, a TV room and plenty of nearby sports.

SEEING THE SIGHTS

Alongside this long beach is one of the town's most interesting attractions, the huge **Paseo Marítimo** seaside walkway. In addition to the many cafés and pizza shops right on the beach, the paseo also is a great place to watch the last remaining fishermen return in their brightly colored boats from a long night at sea.

From the walkway, you can also visit an interesting recreational area called the **Puerto de Fuengirola** that has been built to resemble a castle. The attractions at the port include a small children's amusement park called **Parkilandia**, *open daily and charging about 350 ptas per ride.*

The inner courtyard and harborside sections of the port contain several restaurants and pubs in all price ranges that are loaded with tourists and sometimes offer live music on their terraces. On Sundays from 10am until 4pm the area also hosts a typical outdoor market, selling dried nuts, garments, and handicrafts. A few boat cruise excursions and tourist train rides are also available from this general location.

If you are looking to do a bit of shopping, follow the boutique lined **Calle de Jacinto Benavente** up from the Puerto and northward into the heart of the city. There is also a small but pleasant municipal **zoo** located on the nearby Camino de Santiago road, *open from 9am until 1pm and again from 3pm until at least 7pm daily with a 350 ptas admission charge.*

NIGHTLIFE & ENTERTAINMENT

Along the **beachfront**, you can check out **Harpoon Louie's Bar**, **Discoteca TNT Dinamita**, and **Bonnie & Clyde's Bar**. Around the **Puerto de Fuengirola**, the busiest places to hang out are **Ku Damm Berlin**, **Harry's Bar**, and **La Ola**.

PRACTICAL INFORMATION

- **Main City Tourist Office**, *Turismo, Avenida Jesus S. Rein, Tel. (95) 246-7457*
- **Regional Bus Info**, *Portillo, Tel. (95) 247-5066*
- **Municipal Police**, *Tel. 092*

Major Local Festivals

Contact the local Turismo office, *Tel. (95) 246-1891,* for more details.
- **Fiesta Marítimo**, *16 July, Beachside Fair and Flamenco*
- **Fiesta Rosario**, *mid-October, Outdoor Fair and Flamenco*
- **El Jabegote**, *12 October, Processions*

MARBELLA

This bustling resort area was originally settled by Moorish, and then Roman civilizations, due to its prime seaside location at the base of the **Sierra Blanca** and **Sierra de Ojén** mountain ranges. With the arrival of aristocratic Europeans and Arabs, who built vast mansions and deluxe hotel projects along the beach back in the late 1950's, **Marbella** has become one of the world's top vacation destinations.

While thousands of hard working Spaniards live and work within the city limits, it is the obvious presence of these foreign millionaires that has shaped this city's current reputation as a playground for the rich and famous. Besides the dozens of sandy crescent-shaped Mediterranean beaches along the Paseo Marítimo and Avenida Duque de Ahumada, there are several hidden attractions well within walking distance from the city center. Many of the most impressive sights are in the old quarter that surrounds the highly charming Plaza de los Naranjos.

The city also offers a fantastic array of night life, shopping, and dining possibilities.

ARRIVALS & DEPARTURES

By Bus

There is a circular bus route run by Portillo offering inexpensive daily service to Marbella from several Costa del Sol resort areas and nearby cities. The city's main bus station is located on Avenida Ricardo Soríano, 21, that is on the main drag in the commercial center of town. From here you can walk to most attractions, or take a taxi for about 430 *ptas* to almost any hotel or sight in the city.

By Car

The best way to drive to Marbella is to follow the high speed N-340 Autovia de Mediterraneo highway west for 56 km (35 miles) from Málaga. There are hundreds of metered parking spaces and public lots along the streets of town, some of that are fairly close to the beachfront. Don't even think about parking illegally in Marbella or you are almost assured to get either a serious ticket or perhaps even towed to an impound garage!

By Train

There is no good train service to this area. Your best bet is to take a Renfe train to Málaga and reach this city via connecting regional bus service.

ORIENTATION

Marbella, population 85,000, is on the **Mediterranean Sea** in the western Costa del Sol zone of the **Andalucía** region. By road, the city is about 601 km (373 miles) south-southwest from Madrid, and only about 56 km (35 miles) southwest from Málaga.

WHERE TO STAY

Expensive

HOTEL PUENTE ROMANO, *Carretera de Cadiz - Km. 177. Tel. (95) 282-0900, Fax (95) 277-5766. US & Canada bookings: (Leading Hotels), Tel. 800/223-6800. Low season rack rates from 24,200 ptas per double room per night (E.P.). High season rack rates from 42,900 ptas per double room per night (E.P.). All major credit cards accepted.*

The Hotel Puente Romano is simply the best and most luxurious resort hotel along the entire Costa de Sol. Originally built back in 1976, this super deluxe five-star hotel is comprised of 26 low rise Andalucian style lodges set amidst 10 acres of lush semi-tropical gardens. Tranquil, refined, and relaxing, this superb vacation paradise is situated just off a fine sandy beach halfway between the posh towns of Marbella and Puerto Banus.

The accommodations offered at the Hotel Puente Romano include 229 extremely spacious rooms and lavish suites that all have private terraces and feature dual basin marble bathrooms stocked with French hair and skin care products, remote control satellite televisions with movie channels, powerful air conditioning systems, electronic mini-safe, fully stocked mini-bar, hair dryer, direct dial telephones, plush cotton bathrobes, brightly colored furnishings with designer fabrics and wonderful beds.

Guests here are free to relax all day at one of three fantastic outdoor swimming pools (two are heated), or take advantage of a seemingly endless array of services and facilities including an award winning tennis club with ten professionally surfaced courts and a great team of pros, a state of the art health and fitness center, massage and aromatherapy, a beach front water sports area, two saunas, a children's game room, child care, a range of excursions, horseback riding, temporary membership privileges at over 20 nearby championship golf clubs, a high-season supervised kids club, 24-hour room service and lots of lounges and sitting rooms to relax in.

The property also features three dining areas including the casual El Puente restaurant for buffet breakfast as well as al la carte afternoon and evening meals, the La Plaza French restaurant, and the Beach Club dining terrace which serves an amazing buffet lunch and in the evenings is transformed into Roberto's gourmet Italian restaurant. Guests year-round can enjoy cocktails at the La Cascada piano bar, while in the summer months an opulent nightclub known as Regine's opens its doors for dancing. This is truly a one of a kind resort that receives my highest rating of any seaside hotel in Spain. Selected as one of my Best Places to Stay (see Chapter 13).

MARBELLA CLUB HOTEL, *Boulevard Principe Alfonso von Hohenlohe. Tel. (95) 282-2211, Fax (95) 282-9884. US & Canada bookings: (Leading Hotels), Tel. 800/223-6800. Low season rack rates from 26,000 ptas per double room per night (E.P.). High season rack rates from 51,500 ptas per double room per night (E.P.). All major credit cards accepted.*

The Marbella Club is one of the finest hotels in all of Spain. This delightful five-star property is right on the sea, located halfway between downtown Marbella and Puerto Banús. It proves that paradise really does exist along the Costa del Sol. Originally built in the 1950's as a private beach front estate for the family of owner Prince Alfonso Von Hohenlohe, this fine resort maintains an exclusive, yet welcoming ambiance. Every aspect of the accommodations, cuisine, facilities, amenities, and service has been designed to assure the highest standards of comfort for each and every guest.

The Marbella Club has 119 beautifully designed rooms and suites which are situated in smallAndalucían-style buildings covered in bougainvillea. They either face onto peaceful subtropical gardens or, preferably, onto the great beach. All of these sun drenched accommodations have air conditioning, huge private bathrooms, remote control satellite television, private patios, mini-bar, mini-safe, direct dial telephone, European skin and hair care products and the finest furnishings that money can buy. The super deluxe suites are even more luxurious, and may have Jacuzzis and spectacular ocean view terraces. For guests who require additional space and privacy, there are ten two and three bedroom villas that contain all of the above elements as well as a private pool.

The countless world class facilities at the resort include a brand new private beach club, tranquil sun decks surrounded by lounge chairs, water sports equipment rentals, two massive swimming pools, sauna and fitness area, peaceful gardens, outdoor pool side bars, business meeting rooms, available baby-sitting services, optional massage, and nearby tennis, golf, and horseback riding clubs. For special events, the front desk staff can arrange fantastic private sightseeing trips via deluxe limousines to such destinations as Ronda, Gibraltar, Granada, and Tangiers. Also available from the hotel are unique instructional tennis and golf programs with world famous champions and professionals. Dining here is an absolutely amazing experience, with the some of the finest cuisine in Spain served in majestic style either indoors in the opulent Winter Garden restaurant, outdoors upon the more casual terraces of the main dining room and beach club, or in your room via 24-hour room service. There is even a wonderful bar where you can enjoy cool relaxing cocktails or a glass of fine champagne. All of the internationally trained staff are polite, and some will even remember your name after the first day you are there.

The ambiance here is refined and club-like. Some of the more reserved movie stars and visiting heads of state who frequent this hotel tend to dress formally, while the ever growing percentage of younger couples and families arriving here dress fairly casually. Whether you're looking for the perfect deluxe romantic hideaway, a great business conference location, the ideal base from which to enjoy sporting activities, or just a fine resort to unwind from everyday life in the fast lane, this is definitely a good place to consider. Make sure to ask about the specially priced golf, tennis, and weekend packages. Selected as one of my Best Places to Stay (see Chapter 13).

CORAL BEACH HOTEL, *Carretera de Cádiz-Km. 177. Tel. (95) 282-4500, Fax (95) 282-6257. US & Canada bookings: (I.L.C.), Tel. 800/ SPAIN44. Low season rack rates from 26,000 ptas per double room per night (E.P.). High season rack rates from 33,000 ptas per double room per night (E.P.). All major credit cards accepted.*

The four-star Coral Beach Hotel is Marbella's most relaxed an unpretentious deluxe seaside hotel. Located just a couple of kilometers down the beach from both Puerto Banús and central Marbella, It has a modern Mediterranean design with terraced wings which form a "U" shape that faces directly onto a fantastic swimming pool and nice beach. As a great choice for sun and sand lovers of all ages (children are welcome here!), the Coral Beach Hotel has become a favored hotel for casual couples, singles, and families from places like Stockholm, Oslo, Munich, and London.

The property boasts 170 large and beautifully furnished rooms and suites that all have powerful air conditioning, dual basin marble bathrooms, fully stocked mini-bar, mini-safe, regional original artwork and handmade tapestries, satellite television, direct dial telephone, electronic mini-safe, tropical rattan furnishings, superb bedding, sofa beds in some cases, executive style desks and great terraces with either pool or sea views. The entire interior of the complex is embellished by lavish semi-tropical gardens and man made ponds that are covered by a glass domed sunroof and are inhabited by turtles and Japanese cod fish.

Facilities available to the guests include a beach club, two swimming pools, Jacuzzis, sauna, a nice little health and fitness center, plenty of free parking, a kids game room, tour desk, rental car kiosk, beauty salon, babysitting, a newsstand, business meeting rooms, and a few really good al la carte and half board restaurants (make sure to have a dinner at their great Florencia restaurant). Clients can also make arrangements for nearby golf, tennis, and casino outings, as well as excursions run by local tour operators.

The staff here is comprised mostly of young and friendly employees who provide personalized service with a smile and great suggestions for local night life and nearby dining establishments. Of all the large resorts on this part of the coast, this is where I prefer to stay, and I think that if you are coming to Spain without a Rolls Royce, Ferrari, or a 30 meter yacht, you will love it too. The hotel does however close each year during a few months in the winter.

MELIA DON PEPE, *Carretera de Cádiz-Km. 189. Tel. (95) 277-0300, Fax (95) 277-9954. US & Canada bookings: (UTELL), Tel. 800/44 UTELL. Low season rack rates from 28,000 ptas per double room per night (E.P.). High season rack rates from 45,700 ptas per double room per night (E.P.). All major credit cards accepted.*

Located just outside of town on a nice sandy beach area, this huge five-star modern hotel is a favorite among large groups arriving from all over Europe on package tours. The Don Pepe has some 204 air conditioned double rooms that all have private bathrooms, satellite television, mini-bar, mini-safe, and direct dial telephones. Many of the higher priced rooms also offer sea view terraces. The hotel's facilities include a good beach area with water sports, indoor and outdoor swimming pools, two tennis courts, game room, sauna, tour desk, rental car desk, gift shop, beauty salon, piano bar, business meeting rooms, nearby golf, and two restaurants. Service here is not all that good, so don't expect much in the way of personalized attention.

Moderate
HOTEL EL FUERTE, *Avenida El Fuerte. Tel. (95) 286-1500, Fax (95) 282-4411. Low season rack rates from 12,900 ptas per double room per night (E.P.). High season rack rates from 15,900 ptas per double room per night (E.P.). All major credit cards accepted.*

The towering facade of the Hotel El Fuerte is situated right off the Avenida Puerta del Mar, just steps away from downtown Marbella's beach front. This bargain priced yet somewhat posh hotel contains 263 air conditioned rooms and suites which have private bathroom, mini-safe, satellite television, in-room music system, balconies, comfortable furnishings, and either city or beach views depending on price and availability. The clientele here range from vacationing Northern Europeans during the summer, to somewhat older guests who stay for longer time periods during the low seasons. There is a good amount of services and facilities for this price range including a huge health club with aerobics programs, indoor and outdoor swimming pools, sauna, massage rooms, Turkish baths, beauty salon, tennis, squash, parking, meeting rooms, two medium priced restaurants, bars, and a pleasant beach area. This is good choice in this price category, and you don't need a car to sightsee in town.

PYR MARBELLA, *Avenida Principal, Puerto Banús. Tel. (95) 281-7353, Fax (95) 281-7907. Low season rack rates from 8,500 ptas per dbl studio apartment per night (E.P.). High season rack rates from 15,000 ptas per dbl studio apartment per night (E.P.). All major credit cards accepted.*

Located about a six minute walk from the beaches and harbor front, the Pyr is housed in three medium sized tower buildings at the edge of Puerto Banús about seven kilometers (4 miles) from downtown Marbella. Popular with German, Dutch, and Scandinavian package tours, this aparthotel offers 319 air conditioned studio and one bedroom units which all have marble flooring, private bathroom, satellite television, am-fm radio, mini-safe, balcony, direct dial telephone and fully equipped kitchen areas. The hotel also offers an excursion desk, squash, tennis, outdoor swimming pool, boutiques, garage, free outdoor parking, meeting rooms, restaurants, a bar, and plenty of nearby golf. With the recent addition of a Swiss Hotel School on the premises, this hotel provides good service and accommodations for those who prefer to do some of their own cooking.

PRINCESA PLAYA, *Avenida Duque de Ahumada. Tel. (95) 282-0944, Fax (95) 282-1190. Low season rack rates from 10,000 ptas per dbl studio apartment per night (E.P.). High season rack rates from 13,500 ptas per dbl studio apartment per night (E.P.). All major credit cards accepted.*

With its beach front location in the heart of downtown Marbella, the three-star Princesa Playa is among the busiest mid priced aparthotels in town. Here you can choose between some 100 basic but comfortably sized studio and one bedroom apartments that offer either city or sea views depending on price. All units have air conditioning, satellite television, terraces, mini-safe, and nice interiors. There is also a swimming pool, sun deck, restaurants, bars, shopping center, parking, meeting rooms and plenty of lounge chairs for rent on the beach.

Inexpensive

HOTEL LIMA, *Avenida António Belon, 2. Tel. (95) 277-0500, Fax (95) 286-3091. Low season rack rates from 6,325 ptas per double room per night (E.P.). High season rack rates from 8,200 ptas per double room per night (E.P.). Most major credit cards accepted.*

Located on a shady tree lined street just one block from the beach in downtown Marbella, the Lima is a nice low priced, two star hotel. It offers 64 clean and well maintained rooms with elevator access, nice yet simple private bathrooms, dark hardwood furnishings, direct dial telephones, color televisions, heating, and partial seaview balconies in many cases. Although facilities are limited to a restaurant, bar, TV room, and parking the hotel is still a good selection for this location and price.

HOSTAL ENRIQUETA, *Calle Los Caballeros, 18. Tel. (95) 277-0500, Fax (95) 286-3091. Low season rack rates from 4,000 ptas per double room per night (E.P.). High season rack rates from 5,000 ptas per double room per night (E.P.). No credit cards accepted.*

If you are looking for less expensive but still decent accommodations in downtown Marbella, this small whitewashed pension just off the Plaza de los Naranjos may fit the bill. This little place contains 23 single and double rooms which have either shared or private bathrooms, balconies, direct dial telephones, and heating. There is also a small restaurant, TV room and parking. Not at all luxurious, but good value in this city.

WHERE TO EAT

Expensive

ROBERTO'S (HOTEL PUENTE ROMANO), *Carretera de Cadiz kilometer 177. Tel. (95) 282-0900. All major credit cards accepted.*

The are plenty of great places to enjoy a romantic gourmet dinner in Marbella, but Roberto's is easily at the top of my list. This dinner-only venue serves some of the most incredibly delicious, regional Italian specialties outside of Italy. Each evening a gifted local pianist plays soft jazz and classical music to the well dressed patrons who are seated at a couple of dozen cozy candlelit tables beneath an impressive exposed wood beamed ceiling. The moment you arrive at the front door you will be greeted by the restaurant's ever-present maitre d' (Angelo Cardona) who will make you feel right at home here.

Among the superb items typically found on Roberto's extensive and rather innovative menu are tartar of fresh salmon, eggplant with fresh mozzarella cheese and basil, melon surrounded by parma ham, a rich minestrone soup, black pasta with capers and clams, amazing capelli and lobster served inside a lobster shell, braised sea bass with calamari mousse, gilthead sautéed in virgin olive oil, veal cutlets spiced with fresh rosemary stalks, chicken breast filet with homemade pate, osso buco and a full range of sumptuous desserts and specialty coffees. Expect dinner for two to cost around 7,500 *ptas* plus wine, and reserve a table at least one day in advance.

THE GRILL AND WINTER GARDEN RESTAURANTS (MARBELLA CLUB HOTEL), *Boulevard Principe Alfonso von Hohenlohe. Tel. (95) 282-2211.All major credit cards accepted.*

Award winning executive chef Enrique Martell Lopez, originally of Sevilla, continues to create impressive lunch and dinner menus at these two fine gourmet restaurants. Whether you decide on a romantic little corner table in the opulent Grill restaurant, or to settle in for a more casual meal at the Beach Club or Winter Garden restaurants' terraces, get ready for a real culinary treat!

Their huge menus of mouth-watering dishes change each season, but on my last visit there was pheasant consommé with truffle, gazpacho, lobster mousse, terrine of foie gras, oysters with fresh lemon, Beluga caviar with fresh cream bilinis, green fettucini with salmon cream sauce, spinach mousse with oysters, filet mignon in cucumber sauce, partridge *Toledo* style, paella, chateaubriand with bernaise sauce, lamb filet with ratatouille, their famous fish basted in rock salt, langostinos with mustard sauce and a dessert trolley that will make your eyes pop out of your head. Special buffet lunches, price fixed luncheons (for about 3,800 *ptas* with three courses) and beach barbecue dinners are offered seasonally, and contain many of the above items as well as beautifully prepared salad bars and daily roasted or grilled specialties. If you're diet conscience, just advise the wait staff in advance, and they will be glad to prepare salt free, low fat, low calorie, or even vegetarian meals just for you. A threecourse dinner will cost around 6,250 *ptas* per person plus wine.

Moderate

LA PESQUERA, *Plaza de la Victoria. Tel. (95) 277-8054. Most major credit cards accepted.*

Ramon Mesa's new restaurant (one of three he owns in Marbella), located just a block from the *Plaza de los Naranjos* in the heart of the *Marbella's* old quarter, is a great place to enjoy some of the freshest seafood along the Costa del Sol. By about 9pm, all of the 50 or so indoor and outdoor tables are completely full with local residents from all walks of life. Their three page menu feautures dozens of fantasic items such as smaked salmon, Melon with smoked ham, *Motril* prawn cocktail, mixed salads, lobster salad, fish soup, grilled local red mullet, seafood croquettes, shrimp with garlic, marinated mussels, seafood paella for two, grilled swordfish, baked hake, chicken with garlic, grilled entrecote, and over two dozen varieties of fresh local seafood served in every imaginable way starting at just 3,000 *ptas* per kilogram. They also have a nice assortment of fresh fruits and homemade desserts, as well as a great wine list featuring bottles of red and white vintages from around Spain that start at only 800 *ptas* per bottle and up. This is a great casual place to enjoy a fine meal and lots of typical old world ambiance. A great three course dinner here will cost around 2,850 *ptas* per person plus drinks.

OH BONITO, *Avenida Antónío Belon, 4. No telephone. Visa and Mastercards accepted.*

Located only a couple of streets away from the beach in downtown *Marbella*, this delightful little Chinese restaurant is clean and comfortable, and the prices are inexpensive. The friendly staff here can help you to select the day's finest items including spring rolls, fried won tons, prawn brochettes, delicious shark fin soup, hot and sour soup, shrimp fried rice, vegetable chop suey, shrimp in hot sauce with peanuts, filet of sole with lemon, roasted spare ribs, stuffed mushrooms, chicken with almonds, beef in curry sauce, Peking duck, and plenty of lunch and dinner specials starting at just 775 *ptas* a person including dessert and coffee. A great choice! Expect a three course dinner to cost around 2,150 *ptas* per person plus drinks.

DA PAOLO, *Muelle de Ribera, Puerto Banús. Tel. (95) 281-2797. All major credit cards accepted.*

This casual little Italian restaurant on the harbor of *Puerto Banús* offers some of the coast's best moderately priced International menus. While sitting in the covered terrace or in the humble interior dining room, you can watch the Rolls Royces unload passengers into the yachts while enjoying refreshingly good meals. Some of my favorite items on their five page menu include fresh vegetable soup, French onion soup, smoked salmon, endive and avocado salad, mushroom omelettes, steak sandwiches with french fries, chicken kebobs, grilled entrecote, fettuccine with four cheeses. Not fancy or gourmet, but still good for this area. Expect a three course lunch or dinner to cost around 2,250 *ptas* per person plus drinks.

Inexpensive
   PIZZERIA PICASSO, *Muelle de Ribera, Puerto Banús. Tel. (95) 281-3669. All major credit cards accepted.*
   As far as inexpensive restaurants in the Marbella are go, this is certainly one of the best. Located on the posh harbor-front at Puerto Banús, this relaxed Italian restaurant has a large dining room complete with open air sitting areas, faux Roman columns, marble table tops, and plenty of places to glimpse at the attractive people walking along the harbor. Their huge three page menu is loaded with Italian influenced items that are well prepared and include over 18 types of pizzas that average 900 *ptas* each, salad Nicoise for 650 *ptas*, fettucini Alfredo at 700 *ptas*, 1/2 rack of ribs for 800 *ptas*, roasted chicken at 925 *ptas*, calzones for 875 *ptas*, and peach melba at 625 *ptas*.

SEEING THE SIGHTS
   Approximate duration (by foot) is about 5.5 hours, including town, museum, and beach visits.

   My favorite place to begin a visit to this city is over at the water-spouting fountain in the center of the **Parque de la Alameda** just off the Avenida Ricardo Soríano. This centrally located park is typically filled with the town's older residents who spend much of their time feeding the birds and having long conversations with their friends here. After a good rest in the shade, walk up the avenue until reaching the far edge of the park. At this point you will turn right onto the Avenida Puerta del Mar, where unusual modern fountains and metal sculptures line the path towards the seafront.
   All of the beaches that line this area along the Avenida Duque de Ahumada oceanside promenade (often referred to as the **Paseo Marítimo**) are packed by mid-June, and offer beach chairs and sun umbrellas for rent by the hour. The small outdoor beach cafés and restaurants provide a great location for people watching.
   When you've finished enjoying a cool drink, bear right along the promenade for a few blocks until you reach the small **Puerto Deportivo**

boat basin. Besides being home to many small yachts, the port area also contains many bars and disco/pubs that get packed by midnight each weekend evening. From the port area, turn left to head west along the sea front for a few blocks. Make a right onto Calle Faro and then bear left onto the Avenida de España.

On your right hand side is the lovely **Parque de la Constitución**, where you can find beautiful trees and dramatic *azulejos* (ceramic) covered benches to sit upon. The lovely auditorium pavilion in the center of the park is the host of several seasonal concerts and ballet performances sponsored by the city. From the park, return to Avenida de España and continue to follow it in the same direction until it ends at a curve, where you will bear right onto Avenida de Arías Maldonaldo. At the end of this street, make a right turn onto Avenida Ricardo Soríano where you will wander past many department stores and small shopping plazas.

Follow this wide and noisy avenue for about 12 blocks until turning left onto Calle de Huerta Chica. This will bring you into the **Casco Antigua de Marbella**, the old quarter of the city. All of the lanes found in this area seem to be packed with antique whitewashed houses, many of which are covered by bougainvilleas. If you take the first right you will soon find yourself cutting through the tiny Plaza de Victoria to end up on the boutique-lined Calle de Estación. Another block or so up this street you are led past the orange trees that have become synonymous with the fantastica **Plaza de los Naranjos**.

Originally the center of town during previous centuries, this wonderful public square still contains many monumental structures that have been beautifully preserved. Among the most remarkable are the whitewashed 16th century **Ayuntamiento** (City Hall), with its sun-dial and wrought iron patios and the smaller **Casa del Corregidor** mansion that dates back to the 17th century. The center of the plaza is transformed each afternoon and evening into an outdoor café and restaurant zone Locals and tourists alike spend hours here eating and drinking beneath the stars. Most of the tiny streets that radiate from the plaza are stunningly lit at sunset, and are brimming with clothing stores and small traditional bars.

On a small street called the Calle del Hospital de Bazan, not far from this plaza, is the beautiful 16th century palace of former nobleman, benefactor, and mayor of Marbella, Don Alonso de Bazan. He donated this structure and adjacent hospital to the people of this city. Inside his enchanting mansion is the home of the **Museo del Grabador Español Contemporáneo**. This great museum features etchings and other artwork from such masters as **Dalí**, **Miró**, and **Picasso**. *The museum is open Sunday and Monday from 11am until 2pm, and Tuesday through Friday from 11am until 2pm and again from 5:30pm until 8pm. Admission is 400 ptas per person.*

Spend at least an hour wandering around this incredible ancient area; keep your eyes open for Roman walls and Moorish fortress vestiges that are found alongside the old whitewashed houses in this quarter. Also nearby is the 16th century **Iglesia de la Encarnación** church that is worth a quick glimpse inside.

The tranquil **Parque Arroyo de la Represa** park, while not really close enough to the town center for many visitors to walk to, can be reached by taxi for about 370 *ptas* from the center of town. Inside the park you can visit one of Europe's largest collections of Japanese Bonsai plants at the **Museo de Bonsai**. *The museum is open from Tuesday through Sunday from 10am until 6pm and costs 400 ptas to enter.* Also in town is the world-famous **Manuel Santana Tennis Club** that features championship events and expert instruction.

NIGHTLIFE & ENTERTAINMENT

Just to the left Parque de la Consititucion are a few side streets such as **Calle Pablo Casals** that are full of tiny bars and pubs where most of the night crawlers tend to show up by about 1am. Among the best places to head for are the **Saxo** dance club or the **Havana Bar** on Calle Ortega y Gasset, and the **Atrium** bar on Calle Gregorio Maranon. Those looking for a disco where the rich and famous hang out (and pay a stiff cover charge plus over 1,200 *ptas* per beer!) should head for either the art deco **La Notte** club on the mountain road just across the way from the Hotel Puente Romano, or **Regine's** disco at the Hotel Puente Romano itself. You can also check along the **Puerto Deportivo** and beachfront **Avenida Duque de Ahumada** areas for some other possibilities.

For me, the most fun are the more traditional bars and pubs in the old quarter around the **Plaza de los Naranjos** plaza which get packed just after 9pm. Stay far away from those handful of posh looking "VIP" clubs with names such as "Milady" which are actually huge brothels.

SPORTS & RECREATION

For Málaga & Costa Del Sol
Amusement Parks
• **Tivoli World**, *Benalmádena Costa, Tel. (95) 244-2848*
• **Parkilandia**, *Fuengirola, Telephone Unlisted*
• **Parque Acuático**, *N-340, Mijas, Tel. (95) 246-0604*
• **Atlantis Parque Acuático**, *Torremolinos, Tel. (95) 238-8888*

Bicycle Rentals & Excursions
Check with your hotel or local Turismo office for details.

Bowling
- **Palmeras Bowling**, *Fuengirola, Tel. (95) 246-0641*
- **Martin Crooke**, *Málaga, Tel. (95) 222-5778*
- **Servio Veinte**, *Marbella, Tel. (95) 281-7200*
- **Montemar**, *Torremolinos, Tel. (95) 238-7459*

Bullfights
- **Plaza de Toros Malagueta**, *Málaga, Tel. (95) 221-9482*
- **Plaza de Toros**, *Benalmádena, Telephone Unlisted*
- **Plaza de Toros**, *Fuengirola, Telephone Unlisted*
- **Plaza de Toros**, *Puerto Banús (Marbella), Tel. (95) 281-0389*
- **Plaza de Toros**, *Marbella, Tel. (95) 277-3593*
- **Plaza de Toros**, *Mijas (Fuengirola), Tel. (95) 248-5248*

Boat Rentals
Check with your hotel or local Turismo office for details.

Casinos
- **Torrequebrada**, *Benalmádena, Tel. (95) 244-2545*
- **Nueva Andalucía**, *Marbella, Tel. (95) 281-4000*

Golf
- **Torrequebrada Golf**, *N-340, Benalmádena Costa, Tel. (95) 244-2742. 18 holes, par 72*
- **Mijas Club**, *Mijas, (Fuengiola), Tel. (95) 247-6843. 18 holes x 2, par 72*
- **Club de Campo**, *Málaga, Tel. (95) 238-1255. 18 holes, par 72*
- **Las Brisas**, *Nueva Andalucía (Marbella), Tel. (95) 281-0875. 18 holes, par 72*
- **Golf Aloha**, *Nueva Andalucía (Marbella), Tel. (95) 281-3750. 18 holes + 9 holes, par 72*
- **La Quinta**, *Nueva Andalucía (Marbella), Tel. (95) 276-2141. 18 holes + 9 holes, par 71*
- **Guadalmina Golf**, *San Pedro (Marbella), Tel. (95) 288-3375. 18 holes x 2, par 72*
- **Rio Real Golf**, *Marbella, Tel. (95) 277-3776. 18 holes, par 72*
- **Los Naranjos**, *Nueva Andalucía (Marbella), Tel. (95) 281-5206. 18 holes, par 72*
- **Club de Golf Nerja**, *Nerja, Tel. (95) 252-0208. 9 holes, par 54*

Gyms & Health Clubs
Check with your hotel or local Turismo office for details.

Horseback Riding
• **Hiturga Travel**, *Torremolinos, Tel. (95) 287-4195*

Outdoor Markets
   Check with the local Turismo office for detailed locations and dates.
• **Benalmádena**, *Friday*
• **Fuengirola**, *Sunday and Tuesday*
• **Málaga**, *Sunday*
• **Marbella**, *Monday*
• **Torremolinos**, *Thursday*

Parachuting & Hang Gliding
• **Club Vuelo Libre**, *Villa de Abdalajis (Málaga), Tel. (95) 248-9171*
• **Marbella Parapente**, *Marbella, Tel. (95) 278-4043*

Scuba Diving
• **Centro Buceo**, *Benalmádena, Tel. (95) 256-2365*

Tennis
• **Torrequebrada Tenis**, *Benalmádena, Tel. (95) 244-1007*
• **Club Doña Sofia**, *Fuengirola, Tel. (95) 247-5084*
• **Aquarius Tenis**, *Mijas (Fuengirola), Tel. (95) 283-3940*
• **Club Sol Tenis**, *Mijas (Fuengirola), Tel. (95) 283-0830*
• **Club de Tenis**, *Málaga, Tel. (95) 229-1092*
• **Real Club**, *Málaga, Tel. (95) 229-1092*
• **Club Manolo Santana**, *Marbella, Tel. (95)277-0100*
• **Don Carlos Tenis**, *Marbella, Tel. (95) 283-1739*
• **Club de Tenis**, *Torremolinos, Tel. (95) 243-5125*
• **Don Pablo Tenis**, *Torremolinos, Tel. (95) 238-3888*

Zoos & Aquariums
• **Zoo Municipal**, *Camino de Santiago, Fuengirola, Tel. (95) 247-1590*

EXCURSIONS & DAY TRIPS
PUERTO BANÚS
   About 7 kilometers (4 miles) further along the coast (west of Marbella) you will come to a tiny, famous subdivision known as **Puerto Banús**. This super luxurious village is named for the giant **Puerto Deportivo José Banús** pleasure- craft port and commercial shopping zone that attracts some of the wealthiest people in the world to its tiny lanes. A small two block long village surrounds a sheltered harbor for 915 yachts which is lined by a private street called the **Muelle de Ribera**. The parking spots

along the Muelle can be accessed only by those residents who own condos or yachts in the harbor, so the cars along here are generally Rolls Royces, Porches, Mercedes, and Ferraris owned by the Arab and European millionaires who live here. Fortunately, the street is open to pedestrians, and thousands of visitors roll in each weekend to window shop in the over 100 glamorous designer boutiques, and eat meals in the many harbor-front restaurants. A newly opened **Centro Comercial de Costa del Marbella** at the back end of town has also joined the fray and offers several more high end shops, department stores, and fast food restaurants.

There are two wonderful beaches that border the village. One almost desolate beach is in front of the impressive Gray D'Albion condo complex on the west edge of the harbor, while another windy beach with sun chair rentals and a beach bar lies across from the eastern edge of the harbor. During the night, provocatively dressed young German and Scandinavian women can be found chasing rich older men into the many bars and discos around the **Plaza de la Comida** and along the harbor-side clubs. A five minute ride further west along the **N-340** will lead past the **Nueva Andalucía** subdivision that features a **Casino** and over five championship golf courses.

Directions

If you head down the N-340 (known locally as the Carretera de Cádiz) highway west from Marbella for about 7 kilometers (4 miles), you will find signs leading to Puerto Banús. Parking is not allowed along the village streets, so you can either enter the public lot on the Camino de Ribera about two blocks behind the port and pay 150 *ptas* per hour, or park along the Muelle de Levante on the east edge of the village and tip the unofficial but still uniformed attendants about 125 *ptas*.

Daily bus service is available over 18 times daily in both directions via the Marbella bus station on Ave. Ricardo Soriano for 90 *ptas* each way. Taxis are also available to take you here for about 1,200 *ptas* each way from the heart of Marbella.

Nightlife

Check out the bars and clubs in the **Plaza de la Comedia** and along the small side streets adjacent to the harbor itself. One of the more popular bars along the harbor is **Sinatra**. Be careful around town, as a new crop of topless dancing clubs and champagne bars are loaded with innocent looking ladies of the night that are disguised as lonely tourists.

PRACTICAL INFORMATION

• **Main City Tourist Office,** *Turismo, Calle Miguel Cano, 1, Tel. (95) 277-1442*

- **Train Station**, *Renfe, Tel. (95) 236-0202*
- **Bus Station**, *Ave. Ricardo Soríano, 21, Tel. (95) 235-0061*
- **Traffic Police**, *Calle San António, 29, Tel. (95) 277-2549*
- **Municipal Towing Garage**, *Tel. (95) 277-3692*
- **Hospital Europa**, *Ave. Severo Ochoa, 22, Tel. (95) 277-4200*
- **Municipal Police**, *Tel. 092*

Major Local Festivals

Contact the local Turismo office, *Tel. (95) 277-1442,* for more details.
- **Semana Santa**, *April, Strange Processions*
- **Fiesta San Bernabe**, *June 11, Processions*

RONDA

The historic and picturesque city of **Ronda**, population 33,567, lies 147 kilometers (91 miles) southeast of Sevilla, making it a good long day trip possibility from either Marbella or Sevilla. As perhaps Spain's largest Pueblo Blanco (a traditional mountain top village of whitewashed houses), it attracts thousands of visitors from around the world each day. Known to Spaniards as the birthplace of modern bullfighting, this is where the famed Romero family founded the first school for matadors and created many of the rules and customs that are still observed throughout Spain today.

The city is divided into two sections by a large chasm known as the **El Tajo** that plunges over 100 meters (330 feet) and can be crossed via a wonderful 18th century **Puente Nuevo** arched bridge. This was the spot made famous in Ernest Hemingway's masterpiece "For Whom the Bell Tolls" in which he describes how countless prisoners captured during the Spanish Civil War were executed by being thrown into the ravine from here. On either side of the gorge, who's cliffs are lined with traditional houses resting close to the edge, are two distinctly different sections of the city. The 15th through 20th century **El Mercadillo** quarter rests on the near side, while the more enchanting 8th century Moorish **La Ciudad** section can be reached by crossing the bridge.

ARRIVALS & DEPARTURES

To get here by car, take the high speed N-340 coastal route until reaching Marbella's San Pedro de Alcantara suberb where you will then take the twisting route C-339 northwest for about 49 kilometers (31 miles) until reaching the town and follow signs towards the "Centro."

The most direct bus route here is via Marbella and onwards through several connection possibilities at major resort towns along the coast, with service provided by the Portillo bus company at least four times daily in each direction, and costs around 950 *ptas* and up round trip.

All the above listed excursion companies run bus tours here throughout the year for approximately 3,300 *ptas* per person for a half day trip with guide and admission prices to museums included.

WHERE TO STAY

Expensive

PARADOR DE RONDA, *Plaza de España. Tel. (95) 287-7500, Fax (95) 287-8188. US & Canada bookings (Marketing Ahead), Tel. 800/223-1356. Low season rack rates from 15,000 ptas per double room per night (E.P.), High season rack rates from 18,500 ptas per double room per night (E.P.). All major credit cards accepted.*

Rising up above a cliff overlooking the famous gorge of Ronda on the border between the two most picturesque districts of Ronda, this amazing parador is a superb place to stay. This modern yet romantic hotel, completed just a few years ago, was constructed within the walls of the city's 17th century former town hall. The Parador de Ronda has been lovingly designed by Martintegui Caceres using a dramatic mixture of modern designer furnishings, classic Spanish fabrics, as well as exotic hardwoods and marbles.

Most of the parador's 78 deluxe rooms and giant suites feature marbled tiled private bathrooms stocked with soaps and shampoos, hard wood flooring, cast iron lighting fixtures, Andalucian carpets, mini-bar, electronic mini-safe, executive style desks, direct dial telephones, remote control cable television, hair dryers, extremely comfortable double bedding, an additional sofa bed, plenty of closet space, and in most cases either a fantastic oversized private balcony (top floor rooms only) or a huge picture window overlooking incredible views over the city and the nearby mountain lined countryside. There are also a few super luxury duplex suites which are among the finest in the country.

The property also offers a great Adalucian style gourmet restaurant with fine cuisine, inexpensive garage parking, complete elevator access, international currency exchange services, elaborate lounge and sitting areas with large panoramic windrows, a small yet relaxing outdoor swimming pool and sun deck, lots of business meeting and reception rooms, a cafe, baby-sitting, a tour desk that can help arrange all sorts of private excursions including horseback rides to delightful nearby sights and a great young staff. Selected as one of my Best Places to Stay (see Chapter 13).

HOTEL REINA VICTORIA, *Calle Jerez 25. Tel. (95) 287-1240, Fax (95) 287-1075. Low season rack rates from 13,125 ptas per double room per night (E.P.), High season rack rates from 16,800 ptas per double room per night (E.P.). All major credit cards accepted.*

This historic building was constructed at the turn of the century by a British rail company and now offers 90 old world rooms and suites with classic Spanish furnishings, air conditioning, private bathrooms, televisions, and, in some cases, nice little balconies. The hotel also has parking, a restaurant, business meeting rooms, and an outdoor swimming pool. A reasonably good choice, but certainly not the best in town anymore.

Moderate
HOTEL LA ESPANOLA, *Calle Jose Aparicio 3. Tel. (95) 287-1051, Fax (95) 287-8001. Year round rack rates from 9,000 ptas per double room per night (C.P.). Most major credot cards accepted.*

This nice family owned and operated hotel is situated just a few steps from the Plaza de España. It offers 26 small yet charming rooms that all have antique style furnishings, private bathrooms, direct dial telephone, and television. The hotel also has a breakfast room, a full service restaurant, nearby parking and a nice staff.

Inexpensive
HOTEL EL TAJO, *Calle de Cruz Verde 7. Tel. (95) 287-4040, Fax (95) 287- 5099. Year round rack rates from 6,420 ptas per double room per night (E.P.). Most major credit cards accepted.*

This simple three-star hotel with Moorish interior design elements is located just a half block away from the *Calle de Espinel*, Ronda's famed main shopping street. The hotel towers about 5 floor above the street and features 100 nice basic rooms with private bathrooms, heating, direct dial telephones, simple furnishings, and television. The hotel also offers a breakfast room, a full service restaurant and nearby parking.

HOTEL POLO, *Calle Mariano Soubiron 8. Tel. (95) 287-2447, Fax (95) 287-2449. Low season rack rates from 6,500 ptas per double room per night (E.P.). High season rack rates from 9,000 ptas per double room per night (E.P.). All major credit cards accepted.*

The Polo is another nice, simple, three-star hotel about two blocks away from the *Plaza de España* on a quiet side street. The hotel has several dozen nice little air conditioned rooms that feature blue tiled private bathrooms, double beds, sound proof windows, telephones and televisions. There is also a restaurant on premises and a nearby parking garage.

WHERE TO EAT

Moderate

RESTAURANTE DE PARADOR DE RONDA, *Plaza de España. Tel. (95) 287-7500, Fax (95) 287-8188. All major credit cards accepted.*

This parador's beautiful cliff view restaurant has easily become the best place to enjoy gourmet cuisine in Ronda. Surrounded by huge windows with incredible views out over the Sierra de las Nieves mountains, the dining room here is beautifully designed to impress its fortunate clients. On my recent visit here I sampled several of the chef's fantastic creations that range from classic Analucian dishes to delightful fusions of Europe's most famous main courses. Among the wonderful items offered are gazpachos, braised wild partridge, stewed ox tail, roasted loin of red deer, beef tenderloin, grilled lobster, partridge pate, rabbit casserole in rice, an amazing poached turbot with roasted sweet garlic sauce, roasted red mullet fillets, and one of the best dessert trays in the region. Service here is exceptionally good, and a full three course meal will set you back about 3,700 *ptas* per person plus wine.

RESTAURANTE PEDRO ROMERO, *Calle Virgen de la Paz 18. Tel. (95) 287-1110. All major credit cards accepted.*

Located just steps away from the Plaza de España, this rather good local specialty restaurant is quite famous for having delicious Andalucian cooking. The restaurant has a nice whitewashed interior complete with traditional Moorish style elements and offers high quality cuisine at good prices. Their best dishes include mixed salads, endive with Roquefort cheese, prawn cocktails, black sausage, escargot in garlic, fish soup, bull tail stew, duck cooked in Malaga wine, roasted rabbit, partridge in white wine sauce, and entrecote steak. Dress any way you like, and get here around 9pm for a nice dinner. A three course dinner will cost around 2,650 *ptas* per person plus drinks.

Inexpensive

BAR LA PAZ, *Calle de Espinel 77. No Phone. Cash only - no credit cards accepted.*

The La Paz is one of the best simple and clean luncheonette style restaurants in the entire city. While far from fancy, this little snackbar offers its clients a full range of traditional Spanish items which are lovingly prepared and served. Among my favorite items here are the shrimp with garlic at 500 *ptas*, the cheese omlettes for 250 *ptas*, the salads starting at 300 *ptas*, calamari for 500 *ptas*, burgers at 500 *ptas*, tuna sandwiches for 350 *ptas*, and the ice cold drinks and beers for under 175 *ptas*. The La Paz is open daily (except Sunday) from 11am until 10pm.

SEEING THE SIGHTS

Approximate duration (by foot) is about 6 hours, including town, museum, and palace visits.

The El Mercadillo Quarter

The best entry point to the heart of town is through the **Plaza de España** square in the El Mercadillo area that sprung up after the Christians had taken control of the city. The first thing to do once you arrive into town is to immediately pop inside the friendly but understaffed Turismo tourist office just off the Plaza de España and pick up a free walking map. From here you are just steps away from the brand new **Parador de Ronda** (a magnificent hotel built inside the former town hall).

After taking a peek inside the parador, take a left turn onto the Calle de la Virgen de la Paz and walk a few hundred meters until passing the exterior of the round 18th century **Praca de Toros** bull ring. Built in 1784 by the Royal Equestrian Society, this is where members of the Romero family and their school mastered the art of bullfighting. This bull ring is one of Europe's oldest such venues. Also in the complex is a great little **Museo Taurino** bullfighting museum of old posters, photos, and *matador* costumes. *The bull ring and museum are open daily from 10am until 7pm in the Summer and daily from 10am until 2pm in the winter, and cost 275 ptas to enter both.*

Just a few steps past the bull ring on the left side of the street is an entrance to the panoramic **Alameda de Tejo Jose Antonio** which has several gardens and walking paths overlooking the gorge below. The gardens can be visited for free daily between sunrise and sunset, and provide a great place for a picnic while being surrounded by beautiful fountains and wild birds.

After you're finished with the park, return to the Plaza de España square.Now turn around and retrace your steps along the Calle de la Virgen de la Paz. Just after you pass the bull ring, cross the street and turn left onto the bustling **Calle de Espinel**, a charming street lined with boutiques. At the next corner on your left side you can't help but notice the quaint **Plaza Franco** where many of the city's residents go for a coffee or beer after work with their families.

The Old La Ciudad Quarter

Now return to the Plaza España and turn left to cross over the **Puente Nueva** bridge. The bridge was built in 1793 by architect Jose Martin de Aldehuela to replace an earlier bridge which collapsed in 1735. Cross the bridge and and walk above the ravine and head straight into the more interesting La Ciudad quarter. With it's roots based squarely on the

Moorish heritage of the city (the Christians returned to rule the city after winning a ten day seige during sucessful Reconquest of 1485), this section is full of atmospheric winding lanes and beautiful old Moorish, Gothic, and Renaissance mansions.

Just after crossing the bridge head directly along the Calle Arminan, and about 75 meters (74 yards) later turn left onto the Calle de Santo Domingo. Follow this curvy cobblestone lane until it reaches a fork in the road where you will bear left. Just after the fork you will see a superb mansion on the left side of the road which is the 15th-18th century **Casa del Rey Moro**. Although named as the residence of a Moorish king, this unusual structure has few of its original Moorish elements intact and is actually a Renaissance structure. The facade features cast iron grillwork with royal crests as well as a wonderful tower. The house is privately owned by a young German and Colombian couple who hope to convert it into a deluxe hotel by the year 2002. While the house itself is not open to the public, its lavish terraced **Jardines de Forestier** gardens, designed by French architect Jean Claude Nicolas Forestier in 1912 are. The gardens have several levels of fine ceramics, flowering plants, and panoramic lookout points and feature a dramatic cave path down 236 steps to an old water well known as *"La Mina."* A cafe is also available at the gardens for those desiring cold beverages and snacks. *The gardens and water "mine" are open daily from 10am until 6pm and cost 500 ptas per person to enter.*

Another 30 meters along the same street is the dramatic 14th to18th century **Palacio del Marqués de Salvatierra** palace. Built by the Moors and redesigned for a local noble family who still uses the property as their summer home, this house's bizarre facade features a Pre-Colombian style stone carving of two Aztec Indian couples, a bold Italian style columns, and a fine wrought iron balcony. Inside you can find highly decorated rooms with beautiful furnishings and interesting ceramics. *Guided tours are offered Monday through Wednesday and Friday through Saturday at 11am, 2pm, 4pm, and 6pm, Sunday at 11am and 2pm, for 300 ptas per person.*

Now from the front door of the Palace tuen left onto the Calle de Marqués de Salvatierra. When this street ends a few blocks later, make a left turn down the Calle Arminan, and a couple of short blocks later turn right into the Plaza de Duquesa de Parcent (also known locally as the **Plaza de la Ciudad** square. The square is home to several monumental structures including the the 16th century **Iglesia de Santa María de la Encarnacion** church that was built atop the ruins the city's former mosque. Although the first church constructed on this site was destroyed by an earthquake in 1580, and new building was soon stated and was finally completed in the 18th century. Inside the church you will find relics of the original mosque's mihrab near the entrance, along with Gothic and

Baroque elements. The tower that adorns the church was built around the mosque's original minaret. *You can enter the church and its silver treasury section daily between 10am until 7pm for 200 ptas per person.*

After leaving the church you will keep walking alongside the front of the church towards the rear of the plaza where you will then turn right onto the Calle Manuel Montero. A short distance later you will end up in the orange tree lined **Plaza de Mandragon**. On the left hand side of the square, you can't help but notice the entrance for the **Palacio de Mondragon** palace, which is now the home of Ronda's fine little **Museo de la Ciudad** local history museum. The mansion is supposed to be a former Moorish palace of King Torto (the one eyed King) Abomelik, and sometime shortly after 1485 was the home of King Fernando. These days the palace contains two floors worth of bilingual exhibitions about cave dwelling, megaliths, ancient metal tool making, and muslim burial rituals. The highlight of your visit here is sure to be the amazing Mudejar-style decorations and two wonderful patios with excellant views of the nearby Sierra de las Nieves mountains. *The museum is open daily from 10am until at least 5pm, and costs 200 ptas per adult and 100 ptas per student.*

After departing the museum, continue along the same street for a short while until the next little corner where you will first bear left onto the Rueda de Gamerosand a few steps later turn right onto the Calle Tenerio where you will pass alongside a nice little square with a scenic lookout point. Further along the Calle Tenorio at building #20 is the small **Casa de Juan Bosco**, a traditional Ronda house where you can visit it's ceramic lined interiors and have a peek at one of the finest mosaic fountain courtyards in town. *The house is open daily from 10am until 2pm and again from 4pm until 6pm and costs 100 ptas per person to enter.*

Continue along the same street, bearing left as it forks, and at the next intersection take a left left down the Calle Arminan for a couple of blocks until bearing right onto the Calle de Santo Domingo. Just on the left side, past the **Palacio del Marqués de Salvatierra** palace, is a small road that curves as it descends past a stone gateway and continues down towards the 17th century **Puente Arabe** bridge. Just after reaching the beginning of the bridge you will turn right down a set of stairs and follow the path towards the nearby 13th century **Baños Árabes** Moorish baths and saunas. The baths are among the best preserved of their type remaining in Europe and contain star shaped holes in their ceilings that are supported by columns and Moorish arches. *The baths' entrance is a bit hard to find, but it is open for free from Tuesday through Saturday from 10am until 2pm and again from 4pm until 7pm, Sunday frrom 10am until 2pm.*

Now return to the Puente Arabe bridge and cross over it. A few steps later you will turn left down the Calle Escollera and keep your eyes out for an entrance to a nice public terraced garden on the left. Once again return to the end of the bridge and turn left at the Iglesia de Padre Jesus church and fountains to head up along the Calle Santa Cecilia. Follow this long narrow street several blocks until it merges with the Plaza Carmen Abela where you will soon take a left turn onto the **Calle de Espinel** to return back to the Plaza de España.

NIGHTLIFE & ENTERTAINMENT

The few good local bars with fun music and inexpensive drinks include **Bar Baco** at Calle Molino 2, **Johnny Maracas** on Calle Padre Soubiron 4, the **Bolero Bar** on Calle Jerez 13, and the **Dulcinea** at Calle El Nino 4.

PRACTICAL INFORMATION

Major Local Festivals

Contact the local Turismo office, *Tel. (95) 287-1272*, for exact details.
• **Fiesta Reconquista**, *Late May, Processions and Festivals*
• **Cante Grande**, *August, Singing Festival*
• **Corrida Goyesca**, *Late September, Bullfights and Parades*

19. GIBRALTAR

Known simply as "The Rock" for centuries now, **Gibraltar** is one of those strange yet fascinating destinations that doesn't fit comfortably into any single category: not fully English, not quite Spanish, embracing both the old and the new in a distinct blend. Anchored off the southern coast of Spain, Gibraltar is a British possession. Easily accessible from Spain, this island is a fun excursion.

If you've got the time, take a side trip here and explore this tiny rocky outcrop guarding the entrance to the Mediterranean Sea.

Gibraltar's Unusual History

This small limestone peninsula jutting out into the straits and separating Africa from Europe, was once inhabited by Neanderthal man. We know this from discoveries of two prehistoric skulls, among other archaeological evidence. Additional remains have been discovered here pointing to the area's former settlement by **Phoenicians**, **Carthaginians**, **Greeks**, and **Romans**. It wasn't until the year 711 that the **Moors** landed here, who by the 11th century began building defensive fortresses along the coast to ensure their rule here for the next 400 years. By 1068, a city had been built on the Rock by the Arab leader Al Mumin.

Due to its strategic location at the merging point of the Atlantic Ocean and Mediterranean Sea just 24 km (15 miles) north of the African coast, Gibraltar's history has mostly been a succession of one miliary conquest after another. In 1309, the **Spanish** launched a surprise invasion here and occupied the island for two dozen years. Then the Moors, led by **Sultan Abul Hassen** of Fez, returned to besiege the Spanish troops for several months until claiming victory in 1333.

Embarrassed and bitter, the Spaniards came back to constantly besiege the Rock until 1462, when they finally won a decisive victory and reconquered Gibraltar, creating a large base for naval operations and ending Moorish rule here forever. This did not, however, stop the continuous attacks by pirates and barbarians.

After the War of Spanish Succession broke out in 1701, England began to eye this small territory for its own needs, and on July 24, 1704, the joint Anglo-Dutch fleet with its 1,800 troops captured Gibraltar and claimed it for Britain, much to the displeasure of Spain. Additional attempts to reconquer the Rock by Spanish rulers and their allies led to another series of devastating attacks, including **The Great Siege** of 1779 which lasted for well over three and a half years without success. Much of the old town was left in ruins. Although Gibraltar officially became British after the 1713 signing of the **Treaty of Utrecht**, and then became a Crown colony in 1834, the Spanish still consider it as part of their territory and hope to regain it someday.

During World War II, with the constant sighting of Nazi submarines in the Straits of Gibraltar, the non-military population was evacuated to England, Jamaica, and Madeira. Almost all of the residents who left returned after the allied victory. In the late 1960's, Franco decided to cut off Gibraltar by sealing its border with Spain, and it was not until 1985 that it was finally reopened (but still controlled) to anyone with a valid passport.

Today, dozens of small electronics shops and clothing stores now line the downtown sector and offer cheap tax-free consumer goods that have been attracting thousands of day-tripping Spaniards ever since they opened. Even though the people who call this small chunk of land their home come from a mixture of Spanish, Arab, Portuguese, Italian, and English bloodlines, most do not wish to become independent, nor fall back under Spanish rule. Since the British military has carved over 48 miles of tunnel roads deep within the limestone mountain itself, and have built highly sensitive military intelligence, submarine, and perhaps tactical missile bases here, they're also in no rush to see Spain get their hands back on Gibraltar.

The British Ministry of Defense has been scaling back its presence over the past few years, and has cut back the number of soldiers stationed here by at least 60 percent, leading to a severe economic problem. Local government officials have tried to solve the resulting rise in unemployment by creating an international haven for tax exempt companies, banking institutions, insurance companies, and automobile export brokers. The effects of this new reliance on commerce has had some effect on the average worker's lifestyle, but seems mostly to have benefited smugglers, multinational corporations, offshore shell companies, foreign office workers, and dubious ex-patriots looking to make fast money.

Another interesting part of the Rock's ongoing history is that its port is constantly used as a gateway for the smuggling of tax-free cigarettes (and supposedly narcotics) into several nearby Spanish coastal resorts. Each night after about 10pm, you can see dozens of small powerboats leaving from Catalan Bay loaded with contraband shipments headed for border towns and cities like Algeciras. This has led to a continuation of bad relations with Spain, and nationalistic tendencies on the part of Madrid's more aggressive politicians.

ARRIVALS & DEPARTURES

By Air

Due to political complications arising from their bad relationship with Spain, as well as a rather limited airport area, only flights originating from England are currently permitted to land here. One interesting point is that since the airport's runway is bisected by Gibraltar's main highway, this road may be closed for up to 45 minutes when flights land or take off.

Gibralter's major carrier is known as **GB Airways** and its fleet of eight jets have just been refranchised to their partner, British Airways. It is likely that daily service to and from England will continue or perhaps be slightly expanded. Another airline called **Dan Air** also offers flights to and from Britain.

Currently the daily schedule includes flights to and from London and Manchester, with worldwide connections. From the airport to almost any hotel or sight, expect to pay somewhere around four or five pounds by taxi.

By Bus

To reach Gibraltar by bus, there are a multitude of scheduled bus services, usually via a change of bus in Algeciras, between major Spanish cities like Málaga, Sevilla, Granada, Cádiz, and Madrid. From the Algeciras bus station (or the nearby train station) you must transfer to one of the local buses leading to the border town of La Línea. Buses leave from there every half hour or so for about 900 *ptas.*

By Car

The best way to drive to Gibraltar is to take the major N-340 Autovia de Mediterraneo highway west for 100 km (62 miles) southwest from Torremolinos. A valid passport is mandatory to be admitted to and from the territory's customs and immigration check points. If you needed a visa to enter Spain, you must check in advance with your consulate to make sure it is still valid to re-enter Spain when you depart Gibraltar.

Since the Spaniards love to harass anyone crossing into or out of Gibraltar, they create artificially long delays on both sides of the border. Either you can park your car in Spain and walk across the border with no delay, or drive across and be confronted with long lines that can take upwards of two hours to cross over, especially but not limited to the morning and early evening rush hours. Be advised that no special permits are needed to drive into Gibraltar, and that anyone offering to sell you one is trying to rip you off! Parking is extremely limited in Gibraltar, and unless you're staying at a hotel with a garage, do not even think about looking for a parking spot here during the high season.

By Train

There is no direct train service between Gibraltar and anywhere else. The closest daily scheduled train service to here connects the nearby Spanish city of Algeciras with other major Spanish cities, including Madrid and Córdoba. A bus can be taken from this train station to the Gibraltar border area (see above).

Customs & Immigration Regulations: Entering Gibraltar

Since almost nothing needs to be smuggled into Gibraltar, the customs and immigration officials here only want to see your valid passport for admission. The official regulations call for UK and European residents over 17 years old who have left the colony for more than 24 hours to bring back no more than 200 cigarettes or 100 cigarillos, or 50 cigars, or 250 grams of smoking tobacco. If you are not from the UK or Europe, the allowance is doubled. All persons over 17 years of age entering Gibraltar after being away for at least 24 hours are also allowed up to 50 grams of perfume, one liter of liquor, or two liters of wine.

The total amount of all items being imported must not exceed 32 pounds sterling per person.

DON'T BE FOOLED - NO SPECIAL ENTRY PERMIT REQUIRED!

Remember, special permits or visas are not needed to bring your car here, only a valid driver's license (from any country), a current insurance card (the rental papers from a rental car are acceptable), and that's all! If anyone stops your car before reaching the customs booth, don't be tricked into buying a phony entrance permit.

Customs & Immigration Regulations: Re-Entering Spain

The customs rules for re-entering Spain are the same for entry from any foreign country, so check Chapter 6, *Planning Your Trip*, for full details. Since cigarette and consumer goods are commonly smuggled into Spain, expect a full inspection of your car or luggage. This is also a form of harassment by the Spanish customs officers, owing to the ongoing dispute with Great Britain over sovereignty of the island.

Also be careful to make sure that if you entered Spain on a visa, that your visa is valid for multiple re-entries, or else you may not be allowed back into Spain.

ORIENTATION

Gibraltar, population 31,400, rests off the southern coast of Spain in the Straits of Gibraltar. The drive here is about 702 km (428 miles) southwest from Madrid, or only about 100 km (62 miles) southwest from Torremolinos.

This tiny landmass of only four square km (2.5 square miles) is overshadowed by its centerpiece (the actual "Rock" itself), a huge Jurassic limestone mountain which rises 426 meters (1,405 feet) above sea level.

Since this strange outcrop is so close to the Spanish coastal resorts of the Costa del Sol, it makes an interesting diversion for a couple of nights. The official language used is English, although many Gibraltarians can be overheard speaking in Spanish to each other. Since the vast majority of the shopping and cuisine here is far from impressive, it is the abundance of excellent natural, cultural, and historical attractions within minutes of each other that should be the focal point of your visit.

The currency used here is the **Gibraltar pound**, exactly equivalent to the British pound. But almost all local establishments will accept Spanish *ptas* at an acceptable exchange rate. At press time, the pound is worth approximately $1.62 US, $2.15 Canadian, or roughly 230 Spanish *ptas*.

GETTING AROUND GIBRALTAR

By Bus

Most of Gibraltar can be traveled by public buses that run from about 8am until 9pm each night. The fare is 45 pence (or 95 *ptas*) for each ride, and can even take you from the border to many of the area's attractions.

By Cable Car

A special cable car ride run by **MH Bland & Co.**, *Tel. (350) 778-26*, goes from the Alameda gardens near the south end of Main Street and heads up to various points in the upper and middle rock for about 6 pounds round-trip. Call for exact scheduling information.

By Taxi

Taxis can be found at stands near the airport, border, Southport Gate, and the Piazza. Expect a typical local ride to cost from 2 to 6 pounds, and sightseeing to range from 5 to 30 pounds, depending on the route you select.

WHERE TO STAY

Expensive

THE ROCK, *3 Europa Road, Gibraltar. Tel. (350) 730-00, Fax (350) 735-13. US & Canada Bookings: (UTELL), Tel. 800/44UTELL. Year round rack rates from 75 pounds per double room per night (E.P.). All major credit cards accepted.*

With its excellent location high above the west coast of Gibraltar, but still just steps away from every major attraction, this wonderfully relaxing five-star hotel offers spectacular accommodations at surprisingly low prices. From the moment you arrive, the staff of young and highly trained employees pamper you with great enthusiasm. Over the years since its opening in 1932, English-style ambiance and Swiss-style attention to detail has made this the finest hotel in the colony.

All of The Rock's air conditioned garden and bay view guestrooms contain fine furnishings, deluxe private bathrooms, remote control satellite televisions, and collections of fine art. The top floor suites are among the most luxurious in the world, and contain pretty picture windows, private bay view patios, giant marble bathrooms, mini-bars, an electric trouser press and fantastic sitting rooms. The vast selection of services and facilities here include free parking, breakfast in bed, babysitting, a 24-hour concierge desk, express laundry and dry cleaning, overnight shoe shine and a full size pool and garden terrace.

Choice international cuisine is served with live piano music in the romantic Rib Room restaurant, or on the lovely outdoor Wisteria Terrace when weather permits. A huge buffet breakfast and afternoon tea are offered as well. This is a truly remarkable hotel and gets my highest recommendation.

WHITES HOTEL, *2 Governor's Parade, Gibraltar. Tel. (350) 705-00, Fax (350) 702-43. Year round rack rates from 65 pounds per double room per night (E.P.). All major credit cards accepted.*

This nice and centrally located modern business style hotel is only a two minute walk from Main Street. It offers 126 nicely decorated rooms and suites with air conditioning, private marble bathroom, color television, direct dial telephones, and large windows. Facilities here include a rooftop sun deck and outdoor swimming pool, health club, nearby parking, sauna, business meeting rooms, room service, boutiques, a restaurant and a bar.

CALETA PALACE, *Catalan Bay, Gibraltar. Tel. (350) 765-01, Fax (350) 710-50. Year round rack rates from 65 pounds per double room per night (E.P.). All major credit cards accepted.*

This is Gibraltar's largest hotel, and it occupies a unique location on the edge of Catalan Bay's crescent beach. This family owned and operated property is both modern and tastefully designed, and offers 200 air conditioned rooms with satellite television, comfortable furnishings, direct dial phones and private bathrooms. The pricier Executive seaview rooms also offer small refrigerators, additional amenities, and lots of extra space.

The hotel has two restaurants, a nice pool with bar service, beach chair rentals, an excursion desk, plenty of parking, and business meeting facilities.

Moderate

BRISTOL HOTEL, *10 Cathedral Square, Gibraltar. Tel. (350) 768-00, Fax (9350) 776-13. Year round rack rates from 55 pounds per double room per night (E.P.). All major credit cards accepted.*

This is a nice family style hotel just down a quiet block from Main Street in the center of downtown Gibraltar. This friendly property boasts 60 interior and exterior-view rooms with air conditioning, private bathroom, wall to wall carpeting, am-fm radio, direct dial telephones, hair dryer, mini-refrigerators and satellite television.

Facilities include an indoor garage, outdoor pool, quaint garden, English pub, breakfast room, safe deposit boxes, and a great staff ready to serve you, especially George. Ask for one of the top floor seaview rooms! A great choice for this price range.

CONTINENTAL HOTEL, *1 Engineer Lane, Gibraltar. Tel. (350) 769-00. Fax (9350) 417-02. Year round rack rates from 55 pounds per double room per night (C.P.). All major credit cards accepted.*

This small and cozy three-star hotel is a good choice for those who are looking for reasonably priced accommodations near the heart of the downtown area. The Continental's 17 single and double guestrooms all have simple but comfortable furnishings, air conditioning, private bathrooms, and cable television. The hotel's lobby also has a cafeteria-style restaurant.

WHERE TO EAT

Moderate

STRING'S, *44 Cornwall Lane, Gibraltar. Tel. (350) 788-00. American Express accepted.*

String's is one of my favorite little restaurants in the downtown sector. Here you can enjoy tasty international cuisine in a casual yet elegant setting while being served by friendly waiters who will recommend the day's best dishes. Items typically offered include a fine seafood soup, mussels with garlic lemon butter, grilled sole, English game pie, rack of lamb, and sumptuous desserts. Expect a three course dinner to cost around £11.70 a person plus drinks.

THE VICEROY OF INDIA, *Horse Barrack Court, Gibraltar. Tel. (350) 703-81. Most major credit cards accepted.*

I was thoroughly delighted by how good the food and service was at this colorful Indian restaurant just off of Main Street. The menu features such mouth- watering (and quite spicy if requested) specialties as Indian salads, whole wheat Paratha, Garlic nan, vegetable samosas, meat kebabs, vegetable curry, aloo palak(potatoes and spinach), chicken tikka masala, lamb korma, Madras fish curry, swordfish tandoori, bhuna prawns, tandoori shrimp, and plenty more. Expect a three course dinner to cost around £8.70 a person plus drinks.

THE CLIPPER, *Irish Town, Gibraltar. Tel. (350) 797-91. Most major credit cards accepted.*

With its wonderful location right in the heart of Irish Town, this popular bar and restaurant serves up great pub fare. The casual and spirited patrons dine amidst a traditional interior, surrounded by fun loving locals enjoying a few pints of beer. Their menu features assorted salads, steak and kidney pies, thick steaks, lasagne, and a host of daily specials. A hearty lunch here will cost around £8.50 a person plus drinks.

Inexpensive

SMITH'S FISH AND CHIPS, *295 Main Street, Gibraltar. Tel. (350) 742-54. No credit cards accepted.*

This is the best place in town to eat authentic fish and chips, as well as other typically English fare. Although known as a takeout place, a handful of stools are available for those who wish to eat inside. The personable Mr. Phil Smith of Liverpool offers huge portions of crispy batter fried haddock and chips for £2.95, cod and chips at £2.95, scampi and chips for £3.95, Cornish pasties at £1.95, and several other items, all well prepared, delicious, and inexpensive.

BUDDIES PASTA CASA, *15 Cannon Lane, Gibraltar. Tel. (350) 406-27. Most major credit cards accepted.*

If you're in the mood for an inexpensive and casual sit-down Italian meal, Buddies is a good bet. They have lunch and dinner menus that include daily soup at £2.25, herb topped garlic bread for £1.95, mixed salads at £1.95, shrimp and pasta salad for £3.95, lasagne at £5.25, pasta with pesto appetizers for £2.45, three colored fusilli at £5.25, fettuccine Alfredo for £4.75, spaghetti Carbonara at £4.95, pasta with tuna and tomato sauce for £5.35, apple tarts at £2.65, cheesecake for £2.65, and cappuccino at only 95 pence.

COLLIN'S TAKE AWAY, *The Piazza, Gibraltar. Tel. (350) 779-27. No credit cards accepted.*

If you're out past midnight, this is one of the few places in Gibraltar to grab a quick bite. Among the dozens of items available to go here are fish cakes for 40 pence, mushy peas at 40 pence, lamb samosas for 70 pence, Cornish pasties at £1.40, steak and kidney pies for £1.60, cheese-burgers at £1.60, cod and chips for £2.50, and roasted half chickens for £1.60.

SEEING THE SIGHTS
TOUR 1

The Coastal Tour.
Approximate duration (by car or taxi tour) is about 3 1/2 hours, including park visits.

As you enter Gibraltar and pass the airport, bear left at the traffic circle to reach **Devil's Tower Road**. Just a few minutes up, you will pass by the edge of **Eastern Beach** and bear right onto **Catalan Bay Road** as it begins to follow the eastern coastline. You'll see Catalan Bay, a former fishing village that was settled by immigrants from Genoa, Italy. The village's small but refreshing public beach now is home to the seaview **Caleta Palace Hotel**; the beach is also a base for much of the nighttime cigarette smuggling operations. The shoreline road now leads on past the small hamlet of **Little Sandy Bay** before passing a bizarre series of iron sheeted water catchments that have been cut into steep sides of the limestone cliff and are used to gather the rain needed to supply Gibraltar's reservoirs.

Next the road will pass through **The Rock** via a dark and eerie tunnel that was cut straight through the solid limestone by Canadian engineers, along with another 30 km (9 miles) of additional top secret military roads and bunkers built during World War II. The same road continues along the eastern coast while passing by a huge incinerator and several vintage pill boxes that are all connected to each other by a series of tunnels.

If you look carefully at the top of The Rock you can still see the silhouette of the old Rock **Gun** that can swivel 360 degrees to shoot targets off the coast in any direction. The street now curves towards the south tip of Gibraltar, and you should park your car in the lot in front of the **Europa Point Lighthouse** that has been operating since 1841. The lighthouse stands 49 meters (156 feet) above the high tide water line. From the small promenade near the lighthouse, take a good look across the straits to see the coastline of Africa (a brass plaque tells you that it's only about 15 miles away). The massive guns that once shared this sight with the lighthouse have since been removed.

A bit further down, the same road changes its name to **Europa Road** and curves to the right to reach the town of **Europa Flatts**, where many of the remaining British military personnel live. Some of this zone is well

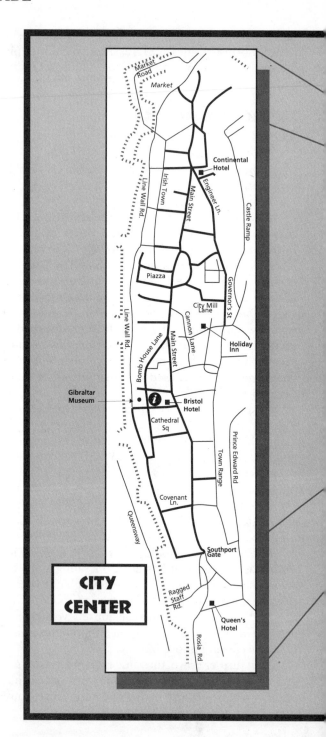

CITY CENTER

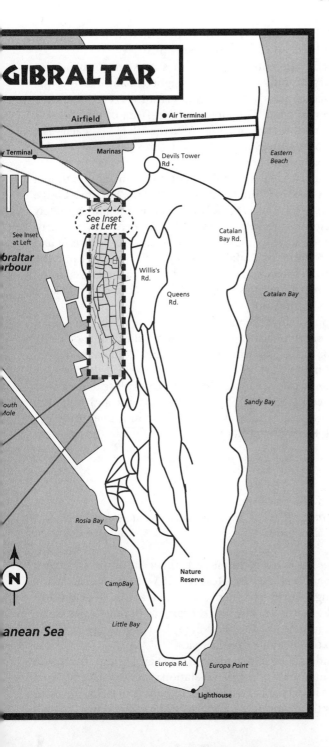

GIBRALTAR

Airfield

Air Terminal

y Terminal

Marinas

Devils Tower
Rd.

Eastern
Beach

See Inset
at Left

See Inset
at Left

braltar
rbour

Catalan
Bay Rd.

Willis's
Rd.

Queens
Rd.

Catalan Bay

outh
Mole

Sandy Bay

N

Rosia Bay

Nature
Reserve

CampBay

anean Sea

Little Bay

Europa Rd.

Europa Point

Lighthouse

marked as being off-limits, but one sight that can be viewed here is the one story whitewashed **Shrine of Our Lady of Europe**.

Although sacked and rebuilt several times, this small chapel for fishermen and sailors was built on the former sight of a Moorish mosque in 1462 by the Spaniards, and contains a wonderful 15th century rendering of the *Madonna and Child*. The mosaic just in front of the church's main entrance is of unknown age and origin. On the 5th of May each year, the community celebrates the **Europa Day festivities** here. *The church is open most of the time, and admission is free.*

Now Europa Road curves to the left and cuts through another tunnel to follow the western coast of Gibraltar. After passing the **Parson's Lodge** defensive battery, bear left onto **Rosia Road** to find the appropriately named **Bleak Beach** and then **Rosia Bay.** This peaceful bay is where Admiral Lord Nelson's flagship, the *H.M.S. Victory*, anchored after it had helped win the 1805 Battle of Trafalgar. Along with the ship came the bodies of several dead soldiers who were buried in Gibraltar, as well as the corpse of Admiral Nelson that was preserved in a cask of rum and later sent to rest in peace in England.

Near the bay you will find the massive steam-driven **100 Ton Gun** at **Nelson's Anchorage**. Built back in 1872, this unusual example of Victorian engineering was capable of firing a 909 kilogram (2,000 pound) shell with a range of 14 km (9 miles). *The gun and its adjacent gift shop are open from 9am until 4pm on weekdays.* From here, find a good place to park near the beautiful **Alameda Gardens**. This enchanting park and botanical garden is studded with exotic plants, statues, and a central delightful plaza known as **The Dell**. From the gardens, follow the signs to the cable car station via foot.

TOUR 2

The Upper Rock Cable Car Tour.

Approximate duration (by cable car and foot) is about 3 hours, including park, cave, and Ape's Den visits.

The top of The Rock is also home to a small but impressive park known as the **Upper Rock Nature Reserve**. If you have time, take a leisurely stroll through the reserve's dense flora and fauna to see countless species of wild birds, lizards, snakes, and the famous Barbary Apes. Since most people have limited time to spend here, I strongly suggest taking advantage of the excellent cable car excursion.

The cable car rides along a high tension cable and brings tourists on a scenic ride up the mountainside with two stations to enter and exit from. The best experience in the park and its adjacent sights can be had by using the cable car to view the major sights, and also walking a bit down the road from each station to see other, less crowded natural and man-made attractions.

From the Top Station, it's a nice walk down to the **Saint Micheal's Caves**, which were the large natural caverns filled with stalactites and stalagmites that once housed an impenetrable emergency hospital during World War II. These days it is possible to enter the **Cathedral Cavern**, the sight of regularly scheduled concerts, fashion shows, and other social events. The Tourist Office can also issue permission for experienced cave crawlers to get further into the so called **Lower Caves**.

Further down the mountain, the road curves around towards the **Ape's Den** near the cable car's Middle Station. This is supposed to be the best viewing area to see the some of the 160 North African monkeys that have been in Gibraltar since the 18th century. Tamed by decades of human contact, these **Barbary Macaques** are the last wild monkeys left in Europe. In the late afternoon at about 4pm, the macaques are fed by the reserve's staff.

Other possible walks include a good hike north along **Queen's Road** to see the Upper Galleries that the British military blasted out of the limestone mountain to house batteries of powerful gun emplacements in the 18th century. A museum with wax figures now explains how life was lived here during the Great Siege.

On the way back down to town, a side trip onto **Willis's Road** will lead interested visitors to the remains of the 14th century Moorish **Tower of Homage** and other adjacent castle ruins that date back at least nine centuries. From the castle, head down **Castle Road** until making a right turn onto **Engineer Road** and walking into the downtown zone. When the wind or rain is too strong for the cable car to operate, a taxi will be glad to take you to these sights instead.

The cable car tour includes admission to the reserve and the caves, and operates Monday through Saturday (weather permitting) from 10am until 7pm; the round-trip ticket with Micheal's Caves and Ape's Den admissions costs about £5 per person. The Upper Galleries are open daily from 10am until about 6pm and admission is about £1. The castle keeps the same hours and costs about 70 pence to get in.

TOUR 3

The Downtown Gibraltar Tour.
Approximate duration (by foot) is about 3 hours, including museum visits.

The best place to begin a tour of downtown is at the **Trafalgar Cemetery** on the south end of the city. The cemetery was named after the soldiers of Admiral Lord Nelson who perished after the Battle of Trafalgar and are buried here. Rising up the slopes of The Rock from this general area, you can see the 16th century **Charles V Walls** that were constructed by the Spanish King Carlos V to defend the residents from pirate attacks, and also to separate the Moors and Christians from each other. The walls connect further down to the beautiful 16th century **Southport Gate** with its small exhibit of a heroic soldier and a couple of cannons.

After passing through the gate, the road becomes known as **Main Street**. On this commercial street and the small lanes that intersect it, there are some decent tax-free boutiques, several pubs, fish and chips restaurants and a few attractions. These include the **Governor's Residence**, formerly a Franciscan convent and now the sight of a continuous changing of the guard; the 19th century **Anglican Cathedral of the Holy Trinity**; the peaceful **Piazza** square; and finally, the town's former sight of public executions known as **Casemates Square**.

One of the lanes just behind the end of Main Street off the Piazza is called **Irish Town**, and it is where much of the nightlife action takes place after dark. Another small street called **Bomb House Lane** leads to the west of central Main Street. Here you will find the impressive little **Gibraltar Museum**, which contains collections of old cannon balls, ancient artifacts, relics from local shipwrecks, and plenty of historical paintings and photos. The small building houses the well- preserved 14th century Moorish baths with their original Arab arches.

The museum is open Monday through Friday from 10am until 6pm and Saturday from 10am until 2pm. Admission is just £2 per adult and £1 for kids under 12 years old. Also included in the admission fee is a free 15 minute video called The Gibraltar Story that details the area's history and points of interest. The video is shown each half hour from 11am until 5pm in the museum's small theater.

Another walk worth taking is over to the old fortified Line Wall Road esplanade, a few blocks west of Main Street. Here there are numerous 9th century defensive positions and bastions including the **Wellington Front**, **Prince Albert Front**, and the **King's Bastion**. Although now a bit inland, this whole area was once on the waterline, but has been landfilled to extend the valuable surface area of Gibraltar. During the Great Siege of 1779-1783, floating Spanish gun batteries pounded The Rock from their positions off this part of the coast. In a defiant act of revenge, British Sergeant O'Hara invented a method of firing red hot cannon balls (known as Hot Shots) from guns in these bastions, and was able to burn and sink the floating Spanish batteries once and for all.

A short stroll northward to the new **Marina Bay** development near the airport will take you past many shops and fine dining establishments.

NIGHTLIFE & ENTERTAINMENT

Most of the action takes place on Friday and Saturday nights after 10pm in the section know as **Irish Town**. You'll find everything from typical dark Irish-style pubs like **Corks Pub** and **The Clipper** to the heart-pounding **Kiss Disco**, which has a small cover charge on some nights and offers more potential for singles to meet each other. Nearby on Reclamation Road is **The Buccaneer** bar and outdoor patio, offering great drink prices, a small dance floor, and home-made snacks.

A few blocks away on Parliament Lane is the **Star Bar**, with London theater curiosities and live music or karaoke on weekend nights. The locals tend to frequent **Cool Blues** on the edge of Main Street, where they listen to English and American hot new tracks. There's also the **International Casino** on Europa Road, where you can play roulette, blackjack, slots, or bingo. They also have a restaurant and bar, and no passport is needed to enter (proper attire is requested but not always required).

EXCURSIONS & DAY TRIPS

Several travel agencies on Main Street offer cheap last-minute specials on bus tours to Andalucían cities such as Sevilla and Ronda, as well as Portuguese beach resorts. For more local sightseeing, try a 2 1/2 hour sail aboard the *Fortuna* clipper from its base at Watergardens Quay (about £17 per person), *Tel. (350) 745-98*. Jet Skis and scuba diving can be arranged by Dive Charters Gibraltar, *Tel. (9350) 424-67*.

PRACTICAL INFORMATION

- **Country Calling Code from Spain**, *Tel. 567*
- **Tourist Office**, *Gibraltar Information Bureau, 6 Convent Place, Tel. (350) 700-71*
- **Gibraltar Airport**, *Tel. (350) 730-26*
- **Dan Air**, *Winston Churchill Avenue, Airport, Tel. (350) 417-37*
- **GB Airways**, *Cloister Building, Irish Town, Tel. (350) 793-00*
- **Gibraltar Customs**, *Tel. (350) 788-79*
- **Gibraltar Police**, *Tel. 199*
- **Gibraltar Firemen**, *Tel. 190*

SAVE MONEY WITH THE PRIVILEGE KEY CARD

*The **Privilege Key Card** is available upon check-in at most Gibraltar hotels. This blue and white fold-out pass allows visitors to receive free admission to many popular museums and attractions, as well as a 5% discount at over 30 participating retailers, restaurants, and night spots. Be sure to ask your hotel's front desk to give you one of these money-saving cards.*

20. SPANISH GLOSSARY

COMMON QUESTIONS

¿Habla usted Inglés?	Do you speak English?
¿Dónde está el oficina de Turismo?	Where is the tourist office?
¿Como se llama?	What is your name?
¿Como está usted?	How are you?
¿Qué pasa?	What's going on?
¿Qué hora es?	What time is it?
¿Puede usted ayudarme?	Can you please help me?
¿Puede indicar-me a....?	Can you direct me to......?
¿Qué carretera está para....?	Which is the road towards....?
¿Dónde está la parada de autobus?	Where is the bus stop?
¿Dónde está la estacíon del tren?	Where is the train station?
¿Dónde está la estacíon del metro?	Where is the subway station?
¿Dónde está la estacíon del tren?	Where is the train station?
¿A qué hora sale a?	What time does it leave?
¿A qué hora llega a?	What time does it arrive?
¿Tiene usted una habitcacion?	Do you have an available room?
¿Dónde está los servicios?	Where is the bathroom?
¿Qué es esto?	What is this?
¿Cuánto cuesta?	How much does it cost?
¿Admite usted tarjetas de creditio?	Do you accept credit cards?
¿Admite usted el cheque de viaje?	Do you accept traveler's checks?
¿Tiene usted.....?	Do you have any.....?
¿Cuándo estará preparada?	When will it be ready?
¿Dónde está la playa?	Where is the beach?
¿Dónde hay un buen restaurante?	Where is there a good restaurant?
¿Dónde hay un buena discoteca?	Where is there a good disco?
¿Desea usted bailar?	Do you want to dance?
¿Qué desea usted beber?	What would you like to drink?

NUMBERS

uno	1
dos	2
tres	3
cuatro	4
cinco	5
seis	6
siete	7
ocho	8
nueve	9
diez	10
once	11
doce	12
trece	13
catorce	14
quince	15
dieciseis	16
diecisiete	17
dieciocho	18
diecinueve	19
veinte	20
veintiuno	21
veinteidos	22
treinta	30
cuarenta	40
cincuenta	50
sesenta	60
setenta	70
ochenta	80
noventa	90
ciento	100
ciento uno	101
ciento dos	102
doscientos	200
quinientos	500
mil	1000
mil y quinientos	1500
dos mil	2000
un millon	1,000,000

DAYS OF THE WEEK

lunes	Monday
martes	Tuesday
miércoles	Wednesday
jueves	Thursday
viernes	Friday
sábado	Saturday
domingo	Sunday

MONTHS OF THE YEAR

enero	January
febrero	February
marzo	March
abril	April
mayo	May
junio	June
julio	July
agosto	August
septiembre	September
octubre	October
noviembre	November
diciembre	December

COLORS

blanco	white
negro	black
azul	blue
verde	green
rojo	red
amarillo	yellow
plata	silver
oro	gold

TIME

día	day
media-día	noon
tarde	afternoon
noche	night
ayer	yesterday
hoy	today
esta noche	this evening
mañana	tommorow
ahora	now

USEFUL WORDS

sí	yes
no	no
vale	okay
bueno	good
mal	bad
entrada	entrance
salida	exit
abierto	open

cerrado	closed
señora	Mrs.
señorita	Ms.
señor	Mr.
médico	Dr.

GREETINGS

Hola	hello
Adiós	goodbye
buenos días	good morning
buenos tardes	good afternoon
buenos noches	good evening
¿como está usted?	how are you?
me lammo es...	my name is...
por favor	please
gracias	thank you
muchas gracias	thank you very much
de nada	you're welcome
lo siento	I'm sorry

DESCRIPTIONS

pequeño	small
grande	big
menos	less
más	more
cerca de	close
lejos	far
caliente	hot
frío	cold
esto	this
eso	that
precio	price
barato	cheap
caro	expensive
con	with
sin	without
aqui	here
alli	there
antes	before
después	after

QUERIES

cuando	when
como	how
cuánto	how much
qué	what
a dónde	where
por qué	why
No comprendo	I don't understand

DIRECTIONS

izquierda	left
direcha	right
derecho	directly ahead
este lado	this side
otro lado	the other side
dentro	inside
fuera	outside
hasta	until
próximo	the next
último	the last
a través	through the
me he perdido	I'm lost
¿donde esta?	where is?

TRANSPORTATION

coche	car
autobús	bus
tren	train
taxi	taxi
avion	airplane
metro	subway
fluvial	ferry
estación	station
aeroporto	airport
primera clase	first class
segunda clase	second class
ida y vuelta	round trip
billete	ticket
equipaje	luggage
carretera	road
puente	bridge
peaje	toll
garaje	garage
estacionamiento	parking
gasolina	gasoline
sin plomo	unleaded gas
gasoleo	diesel
peligro	danger
mecánico	mechanic
semáforo	traffic lights
cruce	intersection
cruce circular	traffic circle

SERVICES

policia	policemen
médico	doctor
hospital	hospital
farmacía	pharmacy
correos	post office
banco	bank
cambiar	exchange
hotel	hotel
restaurante	restaurant
servicio	bathroom
teléfono	telephone

ACCOMMODATIONS

cortijo	farm house
parador	government-owned inn
hotel	hotel
residencia	budget inn
albergue	quality inn
hostel	minor hotel
pensíon	guest house
albergue de juveniles	youth hostel
apartamiento	apartment
villa	villa
habatacíon individual	single room
habitacíon doble	double room
con baño particular	with private bath
con dos camas	with 2 beds
con cama matrimonio	with a king-size bed
aire acondicionado	air conditioning
calificacion	heating
lavandería	laundromat
ascensor	elevator
llave	key
cambiar	exchange

SPORTS & ENTERTAINMENT

tenis	tennis
golf	golf
billares	billiards
piscina	swimming pool
playa	beach
barco	boat
barco de vela	sailboat
esquiar	skiing
esqui acauático	water ski
squash	squash
equitacion	horse riding
pescar	fishing
bicicletas	bicycles
sauna	sauna
casino	casino
cinema	movie theater
plaza de toros	bullfighting ring

SIGHTS

ciudad	city
pueblo	village
centro del ciudad	city center
barrio	neighborhood
judería	old Jewish neighborhood
plaza	a town square
plaza mayor	the main town square
puente	bridge
edificio	building
patio	patio
paseo	prominade
castillo	castle
alcázar	Moorish-era fortress
palacio	palace
ayuntamiento	town hall
catedral, se, seo	cathedral
cartuja	monastery
convento	convent
iglesia	church
costa	coast
montaña	mountain
fuente	fountain
jardine	garden
lago	lake
rio	river
faro	light house
ruinas	ruins
mirador	scenic lookout point
calle	street

mercado	marketplace
parque, alameda	park area

BEVERAGES

botella	bottle
media botella	half bottle
garrafa	carafe
café solo	espresso
café con leche	coffee with milk
cortado	cafe au lait
chocolate	thick hot chocolate
te	tea
leche	milk
cerveza	beer
cava	sparkeling wine
vino tinto	red wine
vino blanco	white wine
vino rosado	rosé wine
agua	water
agua mineral	mineral water
agua con gas	water with bubbles
agua sin gas	water without bubbles
hielo	ice

FOOD & RESTAURANT TERMS

bien pasado	well done
a punto	medium done
poco pasado	rare
menú	menu
camareroo	waiter
lista de vinos	wine list
la cuenta	the bill
desayuno	breakfast
almuero	lunch
cena	dinner
cuchillo	knife
tenedor	fork
cuchara	spoon
taza	cup
plato	plate
servilleta	napkin
cenicero	ashtray
tapa, pincho	tiny portion
ración	larger sized portion

bocadillo	sandwiich
meú del día	daily special
platos combinados	combination plates
vegitariano	vegetarian
pan	bread
tostado	toast
mantequilla	butter
sal	salt
pimenta	pepper
azúcar	sugar
aciete	oil
aceitunas	olives
vinagre	vinegar
mostaza	mustard
sopa	soup
fruta	fruit
ensalada	green salad
ensalada mista	mixed salad
huevos	eggs
huevos revueltas	scrambled eggs
huevos frito	fried eggs
tortilla	omelet
tocino	bacon
hamburguesa	hamburger
patatas fritas	french fries
bocadillo	sandwich
empanadillo	filled pastries
carne	meat
bistek	steak
cochinillo	roasted pig
cerdo	pork
ternera	veal
pato	duck
jamón	ham
jamón Serrano	smoked ham
chorizo	cured sausage
callos	tripe
cordero	lamb
conejo	rabbit
perdiz	turkey
pollo	chicken
mariscos	seafood
pescado	fish
bacalao	cod
atún	tuna
linguado	flounder
merluza	hake

trucha	trout	tomate	tomato
pez espada	swordfish	frutas	fruits
rape	monkfish	naranja	orange
rodaballo	turbot	plátanos	bananas
salmón	salmon	limón	lemon
lenguado	flounder	melón	melon
sardinas	sardines	sandia	watermelon
camarones	shrimp	fresas	strawberries
gambas	jumbo shrimp	piña	pineapple
langosta	lobster	cerezas	cherries
langostinos	prawns	pera	pear
cangrejo	crabs	melocoton	peach
centollo	spider crab	uvas	grapes
pulpo	octopus	manzana	apple
calamares	squid	ciruelas	plums
vieiras	scallops	toronja	grapefruit
ostras	oysters	pasas	raisins
mejillones	mussels	frambuesas	raspberries
legumbres	vegatables	postre	dessert
arroz	rice	queso	cheese
cebolla	onions	pastel	cake
pimientos	peppers	torta	tart
patatas	potatoes	helado	ice cream
zanahorias	carrots	chocolate	chocolate
espinaca	spinach	arroz con leche	rice pudding
setas, campiñones	mushrooms	flan	caramel pudding
pepino	cucumber		
ajillo	garlic		

COOKING METHODS

judias	beens	plancha	grilled
lechuga	lettuce	al horno	baked
garbanzos	chick peas	asado	roasted
lentejas	lentils	curado	smoked
alcachofa	artichoke	frito,	
col	cabbage	al la Romana	fried
apio	celery	cocido	stewed
pepino	cucumber	guisado	casserole

INDEX

TRAVEL NOTES